Caring for Older Europeans

Comparative studies in 29 countries

George Giacinto Giarchi

Published by
Arena
Ashgate Publishing Limited
Gower House
Croft Road
Aldershot
Hants GU11 3HR
England

Ashgate Publishing Company
Old Post Road
Brookfield
Vermont 05036
USA

British Library Cataloguing in Publication Data

Giarchi, George Giacinto
Caring for Older Europeans:
Comparative Studies in 29
Countries
I. Title
362.6094

Library of Congress Catalog Card Number: 95-80344

ISBN 1 85742 229 5

Typeset in 10 point Palatino by Poole Typesetting (Wessex) Ltd and printed in Great Britain by Hartnolls Ltd Bodmin

CARING FOR OLDER EUROPEANS

DEDICATION

To two inspirers: Jean Monnet, Honorary Citizen of Europe, and my father-in-law, James Henri Norbury, better known as Harry, aged 88 – to the end a much loved member of our household – who shared Monnet's European sentiments on unity at our table:

We are not on different sides of a problem,
but on the same side of the table with the
problem in front of us.

Jean Monnet

Contents

Part IV: Eastern Europe

Part V: Southern Europe

List of tables and figures

Tables

Figures

Foreword

Robert Leaper

One result of the 1993 European Year of Older People has been an increased interest within Britain in the ways in which health and social issues function in other European countries. It seems important to get behind the very generalized studies produced by, for example, the EC Commission on ageing and older people (Walker et al., 1993), to look more closely at the actual operation of services at national and local levels.

There have already been modest attempts of this analysis of local practice in the journals *Social Policy and Administration* (Leaper, 1993) and *European Social Policy*. These have been followed by a new journal, *Social Work in Europe*, which has so far dealt only with children and young people, but which must surely expand its coverage to older people as well.

Nothing so far published, however, has been as ambitious or as encyclopaedic in its coverage as this book. George Giarchi has gathered in a single volume a vast amount of material from 29 countries within what he has called 'greater Europe'. The contents are a gold-mine from which researchers, teachers and students of this subject matter will dig out essential basic material, either for deeper studies between a limited number of countries or on trends over most European countries. In a very volatile setting the information gathered here is not only as up to date as anything can be in the circumstances, but it also provides a framework within which the interested reader can make any required updatings or adjustments.

Readers may well question the basis of the categorization of countries made in the book, and several other groupings of countries are possible. No 'clusters' are ever permanent in this field of study and those offered here may well prompt the reader to consider carefully why and how similarities between nation-states are validated.

I draw readers' attention in particular to the treatment of what has come to be called 'community care' and to its translation into practice both in the UK and in other countries where similar – and rather obvious – aspirations for care for dependent elderly people are confronted with the challenge of translation into daily practice. There are semantic and cultural questions to be explored here, as much as economic and administrative constraints. The temptation to extrapolate from one's own national model has to be resisted, and George Giarchi gives his readers a brave lead in that direction.

References

Leaper, R. (ed.) (1993), 'Age Speaks for Itself in Europe', *Social Policy and Administration*, Vol.27, No.3.
Walker, A., Alber, J. & Guillemard, A.-M. (1993), *Older People in Europe – The Public Dimensions*, Brussels: EC Commission.

Acknowledgements

I am indebted firstly to Clare my wife, our two daughters Imelda and Emma-Clare and our son Simon, for their support and encouragement over the three years that it took to write this book. I wish also to thank Liz Thompson for her technical assistance with my data base and word processor, as well as Karen Williams, Cher Cressey, Geraldine Waters, Cecile Borelle and Ann Thorne for their help and clerical assistance in the office of the Department of Applied Social Studies at the University of Plymouth. Special thanks are also due to Sharon Hooper, who typed the Bibliography, and to Peter Gilbert for drafting the diagrams and his helpful suggestions.

I am grateful to the many publishers and authors from whose books I have gained so much insight into the care of older Europeans. In particular, I'd like to say how impossible it would have been to complete this major study without the research findings of several mainstream European publishers and research centre staff: the European Centre for Social Welfare Training and Research; the Centrum voor Bevolking en Gezinsstudie Eurolink; the Hoger Instituut voor de Arbeid; the European Foundation for the Improvement of Living and Working Conditions; Age Care Research Europe; the SAGO centre in Florence; the EU Social Fund; the ESRC UK, and Eurolink-Age. In addition, there are the various members of the British Society of Gerontology, of which I am a proud member. Above all, there are the many hundreds of older people themselves, without whom this study would not have been possible, into whose European homes I was made so welcome, and with whom I have spent so much time discussing the issues that are central to this book.

It is customary to subscribe to Shanas's (1968) emphasis upon the use of collaborators when carrying out comparative studies. I accept that they are essential, and I have worked with them myself and have acknowledged some above, but the researcher must also be personally involved within the various cultural settings in the best tradition of the eminent anthropologists.

Armchair studies are no substitute for firsthand experience. I have been fortunate in interviewing hundreds of Europeans in my ESRC (Giarchi, 1990a) and EU (Giarchi et al., 1992) studies. There is little ethnography in this book, because it sets out to provide overviews and a panorama of the care of elderly people in greater Europe; space did not allow for much more. But the salient frame or window through which I gazed was constructed in my mind during my wanderings in the streets and hills of Europe, which takes me to my final word of thanks – to the many European households which provided me with hospitality at grassroots level, where the real action is.

Permission to reproduce Todd's map of European family types has been gratefully received from Basil Blackwell, Oxford.

Introduction: Setting the scene

The need to locate the study in greater Europe

The focus in this study is upon the care of older people in greater Europe and not restricted to care of older people in the European Union (EU). Recently, updated information regarding services, the quality of care and the conditions of older people in most countries within the EU are more readily available, especially since the 'European Year of Older People and Solidarity Between Generations' in 1993. However, earlier publications on the care of older people have generally been confined to the EU, with isolated chapters on other countries. The task of addressing the provision of care for older people in Europe as a whole is called for. Aware of the daunting nature of this task, this chapter provides an overview of the types of care provided for older people in greater Europe, before setting out to deal with the care of older people in each of the 29 countries. Five introductory issues will provide the background to this study:

1   the demography of old age within the continent;
2   the geopolitical settings;
3   the material, social and spiritual deprivation facing many older Europeans;
4   the response of welfare and the provision of formal care;
5   the provision of informal care provided to meet the need for home care.

Before dealing with these factors, an observation must be made regarding terminology. Throughout this text the term 'older people' is used, rather than 'the elderly'. This is in keeping with the former's more common usage in the past decade, and more particularly in response to the wish of older Europeans themselves, as reported in the recent *Eurobarometer Survey Report* (1993).

1

When dealing with 'care' in this book I wish to include social welfare in terms of income, housing, health and social support, both formal and informal, in multicultural urban and rural settings. Although in most sections I will necessarily be discussing the care provided for frailer older Europeans, I appreciate that four out of five older Europeans are not frail.

The demography of 'old age' in Europe

One in five Europeans will be a pensioner by the year 2040, according to Handy (1989), in a Europe that is melting away like snow in the sun (see Simons, 1992, p.50). Statistics published by the Centre for Policy on Ageing (CPA, 1989, p.2) calculate that by the year 2025 the proportion of children aged 0–14 (18.3%) in the general population will be almost identical to that of people aged 65+ (18.4%). The age pyramids of the statistical figures are turning into demographic pillars (ILO, 1989). The demography impacts upon the costs of care and of welfare. By the year 2015, approximately 41% of the European Union's total medical expenditure will be spent on the health care of persons aged 65+. Currently pensions represent approximately 9% of Gross Domestic Product (GDP) in the countries of the EU (ILO, 1989). The Organization of Economic Co-operation and Development (OECD, 1988a) stated in 1988 that in ten large member countries health expenditure per capita was more than four times as high for the over-65s as for the rest of the population. After pensions, health is the second-largest item of OECD expenditure.

Table 1 presents the overall estimated percentages of older people in Europe, comparing available data with the projected 2025 statistics. These estimates, along with those of Grundy and Harrop (1992), show that the welfare and health problems facing older Europeans constitute an immense challenge. By the year 2025 the increase in costs will be considerable for the poorer countries in Eastern Europe, especially Poland (7.1% increase), Hungary (5.6% increase), Romania (5.0% increase) and Bulgaria (4.7% increase), particularly with regard to those aged 75+ (see Grundy and Harrop, 1992, pp.15–30). Although the proportions are estimated having been gathered from more than one source, they provide an approximate overview of the demographic increases/fluctuations of older populations within greater Europe in recent years up to 2025. The statistics for Russia, Belorussia, Estonia, Latvia, Lithuania, Ukraine, Moldavia, Georgia, Azerbaijan and Armenia are not available at this transitional stage of political unrest.

At this juncture it is not possible to compare the proportion of older people in the various countries within precisely the same years because of lack of information. None the less, Table 1 provides benchmarks, and is

**Table 1   The ranked proportions of older people in Europe in the
second half of the 1980s or early 1990s, and the projected
proportions by 2025**

	1989/1990 (unless otherwise stated) (est. %)		2025 (est. %)
Sweden	(1987) 18.4	Switzerland	23.8
Norway	16.4	Sweden	22.2
Denmark	15.6	Denmark	22.2
UK	15.6	Netherlands	22.2
Germany	15.3	Luxemburg	21.3
Austria	(1987) 15.2	Finland	21.0
Switzerland	(1987) 14.8	Germany	20.4
Belgium	14.8	Norway	20.2
Italy	14.5	Belgium	19.8
France	14.0	Austria	19.7
Greece	(1989) 13.7	Italy	19.6
Luxemburg	13.4	France	19.3
Hungary	13.4	Hungary	19.0
Spain	13.3	UK	18.7
Finland	(1987) 13.2	Greece	17.8
Portugal	(1988) 13.1	Malta	17.7
Netherlands	12.8	Yugoslavia[1]	17.3
Republic of Ireland	(1987) 11.3	Poland	17.1
Bulgaria	(1987) 12.0	Iceland	17.0
Czechoslovakia[2]	(1987) 11.3	Bulgaria	16.7
Iceland	(1988) 10.5	Czechoslovakia[2]	16.2
Malta	(1988) 10.1	Cyprus	16.1
Poland	10.0	Republic of Ireland	16.0
Cyprus	(1985) 9.9	Spain	15.7
USSR/CIS[3]	9.6	Portugal	15.7
Romania	(1985) 9.5	USSR/CIS[3]	14.8
Yugoslavia[1]	(1988) 9.1	Romania	14.5
Albania	(1985) 4.9	Albania	9.8
Turkey	4.2	Turkey	8.4

Notes:
[1] The former Yugoslavian territories
[2] The former Czechoslovakia
[3] The former USSR territories
Sources: CPA (1989); Eurostat (1991a); UN (1991); *Economist* (1993)

useful in providing an estimate of the growth of the ageing populations throughout the continent of Europe by the year 2025.

Framing the geopolitical picture of the greater European setting

It is essential to compare the modes of care of older people within a meaningful framework, which ought to take cognizance of the geography of greater Europe. Davy (1990, p.141) states that 'Any mental map of greater Europe is bound to be confused.' On the basis of Lipset and Rokkan (1967), the later study of Rokkan and Urwin (1983) and recent historical events, it is possible to identify the salient macro developments which help the social gerontologist to piece together the context of the panoply of need and welfare provision in Europe. The cleavages and cultural divides that separate Europe into long-standing entities need to be acknowledged.

North/South and East/West cleavages

Some pertinent points can be made by drawing upon the Euroanalysis presented by Lipset and Rokkan (1967), Rokkan and Urwin (1983) and Hobsbaum (1990). These authors direct attention to the nature of the European divisions between North and South, and between East and West.

Firstly, as a result of the Reformation and the Counter-Reformation, Europe was split ideologically. North and South were fiercely entrenched within closed belief systems for over four hundred years. At the same time, a divided Christendom weakened the Churches, whilst increasing secularization. The provision of care progressively passed from the monastery cloisters to the decision-makers and power-holders in palace courts. Today the secular revolution has turned full circle and invited the Churches to be part of the plural systems of care provided for older Europeans in most of Europe. Although congregations have waned, their social outreach has increased (see Giarchi and Sharp, 1993).

Secondly, after the French Revolution had run its course, rule by divine birthright and care by religious calling were largely supplanted by a totally new development. State bureaucracy progressively took over, providing professionals in place of the clergy as social carers. The Churches reacted and formulated a mission to the sick and an option for the poor and social welfare, chiefly through Caritas and the many Protestant welfare agencies. Their contribution will be referred to where relevant in Parts I–V. Caritas is probably the largest voluntary organization in the Southern European countries, and one of the largest in the Central European countries.

Thirdly, the South resisted the nation-builders. However, in the North the Protestant Church collaborated with them. Exceptionally, peripheral concentrations of Catholic minorities, such as in Ireland and Holland, resisted the interference of central controls, creating alternative, localized, parish-based systems of care. The formal seal of approval and caring credentials were no longer episcopal, they were now legitimized by the secular authority, as care progressively became a responsibility of the state. Bureaucracies reached down into communities which were once almost a law unto themselves. Hitherto, religious and family status had mattered most, but the nation-state gradually took over and meticulously attempted to systematize caring arrangements and organize life's major functions. The state became responsible for caring and healing. The supreme example of the all-embracing new tutelage was that of France. For example, the independence of the French *communes* and the local caring arrangements came under Napoleon's mammoth bureaucratic system. That vertical bureaucratized control, exerted by the *départements*, set the model for most Western European states.

Fourthly, the Industrial Revolution further extended the bureaucratic controls, particularly in the North of Europe, where both Protestantism and industrialism reinforced the entrepreneurial and administrative systems. Industrialization accelerated the shift and the regulation of local care and service provision from the peripheral regions to the industrialized and now mainly Protestant cities of a more progressive and affluent North, where the first major industries first took off. Welfare provision was rudely shunted from the market towns to the city centres. The charitable organizations also moved with the masses to these high-density urban areas, hoping to draw upon the heavy concentration of resources so as to alleviate the misery of increasing numbers of the poor, who faced multiple deprivation within the crowded and congested industrialized zones. As a consequence, there was a shortfall in updated services in rural areas, setting the scene for today's rural deprivation throughout Europe. Rural sparsity and inaccessibility, as a result of heavy concentrations of services in urbanized centres, became critical factors in the delivery of health and social services, as they continue to be in contemporary Europe, which will be documented in Parts I–V.

Fifthly, there was another revolution which altered the face of welfare and consequently of care of the old in Europe, which was centred upon Russia. The Russian Revolution was to propose an alternative welfare state to that of capitalist Europe. After World War II, Eastern countries were to be separated, not only ideologically but also in geopolitical and socio-economic terms, from the rest of greater Europe. This drastic cleavage was to impact disastrously upon the older people of Eastern Europe behind the Iron Curtain, as Part IV will demonstrate, country by country.

The Eastern European states of the former German Democratic Republic, Poland, the former Czechoslovakia, Hungary, Bulgaria and Romania were forced to adopt totalitarian welfare state systems (as was Albania, that stray communist regime in the South). Only with the advent of *perestroika* (1987) was the curtain raised, and more flexible welfare systems became a welcome possibility. Sik and Svetlik (1988, p.275) refer to the 'omnipotentiality of the state' in the Eastern countries dominated by a planned economy. After the 1917 revolution, the older Russians, and to a lesser extent the older people of the occupied Eastern countries after World War II, were socialized into regarding the state as omni-provider. The reality, as I shall show in Part IV, was quite different (see also Laczko, 1994).

The older people of the former Eastern Bloc countries were, after all, the first youths indoctrinated into thinking that the state was the sole provider. They were also the first socializers and educators of the communist ideals in their own households/families. Within the span of a single lifetime they were to experience illusion and then disillusionment.

The Central European core

It is customary in most studies of social systems in Europe not to acknowledge Central Europe. Some simply refer to Northern, Southern, Western and Eastern Europe, as for example in *The Coming of Age in Europe* (Davis, 1992) and in Bailey's *Social Europe* (1992). However, Central Europe does exist as an entity, as discussed by earlier seminal writers, amongst the first of whom was Delaisi (1929), and later Seers (1979). Other studies refer to Central-Eastern countries (see Schöpflin and Wood, 1989; Laczko, 1994).

On the basis of earlier seminal studies by Lipset and Rokkan (1967), Rokkan and Urwin (1983) and later commentaries by Wijkman (1990) and Davy (1990), it is clear that certain European countries constitute a 'golden egg' or 'golden triangle' at the geographic centre of Europe. The European epicentre is an economic cluster of countries, most of which now constitute the more affluent EU nations.

However, within the 'golden egg' (Rokkan and Urwin, 1983) there is a geographic and recognizable Central European area, which has existed for centuries; it could be described as the 'yolk'. Germany is centre-stage. Wijkman (1990, p.95) refers to a 'core Europe', of which Germany is the pivot. As Burgess (1986, p.23) demonstrates, Austria, Switzerland and West Germany are the three acknowledged central federations (with East Germany now added in). To the west of this spine are the seaward peripheral countries, and to the east of it are the landward peripheral countries. Too many studies simply lump one country with another in a vague geopolitical vacuum.

Examining the shifting maps of Europe, the former territories that now make up Switzerland, Austria and Germany have constituted a centre of one kind or another since the early La Tène civilization which stretched northwards from where Switzerland now stands. This was followed by the uneasy unity of the Roman Empire, which was succeeded in turn by the rise and fall of various dynasties within and around the well-established confines of the Holy Roman Empire. The European maps of 1648, 1748 and 1798 indicate that the frontiers of the central territories west of the Danube and north of the Alps remained broadly the same until the demise of the Holy Roman Empire in 1806. The old confines of the German Confederation of 1815 roughly covered the major, more central terrain which now constitutes the heart of Europe, excepting the western cantons of Switzerland. The German Minor States, the Viennese Habsburg dominion, the Moravian and Bohemian lands, and the Tirolean territory bordering on Bavaria had in the main conserved the confines of the old Roman Empire. The powerful Austrian Habsburgs and Metternich and Bismarck, guaranteed the centrality of Germany and Austria, with Hungary and the Czech and Slovak territories as reluctant adjuncts.

The lingua franca of Central Europe was once German (see Schöpflin and Wood, 1989, p.1), which is instructive amongst other historic, political and economic reasons for placing Germany at the centre of what could be regarded as *mitteleuropa*. The German historic links and central geographical location along with Switzerland and Austria have also added weight to including them in the centre of mainland Europe.

I am well aware of the fact that Croatia, Slovenia, the Czech and Slovak Republics and Hungary are referred to as Central and at times as Central-Eastern European countries by some Europeans. Historically, they have been interrelated during the recurrent central political struggles and culture conflicts of mainland Europe (see Hankiss, 1990; Graubard, 1991; Schöpflin and Wood, 1989). But, given the reluctance of the Czechs and the Hungarian Magyars to be part of the Austro-Hungarian Empire and the split between the Slovaks and the Hungarians (see Fernández-Armesto, 1994, pp.151–9 and 248), an argument could be put forward not to include them in a centre from which they strove to break away. There is, moreover, their connection with the other Eastern Bloc countries.

The Czech Republic stands where the former Bohemia was once part of the central areas identified as Europe's ancient hub. Its centrality historically and geographically is evident, but at present, because of its recent historical links with Eastern Europe, its caring systems are discussed along with those of the other former Eastern Bloc countries of Poland, Bulgaria and Romania. Future political configurations and welfare developments may well include the Czech Republic and perhaps Hungary and Poland.

The stray, former communist country of Albania is strictly a Southern country, so it is included in Part V of this study, as is also its neighbour, the former Yugoslavia. Whatever the reconstruction of mainland and Central Europe, the fivefold framework for this study of caring arrangements in greater Europe would appear to be appropriate, at this point in time. After all, Hankiss (1990) and Deacon (1992c) simply regard the former Eastern Bloc countries as constituting a 'new Eastern Europe'. There is no clear consensus to determine the delineation of liberated Europe. As Schöpflin (1989, p.19) has said, 'in the search for a Central Europe the content of the Central European identity remains inchoate', as nations gravitate inwards.

It is clear from Table 2 that the highest proportions of older Europeans are at the heart of mainland Europe, and that the proportions in the Northern and Western European countries are greater than those in the Southern and Eastern European countries. According to the estimates of the CPA (1989), by the year 2025 the Central, Northern and Western European countries will continue to maintain the largest proportions of older people, and as a consequence it is also clear that the burden of care for them will continue to be greatest in the Central, Northern and Western countries.

Having discussed the geographic focus of the greater European setting adopted in this study, the general deprivation facing millions of older Europeans can now be identified. It is against such a bleak backdrop that their care will be set in Parts I–V.

Material, social and spiritual deprivation in the life of older Europeans

Central to the notion of deprivation is 'quality of life'. Three forms of deprivation may affect older Europeans:

1   material deprivation;
2   social deprivation;
3   spiritual deprivation.

Each of these requires explanation and application to the conditions of life facing older European people.

Material deprivation

With regard to material deprivation, Walker (1992b), Doyal and Gough (1991), Townsend (1987), Pacione (1984) and Moser (1970), amongst many others, have underscored the general indicators of material deprivation, which for older people are mainly related to the elements of life quality such as health, level of income, standard of living, housing, mobility, availability of and accessibility to services, and the nature of the environment. These are interrelated and usually constitute a mix of various miseries, best described as 'multiple deprivation'.

Table 2   The clusters of countries within greater Europe, and the average proportions of older people within them, *c.* 1990 and estimates by 2025

Northern Europe
(average proportion: 14.8% *c.* 1990/2025: 20.5%)
Iceland, Finland, Norway, Sweden and Denmark

Western Europe
(average proportion: 13.7% *c.* 1990/2025: 18.8%)
Republic of Ireland, UK, Netherlands, Belgium, France and Luxemburg

Central Europe
(average proportion: 15.1% *c.* 1990/2025: 21.3%)
Germany, Austria and Switzerland

Eastern Europe
(average proportion: 11.1% *c.* 1990/2025: 16.4%)
Poland, Romania, Bulgaria, Hungary, the former USSR and the former Czechoslovakia

Southern Europe
(average proportion: 10.3% *c.* 1990/2025: 15.3%)
Portugal, Spain, Italy, Malta, the former Yugoslavia, Albania, Greece, Cyprus and Turkey

---

Material deprivation can best be examined in terms of a polluted environment, poor housing conditions, inadequate income (being below the minimum standards of living) and ill health.

Polluted environment   The ecological setting is the starting point of any study dealing with deprivation. Large areas of industrialized greater Europe and many of its cities are spoiled environments. As a result, the quality of life for older Europeans is inevitably impaired, particularly within the inner cities. In addition, the health and general wellbeing of rural older people living near the polluted temperate rainforests may be affected, as well as those dwelling within those vast stretches of arable land that are saturated with insecticides. Although the cities and countrysides of North-west and Central Europe are often unhealthy places for older Europeans, those of the Eastern European countries cause even greater concern for ecologists and social gerontologists.

Thompson (1991, p.37) identifies Eastern Europe's 'dark dawn' – the acid rain dumping ground of the West. He aptly describes how 'the iron curtain rises to reveal a land tarnished by pollution'. Millions of older Europeans are trapped within Europe's 'long shadow', stretching from the Elbe to the Balkan Mountains in southern Bulgaria. A dirty triangle casts its lethal shadow across Eastern Germany, the former Czechoslovakia, Hungary, Romania and Bulgaria. In Poland, 600,000 acres of woodland have been ruined by pollutants carried by the winds from as far away as the UK and the German industrial cities. Close to 1 million acres, according to Thompson (1991, p.45), have been blighted and damaged almost irretrievably.

Damage to the environment necessarily damages the health of the more vulnerable inhabitants. Smoke laden with cadmium, fluorides, organic solvents, lead and other damaging elements badly affects the frailer inhabitants, like the older people. Whereas fluoride thickens their bones, cadmium thins them; the lead may cause anaemia; the organic solvents dull the brain and severely damage the liver. Illnesses and discomfort affect so many older Eastern Europeans. Thompson (1991, pp.44–54) reported that:

1   the incidences of bronchitis and eczema had increased significantly in Eastern Germany due to health hazards posed by reckless industrialization schemes;
2   one-third of Poland's population lived in 'ecological hazard areas';
3   half of Czechoslovakia's drinking water was unsuitable for consumption;
4   173,000 acres on the borders between Germany and Czechoslovakia were heavily polluted, where the conifers were dead, and the area showed up as orange on the satellite pictures;
5   one in ten Hungarians had no access to drinking water;
6   Bucharest, Romania's capital, had no sewage treatment plant, and almost all the country's sewerage failed to work properly;
7   industrial waste polluted almost 70% of Bulgaria's farmland and 60% of its river water;
8   in Slovakia, power stations burnt coal with a high arsenic content and deposited tons of arsenic within a twenty-mile radius, so that the frailer people living near were more prone to cancer of the skin;
9   in Hungary the nitrate fertilizers had seeped through to the water wells in many areas – the nitrate prevents the blood from carrying oxygen efficiently.

Housing conditions   Housing conditions are a critical environmental factor in relation to the quality of life. Determining the state of housing involves a great deal more than assessing the terms of owner-occupancy, rented and public housing or social and service housing. The condition of the housing needs to be identified, as it will be in Parts I–V. We are also accustomed to rate owner-occupied houses in the UK as top of the league in terms of general housing conditions, whereas in Southern Europe the worst and greatest proportion of poor accommodation is that of the owner-occupied dwellings, and in Europe as a whole the owner-occupied rural houses are often rundown unhealthy properties. According to Eurostat (1991b, p.117), owner-occupancy is highest (70%+) in the Republic of Ireland, Spain and Portugal, where housing conditions are amongst the worst, in contrast with the superior housing in the more affluent countries, where rented private accommodation is higher proportionately, and where owner-occupation is approximately 40%, such as in Western Germany and the Netherlands. In the EU as a whole, owner-occupancy is about 50%. My research in the Republic of Ireland, Italy, Germany and the UK, as well as the findings of Potter and Zill (1992, pp.117–18), indicate that there is a North–South divide in terms of older people's satisfaction with housing. Although people are living in inadequate older houses in the Northern inner urban areas and in the Southern more remote rural areas, there is greater satisfaction with housing conditions in the North than there is in the South.

Income Many older Europeans suffer from the lack of an adequate income. According to a Eurolink-Age report (1989, p.3), approximately 57% of women over 65 and approximately 67% of men over 65 fall into the lowest income group in ten countries in Western Europe, all but two of which are the most affluent nations. Walker (1992a, p.161) points out that pensions form the bedrock of income in old age. Over 95% are dependent upon pensions in the relatively prosperous Economic Union (Walker, 1992a, p.5). In the Northern countries of the EU pensions are the largest item of welfare expenditure (Walker, 1992a, p.162); 45% of the total expenditure on social security in the EU is allocated to older people and widows. However, this is unevenly spread; for example, Walker (1992a, p.162) states that the Republic of Ireland, Spain, Greece and Portugal spend less than half of the EU average old age benefit expenditure per capita. Expenditure levels in the UK, Belgium and the Netherlands are around the average, whereas the former Federal Republic of Germany, Italy, France and Denmark have the highest expenditures, well above the average.

The evidence indicates that the needs of older people will increase into the next century as public expenditure is stretched by the increase of the frailer over-80s who are the major consumers of health and social services. Eurolink-Age (1989, p.4) cites a set of statistics from the OECD (1988a) which shows that in the major European countries it will be necessary to increase public expenditure by some 34% to meet the growing demands for more intensive and specialist care by the year 2020. Clearly, the needs within the Eastern European countries will be even more expensive to meet.

The situation in the countries outside the European core, particularly in Eastern Europe, Belorussia, and the Baltic countries, is especially critical for the vulnerable (Laczko, 1994). Even in the European core countries the economic conditions for the older citizens are relatively bad. This has been so since the 1980s (see Eurostat, 1990). In the OECD countries, since 1982 (in spite of some improvements in terms of increased incomes) the incidence of poverty remains a matter of great concern (Holzmann, 1986, p.48). In particular, 'progressive poverty' increases as older people become frailer and more vulnerable, both psychologically and physiologically.

Laczko (1989) cites the proportion of older people dependent upon social assistance. He draws upon a larger EU-sponsored study by Room et al. (1989). He and his colleagues address 'the new poverty' facing significant numbers of older people in the EU, who number one in seven of the general population. Alongside the demographic trend of an increase in dependent and frail persons over 85 years of age is the disproportionate number of older people suffering from social and material deprivation (Greengross, 1988, p.1). However, dependence on social assistance is only one indicator of poverty, as demonstrated by Laczko (1989), Walker (1986), Lawson (1979) and Mastenbroek (1986). By way of example, Walker adds that, in spite of the fact that relatively fewer people in the Netherlands receive social assistance, a high proportion still have very low incomes. Ironically, the USA, which is the most progressive nation of the technological West, and over the years the most affluent, has the highest poverty rate amongst the older population (Laczko, 1989; Hedstrom and Ringen, 1987). Even when economic improvements occur, and there is 'take-off' after recessions, the poor are left well behind (Milano, 1989). The economic gap widens between the retired population and the younger population in paid employment, particularly in terms of pensions. It cannot be assumed that in the richer countries the older population receive relatively better pensions within their own economies. Laczko (1994) describes the growing pensioner populations in Bulgaria, the Czech and Slovak Republics, and those of Hungary, Poland and Romania. The workers under the old regime retired earlier than in the other parts of Europe, but nevertheless had to continue working to make ends meet. Under the new regimes the situation is generally not much different; in fact an increasing number have a job in the 'shadow economy' (Laczko, 1994, p.19). Governments are tight on pensions.

The cost of providing pensions is a matter of great concern in Europe. One of the best means of calculating the comparative expenditure on state pensions in relative terms is on the basis of government spending as a percentage of GDP. The ILO report *From Pyramid to Pillar* (1989) and the OECD (1988c) discussion document *Reforming Public Pensions* present the expenditures of most European governments on pensions during the period 1975–85 (see Table 3). The diverse spending levels demonstrate how wide a range there is in the values of state pensions within the listed countries. It is clear that the levels of expenditure on pensions by the state in Eastern

European countries compared favourably with those of the Western countries, but in waning economies with huge fluctuations in the inflation rates. As shall be seen later, they relied heavily upon the family/kinship networks to provide older people with care – money, not welfare systems, was made available to enable them to cope at home. As shall be seen later, this is akin to the Continental incremental system as in the Southern European countries. Older people in the poorer Southern countries have less state welfare support. Older people in the Northern countries receive less income because their governments have generally provided more state support. As shall be seen in Parts I–V, the dismantling of the state systems in Northern and Western Europe has significantly altered the situation and aggravated the increasing deprivation amongst older people (see Walker et al., 1991). The dismantling of the welfare states has created a corresponding need for increased state pensions, so that the older people are able to buy in care; only those who can afford to pay for welfare will be assisted. Walker (1993, p.15) reports that only 13% of the older population in Europe as a whole regard their pensions as completely adequate; however, the majority of older people in the Netherlands and Germany state that their pensions are adequate or completely adequate.

The comparisons in Table 3 ought to be read in conjunction with the data presented in Table 4 with regard to the net replacement ratios in the EU countries. Walker (1992a, p.162) refers to the expenditure as a proportion of GDP on EU pensioners' benefits and pensions, ranging from 10.7% in Italy, to 9.7% in France, to 8.4% in the UK and to 4.9% in the Republic of Ireland. Whatever the range between countries, the largest share of social benefits is committed to older people and their survivors in most EU countries. In the EU, over 80% is devoted to old age benefits. The relative value of pensions must take into account the replacement ratio. Table 4 presents the comparative data within the EU regarding the replacement ratios' gross and net gain. The ECU (European Currency Unit) provides a standard measure of the value of the pension outside the individual country, whereas the PPS, the 'Purchasing Power Standard', provides a measure of the value of the pension within the individual country. A reply to a European parliamentary question published by the European Commission 26 May 1989 (see Eurolink-Age, 1990) is often cited to illustrate the importance of discovering the PPS. At that time the Commission contrasted the net worth of the monthly pension in Luxemburg and in the Netherlands in terms of the PPS and the ECU. Whereas the monetary value of the monthly payment in Luxemburg was 41 ECUs more than that in the Netherlands, the value of the pension in the Netherlands in terms of the PPS exceeded that of the Luxemburg monthly pension by a margin of 31 ECUs. The value of the pension in ECUs was higher in Italy than in France, but lower in terms of the PPS. It was higher in ECUs in the Republic of Ireland than in the UK, but it was lower in terms of PPS than in the UK. To

Table 3   Ranked pension expenditure as a percentage of GDP in 1975, 1983 and 1985, and yearly average during the decade 1975–85

	1975	1983	1985	Yearly average 1975–85
Norway	8.0	8.2	8.0[1]	7.4[2]
Sweden	7.3	11.6	11.2	10.3
Denmark	6.8	9.3	8.5	8.5
Finland	6.1	7.0	7.1[1]	7.0[2]
Republic of Ireland	4.8	5.4	5.4	4.6
UK	6.0	6.8	6.7	6.9
Netherlands	8.9	11.1	10.6	10.5
Belgium	10.5	n.a.	n.a.	11.5[3]
France	10.1	12.5	12.7	11.6
Luxemburg	8.5	9.8	n.a.	9.2
Switzerland	7.7	7.9	8.1	8.0
Austria	12.5	14.3	14.5	13.6
Germany	12.6	12.2	11.8	12.4
Greece	4.8	9.2	10.7	7.0
Italy	10.4	15.1	15.6	12.8
Spain	4.3	8.4	8.6[1]	6.1
Portugal	4.1	7.4	7.2	6.0
Czechoslovakia	7.8	10.8	n.a.	9.3
Hungary	6.8	10.1	n.a.	8.5
Poland	4.6[4]	7.0	n.a.	5.8
Bulgaria	7.2	8.6	n.a.	7.9

Notes:
[1](1984)
[2](1975–84)
[3](1975–82)
[4](1980)
Sources: ILO (1989) and OECD (1988c)

compare pensions within Europe is problematic because of these factors, especially when a particular country (such as Germany) suffers inflation, whilst another (such as the UK) experiences recovery.

Table 4 Gross and net replacement ratios for compulsory retirement pensions

	Gross annual amount of pension (ECUs)	Gross replacement ratio (%)	Net annual amount of pension (ECUs)	Net replacement ratio (%)
Luxemburg	13,238	67	11,301	78
Italy	12,320	78	10,605	89
Germany	11,432	53	10,698	77
France	9,876	69	9,415	88
Spain	9,590	90	8,650	97
Belgium	8,049	47	8,049	73
Denmark	7,801	34	7,545	60
Greece	7,473	98	6,978	107
Netherlands	6,275	33	5,982	49
UK	4,639	33	4,623	44
Republic of Ireland	4,219	29	4,044	42
Portugal	3,138	77	3,138	94

Note: Person with dependent spouse – full-contribution career workers in manufacturing industry with average wage
Sources: Based upon the European Commission's published reply to a parliamentary question put by Mr E. Newman (S-UK) (Written question No.792/92 OJ C16/5 26.5.89); see Eurolink-Age, 1990, p.16

Unfortunately, 'harmonization' within the EU does not extend to pensions. They remain disjointed, diverse, complex and discriminatory. The burden of payment also varies enormously between countries, as Parts I–V will demonstrate in some detail. Outside the EU the situation in greater Europe is even more disparate and confused. The largest share of contributions from public funds varies between 78% in Denmark and 14% in the Netherlands. Employers' contributions also vary significantly, from 53% in Italy to 11% in Denmark. Employees' contributions vary between 36% in the Netherlands and 4% in Denmark (see Eurostat, 1991a, p.81).

As stated already, income is clearly the single most important factor in the lives of older Europeans – for many of them, the pension and accompanying benefits are their major source of income. In spite of this, even in the more affluent countries – such as Belgium, the Netherlands and Italy – 20–25% of the older population are at least relatively poor, according to Fogarty's report (1986). More recent studies do not substantively alter Fogarty's major observations. For example, Walker (1992a, pp.177–8) states that in the majority of EU countries the poverty rate among older people remains above the average for the whole population. Efforts to reduce poverty amongst the older sectors of the population have been most successful in the Netherlands and least successful in Portugal. According to two recent reports of the EC Observatory on Ageing and Older People (see Walker et al., 1991 and 1993) income inequalities continue to widen amongst the EU's older population. This is especially true of those older pensioners who do not have the additional private pension arrangements of the younger pensioners, and who depend more on flat-rate state pensions. In addition, there are at least 26% more older women than men in the bottom income group (Walker, 1992a, p.178). If this is the case in the more affluent countries of the EU, how much greater are the levels of deprivation in the countries that lie beyond the pale in the former Eastern Bloc communist countries?

Since 1989 in the major former Eastern Bloc countries, incomes of older people have fallen substantially. Benefit adjustments do not exist, and pensions have not been protected against inflation (Laczko, 1994, p.25).

Minimum standards of living   Apart from ecological concerns and rundown housing, as a consequence of other diverse conditions of material deprivation many older people fall well below the minimum standards of living. However, before noting these, there are some positive factors: Fogarty (1986, pp.25–42), in his study of the needs of older Europeans in ten countries (Ireland, the UK, France, Belgium, Germany, Italy, Denmark, Luxemburg, the Netherlands and Greece), states that most older Europeans in these countries do not fall markedly below the minimum acceptable standard of living established within each country. One factor of deprivation, and an indicator which is not referred to in the social science literature, is 'information deprivation' (Giarchi, 1990c) – the lack of sufficient information concerning benefits and rights, and the poor quality of such information when it is available. Information is critical. No matter how creditable and appropriate the benefits and rights system of a country for its older citizens, the lack of information or its poor quality blocks access. Research in this domain is sorely needed. I make reference thoughout Parts I–V to the gross extent of 'information deprivation', particularly in rural areas.

Laczko (1994) describes the weakness of the economies in Hungary, Poland, Romania, Bulgaria and Russia when explaining the large numbers of older people living below the subsistence minimum. About half of pensioners in Hungary are below the subsistence minimum, for example. Most of the above countries have not introduced major pension reforms.

Poor health   Life expectancy and quality of life vary across Europe, principally in accordance with the degrees of pollution, housing conditions and levels of income relative to costs of living (see Table 5). Clearly the life expectancy at 65 is higher amongst women throughout Europe than it is amongst men. The margin in terms of life expectancy at birth and at 65 is greater in the Northern, Western and Central European countries than in the Eastern European countries. Also, the recent war in former Yugoslavia will result in a worsening of the quality of life and life expectancy for the Bosnians and Serbs.

Although less than 10% of persons over 65 in the EU countries are

Table 5   Life expectancy of women and men at 65 in the late 1980s and early 1990s

	Women	Men	Difference
France	19.8	15.4	4.4
Switzerland	19.5	15.3	4.2
Sweden	18.9	15.0	3.9
Netherlands	18.9	14.3	4.6
Iceland	18.9	15.6	3.3
Spain	18.8	15.4	3.4
Norway	18.5	14.4	4.1
Italy[1]	18.5	14.7	3.8
Belgium	18.2	14.0	4.2
Germany	18.0	14.2	3.8
Denmark	17.9	14.2	3.7
Portugal	17.8	14.5	3.3
Austria	17.7	14.5	3.2
UK	17.5	13.6	3.9
Finland	17.5	13.4	4.1
Luxemburg	17.2	13.1	4.1
Greece	16.9	14.5	2.4
Malta	16.8	13.7	3.1
Poland	16.2	12.5	3.7
Republic of Ireland	16.0	13.0	3.0
Former Yugoslavia	15.5	13.1	2.4
Hungary	15.4	12.2	3.2
Former Czechoslovakia	14.8	11.6	3.2
Bulgaria	14.6	12.7	1.9

Notes:
[1]Life expectancy at 60+ years
Life expectancy figures at 65 for Romania and Albania during this period were not available.
Sources: Eurostat (1991a); UN (1991)

reported as being in good health, evidence so far indicates that in Northern, Western and Central Europe there is less reported illness amongst the over-65s than in Eastern and Southern Europe (see Potter and Zill, 1992; Dumon, 1991; Nijkamp et al., 1991a). Most texts on the health of the older Europeans indicate that, although women live longer, they also have a disproportionate number of illnesses and more disabilities than the men who live until the age of 75 (see, for example, Wells and Freer, 1988; Jani-Le Bris, 1992). The majority of older people are not mentally ill, depressed or confused (Murphy, 1986). There are considerable differences between estimates of those suffering from dementia – in Europe it is reported as affecting up to 6.3% of the over-65s, rising to almost 18% in the over-80s (see Wells and Freer, 1988; WHO, 1982; Anderson, 1992).

In addition, the health of the older population appears to be improving outside the Eastern European countries, judging by the reports on the Republic of Ireland, Italy, the Netherlands, Belgium and France, as cited by the ILO (1989), Anderson (1992) and Jani-Le Bris (1992).

Social deprivation

In addition to material needs there are the social needs, which are inextricably intertwined. Isolation from other people and from formal as well as informal care are abiding realities for numerous older Europeans. Greengross (1988, p.2) has drawn attention to the multiple forms of isolation generally facing underprivileged older people in Europe. She points out that many older Europeans are isolated from:

1   their families due to greater mobility;
2   their neighbourhood within inward-looking households;
3   the younger generations, with their own networks;
4   social interaction, entertainment and leisure pursuits;
5   the provision of health and social services;
6   local forums for discussion.

Wall (1989) observes that throughout Europe the proportion of persons residing alone is greater amongst older women than older men. Men over 75 years of age are more likely to be living at home, where they are cared for by their wives or partners. A disproportionate number of European women aged over 75 are living alone, often suffering from multiple loss. Wall (1989, p.129) cites the proportion of females of more than 60 years of age who are living alone in West Germany (53%), the UK (45%), Sweden (44%), Finland (44%) and France (43%). In contrast, fewer older people live alone in Southern or Eastern Europe. There the family is a more significant support system, providing shelter and family care.

There are also the older rural population, facing isolation, cut off from public transport, social, welfare and health facilities (Giarchi, 1987a; 1990b). The need for a qualitative study of the rural in comparison with the urban has been well exemplified by Wenger (1984; 1986; 1989). The qualitative differences between the rural and the urban need to be taken into account when attempting to explore the standard of life facing older people. Older people are isolated from health and social services, from legal advice/information centres, from shops, banks and post offices, and are less likely to have a car. The more isolated they are, the more their property, their health and social life deteriorate, which is best described as the result of 'distance decay'. As will be clear when dealing with the older rural population in Parts I–V, younger people leave their ageing parents and relatives behind when seeking job opportunities in the cities.

The worst forms of social deprivation have to do with sexism, racism, ageism, and class discrimination, as well as discrimination against persons with disabilities. With regard to ageism, Wells and Freer (1988, p.211) explain:

> It is the beliefs and attitudes of other people which present more of a problem in the promotion of self-care. Many people believe that all older people are affected principally by the ageing process, and are therefore unable to change or learn or develop in any way.

This ageist attitude is pervasive in Europe, as has been made abundantly clear in de Beauvoir's (1970) commentary on old age in Europe. Guilt is also experienced concerning the neglect of older people, which is assuaged by cosseting and comforting them; once spoon-fed, people may 'turn off' and vegetate. Also, policies of providing work for younger workers but not for older ones in a society where it is judged that there cannot be 'full employment' is ageist (see Evers, 1988, p.21 for a fuller discussion). This is also backed by the ominous statement in current European discussions that 'full services' cannot be provided for older people. Access to jobs and to services is reduced by age barriers, creating modes of social exclusion. Ageism has also affected the older workers' self-worth – they are often conditioned to regard themselves as disposable. Age discrimination in the employment sector in Europe has not been tackled by Europeans. Only France has legislation with regard to age discrimination when advertising or selecting employees (Drury, 1993, p.60). The EC *Community Charter of the Fundamental Social Rights of Workers* (European Commission, 1989) simply deprecates 'every form of discrimination'. However, the European parliament has passed some notable resolutions against age discrimination:

1 'Employers should not discriminate against older workers in their

recruitment policies; it is undesirable to mention upper age limits in job advertising.'
2   'The Commission and other Community institutions should cease age discrimination in their own recruitment policies.' (European Commission, 1989)

An important precedent had already been established when a European Court judgment prevented women state employees in the UK from being forced to retire at 60. However, the EU itself maintains age discrimination practices: it sets a maximum age limit for posts within its own bureaucracy. In Spain, driving licences are withdrawn from people at 70. In Belgium, candidates for political election cannot stand for election after 65.

With regard to sex discrimination, there has been a great deal of interest amongst researchers on the topic (see Glasner, 1992) but little comparative material has been drawn together with regard to sexism affecting older women. Fogarty (1986) and the European Commission (1988) depict the continuing difficulties faced by European women generally. Only 26% of men and 27% of women aged 55 years of age and over were perceived to have equal roles. There was a negative correlation between age and equality: the older women became, the more they were discriminated against. Danish, UK and Spanish women had more equal roles in families than women in Luxemburg and West Germany. Twenty-nine per cent of European women did more housework than their male partner; of these the Irish and the Spanish women were more fortunate in having partners who shared more of the housework than their counterparts in other European countries.

More important than domestic roles in the family is the issue of equal pensions for men and women in Europe. The European Commission (1988, p.494) published a proposal for the equal treatment of men and women in statutory and occupational social security schemes: 'When a pensionable age is determined for the purpose of granting old age and retirement pensions it shall be identical for both sexes.' This was chiefly directed against Belgium, Greece, Italy, Portugal and the UK, where men have had a higher pension age than women. Later, the European Court of Justice (17 May 1990) declared that men and women must be treated equally with regard to occupational pension schemes (implemented on 1 January 1993). Equal treatment for many ethnic groups – especially older 'foreigners' – has been more difficult to legislate for in a Europe whose centre is attracting millions of migrants, and subsequently their families.

Rex (1992) reminds us on the basis of Eurostat (1990) statistics that there are 12,505,305 migrants in the EU, of whom 4,763,243 are EU migrants and 7,742,062 are non-EU migrants. Eurostat (1991a, p.18) indicates that, of the 'extra-EC foreigners', the two major ethnic groups amount to 28% from Africa and 24.4% from Turkey. Four-fifths of the extra-EC foreigners are living in three countries: 3.2 million in the former Federal Republic of Germany; 2.1 million in France, and 1 million in the UK.

The EU formulates its communications on ageing as if there were no non-white ethnic minorities in Europe. Europe is not only multi-cultural, it has also built up its wealth over the centuries on the backs of the mainly black slave trade. Today the exploitation of black and ethnic white minority groups continues, and they suffer from racial disadvantage at the hands of established white Europeans. Moreover, as Foot (1965) demonstrated years ago, the political parties see immigration as a problem only because of the latent racial prejudice which they harbour. The more recent history of greater Europe is one of nationalism and intra-state race conflicts. Little has been written about black older people (see Fenton, 1987). When the UK negotiated entry into the Common Market the major concern was whether it would be taking its black Commonwealth population with it into Europe (Haynes, 1983).

Contemporary Europe has not shaken off the racism that has dogged its sometimes shameful history – scarcely any country in greater Europe has a clean ethnic record. Racism is endemic within a continent with no less than 103 different 'tribes' (see Fernández-Armesto, 1994).

Disability is not an inevitable result of being older. Most older Europeans are not disabled (see CPA, 1993): for example, the fully able constitute 70% in Belgium and probably 73% in France, and in the UK approximately 80% of those aged 75+ are not severely disabled. Anderson (1992, pp.66–7) cites studies in the Netherlands, the former West Germany, Belgium, the Republic of Ireland, France and the UK which show that the majority of persons aged 75+ have no significant incapacity. Yet most European countries have health and social care departments which usually bear such titles as 'The Department for the Elderly and Physically Handicapped' or 'The Department for the Elderly and Disabled'. In my interviews with older Europeans in the UK, the Republic of Ireland, Germany and Italy, most complained about this practice of lumping older and disabled people together.

We know very little about class discrimination with regard to the older generations of Europe. In addition to material and social deprivation there is spiritual deprivation, which also affects many older Europeans.

Spiritual deprivation

Spiritual deprivation is associated chiefly with the negative and often anomic response to denial of basic rights, freedom of expression, self-fulfilment, self-determination, sexual relationships and religious freedom. The stripping of the self – as explained by Goffman (1961), for example – and psychological abuse are extreme forms of spiritual deprivation. They are an affront to the inner self and the dignity of the human being. These forms of deprivation are often associated with depression and stress, and may drive older people to suicide (Pritchard, 1992). In Parts I–V the suicide rates of the older population in Europe will be discussed where appropriate. Significantly, McLaughlin (1985) makes a distinction between 'deprived places' and 'deprived people'.

The welfare system of care and its administration within greater Europe

This section and the next could come under the heading of 'the mantle of care', which is the term used for care systems in both the Netherlands and Flanders. The quality and availability of services to older Europeans are dependent upon the nature of the delivery systems and the type of care shown. The underlying philosophy of care and welfare is crucial, as is the 'culture of care' in each country. Here I will attempt to give an overview of the ideology determining modes of care. The culture of care will be touched upon in the next section.

The salient ideal European welfare systems

This is not the place to discuss in depth the debate about welfare in Europe, past or present. However, it is necessary to identify three types of welfare which have operated within Europe, and catered for Europeans' socio-economic and health needs: 'market welfare'; 'state welfare', and the 'welfare society', with its emphasis upon the role of society within the process of caring.

The debate about welfare in terms of the opposition between individualism and collectivism has already been widely discussed by many writers for many years, such as George and Wilding (1976; 1984), Room (1979), Gamble (1979), Friedman (1978), Friedman and Friedman (1980), Taylor-Gooby and Dale (1981), Bosanquet (1983), Mishra (1984) and Taylor-Gooby (1985). On the one hand, Hayek (1944), the prophet of the New Right, argued for uncompromising individualism, in contrast to Schumpeter (1942), the prophet of the 'old left', who argued that a socialist collectivism was inevitable. The idea of 'a middle way' between these options was first put forward in Switzerland by Röpke (1943). He formulated his way about the same time as Hayek (1944) and Schumpeter (1942) discussed their notions of the way forward for social welfare in the West (see de Laubier, 1985). The terminology used here of a 'welfare society model' or community welfare society was not used by Röpke, but by those who regarded society as evolving towards a welfare model. It was seen to be moving away from welfare state provisions towards more and more collaboration and coalitions between the formal professional, voluntary and commercial providers of social and health services and the informal caring sectors of society (see Taylor-Gooby, 1985). This is in keeping with commentaries of Hadley and Hatch (1981) and Bayley (1973), who have all argued for citizen participation. Halsey (1981), and many others such as Webb and Wistow (1982), refer to the transition from a 'welfare state' to a 'welfare society' as a response to the crisis of welfare, rather than the crude response of a monetarist welfare system.

In contemporary Europe the choices between privatized and public welfare are opening up as services move increasingly towards more and more public/private welfare mixes for the older population, even amongst the Scandinavian countries. The mixes are usually represented by the 'triangle of care'. I wish to go further by identifying 'the process of the triangulation of welfare' within Europe, as I will now explain.

The formal triangle of welfare provision and care in Europe

The theorists provide us with models of the delivery of welfare or the process by which care and health needs are catered for. It is opportune to cite them here in the context of caring for older Europeans. The 'triangle of welfare' provides the basis of such a model and is referred to principally by Rose (1985), Gershuny (1986), Evers (1988), Attila (1989) and Svetlik (1992a).

These authors locate the principal sectors of care within a three-way system within which the state, the market and the family are each located at the three corners of the triangle of care/support. But 'the family' as such does not exist: there are only 'families', and they are situated at the micro level and are not of the same genre as state, market and civil society. The involvement and interventions of the state, the market and civil society in the 'life-world' of older Europeans create three spheres of influence. In the interactive process the socio-political pressures and means of central controls (the state), the economic forces (the market), together with the vagaries and flux of national, regional and local civil and religious ways of life (society), impact on older people's perceptions. These affect the government's legal, health and welfare structures, the nation's economic exchange systems and the ritual and roles people indulge in within both their public and private spheres of everyday living. (For the sociological implications see Giarchi, 1996.) A few comments here will suffice to explain the dynamics created by the interrelationship between the state, the market, civil and religious society and older Europeans within their households.

The various chapters in this book show in concrete terms what formal services are provided for older people within the triangle of care. As each part of the study states, this triangle constitutes a mantle of care, which conditions to a large extent the health, quality of life, social and therapeutic support and social lifestyle of Europe's older citizens. But, older people are in competition for resources with other groups in society, especially the younger populations. Older Europeans are generally unable to succeed (see Hugman, 1994). In the evolutionary process of life within Europe over the centuries, weaker people in society have not enjoyed either status or their just share of resources. De Beauvoir (1970), Minois (1987), Bytheway (1995) and Giarchi (1996) have shown how ageist Europe has been and is towards the older generations.

In spite of the lack of influence of older people, they are not wholly passive. The emergence of the 'Gray Panthers' in the USA and in Germany is indicative of the solidarity that is building up amongst older people. They, in turn, can alter and influence state intervention and the market. Giddens (1990) refers to the 'reflexivity' within society, which in simple terms means that changes are not independent of people's interaction and reaction to socio-economic forces and tradition. Within the monitoring of the nature of society and the reconstruction of life, civil movements may emerge to side with older people. Indeed, with the expansion of an older electorate, the socio-political influence of older people may shift the balance of care and the allocation of resources. However, as this book shows, there is not much evidence of major shifts in favour of older people. European taxpayers are unwilling to contribute towards the welfare of their older populations. An inter-generational conflict now exists (Therborn, 1995).

The three-way interaction of the mega forces upon older people has to be represented by the response of older people. We are witnessing a more concerned older electorate, which is largely defensive, as it battles with the onslaught of the New Right. The dynamics of the whole top-down/bottom-up process of European care between the state, the market, civil and religious society, and older people are represented within Figure 1. The dynamics are referred to as 'the triangulation of welfare'. This operates at three levels, as illustrated in Figure 2 and explained below. The outcome may well be one of 'strangulation', where welfare is cut off, and support denied to older generations because of ageist discrimination. The latter will be dealt with later in this chapter.

1   At the *macro level*, there are three major sources of provision and interaction:

- the central state;
- the market;
- civil and religious society.

2   At the *mezzo level*, there are three possible mediating modes of provision and interaction:

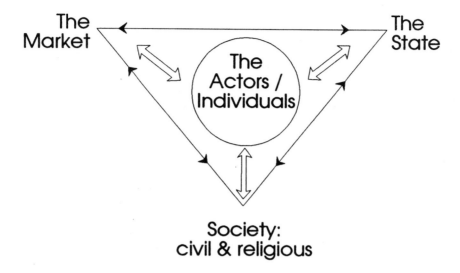

The
Market

The
State

The
Actors /
Individuals

Society:
civil & religious

Figure 1   The triangulation process of welfare
Source: based on Abrahamson, 1991, p.35

- the local state;
- private, commercialized, regional schemes;
- regional community associations; the diocese or regional religious centre; non-state organizations; regional voluntary headquarters.

3   At the *micro level,* there are at least three localized sources of possible provision and interaction:

- statutory social and health community services/offices;
- private caring agencies;
- voluntary caring organizations/bureaux; caring co-operatives; vocational (Church/religious sect) caring agencies/advocacy groups.

These distinct sources of provision provide the basis of a transnational comparative analysis of modes of care for older people at the centre of greater Europe, and the peripheral corners of any one country within it.

At the micro level, the statutory authorities, municipality or commune may simply be the extended centrist hand of government; or powerful, semi-autonomous local units; at the mezzo level may be federalist or centralist

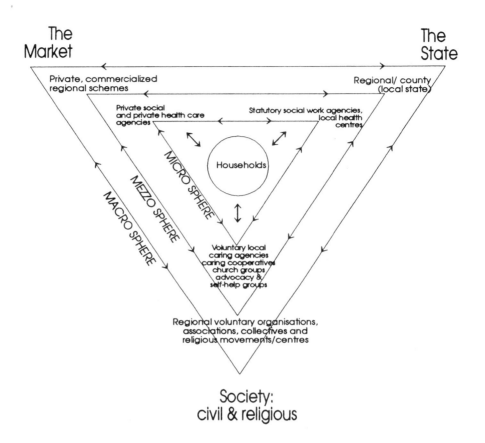

The
Market

The
State

Private, commercialized
regional schemes

Regional/ county
(local state)

Private social
and private health care
agencies

Statutory social work agencies,
local health
centres

Households

MICRO SPHERE

MEZZO SPHERE

MACRO SPHERE

Voluntary local
caring agencies
caring cooperatives
church groups
advocacy &
self-help groups

Regional voluntary organisations,
associations, collectives and
religious movements/centres

Society:
civil & religious

Figure 2   The triangulation process of welfare at three levels

bureaux – the former encourage and support subsidiary agencies locally, as
will be shown particularly in most of Central Europe and in many areas of
Southern Europe.

There is a 'nearer-to-home' triangulation (see Figure 2) between the local
state or municipality/commune statutory sector, the voluntary/Church
organizations and the private agencies. These are non-contiguous, but
respectively parallel the central state bureau, the civil society and the market.
As shown in Figure 2, these constitute an identifiable separate inner triangle
of infrastructural care with its variable, local triangulation process. These are
critical elements in the delivery of care for older people. Clearly, much will
depend upon the local culture of care and local politics. The system may be
synchronic or asynchronic (see below), depending upon the type of welfare

adopted by the state, the people and the market. The administrative systems in Europe are set within the triangle of welfare, and are affected by the interactions or blockages that may arise between them. However, overall is the mega state structure, which will ultimately determine the nature of care delivery and welfare at the macro, mezzo and micro levels.

The mega systems of welfare/care

There are four mega welfare structures which are discernible in Europe that require some explanation. These provide an overall context in which the macro-mezzo-micro modes of intervention dispense care and provide for older Europeans. Except for type (1), most countries do not fit the descriptions exactly. The types provide benchmarks along a welfare continuum against which the tendencies and policies of welfare affecting older people may be identified:

1　The *paternalistic*, which is epitomized by the totalitarian Leninist welfare systems, chiefly affecting the Eastern European countries dealt with in Part IV.
2　The *synchronic*, whereby the state operates as co-ordinator, facilitating the intervention of the other welfare sectors (Svetlik, 1992a, pp.214–15). Here the state plays a leading role as orchestrator in mixed economies of welfare and care, as, for example, most of the time in most of the countries described in Parts I and II.
3　The *asynchronic*, which operates when the welfare agencies and the state function in partnership, adopting a 'self-co-ordinated welfare pluralism' (Svetlik, 1992a, p.215). These create a 'citizen's culture', whereby the electorate have rights as 'users' backed by a communitarian philosophy. Examples of this model exist chiefly in the areas covered by Part III – Switzerland and in many of the western German *Länder* – and in some countries described in Part V, such as Italy and Spain, where co-operatives of care exist.
4　The *anarchic*, where the market takes over in a *laissez-faire* welfare system, which is money-led and adopts a 'customer culture'. Countries such as Luxemburg and the UK are shifting in this direction, as are some CIS countries, which are careering headlong from the paternalistic, totalitarian welfare system at one end of the continuum to the other extreme of a 'market welfare model'.

Social services in the UK and some academics use the terms 'customer culture' and 'user culture' interchangeably. As can be deduced from (3) and (4) above, they are distinctly different, because customers' rights are based upon a market exchange model, whereas the rights of users of services (whether the older people pay in part or not) are based upon a citizenship model.

The mega systems are either centralized or decentralized, which is of immense importance in deciding how care is delivered in greater Europe. The systems are either monocephalic or polycephalic (see Table 6), as suggested by Lipset and Rokkan (1967) and Rokkan and Urwin (1983). The monocephalic structure means that the decision-makers and resource-holders are located centrally within unitary and more mechanistic bureaucratic systems, whereas the polycephalic structure means that deci-sion-making is pluralist, dispersed and closer to the people within more organic systems at the infrastructural levels (for examples see Julliard and Noin, 1976; Rokkan and Urwin, 1983). As shown in Table 6, most of Europe is in a state of flux, creating uncertainties for millions of older people.

Eastern European countries are in the initial stages of political and socio-economic changes. The former East Germany is moving laboriously from its centralized communist regime to the polycephalic structure of the former West Germany within the reunification process. In the territories of the former Yugoslavia, uncertainties and the trauma of war, multiple losses and ethnic strife will make it difficult to assess the quality of care for older people for some time to come. In crises the monocephalic structure takes over.

Local authorities and the shift to community care systems

Batley and Stoker (1993) provide data regarding the number and population size of basic European authorities. It would appear that the more northerly countries generally have smaller numbers of authorities with a larger popu-lation, and the more southerly countries a larger number with smaller popu-lations. However, the latter have provided less services for older people, whilst the former have provided more formal services. Because of the dismantling of the welfare state, these are now badly under-resourced, with the possible exception of Denmark. European welfare and health care services are in financial crisis, so that care is largely money-led rather than needs-led. At the very time when the care systems are stretched, older people are also in dire financial straits, caught – as are the services – in the grip of a long-term recession. Alongside the increase in their numbers is their increased poverty: they are the new poor.

As part of the rationalization of social and health care, in the face of increasing costs, most of the governments of Europe are in the process of de-institutionalizing the care of older people and concentrating on supporting them within the community instead. As Parts I–V will show, most of Europe has been providing community care for over a decade.

In this introduction, it is opportune to note the view of some commenta-tors that 'community care' policy is a shambles and that 'community' is a

Table 6   The monocephalic and polycephalic European administrative systems

Parts of Europe	Monocephalic	In flux or Transitional	Polycephalic
1 Northern			
	Iceland Denmark	Norway→ ←Sweden→	Finland
2 Western			
	UK Republic of Ireland	←France→ ←Luxemburg→ Netherlands→	Belgium
3 Central			
		East Germany→	West Germany Austria Switzerland
4 Eastern			
		←Russian Federation[1]→ ←Bulgaria→ ←Romania→ Poland→ Czech Republic→ ←Slovak Republic Hungary→ ←Belorussia→ ←Estonia→ ←Latvia→ ←Lithuania→ ←Ukraine→ ←Moldavia→	
5 Southern			
	Turkey	Portugal→ ←Malta→ ←Cyprus ←Slovenia→ ←Bosnia→ ←Serbia→ Macedonia→	Spain Italy Greece *continued*

Table 6   The monocephalic and polycephalic European administrative systems – *continued*

5 Southern		
continued		Montenegro→
	Albania	

Note:
[1]Up to the Urals
Key: regarding countries in transition:
←towards centralization
→towards decentralization/multiple centres
← →uncertainty as to which direction systems are going
Source: partly based on Lipset and Rokkan (1967); Rokkan and Urwin (1983)

vacuous term (see Bulmer, 1987b, p.214). These criticisms are echoes of the old Stacey (1969) debate of the 1960s, when 'community' was regarded as a myth. Without taking up the debate, suffice it to make one point very clear at the outset: when I refer to 'community care' in the course of dealing with the care of older people in the various countries of Europe, I understand it to mean what the UK White Paper *Caring for People* (Department of Health, 1989, p.9) expressly referred to, in response to the question 'What is community care?' The statement is worth quoting in full:

> Community care means providing the right level of intervention and support to enable people to achieve maximum independence and control over their own lives. For this aim to become a reality, the development of a wide range of services provided in a variety of settings is essential. These services form part of a spectrum of care, ranging from domiciliary support provided to people in their own homes, strengthened by the availability of respite care and day care for those with more intensive care needs, through sheltered housing, group homes and hostels where increasing levels of care are available, to residential care and nursing homes and long-stay hospital care for those for whom other forms of care are no longer enough.

Some of the doubters go so far as to pose the question 'Community care or home care?' As is clear from the above statement, community care is a great deal more than home care in the UK policy statement, as it is with almost all European practitioners.

Some countries refer to 'open systems' of care or 'extra-mural care', as shall be shown when I review the many European systems of care. Upon examination, their policies concur substantively with the notion of community care as expressed in the UK White Paper (Department of Health, 1989). Collaboration between statutory and voluntary agencies, professionals, carers and users of the service is the centrepiece of most efforts to provide optimal services for older people in many European countries. The concept of 'community' survives in spite of 'community bashing'. At this introductory level, it is profitable to draw attention by way of example to the German word *Gemeinwesen*, which the Germans and Austrians understand as the 'gestalt of a local community' (Muller, 1993). The *Gemeinschaft* of Tönnies (1955) has been replaced, not because the Germans reject the notion of 'community', but because the Nazis had misused the term, so the more ancient term *Gemeinwesen* has been resurrected by them.

The role of the European Churches and religious agencies will be considered in the overview of community care of older people. As Parts I–V will demonstrate, the Church organizations continue to play a significant role in providing care for older Europeans. Hence the need for the next section.

Voluntarism and vocationalism

Side by side with the *voluntarism* of the largely Protestant nations of Northern Europe is the *vocationalism* of the largely Catholic nations of Southern Europe. The dominance in these Southern countries of the Catholic community action principle of 'subsidiarity' (which will be expanded later in this study) clearly demonstrates that salient qualitative differences regarding the culture of care exist in general between the South and the North. For hundreds of years prior to the Reformation, the monastic monasteries had provided care as an answer to the 'call' of Christ (described as 'vocation'), but only when the family network could not cope. Many of Europe's largest hospitals and clinics are still running under the aegis of the Church – in Malta, Ireland, Belgium, Luxemburg, the Netherlands, Austria, France, the former West Germany, Poland and the Mediterranean countries.

Vocationalism was shared not only by the religious orders, but also by parish-based lay workers. Many Protestant agencies were also to be motivated by vocationalism, which was to be integrated into their mission statement, especially in Germany. Although the Protestant denominations did have their lay workers – and their social workers continue to be significant today, as the Salvation Army or the Children's Society in the UK, or the Evangelical social service centres in Germany – the notion of 'vocationalism' has not generally been used as a category distinct from 'voluntarism' in the countries of the North. However, Southern European scholars distinguish between professionalism, voluntarism and vocationalism. It is of interest that the term 'vocational organisation' was used by Beatrice and Sydney Webb in 1917, when writing their study *Vocational Organisation in Great Britain* (see Kennedy, 1981, p.191). The importance of the distinction will become more apparent later. Jones (1985), Rodgers et al. (1968) and others describe such organizations as 'confessional', in that they are perceived as essentially founded upon religious belief.

Rokkan and Urwin (1983, pp.130–1) group the mainly Protestant countries of the North and the mainly Catholic countries of the South along a North–South axis. The socio-religious and administrative structures may also be grouped along a West–East axis. Western Christian beliefs contrast with the Orthodox religions and more Muslim groups, as one travels across the Continent in a south-easterly direction.

The more monocephalic Protestant nations of Northern Europe, especially the Scandinavian countries, have formulated social policies and adopted welfare systems which have not included family policies related to community care. This contrasts with family policy in Central Europe, as epitomized most in Germany, and the care systems in which families in Southern Europe play a central role. But 'for how long?' is the ever-recurring question in country after country, as Parts I–V indicate.

At this stage, it is opportune to refer to and explain the European principle of 'subsidiarity'. This welfare notion of the 1930s was described at the time of the formulation of the *EC Social Charter* as the EU 'buzzword'. Jacques Delors, the then Commission President, when faced with the criticism that the EU was becoming too centralized, instructed Commission officials not to propose procedures without taking account of the principle of subsidiarity.

The principle of subsidiarity has a central place in caring systems in Central and Southern Europe, and is progressively being adopted elsewhere. As shall be shown, it is highly relevant to the various caring systems for older people, both secular and religious. Subsidiarity is at the centre of poly-cephalic welfare systems such as in Italy, Switzerland, Austria, Germany and Spain. It means fundamentally that the response to need should first be made within the immediate world of the clients: at first, with family or relatives. Failing these, they are next expected to call upon informal helpers, either neighbours or friends. Should they not be able to provide support, assistance should be sought from the voluntary Church or lay organizations. In the event of these agencies or organizations not being able to help, the next step is to approach the welfare organizations and the statutory personal social services. The state is the last port of call.

Informal care in Europe, or 'the crazy quilt of care'

Informal care for older Europeans is principally provided by the family throughout Europe, as will be demonstrated in Parts I–V. Balbo (1982) describes informal care – because it is largely domestic and carried out by women – as 'the crazy quilt of care'. All too often that quilt is turned so easily into 'guilt', as women are constrained to care by an oppressive sense of familial obligation in a patriarchic European society. In all countries except Denmark, the governments are advocating a return to family care. The

European household increasingly, in a very real sense, constitutes an alternative 'household welfare' ('the informal household production' of care, see Gershuny, 1986). The care provided for older people by the family remains a central EU pillar of informal care, supplemented by the states' travel subsidies, housing benefits, 'closer-to-home' schemes and cheaper housing arrangements. Informal care is determined to a large extent by the localized cultures of care (Evers and Wintersberger, 1988b), and by Todd's (1985) five European family types, set out below (see also Figure 3).

The traditional European family types

1 *The exogamous community family:* This consists of various family households living together. The older people are less isolated and enjoy the status of elders. Here there is a collective sense of responsibility. This type of family traditionally exists in the Eastern European countries of the former USSR, Finland, Hungary, Bulgaria, Albania and the former Yugoslavia. It also exists in the Southern European countries of central Italy, parts of central and southern France and southern Portugal.

2 *The authoritarian family:* This consists of hierarchical families headed by the male. The first son inherits and occupies his parents' house. He has the prime responsibility to care for them. This type of family traditionally exists in the Northern European countries of Norway, Iceland and Sweden; in the Central European countries of Germany, Switzerland and Austria; in the Western European countries of Scotland and Ireland, Belgium and parts of eastern and southern France, and in the Southern European countries of Turkey and northern Spain.

3 *The egalitarian nuclear family:* This type of family has a matriarchical bias, but is counterbalanced by male chauvinism, which is a characteristic in many Latin regions. Older men have more freedom than older women. This type of family traditionally exists in the Eastern European countries of Romania and Poland; in the Western European countries, such as in most of France, parts of Western Germany, and in regions lying along the Belgian and French borders, and in the Southern European countries of Greece, Corsica, Sardinia, Crete, Malta, and in parts of Portugal and northern and southern Italy.

4 *The absolute nuclear family:* This type of family offers older people greater autonomy and life apart from their dependents. The older women have more freedom. This type of family traditionally exists in the Western European countries of the Netherlands, Denmark, England, Wales and in parts of the north-west of France.

5 *The endogamous community family:* This type of family is essentially Islamic, originating in North Africa, the Middle East and Turkey. The male dominates a polygamous plural household that is extended and

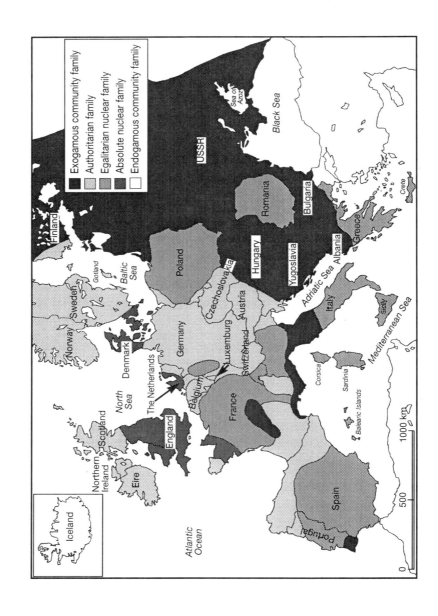

Figure 3 The families of Europe

Source: adapted from Todd, 1985

Legend:
- Exogamous community family
- Authoritarian family
- Egalitarian nuclear family
- Absolute nuclear family
- Endogamous community family

strives to be independent, finding its strength from within its multiple relationships and the support of nurturing women. Here the older males are held in high regard, whereas the older women have servile roles.

These types have been affected by the advent of modernity. To what extent and in what ways they have affected informal care has yet to be adequately researched. Parts I–V will provide some insight into the contemporary family scene in terms of the informal family caring arrangements for older Europeans.

The informal care of older people

There are two main domains of informal care which are critical factors in the support provided for older Europeans: firstly, individual informal care, and secondly, informal 'circles of care'.

Individual informal care   According to Atkin (1992, p.30), informal carers are of six types: spouse carers, parental carers, filial carers, sibling carers, child carers and non-kin carers. In contrast to those who are within 'the community care industry', these carers are the unwaged helpers of millions of Europeans. Most carers of the older population are women: at least two-thirds of them. Theirs is truly 'the crazy quilt of care'. In the UK a third of the carers are men, as cited by Arber and Gilbert (1989b, p.80). The greater burden falls upon women in most of Europe. Glasner (1992, p.79) reminds the social gerontologist that six out of ten Europeans still do not accept the equality of husbands' and wives' roles.

The wives and mothers carry the greatest burdens of household and familial care (Ungerson, 1990). Ironically, those relatively few men who do care for older people (at least in the UK) are better supported and given more respite than their women counterparts (Parker, 1992). The demands of caring for the older spouse rob thousands of European wives of sleep and leisure. As is clear from many studies, wives in the UK and Denmark have the least negative attitudes towards women's roles, whereas wives in Luxemburg and Germany have more negative attitudes towards their roles, which reflects Todd's (1985) more egalitarian traditional family systems of England and Wales, and the more authoritarian traditional systems in Germany, Luxemburg, Scotland and Ireland. The older parent carers of adult disabled offspring carry a great burden also, often lasting a lifetime, which follows them into their own years of frailty. The filial carers, usually daughters, have to carry the greatest burdens in caring for their old parents, especially when the carers stay with their parents. They often have to balance caring for a parent against other family duties. The sibling carers usually exist in societies where there is a higher percentage of unmarried people. The non-kin carers are the friends and neighbours, described by some, such as Griffiths (1988) in the UK, as the 'bedrock of care'.

Willmott (1986, p.105), on the basis of previous research in the UK, has identified four major provisions of individual home care:

1   *Personal care:* This is the more intimate form of care. It is often described as 'tending' (after Parker, 1980). It usually consists of toileting, washing, bathing, lifting, feeding, and assisting the incontinent and those who have difficulties because of soiling.
2   *Domestic care:* This consists of cooking, laundering clothes, house-cleaning and ironing.
3   *Auxiliary care:* This consists of practical help, such as escorting persons with mobility difficulties, shopping, collecting prescriptions and doing odd jobs in the house or garden.
4   *Social support:* This consists of sitting, listening to music together, chatting and sharing meals or table games.

These modes of household care are identifiable within the various countries described in Parts I–V.

Informal circles of care   It is customary for the social gerontologist to refer to informal carers as constituting supportive 'networks'. However, the collective support in communities may also be described as family, friend-ship or neighbourhood supportive 'circles'. I prefer to confine 'networks' to formal support and to speak of 'circles' when referring to informal support arrangements. This is not the place to enter into the sociological and psycho-logical reasons for the usage of the term 'circle', which was first used by Simmel (1908). 'Networks' suggests formalized and organized ties, as the term does in technology and electronic communications. Because informal ties are quite different, it is preferable that they are not described as 'networks'.

Needs, household composition and arrangements

In spite of these limitations, on the basis of the most recent available statistics and studies, it appears that older women within Europe as a whole are usually in greater need than older men. Firstly, they live longer, so married women are more likely to be widowed at a younger age. Secondly, there are two common features of the older population in Europe as a result of these factors:

1   Older men are more likely to live at home, and are less likely to live alone.
2   Older women are more likely to be in care, and those who are at home are likely to be alone.

Having provided the basic European statistics, Wall (1989) adds that there is a recent trend towards smaller, less complex households in Europe as a whole (p.135). This comment is of considerable importance to the future welfare policies for older European families/kinship groups living in households.

Apart from these common features, there are significant differences between the older populations in Northern, Western and Central European countries and those of the Southern and Eastern European countries. Firstly, in Northern, Western and Central Europe, more older couples are likely to be on their own, especially in Germany, where virtually half the older population live alone (see Potter and Zill, 1992, p.119). The women are more likely to be in homes for the aged and other institutions, and to be widowed at a younger age. Moreover, in Southern and Eastern Europe, women and men are less likely to be on their own, and both women and men are less likely to be in institutions. As cited by Potter and Zill (1992, p.121), the largest proportions of older people living in extended households are in the Southern European countries. The countries with the most older people in extended households in rank order are Portugal, Italy, Greece, the Republic of Ireland and Spain, with France following close behind.

Conclusion

Taking account of the social cleavages and the related macro-mezzo-micro factors outlined above enables the social gerontologist to recognize the major European divergencies. Against this backdrop, the survey of the care of older Europeans presented in Parts I–V will be set out under the following headings in each chapter:

- Demography
- Socio-political and administrative background
- Social security: pensions and benefits
- Housing
- Health care
- Mental health care
- Institutional care
- Personal social services
- Voluntary care agencies and support organizations
- Informal care
- Leisure pursuits and education
- Rural aspects
- Conclusion

Part I

Northern Europe

The five Northern European states of Iceland, Finland, Norway, Sweden and Denmark have been tied together by geography, similar language, culture and religion for hundreds of years. In the post-war years, the major Scandinavian nations have adopted very similar state-driven welfare and health care policies for older people.

In more recent years, Iceland, Sweden, Finland and Norway have moved towards a greater balance between the state, the market and civil society. However, Denmark continues to maintain a welfare state but even here there are signs of a gradual shift towards a welfare mix for older Europeans.

1   Iceland

Demography

Although only 10.5% of people in Iceland are aged over 65, by the year 2025 it is estimated that the proportion of older people will increase by about 6.5% (see CPA, 1989, p.75). This will be one of the largest increases in Europe. The life expectancy at birth of Icelandic men (74.6 years) is the highest in Europe, and that of Icelandic women (79.7 years) is the fourth-highest (Eurostat, 1991a; UN, 1986 and 1991). At 65, Icelandic men can expect to live another 15.6 years and Icelandic women another 18.9 years.

Socio-political and administrative background

This island nation has lagged behind the other Scandinavian countries, partly because of its geographic isolation and partly because its island economy and smallness have tended to establish a welfare society system, rather than a welfare state system. The dominant social norms stem from the Scandinavian Evangelical Lutheran values of stewardship and ministry to the needy encapsulated in the sixteenth-century writings of Guðbrandur Thorláksson, an influential Icelandic bishop who served his flocks for 56 years. His school catechism was of importance in providing an island value system in which the Protestant ethic engendered a more personal moral imperative of individual acts of charity rather than collective social responsibility. Although the majority of people do not belong to a Church, the traditional Icelandic values endure, especially that of self-reliance, which has had considerable influence in shaping Icelandic policies *vis-à-vis* the lives of older people.

41

The legislature and running of the affairs of older people resides with the 60-member parliament (the Althing), who are in office for four years. Its six-plus cabinet and Prime Minister must have majority support in parliament.

The Icelandic Independence Party usually dominates parliamentary proceedings. It is centre-right, which reflects the less socialist welfare policies that have shaped the lives of older people in Iceland, and mirrors the rural conservatism of the island. The value of personal, individual, religious experience conserved by the Icelandic Evangelical Lutheran Church and the impact of pietism have helped to maintain Iceland's centre-right political responses to social and welfare issues.

The administration of the island is centred upon Reykjavik. Side by side with the welfare services are the Church 'provostries', which are subdivided into parishes. These form the local administrative bases for the delivery of health and social care on the island. Under parliamentary rule are the *kaupstadhir*, which run the administration and consist of 14 independent towns, and the *syslur*, which consists of 23 counties. The counties are divided into the 215 rural communes (the *hreppar*). Elected councils administer the affairs of the people at county, town and district levels. Local government decides upon the social and health needs of the older people.

The OECD's economic survey of Iceland (1988b) indicates that from 1980–6 the highest expenditure by the government has been on health (20.5% in 1986), then economic affairs (19.5%), then social security and welfare (16.7%). Health expenditure has been about four times that of housing and community planning (4.7%).

For most Europeans, Iceland is out of sight and out of mind, being the most peripheral of the European countries – indeed, in many atlases Iceland does not appear in Europe at all. Iceland's island welfare system leans towards the welfare state systems of the other countries within the Scandinavian North, but is less progressive and universalist than its Scandinavian counterparts. Health insurance is compulsory, and the government is generous in its quota spent on health, which is approximately 43% of GDP. However, Iceland lags behind the more egalitarian and better-resourced welfare systems of Norway, Sweden and Denmark. Iceland's social security spending as a percentage of GDP is less than in all the EU countries except Spain and Portugal (see OECD, 1988b, p.51; Eurostat, 1991b, p.82).

Social security: pensions and benefits

The Centre for Policy on Ageing (CPA, 1989, p.75) describes the Icelandic social security pensions system as 'most comprehensive'. The pension is made up of the contributions of the government and the employer. Only three years' residence is required for the minimum pension, and it is paid at 67. As in other systems, the full pension requires 40 years' residence. After 25 years, fishermen and other seamen receive their pensions at 60. Each spouse receives 90% of the single person's pension. Older people may defer their pension for five years. This arrangement encourages active older people to continue in employment, because they receive an annual increment over those years. This generous scheme also allows for an adjustment each quarter in accordance with the wages index.

Housing

According to the CPA (1989, p.75), under 3% of older people live in sheltered accommodation and 89.4% live in ordinary accommodation. Rent subsidies and improvement loans have helped to maintain a high standard of housing. Over half of the existing housing stock has been built since World War II. In common with other Scandinavian countries, the policy is to maintain the highest standard of shelter and comfort in the cold and often severe climatic conditions. Fifteen per cent of the people do not live in towns or villages. About 80% of houses are owner-occupied (see Kristinsson and Matthiasson, 1979, pp.170–5). Self-reliance is a feature in a country where people have always had to survive the long winter months on their own against the polar elements, hence the government's emphasis upon high-quality housing.

Health care

Iceland has probably the highest standard of public health in the world (Kristinsson and Matthiasson, 1979, p.174). Icelandic people's life expectation at 65 years is particularly high and one of the highest in the world (Eurostat, 1991a; UN, 1991). Perhaps the clean environment combined with the very high standard of living make it a very healthy haven for its older people. At 60, life expectancy is approximately 19 years for men and for women approximately 23 years (CPA, 1989, p.75) – only Swiss women at 60 come near the longevity of Icelandic women. Comparing the Icelandic life expectancies with those of the latest EU Eurostat statistics (1990; 1991a; 1991b) reveals the very wide gap between Icelandic life spans and those in the most prosperous EU countries.

Communications are vital if the users are to have access to the health services. The local radio stations provide health education programmes and communicate with the older population during the severe winters. There are nine major broadcasting stations. Obviously, the telephone network is also of vital importance in emergency situations. As far back as 1974, there was approximately one telephone to every three persons. At least one in every five households has a television. These means of communication have made an enormous difference to the lives of the older population, who suffered a great deal in the past from isolation during the family's working day (*Encyclopaedia Britannica*, 1979, Micropaedia, Vol.V, p.278).

Hospital care and medical services

The ratio of doctors to patients is 1:689, which is approximately the same as that of Luxemburg. The ratio of hospital beds to patients is also one of the highest in Europe, 1 per 68 persons – about three times that of the highest ratio in the rest of Europe (Luxemburg) and almost five times that of the lowest (Portugal). Hospital services are free of charge, and other medical services are provided at a very low cost.

Nursing

The nursing outreach services nowadays have fewer difficulties in reaching the older population in the remoter parts. The hazards of travel have progressively diminished because of improved roads and better transport. Most of the older population are within easy reach of the health and social services in their capital. There are no railways, but the bus services are excellent.

Mental health care

The mental health of older people is catered for within psychiatric nursing homes.

Institutional care

In common with the other Northern European countries, the proportion of persons in residential and nursing homes is higher than in European countries as a whole, standing at approximately 9% (Anttonen, 1991, p.79). Almost all of these institutions are provided by the municipality. About 2% live in purpose-built pensioners' flats and in sheltered housing (CPA, 1989, p.75). These are comparable to mainland establishments in Western and Northern Europe in terms of their management and facilities.

Personal social services

Personal social services have existed in Iceland since 1957 (Jònsdòttir, 1986, p.279).

Social workers

In 1970, there were only ten social workers in Iceland; today there are over a hundred. Private social workers existed in Iceland long before most other countries in Europe privatized their social and health services. Most social workers are engaged in preventative work. A large proportion are employed as therapeutic clinicians. Most of the older population hardly ever come into contact with social workers.

Services

There is no information available regarding day care, state-provided meals-on-wheels, or practice innovations for older people.

Voluntary care agencies and support organizations

Voluntary agencies do more for older Icelanders than do the state social services. Parishes of the National Church of Iceland centred upon Reykjavik provide care for older people. Meals-on-wheels and assistance with transport are sometimes provided by parish groups. The major lay agency is the Icelandic Organization for the Care of the Aged (Oldrunarrao Islands). Established in 1981, it is an umbrella group of 43 member organizations, and also serves as an advisory body to the Icelandic Board of Health and Social Security.

Informal care

The social science literature upon the familial and kinship care of older people in Iceland is almost non-existent. The CPA (1989, p.75) indicates that there is not much difference demographically between the island of Malta in the warm Mediterranean and the island of Iceland in the cold North Atlantic Ocean. However, the life expectancies at birth of males (approximately 74 years) and of females (approximately 80 years) in Iceland are higher than that of males (approximately 73 years) and females (approximately 78 years) in Malta. There is no means of assessing why this is so, and no data are available on the extent and nature of caring arrangements at home.

Leisure pursuits and education

At present very little has been published regarding the leisure pursuits and educational opportunities available to older Icelandic people. The national folk traditions of the saga writers and the rich Viking folklore, together with the rich heritage in storytelling, are conserved by the older Icelanders, while swimming in the naturally heated pools and their interest in fishing offer the more active older people outdoor seasonal pursuits.

Rural aspects

Although over 80% of the population lives in urban areas, most of Iceland is rural, but studies of families within the sparsely populated remoter parts of the country are not available.

Conclusion

The literature on the subject of care of older people in this country with just over 0.25 million inhabitants is scant. The geographic isolation of Iceland, much at the mercy not only of the cruel elements but, historically, of invaders, may also help to explain the lag in major social developments. It was pillaged and subjugated by outsiders, especially at the hands of the larger Scandinavian countries, Norway and Denmark. Also, European movements and ideas have been slow to be imported to Iceland – for example, it took Christianity hundreds of years to reach Iceland in the tenth century, the nation only officially became Christian as late as AD 1000, and it took half a century before a bishopric was created in 1056.

The Scandinavian welfare state has not taken hold in Iceland, as it has in its sister countries, perhaps because of the remoteness and isolationism mentioned above, although shared Scandinavian values remain a strong link. Life has been harsh for the older population in the past, but the advent of modern communication systems and facilities have boosted the quality of their life considerably. Links with the other Scandinavian countries have also been formative in assisting the Icelanders to establish supportive social care and effective health systems based upon sound welfare values, although these have been muted by Iceland's more conservative value system. The triangle of care would appear to be well balanced between the central state and local state systems in an island community where large sums of money are invested by the state in health at local levels. None the less, the administration tends to be monocephalic (see Table 6). Not much is known about the extent and nature of the voluntary care systems, nor of the informal circles of care and neighbourhood support. However, enough has been stated to indicate how important it is to establish European research links with the Icelandic Gerontological Society (Oldrunarfraedafelags Island) in Reykjavik. Contact would help to identify the support systems and general conditions, which may help to explain the higher life expectancy in Iceland in contrast with that of other more affluent European countries with so-called 'progressive' social and health care systems.

2 Finland

Demography

According to the data presented in Table 1, Finland ranks fifteenth amongst
the greater European nations in terms of proportions of older people. It will
also have an increase of 7.8% in the older population by the year 2025, on the
basis of the projections. The life expectancy at 65 for women (17.5 years)
ranks fourteenth, and that for men (13.4 years) ranks seventeenth out of the
24 major European countries (see Eurostat, 1991a; UN, 1986 and 1991).

Socio-political and administrative background

The first priority of the Finnish state since the 1960s has been to establish a
redistribution of wealth. Alestalo and Uusitalo (1986, pp.199–205) describe
the adoption of the German principle of *Sozialpolitik* from 1874 – in effect the
belief that the pivotal function of social policy is to lessen class conflict. After
World War II the Communist Party was legalized. An extensive entente with
the USSR created and fostered closer market links. However, there was a
great deal of ambivalence towards a Soviet state that had threatened
Finland's nationhood. At the same time, the strong cultural links with
Sweden have engendered a sharing of ideas regarding welfare. However, a
four-way conflict between the Communist Party, the Agrarian Party, the
Social Democrats and the Conservatives has tended to halt the progress of
the welfare state, so that the development of social policy in Finland lagged
behind that of its Scandinavian neighbours. At first, the Communist Party
along with the Social Democrats and the Agrarian Party created a left-of-
centre government which set out to 'provide maximum social security for

49

every citizen'. By the 1950s the hard edge of the Marxist model was softened by the adoption of a Beveridge type of welfare (see page 129). It took until the late 1970s before Finland's social security system was established and universal coverage created.

Legislative powers reside with the parliament (the Eduskunta), consisting of 200 members who are elected for four years. Executive powers are shared by the President and Council of State. The President is elected for six years, providing continuity, and can dissolve parliament. Policy regarding older people has been decided mainly by coalitions made up of eight parties, but with a strong representation by the left-of-centre.

For reasons explained earlier, social welfare developed relatively late in Finland, compared to the earlier developments and subsequent progress in other Northern, Western and Central European countries. None the less, the development of welfare arrangements has increased considerably since the mid-1960s (see Alestalo and Uusitalo, 1986; Satka et al., 1986, p.115). Social expenditure as a proportion of GDP is around 25%: higher than that of Portugal, Spain, the Republic of Ireland, Italy and the UK (see Eurostat, 1991b, p.82). In addition, unlike other European economies, there has not been a significant cutback in health and social care resources. In fact, as the recession has bitten deeper, the state has supported the more vulnerable groups even more. The popular support for welfare has coincided with the political conviction that the country has suffered more acutely when welfare needs have been disregarded. Serious decreases in welfare and health care have also created more serious problems in the medium and long term.

At the largest European conference on the family ever staged in Europe, held in Malta in 1989, Taja Halonen (1990), the then Minister of Social Affairs and Health in Finland, made a statement about the new partnership between the public and private sectors in the care of older people. In spite of her assurances that there would be an integration or mix of provision which would not create a two-tier system of care, the fact was that there were two systems pulling in two directions – the 'home care private market' was attracting those who could pay, and the queues were getting longer at the public clinics. The 54% of women employed in the public sector were concerned that a money-led system was causing injustices. 'Joint responsibility' of the state and the market required harmonization, but the situation was one in which social injustice was all too apparent, when choice carried a price tag. The welfare state backed by a multi-party system was facing the need to secure fairer arrangements for older people and for other vulnerable groups in Finland (Anttonen, 1991, p.68).

The Social Welfare Act 1984 ensures 'income security' for all older people. Welfare adminstration is provided at three levels: central, regional and local. At central level, the state's administration consists of the Ministry of Social

Affairs and Health and the National Board of Social Welfare. At middle level, the Department of Social Affairs and Health operates through the Provincial Boards within each of the twelve provinces (*laanit*). Each *laanit* is under a governor (the *maaherra*). Health and social care are provided by the munici- palities, but under the regional administration. The municipalities some- times only number some 500 inhabitants, so that the smaller ones form federations – 461 municipalities implement policies within 77 federations (see Brauns and Kramer, 1986, p.117). The system is polycephalic. The provi- sion of care has been more effectively secured within a decentralized local system with services closer to the households of the older population.

Social security: pensions and benefits

It is obvious that an adequate income is a prime requirement in the lives of the retired. The welfare model that preceded today's more service-oriented system in Finland was a 'social insurance state', as Anttonen (1991, pp.66–7) points out. One means of topping up the income of the older population was to introduce statutory earnings-related pension schemes. The movement was from a residual post-war model to an institutional and industrial achieve- ment model.

The state's priority in policy-making has been to support the redistribu- tion of wealth amongst the older Finns through the integrated pension schemes, as discussed above. Unfortunately for the very old, there has been a snag: the earnings-related pension was not introduced until the 1960s, so that many older people are currently excluded from the better pension arrangements. Alestalo and Uusitalo (1986, pp.228–9) indicate that inequal- ity of disposable income is larger amongst pensioners' households than amongst any other socio-economic groups in Finland. This is illustrated by the fact that the proportion of the older population in the lowest 10% groups is twice that for the total Finnish population. In contrast, there is a signifi- cantly higher proportion of occupational pensioners within the higher income 10% than there are workers and lower-income white-collar employ- ees; their income per capita is also proportionately higher.

There are a number of pension schemes in Finland. The five main ones are as follows (Ma Mpolo, 1982, pp.144–5):

1   A universal flat-rate provision exists for all residents in Finland. People are eligible at 65 but must have been resident in Finland for at least 5 years. The pension is funded by contributions from the insured person, the employers and the state. This was originally set up in 1937 under the National Pensions Act (see Satka et al., 1986; CPA, 1989; Anttonen, 1991,

pp.66–8). In spite of adaptations, this has lagged behind the nation's average wage/salary levels.

2   An earnings-related occupational pension covers most private sector employees, and contributions are recovered from the employer. The employee is eligible at retirement. The Employees' Pensions Act 1983 establishes eligibility (see CPA, 1989, pp.57–8).

3   A pension exists for the self-employed. The Self-employed Person's Pensions Act 1983 determines the pension requirements (see CPA, 1989; Anttonen, 1991, pp.66–9).

4   A public sector pension exists for central and local government employees. They are eligible at 63, and also at a lower age for certain privileged public service staff.

5   A special scheme exists for temporary employees (under the Temporary Employees' Pension Act 1983).

For public sector employees the maximum pension after 40 years amounts to 66% of the highest salary/wages level in the previous four years; for the rest of the occupational pensions it amounts to 60%. The larger the earnings-related occupational pension, the lower the national pension. The size of the contributions for the occupational pensions, for public sector workers and the self-employed, is reviewed twice annually and adjusted in relation to prices and related incomes. The irony is that the pension system is financed by private Finnish pension trusts, to whom the funds and subscriptions are directed for investment on the market.

As in most Northern, Western and Central European countries, a means-tested 'assistance allowance' and housing allowance exist for older people in need. A special feature is the extra 'helplessness' supplement at 80, which is further increased at 85. Some municipalities have introduced paid family care, whereby adult foster care is provided for older people. Unlike the provision of family care for older people in Belgium, these schemes have not been successful to date.

Housing

Almost 60% of those aged 60+ live in towns or cities (Ma Mpolo, 1982, p.140). Housing for the older Finnish population does not appear to be of the same high standard as in the other Scandinavian countries, nor are the services for them on a par with the quality of care notable in Norway, Sweden and Denmark (see Anttonen, 1991, pp.64–5). In many respects, the country had tended to relate more to the former USSR than to the more affluent European nations. This may have had an effect upon the building standards and the creature comforts of housing for the older population. According to Heikkinen et al.'s (1983, p.74) socio-medical study, it would appear that the older urban people in Tampere, Finland's second-largest city, generally seem to have suffered worse conditions than their counterparts in other European cities. Older people in Louvain, Brussels, West Berlin, Florence and Belgrade appear to have had more space in which to live their domestic lives, and a higher standard of household facilities.

Alestalo and Uusitalo (1986, p.235) cite the official housing statistics, indicating that the government provides state loans for housing improvements, which cover on average approximately a quarter of production costs for owner-occupiers and about half of the production costs of rented accommodation. None the less, the housing allowances only benefit a relatively small proportion of the older population. The allowances favour the middle class, who constitute most of the home-owners. Since the 1980s, the Finnish state has been intent upon redressing the imbalances in the quality of life between social groups by improving services for the older population, so one priority has been to build service flats for them, close to service centres or to residential and nursing homes.

From the mid-1980s the number of housing units for those aged 65+ has exceeded the places for older people in institutional care (Anttonen, 1991, p.69). Alongside this building programme, there is also the refurbishment of properties and general improvement of the housing conditions of older Finns. The CPA (1989, p.58) describes the Finnish sheltered accommodation as being situated near service centres, with support workers providing social and health care, an emergency call service, sauna, bathing and pedicure services, as well as transport, laundry and educational or leisure programmes.

In addition, the integrated model village has been adopted (of which the settlement in Kannus is a Finnish prototype) where the younger and older generations live and support one another within a 'village' of about thirty households. At the centre of the housing complex there is a 'village house'. This model is not simply Finnish, it is also Italian. (The first Italian *villaggio famiglia*, with about 15 households, was established in 1987 in the north at Sorbolo di Follo, as described by Giarchi, 1990a.) Both the Italian and Finnish models are built upon the principle of integration.

Because of the policy to provide state residential care on a large scale and the philosophy of state responsibility for a comprehensive universal system of care, the state did not have 'home care allowances' in place until as late as 1981. The informal household helpers are now given monthly allowances by the municipalities, as agreed within a contract between the carer and the Social Welfare Board.

Health care

Hospital care and medical services

Health and social care for the older population are run by the municipal authority. The administration of health and social care, however, are separate. In Finland there is 1 doctor per 978 inhabitants, which is a lower proportion than in Denmark and the other EU countries (see OECD, 1988d, p.88). Alestalo and Uusitalo (1986, p.231) indicate that the number of doctors per 10,000 population is one of the lowest in Europe. However, the same authors state that the hospital bed/patient ratio is the highest of the Scandinavian countries. This ratio is about 13.9 beds per 1,000 inhabitants (*Encyclopaedia Britannica*, 1979, Micropaedia, Vol.IV, p.143; Eurostat, 1991b, p.88).

Nursing

The level of community nursing in Finland is lower than that of Denmark or Norway (CPA, 1989, p.57); however, it is still impressive. The dual service of the district nurses working in tandem with the home helps is run by the local authority.

Mental health care

Counselling is available for older Finnish people. The suicide rate of those aged 75+ is the eighth-highest in Europe (Pritchard, 1992, p.125), giving cause for some concern nationally. The 461 municipalities cater for the mentally ill under the Ministry of Social Affairs and Health.

Institutional care

In spite of imaginative provisions, gaps in provision still exist in certain regions. Older people are often cared for in hospital wards or those of health centres (Anttonen, 1991, p.69). Institutional care of older people was the major type of formal care until the 1990s. Until recently, it was the state which provided care as its prerogative – 11.5% of those aged 65+ were in institutional care in Finland in the 1990s (see Anttonen, 1991, p.69). The old poorhouses in Finland were refurbished and turned into semi-hospital units for the care of older people in the 1950s. Like all other Northern and Western European countries, institutional care in Finland was well-resourced. The Finns speak of 'natural helping' when referring to informal care. When the family or household cannot cope any longer, institutional care takes its place, providing professional help. This formal care is largely state-supported within the local health services provided by the municipal authorities. About 8% of the older population are cared for in about 529 Finnish institutions, providing 31,250 places in state-run communal or nursing homes (see Anttonen, 1991, pp.68–9); about 18% of these places are in private institutions. De-institutionalization is cutting back on these numbers, with the provision of alternative extra-mural modes of care. It has been calculated that about one-seventh of older people in Finnish institutions should not be there. The CPA (1989, p.58) cites the Finnish policy recommendation that 10% of the places in Finnish homes be allocated to short-term care. Homes are merging with older people's service centres in providing support services.

Hytti (1983), Koskiaho (1988) and Anttonen (1991) describe the extent of institutional care in Finland. In line with the universal experience, every ten years the proportion of Finnish people aged 65–75 in institutional care doubles; this doubles again in the next decade, and almost doubles yet again every five years after the age of 84. By 1983 the number in service flats and other extra-mural special housing innovations referred to above had raced ahead of the number in institutions. There are about 10,000 more older people in the alternative modes of provision than in the traditional nursing homes, on the basis of the findings and statistics provided by the Finnish writers cited above. Alestalo and Uusitalo (1986, pp. 229–30) refer to the same shift from institutional care to service housing. A small but increasing percentage of these alternative housing units are private. However, given the demographic explosion and the life expectancy of 13.4 years for men and 17.5 years for women at 65 years of age, there is still cause for concern.

Staffing levels are difficult to assess, but on the basis of figures provided by Official Statistics of Finland (1983), the employees serving the older population constituted about 9.2% of the bulk of welfare workers. This was in keeping with the low staffing levels of almost all European countries at that time. Today the staffing level of state employees has dropped even further.

In terms of expenditure across the various branches of social and health care, Alestalo and Uusitalo (1986) indicate that well over a quarter of health and social care expenditure is spent upon older people; the major expenditure, as elsewhere in Europe, is upon health care. The CPA (1989, p.57) indicates that patients aged 65+ account for over 40% of hospital care in central hospitals and over 80% in primary health care health centre hospitals.

Personal social services

Only with the Social Welfare Act 1984 was social work recognized as a professional activity in Finland (Brauns and Kramer, 1986, p.119).

Social workers

Many social workers are employed within the municipalities, where they provide the older population with support. There are about 7,000 social workers in the country.

Meals and day care services

Unfortunately, Anttonen (1991), in one of the most comprehensive texts on care of older people in Finland, does not describe the social services provision. It would appear on the basis of available sources that it is the middle class who are the chief beneficiaries of what little social services do exist (see Alestalo and Uusitalo, 1986, pp.242–3).

Home care/help

The Municipal Home Help Act 1966 first legislated for home helps to serve the older population. Simonen (1990) provides the major study on home helps in the English language. There are probably about 5,000 municipal home helps providing about 70% of the home care service for those aged 65+, based upon the data provided by the CPA (1989, p.58), Anttonen (1991) and Simonen (1990). The home help provided by the municipal authorities reaches about 20% of the local older population (Anttonen, 1991, p.70). The average time spent caring is approximately 1.6 hours per week. There appears to be a charge attached to the service in some Finnish areas, but not in others. According to the CPA (1989, p.57) a third of the Church of Finland's 598 parishes provide auxiliary services, home help and nursing in collaboration with the municipalities. The provision of home help in Finland is on a smaller scale than in Sweden, Denmark and Norway (see Alestalo and Uusitalo, 1986, p.230) but, according to the CPA (1989, p.58), the part-time home helps are more professionalized in Finland than in other Scandinavian countries.

Voluntary care agencies and support organizations

In addition to the municipal provision, 30% of home help is provided by the voluntary organizations and the Churches. As stated above, a third of the

Church of Finland's parishes provide home helps in partnership with the municipalities; another third of these parishes provide home nursing care (see CPA, 1989, p.57). However, Anttonen (1991) says that the Church of Finland's provision has decreased in recent years. There are two other major voluntary services which certainly have not diminished. Firstly, there is the Central Union for the Welfare of the Aged (Vanhustyön Keskusliitto Ry). It constitutes a voluntary co-ordinated alliance of 16 voluntary organizations serving the aged. This union implements and evaluates special extra-mural services for older people throughout Finland. The venture jointly provides quality residential care, imaginative sheltered housing plus advice and support, as well as publications and an influential journal. Secondly, there is the Red Cross, with its headquarters in Helsinki, which fills many gaps in municipal extra-mural nursing.

The decentralized services at municipality level are backed up by the service centres for older people. These provide community facilities for the older population within neighbourhoods – saunas, laundries, hairdressers, chiropody services and meals – at cheap rates. There are over sixty such centres in Finland, half of which are run by the municipal authorities and half by the Evangelical Lutheran Church or voluntary and private agencies. They also provide a visiting service for the housebound and bedridden in the neighbourhood. However, these services are not only relatively few in number, they are also complementary facilities – they do not provide substitutes for the more organized and better-resourced state provision (see Anttonen, 1991, p.76). The voluntary sector is marginal in Finland because the welfare ethos of state provision has been a dominant feature. In addition, the women who make up the majority of formal carers support the notion of state provision and are opposed to the practice of unpaid work so common outside of the Scandinavian countries.

Informal care

Todd (1985, p.46) makes the point that, although Finland is Scandinavian, it is culturally separate from Sweden and Norway because the family structure in those nations is authoritarian, whereas that of Finland has traditionally been that of the exogamous community family. The Finnish family is splitting up into nuclear units, and more and more members are living alone, including older people (see Anttonen, 1991). As far back as 1983 the evidence offered by Heikkinen et al. (1983, p.84) suggests that 45% of men and 73% of women aged 85–9 were 'often alone'. The OECD trends (1992, pp.24–6) indicate that shrinking households and older people who live alone have been an ever-increasing phenomenon, and 'particularly high in Finland' (p.15).

According to the Luxemburg *Sozialporträts Europas* (Luxemburg Grand Duchy, 1991a), after Germany, the largest percentage of older people (65+) living alone are in Finland.

The *Finnish National Report for the World Assembly on Aging* (Ministry of Social Affairs and Health, 1982) stated that 'the family continued to be the most natural and closest source of support for old people'. However, the exodus of younger people to the cities and abroad to seek a better living and escape from the severe conditions has increased since 1982 and further isolated many older people in the countryside. The same report cited a survey which estimated that about 25% of the offspring of older parents had left their localities. This may have increased by some 15% to date: the traditional exogamous families are breaking down, especially where people move to the cities to find work. The Finnish household has never been smaller, with only 14% of older men and 8% of older women living with four or more people. In addition, approximately one in three older Finnish people live alone. Many older rural people are bewildered and confused by the significant change in size of household; but in the cities less so. However, only about 8% of the men and 12% of the women feel lonely. Their lives are very active, backed by a government policy of integration in keeping with the traditional social values of Finland. The CPA (1989, p.57) states that in 1985, 70% of those aged 65 and over were economically active. Halonen (1990) reports that combining work and care are dual ideals within the Finnish family. An increasing number of older women also enable the younger mothers to work, some older women maintaining their independent lodging nearby.

The older people in particular expect the state to provide universal care, which has been described during their lifetime as 'the social service state' or 'caring state'. However, Finland is discarding its purist socialist policies more slowly and circumspectly because of the support of its people for the retention of 'the social service state'. The state is now passing the burden of care on to the family, but at the same time the proportion of women in work in Finland is higher than in any other Western country (Anttonen, 1991, p.73), so clearly the burden of care cannot be so easily passed on to women as it is in many European countries. Halonen's (1990) social policy report on family care is notable for the absence of any reference to home care for older people. Awareness of this reversal in policy has not yet fully registered.

In addition to the significant increase in the proportion of women in full-time work, the supply of potential younger carers is being sharply reduced, because of the drop in the birth rate. At the same time, the Finnish social policies are moving in the direction of welfare mixes. The numbers of institutions are also being reduced.

Halonen (1990, p.163) stresses that the Finnish government's current policy is to emphasize the participation of clients and support for self-help, but as in the case of the 1982 World Assembly report referred to earlier, the call to care for one's aged relatives may fall short of the need for more informal home care. The underdevelopment of familial and kinship care has been a result of the European social changes accompanying modernization (Anttonen, 1991, p.73).

Leisure pursuits and education

In addition to the service centres there are also an increasing number of clubs for older people in Finland. Neighbourhood clubs are organized by the older people themselves, where people may drop in for meals, for a chat and to read the newspapers or magazines, as described by Anttonen (1991, p.77) and the CPA (1989, p.58). These clubs are in effect self-help centres. Also, as in many parts of Europe, educational courses for older people, which are usually organized in the summer, are run within certain universities and colleges. Maintaining contacts at local level requires back-up, maintenance of rooms, etc., and subsidies keep these ventures going. The importance of state subsidies to local ventures is of particular relevance to services as well as centres in rural Finland.

Sjoholt (1988) describes the low-population density areas in Scandinavia, especially the virgin-forested localities of northern Finland, as 'extreme peripheries'. It is not the harsher climate nor the fragmented topography and great distances which determine the quality of life of the older inhabitants so much as the social parameters. As Harvey (1973) established years ago, the physical world is determined by social class and those who control the socio-economic dimensions of life. The older population in the remote rural areas are not so much the victims of the elements as victims of the low priority given to their needs by those who control the provision of housing, and determine the infrastructure of social and health care. For many, urbanization is still a first-generation experience.

Rural aspects

Before concluding, something must be said about Finland's rural municipalities. Finland was the only European country where the number of farms increased after World War II until the 1950s (Alestalo and Uusitalo, 1986, p.203); in fact 100,000 new small farms were set up in the rural areas of Finland in the immediate post-war years. The rural electorate is politically influential: for example, the Agrarian Party and the Farmers' Union have favoured flat-rate social security systems, whilst the Social Democrats and the Conservatives have favoured earnings-related benefits. The political split in the Finnish pension system also reflects the rural/urban split. Urbanization in the 1950s saw the exodus of younger families to the cities and towns, as has been the case in many other parts of Europe; none the less, like France the rural areas still constitute a major area of concern in terms of underdevelopment and deprivation. The older population are amongst the first victims of rural poverty; unfortunately for them, the Agrarian Party has lost ground in the fight for more welfare and health resources in the Finnish countryside.

Conclusion

It is commonplace to emphasize the significant role played by the Scandinavian health and welfare services. As has been demonstrated, Finland's formal services do not measure up to the high expectations usually associated with countries in Northern Europe. The evidence demonstrates that Finnish welfare systems are increasingly unsteady. The electorate and the major parties, whether of the left, the centre or the right, appear to be committed to the rhetoric of a state welfare system, but in spite of Alestalo and Uusitalo's (1986, pp.275–6) earlier assurances, the reality is that social and health care services are beginning to show signs of shifting towards a pluralist welfare model. This is facilitated by the polycephalic infrastructure (see Table 6). Care is increasingly passing from the centre to mezzo-micro levels of delivery. There are blurred edges to the Finnish portfolio of public services, and the signs are that statements of state welfare intent will be further obscured. However, the feminization of the welfare state has to be taken into account; the influence of women is considerable: in the early 1990s, women occupied one-third of parliamentary seats which constituted 54% of public sector employees and about 35% of Finland's total employees. The feminization of state welfare in Finland has provided and will continue to provide a brake, preventing a full swing to privatization, but it remains to be seen whether welfare costs will prove too great to manage.

Anttonen (1991, pp.73–4) cites a study by Sihvo (1988), written in Finnish, which shows that there were 275,418 households with 319,605 older people or other dependent adults needing household care. If these households had not provided informal care, they would have required two daily visits by municipal home helps throughout a full working year; 43% of those who needed assistance were provided with some home help; 6% had meals brought to them; 12% were assisted by the social centres, and 80% were helped in one way or another by the social services. The care was partial, and would have been inadequate without informal care: 29,000 households did not receive the help they had requested, and 45,000 declined the services offered. In the case of those in need who lived alone, as many as 93% received some municipal assistance, but one in two received help from kin, and one in four from neighbours and acquaintances.

Enough has been said to indicate that the informal sector in Finland is indispensable. Certain difficulties stand in the way of a full-blown, paid-up informal army of carers. Will the welfare state be flexible enough to adapt to change? The need to respond will have to take account of the changing social scene within the Finnish family, and the shifting demography, in which those aged 80+ will treble in numbers within the next twenty years. The proportion of Finnish persons aged 15–64 which provide the pool of carers is progressively decreasing and will possibly be the lowest in Europe by the year 2025, according to Ermisch's (1990, p.45) projections.

3 Norway

Demography

According to the data presented in Table 1, Norway has the second-highest proportion of older people in Europe. As shown in Table 1, the projected proportion of older people in Norway by the year 2025 will be as high as 20.2%, but this figure will only rank eighth: the proportion of older people will probably only increase by 3.8%. This increase may be relatively small, but when seen as an additional burden on the already critical situation facing the state, it could add up to the proverbial 'last straw'. The increase will stretch the nation's resources to crisis point. Solitary older women are a major concern: Norwegian women are more likely than men to live alone. Of those aged 65+, there are almost twice as many married men as women (see CPA, 1989, p.116); 90% live within their own households. The life expectancy of women aged 65 is 18.5 years, which ranks seventh in Europe; that of men is 14.4 years, which ranks tenth (UN, 1991; Eurostat, 1991a).

Socio-political and administrative background

Norway is governed by a constitutional monarchy: the king acts as head of government and selects the cabinet. The Storting, the parliament, consists of 150 members. It may vote against the cabinet when faced, for example, with major welfare decisions which may affect older people. As with Finland, the affairs of the older population have been decided upon by political coalitions. A moderate socialism is opposed by a moderate conservatism.

According to Kuhnle (1986, pp.120–4), social care in Norway has a long history, going back to the twelfth century. Of note was the arrangement (the *legdordning*) which provided accommodation on a rota basis for older people who had no kin.

Kuhnle (1986, p.160) refers to the 1970s, when the Norwegian welfare system was in effect a myth (*myten an velferdsstaten*). It was accused of establishing a client-creating society. However, from the 1970s to the 1980s, the system had proven itself and the older population in particular were prime beneficiaries. In the 1990s, the cost of welfare, not the quality, has come under fire. In the mid-1980s 33 billion kroner were allocated to expenditure on the older population alone (9% of GDP), as indicated by the CPA (1989, p.116). In the bleak days of the early 1990s, the anticipated rises in costs have put the brakes upon welfare provision. Kuhnle (1986, p.161) predicts that 'the Norwegian welfare state will soon encounter serious challenges. This is emphasized by the likelihood of an increase of the population aged 65+.'

Nowotny (1986, p.15), in an early text on the advent of plural welfare within the Nordic setting, refers to the welfare myth of the Scandinavian system. For years the 'public time' of the state administration has taken precedence over the 'private time' of household carers. That was the official line of government and has been an ideal that has epitomized the Scandinavian model internationally. However, the women in the home have been keeping the system going: a domestic welfare system has been unrecognized and unrewarded. Women carers have been used as much within Norway as anywhere else. The new social contract between the state and the private sector could well worsen the injustices that have beset the care of older people in Norway. Women's employment has become a major social issue, but they might simply be working to pay for care for older relatives. The state is now turning its back upon women yet again, only this time in a sense the state is coming out into the open and declaring that there is no alternative to a money-led system. Its assurances that those unable to pay will not suffer are vague promises. The indications are that yet another pretence is at work. The market is exerting increasing influence within the triangle of care, although the state supports a synchronic system. In effect this could be creating a market in care, which potentially could become as anarchic as any of the more extreme capitalist non-Scandinavian systems.

The administration of welfare in Norway veers towards being polycephalic (see Table 6), but some intrusion of the central state in the municipalities has been noted by commentators. Health and social care are managed by the 454 municipalities (*kommuner*) and the counties (*fylkeskommuner*). The municipalities have been of importance as political institutions since the 1830s (see Sjoholt, 1988, p.79). There used to be 750 of them, enjoying more freedom, before many were amalgamated and put under the authority of the elected county councils. Just as in many other countries of Europe, the older rural population generally suffer most from being the victims of 'distance decay', removed as they are from hospitals, health clinics and social services.

The National Council for the Elderly in Oslo acts as a national advisory body to the Ministry of Health and Social Affairs with regard to social and health care. It also provides information and expert advice to those older people involved in care. In practice, since 1970 it has constituted a workable national forum for the older population.

Social security: pensions and benefits

With regard to pensions, the Norwegian Poor Law 1845 first provided a relatively generous support system for the older population (Kuhnle, 1986, p.120). However, Norway was one of the last nations in Northern and Western Europe to introduce a pension scheme. In 1930, in terms of social insurance provision, the country was near the bottom of Europe's major countries (Kuhnle, 1986, p.121). However, by the start of World War II, Norway had one of the leading welfare systems in Europe. A compulsory old age pension (*alterstrygd*) had been introduced in 1936 and allowances had been established for the blind and the crippled.

The post-war social security system was set up in Stockholm by the Norwegian Central Federation of Trade Unions in 1944. The previous income-based means test was replaced by a flat-rate old age pension, which was passed by law in 1957 and implemented in 1959 (see Kuhnle, 1986, p.123). A general invalidity pension was created in 1961. In 1966 the Norwegian National Insurance Scheme was established. It replaced all forms of previous pensions. It was revised in 1971. In 1973, the pension age was reduced from 70 to 67.

Today, there is a two-level state pension scheme for those aged 67+. Firstly, the 1971 National Insurance Scheme guarantees retired Norwegians a basic universal pension (*grunnpensjon*) and a compensation benefit (*kompensasjonstillegg*), whatever their income. This pension requires at least a three-year period of residence. The full pension requires residence in Norway for at least 40 years since the age of 16. Those who are on the minimum pension are exempt from taxation. Secondly, there is the earnings-related scheme (*tilleggspension*), which covers all residents and the self-employed who earn above a specific amount. Substantial tax reductions have also been provided for the pensioners, especially during the 1980s. Special pension schemes exist for specific occupational groups, such as reindeer-herders, seafarers, railway staff and public employees. The schemes are maintained by funds which are obtained from the insured, employers, the municipalities, the counties and central government. A supplementary top-up (the *saertillegg*) is provided for those who are not eligible for the earnings-related pension. The amount is dependent upon the previous earned pensionable income and the number of pension-earning years and is indexed to prices and salary levels.

About 34% of those aged 60+ (approximately 44% of men and 25% of women) were economically active in the mid-1980s (see CPA, 1989, p.116; Laczko and Phillipson, 1991, p.58). With the increased pressure upon the Norwegian welfare system the postponement of retirement has been encouraged.

The welfare state can no longer meet the demands of maintenance and care of the older population without a restructured system. The plural mix to which most Norwegians have been ideologically and politically opposed appears to be the only solution. In the political scramble of the mid-1980s the opposing parties were agreed that the higher income groups should receive less generous state pensions and the lower income groups should receive more generous ones. However, the very real danger has been that the upper and middle-income groups have opted increasingly for additional private insurance systems, so that pressure has been exerted by the more affluent Norwegians to free themselves from the National Insurance Scheme and the financial obligations of membership.

The assistance grant is a social security benefit for those who need special home care, nursing or domestic help. It is also available when helpers are prevented from undertaking employment. However, the level of assistance, even during the better days of the mid-1980s, was only about 5% of the average gross earnings of a full-time Norwegian industrial worker. Unlike the care of older people, assistance for care of disabled people is a legal right (see Hatland, 1986, p.54). The decision over eligibility is taken centrally by the Social Insurance Administration and not by the municipalities. At least 62,000 grants are made every year. Travel concessions entitle older people to a 50% travel discount. On the basis of a means test, they are also entitled to allowances for the installation of telephones.

Housing

Housing has been high on the political and social agenda for many years in Norway, and establishing appropriate accommodation adapted to the needs of the older population has been one of the most important social issues in the post-war years.

Norway has had a credit system for housing dating from 1894, when a Housing Loan Fund (*huslanefondet*) made funds available on the basis of social need. The Housing Directorate was founded in 1946, as was the Norwegian State Housing Bank. The latter has provided loans for the housing needs of older residents in the urban areas, and the Smallholding Bank has catered for those living in the rural areas. Service flats are provided by the municipality and are financed by the Norwegian State Housing Bank: 10% of those aged 70+ live in purpose-built flats. Some of these are built by housing organizations, such as the people's housing savings clubs. The policy is to increase the availability of these houses and to decrease the supply of institutional beds. There has been no income or property means test for applicants approaching the Norwegian State Housing Bank for a housing loan (Kuhnle, 1987, p.93). However, the older person must be able to raise 20–30% of the necessary capital to cover the costs. Interest on the loans for much of the 1980s was about 12%.

The improvement and provision of adapted housing has been a major policy of the Norwegian government, especially since the 1960s. Improvements in housing have been made possible since 1969 by the ready availability and favourable terms of State Housing Bank loans. The loans and the adaptations are available for all types of tenancies, whether public or private, and all owner-occupied dwellings. Housing benefits have also been granted to persons aged 60+. These were introduced in 1965 and extended and improved in 1970. These allowances cover fuel costs, loan repayments and taxes.

Health care

With regard to health, sickness insurance was introduced for fishermen and seamen in 1936. Three years later, a universal sickness insurance was made compulsory for all citizens (see Kuhnle, 1987, p.121) before Beveridge's UK scheme. In 1971, sickness and health insurance was incorporated into the 1966 National Insurance Scheme.

Hospital care and medical services

As early as 1969, updated hospital services at county level were introduced, funded by generous grants for costs associated with hospital expansion. Hospital treatment is free and cash benefits are not reduced during hospitalization. The Norwegian Primary Health Services Act 1982 states that every resident 'has a right to necessary health services in the municipality where he lives or temporarily stays' (see Hatland, 1986, p.57). The Act (effective from 1984) made municipalities responsible for the non-hospital health services. Between 1982 and 1983, central government increased its contributions to municipal home help care and home nursing.

The number of beds in hospitals and nursing homes is about 50,000 (see

Kuhnle, 1986, p.150). There are 123 beds for every 10,000 inhabitants in Norway, and about 2.1 doctors per 1,000 inhabitants. Most EU countries have a higher doctors' ratio. However, Oslo has one of the highest ratios: 1 doctor per 302 persons (see Kuhnle, 1986, p.150; Eurostat, 1991b, p.88). The doctor/patient ratio has been 3 per 1,000 inhabitants. The costs of running the Norwegian health services have been considerable; in 1980 they constituted about 40% of the nation's total social security expenditure and 9.3% of GDP.

Nursing

There is evidence that, even in the halcyon days of the welfare state, nursing care was not meeting the needs of the older Norwegian population. Waerness (1990, p.113) cites the mid-1990s Scandinavian research which indicated that 12% of those aged 65+ reported that they were in need of nursing. Also, the numbers of community nurses are decreasing.

Mental health care

Although there has been a recent awareness of the need to provide for people suffering from psychiatric illnesses, there has not been any major innovation in terms of provision for the mentally ill and older Norwegians (Kuhnle, 1986, p.151). In 1970 a major study, *Myten an velferdsstaten* ('The Myth of the Welfare State'), argued that the state was creating anxiety and increased problems of loneliness (see Lingås, 1970). There was no major reorganization or radical response to its disturbing observations. There are no statistics available regarding the types and incidence of mental illnesses affecting older Norwegians, except that the suicide rate of Norwegians aged 75+ is ranked tenth in Europe (Pritchard, 1992, p.129). On the basis of Gibson's (1992, p.94) commentary on Norway's family support for older Norwegians, home carers of older people with Alzheimer's Disease are paid by the government at the equivalent rates for home helps. There are homes for people with dementia, and psychiatric nursing homes, half of which are filled with people aged 70 and over (CPA, 1989, p.117).

Institutional care

With regard to institutional care, in 1980 there were 655 homes with a total of 14,042 beds. A few years later there were 27,404 beds in 630 nursing homes

(Kuhnle, 1986). These beds catered for those aged 70+. The CPA (1989, p.117) states that there are 6.5 nursing home units per 100 persons aged 70+. There are also residential homes for self-reliant older people: 3.4 units per 100 persons aged 70+. The majority of patients in psychiatric nursing homes and homes for dementia patients are aged 70+. Most recent institutions provide both nursing and residential care, as indicated by Kuhnle (1986) and CPA (1989, p.117). The homes are maintained by the municipalities. Short-term stay and respite care have been available for some years. Norwegian homes have been renowned for their hotel-like facilities, providing *en suite* accommodation long before most other European countries. The costs of nursing home and residential care are shared by the municipalities and the National Insurance Fund.

Personal social services

With regard to social services, high costs of services on the older population is a major Norwegian concern. However, municipal social services have had a relatively short history in Norway. For many years personal social care was largely left to the Norske Kvinners Nasjonalrad, a voluntary women's organization. The Protestant ethic has emphasized familial care and bolstered the notion of the nurturing role of women. The polycephalic structure of the welfare state increasingly devolves decision-making to local social workers.

Social workers

Hildeng (1986, pp.425–6) states there was no state social work education in Norway until 1949. Strangely enough for a socialist welfare culture, the US social work provision and casework approach were first adopted, because the earlier influential social work educators were trained in the USA.

Social workers within the municipalities are responsible for the administration of welfare as well as for the modes and extent of intervention. They are civil servants, who are responsible for safeguarding the citizens' social rights, which is particularly important for the vulnerable and more disabled or deprived sectors of the older population.

There has been a long-standing shortage of social workers for older people in the northern parts of the country, which are more rural. Social work provision is more marked in and around Oslo, as indicated by Hildeng (1986, p.432). The restrictions in financial resources have shifted the casework orientation of the social workers to that of brokers and liaison workers, linking the older population with the relevant providers of formal and informal care.

Home care/help

The 'home nursing service' run by the 454 municipalities is free, and mainly caters for those aged 67+ (see CPA, 1989, p.116). With regard to home help, the main statutory provision for social care within the municipalities is contained in Article 8 of the Norwegian Social Care Act 1964, which states that it is the duty of the local authorities 'to strengthen the social protection for the residents of the municipality'.

The direct care provided by the public sector for the older population in Norway is mainly through home help and assistance grants. Hatland (1986), Kuhnle (1986; 1987) and CPA (1989) comment upon them. At least 18% of the older population receive some form of home help (see Kuhnle, 1986, p.149; 1987, p.77). Hatland (1986, p.54) states that there are about 43,000 home helps, 27% of whom are related to the users. The 'social home help services' are provided by the municipalities. A small charge for home help is made. Most of the home helps are untrained, and about one-third are related to their clients (CPA, 1989, p.117). Home help mainly consists of special cleaning services, meals distribution and snow removal.

From the outset the home help service has been based upon the role of the housewife, as stated by Waerness (1990, p.124). This complaint by many critics has also been accompanied by the observation that the major reason for cutting back on institutional care and providing more home care was simply expediency in the face of rising costs. The welfare principles of a Scandinavian value system have been pushed aside, according to many feminist observers. The evidence provided by Waerness (1990, pp.124–5) supports the view that the government relied until relatively recently upon middle-aged and older women to provide home help. The situation has recently been changed because the 'reserve army' of these women is diminishing, so that younger women and men have been recruited to fill the gap.

Voluntary care agencies and support organizations

With regard to voluntary work, Norway, in common with the other Scandinavian countries, has pursued a social policy of public provision which at first virtually excluded alternatives. Of the relatively few voluntary organizations which do exist, the Norwegian Red Cross is the major agency, providing alternative home care for the older population.

There is an increase in private and voluntary provision in certain services for older people. Over 45% of all Norwegian day care is voluntary or private, but the municipalities provide 80% of their running costs, mainly for the voluntary agencies (Hernes, 1986, p.47). Caring contracts were being applied in Norway in the early 1980s, which were first tested in five municipalities of a Norwegian county (Hatland, 1986, p.58).

Informal care

Ermisch (1990, p.45) points out that the ratio of potential carers to the population aged 65+ will reduce by almost 3% by 2025. Whatever the gender factor in care, the availability of carers will be less, as also will be the number of formal carers, when the proportion of younger people drops even further in Norway. Care (*omsorg*) in Norway has been very much a state welfare provision. The care of older people has been significant, as has state expenditure on formal services in one of the most universalist systems in Europe.

About 50% of all public sector carers are women, and, as Hernes also states, about 80% of all women in Norway and Sweden are public employees (the 'family going public': Hernes, 1986, p.44); the majority of their clients are also women. Women have also made their way into the political arena, as they have done in Sweden and Finland: about 35% of the parliamentarians in Norway are women. The coalition of formal and informal female carers, of women clients and of women politicians has constituted the major thrust behind the development of some of Europe's best social and health care systems and caring arrangements. However, because of the recent cutbacks resulting from the deep recession and chronic European economic crisis in the early 1990s, many of the Norwegian social and health care provisions have been questioned and altered. Substitute caring arrangements have been made.

Hatland (1986, p.56) points out that the burden of informal care falls disproportionately upon middle-aged women. The number in this group will decrease and will be further diminished by the lack of motivation to provide care exhibited by the growing number of 'strong feminist groups'. The family does not step in to provide household care as it does in the Southern and Eastern European countries, and the voluntary agencies do not step in as they do in Western European countries (Hatland, 1986, p.53). State support systems – chiefly institutional care – are the major options. This policy has changed, but has the culture of care? Any transfer of the burden of such support to families is feared by most Norwegian women; the burden would fall disproportionately upon them, because 'family' means 'women' in this instance.

It is clear that families in Norway, alongside other Scandinavian countries, have provided less support for older people than is provided in the Western, Central, Eastern and Southern countries of Europe. Older people expect the state, not the family, to provide for their needs in retirement. If the welfare system cannot (as feared) respond to the needs of older Europeans, what is there to turn to in a nation where the caring ratio is unbalanced and voluntary care is relatively scarce? The National Council for the Elderly in Oslo, which supports 20 organizations, attempts to extend the voluntary sector, but it faces the need for a sea change in people's expectations.

Leisure pursuits and education

There are service centres for older people, financed by the municipalities and organized by the local education departments. They are usually open four days per week, and usually provide crafts, excursions, educational courses, exercise, meals-on-wheels, chiropody, a visiting rota, advice, counselling and hairdressing (see CPA, 1989, p.117). Some centres publish their own local newspaper. Older people are involved in user management groups. These centres have to be distinguished from day centres, which are usually based in nursing homes. The service is free, except for medication and meals. This provision is mostly concentrated in Oslo and the surrounding urban areas. Older people who are not granted assistance have the right to appeal to the regional commissioner, who can overturn prior decisions. University of the Third Age courses were established in Oslo in 1984 and have increased in number since.

Rural aspects

With regard to the provision of services in rural Norway, some south-west morainic and moorland areas and extensive tracts of northern Norway are remote. Here the older population are more deprived than the better-served population in the urban areas, especially around Oslo. Sjoholt (1988, p.71) refers to emigration in the remoter rural areas of Norway. The infrastructure of care is especially meagre in these areas. As late as 1979, there were 700 places which had no roads or ferry links with the outside world (Sjoholt, 1988, p.74). There are delays in setting up TV and radio networks. Social services are lacking in many areas of the north. The old integrated household economy in the remoter areas of Norway has tended to resist plans to improve communication with the urban officialdom. It must also be noted that many urban areas are first-generation urbanized societies, where independence is conserved amongst families, where traditions come first, and where formal care may be an unwelcome intrusion.

Conclusion

Care by informal carers has gone unnoticed for many years, but without the private time women have put into home care, many older people would have lacked total care. For years the 'public time' of state administration had taken precedence over the 'private time' of household carers. However, the state can no longer keep up the pretence of public care. It now synchronizes a plural welfare system. A social contract between the Norwegian state and the private carers is now in the process of destroying the myth of universal state welfare. Even in Norway, the service culture has been twinned with the enterprise culture. A bargaining economy is at work in Norway (Hernes, 1986, p.43). One-third of Norwegian privately-owned health institutions are publicly financed. Private entrepreneurs are advised to buy their necessary equipment on cheap public loans, whilst Norwegian women undertake part-time work and full-time care to make up what is wanting in both the production of goods and welfare. If the state shifts its responsibilities yet more in the direction of home care, Norwegian women will be overstretched, both as workers and as domestic providers. The danger is that as the infrastructures of care are extended and diversified, anarchic elements may enter in as the market intrudes. Women carers may be relied upon increasingly as cheap labour. However, family members and contemporary values do not appear to welcome the encroachment of a market welfare system and are likely to resist privatization of care provided for older Norwegians.

4　Sweden

Demography

The proportion of older people in Sweden has ceased to accelerate as fast as it did in the mid-1980s (see Sundström, 1988, p.167), but as shown in Table 1, Sweden in recent times has had the highest percentage (18.4%) and the second-highest projected proportion of older people in Europe (22.2%) by 2025 (see CPA, 1989, p.139; UN, 1991). The caring ratio is also very low, due to the dropping birth and marriage rates, as well as the increasing number of women in employment. The burden of care of the older population will not increase as greatly as it is likely to do elsewhere in Europe. The projected increase by the year 2025 in the proportion of those aged 65+ in Sweden is likely to be 3.8% (CPA, 1989, p.139; Eurostat, 1991a; UN, 1991). This is considerably lower than the projected increases in Iceland, Finland and Denmark.

About seventy per cent of women aged 16–74 years are in paid employment, half of whom are part-time employees (Lagergren, 1986, p.27). According to data cited by Tornstam (1992, pp.138–9), roughly half of all retired Swedes live with a spouse, and only 6% with offspring or another relative. In 1980, 36% of the older population lived alone and 5% were in institutions. In the second half of the 1980s the numbers of those living alone had risen dramatically: at least 44% of older women and 15% of older men were living alone, and the proportion of older people in institutions was one of the highest in Europe – 7.5%. The life expectancy of older women at 65 is 18.9 years, which ranks third in Europe, and that of older men at 65 is 15 years, which ranks fifth (Eurostat, 1991a; UN, 1991).

Socio-political and administrative background

Sweden has a constitutional monarchy. However, a 'middle-way' socialism has catered for the welfare of older people, particularly since World War II. Olsson (1992, p.20) describes this 'middle-way' as an 'extremely broad-based liberal system'. The monarchy is symbolic, but interestingly enough, in spite of the strength of the feminist lobby, the monarch is decided upon by direct patrilineal descent. The parliament (Riksdag) consists of 350 elected members. The Social Democratic Labour Party has been the major force in running the affairs of the country and deciding upon the social and health care of older people in what was chiefly a monocephalic system. Power to enact laws is jointly vested in the King in Council and the Riksdag. Local lawmaking does not exist. In Sweden there are 23 county governments (*landsting*), each made up of about 300,000 inhabitants, which are responsible for health care in addition to hospital care. The county governments are further subdivided into 284 municipalities (*kommun*), consisting of 10,000–60,000 inhabitants; the municipalities are responsible for social care. As Lagergren (1986, pp.29–30) explains, the Swedish citizen (in keeping with the notion of a social democracy) is responsible for the care of others, but through the apparatus of the state which represents the citizens. The citizen carries a 'public' responsibility.

However, the Swedish state exerts considerable control over family life – but in relation to child care, not the care of older people. This child welfare control was referred to as 'gross violation of the integrity of the citizen', as cited by Adams and Winston (1986, p.206). The authors proceed to say: 'Forty years of Social Democratic dominance have shaped national policies *vis-à-vis* the family. The state, rather than the family, provides a welfare cushion. Hence the family disposes of relatively fewer resources to meet its own needs.' The welfare cushion usually consists of the excellent comforts of Swedish nursing and residential homes. According to Selby and Schechter (1982, p.45), this has led to older people being treated as inactive and passive. This, together with the high proportion of people in institutions, has created greater dependency and lower standards in the quality of life of older Swedes (Johansson and Thorslund, 1992, p.58). It comes as no surprise that the culture of care tended to be one of domestic control and confinement, however comfortable the beds and chairs and however enjoyable the meals. The situation is now changing as Sweden turns from a policy of institutional care to one of open care and more autonomy for older people.

In the 1960s and 1970s the policy began to shift from the 'institutional way' to more 'home-based care'. Home care accelerated, and social and health care within the household began to eclipse institutional care. Institutional care became more 'home-like' as nursing homes were reduced in size. During the 1980s, diversified modes of care were developed and plural welfare began to replace the monopoly of state welfare. The high-quality care provided for older people could not have been maintained without high taxation (Lagergren, 1988).

Sweden's welfare system is now at a standstill because of the heavy costs. But what can the state put in place of one of the world's most comprehensive state systems? The problem for Sweden is that it cannot look to families to provide sufficient care to make up the yawning gap that will appear in the next twenty years between the increasing needs of the older population and the cost of state welfare and of universal health provision. The Swedish Institute (1989b, p.4) sums up the crisis facing the planners:

> Expansion is unlikely. Firstly, such an expansion of services for the elderly would demand an increase in taxation and today there is virtual political consensus that the present high taxes cannot be raised further. Secondly, the most significant, is the fact that the increase in staffing numbers which an expansion would necessitate simply cannot be realized.

According to the same source, there would need to be an increase of between 80–100% in staff levels to keep up with the projected needs of the older population. At the same time, care systems are in flux.

From the beginning of the twentieth century the Swedish objective has been to create a 'social democracy'. This was influenced by the social welfare ideas of notable Scandinavian welfare leaders such as the Myrdals before World War II, and after the war by Beveridge's UK model (see page 129). Olson (1986, pp.4–18) describes the development of the formal caring service systems in Sweden from the mid-nineteenth century onwards. From the start the administrative structures took the need to provide infrastructures of care and welfare provisions into account. At the time the county councils were founded in 1862, the 25 representative regional bodies for in-patient hospital services were also created. The 23 counties are responsible for the health services under the National Board of Health and Welfare. The county health service is usually organized at three levels. Firstly, there is primary care, with doctors, assistant nurses, district occupational therapists and district physiotherapists. Secondly, there are the county medical services, which mainly constitute hospital care. Thirdly, there are the regional medical services, which are planned jointly by adjacent county councils (Johansson and Thorslund, 1991, p.31).

Social security: pensions and benefits

The Swedish universal, compulsory old age and invalidity pension was introduced in 1913. With its introduction, poor relief progressively diminished. It was down by 50% in the early part of the century until it had almost expired by the 1980s. The general old age pensions of 1913 constituted the *demogrants* – granted to all, irrespective of social class and level of income. The older Swedish population were amongst the first beneficiaries of the welfare state, which reflected major aspects of the Bismarckian welfare model.

The current universal flat-rate pension (*folkpension*) was introduced in 1948; this trebled the real value of the old pension. The earnings-related compulsory supplementary pension for employees and self-employed alike was added in 1959; in 1976, the part-time employees' pension and lower age of retirement extended income support provision for the older population.

The partial pension scheme deserves further comment, because it was a notable Swedish contribution to the welfare of the older population in Europe. Whereas the other pensions are payable at 65, the partial pension scheme is a flexible system whereby people may retire between the ages of 60 and 64. The conditions are that employees may receive a partial pension if they are employed for five hours or less per week, or work part-time for a maximum of 17 hours per week; the partially retired receive 80% of their original income. There is a special scheme for public sector employees, and an occupational scheme for private sector employees.

Expenditure on basic and supplementary benefits has constituted at least 50% of the total public expenditure on income maintenance in Sweden for at least thirty years (see Olson, 1986, p.18). In addition, on the basis of the OECD's (1988c) statistics, Sweden spends 60% of its GDP on social and public services as well as upon income transfers (in contrast with the UK's 45%). The welfare values of the state in Sweden owe a great deal to the feminization of the state, in common with Finland.

For most of the older population there are two parts to their general pension, as described by Tornstam (1992, p.138): there is a basic pension and an additional pension, which is earnings-related. Because the latter was introduced relatively recently, the oldest people often have poorer pensions. One out of every five pensioners in Sweden feels financially hard-pressed. Their income is insufficient to maintain a decent standard of living, as recorded by Dooghe (1992, p.156) and researched by Sheppard and Mullins (1989). At the same time, this must be counterbalanced by the fact that the older Swedish population have generally been better off financially than most other older people in Europe. However, such pre-eminence is now severely questioned.

For many years in Sweden it has been the citizen's social duty to subscribe to the notion of the universal welfare state and to finance these services through taxation. Spicker (1991, p.22) would describe this as a 'solidaristic philosophy', which strives to protect people in unequal circumstances. However, one must take into consideration some of the points made earlier, when discussing the informal care provided within households and neighbourhoods. Rightly, Thorslund and Parker (1992, p.8) state that informal carers in Sweden provide about twice as much care as is provided by the public agencies. The benefits of the Swedish welfare state have been commented upon favourably by the majority of commentators. However, the Swedish formal care systems were not without their critics. For example, Huntford (1972) described Sweden as 'a totalitarian state masquerading as a democracy, whose care from the womb to the tomb has been ineffective'. The effect of the weakening Swedish domestic economy in the early 1990s upon the much-vaunted Swedish welfare state prompted Thorslund (see Thorslund and Parker, 1992) to declare 'the party is over'. The weakened krona (SEK) in turn has devalued the Swedish pension. The increase of the price of food has shot to the highest levels in Western and Northern Europe. Food in Sweden is costly for pensioners: between 25–30% more than the average EU countries (Brasier, 1992).

Housing

As the CPA (1989, p.139) points out, 87% of the older Swedish population live in ordinary housing, 3% in pensioners' flats, and 2% in sheltered housing. More than half of ordinary pensioners are owner-occupiers (Johansson and Thorslund, 1991, p.33). The service apartments (the *service-hus*) have been a recent development, much like those elsewhere, such as in Belgium. The Swedish government has been a European frontrunner with regard to innovative housing arrangements. It provided public loans and interest subsidies for housing construction in 1948. Since the 1950s, over 90% of newly-constructed houses have been subsidized by the National Housing Board (Bostadsstyrelsen), as cited by Olson (1986, p.26).

Modern Swedish houses tend to be smaller units: about one-third are single-person accommodation. Compared with the household situation in 1960, by the mid-1980s approximately five times as many men and six times as many women were not living with their offspring (see Lagergren, 1986, p.31). Today, almost all retired persons live independently, either alone or as a couple on their own, according to Tornstam (1992, p.138).

Several types of accommodation have been tried out in Sweden to meet the need of the older population to be independent. Johansson and Thorslund (1991, p.33) identify two forms of housing for those who cannot manage on their own at home. Firstly, there is 'congregate housing with full board and lodging'. This consists of very small apartments which are serviced and supervised round the clock. They provide some 43,000 beds. Secondly, there are 'congregate housing facilities with individual apartments in service houses'. Day centres are often attached to these apartments.

Municipal housing allowances for pensioners were introduced in 1954. After an experimentation period from 1968 to 1974, interest subsidies were reintroduced. Selby and Schechter (1982, p.61) over a decade ago pointed to the tendency of elderly Swedish households being generally in disrepair. Olson (1986, p.26) cites the housing construction loans, interest subventions, tax deductions for interest paid on housing loans and housing allowances that subsidize rents for low-income earners. Those with lower pensions have usually been compensated for in several ways, for example Tornstam (1992, p.138) cite the 21% of retired men and the 42% of retired women who receive extra benefits to cope with their accommodation costs. Olson (1986, p.27) states that over the years housing allowances for pensioners have continued to increase in real terms.

Health care

The county councils are responsible for the delivery of health and medical care (Johansson and Thorslund, 1991, p.30). This involves 23 counties and the three municipalities of Malmo, Gotland and Gothenburg. The county's health services are mainly organized at three levels, according to Johansson and Thorslund (1991, pp.30–1):

1   At primary care level there are the district doctors, district nurses, assistant nurses, district physiotherapists and district occupational therapists. Day care and local nursing homes are within the primary care system. The district boundaries are conterminous with those of the municipal social services.
2   At county level there are the county hospital and several local hospitals.
3   At regional level there are the more specialized regional centres of health care, training and research.

Hospital care and medical services

Thorslund and Parker (1992, p.6) point out that long-term medical care was the responsibility of the counties before the 1992 parliamentary reforms. Each county has a large county hospital and several smaller local hospitals (Johansson and Thorslund, 1991, p.31). There are about 49,000 beds for somatic long-term care. Often the Swedish geriatric departments (the *langvardskliniker*) are linked to general hospitals. Their aim is to rehabilitate (see Swedish Institute, 1989a, p.2).

Sweden has 2.5 doctors per 1,000 inhabitants (OECD, 1987). Compared with the other EU countries, this ratio is greater than that of France, Ireland,

Luxemburg, the Netherlands, Portugal and the UK, equal to that of Germany, but less than that of Belgium, Denmark, Greece, Spain and Italy (see Eurostat, 1991b, p.88). Sundström (1988, p.172) refers to the lack of doctors in the rural areas of Sweden (see Sjoholt, 1988), where older people are diversely affected and usually worse off than their urban counterparts. Long-term care clinics or geriatric clinics provide approximately 14,000 beds for short-term recovery, respite and rehabilitation programmes. Older people take up one-third of all medicines (Johansson and Thorslund, 1992).

Nursing

Home health care in Sweden has been provided exclusively by visiting nurses, according to Sundström (1988, p.172). About 13% of 65–84-year-olds, on the basis of Sundström's sources, are probably in contact with a visiting nurse. According to the Swedish Institute (1989b, p.2), the number of district nurses has trebled since the mid-1970s: there are about 49,000. However, the nursing service as a whole is unevenly staffed and inadequate, which was also the case in the pre-1992 era of so-called 'plentiful' state care. A 'night patrol' call and emergency service is provided by a home help and a nursing assistant, who provide care for older people during most of the night.

Mental health care

The older population take up half of all mental health care in Sweden and one-third of all medicines. Sweden has more mental health hospital beds than anywhere in the world. Psychiatric care is often linked to the county or smaller hospitals. However, at least 30–35% of patients in psychiatric beds need not be there (see Johansson and Thorslund, 1991, p.31).

Institutional care

According to the Swedish Institute (1989b, p.2), there are some 900 municipal old people's homes (*alderdomshem*) in Sweden, with approximately 44,000 places. Central nursing homes provide a total of about 15,000 beds for ill and frail older people; these are large, providing some 100–200 beds, and are usually adjacent to hospitals. Local nursing homes provide a total of approximately 21,000 beds; these are smaller, with only 40–60 beds in each (see Johansson and Thorslund, 1991, p.31).

As Sundström (1988, p.179) has indicated, there is a heavy over-representation of the never-married and of persons from the lower social classes in institutional care. Institutional care was regarded as the best type of provision for older people from 1960 until the late 1980s, as described by Johansson and Thorslund (1992). The number of beds within residential and mental health care establishments doubled. The policy is now to decrease institutional care and increase serviced social housing and extra-mural care. By 1988 the number of old people in these homes had decreased by 2,000 (see Swedish Institute, 1989b, p.2). However, the number of institutions has since remained much the same. The changes will take some time to materialize.

There has been a gigantic turnaround in policy. Today there are at least 45,000 apartments or service houses (see Johansson and Thorslund, 1991, p.33). However, there are still about twice as many residents in the old people's homes (mostly in single rooms) as there are in the apartments of serviced houses (Sundström, 1988, p.175). The first change will be to decrease the proportion of those aged 65–79 who are resident in nursing homes, and to increase their number in the apartments within serviced houses. The long-term care wards, once under the auspices of the county councils, are now under the auspices of the municipalities. Decisions regarding admissions are now made locally. There are 36,000 beds in Swedish nursing homes (the *sjukhem*), according to the Swedish Institute (1989b, p.3). There are three types of nursing homes. Firstly, there are the central nursing homes, which are usually annexes to a geriatric nursing department. Secondly, there are the nursing homes which are independent of the hospitals and are organized within the primary care system. Thirdly, 4% of the long-term care beds are in private nursing homes, and 2% of places are in old people's homes (see Swedish Institute, 1989b, p.4).

As well as the traditional long-term hospital wards, the old people's homes and the nursing homes, there are the group dwellings (the *grupp-boende*). These often cater for persons with special needs – for example, persons with dementia. The group dwellings consist of small housing collectives of about 6–8 persons. There are just over 1,000 older people living in this type of dwelling. It will take time for the innovation to provide a significant alternative to more traditional types of institutional care.

After 1992 the municipalities have taken on long-term medical care as an additional responsibility, including the administration of nursing and home medical care. The subsidies to the localities are determined by: the number of older residents; the number taking early retirement, and the number of older people living alone. Before the economic crash of the early 1990s the rural areas received additional sums; since then the tendency has been to prioritize resources where there are more users within urban areas. In Swedish law, citizens have the right to equal conditions and benefits; however, since the 1992 reforms the regional diversities have inevitably created geographical disparities.

Long before the idea of purchaser/provider splits was floated in the UK, the Swedes were setting up primary care centres to provide treatment or purchase hospital services when the care centre did not have the appropriate facilities and expertise.

Hospital day care appears to be scant (see Sundström, 1988, p.174), but ironically, disproportionate numbers of hospital beds are taken up by older patients, as stated earlier. Lagergren (1986, p.31) observes that about two-thirds of bed stays in somatic medical care in Sweden are taken up by persons aged 65+. In a country where marriage and family patterns have been changing dramatically in recent years, Lagergren reminds the providers of care that the single divorced have a higher mortality rate, are often more susceptible to ill health, and are more likely to be users of social and health services.

Personal social services

Social services are run by 284 municipalities, which together with the county councils are obliged to ensure that older people receive the help they need (Johansson and Thorslund, 1991, p.30). Lagergren (1986) and Nilsson and Wadeskog (1988) are unsure about the future of the formal services in Sweden. Nilsson and Wadeskog (1988, p.53) state: 'We envisage social service production becoming more and more informalized over the coming years.' This remark must be borne in mind when outlining the formal services available for the older population in Sweden, added to which there are also the repercussions flowing from the deep recession of the early 1990s.

The Swedish form of personal social services can be traced back to 1862–3, when social service welfare was established within the municipalities, as described by Ricknell (1986, p.480). Social care of older people has a similarly long history. Formal training of social workers began in 1910, when social workers were introduced to care for vulnerable groups such as the older population. At the end of the 1960s a national drive initiated by the government helped to revitalize the local services with the slogan 'Putting decisions closer to the people', anticipating the 'closer-to-home' approach in the UK by over twenty years.

The current social care services have been provided for most of Sweden's post-war period, on the principle that the state should respond to the needs of its citizens. It was a time when the professionalization of care was set up in preference to informal, voluntary care and private care. However, the principles of state welfare have worn thin, so that the varied services in kind began to decline in the late 1980s.

Social workers

The responsibility for social work resides within the Social Welfare Department; 284 municipalities are responsible for the delivery of social services. Social workers in Sweden rarely do any direct work with older people outside the hospitals. According to Sundström (1988, p.180), there are about 2,200 qualified social workers in Sweden, many of whom are involved indirectly with older people in making assessments and providing professional supervision.

Meals services

Meals-on-wheels have only been available for less than 1% of the older population, and are provided by only 6 out of 10 municipalities in Sweden. This is surprising, given that this service is usually one of the larger organized services in most industrialized countries.

Day care

Sundström (1988) states that day care is provided in 80% of the municipalities, whose facilities are much the same as in the UK. However, Nilsson and Wadeskog (1988, pp.40–1) cite the general contraction of social services in Sweden. Where services do exist, the older people in Sweden are particularly dissatisfied with the social service approaches to their care.

Home care/help

The provision of home care for those 'at risk' aged 80+, and appropriate long-term health care for the older chronically sick, are the immediate challenges for the Swedish welfare and health authorities. Every municipality provides home help. There are also night patrols by nurses and home helps in the Swedish municipalities.

With regard to home help, on the basis of the data provided by Tornstam (1992, p.139), probably about 6% of the older population receive home help, on average for about 205 hours per year. As Thorslund and Parker (1992, p.4) point out, the demand for home helps increased significantly during the 1980s; in fact, in 1969 home help amounted to a total of 35 million hours, which had increased to 94 million hours by 1988, as cited by Johansson and Thorslund (1991, p.32). Sundström best describes the development of home help in Sweden. Other writers have tended to overlook the problems faced within the Swedish home help system. Sundström (1988, p.170) describes the slow beginnings of home help care – firstly, because of the lack of labour. The municipalities depended upon middle-aged houseworkers, paid on an hourly basis. From the 1960s to the mid-1980s, the Swedish (and Norwegian) government paid family members as home helps, but the number has steadily been on the decline. Secondly, the Swedish home helps lack status. The introduction of training and the establishment of full-time as well as part-time home helps are attempts to enhance their image, but in spite of this the ratio of home helps to older households failed to increase after the mid-1980s, according to Sundström (1988, p.171). Before the 1992 reforms, municipalities recovered 35% of their costs from the National Board of Health and Social Welfare, and another 5% from clients' fees.

The provision of home care is increasingly driven by budgetary and regional criteria and not by need. Before the 1992 reforms, 40–44% of those aged 80+, 13–17% of those aged 65–79 and about 27% of households with 1–2 older persons had some home care, on the basis of statements by Thorslund and Parker (1992) and Sundström (1988). Given the 'unwillingness of the home help administrators', as cited by Sundström (1988, p.171), to spend money on home helps, and escalating costs of any form of home care, it is hardly likely in the harsher economic climate post-1992 that there will be more home help for the older population.

Other services

Under social welfare management, as described by Thorslund and Parker (1992, p.3), transport services, food preparation, snow clearance and technical aids have provided state welfare for the older population during the halcyon days of socialist welfare. These services are described as 'benefits in kind'. In addition, respite provision, case management groups, alarm systems and other responsive services have been amongst the best-quality services in Europe. Cheap fares on the municipal transport services (*fardtjansten*) and in some instances free travel for shorter journeys are referred to by Sjoberg (1985) and by Sundström (1988).

Voluntary care agencies and support organizations

As stated above, the social services are contracting in Sweden, and with them the care of older people; co-operatives are taking their place. Various local initiatives at grassroots have been created and fill the social work gaps that exist between the formal and the informal carers, which Nilsson and Wadeskog (1988) name 'the fourth sector'. They are described as 'self-reliant groups' in the same way as the co-operatives are in Germany.

Unlike the situation in most European countries, Sweden has little place for voluntary work within its strategy of extra-mural care, as observed by many Swedish authors, such as Thorslund and Parker (1992, p.8). Over the years the Salvation Army and the Red Cross have provided various forms of care for the older population, but generally volunteering has been minimal and usually consists of social contacts. Where volunteers do get involved, it usually consists of organizing social events (Johansson and Thorslund, 1992, p.34). In fact, the labour unions have resisted volunteering, because it has been seen as a threat to existing jobs. However, expediency now dictates differently in the climate of deep recession and mounting costs. Just as in the UK, there are a growing number of younger retired persons providing care and services for the older population. A new Swedish organization, the 'Ageing is growing' organization, has begun to attract older volunteers (see Thorslund and Parker, 1992, p.8).

Some 30% of the older Swedish population are members of various pensioners' organizations (see Swedish Institute, 1989a, p.4). In almost every municipality there are pensioners' councils, which act in an advisory capacity to the authorities regarding the running of the services, as described by the CPA (1989, p.140).

With regard to the carers, Johansson and Thorslund (1992) and Thorslund and Parker (1992) refer to the care leave policies that have been legislated for within the social insurance system. It remains to be seen whether this innovation will also founder upon the economic rock of hard-headed expediency. The support of the formal sector for voluntary units has been almost non-existent in Sweden. Another alien element in the new plural mix is that of private welfare and health care provision. Private agencies are now beginning to operate within the welfare strategy. For some time to come, in the wake of the new mix of welfare, there will necessarily be a lag in both awareness and ability to cope with a plural welfare system. Few countries can be as ill-prepared as Sweden for the transition from a universalist welfare system to a plural welfare system, and the mix between the public, private and voluntary services of care.

Informal care

Care is not a private matter in Sweden. The offspring have no legal responsibility to care for their aged parents, but there is a collective responsibility, which strives to secure the good of others. This collective altruism is founded upon an institutionalized concept of social citizenship (see Leibfried, 1991, p.23).

Families within the northern Scandinavian countries have traditionally been authoritarian nuclear families (Todd, 1985, p.54). However, Scandinavian families have altered dramatically under the impact of the liberation of women as well as the liberal views within socialist-inspired movements which regard families as extended welfare units of the state. There is evidence that the Swedish people prefer to turn to the family when they have small problems, but to the formal carers when they have large and long-term problems (for example, see Platz, 1989; Tornstam, 1992).

Hernes (1986, p.46) points out that more and more Swedes rank state care above family care: whereas in 1969 only 16% of older people preferred help from the state or the municipality, in 1981 58% preferred state intervention to family care. She adds that, according to surveys, most women prefer impersonal, abstract and bureaucratic care to care within the family. The state has created a substitute care culture, and most Swedish people have now been socialized into the welfare society with a different set of expectations from those of earlier generations. Also, the Scandinavian countries along with the Western and Central European countries have a significantly high percentage of solitary older people. The marriage rate has been decreasing dramatically whilst the 'singles culture' has been increasing rapidly. At the same time, Swedish women aged 49–67 are a shrinking 'caretaker pool' (see Hernes, 1986, p.46); 80% of Swedish women are in paid employment (Swedish Institute, 1989b, p.4). They have also been accustomed to the state taking over. Women have received considerable support from the welfare state in their days of motherhood, ranging from the most generous post-natal cover in Europe, whereby the father may stay at home to nurse children without loss of income, to an adequate pension which is not dependent upon their employment record. Half of the carers of the chronically sick, the disabled, the children and the older population are also in paid employment.

The Swedish government supports informal care in certain situations: for example, in family crises a family member may stay off work for 3–10 days to care for the older person involved, and the leave is paid for by the employer. When the care needed is long-term, the carer can claim economic support from the municipality or county, according to Johansson and Thorslund, 1991, p.34). In some cases the family member may be employed by the municipality or county as carer; about 9,000 such persons are so employed, as cited by the same authors. If the carer is over 65 he or she cannot be employed as a carer. However, a cash payment is made to the older person in need of care in order to buy in care; 20,000 families receive such cash allowances (Johansson and Thorslund, 1991, p.34).

In addition, older people are moving from their familiar family circumstances to alien cities and townscapes. Nilsson and Wadeskog (1988, p.33) draw attention to the emigration of older people to central Sweden and the dislocation of older people's lives as more and more older Swedes live solitary and fragmented lives. The abuse of alcohol also features as an increasing problem for the solitary older person; detecting the abuse within the single-person household is difficult.

In Sweden nowadays, the family is expected to take on more and more care of older relatives. For the most part, informal home care will be offered to the older person, but many family members will only undertake this reluctantly. This is not to say that family ties do not exist: for example, 46% of the older population either visit or are visited by their offspring each week (see Tornstam, 1992, p.143), and probably 54% of older Swedes live within 15 kilometres of their offspring. Until now, Swedish families have had the state to underpin their home care; will they be able to cope with a severely reduced level of support?

Leisure pursuits and education

Older Swedes are provided with private, government-subsidized adult education run by associations. In addition, special courses are run for older adults at *folk* high schools. Social and leisure activities are also made available by the municipalities. Programmes are organized locally for older people which may consist of study groups, or dance, theatre and film shows, as well as tours and outings. Discounts are provided for older cinemagoers and older students on educational courses.

As stated earlier, about 30% of older people in Sweden are members of pensioners' organizations (Swedish Institute, 1989b, p.4). They also have an active voice in the planning of local services and activities (see CPA, 1989, p.140). Pensioners' councils have been established to advise municipal authorities on social and health issues of public concern. Significant amongst the organizations providing educational and social events is the National Organization of Pensioners (Pensionarernas Riksorganisation).

Rural aspects

Sweden is the fourth-largest country in Europe, with very remote rural areas in harsh environments. Regarding the rural areas, the policy of the Swedish system is to secure comfortable housing for older people and to encourage and support the transfer of the older population from the remoter areas to the more concentrated settlements where the infrastructures of care are better-resourced. The municipal planning institutions play a large part in this, as described by Sjoholt (1988, p.77). Central places are designated as 'support points' (the *stodjepunkt*), which are mainly located in the more populated areas. However, as Stahl and Ahlund (1992) show, in recent studies conducted by the University of Lund, housing and transportation in rural areas have created huge difficulties for the older Swedish population in four municipalities in sparsely populated areas of the south.

Conclusion

The weakness of the Swedish currency in the early 1990s has weakened the provision of health and social services. The care of older people has been expensive in Sweden. Not long before the economic crash, Sundström (1988, pp. 167–8) pointed out that old age accounted for about 40% of social costs in Sweden. Years beforehand, Alva Myrdal (1935) made a gloomy forecast that the growing number of old people 'would poison the whole social atmosphere' from the 1970s onwards. This did not occur, but the poisoned chalice of expediency in the hands of a conservative government has brought deep gloom to the Swedes. The much-vaunted Swedish economy has been dealt a severe blow, resulting in major long-term changes from a welfare state to a mixed welfare system, within which there will necessarily be untried programmes and a public totally unprepared for the major social care upheavals entailed.

The services taken for granted by the electorate for more than thirty years are no longer guaranteed in the medium or long term. The welfare and health care systems in Sweden are in crisis. The triangle of care was dominated by the welfare state for almost forty years. The local state effectively orchestrated the services at county and municipal levels. The welfare interventions of the Swedish Church and the voluntary agencies were uneasily integrated into the country's service strategies. The triangulation of care was therefore torn apart when the state shifted officially from a monopoly of state welfare to a plural system of care in 1992. As shown in Table 6, Sweden's welfare system is in transition, torn between monocephalic and polycephalic structures.

The immediate effects of this U-turn in Sweden have had considerable consequences for the older population, their families and households, their formal carers, and for the local and state welfare systems. Some of the main consequences are highlighted by Thorslund and Parker, 1992, pp.9–12).

Firstly, in an enterprise culture the poorer older people lack the ability to pay for high-level standards of state welfare and health care. Secondly, there will be marked differences between poorer and more affluent older consumers, as well as between the urban and rural older populations. Thirdly, within families and households, the burden of care upon the informal carers will be felt more than elsewhere in Europe. Lagergren (1988) states that maintaining the current high levels of care in Sweden would absorb the entire young population entering the job market by the year 2000. The culture of informal care in Sweden exists, but to a far lesser extent than in most European countries. Moreover, Swedish people have taken a monopolistic system of all-embracing care for granted over many years. Fourthly, with regard to the social care and state welfare apparatus, the universalist system is breaking down into multiple-tier systems within regionally diverse municipalities. In addition, third-rate systems are inevitable within the more deprived rural areas. Finally, the costs for social and health care have been met entirely by taxation in Sweden. In recent years, the electorate have complained that taxes are far too high. The deep recession of the 1990s means that there will have to be less taxation, and therefore fewer services. It remains to be seen to what extent the erstwhile welfare provision for older people will survive, as the role of the state is diminished, and monocephalic structures are weakened. The Swedish welfare system is now in flux and older people face confusion and uncertainty.

5 Denmark

Demography

Denmark has the third-largest proportion of older people in greater Europe, judging by the 1990 statistic as shown in Table 1. It will probably maintain its position by the year 2025. Its proportion of older people to the general public is likely to increase by about 6.6% by the year 2025 – according to the CPA's projection, the proportion of the population aged 65+ will be as high as 22.2%; along with Sweden and the Netherlands, this proportion ranks second, just behind Switzerland (see CPA, 1989, p.49) and above such countries as Luxemburg and Finland. The CPA (1993, p.61) stated that the proportion of women aged 80+ was twice that of their male counterparts in 1990. The life expectancy of women at 65 is 17.9 years, which ranks eleventh in Europe; that of men is 14.2 years, which ranks twelfth (UN, 1991; Eurostat, 1991a).

Socio-political and administrative background

Legislative authority in Denmark rests with the crown and with parliament (the Folketing). Their jurisdiction covers the Faroes, Greenland and Denmark. The monarchy exercises executive power through the 19-minister State Council, headed by the Prime Minister. The Social Democratic Party has had the greatest say regarding the welfare and health policies affecting older people in Denmark.

The history of welfare in Denmark has been discussed elsewhere by Johansen (1986). Formal care for the older population goes back to the paternalism of the Poor Relief Reforms of 1798, 1802 and 1803. Later, sickness insurance funds were introduced in the 1820s and 1830s. However, most of nineteenth-century Denmark was overcast by the shadow of the work-houses, which carried with them the stigma of poor relief and the loss of political rights. As in the UK, the categories of the 'undeserving and deserving poor' created stigma for many older persons along with other needy groups. Only in 1891, when the Old Age Relief Act was enacted, were the older population excluded from the poor relief system. Municipalities were to contribute three-quarters of total living costs for those aged 60+ by the introduction of a means-tested non-contributory payments system. It was to be the harbinger of today's more universal welfare system.

In 1892 the Sickness Insurance Reform made it possible for those with limited means to make use of subsidized health care. These systems were monitored by state commissions. Such welfare schemes were in place long before the much-vaunted Bismarckian social reforms (Johansen, 1986, p.299), and they were pushed forward by the peasantry. The 1922 Old Age Pension Reform followed, then the famous Social Reform in 1933, which introduced universal benefits as a citizen's right. The stage was set for the post-war democratic state welfare system. Social welfare for all (universalism), social rights and citizen entitlement (flat-rate benefits and free social services) were set up in one of Europe's most equitable and efficient state welfare systems.

Johansen (1987, p.195) describes the administration of welfare within the counties and municipalities. The 14 counties (*amter*) are run by their county council (the *amtsradet*). Within the counties, the Social Welfare and Health Committees (Social og Sundhedsudvalg) are responsible for monitoring and supervising social security. The counties run the hospitals and the social centres (the *socialcentre*). Within the 275 municipalities, the Municipal Social Welfare Committees (Socialudvalg) come under the local councils (the *kommunalbestyrelsen*), half of which have only 10,000 inhabitants. In the context of the care of older people, these provide most of the social security benefits, public general pensions, rent subsidies and housing allowances. The Social Service Department (the Socialforvaltningen) executes the decisions made by the Municipal Social Welfare Committees.

At central government level, the Ministry of Social Affairs (Social-ministeriet) has three special divisions: the National Social Office, the National Social Security Office and the National Social Board of Appeal.

The Aeldrekommissionen, a Danish parliamentary commission, acts in an official advisory capacity and publishes reports which have influenced policies for the older population since the early 1980s. As far back as 1980, the principle of maintaining people in their own homes rather than in residential care was advocated by the commission. Within the last decade, several years before the UK's community care policy took off, the Aeldrekommissionen was instrumental in bringing about the U-turn in policies which led to the contraction of residential and nursing home care and the expansion of home care. The need for home care services has initiated the privatization, decentralization and de-bureaucratization of caring arrangements (Abrahamson, 1989; 1990; 1991). Services have been purchased in the market; have been provided closer to the older population within their own localities and neighbourhoods, and have been provided by voluntary and self-help institutions rather than by the municipalities. These welfare state arrangements have worked well.

Denmark's politicians and electorate have regarded the dismantling of the welfare state in other European countries with great unease. Symptomatic of this loyalty to Scandinavian value systems was Denmark's opposition to the Eurocrats' vision of standardized EU systems. Denmark, the first Scandinavian country to enter the EU, was also the first member country to seriously question the administrative and political structure of the EU, hence its historic rejection at first of the Maastricht Treaty on 3 June 1992. The 'no' vote was essentially a reaction to top-heavy bureaucratization in Brussels.

However, things are not perfect in Denmark. There is a great deal of confusion over the lines of responsibility and authority in the health care sector. For example, Hunter (1986, pp.19–20) notes that GP services are the county's responsibility, but most primary care – such as home nursing, the former nursing homes, public health nursing and some rehabilitation services – are the responsibilities of the municipalities. Physiotherapy is the responsibility of the county, but the care of older people is the responsibility of the municipality. Also, the catchment areas for hospitals, districts for GPs, public health nurses, home nursing services and the former nursing homes do not match. In 1988 the sharp division between the hospital services and other health and social services was rectified, with the move towards a mix of health and social care at municipal level (Ramhoej, 1992, p.16).

Social security: pensions and benefits

The single most important piece of post-war Danish legislation was the 1956 pension scheme, which introduced the 'full old age pension' (*den fulde folkepension*). Shortly afterwards the general widows' pension was introduced. In 1961 the old tag of the 'undeserving poor' was eliminated by the Public Assistance Act.

Danish pensions are substantial but about half of the pensioners have no other source of income. According to the Ministry of Social Affairs (1990), the pension in Denmark roughly equals the total sum allocated to sickness benefits and unemployment benefits, as cited by Abrahamson (1991, p.52).

Three major state pension schemes were set up in October 1984. Firstly, there is the universal flat-rate pension (the *folkepension*) for all resident nationals. Secondly, for employees there is the employment-related occupational pension scheme (the *arbejdsmarkedets tillaegspension*). Thirdly, for those who are members of an employment insurance fund, there is the voluntary early retirement pay scheme (the *fortidspension*) for those aged 60+. All three funds are financed by payments from the insured person; from the employer for the employment-related scheme, and from the government to cover any deficit incurred in the universal and voluntary early retirement schemes. Eligibility for the universal flat-rate pension is fixed at 67 years of age. Entitlement to a full pension requires at least 40 years' residence. For those residing for a shorter period the pension is calculated in fortieths of the full pension multiplied by the number of years of residence. Entitlement to the employment-related pension is acquired at 67 years of age; 40 years' contributions are required for the maximum pension. A flexible formula has been introduced for immigrants, expatriates and refugees, whereby their years of residence outside Denmark are regarded as years of residence within Denmark.

Eligibility for the voluntary early retirement pension requires that a person be aged 60–66 and have been a member of an unemployment fund for a minimum of 10 years within the last 15 years. This pension adds up to 90% of insurable earnings for the first $2\frac{1}{2}$ years, 80% in the following 2 years and 70% from then onwards. All of these are subject to an upper limit.

In addition to these three main schemes, persons aged 60+ may reduce their working hours and receive state compensation (see CPA, 1989, p.50). Early pensions may also be granted for social or health reasons. There is also a means-tested supplement. All pensions are taxed as income.

Abrahamson (1991, p.53) states that many who have both their state pension and occupational pension end up with an income of 75–90% of their prior salary. He states that there is a growing divide between these more affluent pensioners and those who are simply on the basic state pension. One-third of the employed have private pensions (Wilderom and Gottschalk, 1991, p.117). There is a considerable gap between them and the vast majority of older people who are dependent upon the state pension. An upper-bracket of more affluent older people exists.

In comparative terms, Danish old age benefits as a percentage of overall benefits rank seventh amongst the EU countries (Eurostat, 1991b, p.84). The purchasing power of benefits in Denmark ranks fourth within the EU (Eurostat, 1991b, p.83). On the basis of these rankings, Denmark does not match the pensions of other major European countries. Abrahamson (1991, p.37) regards the Danish old age pensions as inadequate. He states that the recipients of the Danish pension are split into two: most have an income of between 40–50% of their former earnings, and others have between 75–90% of their former salaries (pp.52–3). However, in terms of housing benefits, provision for a majority of the older population is much more significant.

Housing

From the late 1970s and early 1980s the policy has been to enable older people to live in their own homes rather than enter institutional care, as emphasized by Norregaard (1986, p.14). He also adds that most Danes prefer to live in their own homes. Housing subsidies and improvements to houses have been massive. As in Norway, there are generous allowances for pensioners living in rented and owner-occupied accommodation, providing financial support for expenses including rent and repairs. There are also allowances for heating costs and home alterations (CPA, 1989, p.50). In comparative terms, the housing benefits in Denmark rank second amongst the EU countries (Eurostat, 1991b, p.84).

Special public housing designed to meet the needs of older people, such as service flats and sheltered accommodation, form part of Danish housing policy. As will be explained on page 99, after 1988 no nursing homes were to be built. Instead, sheltered housing, housing collectives and adapted flats are now subsidized and given the same financial status as the nursing homes.

On average, about half of the older population own their own home. However, ownership as well as housing conditions for older people in Denmark are uneven: three-quarters of the older population in rural areas own their home compared to about one-quarter in the urban areas. Abrahamson (1991, pp.53–4) provides an updated picture of the housing situation facing the older urban residents. In Copenhagen 15% own their own homes; about half have to cope with stairs and about one-fifth of the houses are below modern standards. Citing Danish research, Abrahamson concludes that the living standards of the older population are below those of the general population.

Norregaard (1986, pp.14–15), in an earlier study, identifies, in approximate terms, the 1% of older Danish people who live in rented single rooms; the 49% who live in single-family houses (some with gardens); the 10% who live in agricultural properties, and the 40% living in flats. He refers to 9% of the older population who find it difficult to go up stairs, and 2% who cannot climb them, but still live above the ground floor.

About a quarter of older people in Denmark find that their home is too large, but those who have lived in their homes for twenty years and more are reluctant to move. High heating costs and expensive maintenance have created financial burdens for older residents in older and larger accommodation – a problem shared by the older population in many parts of Europe, as illustrated elsewhere in this study.

Platz (1989, p.23) describes similar findings regarding the housing conditions of the older population: 25% live on the second floor without a lift, and 11% have no bath in their home. These conditions have prompted the Danish authorities to prioritize housing adaptations and increased housing benefits. By the year 2000 about 30% of older couples and about 60% of single older persons will not own their own house, on the basis of data cited by Abrahamson (1991, p.56).

In order to provide for these vulnerable people, the Housing for the Elderly Act 1987 blocked the building of any more municipal old people's homes and entitled the municipalities to provide subsidies for the building of 'old age flats' adapted to their needs and possible disabilities. Unfortunately, very few municipalities have implemented the scheme, and where they have done so, relatively few flats have been constructed.

Wilderom and Gottschalk (1991, pp.118–20) describe the four major types of housing provision used by older people, two of which can no longer be constructed. Firstly, there are the 'service flats' (*lette kollektivboliger*) which cater for 3,800 older people. By law they could not be built after 1989. These are suitable for disabled persons, and are served by home helps and district nurses. The pensioners pay 15% of their income as rent. Secondly, there are the 'sheltered houses' (*beskyttede boliger*), which are partly nursing homes and partly service flats. They cater for 6,800 older people with permanent diseases. The municipalities decide who should occupy these purpose-designed flats. Here too, the pensioners only pay 15% of their income as rent. Thirdly, there are the 'pensioners' flats' (*kommunale pensionistboliger*), which cater for 30,000 older people. These are older properties which have no bathrooms and no elevator, and no more of these could be made available after 1987. Once again the pensioners only pay 15% of their income as rent. Fourthly, there are the 'flats for disabled persons in non-profit housing' (*aeldreegnede boliger i almennyttigt byggeri*), which cater for 20,000 older people and are suitable for disabled people. There are elevators in these flats. As in the previous cases, the pensioners only pay 15% of their income as rent. The municipality decides upon occupancy.

Home improvements (*boligaendringer*) are available to install an elevator and to adapt a house for the disabled. The Urban Renewal Act 1989 provided the homes of many older people with central heating, alarm systems and elevators where necessary. There are no charges for these.

Health care

The older Danes are very active. Of men aged 65–69, approximately 24% are in paid employment, as are 9% of women in the same age band. Of men aged 70–74, 12.7% are in paid employment, as are 2.6% of women within the same age band. About 85% of the older population in Denmark are mobile both within and outside their homes, according to Abrahamson (1991, p.54). About 10% of persons aged 80+ need help with personal care on a daily basis;

Wilderom and Gottschalk (1991, p.115) state that 11% are fully disabled. However, recent research in Denmark, cited by Abrahamson (1991), indicates that only 10–15% of the older Danes report that their health is bad; at least half say that their health is 'good', and the rest state that it is 'pretty good'. A major concern for the health authorities is the number of older people who live alone: their proportion has risen from one-third in 1962 to about 50% in the early 1990s.

Hospital care and medical services

There are 2.6 doctors for every 1,000 inhabitants in Denmark (Eurostat, 1991b, p.88), the fifth-highest ratio in the EU. Staff in day centres and occupational therapy and other related personnel increased from 3,147 in 1983 to 4,560 in 1989 (Wilderom and Gottschalk, 1991, p.117). Hospital and medical consumption is the lowest in the EU, after the UK.

In comparison with other countries, the health of the older Danes is not as impressive as might be expected for a nation with one of the highest reputations for its welfare and health services. For example, the life expectancy at birth of men ranks ninth and that of women tenth in the EU. Death by cancer amongst Danish women is the highest in the EU.

Nursing

There were about 3,450 nurses in Denmark, according to the Danish Statistical Department (1988, pp.26–7), which, according to Wilderom and Gottschalk (1991, p.117), has increased to 4,560. They provide evening and night cover. Nursing care has been criticized in Denmark because the nurses are too busy to provide social and psychological care (see Abrahamson, 1991, p.55). These nurses serve about 159,279 patients within their own homes (Norregaard, 1986, p.28). There are about seven times as many home helps as home nurses. The nurses appear to serve the more aged older people, judging by the data provided by Norregaard (1986, p.27): 12% of those aged 65–79 and 29% of those aged 80+ are served by the home nurses. District nurses patrol the area in radio cars, usually chauffeur-driven (Young, 1986, p.15). In contrast with home help, 'visiting nursing' is always free (see Ramhoej, 1992, p.16).

Mental health care

Stromgren (1985, p.58) states that four medium-sized hospitals for mentally ill persons serve the entire Danish population; these are located near general hospitals, and also serve out-patients. Basic training in psychiatric nursing does not exist in Denmark. Forty per cent of hospital admissions in Denmark are of psychiatric patients. Stromgren (1985) expresses concern about the older mentally ill: they lack the provisions of the older population in most of the Western European countries.

Suicide rates amongst Danish women and men in general are the highest in the EU. The suicide rate of those aged 75+ ranks seventh out of 16 European countries, as cited by Pritchard (1992, p.129). Hunter (1986, pp.18–22), in an insightful commentary, draws attention to major issues which may damage the effectiveness of the health care of older people, some of which appear to affect its delivery more immediately. Firstly, there is a lack of co-ordination at central and regional levels; secondly, there are problems of communication between secondary and primary health care, and thirdly, there are difficulties in the shift to decentralization from what has been a more centralized welfare state system. The rather haphazard development of the Danish health services in the past underlies these major concerns.

Ramhoej (1992, p.24) refers to the psychiatric departments at the municipal hospital 'psychiatric emergency section', which has been set up as a pilot in Copenhagen, and is open around the clock. In addition to younger patients who have benefited from the unit, older confused or difficult patients (perhaps suffering from Alzheimer's Disease) plus their distraught carers can call upon the unit for help outside of hours.

Institutional care

In 1977, 7% of Danes aged 65+ lived in an institution (Norregaard, 1986, p.15). In the decade 1977–87, the proportion of those aged 75+ in nursing homes (*plejehjem*) dropped by 4.1%, according to data cited by Abrahamson (1991, p.50). There are about 47,000 older people in 1,200 Danish nursing homes, which now represents 6% of the older population, according to Pedersen (1992). He points out that the ratio of highly-trained nurses has been one to one. Thirteen per cent of those aged 80–84 are in nursing homes, and one in three of the patients in these homes are aged 85+, as stated by Norregaard (1986, p.6). The people in the homes receive their full pension: they keep their savings, as reported by Pedersen (1993). There are no waiting lists to enter the nursing homes, except in Copenhagen. Even here, the longest wait is seldom more than six months. However successful the nursing home programme appears to have been, the state has decided to end this type of provision, but clearly this cannot be done overnight. It must be said that the standard of nursing care is not as high as in the UK. Only half of the staff in nursing homes are qualified (Wilderom and Gottschalk, 1991, p.113). Costs are also rising, and are prohibitive.

As Pedersen (1993) points out, the new legislation formulated in the Housing for the Elderly Act 1987 put a stop to the building of any more nursing homes. The Act stressed that institutional care and home care were not to be regarded as totally separate, but as services on the same continuum of care. From the Act's implementation in 1988, no more nursing homes were to be built. In some areas the local authorities have already closed down their nursing homes and substituted dwellings suitable for older people, whose nursing needs are served by the home nurses and home helps. In other words, institutionalization has ceased to be a major provision because of this dramatic change. In some ways it resembles the brave Italian decision to close down its psychiatric institutions.

The 'old age dwellings' which are to replace the nursing homes receive a subsidy of 80% from the state, 18% from the municipality and 2% from the inhabitants. If they are unable to pay, the state steps in to do so on their behalf. Although the response has been uneven, 7,000 'old age dwellings' have been constructed since 1987, as reported by Pedersen (1993). The policy is to build them in the area where the people already reside. Leeson (1993) describes the 'congregate housing' which is now replacing the former nursing homes. These consist of 12–20 houses with a common service centre to provide care when needed. District nurses and home helps work from the centre. The residents consist of a mix of older and younger people.

Respite or short-term care (*daghjem og dagcentre*) is well-organized and well-established in Denmark.

Personal social services

There is no stigma in approaching the social services in Denmark because the users of the social services are not just the poor, as is well described by Jamieson (1991b, p.116). The Danes are socialized into the ethos of state welfare provision, and their social services are amongst the best in Europe.

Social work (*dagcentre*) services are separate from health care provision. The Danish social services receive more money than the health services. However, as Young (1986, p.16) observes, health and social services are highly integrated, although Hunter (1986) observes that the integration is sometimes patchy. Like health, social services are subsidized by government grants and subsidies. Older people seek assistance from the Social and Health Administration in the municipality.

Social workers

There are about 5,200 social workers (*socialraadgivere*) in Denmark, about 13% of whom are private (see Sorensen, 1986, p.95). The client has a right by law to be seen by a social worker when seeking assistance from the municipality (see Ramhoej, 1992, p.5).

Meals services

Older people only pay 40% towards the costs of 'meal distribution' (*madud-bringning*) (Wilderom and Gottschalk, 1991, p.121). Often the home help provides the meal at the older person's home.

Day care

There are about 158 day centres (*dagcentre*) with a total of about 5,600 places, as cited by Norregaard (1986, p.28). Day care and innovatory short-term care are available as alternatives to residential or nursing care. The policy of committing fewer and fewer older people to old people's homes has been supported by alternative community care provisions, such as a 24-hour day care service (Abrahamson, 1991, pp.49–50). The number of older people using this service on a regular basis is about 49,088, as cited by Abrahamson (1991).

Many converted older people's homes are used as centres (Ramhoej, 1992, p.16) which offer cafeteria lunches to the older local population. This has proved to be a better alternative to meals-on-wheels.

Home care/help

About 6% of the older population receive home help (*hjemmehjaelp*) (Pedersen, 1992). There are about 29,489 home helps in Denmark (Wilderom and Gottschalk, 1991, p.121). The service is financed by the state and the munici-pality. Training for them has been obligatory since 1976, amounting to a total of 30 full days. According to Olsen and Gregersen (1988), the division of home help time given by the formal services, in rank order, consists of cleaning, shopping, cooking, and washing clothes. These services are provided for some 18% of the older population, as cited by Pedersen (1993).

'Permanent domestic assistance' is free (Ramhoej, 1992, p.16). As mentioned earlier, the home helps are also attached to the new 'congregate housing'. The service varies from a couple of hours' cleaning a week to full day care. Talking, advising and counselling occupy very little of the time allocated to the older population. According to Jamieson (1991b, p.116), 20% of those aged 70+ receive home help. One innovation has been the introduction of teams of home helps, which Abrahamson (1991, p.55) states has been very well received and apparently successful. The service is provided and organized within districts from home care centres, and supervised by a senior district nurse, as described by Young (1986, p.15). Considering the fact that 53% of the older Danish popu-lation live alone and that 23% of those with offspring have not seen any of them nor relatives in the past week, the home help service is a lifeline for many more isolated older people (see Platz, 1989, p.23, as cited by Abrahamson, 1991, p.55; also Wilderom and Gottschalk, 1991, p.121).

The proportion of the older population receiving home help is large. Wilderom and Gottschalk (1991, p.121) state that the following are in receipt of this form of assistance: 15% of persons aged 70–74; 28% of those aged 75–79; 44% of those aged 80–84, and 61% of persons aged 85+.

Other services

Respite care (*daghjem og dagcentre*) and home improvements (*boligaendringer*) are also available to older people and their carers.

Voluntary care agencies and support organizations

The voluntary sector is weak in Denmark, and there are few voluntary agencies. A handful of voluntary organizations provide care, such as Falk (named after its founder), which is a 24-hour agency that responds to emergencies. There is also Dane Age and the Senior Tjenesten (see Leeson, 1993), voluntary agencies which collaborate with the local authorities to build self-help accommodation.

There are many relatively small pressure groups. These mostly exist as minor pensioners' clubs at municipal and national levels. There are four major voluntary pressure groups. Firstly, there is the Aeldresagen (EGV), which is a national organization with many local branches dealing with the formulation of local and national goals for older people; it also provides a travel bureau for them. Secondly, there is the Pensionisternes Faellesrd, which has four regional centres for pensioners. It has a formal right to negotiate in legal matters with the Ministry of Social Affairs in Denmark. Thirdly, there is the Pensionisternes Samvirke, which runs local clubs and also presents the views of pensioners to parliament and the Ministry of Social Affairs. Fourthly, there is the Omsorgsorganisationernes Samvirke, which is an umbrella agency for clubs, organizations and institutions that deliver services for older people.

Informal care

Informal carers continue to provide support for older people within the community. However, the provision of individual informal care and neighbourhood/kinship circles of informal care have been contracting.

Much of what is contained in the UK White Paper, *Caring for People* (Department of Health, 1989), with regard to creating more home care and less institutional care was substantively contained a decade earlier in the statements of the Danish Ministry of Social Affairs in the 1980s (see, for example, Abrahamson, 1991). But there are signs that informal care is declining in Denmark due to the growing numbers of women in paid employment.

The maintenance of older people within the community has been a salient policy in Denmark for more than a decade. Uldall-Hansen (1980, p.74) refers to the objectives in Denmark of keeping older people 'for as long as possible in their own homes'. The new ideas regarding the care of older people were given added impetus in the early 1980s from the Elderly Commission (the Aeldrekommissionen), as described by Abrahamson (1991, p.49). This influential commission advocated that those aged 67+ live in their own homes for as long as possible. Also, in an uncanny way the Danish statements reflected and often were identical with policy statements a decade later in the UK. Norregaard (1986, p.14) says: 'In the last few decades, social policies and housing policies have been aimed at enabling the elderly to remain in their own homes for as long as possible.' Holstein et al. (1991, p.39) also refer to the guiding Danish principle for older people: 'as long as possible in your own home'. They date the principle back to the early 1970s. But to what extent are they supported there by family or kin?

Not much emphasis is given in Denmark to kinship care of older relatives (Jamieson, 1990, p.14). The proportion of the older population living with their family or relatives is declining dramatically: in 1962 there were 21% (Stenhouwer, 1970), but by 1986 this was considerably reduced. Norregaard (1986) in the Danish report of the European Foundation for the Improvement of Living and Working Conditions stated that almost 14% of the older population live with one of their unmarried offspring or with a brother or sister. Norregaard (1986, p.15) admitted that 'the household as a caring unit is on the whole weak and becomes weaker as time passes'. By 1988, Holstein et al. (1991) calculated that the proportion of older people living with their offspring was probably as low as 4%. The caring potential of the family has been considerably diminished. Indeed Wilderom and Gottschalk (1991, p.129) state that there is less potential for informal care because of the integration of women in the labour market, and greater mobility, which separates offspring from their aged parents.

On the basis of the CPA (1989, p.49) statistics, 19.5% of men and 12.3% of women aged 65+ live in the rural areas of Denmark. Schwelder (1985) refers to the mass exodus of Danish people from the rural areas, especially from the islands, and the weakening of the traditional family as households break up and older people are left behind. Here there are considerable gaps in research material.

With regard to the formal systems of care in rural Denmark, transport is less of a problem, as is isolation from major centres. For these reasons there have been fewer transport subsidies in Denmark than in Sweden, Norway and Finland (see Sjoholt, 1988, p.87). Research in the English language into the provision of care in the rural areas has yet to fill the gap in Scandinavian research.

Leisure pursuits and education

The Social Assistance Act 1974 authorized municipal authorities to create clubs and establish study groups, entertainments, excursions, educational programmes and holidays. The Danish *folk* high schools/adult educational colleges provide two-week residential courses. Grants for fees make it possible for less affluent older people to make use of the courses. Those aged 67+ are entitled to a 50% reduction of admission fees to galleries and museums; there are subsidized holidays for those on low incomes. About 13% of older people participate in educational activities (CPA, 1993, p.69), and there are four special pensioners' high schools.

Rural aspects

Population density in Denmark is not as low as in Norway and Sweden. The migration of younger people to the towns and cities often results in older people being left behind, which is a common European phenomenon. Up to the nineteenth century the rural system was centred upon the nucleated village and the common-field system, which engendered communal values. This may help to explain the more collectivist philosophy that characterizes Danish society and inspires its welfare state. Little can be stated at this stage about the care of older people in rural Denmark because of the lack of data.

Conclusion

Allowing for some discrepancies, the Danish welfare state has built up one of the world's most impressive systems of care for older people. It also provides generous benefits provision. The social reformer N.F.S. Gruntwig is quoted by Stovall (1980, p.15) as saying that: 'Few have much and too many too little.' The Danish welfare system has striven to alter the imbalance by holding on to a welfare state model. Approximately 10% of GDP is devoted purely to the care of the older population in Denmark, which is 37% of total government social expenditure (Abrahamson, 1991, pp.50–1). The synchronic plural welfare system adopted by most Northern and Western European countries is becoming more acceptable within Denmark. But, none the less, a monocephalic structure appears to prevail and to centralize most of the provision of care.

Danish institutional care provision is winding down. Home care is increasing: the new policy is to provide, first, more state home help on a 24-hour basis; second, a 24-hour basic home nursing service, and third, specialized housing for older people (see Pedersen, 1993). Older Danish people still expect the state to provide for them (from the cradle to the grave). It only remains to be seen if the taxpayers are able and willing to support the universalist welfare system within the next thirty years, when Denmark will have the second-highest proportion of older people in greater Europe.

Part II

Western Europe

The welfare system and formal health and social care services in Western Europe generally provide a basic support system for most older people within the triangle of care at macro, mezzo and micro levels. These will be identified and described, beginning with the Republic of Ireland, then the UK, the Netherlands, Belgium, France and Luxemburg.

Contrary to popular opinion and the self-criticism that often characterizes Western Europeans, informal home care of the older population is generally more evident in these six Western European countries than in Central and Northern Europe. Certainly the older women in Western Europe generally appear to enjoy a healthier life and a higher quality of life within their families than do their Southern and Eastern European counterparts. On the basis of research, older people in Western Europe enjoy greater autonomy and freedom to determine their lifestyle than older people do in these other countries.

6 The Republic of Ireland

Demography

In many ways, the Republic of Ireland stands out on its own within the EU and Western Europe because of its high fertility rate. However, there will be a 4.7% increase of the Republic's older population by the year 2025 (see CPA, 1993, p.129); 37% of the population is under 19 years of age (CPA, 1993, p.127). As shown in Table 1, the Republic of Ireland has the lowest percentage of older people amongst the countries of Western Europe. Households in Ireland have an average of 3.6 persons per household. However, the republic also has the second-lowest level of one-person households, after Greece, in the EU (see Eurostat, 1991b, p.22). One might be tempted to think that the formal provision of support and care by the state has few gaps to fill but, on the negative side, the care of older people is often eclipsed by child care.

Although the increase in the numbers of older people generally is relatively low, as Carroll (1991, p.238) points out, the proportion of those aged 75+ is projected to increase by 20% and those aged 80+ to increase by 28% by the year 2006. By then the number of older people living alone is expected to have increased by 31%, and there will probably be a 54% increase in the number of older women living alone. The dramatic fall in the birth rate since 1973 (see Leaper, 1991, p.186) helps to explain the projected demographic bulge in the second decade of the twenty-first century.

The life expectancy of Irish women at 65 is 16 years, which ranks twentieth in Europe; that of men at 65 is 13 years, which also ranks twentieth (UN, 1991; Eurostat, 1991a). Clearly, the health of older Irish people is a matter for some concern.

Socio-political and administrative background

The Republic of Ireland (Poblacht na h-Eireann) is run by a parliamentary democracy. The parliament (the Oireachtas) passes and promulgates bills which are signed by the President of Ireland, who is the head of state. The government is headed by the Prime Minister (the Taoiseach). There are two houses of the Oireachtas – the House of Representatives (the Dail) and the Senate (the Seanad). The majority vote in the Dail is critical when major decisions have to be made. There are 145 members in the Dail and 60 members in the Seanad; the latter may delay and suggest amendments to bills passed by the Dail, but older people's lives are largely in the hands of the deliberations in the Dail. The government consists of no less than 7 and no more than 15 members, headed by the Taoiseach. The policies that have affected older people have been formulated by either the Fianna Fail Party or the Fine Gael Party, both of which have eclipsed the Irish Labour Party. Socialism has had minimal impact upon the welfare system.

The Republic of Ireland consists of 31 major administrative counties. Four of these consist of the cities of Dublin, Cork, Limerick and Waterford, and there are 27 other rural counties. A county borough council is elected for the cities, and a county council for the 27 rural areas. In addition, there are a number of smaller boroughs with directly-elected borough councils. Each local authority has a manager who is in charge of the day-to-day administration.

County councils are responsible for health, housing and public assistance services. By means of subsidies, rents may be reduced by their authority to affordable levels for the older tenants. Browne (1990) cites the Irish Housing Act 1966, which made special centralized provision by grant aid to provide for older people. Non-county boroughs, urban districts and towns have had more limited powers.

Social security: pensions and benefits

With regard to social conditions, the older population have incomes which are about half of the income of other Irish social groups (see CPA, 1989, p.82). This must be set against the fact that the Republic of Ireland has the second-lowest disposable national income per head in the affluent EU (Eurostat, 1991b, p.67). The country stands out amongst the countries of Western Europe as more akin to the social conditions of Spain, Portugal, southern Italy and Greece. In the early 1980s the public began to realize that many older single people were amongst the country's poorest. Power's report (1980) shocked Ireland into the realization that charity is not enough. For example, 12% of the older population who were dependent upon social security were in 'absolute poverty'. Today approximately 17.5% of older Irish people live alone (Rosdorff and O'Shea, 1991, p.219). In terms of the breakdown of social protection benefits for the older population, as a percentage of overall benefits, the republic has the lowest provision in the EU (Eurostat, 1991b, p.84).

Leaper (1991, p.186) states that the Irish social security system is a mixture of UK state administration and the Continental system of independently-administered group coverage. There is a dual contributory pension scheme for both sexes, consisting of a retirement pension at 65 and an old age pension from 66 (see CPA, 1989, p.81). Public pensions are about 5.4% of GDP. Between 1966 and 1985 the contributory pension for older couples almost doubled in real terms; in contrast, the non-contributory pension only increased by 60%. There are therefore the 'have-much pensioners' and the 'have-much-less pensioners'. Given the 12% in absolute poverty and these less well-pensioned persons, there are many retired people in severe need.

Social insurance for pensioners was also granted to the self-employed in 1988. There are also many more benefits in kind than there are in many of the EU countries and in greater Europe as a whole, as will be illustrated below.

My Irish study in Cork (Giarchi, 1990a) cites the official Irish government leaflet on benefits, 25/7 (1987), which states: 'British old age pensioners [living in Ireland] should always apply for some non-contributory pension.' Retired Irish people who have been working in England, Wales or Scotland and then retire to Ireland on a UK pension lose out because the prices are more inflated in the republic and the UK pound has recently suffered a lower exchange rate. Hence many Irish pensioners who return to the republic are worse off than they anticipated.

After Power's report (1980), Irish welfare attempted to make up the huge leeway between the poor and the comfortable older population: those living alone are now in receipt of better benefits in kind. From the end of November until the end of March they receive five fuel tokens at the Post Office; 300 free units of electricity in the winter and 200 the rest of the year; free telephone rental and a free black and white television licence. Everyone aged 66+, irrespective of income, travels free on public transport (see Leaper, 1991; Giarchi, 1990a; National Social Service Board, 1989).

Housing

The larger proportion of the older population live in the worst housing. In an attempt to redress the situation, local authorities allocate 12% of new housing to older and disabled people (Carroll, 1991, p.239), amongst other target groups. Their rents are subsidized in accordance with the ability to pay. Such provision is a priority on the basis of the report of the Inter-departmental Committee (1968), which stated amongst its 94 recommendations: 'That it is better, and probably much cheaper, to help the aged to live in the community than to provide for them in hospitals or other institutions.' A permanent liaison committee and co-ordinating officer facilitate the co-ordination of public services. It is recommended that the officer be the Chief Medical Officer for the area.

Between 1972 and 1987 the local authorities provided 12% of new dwellings for older or disabled Irish people (CPA, 1993, p.134). Also, the local authorities introduced sheltered housing for older lone people and older couples on their own in larger urban areas, supported by home helps and meal provision, medical and social services, according to need.

Recent Irish welfare policies have stressed co-ordination between housing and supportive health care for older people. The government working party on services for older people, in *The Years Ahead* report (Ministry of Health Working Party, 1988), advocated collaboration and liaison between the authorities and the various social service workers, health and voluntary agencies. Housing authorities also provide 80% of the cost of voluntary housing projects (CPA, 1993, p.134). Sheltered accommodation, backed by the assistance of health and social care authorities and agencies, is now a priority. Warden facilities are highly recommended, as well as sheltered units and day centres. Such measures are designed to prevent or delay the entry of older people into some form of residential or nursing home.

Although the improvements in housing provision for older people in Ireland have been creditable, they have not provided enough accommodation to meet demands, nor have they acted swiftly enough. More needs to be done. As cited in my Cork study (Giarchi, 1990a), the city's Housing Department has provided 8,316 housing units since the 1950s. However, over a period of almost 30 years only 15% of these were for older people, who in disproportionate terms occupied the worst housing, as was the case in Dublin. Fortunately, SHARE, a local housing association, built 250 houses for single older people in the Cork area with what must have been the lowest rental in Ireland: in 1987 the weekly rent was I£1.60.

SHARE is run by secondary school pupils, but its work compares favourably with that of any housing association anywhere. The association was first conceived in the early 1970s to provide care for the older residents in the marsh area of Cork, a notoriously damp area in which the city's oldest housing is situated. As stressed by Dooghe (1992, p.172), a disproportionate number of older people occupy the oldest housing in inner cities. Through SHARE's initiative, the housing needs of some 250 or so older people were met. It is worth explaining SHARE's work more fully, because it is a unique venture by any standards.

By 1977, a small idea which started in a classroom had become a big city project; by 1987, it had become a national scheme, which is described in greater detail elsewhere by Giarchi (1987b). Annually, hundreds of thousands of Irish punts come from charities, firms and street collections organized by the pupils. Today, hundreds of furnished flats with alarm systems, backed by a community laundry system, and a central city dual-registered sheltered complex in Cork are provided by SHARE. The local authority provide 60% of the costs, and SHARE provides 40% and administers the scheme. The association is a multi-million-punt project. Its management is directed by the secondary school pupils themselves, and adult employees under the direction of the young committee maintain an association which is truly professional.

By Western European standards, Irish households in general are badly equipped: they are bottom of the league table for phones and central heating in the EU; they are in the last three or four for other amenities such as dishwashers, washing machines, internal WCs and bathrooms or showers on the premises. To worsen matters, the republic had the sixth-highest increase in rents between 1980 and 1986 (Eurostat, 1991b, pp.117–22). The older Irish people's homes are the least well-equipped in a nation where upgrading and refurbishment need to be undertaken on a widespread basis. SHARE may capture the imagination, but a national housing programme is urgently required, and more housing associations need to be involved in providing decent homes for the older population in particular: there are only 1,500 sheltered housing units and fewer than 50 warden schemes in Ireland (see Rosdorff and O'Shea, 1991, p.230).

Health care

With regard to structure and management of the health and social services, Curry (1980) and Hunter (1986) describe how the Health Act of 1970 introduced the eight Health Boards under the Minister of Health heading a Department of Health. The Hospital Planning Office assists the department in the provision of homes, clinics and hospitals. The National Health Council regulates hospital staffing.

The Health Boards are divided up into three programmes:

1   the Community Care Programme;
2   the General Hospital Programme;
3   the Special Hospital Programme.

These are headed by a programme director. It is recommended that the post be filled by a doctor.

Amongst other tasks, the Community Care Programme has been set up to maintain older people in the community and to develop programmes of care for them. Community Care Areas are set up with populations of 100,000–120,000 people. Unlike the UK and many other European countries, personal social services, community work and welfare come under the heading of health. The work is essentially multidisciplinary and aims at being highly integrated. On the basis of the Rosdorff and O'Shea statistics (1991, p.230), there are 1,154 public health nurses, 101 home help organizers, 127 occupational therapists and 106 speech therapists. These make up the Community Care Programme team in the eight Health Boards. There are also social workers, community workers and chiropodists, for which statistics are not available.

Hospital care and medical services

The General Medical Service was set up in 1972 following upon the Health Act 1970. Since 1972 there are three categories of patients who are eligible for health services, so that three types of reimbursement exist:

1   'Full eligibility': those within the lowest income level, who are means-tested and receive free medication, described as the 'medical card-holders' (40% of the population).
2   'Limited eligibility': those within the middle-income levels, who have access to a more limited range of free services and hospital care. They pay an earnings-related subscription. They are entitled to free in-patient and out-patient treatment, and receive a partial refund for the costs of medication. They may join the Voluntary Health Insurance Scheme (VHI) for the services to which they have no free entitlement (approximately 55% of the population).
3   'Above the threshold of limited eligibility': those with higher income levels, who have access to maintenance services in hospitals. They may also pay into the VHI scheme.

General hospital care for older people is well-resourced. For example, in Cork there is a special geriatric assessment centre with 30 beds, backed up by a custom-built rehabilitation unit for older patients and a large day hospital. The emphasis on hospital care has been a feature in the Irish system for many years. For example, there are 14 hospitals in the Cork area, four of them large (two run by religious orders), providing 1,950 beds (1,200 acute), in a city of only 140,000 people and 520,000 in the total county catchment area.

The republic has the sixth-highest proportion of hospital beds in the EU. There has been concern that older people are being admitted inappropriately to the hospitals. Regarding hospital care, the Ministry of Health Working

Party (1988) reported that 25% of admissions and over 40% of acute bed stays involved older patients, although they constituted only 11% of the population. Many should not be in hospital: my study in Cork (Giarchi, 1990a) and the report of the Dublin Hospital Initiative Group (1990) have indicated that about 40–46% of older patients are inappropriately placed in the hospitals. An examination of the *Cork Examiner* over a period of twenty years indicated that bottlenecks and jams in the hospital emergency admission service for older patients were a matter of continuous grave concern (Giarchi, 1990a). However, the reason was not that there were too few beds, but that patients were retained too long and admission criteria had not been agreed.

The current policy is to provide small community hospitals closer to the people, which is in keeping with policies in almost all of greater Europe. Both the Eastern Health Board and the North Western Health Board had already been committed to the community hospital model.

The Ministry of Health Working Party (1988), in its report, *The Years Ahead*, recommended 50–60-bed community hospitals should act as community centres, providing:

1 local assessment and rehabilitation;
2 convalescent care;
3 respite care for carers;
4 facilities for housing very frail, highly dependent or terminally ill persons, who are unable to be cared for at home;
5 information and support for carers at home.

Another problem in Ireland is the lack of specialist doctors for older patients. There are only 11 in the whole Republic of Ireland: 6 in Dublin and 2 in Cork (see Giarchi, 1990a; Carroll, 1991). They do not make domiciliary visits; had they done so in Cork, for example, certain inappropriate admissions would not have taken place. There are 6 day hospitals in Ireland with the capacity of serving only about 200 older people, as cited by Rosdorff and O'Shea (1991, p.230). They are very similiar to those in the UK, providing treatment and rehabilitation for the frailer older population.

It must also be noted that the number of GPs in the area has been low by European standards. Tussing (1985) points out that the republic has the second-lowest proportion of doctors in Western Europe. There were 1,800 GPs in 1989, of whom 1,500 were registered with the Health Boards to serve patients with medical cards. By 1991, when Leaper commented upon the Irish system, the number of GPs had grown to about 2,300, of whom 1,400 served medical cardholders. There are twice as many cardholders in Cork as in Dublin, which is one reason why this chapter focuses upon Cork in some detail when describing the formal Irish systems of care. The more recent Eurostat statistics (1991b) indicate that the republic has fewer doctors per

1,000 population than any of the other EU countries. With the exception of Portugal, it also has less dentists per 1,000 persons.

The sick have a choice of medical practitioners within their locality. So the same doctor attends to patients who pay and those who do not, both receiving care without discrimination. The former system segregated those who attended the surgeries (the payers) and those who attended the dispensaries (the non-payers). Today, there is no segregation and the doctors are paid on a capitation basis, which replaced the old fee per consultation system which prevailed up to 1989.

Pharmacists in Ireland are often substitute doctors, consulted, especially by older people, regarding their ailments and the appropriate medication or remedies. The republic has the fourth-highest number of pharmacists in the EU per 1,000 inhabitants, according to Eurostat (1991b, p.88). In my Cork study (Giarchi, 1990a) I reported that the GPs were very concerned that 18–20% of their patients did not comply with their prescriptions.

Prior to 1966, most of the doctors ran dispensaries. Today, there are well over 1,200 pharmacists formulating and dispensing the GPs' prescriptions. However, in the rural areas the GP may dispense if the nearest pharmacist is more than three miles away. There are probably about 389 such dispensing doctors in the republic (Curry, 1980, p.158). In my Irish study there were 82 dispensing doctors in the rural areas of the Southern Health Board (Giarchi, 1990a).

Prior to 1989 there appeared to be a tendency for the GPs to admit older patients to hospitals too readily. Today there is an awareness of the need to keep people in their own homes for as long as is possible. Doctors' capitation fees increase in accordance with the age of the patient and distance; the highest capitation fees are paid for those aged 65+ (Carroll, 1991, p.240).

Nursing

According to the Eurostat data for the early 1980s (see Giarchi, 1990a), there are more nurses per 10,000 population in Ireland than in any other European country. They are mainly employed in the hospitals. The community care nursing provision is not as well-resourced. The community nurses are known as Public Health Nurses (PHNs). They are deployed by the Programme Director for Community Care. Only 40% of their time is spent caring for older people, the rest is spent with younger families (see Rosdorff and O'Shea, 1991, p.229).

A commentary on Cork's system may provide a picture of the workings of the PHNs in community care in the second-largest Health Board in Ireland, which in many respects vies with the capital (there is an old saying in the south: 'Limerick was; Dublin is; and Cork will be the greatest of the three.')

Also, the Southern Health Board, centred upon Cork, covers the largest cross-section of rural Ireland.

As far back as 1984, the Health Board in Cork concluded, on the basis of unmet needs, that 39 more PHNs were required; yet in 1987 the Health Board could only request an additional 8 PHNs due to the lack of funds. The recommended ratio of PHNs to the general population in the republic is 1:2,000; nationally it is 1:3,065 (see Carroll, 1991, p.244). In Cork, it is 1:5,500 (Giarchi, 1990a). The problem is that Ireland has the highest child dependency rate in Europe: 30–31% are under the age of 14, and the PHNs spend 75% of their time with them. In addition, the nurses work from 9 am to 5 pm on a five-day working week. They seek to provide nursing cover until 10 pm, in addition to a weekend service. The Health Board introduced the idea of one in four PHNs caring for the older residents within high-density population areas. In addition, the nurses were not attached to the GPs, but worked from health centres. A primary care team did not really exist, the referrals to the PHNs coming more and more from the hospitals and less and less from the GPs, once again pointing to the pre-eminence of the overarching, top-heavy hospital system. The high-status Irish hospital is the gravitational centre of care. It tends to orchestrate community nursing care.

Home care/help

The home help service is attached to the PHN system rather than the social work system, hence its inclusion here and not under 'Personal social services'.

The home help service was initiated in 1972 under Section 61 of the Health Act. There are many, but they are neither well-trained nor well-paid. In 1987 there were 1,414 home helps in the Southern Health Board. The board only paid them a nominal I£0.75 an hour, regarding them as volunteers, not employees. Recipients in County Cork did not pay for the service, unlike those in the other half of the board's territory in Kerry, and payment schemes are increasingly being introduced to help towards costs everywhere.

Mental health care

Psychogeriatric care has become a matter of concern in recent years in Ireland. The dementias and depression affect about 20% of those aged 85+, as stated in the report of the Southern Health Board (1987, p.47). The republic has the highest proportion of psychiatric beds in the EU (Eurostat, 1991b), but interestingly enough, it has a ratio of only 85 suicides among those aged

75+ per million inhabitants, the lowest in the EU (see Pritchard, 1992, p.129). The Health Boards have been slow to appoint psychogeriatricians. When I was writing my report in Ireland in 1988–9, there was no psychogeriatrician in Ireland's second city, there were only 15 beds for senile dementia patients, and there was no adequate respite care system.

Since the 1950s, Ireland has invested in a 'liaison psychiatry service', which has consisted of out-patient short-stay units, usually attached to the hospitals (Walsh, 1990, p.152). These cater for all ages. The policy has been to integrate psychiatry into general medicine, providing short-term care in the general hospitals. Specialist out-patient psychiatric clinics have been running, not so much as part of the community care plan, but rather as extended hospital care. The major focus is upon the hospital. As Walsh (1990, p.161) points out, there are probably about fifty psychiatric social workers in the entire republic.

Intensive care within the community has been minimal. Community Psychiatric Nurses link hospital care with home care. Psychiatry comes under 'special hospital programmes', the fourth remit of the Health Board.

Institutional care

The provision of residential nursing care had been hampered in Ireland until the 1960s because long-stay geriatric care afforded the sole means of providing long-term care. To reduce the numbers in geriatric hospitals, 30 welfare homes were created under the Health Act 1970. The distinction was made between 'welfare beds' – providing social care – and 'nursing beds'. Just as there is a major dispute in many parts of Europe over the distinction between social and health care, there is ongoing debate about the distinction between welfare and nursing care in Ireland. It may help to clarify the situation by listing the types of welfare and nursing care provided.

There are five major types of institutional care other than acute hospital care in Ireland:

1　Health Board geriatric hospitals or homes. These mainly provide geriatric long-term care, mostly for the more chronically sick.
2　Long-stay district hospitals. These mainly provide short-term care, mostly for older people.
3　Health Board welfare homes. These provide non-nursing care for those who cannot be cared for at home. Most of the residents are aged 75+.
4　Approved nursing homes. These are private or voluntary. They receive a

subsidy from the Irish Exchequer. The residents are mostly aged 75+. Only about one-third are chronically sick.

5 Non-approved nursing homes. These are either private or voluntary. Although not subsidized, they have to conform to minimum standard regulations if they are run for profit. There is some concern about the standards of the voluntary non-profit homes, so new regulations are being introduced to secure the minimum standards.

State nursing homes receive a percentage of their running costs from the state, the remainder of which is paid by the residents. Sheedy (1985) comments upon the stigma and inconvenience attached to being cared for in the state sector. As far back as 1980, Powell and Powell focused upon the needs of older people who were in need of care but were 'too fit for hospital care'. The homes run by lay people often take over the residents' entire pension, whereas those run by religious orders usually allow the residents one-fifth of their pension as pocket money (Sheedy, 1985, p.14).

There has clearly been a sharp divide between the state homes and the private ones. Sheedy states: 'There is a generally held belief that the more one pays, the more one is entitled to' (1985, p.19). The mix of private and public residents reveals glaring differences under the same roof. Regimented hospital care does not have any semblance of the place being 'home'. Sheedy (1985, p.10) states: 'The reason for everyone being kept in one not so large room by day was because it was easier to count them', and adds: 'The Board cannot afford to close or prosecute many of these homes as it is dependent on them to alleviate the large numbers of elderly people who need the extra care available in these homes' (p.14). The religious homes are short of nuns, so that closures have begun to increase. In Cork, for example, the well-known Montenotte residential home had to close in 1987 after providing a century of care for older people on poor incomes.

Carroll (1991, p.242), in his assessment of the extended care of the older population in Ireland, cites the 75.7% increase of older people in residential homes by 1988. The policy now, however, is to provide relatively small community hospitals and better facilities to keep them at home, as stated above. The voluntary and private for-profit nursing homes will of course still continue, and now provide over 19,000 beds (O'Shea et al., 1991). The Health (Nursing Homes) Act 1990 provides for much-needed registration, regulation governing standards, and inspection of the system.

As an alternative to residential care, the Irish National Council for the Aged has suggested adult foster care as a possible option. In Chapter 9 the ancient practice of adult foster care will be described and discussed when dealing with Belgium, where the practice originated (see page 190). The Irish managers have described it as 'boarding out – a home from home' (Southern Health Board, 1987, pp. 18–20).

Personal social services

In contrast with the high number of nurses (Giarchi, 1990a), there are only six medical social workers serving the Southern Health Board hospitals. The community care areas within which the social workers operate each contain 100,000–120,000 inhabitants. Their Director of Community Care, referred to earlier, is usually a doctor. There is a National Social Service Council, founded in 1971, which amongst other aims sets out to promote co-operation between statutory and voluntary social services (see Curry, 1980, pp.219–20). No more than 500 social workers serve the boards in the republic, mostly with regard to child care.

In Cork, the social workers openly stated in their interviews with me that they did not have the time to provide care for older people (Giarchi, 1990a); however, community workers did. There were eight community workers employed by the board. In 1975 the then Minister of Health stated: 'my objective is to bring about a shift in resources in favour of community services, in the belief that this will lead to a better health service overall' (*Dail Debates*, 1975). Central to this shift has been the involvement of Irish community workers. They were each given the responsibility for either rural or urban areas. They met regularly to determine and plan caring arrangements and to support voluntary care, especially for older people. They worked within a 'patch' system, as described by Carey and Carroll (1986). The first full-time community work posts were established in Cork in 1971. They remain few in number – approximately 25 are employed by six health boards – but their work for the older population in Ireland is considerable. It cannot be fully understood unless related to the work of the community associations in the urban areas and the community councils in the rural areas.

The community associations/councils, which provide grassroots care and support locally for neighbourhood ventures, were formally approved in 1941. They are subsidized by the Health Boards, and are run by locally elected committee members and their chairperson. They organize visiting groups for older people, and initiate action in neighbourhoods on behalf of groups with special needs, particularly older people. A local voluntary laundry service and meals-on-wheels (or on feet) are organized, along with various other caring arrangements within a very flexible system. Their major events are organized by a community centre – there are eight in Cork city. GPs, PHNs and welfare officers often use the premises for local consultation. Dances and other social events are organized there. A community council, headed by a director paid by the local authority, provides expert consultation and support, especially with regard to legal matters and the management of budgets. Training courses for volunteers are provided by the council, which runs a resource centre for the various voluntary agencies.

Voluntary care agencies and support organizations

The National Social Service Board provides a *Directory of Voluntary Organisations* which lists as many as fifteen national bodies concerned with providing services and support for older people (Giarchi, 1987b). In Cork there are many voluntary organizations providing such support, particularly the AOSTA (Association of Services to the Aged). Several nuns and clergy work alongside the agencies, and sometimes within them. One such parish group, the St Vincent De Paul Society, visits older people in their homes and provides them with clothes and meals.

In the rural areas of County Cork, eight community workers liaise with the rural groups; 14 community councils are also maintained around Cork, and reports on their work and feasibility are provided by the community workers in collaboration and consultation with the local people. Older people are seen as active agents, whose voluntary efforts are a major neighbourhood resource for the community workers.

The Churches are part of the community care strategy. A Social Care Commission has been set up in the dioceses. Some nuns, such as Stanislaus Kennedy, are highly regarded by the agencies and the Ministry of Health as social care experts. The bishops have been behind the creation of old people's self-help support groups in each parish, as well as parish street warden schemes (see Cork Diocese, 1984). In Cork, for example, 168 clergy were visiting 1,686 housebound or bedridden older people, as reported in the diocesan year books within the 64 parishes in 1984. The practice continues.

Informal care

Woods (1990) comments upon Ireland's young population: 46% are under 25. The emphasis is upon family responsibilities: 'The family is central to our policies in the social field. The Irish constitution places special emphasis on the role of the family' (p.178). However, the major concern is not with the care of the older population, but with the increasing number of unemployed youths and single parents, where the main formal resources are channelled. The government relies upon informal carers with regard to the older population, backed by the voluntary and Church workers.

Carroll (1991) refers to the policy statement of the Ministry of Health Working Party (1988). Its first three objectives are:

1   to maintain older people in dignity and independence in their own home;

2   to restore those older people who become ill or dependent to independence at home;
3   to encourage and support the care of older people in their own community by family, neighbours and voluntary bodies in every possible way.

The report acknowledges at the same time that informal care lacks the back-
up of adequate formal care.

There is a major concern about the need for better-supported family or
household care in the more urban eastern and seaboard counties (Carroll,
1991, pp.238–9). But will the concern be backed by resources? There will be a
projected 62% increase of the over-75s living alone in Dublin city and county.
These areas are in the throes of a projected 33% increase of the over-65s and
a 43% increase of the over-75s between 1986–2006. It comes as no surprise
that 78% of the carers of incapacitated older Irish people are women.

In my comparative explorative study of three European areas – Cork
(Republic of Ireland), Plymouth (UK) and La Spezia (Italy) (Giarchi, 1990a) –
I was able to identify the importance of family support for those aged 75 and
over, particularly amongst the middle class in both urban and rural areas of
County Cork. I interviewed a random sample of 74 persons aged 75+ in the
Cork area and compared their responses with those of the other two areas.
The findings showed that 22% of those living either alone or as a lone couple
were visited by offspring, siblings or grandchildren at least once a week, and
27% at least once a month; 28% were visited by relatives at least once a week,
and 17% monthly.

Rosdorff and O'Shea (1991, p.221) state that 78% of the older population
do not need assistance. However, contact with others is an essential element
in most people's lives. Of those who do need help, they cite the 9% who are
assisted by neighbours, friends and volunteers. These more dependent older
people are assisted jointly by spouses (18.4%), daughters (27.2%), sons
(13.4%) and by other relatives (20.8%). The major assistants here are the
family, as in almost every other country in Europe.

What Rosdorff and O'Shea's (1991) citations do not indicate is the contact
that healthy people have with their neighbours. Irish neighbourhood links are
impressive: the proportion of those in contact with neighbours was significantly higher in my Irish study in County Cork than in the Italian and English
samples (Giarchi, 1990a): 57.5% were visited by next-door neighbours during
the week, and 39.7% monthly; 61.6% were visited each week by nearby neighbours, and 37% monthly; 45.3% were visited by friends weekly, and 43.8%
monthly. The neighbourhood circles appeared to be amongst the tightest and
most supportive in Europe. It must be added that Cork is regarded as the
Republic of Ireland's most sociable city.

Recent studies indicate that the family circle is also tight: 68.6% of older
people in Cork were visited by family and relatives each week, and 60.2%

each month (Giarchi, 1990a, p.494). The people contacted were aged 75+, and they were healthy and mobile. The Cork study was carried out about the same time as O'Connor and Ruddle's (1988) Irish study of informal carers. They describe a more supportive familial web of care surrounding older people. In their study, all offspring residing within five miles of their parents contacted them at home at least once a week. In general, 73% of all offspring were reported as visiting them on a fairly regular weekly basis.

In my Cork study there appeared to be a class difference, in that family contact with older relatives was more regular within middle-class families. If the relatives or immediate family lived further away, there was usually the convenience of a family car. In addition, the older middle-class people living away from relatives mixed less with people in their neighbourhood and relied more upon their family ties. The older working-class people often had more contact with a neighbour, especially someone next door, up the stairs or across the road, rather than with any member of the family. When enquiring about possible reasons, it was suggested by social workers and the PHNs that Irish family ties are more tenuous in many instances because of the high rate of emigration. This long-standing factor was also confirmed by Brody's (1973) findings. Many of the poorer older people have had to build up long-term relationships with people beyond the family circle because their offspring or even husbands have sought jobs abroad during the many years of Ireland's deprived history.

However, there are misgivings, even in Ireland, regarding the caring role of the family in the future. Kennedy (1986b, pp.91–100) presents a broad, comprehensive picture of the family in transition in Ireland. She states that urbanized and industrialized society has not only replaced the Irish fireside with the television set, but has also altered the traditional values of the Irish household.

It is possible that Ireland will face a problematic future in the twenty-first century, when, in effect, there might no longer be one accountable family to which the members of a serial marriage or partnership can turn. However, neighbours have for centuries stepped in when the exodus of siblings and offspring have left older people to cope largely on their own. This has been the case particularly in the larger rural areas of Ireland and friendly cities like Cork. However, neighbours will not be able to provide the more intensive household nursing. That is a major problem facing Ireland in the future, especially if the birth rate continues to drop. The younger Irish people of today will be tomorrow's problem.

Leisure pursuits and education

With regard to the leisure interests and pastimes of the older population, many events are organized by the parishes, the community associations and the voluntary agencies. These are not always confined to the older people, but provide a social gathering for inter-generational fun. As part of my methodology, I attended 28 such socials in and around Cork within a period of four weeks, in order to evaluate the quality of the 'sing-alongs' and the involvement of the older participants (Giarchi, 1990a). Older men were under-represented, but the older women were often the life and soul of the party. On more than one occasion, the older women stated: 'I could never have done this had my husband been alive' (Giarchi, 1990a). The men, in contrast, were often to be seen in long silent lines on their own, sitting or standing at the bars during the day, or out walking alone by the River Lee.

The major annual event for older people is their entertainment competition staged in Cork, and now a national event on TV. All the old tunes, jokes and routines are performed in the various community centres and voluntary agency socials. The successful performers go forward to a semi-final, and ultimately a splendid final on stage in the Cork Opera House. All the participants and the audience must wear formal evening dress. There is preparation months ahead and the Opera House is usually fully booked well in advance. The event helps to bring families and friends together throughout the heats as they come to support their relatives, often great-grandparents.

CPA (1989) states that concessions are available on a discretionary basis for persons seeking places on adult educational courses. There are reduced rates for older people (65+) at local authority centres. The community association centres provide premises for many learning programmes.

Rural aspects

Daly and O'Connor (1984) describe the experiences of older people in rural Ireland. Significant numbers of older people have no piped water in their old properties. Many are without a bath, a car, a TV set and a shower. The only facility which they all have is a radio. Nostalgia is strong and loneliness is common for many in the remoter areas. Concern about their security appears to be a major fear, which is usually exacerbated by the media. Many do not feel safe in their homes. Some also feel alienated in a strange world of rapid changes. However, in spite of these negative factors which affect significant numbers of rural older people, the majority of them are generally contented individuals. One factor that affects most of them is the failure to provide for their retirement, which accelerates the downward plunge into poverty. Fortunately, many cope because neighbours are the most vital source of contact for over half of the older rural population, according to the findings of Daly and O'Connor (1984, p.77).

Where there are no offspring or immediate family nearby, contact with more distantly related family members is a feature. Neighbours are also of vital importance, whether the older person has relatives or immediate family nearby (Daly and O'Connor, 1984, p.108). The authors state:

> Neighbours play a vital role in the lives of the elderly people interviewed, especially for those who have no immediate family alive or available. In these instances, neighbours provide an important lifeline to the elderly, either acting as an emergency support service or by providing a range of services which allows the older person to continue to live in the community. (p.108)

One older person made a comment which sums up the appreciation of most regarding good neighbours: 'Who else have I, only the neighbours? You have nobody else if you haven't your neighbours because you are not going to go to a relation of your own because they live too far away' (p.108).

Conclusion

It is clear that since Power's shock report in 1980, many of the most disadvantaged Irish older people have better incomes and provision in kind. It is also clear that formal community care provided for older people deserve Browne's (1990) jibe of being 'shot-gun' measures. There are other considerations that emerge.

Firstly, the major structural problem is the pre-eminence of the hospital system and the underdeveloped community care system. The need for more PHNs, supported by better-paid home helps, is one of the factors blocking a more efficient open care service.

Secondly, the emphasis upon the medical models and the curative rather than the rehabilitative approach is another of the major difficulties. Subsuming personal social services within a community care programme headed by a doctor and employed by a Health Board is indicative of the dominance of the medical model. In some areas the matron of the local hospital determines the community care in the district.

Thirdly, there is an in-built fault line within the Irish system: housing remains the local authority's responsibility, whilst health and welfare are those of the Health Boards. These interrelated vital providers have separate programmes, divided up regionally. In fact, hospital care, community care, and in some instances special hospital care, may be accountable to a centre in another county.

Fourthly, the centralization of administration militates against the flexibility required for community care. Decision-making is centred on Dublin. Co-ordination has been called for by the National Council for the Aged and by the Ministry of Health. The Irish monocephalic structure has militated against allied and well-co-ordinated services by slowing down decision-making.

Finally, there is a need to provide at least four essentials:

1   enough PHNs to provide home nursing;
2   support for the carers, such as respite care or short-term care;
3   specialist assessment and rehabilitation services;
4   more innovative housing schemes or service units.

The 'shot-gun' approach to the provision of care in the republic is now being redressed by the new district care teams, set up in response to the call of the report, *The Years Ahead* (Ministry of Health Working Party, 1988).

7 The UK: Northern Ireland, Scotland, Wales and England

Demography

The demography of old age in the UK is made up of four sets of statistics based upon the populations of Northern Ireland, Scotland, Wales and England. On the basis of the published data of the Statistical Office of the European Communities (SOEC), *Regional Trends* (HMSO, 1988–93), the percentage of persons aged 65 and over has been consistently highest in Wales, followed in rank order by England, Scotland and Northern Ireland. The proportions have been consistently above the EU average.

Northern Ireland and Scotland lie in the bottom half of regional rankings of proportions of older people within the EU, whereas Wales and England are in the top half, in the first ten out of over 50 regions (see *Regional Trends*, HMSO, 1988–93).

Wales has had a significant influx of older people because of the constant immigration to the more scenic areas from the urban areas of Lancashire and beyond. The increase in the Welsh proportion of older people will constitute one of the most significant rises by the year 2001 (see Champion, T. and Townsend, 1990, p.359). In addition, the imbalance of the proportions of children under 15 and of persons over 65 is a matter of concern, with only 2.5% more youngsters than older people. Its percentage of old people ranks fifth out of the EU regions, as can be calculated on the basis of *Regional Trends* (HMSO, 1988–93).

In England, 15.7% of the people are aged 65 or over. In Europe, this proportion was fourth after Sweden, Norway and Denmark in 1989. There are also regions in England where the proportion of older people is amongst the highest in Europe – for example, the south-west (SOEC, as cited in *Regional Trends*, HMSO, 1988–93). However, the life expectancy of older people at 65 does not rate as highly.

Taking the UK as a whole, the proportion of persons aged 65+ in 1990 was 15.6% (Eurostat, 1991a). As cited by the CPA (1993, p.211), this was the highest proportion of those aged 65+ in the EU in 1990. The life expectancy at 65 years of age and over for women is 17.5 years, which ranks fourteenth in Europe, while that of men is 13.6 years, which ranks sixteenth.

The presentation of the demographic data would not be complete without including the populations of ethnic minorities. Of the four provinces of the UK, England is the most multi-cultural: most of the older black Caribbean, South Asian and East African population are to be found in England. Haskey's (1990) documentation has shown that there has been an increase of all ethnic groups in the UK of some 23% between 1981 and 1988. However, until the research carried out by Fenton (1987; 1991), the older black and white minorities hardly found a mention in the literature of social gerontology in the UK. The proportion of the ethnic groups and their older people are:

- Indian (31%), of whom 4% are pensionable;
- West Indian (19%), of whom 5% are pensionable;
- Pakistani (17%), of whom 2% are pensionable;
- mixed (11%), of whom 3% are pensionable;
- Chinese (5%), of whom 4% are pensionable;
- African (4%), of whom 2% are probably pensionable;
- Bangladeshi (4%), of whom 1% are probably pensionable;
- Arab (3%), of whom 1% are probably pensionable;
- other (6%), of whom 5% are pensionable.

These percentages will increase rapidly, notably the Indian, West Indian, Pakistani and Chinese. The second generation are less likely to abide by all the customs and traditions associated with the culture of care of their grandparents, who were born and socialized outside the UK.

Socio-political and administrative background

The Audit Commission's (1986) report, *Making a Reality of Community Care*, had as its main concern the disproportionate cost of keeping 5% of the older population in institutional care. The consequences were that the other 95% of the older population were often deprived of services and resources. This was taken up by the Griffiths Report (Griffiths, 1988), followed by the White Papers, *Caring for People* (HMSO, 1989), *People First* (1990, covering Northern Ireland), and the National Health Service and Community Care Act 1990. The cost of independent residential and nursing care provision had risen through social security payments in this sector from £10 million in 1979 to £1,000 million by May 1989. The new arrangements within the recent legislation aim to shift millions of pounds over into the community care programmes, with a view to keeping people at home to obviate the immense escalation of costs because of the demographic increase in the number of older people, especially frailer people aged 80+. As is clear from many of the accounts of care strategies in Northern, Western and Central Europe, the strategy and policy of 'Care in the Community' was not new.

There are four provinces within the UK: Northern Ireland, Scotland, Wales and England, and community care in the UK does not constitute a level playing field; therefore, as far as possible, this overview of plural welfare, nursing, social services and voluntary organizations and Church involvement will differentiate between them, whenever appropriate.

Northern Ireland is the most deprived of the provinces, the most divided region due to religious segregation, and the most terrorized zone in Western Europe (St Leger and Gillespie, 1991, p.1). The extremes of poverty, the sectarian divisions and the terrorism are mainly to be found in the urban areas of Northern Ireland. However, the older rural population lose out in terms of priority, so that services there are less well resourced. The infrastructure of local care is politically sensitive. The sharp age-old religious divide within localities and within classes and generations fragments the mass concern of older people and dilutes their protests over inadequate pensions and poor-quality services. Although the Churches support ecumenism, neighbours tend to cater for older people of their own faith. Although formally the Churches aim to integrate social programmes, unease exists, especially in the city of Belfast (see St Leger and Gillespie, 1991). The Presbyterian Church, the Church of Ireland and the Catholic Church provide neighbourhood care for older people, but this tends to be within segregated areas and for their own congregations, as is the case with their discrete school system, in spite of ecumenical efforts to destroy divides between people.

Hunter and Wistow (1987, pp.10–11) cite Owen (1979) and Kellas (1975) in support of their view that, in macro terms, Northern Ireland, Scotland and Wales (and some might include Cornwall) tend to encounter the same difficulties of provinces struggling to maintain an independent administrative role (see, for example, Meny and Wright, 1985; Hunter and Wistow, 1987). These difficulties have a severe impact upon welfare and health provision for older citizens in urban and rural areas, particularly the remote and less accessible countryside.

A tension exists between the provincial bureaux in Belfast, Edinburgh and Cardiff and the civil service bureau in London, and senior citizens are caught in the cross-fire of politics. It will be argued that, in the new set-up after 1 April 1993, the onus of the lead role has been placed upon the shoulders of local authorities. However, the decentralization of administration of operations has been accompanied by the centralization of control over resources (Walker, 1993, p.215). Central government's insistence that the major percentage of the allocated budget must be spent in the private sector is evidence of both the residualization of the social services and the maximization of the private sector. Older people now have to dip into their life's savings to pay for what was once a universal provision. Those who have least suffer most: the older people in the peripheral provinces more so than those in the southern regions.

There are some thirty central government departments. Of these, the Department of Health, the Department of Social Security and the Department of Housing are the critical bodies of administration whose policies and deliberations particularly affect the lives of older people.

The UK is a multi-provincial administrative system. There is a Welsh Office under the Welsh Secretary, and a Scottish Office, with its own Secretary of State, whose administrative procedures and programmes contrast with one another and with those of the central Department of Social Security and the Department of Health. The administration in Northern Ireland, under the Northern Ireland Secretary, enjoys considerable independence, but has lost a great deal of it since the 'troubles' began in the later 1960s. The Department of Health for Scotland also plays a critical role in helping to improve the quality of older people's lives. Hunter and Wistow (1987) describe the administration of community care in England, Wales and Scotland. They conclude that there are substantive differences between administrative arrangements and decision-making in Scotland and those of England and Wales because of the separate Scottish legislature. Although the commitment to community care has provided a policy lead in the various provinces that make up the UK, the interpretation and the means used to achieve the policy aims are quite another thing. These major issues and structural diversities in the pre-Griffiths era continue to be a major concern, and determine the varying interpretations of the National Health Service and Community Care Act 1990 (see Means and Smith, 1994; Bornat et al., 1993).

In Northern Ireland there are 26 district councils with very limited powers and few resources. Since 1972 these peripheral UK political structures have been linked incongruously to central government in London, and mediated by a relatively small caucus of politicians and civil servants in Belfast. Because of the peripherality of Northern Ireland and the division over the Irish question, there is more suspicion and greater unease in the urban areas towards officialdom in Whitehall, and more distrust towards city bureaucracy in the Northern Irish villages and hamlets. At the same time, expenditure is mainly directed to where the electorate is most powerful: in the high-density urban areas.

Turning now to Scotland, the Scottish Home and Health Department runs the health services, and the Social Work Services Group, within the

Education Department, runs social services. The personal social services devote 20% of their expenditure to the care of older people – a higher proportion than the personal social services in England.

Taking into account these centre–periphery factors within the UK enables us to be more aware of the differences between modes of care in the four provinces.

Social security: pensions and benefits

Part of the positive UK approach to an enhanced quality of life in retirement and a productive old age has been recognition of the need to increase the income of the older population. Walker (1991, pp.60–1) draws attention to the section in the Beveridge Report entitled 'The Problem of Age'. Apart from the fact that age *per se* is not a problem, Beveridge built his insurance system on the principle of contributions or 'work-testing' rather than of means-testing, so pensions were not regarded as a right. Women were to receive their pension at 60, men at 65. Women are described as the 'poor relations' by Walker (1992b), largely because for much of their lives they have been unemployed. The pensions have been provided within a two-tier scheme. There is an employment-related flat-rate and earnings-related pension, with the possibility of contracting out. There is also the back-up of social assistance.

Walker (1992a, pp.165–6) points out that the flat-rate scheme is designed to combat poverty, whereas that of the earnings-related scheme is aimed at maintaining living standards. In 1975 the UK introduced the State Earnings-Related Pension Scheme (SERPS), which combined the two by introducing a compulsory statutory earnings-related supplementary pension with the option of contracting out into an occupational scheme.

The basic earnings-related scheme covers employees, self-employed and voluntary contributors. From 1988 the option of contracting out into the occupational scheme has been extended to personal pensions. A non-contributory pension plus various allowances provide income for all those aged 80+ provided they have resided in the UK for at least ten years in the 20 years before their eightieth birthday. Pensions are adjusted annually in line with the Retail Price Index.

The CPA (1989, p.155; 1993, p.216) and Walker (1991, pp.63–70) have provided a disturbing picture of the collapse of the value of the pension, and the large numbers of older UK citizens who have poor incomes. In 1985–6, for example, 18% of the retired were claiming means-tested Supplementary Benefit. After 1988, Supplementary Benefit was replaced by Income Support, with weekly premiums for old age and disability. A Social Fund has also been available, offering loans and grants. More than half of the pensioners derive three-quarters or more of their income from the state. Under half obtain at least a quarter from occupational pensions or from other private sources. According to Walker (1991, p.63), the value of UK pensions has deteriorated so badly that present pensions are lower than the relative values of pensions in the nineteenth century. In recent years, 35% of the older population were living below the poverty line compared with 10% of the younger population (Walker, 1991, p.62). As the retired get older, so their income worsens in the UK. There is also no acknowledgement that disabled older people face greater poverty than non-disabled older people in the UK. Walker (1991, p.65) refers to research which has shown that proportionately more disabled people are in poverty or on the borderline than those with no disabilities.

Since the recession particularly, the UK state pension scheme has not kept pace with the rest of Western Europe, still less with Northern Europe and even Southern Europe. Recent Eurostat statistics indicate this: in general the UK spends far less on social protection benefits – the UK comes sixth out of the EU countries, excluding Greece (see Eurostat, 1991b, p.81), using the Purchasing Power Standard (PPS) as the measure. Belgium, Spain, France, Italy and Luxemburg offer their older people more. Baldock (1991b, p.128) reports that as the state moves from universalism to residualism, Whitehall is encouraging private pension schemes. He predicts that the universal state pension will no longer be the principal source of income for the older population in the UK. This is a matter of concern because, on current estimates, most of them will not be able to afford a decent private pension.

Dooghe (1992, pp.154–6), citing recent studies, indicates that the older population in the UK fall into three broad income groups: the poor (31%) – those on or below the established Supplementary Benefit or Income Support level; the low-income (30%) – those whose relative income is above the Supplementary Benefit or Income Support level, but is less than 140% of the benefit level; and those above low-income (39%) – who have an income which is more than 140% of the benefit level.

Older women in the UK are particularly vulnerable to poverty, according to the evidence cited by Dooghe (1992, p.163). He points out that approximately 70% of older UK women living alone who depend upon a state pension are poor; this contrasts with only 55% of men. This significant difference is not universal; for example, the difference is far lower in West Germany, and in Sweden, older men are poorer than older women. About 24% of the older married couples in the UK are poor, in contrast with the much higher proportions of the lone older population.

Women within black ethnic communities are amongst the most vulnerable pensioners, as demonstrated by Norman (1985). Access to information regarding their rights to social and welfare benefits is a particular difficulty.

However, in the areas with the highest black ethnic populations, social security leaflets are increasingly available in Urdu, Gujarati, Hindi, Punjabi, Bengali and Chinese (see Baxter, 1988; George and Young, 1991, p.101).

Housing

Housing, like income, is another basic factor, and closely related to it. Over 90% of older people in the UK live outside institutions. To a large extent their health and quality of life are determined by their housing conditions. Independence and self-reliance go hand in hand with healthy living. Living at home in decent, appropriate and affordable housing is an integral part of self-fulfilment and maintaining one's dignity. Owning a house provides security and is a capital asset. 'Staying put' is an important test of older people's ability to cope and maintain their human dignity and independence. Also, health problems often mirror problems people have with their accommodation. Although the UK's emphasis upon enabling older people to stay in their own homes is a central factor in care policies, there was no reference whatsoever to housing conditions or housing maintenance in the Griffiths Report (Griffiths, 1988), the White Paper, *Caring for People* (HMSO, 1989), nor the National Health Service and Community Care Act 1990.

There are 19,670,982 dwellings in England, of which 15.5% are purpose-built apartments (OPCS, 1992). Several major factors regarding older people's housing need to be addressed: 53% of older people are owner-occupiers (Dooghe, 1992); older people are more likely to live in apartments (Potter and Zill, 1992); 43% of older people are living in rented accommodation (Dooghe, 1992); more than a third of older people live alone (Potter and Zill, 1992), and older couples are more likely to live on their own (Potter and Zill, 1992).

There is great emphasis on and pride in the high proportion of older owner-occupiers – about 44% of older people own their house outright (Allen et al., 1986, pp.21–3). However, the temptation to picture all or most retired UK owner-occupiers as residing happily in manageable properties that constitute a sound, secure capital asset with a healthy marketable value, independent of others, must be resisted. Such a picture, based on generalizations about 'paid up' mortgages, does not take into account the state of the accommodation; the burden of maintenance; the risks for individuals or couples of being alone, and the low income levels already referred to above.

Allen et al.'s (1986) work on the condition of older people's housing, although it was published several years ago, still provides an insight into the housing conditions of older people in the UK. If anything, matters have worsened because of the intervening deep recession and the drop in income that has increased the costs of running a home. Allen et al. (1986, p.25) state, citing the General Household Survey, that three times as many older people still have outside WCs than do younger households. More than half of the older population have no central heating in their homes, whilst nearly two-thirds of younger householders have it. Although 84% of the younger households have washing machines, 41% of the older ones do not. Whereas 77% of the younger households have telephones at home, 39% of the older ones do not (see Allen et al., 1986, p.28). Most of the older people who live in apartments above the first floor do not have lifts. Although the UK in general has the highest percentage of households with basic amenities in the EU (see Eurostat, 1991b, p.121), the older population do not significantly share in the overall high standards of accommodation and modern conveniences.

Allen et al. (1986, p.25), on the basis of available research, state that about two-thirds of the houses of the older population were built before 1939. As pointed out already, older Europeans disproportionately occupy the oldest houses in Europe: this is certainly so in the UK; these houses are more likely to be in disrepair and to lack basic amenities. A significant number of older owner-occupiers are living in larger and older properties, many of which are under-occupied. In effect, many are unmarketable. Those that are in better condition have lost some of their value, especially after the decline in the UK housing market in 1987. With the loss of income, older people have had to put housing maintenance at the bottom of their priorities. Also, from 1 April 1993 those who require long-term residential or nursing care have been forced to sell their house and to pay for their care out of the proceeds.

Dooghe (1992, p.172) states that about 12% of older people live in rented private accommodation, which is almost entirely unfurnished. Ironically, those living in the older terraced private rented housing are less likely to move (Potter and Zill, 1992). Those who are frailer can be at risk. 'Care and Repair' schemes in the UK have enabled many older people to stay in their own homes, but in what kind of accommodation and with what possible hazards?

Over a third of older people rent from local authorities. Since the 'right to buy' council houses was introduced (following the Housing Act 1988 and the Local Government and Housing Act 1989), few of the older tenants have taken advantage of the opportunity, because generally they do not have the will to move nor the means to purchase. The stock of council housing has more than halved, as cited in the census data of the OPCS (1992). Council housing tenure has fallen to 19.8% in England and to 19% in Wales, but in Scotland the tenure is significantly higher at 37.9% (OPCS, 1992).

After the Netherlands, the UK has the highest proportion of older people in social housing, as cited by Potter and Zill (1992, p.115); 68% of the housing stock is provided by councils; 26% is provided by housing associations, and 6% by the private sector (Murray, 1993, p.10).

Firstly, public sheltered housing was introduced in the 1970s following upon Circular 82/69 (Ministry of Housing and Local Government, 1969), as cited by Murray (1993, p.8). Local authority provision of sheltered housing has fallen dramatically, from 14,000 places in 1978 to less than 5,000 in 1987 (Casey, 1990). Completions in England are now around 2,500 annually (see OPCS, 1992, p.148).

Secondly, the subsidized housing associations followed, and made an enormous contribution to accommodating older people in the UK, in particular the Anchor Housing Association and the Hanover Housing Association. By the early 1980s, 22% of the sheltered housing stock was provided by housing associations. Dooghe (1992, pp.180–1) regards England as a pioneer internationally in this sector of provision. Completions in England are now around 1,800 annually (see OPCS, 1992, p.148).

Thirdly, private sheltered housing was introduced, catering for those who could afford it. Murray (1993, p.11) cites the 35,798 private sheltered units which had sprung up all over the UK by 1990, plus the 8,000 specially-designed houses for older people. However, there has been a recent steep decrease in provision. Approximately 5,000 private sheltered houses were built annually in the mid-1980s, according to Walker (1986). Completions in England are now around 1,100 annually (see OPCS, 1992, p.148). Getting these developments into perspective is important: only 5% of the older population live in sheltered housing in the UK (Marshall, 1991, p.36), and there was a drop in the development of housing association projects in the late 1980s, as stated earlier (see also Murray, 1993, p.10). It must be noted that the provision shows signs of climbing back to the 1984 level, but that of local authorities dropped by 48% between 1985 and 1990 (see OPCS, 1992, p.146). Also, there were only 8,258 specialized dwellings for older people in England in 1990 (see OPCS, 1992, p.148). None the less, in under a decade, England has built up the largest proportion of sheltered accommodation in the EU.

The Audit Commission report *Developing Local Authority Housing Strategies* (1992b) has addressed the need to assist those who are not able to cope in their present accommodation, which includes frail older people in particular. Their unmet needs have to be addressed systematically in terms of alternative housing, for example. If they are judged to be at risk, or continued residence in their present home would be seriously detrimental to their health, their accommodation needs should be met within one to two years. It remains to be seen how the Audit Commission's report will affect policy.

The Archbishops' Commission on Rural Areas (ACORA) report, *Faith in the Countryside* (1990), identified the lack of decent and affordable housing as the major social problem in rural England: about 7% of rural houses are unfit for human habitation, according to McLaughlin's (1985) discussion of rural deprivation; this is 0.2% worse than in urban areas.

Regarding the homeless in the UK, it is probable that about 8% are older people; 18% of those sleeping in the street are men aged 60+. About a third of those using lodging houses and hostels are older people (Allen et al., 1986, p.28). The Audit Commission (1992b) put forward, amongst other recommendations, that the homeless 'who through age would be seriously prejudiced' should be dealt with urgently.

Health care

Health service provision in the UK dates back to 1945. The National Health Service Act 1946 launched a universal health care scheme which was the envy of Europe. This was followed by the National Assistance Act 1948, which introduced and promoted institutional care for frail older people. These were provisions as of right on the grounds of citizenship. They were lifted out of the domain of charity and placed under the state's responsibility. The state was firmly placed at the apex of the triangle of care, from which it is being steadily dislodged by values of the New Right in favour of the market. The UK was ahead of the rest of Europe, not only because of these major provisions, but also because the specialism of geriatric medicine had emerged, which by the 1950s had established itself in most of the major hospitals and was gaining credibility in the pages of major medical journals.

The more dominant emphasis upon hospital and professional care in Scotland and the more dominant medical and nursing interests in Wales make the task of establishing a community care strategy with social work taking the lead role much more difficult. Policy diversity rather than policy uniformity have characterized the contribution of the three administrative regimes of England, Scotland and Wales.

Northern Ireland has differed even more from the Whitehall welfare, health and social care models and from the prescriptions of either the Welsh or the Scottish Office. For example, Northern Ireland adopts the Republic of Ireland's Health Board system. The social and health services in Northern Ireland are jointly administered. Since 1972/3 there have been four Area Boards in a highly centralized system, answerable to the Department of Health and Social Services. Within each there is a community care management unit, which is responsible for all the services in the community, excluding mental health and learning difficulties. As Smith (1991b, p.21) says, the social services and the health service operate separately and there is friction between them. The older population, needless to say, are liable to get caught in between. Bridging finance schemes have helped to create more respite care and day care in the north (Smith, 1991b, p.21).

In Scotland, the emphasis in the care of older people is institutional. The medical model appears to have more weight than the social model. Hunter (1991, p.6) points out that Scotland spends more per capita on health than England. In English health authorities the funding levels are 25% below those of their Scottish counterparts. Per capita, Scotland provides more health care than England or Wales. But, as in the Irish Republic, community care revolves around the hospital. Community care is less well resourced in Scotland than in England. According to Hunter (1991, p.6) there are significantly more old and mentally ill persons in Scottish hospital beds than in England or Wales. There are fewer alternatives to hospital care for the mentally ill in Scotland than in England – 31% fewer places/beds. The shift from a hospitalized and more heavily resourced residential sector of care to that of community care in terms of 'closer-to-home' alternative services for the older population, plus more home care, is meeting with more political resistance in Scotland. Well-established resource flows and pathways to care are not so easily changed by the fiat of Westminster.

Providing for the black ethnic communities is part of making a reality of community care. As already indicated above, the special needs of older black ethnic groups will escalate within the next thirty years, and many social and health care providers will be faced with novel demands.

Fenton (1987) and Squires (1991) have compiled some information on the modes of care provided for the relevant groups of older minorities. The general conclusion is that the poorest, most unhealthy and least cared for older people in England are disproportionately black. Of the white minority groups, the Irish migrants are probably the worst off, being largely at the bottom of the social scale, and their cultural needs and identity are often disregarded – they are simply taken to be 'English', like the rest of the white population (see McKeigue, 1991, pp.70–1).

Hospital care and medical services

Rosdorff and Wright (1991, p.327) cite the 74,000 older people who are patients in UK hospitals. However, the majority of older people are not cared for in hospital, but are catered for by the primary care team (p.329). This has been the single most important element in the NHS strategy of care. Central to the primary care team is the GP, whose practice generally consists of some 2,000 patients. On average, about 15% of these patients will be aged 65+, and about 6% aged 75+. However, in the south of England older patients make up 45% of the lists of some practices. The GPs' services are administered by the Family Health Service Associations (FHSAs). There is an increase in capitation fees for the patients aged 65+, and another increase for those aged 75+. The assumption is that older people require more care; the reality is that many stay away from their doctors. Prevention, therefore, is not really possible, because it requires a monitoring system. Within the new 'Working for

Patients' GP contract, an annual check of those aged 75+ is built into primary geriatric care, but many do not take advantage of it.

The strength in the provinces resides in the primary care team. Smith (1991b) refers to many effective examples of integrated care in Northern Ireland at this level. The lead role in care management may fall into the hands of the GPs. Were the forebodings of Aneurin Bevan justified after all, when he expressed the fear that the health services would be led by the NHS practitioners? The fact that social services is to take the lead role will necessarily create tensions, and far from working for the good of the older population, the new strategy of community care may result in more unmet social needs for older people, and the lack of rehabilitation for those who all too often come last in the priority of health care.

The White Paper *People First* (1990), covering Northern Ireland, has the same emphasis on mixed welfare, arms'-length inspection and case management as the White Paper *Caring for People* (HMSO, 1989). The latter will be dealt with later.

Since the 1990 White Paper, the Social Service Director at board level in Northern Ireland has lost all executive powers. Medical and health care retain status and control. As seen with regard to the Republic of Ireland, the Irish hospital and medical models of community care are pre-eminent. Smith (1991b, p.22) is concerned that in the competition for resources the acute hospital will have priority. It is opportune at this point in describing the primary care provision to identify an area of great concern regarding the state of health of older people: although the aged are largely fit, GPs over-prescribe drugs for them. Dooghe (1992, pp.62–6), on the basis of UK research, states that probably three-quarters of those aged 75+ are on some kind of prescribed drugs, and about one-third of them use four to six drugs. Indeed, 20–25% of older patients admitted to acute hospital care in the UK are suffering from adverse drug effects (Dooghe, 1992, p.63).

The District Health Authority is responsible for district nursing, health visiting, chiropody and other ancillary nursing and medical services. The introduction of Health Trusts and GP fundholding is altering the shape of health and nursing care and eroding the notion of a state health care service that is free of charge.

At the primary health care interface, the practice nurse attached to the surgery plays an important role in assisting with injections, etc. The team to whom the older patient now relates is composed of the GP, the district nurse, the health visitor and the practice nurse. The team within the new concept of the 'seamless robe' of inter-agency community care is the wider network of multidisciplinary formal carers, the main ones being pharmacists, clergy, chiropodists, social workers, occupational therapists and physiotherapists. However, the professionals do not really constitute a co-ordinated team for older people, which has been a matter for concern. The recommendation is to develop care management in partnership with social services, basing the target populations on GP practice lists where possible. Under the NHS and Community Care Act 1990, the districts commission/purchase from provider units, which are directly-managed units or NHS Trusts. The mixed and plural model of care is now firmly in place. Indeed, the 'hospice at home' and the 'hospital at home' are being tried out. The whole movement is away from the hospital to the neighbourhoods; from cure to prevention. Time alone will tell whether the idea of neighbourhood nursing, mixed welfare and partnership between the health, nursing, statutory and voluntary agencies and users of the services will materialize.

The policy is to rehabilitate after short-term hospital stays or visits, so that the older person may return home. Long-stay care is the very last resort. Even the UK hospice system is committed to this approach: people do not go into hospices to die, but to learn to live. The hospital in the UK model of community care is also part of the continuum of care, as Gray (1988, p.214) stresses; so too are the residential and nursing homes. They are open systems, sharing in and contributing towards neighbourhood events and activities.

Nursing

Luker and Perkins (1987), in a Manchester survey involving 1,400 persons aged 65+, indicated that district nurses and health visitors had far less contact with older people. The need, as expressed by Luker (1988, p.160), is for a geriatric health visitor. There has generally been a lack of a proper, balanced and truly multidisciplinary team.

As cited by Rosdorff and Wright (1991, p.329) and Baldock (1991b, pp.130–1), the nursing services are inversely related to the availability of informal care. The foremost assistance is provided by the district nurses, whose annual interventions add up to an impressive total of some 16 million visits.

The Audit Commission (1992a) describes the updated community health services under the new scheme of things within recent legislation. The commission points out that community health has not been modelled upon an integrated range of services. The Cumberlege Report (1986) called for neighbourhood teams of nurses focused on small communities of 15,000–20,000. It remains to be seen how privatization will affect the smaller units closer to the users.

Mental health care

Mental health provision in the UK had been largely institutional since the 1820s (see Mangen, 1985a, pp.6–7). Although the institutions are being run down, the bed ratios in the UK and Northern Ireland are the best in Western Europe (Mangen, 1985a, p.23). Many older people had been 'put away' until the 1980s and early 1990s. At the same time, less was spent on mental health care than in any other Western European country except the Republic of Ireland. Like other European countries, the UK has attempted to follow the Italian lead in initiating a mental health community care programme – with disastrous results, because of the lack of planning and unstable funding. Nursing and residential homes continue to provide for large numbers of Alzheimer's Disease cases and other states of dementia, and sufferers are often locked up in private sector homes. Expert care is minimal, and training is of low priority because it is expensive. Gurland et al. (1990, p.263) state that for many older people mental health care is reduced to anti-depressant medication and electro-convulsive therapy. Also, the incidence of dementia cases is increasing. The most common form of Alzheimer's Disease affects about two-thirds of all cases. The CPA (1993, p.224) cite about 50,000 cases in the UK, 20% of whom are aged 80+.

Current policy is to transfer mental health care to the community and to voluntary agencies. The CPA (1993, p.224) refers to the £2.4 million transfer of such money from central funding.

Institutional care

The UK's institutional system of nursing/residential homes has provided care for approximately 5% of the older population in the UK (see Potter and Zill, 1992; Nijkamp et al., 1991c).

With regard to institutional care in the UK, local authority homes were established under the National Assistance Act 1948. They were the main providers up till the 1980s. The so-called local authority 'Part III accommodation' homes increased in number during the 1960s and 1970s. They catered on average for 40–50 older persons. Hammet and Mullings (1991) provide a conspectus of the residential sector in England from 1970–88 (the coverage in Wales is dealt with below). There is an uneven distribution of private residential care within the UK, with most falling within England – 270,046 residential places (on basis of Department of Health, 1988, Table 2). The fact remains that in Wales, as elsewhere in Europe, older people may be referred to homes and admitted because the family wish them out of the way, nursed in homes, when there is no real need for this. For example, Booth's (1985) evaluation of 7,000 residents in 175 nursing homes in Wales found that a sizeable proportion were quite independent and could have managed in the community (see Hirschtfeld and Fleishman (1990, p.486). In the main, the institutional experience had had negative effects upon many of the residents, mainly because of the uniformity of the institutions' regimes, whether they were nursing or residential homes. Even before the UK government's policy of tightening up the admission to homes, the Welsh experience had indicated that staying at home was the preferred option for a significant number of older people.

Institutional care in Wales has been described by Larder et al. (1986), Bochel (1988) and Hammett and Mullings (1991). Residential care rose from 8,306 places in 1978 to 13,652 in 1988 (Department of Health, 1988, Table 4) – a 64.4% increase. The private sector, however, increased less than in the south of England, but more than in the north of England. In the 1980s, when the Thatcher government was 'rolling back the frontiers of the state', the public growth declined and the private homes increased by a colossal 242% (Hammett and Mullings, 1991, p.4). The entrepreneurial venture of running homes for profit during this period was best commented upon by Phillips et al. (1986). There are about 53,206 beds in 2,492 nursing homes and 269,000 places in 10,769 residential care homes (Rosdorff and Wright, 1991, p.327).

It is clear from the evidence provided in this book that the UK government policy of channelling money from the institutional sector to that of community care was simply in line with what was happening in Europe generally, and of course in the USA. It is hardly likely that Europe was following Thatcher. Her privatization of health and welfare were not novel, nor would the privatization of homes have come about had it not been for the recession (see Estrin St Pierotin, 1988). The diversion of funds, from local authorities into the private sector, however, led to an increase in DHSS payments to the private owners from £200 million in 1984 to £1 billion in 1989 and an estimated £1.3 billion in 1990, which jolted the UK welfare state.

Personal social services

Any commentary on service provision in the UK should include services for ethnic minorities. Coombe (1986, pp.219–25) refers to the fact that the older black population is at present a 'young elderly' population, numbering only 79,000 retired persons. She does add, however, that few social services departments have reached policy decisions regarding certain aspects of their care, and they are ill-prepared for the demand for care of older black people by the end of the current decade, when their numbers will increase fourfold (Coombe, 1986, p.219).

However, little can be said on the subject of older black service users at this stage, and this study is the poorer for it. Research into the provision of care for older black and white minority groups has been scant (Fenton, 1987, p.30).

Social care adapted to the needs of Afro-Caribbean and Asian groups is more in evidence where they have been most able to exert pressure within their local constituencies, and where far-sighted social work departments have stood alongside them in protest. This is particularly so in the Midlands and in Newham, London, where the black people have secured themselves a role (albeit somewhat tenuous) in the planning and consultative processes. After considerable pressure, these multi-racial groups have information bulletins and social security leaflets written in Urdu, Gujarati, Hindi, Punjabi, Bengali and Chinese (see Baxter, 1988; George and Young, 1991, p.101). Interpreters for older black people are usually available in the major Asian languages. The number of carers from ethnic minorities is unknown. They will have a critical role to play at the first decade of the twenty-first century. Social service provision for older people is almost exclusively for the white population.

Social services community care largely consists of meals-on-wheels, home help, aids and adaptations, as well as day care. Social workers are hardly involved in direct caring for older people (Sinclair, 1988b, p.80). Rosdorff and Wright (1991, pp.237–9) provide a comprehensive coverage of the UK services available and direct social work involvement.

Meals services

About 48,000 older people are in receipt of meals-on-wheels in the UK – about 1% of those aged 65–74 and 3% of those aged 75+, as cited by Sinclair (1988b). The quality of the meals leaves much to be desired. Researchers have come across stacks of portions in the homes of frailer older people, left to rot, or sometimes given to the dog or cat, as I have also encountered myself in Scotland and England at the time of arranged interviews.

Day care

There are 31,143 day care places in the UK. About 2% of those aged 65–74 and 5% of those aged 75+ attend day centres once or twice a week. Given the number of older people, Arber and Ginn (1991, pp.151–2) say that the level of state provision for older people in the UK is at a low level. Most of these only have one day a week at the centres, and most centres do not operate a seven-day week.

Home care/help

There are at least 560,000 older people served by home helps in England, Scotland and Wales. The service is undergoing massive changes in terms of its philosophy of care and its domiciliary programmes.

Home help is the major social service provision, but it is now less available due to costs; 4% of those aged 65–74 and 19% of those aged 75+ are served by home helps on a once- or twice-weekly basis. In many areas, the home helps are being replaced by 'home care assistants', who mainly provide ancillary nursing tasks, escorting the older person to shops and baths. Increasingly, they have few if any domestic roles within the social services.

Voluntary care agencies and support organizations

Social agencies, such as Age Concern, provide 1,400 centres of care and support in the UK. Help the Aged, a major fundraiser, assists in promoting services to improve the quality of life of older people. Over a million volunteers work alongside older people in the UK – in fact most of them are older people themselves. Pressure groups have also been established, such as the National Federation of Retirement Pensioners Associations. More recently, the Standing Conference of Ethnic Minority Senior Citizens has acted on behalf of the growing number of ethnic minority groups.

Informal care

Northern Ireland, Scotland and Wales are peripheral provinces with similar Celtic origins. This, together with cross-migration, is particularly true with regard to Scotland and Northern Ireland. These share certain features, and the pattern of their informal care is very similar in many respects.

Northern Ireland, with its large proportion of Catholic Irish, has larger families than in the rest of the UK. After the Republic of Ireland, Northern Ireland has the highest percentage of children under 15 in Europe (SOEC, 1988, Table 13.1). The difference between the proportions of children and older people in Northern Ireland is approximately five times as great as the corresponding difference in Scotland, and at least three times as great as that in Wales. Taking stock of the situation in Northern Ireland, St Leger and Gillespie's study (1991) of informal welfare in Belfast probably provides the most comprehensive analysis of informal care in any city in the UK. It is essentially a settings-based study in the best tradition of neighbourhood studies. The authors describe the larger Northern Irish household, quoting the *General and Continuous Household Surveys* of 1984 and 1985. The average household size in the UK in 1984 was 2.59, compared with 3.07 in Northern Ireland in 1985. Whereas in the UK as a whole larger families of six or more persons constituted only 3% of all households in 1984, in Northern Ireland they constituted 10% in 1985. The St Leger and Gillespie study presents a picture of larger families with more human resources to draw upon than elsewhere in the UK. Family members live closer to their parents. Two-fifths of aged parents have relatives or immediate family living within walking distance of their home. Normative and mutual support appeared to be salient features. About half of the older people were seen by offspring or in-laws 'today or yesterday', and four-fifths within the past week.

Class differences do not seem to have been considered in relation to the extent of contact with older relatives or parents – a major flaw in most European studies of the care of older people with the notable exceptions of Shanas et al. (1968), Abrams (1979/80), Taylor (1988) and a few others. These studies indicate that working-class older people are more likely to live near or with their immediate family. In the Cork study (Giarchi, 1990a), those older middle-class people who did not live with or near their immediate family or relatives appeared to be in closer contact with their family than those of working-class origin who lived apart from their kin.

St Leger and Gillespie (1991) state that their findings indicate that the levels of contact with relatives were closer in the Belfast neighbourhoods than those in studies in England and Wales. In the background are the 'troubles' in Northern Ireland, particularly Belfast, in which families become more closely knit during the long-drawn-out terrorist crises, and the conflicts along the ethnic and religious divides.

St Leger and Gillespie (1991, pp.63, 68 and 95) provide several important conclusions in relation to the older people in their Belfast study. Firstly, women have more friends and socialize more than men. Secondly, women rely more upon their families, and particularly upon their children. Thirdly, three-quarters of the carers are women. Fourthly, about equal proportions of disabled older spouses/partners care for each other. Fifthly, although a quarter of the carers are men, they are less likely to carry out toileting, bathing or dressing. Finally, disabled people and those living alone are more likely to be givers than receivers of help.

The major source regarding the rural areas in Northern Ireland is provided by Cecil et al. (1987). As in other parts of Europe, caring is often forced upon one person (Cecil et al., 1987, pp.42–3 and p.110). Their study portrays the high level and comprehensive nature of informal care in the traditional rural areas of the province. Very few older people appear to fall through the meshes of informal care within a twenty-mile radius. The emergent picture of a high density of neighbourhood care corresponds closely with my study (Giarchi, 1990a) in the comparatively rural areas of Cork. As elsewhere in Europe, more personal or intimate care for the housebound and bedridden is mainly provided by close female relatives.

Care is more satisfactory within three-generational families or 'complex families' rather than within 'broken' families; for example, care is provided by offspring for the widowed or lone older people. The emergent picture is one of localized small-scale, self-contained circles of friends and neighbours, with tighter circles of relatives providing either the more personal or informal domestic nursing care. In general, they are also more expressive relationships. Availability, gender and closeness appear to determine the nature of the informal care (Cecil et al., 1987, p.110). Particularly important is the closer interest and greater contact of women with their older kin than that of the men.

McCafferty (1985) examines nine North Antrim and County Londonderry villages. Her study differs from Cecil et al.'s study in that the ties and caring circles are found to be tighter and closer amongst Catholic rather than Protestant families. She attributes this to Catholic values. However, Cecil et al. (1987) did not discover any such differences in their area of study; they note that the kinship ties are significant in both studies. Care by neighbours, though important, is not as significant as kinship support in these rural areas. Working with a smaller sample of persons aged 75 and over, I have discovered that the contact between non-kin and older people who are lower down the social scale in the rural areas (and urban areas) is more frequent than that between relatives (Giarchi, 1990a); this is often influenced by proximity and the length and strength of the relationship. The lack of public transport or the use of a car are also additional factors in blocking contact between persons on lower incomes.

Scotland, like Northern Ireland, according to Todd (1985), traditionally has an authoritarian nuclear family type, contrasting with England and Wales's absolute nuclear family type. It is also part of the Celtic fringe. The west of Scotland has a great deal in common with Ireland as a whole, particularly with the province of Northern Ireland, not only because of its high percentage of Irish immigrants, but also because of the Celtic affinities with Ireland as a whole, and with Northern Ireland because of the links between the Protestant settlement there and its Scottish origins in mainland Britain.

Scotland and Wales, the two mainland UK peripheral provinces, have proportions of older people well above the national European average and that of the UK as a whole. Cornwall, that other part of the Celtic fringe, and very much a peripheral area, largely accounts for the significant high proportion of older people in the south-west. Vast parts of these peripheral areas, which are typically rural, attract the more affluent retired and urban older people.

The European SOEC data, as cited in *Regional Trends* (HMSO, 1988, Table 13.1), indicates that as a region Scotland has one of the highest proportions of older people in the EU and in Europe as a whole. The proportion of persons in Scotland under 15 is only 2.2% more than that of persons aged 65 or over.

With regard to informal care in Scotland, a few studies identify some salient factors. Taylor's report (1988, pp.108–18) on his study of a random sample of 619 older Scottish people in Aberdeen identifies possible risk factors along with some general observations regarding the extent of older people's contact with friends, neighbours or family:

- Those living alone (35%) were disproportionately female and older, being 75 and over. They had significantly more friends than the rest of the sample.
- Those who were childless (20%) were disproportionately middle-class. They had fewer intimates and confidantes, and fewer family living close to them.
- Those who were poor (15%) – those whose income was below the then Supplementary Benefit (today's Income Support) level – had the most visitors and more family members living nearby, a situation very similar to that in the Belfast study.
- Those who were very old, aged 80 and over (15%), were disproportionately female, middle-class and widowed. They did have visitors, but were more housebound. They had fewer family residing nearby, because many of their family, relatives and friends had died.
- Those who had moved within the previous two years (13.7%) were disproportionately from a working-class background. They enjoyed a closer relationship with their family, who were very available.
- Those discharged from hospital during the previous two years (13%), although they did have visits and family nearby, were the most disadvantaged and made greater demands upon their contacts.
- The never-married (10.3%) were mostly women. They had few family members and relatives living nearby, and depended upon contacting a few confidantes.
- Those recently widowed (32.6%) were surprisingly less deprived than those who had been bereaved for more than two years. They did not appear to be without contacts.
- The isolated (23.5%) were generally female and middle-class. Some had no offspring or siblings residing close by.
- The Social Class V older people (8.2%) were the most disadvantaged, but they had the greatest support from their family of all the sample.

The isolated, the never-married and to a lesser extent the childless were identified as those people who were most at risk. Taylor (1988, pp.119–21), on the basis of his analysis, identifies several clusters within his Aberdeen sample:

- The *elderly élite*: these are disproportionately male, the 'young old'; they are generally married and middle-class.
- The *family-shielded*: these too are typically 'young old'; these have

family nearby; they are low on friends, high on family contact, and the majority have a spouse.

- The *supported*: these have above-average family support and are more sociable; they tend to be older, many living alone.
- The *ill and the unsupported*: these are older middle-class widows with restricted activity outside their home.
- The *exclusive couplehood*: these enjoy intimacy through marriage, but they tend to be rather exclusive.
- The *health optimists*: these have many friends, enjoy high morale and have many interests, although often older.
- The *psychologically fragile*: these are low on family, friends and confidence.
- The *socially isolated but defended*: these have few family and few contacts, but are healthy and on better incomes.
- The *'poor souls'*: these are older and middle-class; they are usually female and have above-average family support, but their health is poor and morale is low.

It is clear from the Aberdeen study that family matters to the older Scottish population within a major city. However, it is also clear that when health is poor, as in the case of the 'poor souls', the family cannot compensate. None the less, it is also clear that, when family support is slacker, the older person in poor health would be in an even more desperate state. It is also clear that, when older people have good incomes, they are 'defended' although socially isolated.

These categories are meaningful and revealing in the context of family support and informal care. Their applicability within comparative studies might be worthwhile pursuing in future European studies.

Reduced social contact has negative effects, especially for those with nothing to do, a fall in income, declining health or without a sense of purpose (Long, 1989, p.57). Long's study provides interesting views of what Edinburgh people feel about contacts after retirement. Long (1989, p.64) states:

Neighbours would seem an obvious and immediate source of friendship, yet only half our respondents felt they saw more of the people living locally once they had retired than they had previously. Many kept neighbours at arms' length even if they shared several years of living in the same neighbourhood.

The picture that emerges is sharply in contrast with the family contacts and care by neighbours in Aberdeen and Belfast, part of the reason being that this study deals primarily with the healthier older people who do not wish to be dependent.

There is also the Scottish study of West et al. (1984), in which the least acceptable option for three-quarters of the respondents was to move in with relatives. None the less, in Long's study (1989), family ties for the majority are sovereign. Pursuits with spouse and family, alongside those undertaken alone, are amongst the major pastimes.

In the rural context there is Lishman's (1984) research. Within this short compendium of studies and papers, Watts (1984), whilst practising as a social worker in the Scottish Grampian Region, refers to the problem of the rural incomers who are out of touch with the local neighbourhood care system or informal self-help systems. He also observes that the urban 'good neighbourhood' schemes are less welcome in the rural areas because 'such schemes are looked at with a certain amount of suspicion: the local people would often say that they are not needed and there are already informal caring schemes' (p.146). Local, informal Scottish carers are described as the 'barefoot' practitioners, who, like their other European counterparts, do not welcome the interference of the formal services in their everyday household or neighbourhood care.

Cohen's (1982b, pp.28–30) study of Whalsay describes the Celtic-type households with their close-knit circle of support. Family members set up home close to those with whom and by whom they are brought up. The family household clusters go back to the early years of the twentieth century. Kinship care is clearly dictated by the traditional values of the crofters.

Mewett's (1982) study of Clachan, on the Isle of Lewis, the largest of the Scottish Hebridean islands, also closely examines the kinship relations. Family is sovereign: 'the stereotype of the family is more important than an assessment of the individual' (p.104). Two sets of expectations determine mutual support within kinship relations:

1   a person should act like a relative in order to be thought of as one;
2   the *cardean* (relatives) are obliged to enter into generalized reciprocity with one another.

The meaning attached to 'relative' relates to an expectation not only that they cannot marry each other, but that they must assist each other when needed (p.109). Friends select from the same social type (p.119), which therefore establishes the associations for old age.

There are also other Scottish studies, referred to by Dalley (1984, pp.114–34), which show the importance of domestic familial and neighbourhood networks. There is abundant empirical evidence that domestic care provided by the family is preferable to any type of formal care. Commenting upon responding to the needs generally in the more distant rural areas, Dalley (1984, p.128) observes:

It appeared that greater value was given to dying and being born within the community rather than being taken to hospital. Thus in the case of the elderly, more illnesses were coped with at home than elsewhere because this was valued.

Turning now to Wales, the imbalance of the proportions of children under 15 and of persons over 65 is much the same as that of Scotland, with a corresponding difference of 3.3% more children than older people. Its percentage of older people, however, ranks sixth out of 59 EU regions according to the SOEC (cited in *Regional Trends*, HMSO, 1988, Table 13.1).

The major Welsh studies of Wenger (1984; 1986; 1989) and Bytheway (1987; 1989) extend the bank of information regarding informal care of older people in Europe. Bytheway's 1987 study is of older men made redundant in Port Talbot, and the informal support provided by groups of households to enable them to cope. This rather unique study presents an inside picture of the relationship between caring households within families. Bytheway (1987, pp.179–80) comes up with the original concept of the 'extended household'. This is made up of groups of caring households, not necessarily based upon kinship, which share the following characteristics: contacts are regular and frequent; there is open-door access to the dwelling, and duplicate keys are kept by the caring household.

There are also the 'extended family households' that are interrelated and come together, or are involved one way and another in supporting a family member in need. These have reserves of family assistance. Bytheway (1987, p.180) identifies older people who are in receipt of care and support from more than one extended family household, and also are receiving care from more than one in turn.

In addition to this Welsh urban research, Wenger, in a rural setting, also adds significantly to our understanding of the diversities of European familial support and informal caring arrangements. Her ideas on supportive networks for older people are based upon her surveys of 1979, 1980 and 1982. However, the real strength of her contribution comes from her in-depth longitudinal research into the informal care provided for 30 persons (aged 75 and over) selected from her original 1979 sample of 534 older people. On the basis of this research, Wenger (1989, pp.171 and 179–83) formulates a typology made up of five distinct support networks:

1 The *local integrated support network*, which is made up of close relationships with local family, friends and neighbours, usually founded on long-established local residence and active current or recent community involvement in the neighbourhood/locality. These networks tend to be larger and enjoy high morale.

2 The *local self-contained support network*, which consists of infrequent contacts and arms'-length relationships with local kin, because they

rely mainly on neighbours. The older people in this group are typically of a more retiring nature, with infrequent community involvement. They usually resist help. Social isolation sets in when one of the spouses or siblings dies. They then face greater difficulties. They are prone to succumb in emergencies.

3   The *wider community-focused support network* – typically the older people in this group have developed strong friendships and have contact with some neighbours. There is an absence of local kin. They have a high level of involvement in community activities. They are frequently in contact with their kin by phone. In emergencies, friends and children at a distance help out

4   The *family-dependent support network* typically enjoy close local family ties, but have few contacts with friends or neighbours. They either live close to kin (usually their daughter) or share a household with them. The older people in this network are likely to be frailer and to turn to and be helped by the immediate family when requiring personal care, which is usually of a high quality. Like the older Polish people living with their offspring, these people also feel very lonely because they are often out of touch with their peers. When the care is provided by a non-married daughter, the carer is generally more successful. Whereas siblings ask for help sooner when they cannot cope any longer, the daughters tend only to do so as a last resort.

5   The *private restricted support network*, in which there is sometimes a lack of local kin other than the spouse. Within this network there are no local friends and there is only superficial contact with neighbours. They suffer from a lack of practical informal help and a lack of companionship. Half of these older people will need the help of the statutory services to survive.

It is clear from these Welsh studies that plural and diverse forms of informal care exist. Within these, the family currently provides the most successful form of informal care and support.

A number of writers have carried out thorough, grounded research into the needs of the carers in English settings, as well as their roles and tasks. Some of the major researchers into informal caring, to mention only those from the 1980s onwards, are: Parker (1985), Allen et al. (1986), Bulmer (1986; 1987a; 1987b), Abrams et al. (1981; 1982; 1985), Arber and Gilbert (1989a; 1989b), Twigg (1990; 1992b), Willmott (1986) and Finch (1989; 1990). The older person's views and wishes are central elements in the new equation of care, but carers are usually given only belated recognition within the new UK strategy of care, and are regarded as passive within the sector of home care.

Twigg (1990, p.26), on the basis of research carried out mainly in England, rightly stresses that most care of older people is provided by informal carers.

These carers are regarded as resources (as a support); as co-workers (as collaborators); and as co-clients (as in need of care also). These aspects are elucidated in the Domiciliary Care Project (1986) of the Personal Social Services Research Unit at Kent University, which studied 300 informal carers across ten local authorities (see Challis and Davies, 1986).

The *General Household Survey* (OPCS, 1985) forms the basis of an influential study by Green (1988) on the amount of informal care in the UK, most of which refers to England. One adult in seven cares for a sick, handicapped or older person living in their own or another household; of these, 3% provide 20 hours or more of care each week. This care is valued by the Family Policy Studies Centre (1989) as equivalent to £15–24 billion a year: more than the entire UK annual expenditure on health. Ungerson (1990), and many other feminist writers, has also drawn attention to the immense contribution of daughters and wives in particular to the care of older relatives.

However, there are doubts as to whether the English family, as it exists today, will provide the same care to the same degree tomorrow. Four out of ten marriages break up, and 25% of offspring live in reconstituted families (see Baldock, 1991b, p.133). There is also evidence that considerable numbers of English people would prefer alternatives such as state-supported paid care to care by the family (Finch and Groves, 1983). None the less, family care is still prevalent and resourceful, however reluctant the carers might be.

A statement by P. Abrams at an Age Concern conference, shortly before his untimely death, is cited by Bulmer (1986, p.240), which sums up the growing opinion, not only in England, but in other parts of the UK. He complained about the lack of back-up services, and felt that caring ought to be turned into a 'proper job with paid wages, and we cannot rely on volunteer housewives who simply don't have the time or sufficient numbers to do the work'. The implications of these views will be taken up below.

Arber and Ginn (1991, pp.18–32) describe the 'gender-blindness' within social gerontology. They argue for a paradigm shift away from the 'malestream' assumptions, with regard to the extent of caring in terms of gender and domestic personal care enjoyed by older people. On the basis of the *General Household Survey* (OPCS, 1985), Arber and Ginn (1991, p.146) point out that 93% of disabled older men and 86% of older women manage to perform personal tasks unaided. However, there is a bias towards assisting men with domestic tasks. The bias in favour of men is accentuated (on the basis of the same survey) when taking into account that 37% of able-bodied men report that they receive help, in contrast with only 7% of able-bodied women.

Over two-thirds of carers are women. As Finch (1989) points out, 'it is the proper thing to do' for one's own, expecially if one happens to be a daughter. The argument that family care is disproportionately 'care by women' is driven home when comparing the average care given by spouses for each other. Older men receive almost two-thirds of their domestic and personal care from their spouse, whereas only 28% of older women do so (Arber and Ginn, 1991, p.148). The above disparities worsen when considering that older women's income falls markedly below that of older men. However, when it comes to disability, in England the spouse's personal tasks are usually carried out by the husband or wife. In multi-generational families, it is the daughter or the daughter-in-law who often carries the obligation to care for the frailer older relative, a situation (on the basis of reports and research to date) which is replicated throughout the whole of greater Europe.

Leisure pursuits and education

The Third Age Trust, following upon the French lead, has provided 230 local Universities of the Third Age, with a membership of at least 32,000 (National Association of Teachers in Further and Higher Education, 1994, p.21). The University of the Third Age programme is based upon the basic principle that 'stage' of development and ability, not age, counts. Development of the self and ability have become a central theme in social gerontology. This is reflected in the UK 'Age Well' campaign, promoted chiefly by Age Concern, England. However, only 2% of pensioners take advantage of the educational courses available. The CPA (1993, pp.222–3) document the drop in participation in educational and leisure activities in the UK. As can be seen from the concessionary systems in other parts of greater Europe, they are often less generous.

Rural aspects

This section will consider the rural dimensions of caring at home, of housing needs and of transport for older people, and wherever possible in the provincial settings. Much of what is discussed could have been included within other sections, but the overriding rural dimension and the research data available have suggested that it would be more logical to consider them here together.

The rural provisions of care are difficult to monitor in a fluctuating world of migration, because of 'turn-arounds' and 'counter-urbanization' in some rural areas, and depopulation in others. Also, the rural boundaries are as haphazard as the English hedgerows and as confusing as the perimeters of the Scottish crofts. In addition, there is also a bias favouring urban community care, as reported by the NCVO (1990). The rural areas differ within the provinces which make up the UK. Reaching the older rural population is a major challenge for practititioners, especially for health and social services (Giarchi, 1990b). The problems of distance, so aptly described as 'distance decay', is the most exasperating and most expensive factor facing the authorities, the formal and informal carers, and the older people themselves in their attempts to use health and welfare facilities. This UK overview will take these matters into account.

Moreover, the 'rural areas' are not easily defined. Champion and Watkins (1991, p.7) state that in the face of the complex social science debate it is best to stay with the understanding of the general public that the rural consists of 'small settlements separated by open countryside'. Rural areas are characterized by low-density population, usually by older-than-average age bands, emigration of younger people, and distance-accessibility problems.

Before referring to the geographical rural areas, two points ought to be borne in mind. Firstly, the per capita income is generally lower in remote rural areas than in the urban areas, especially the income and resources available to the established local older population. Secondly, the older male partner is statistically the first to die, often shortly after a move to the countryside at retirement. The older widow is less likely to drive, either because she never learnt, or because she has given it up some years before, which is a common phenomenon in the rural UK (Giarchi, 1990b).

Some observations regarding rural caring arrangements in Wales, Scotland and England will help to provide comparative rural data.

Much of Wales is rural. The problems facing the remoter rural mid-Wales areas have been a matter of political and social concern, part of which was how to meet the needs of the growing number of older people. The Mid-Wales Development Board was set up in 1977 to promote economic and social development in much the same way as the Highlands and Islands Development Board for Scotland. The hope was for more social and cultural infrastructures. However, under the Thatcher and Major governments the policy has been to cut funds and planning projects and substitute marketing aid in place of grant aid. Advice notes from central government increasingly constrain local authority expenditure on housing and transport in rural areas (see Cloke, 1988, p.42). Intervention on behalf of the deprived, such as isolated older rural people, was a discretion that could be exercised by the local authorities. Central government had other ideas, and these are in favour of a market welfare in which private care is sovereign and a needs-led value base non-existent.

Part of the New Right intrusion which has affected the rural people of Wales negatively is the deregulation of buses following the Transport Act 1985, as discussed by Bell and Cloke (1991). They examined the effects in the remote rural areas of North Powys and West Clwyd. Route mileage was affected, and the minibuses did not penetrate the rural hinterland. Although the bus mileage did not alter much, irregular buses created uncertainty; their timetables were difficult for older people to grasp; the possibility of their withdrawal created fear in their minds.

Champion and Watkins (1991, p.20) observe that most rural people depend upon the motor car, but older people make up the highest proportion of non-car-owners and -users. They depend increasingly upon getting lifts. This facility is only available if they have established relationships with locals. The immigrants are less likely to give lifts to the older locals and vice versa. Access to welfare and health services, to Post Offices and shops is essential for older people; many are unable to acquire it. The infrequent bus is no solution, nor are the exorbitant fares for long-distance taxi cab journeys in the remoter parts of Wales. The above remarks indicate that services are not easily accessed, nor are facilities readily available in a peripheral part of the UK. The political climate is bleak, and life for older lone people is often depressing. However, survival has always been a feature, because of the collective support of families and neighbours. Rural Welsh people in the valleys have helped one another in times of depression over many years, which is indicative of the strength of the informal networks.

The formal carers are called upon in emergencies or crises. Wenger (1984) also regards the lack of transport as the 'most serious problem facing rural populations' (p.32). Many of Wenger's interviewees lived more than two miles from a bus route. People in hamlets did not have access to public transport. She came across older people hitch-hiking; others rode bicycles, including a woman of 90. Half the older people had cars: 'forced car owner-ship' lays a heavy financial burden upon older people. Wenger observed, regarding her Welsh sample, that car ownership also declined with longevity. The irony is that, as they get older, people have more need of the car.

With regard to social care, the problems are akin to those identified above in the contexts of centralized services and 'distance decay'. Getting in touch in emergencies is a great problem. In east Cornwall, 14% of rural households had no phone, mostly older people (Giarchi, 1990c). Social services and social security offices are miles away from the villages and hamlets. Social workers reported that they had to drive some 30,000 miles in a year to visit their clients, many of whom were lonely, old and isolated people (see Lennon, 1991). The referral rate of the social services is generally lower per capita than in the urban areas (Giarchi, 1990b; 1990c).

Meals-on-wheels services are being privatized in England within the new Community Care Plan, but viability and profitability excludes many people from the possibility of private provision filling the social care gaps.

With regard to information and advice centres, I coined the phrase 'infor-mation deprivation' in my Cornish study (Giarchi, 1990b). Where there is deprivation, information is usually also lacking. In fact, a major reason for the continuing poverty of some older people is simply that they do not know to whom to turn. Having the facilities and resources to help is one thing, enabling older people to make use of them is another; assistance is only as good as the information given, especially to older residents in the remoter areas of the countryside. A third of Wenger's rural sample did not have a phone (Wenger, 1984). This is a matter of grave concern when the older person is also living in a remote area. Most use a telephone in a neighbour's house; others have to go out and find a telephone kiosk.

The lower the social class of the older rural resident, the lower the chances of access to information regarding the services available. The National Consumer Council (1977) stated that advice and information is the 'fourth right of citizenship'. Many older rural people are denied this right because information leaflets do not reach them.

As is often stated in the research literature and has been repeated in this text, care provided by the family has been and currently continues to be the mainstay of the care of older people. Government planning now leans more heavily upon the informal rural networks, as exemplified by the empirical findings, but they have their limits. The circumstances facing older people in Wales are not dissimilar to those facing older people in Scotland, which will be dealt with next.

In rural Scotland, distance is also a major problem facing the providers of services, especially in the remoter areas of the Highlands. The locals usually cope because of the supportive informal circles of care created over the years, often cemented by the Church of Scotland. Older incomers without local kin have more difficulties in coping because they do not belong to the networks.

In the Highland areas the need for services is greater, but the provision of services is less. Older rural people who have to go into residential institutions may have to move to Oban, Inverness, and even further afield. They are uprooted in their frailty, and usually under severe stress at a time of dramatic changes and upheaval. McCleery's (1991) study indicates that in the Highlands and Islands areas people have to be taken for urgent or serious operations to hospitals in Inverness, Aberdeen and even to Glasgow. Therefore dislocation results in many ways for thousands of older people, whether incomers or established retired people. Reaching them is both expensive and demanding: social workers and nurses are commonly limited to visiting one or two clients a day in very remote Highland areas.

Counter-urbanization has affected the lives of older people in probably 23 districts of Scotland (see Champion, 1981). As I have shown in Western Scotland (Giarchi, 1984), the 'boom' that comes with new ventures tends to bring 'doom' to the vulnerable locals. In the 1970s, the North Sea oil structures, built in Argyllshire, western Scotland, attracted many outside labourers and only a few locals. The new demands upon the scarce local services created a situation where the locals suffered badly and the older population became very disorientated. The new oil developments in the north-western waters will have the same negative effects. In the transitional stages of adjustment, it is the vulnerable people who suffer most. The market has no social conscience.

There are also the more affluent retired immigrants. Their influx in the Highlands and Islands raised the proportion of the population aged 75+ by a staggering 18%. In 1981, more than one in five people were pensioners in 9 of the 21 Highland Statistical Areas (McCleery, 1991, p.157). The cost of living and of houses rose. In fact, the prices in these remote areas were 7% greater than in Aberdeen or Edinburgh (see McCleery, 1991, p.157).

Turning now to England, although pockets of older deprived residents exist almost everywhere, there are designated 'deprived areas' in which the least fortunate older people reside. These areas are typically peripheral; for example, seven out of the nine 'problem rural areas' are located in peripheral England, as analysed by Cloke (1977), with none in the south-east. Another influential rural geographer, McLaughlin (1985), in a national report to the Department of the Environment, identified a quarter of rural households as living in or on the margins of poverty, the worst examples of which were the isolated older people outside the south-east of England.

As stated earlier and repeated in most European studies, a major phenomenon has been the movement and relocation of large older populations to rural areas, but the exodus from the cities is more marked in England, especially within the last ten years. Harper's (1991) studies help towards understanding some of the major elements in these relocations and the impact upon the older population in rural areas. Her interviews with 600 older rural people, 500 of whom were immigrants, indicates that migration is complex and creates different problems for the older incomers. In this study, the migration is part of the counter-urbanization occurring in the south of England particularly. In this instance, the immigrants have moved to the hinterlands of south Hampshire and the West Midlands. Her examples are of older immigrants living mainly in accessible urbanized rural areas. Moving shorter distances into rural areas allows the new residents to make use of the urban facilities nearby.

The second factor, identified earlier, is that of housing, which is central to the experience of retirement in rural areas, and will now be considered in the various parts of the UK.

The social, health and housing departments throughout the UK encourage the frailer and more vulnerable older rural residents to move closer to the social and health delivery centres, and nearer to shops and amenities. The preference is to locate older people, if possible, in the urbanized rural areas, closer to the market towns or the mill towns. The suggestion is often resisted by local old people, especially by those whose families have resided locally for many years. Understandably, the older rural residents seek to remain in their familiar surroundings. Those who agree to move are faced with obstacles. The problem facing the poorer pensioners is that the supply of adequate, affordable housing is greatly reduced in many peripheral rural areas. The older indigenous population face several major blocks to purchasing a house in the accessible countryside nearer to services and amenities.

Firstly, the supply of suitable housing is reduced because of the purchase of local houses as summer residences by second house owners. Secondly, the tourist industry has cut back the number of rented properties available to residents. Thirdly, the housing stock has been reduced because of the sale of rural council houses, the bulk of which are either in accessible or urbanized rural areas. Finally, there is the over-demand by the older immigrants for local houses – their demand is for a wide cross-section of properties from the bottom to the top of the estate agents' price ranges. Only the worst type of unwanted housing is left. The cost of repairing rundown properties is prohibitive.

Turning now to rural transport, Gant and Smith (1991), Giarchi (1990b), the Association of District Councils (1986), McLaughlin (1986) and Champion and Watkins (1991), to mention only a few, have identified the adverse effects the lack of public transport has upon the older population in rural England. The farther away they are from resources, the more their lives suffer: their dwellings, health, leisure pursuits and interests, their contacts and diet generally deteriorate (see Giarchi, 1990b, p.63).

In remote villages of East Anglia, Haynes and Bentham (1982) carried out a study in which they discovered that the closer the villagers were to the GPs' surgeries, the more they consulted their doctors. Also, the doctors were less likely to refer these villagers to specialists than their counterparts whose surgeries were nearer the urban out-patient departments. Clark and Woollett (1990, pp.41–2) refer to a Derbyshire rural study in which non-car-users were three times more likely than car-owning households to face problems of getting to their doctors' surgeries; 79% in Leicestershire who depended upon buses had difficulties. Only 11% in the remoter parts of that county were satisfied with public transport. Giarchi's (1990c) study in east Cornwall shows that the further old people are from the hospitals, the less likely they are to visit sick relatives, or if they are in hospital, the less regular the visits of their relatives and friends from their rural locality. The older people could be described in these instances as the 'rural transport-poor'; they can ill afford to buy a car, however fit they are. Getting a lift is not easy when residing in isolated dwellings or hamlets miles away from villages.

Ambulance teams, Post Office workers, milk deliverers, mobile shop drivers, GPs, district nurses, newspaper deliverers, etc. realize only too well the factor of 'distance decay'; Cornwall even has a helicopter ambulance service. With regard to health provision, the provision is described as 'impure' because health centres are unevenly located and community health services are not uniformly available. Rural health needs are not prioritized. Clearly, the areas where the patients' population density is higher are favoured. In Cornwall, according to McLaughlin (1985, p.22), 19% of rural doctors' surgeries have been closed down, as have 14% in rural Devon. This is not to be confused with the number of GPs in rural areas, which have increased almost everywhere, but have been concentrated in larger and centralized group practices. The single-handed and two-partner practices closer to remoter areas are closing down, so one ought not to be misled by the statistics, which show that there has been a 42% increase nationally in rural GPs (not surgeries) between 1978 and 1987. The increase has come with the increase in 'rural practice allowances' for the GPs (Clark and Woollett, 1990, pp.36–7). The fact is that 23,000 villages have no local surgery. There has been a 6% decline in the number of villages with a surgery and a contraction in the number of non-dispensing surgeries since 1978. The advent of trust status GP surgeries in the early 1990s has also affected the number of surgeries, as they have tended to come together to form rural group practices.

Older people have to travel great distances to their pharmacists to acquire their medical prescriptions. Friends and relatives often have to travel on behalf of them to the pharmacists; when they have neither, problems arise. Again, this penalizes the older residents in the more peripheral areas, particularly in the Celtic fringe. For example, the development of rural pharmacies is thwarted by the Rural Dispensing Committee, because they are not financially viable in remoter areas. The number of rural pharmacist shops has decreased in the smaller villages: only one out of every 200 villages with a population of less than 1,000 is served by a pharmacy (see Clark and Woollett, 1990, p.47). In Surrey, 82 of the 104 villages lack a pharmacy; 77% of villages in Lancashire have no pharmacy, as cited by Clark and Woollett (1990, p.48).

In Gant and Smith's North Cotswolds rural study of older and disabled people (1991), not one of the eight rural parishes had a pharmacy.

Clearly, the older rural population are greatly disadvantaged in these circumstances in many villages, hamlets and in lone dwellings in many parts of rural England.

Conclusion

As this chapter has indicated, the UK is not only multi-cultural, it is also four provinces, in which the older population and the care provided for them are as diversified as are their histories and multi-cultural localities. However, welfare and health care arrangements are tightly controlled by the monocephalic conservatism of Westminster, bolstered by the non-elected quangos which are usually appointed by government, creating centre–centre and centre–periphery tensions.

At macro levels, the links with the centres of administration and planning have been uneasy in all provinces. The Thatcherite era brought with it increased central controls. The rural parts of Northern Ireland, Scotland, Wales and the remoter parts of England mistrust central administration, particularly Whitehall. The provinces also share many infrastructural problems which greatly affect older people: the lack of adequate transport; the centralization of services; information deprivation; lack of affordable and decent housing, and support for the informal carers. The research cited above demonstrates that these problems are shared generally throughout the UK.

At mezzo levels, the post-1993 community care era brought with it a purchaser/provider-led provision of care. Few authorities are able to respond adequately to user needs. Budgets are slim. The policy of enabling people to stay in their own homes and of diverting Department of Social Security funds from institutional care to community care has, since April 1993, been effective in cutting down the number of places in the residential sector, as studies in Devon, Somerset and Cornwall, for example, have demonstrated (Giarchi and Lankshear, 1993; 1994). The impact of the Community Care programme in terms of home care, however, is another matter, which research has yet to fully appraise. Its success is dependent upon the level of collaboration between the carers, the public and private agencies, and the effectiveness and equity of multidisciplinary assessment. The extent to which older people will be able to stay in their own homes will be dependent upon the supply and commitment of informal carers, and the provision of community nurses and other ancillary formal carers. Although older people constitute the major consumers of health and social care, most are healthy. As the CPA (1993, pp.224–5) states, the vast majority of older people in the UK are neither frail nor dependent, and less than 20% of those aged 75+ are severely disabled. However, their needs and steady increase in numbers are significant.

At micro levels there are also difficulties. Some confusion, and in some instances conflict, exists between the public services and the Health Trusts over matters such as what is a 'social bath' and a 'health bath', and what should constitute the skills mix of professionals and others working for older people. There are also problems of establishing criteria for provision. The assessment, monitoring and review of each 'individual package of care' are labour-intensive. The danger is, as in the USA, that many older people will be kept waiting for months and even years because of lack of resources. It remains to be seen if private and voluntary provision can fill the gap. The shrinkage in the supply of informal carers and of the pool of younger people available for training in the next fifty years, together with the drop in the marriage rate and of stable household units, cannot be overlooked.

Services are principally provided for older people who are living alone. The men, however, benefit more: older lone men are twice as likely to receive home care than women. When not alone, men are more likely to be cared for by a spouse. Women carry most of the burden, both as frailer older people and as carers. There is widespread concern that less formal care is now available because of the constraints of the Community Care budget, and because the burden is being passed back to the household members. Unless there is danger to life or limb, they will be expected to support the older person. Such management as exists is in danger of being reduced to 'cost management'. The precarious balance between the welfare state, civil society and the market may prove too difficult to maintain in the UK.

8 The Netherlands

Demography

On the basis of Table 1, the Netherlands will have the second highest proportion of older persons aged 65+ in 2025 (jointly with Denmark and Sweden). The proportion of older people in the Netherlands is relatively low – the country ranks seventeenth in Europe – more than 1.7 million older people are living within 41,000 square kilometres; by the year 2000 there will be 2.2 million in this high-density area (Ministry of Welfare, Health and Cultural Affairs, 1986, p.1). There are twice as many women aged 80+ as men (CPA, 1993, p.173).

In terms of regional variations, the highest proportions of the older population are concentrated in Amsterdam, Rotterdam, The Hague and Utrecht in the west and centre of the Netherlands. The agrarian areas in the same regions also have a higher percentage of older people (Van Poppel and Van der Wijst, 1987, p.108). Many of the retired move into the urban areas to the garden cities, in much the same way as other Europeans seek out their own 'costa geriatrica'. The southern areas have a low percentage of older people.

According to Eurostat (1991a) and the UN (1991) life expectancy at 65 in the Netherlands is ranked joint third in Europe for women (18.9 years) and eleventh for men (14.3 years).

Socio-political and administrative background

The Netherlands is a parliamentary democracy under a constitutional monarchy. Like the other two Benelux countries, Belgium and Luxemburg, the Netherlands is one of the smallest countries of Europe and at the same time one of the most densely populated in the world.

In spite of its size the country has 11 provinces. The parliament is known as the Staten-Generaal. It has two chambers, a larger (the First Chamber), and a smaller (the Second Chamber); the members of the former are elected by the people and the latter by the councils of the 11 provinces. The First Chamber has the power of veto. Older people have to win over the Second Chamber to push through legislation that favours the retired. A large number of political parties and movements are represented in parliament. There are three Christian centre parties (one Catholic and two Protestant) which often unite on issues in opposition to the Labour Party, the Democrats and the Radical Political Party. These two blocs between them have consistently taken the majority of the votes, so that some continuity in policy-making has been achieved, which is especially relevant regarding the services for the older population which are increasingly polycephalic.

The state is committed to decentralization. As part of this polycephalic process the responsibilities of the national government have been pared down. Social policy is shaped by the principle that citizens are primarily responsible for their own wellbeing (Pijl, 1992a, p.2). There are six consultative secretariats, one of which deals with provisions for older people.

The 11 provinces and the municipalities have the same administrative structure. They are run by directly-elected councils (*staten*); these elect the executive; the chair is appointed by the government.

The National Institute for Care and Wellbeing (NIZW), which serves the various agencies for home help, social work, community development, etc., is charged with development work for the entire sector of social welfare. As Pijl (1992a, p.2) explains, it encourages the *sociale vernieuwing* (social restructuring). This has administrative consequences.

The state is now opposed to excessive legislation and administers a scheme in which the municipalities receive a lump sum of money; they then decide where, when and how to spend it, and upon which special needs groups. Also, the state no longer subsidizes organizations, preferring instead to subsidize projects.

Pijl (1992b, p.201) indicates that the Netherlands only published its first policy statement for the older population in 1970; three White Papers on this issue appeared in 1970, 1975 and 1980. The first policy statement aimed to ease their hardships and increase their independence. The second policy statement had the same aim, but put a limit on the number of residential homes, making money available for sheltered housing and home help. The third policy statement aimed to contain the costs of care of older people. Other White Papers in 1986 and 1988 simply repeated much of the same until the White Paper of 1990.

Pijl (1992b, p.202) describes the innovatory proposals of the 1990 Rijswijk White Paper, *Sociaal en Cultureel Rapport*. Its major focus is upon people aged 75+, when major problems begin to appear (but are still confined to a minority). The White Paper sets up seven priorities, which Pijl identifies:

1 re-evaluation of what it means to be older is necessary;
2 a local and national prevention policy must be created;
3 a co-ordinated housing and care strategy must be adopted;
4 a care scheme for the chronically sick older population is needed;
5 training for prevention/participation should be set up;
6 prevention of involuntary loss of work is required;
7 integration of older people's and women's issues within policies is called for.

Integration, and the participation of older people in caring for themselves and for others, are part of the philosophy of care set out within the White Paper.

Social security: pensions and benefits

Social concern has a long history in the Netherlands. Social legislation was first formulated in 1871 (Steijger, 1986, p.406). The state pension (AOW: Algemene Ouderdomswet) ensures that older people enjoy the minimum standard for a decent life (Knipscheer, 1992; see also Laczko and Phillipson, 1991). On the positive side, the pension includes a holiday allowance (CPA, 1989, p.109), and only 1.5% of the older population receive social assistance (Murray, 1993, p.17). In the Netherlands social protection expenditure as a percentage of GDP is the highest in the EU, and the standard of living is the envy of many other nations. On the negative side, evidence shows that a large proportion of the older population in the Netherlands do not share the country's high standard of living. Murray (1993, p.17) accepts this, but adds that, although a high proportion of older people in the Netherlands have very low incomes, the poverty levels are still less severe than those in England.

All persons aged 65+ receive a state pension. The pension is fixed at the 'social minimum'. In the 1980s this declined by 10% (Pijl, 1991, p.98). A married person aged 65+ receives a basic pension amounting to 50% of the net minimum wage. There is a supplement of 50%, if the younger partner has not reached 65. However, not all employees are entitled to supplementary pensions. Since 1 April 1988 the supplementary pension has been adjusted to take account of the income of the partner who is under the age of 65, whereas up to that time it did not. Dooghe (1992, p.153), citing Dutch research, points out that one in six people aged 65+ have to cope with an income at the level of the social minimum; for those living alone it is one in four. At the same time, on the positive side, the share of income ascribed to pensions has grown from 68 to 83% from 1970 until the mid-1980s (Dooghe, 1992, p.153).

In addition to the state pension, there is also an employment-related pension, but 35% of those in employment in the 1980s were not covered by this pension (see Van Poppel and Van der Wijst, 1987, p.112). Indeed, more than half of the older population depend upon the state pension alone. The problem for the Netherlands is that the majority of the frailer and older population, who are in the greatest need, are worst off financially: they are over-represented in the lower income groups (Van Poppel and Van der Wijst, 1987, p.112). If anything, their income levels have deteriorated further since 1988. The older they are, the greater their needs and the less their income, particularly the men in the older age groups and the single women. Driest (1988, p.155) states that only a quarter of those aged 65+ are fairly comfortable financially; as almost everywhere in Europe, the older women are the poorest. Driest (1988, p.153) points out that Dutch women account for nearly 60% of those aged 65+ and two-thirds of those aged 80+.

Also, in the Netherlands the disposable income of the older population is lower after taxation than that of the younger population. The situation worsens further with age, according to Dooghe (1992, p.153). The pensions are organized on a pay-as-you-go basis. Those in paid employment pay for the current pensions. The concern is over the costs of maintaining pensions: these will rise in step with care costs, so that higher premiums will be necessary. Knipscheer (1992, p.152) describes how the 57% of unmarried people aged 65+ in 1960 had risen to 83% by 1970. These are amongst the poorest sector of the population. Van Poppel and Van der Wijst (1987) ask whether the younger population will wish to pay higher premiums towards pensions. This is a central issue because, as will be shown, the Netherlands is moving from a state welfare model to a plural (largely, 'pay if you can afford it') model.

It is clear from the above sources that the inadequate pension means that the many older people in the Netherlands are increasingly impoverished as they become frailer. How then do they survive? In fact, they are reputed to be amongst the best-served and healthiest in Europe. However, the discussion that follows will show how the quality of life and the care of the older population in the Netherlands are fraught with contradictions.

Housing

Quality of life is determined to a large extent by the quality of housing. In addition, housing and social care policies for older people are interrelated. Advances have been made by the housing associations in the Netherlands. Murray (1993, pp.18–19) refers to their response to the housing problems facing the Dutch government. The country has a long history in subsidizing accommodation, going back to 1901, when the introduction of subsidized housing in the Housing Act anticipated that in the UK by some eighteen years. But in 1945 the nation's housing lay in ruins after the bombardments and aerial bombing of the war. Older people were amongst those who were either homeless or living in devastated properties.

Since the 1940s the 840 housing associations provided about 35% of new housing stock at reasonable rents or prices annually (Murray, 1993, p.18). Today there are probably 250,000 housing units designed to accommodate older people, of which between 15,000-25,000 can be defined as social housing (Murray, 1993, p.25). There is very little private housing. Purpose-built blocks (*uitsluitend senioren woningen*) are currently being provided for the more independent older people.

The housing associations may have helped, but the majority of properties are not affected by their intervention. There is one exception, that of Amsterdam, where the city housing department and the housing associations provide half the accommodation for the older population (Murray, 1993, p.27). However, in spite of the increased housing provision in many parts of the Netherlands, many poor older Dutch people – particularly lone women – are forced to live in old dwellings. Murray (1993, p.18) states that the Dutch councils provide only 7% of housing stock, and this share is reducing. The Dutch government, as in the UK, is selling off municipal housing. About 55% of people aged 55+ report discomfort in their homes, as cited by Mastenbroek (1986, p.22). For example, Driest (1988, p.155) paints a gloomy picture of the older residents in bad pre-war housing: the stairs are steep; there are no baths and no showers; no central heating, and rooms are either too small or too large. Home ownership is at 43%; about 22% are living in rented accommodation. It is here that the worst conditions prevail, and where a disproportionate number of older people are trapped. The national statistics for the population in general provide a contrast: 95% of houses have a bathroom on the premises, 66.1% have central heating and 93% have a telephone (Eurostat, 1991b, pp.121–2).

Independent living is a social policy objective for older people in the Netherlands, so that the quality of their homes is a significant factor in maintaining that independence: 92% of older/retired men and 87% of older/retired women live independently in the community; most live in family dwellings.

The housing stock problems cited above, and the policy of maintaining people in their own homes, have led the government to encourage the provision of special accommodation. The costs have also spurred local government to work in collaboration with private agencies. Small dwellings are provided for some older people; others live in special housing, 69% of whom have an alarm system. Serviced dwellings consist of satellite dwellings (homes or apartments built beside or near to residential/nursing homes or service centres, with or without the supervision of a manager) and service flats (which are rented or purchased, but have domestic help and communal facilities).

Innovations in rented or owned service accommodation are amongst the most progressive in Europe. Experiments carried out in close collaboration with the local authorities and the Co-ordinated Work for the Elderly agency have developed 'group housing' with communal facilities; 'collective housing' with separate housing units in one building, and 'communal housing' where everything is shared.

Apart from these more recent developments, a higher proportion of the older population own their own houses in the rural areas; in the urban areas, a higher proportion of them rent apartments. The older rural population tend to stay where they are, whereas the older urban residents tend to move more frequently, because housing costs in urban areas are considerably less than those in the rural or small town settlements, mainly because older people can make use of the individual rent subsidy (Mastenbroek, 1986, p.21).

Just as there appear to be major problems concerning housing, there are also transport difficulties in the Netherlands. Mastenbroek (1986, pp.24–5) discusses these. The need to be mobile has increased with the better health of the older population and higher living standards. At the same time, this coincides with local shopping facilities being scaled down and other primary facilities being centralized. A national working party had to be set up to address the problem (Mastenbroek, 1986, p.24). The less healthy are mainly affected, mostly in winter. With regard to people aged 80+, up to 25% of the women and 13% of the men are virtually housebound in winter.

Health care

The general health of older people in the Netherlands is regarded as being among the best in Europe, and the health services obviously contribute towards maintaining this. However, health expenditure almost doubled between 1975 and 1982, as stated by Pijl (1992b, p.202). She also adds that in 1990, 9.1% of GDP was spent on health services. The health services and related insurance have had a complex and volatile history.

The Health Insurance Act 1966 introduced compulsory health insurance for employees and benefit recipients under 60 years of age. The General Act on Extraordinary Medical Expenses (Compensation) 1968 (AWBZ) extended insurance cover for long-term illness or disability; it included fees for nursing, and residential fees for persons with disabilities, hostels, day centres and home care services provided by private agencies (see Lunn, 1989, p.15). However, the AWBZ subsidy was dependent upon the user's level of income. Under the Health Insurance Act 1966, there was a compulsory contribution towards the health insurance scheme. People with an income above the declared ceiling have to take out private health insurance; 62% of the population were insured by the government scheme, the rest were insured by private health insurance companies. Those in receipt of welfare state benefits were insured free of charge.

Health care policy was reformed in the mid-1980s, and modifications to the above schemes have been introduced. What has remained has been the split between the major basic insurance cover and the additional minor private insurance cover. The changes came about, firstly, through a commission chaired by Wisse Dekker, which published the Dekker Plan in 1987. Market elements of effectiveness and flexibility were to be introduced into a plural welfare scheme. With a change of government, the Dekker proposals have in turn been modified by Simons, the Socialist State Secretary for Health, although the major Dekker proposals have remained. The Simons Plan has now replaced the provisions of the 1987 report. Changes in the delivery of care and health insurance are to be introduced at intervals until the full implementation of the Simons Plan in 1995 (see Pijl, 1992b, p.202). These changes consist of health insurance under which everyone will receive basic cover for 95% of health care services. These services are now designated as 'functions', because home care, home help, residential care and nursing home care may be provided by a private or public agency, on condition that the quality of care they offer is ensured. The other 5% can be insured freely from any private insurance companies. For those older people with a low income the new scheme is cheaper; the care packages are now better tailored to their personal needs than before. The choices that may be made under the Simons Plan, however, have thrown up problems linked to criteria of acceptability that must satisfy the user, the professionals and the local authorities, so that yet another committee, the Dunning Committee, produced its report at the end of 1991 (see Pijl, 1992b, p.204). Four major questions now need to be asked before care is provided:

1   Is the care necessary?
2   Is the care efficient?
3   Is the care effective?
4   Is the cost of care payable by the patient?

These questions are clearly dictated by costs, and the fear is that health care will be budget-led and not needs-led, a far cry from the philosophy of the welfare state.

Health care is not the responsibility of the municipalities in the Netherlands, although the Municipal Public Health Services are in charge of prevention (see Pijl, 1992b, p.206). With regard to health services in particular, there are six hospitals with geriatric units, totalling some 250 beds (Ministry of Welfare, Health and Cultural Affairs, 1986, p.3), but older long-stay patients are cared for in nursing homes.

Hospital care and medical services

Tunissen and Knapen (1991a, p.13) and Murray (1993, pp.24–5) refer to the 198 general and specialized hospitals in the Netherlands, providing over 60,000 beds. About 15,000 beds are occupied by people aged 65+. The Netherlands has 9.6 hospital beds per 1,000 population, which is second only to Luxemburg (Eurostat, 1991b, p.88). Only 1.7% of the older population are in hospital at any one time, but those aged 65+ cost three times as much as the average patient, and those aged 75+ cost five times as much (Tunissen and Knapen, 1991a, p.13). The country still has the largest per capita consumption of hospital services. Since the Reformation, the Netherlands has depended to a large extent upon Protestant religious groups, whose institutional provision provided most of the earlier modes of formal care, later to be supplemented by Catholic agencies within a fast-growing Roman Catholic community.

There are 2.2 doctors per 1,000 inhabitants, the fourth-lowest ratio in the EU (Eurostat, 1991b, p.88). Under-usage of the GP is cited by Mastenbroek (1986) on the basis of Dutch research. Fewer and fewer GPs are making home visits, and the country also has the lowest ratio of pharmacists in the EU (Eurostat, 1991b, p.88).

Nursing care

Pijl (1992a, p.16) refers to the 60+ community nursing agencies in the Netherlands, consisting of about 11,854 nurses and nursing assistants. These agencies are made up of several teams. The community nurses and the home helps both belong to the National Association for Home Care (LVT).

More than two-thirds of a district nurse's visits are spent dressing wounds, washing patients and giving injections (Mastenbroek, 1986, pp.36–7). About 72% of their clients are older people (Van den Heuvel and Gerritsen, 1991, p.220). Costs are covered by the AWBZ. District nurses are used more in the south. Reports indicate that there are role conflicts between the home helps and the district nurses.

Home care/help

Home help was formerly a function of the social services; it is now administered within the health care system. The home help services work closely with the district nurses; however, there may be a clash of expectations regarding what these have to offer the users. There are some similarities in procedures between the home care and health care tasks, and in agreed criteria and defined responsibilities between nursing tasks and those of the home help service.

With regard to home care, Mastenbroek (1986, pp.27–32) and Van den Heuvel and Gerritsen (1991) state that 15% of all households with a member aged 75+ are assisted by the home help service (Gezinsverzorging). This service is provided by private organizations, but is also supported financially by the state. There are about 233 such organizations served by some 105,800 'direct' workers; Pijl (1992a, p.16) states that they constitute about 40,300 full-time equivalent jobs. The home helps are organized regionally: the home help agencies supervise home care, and hire paid workers, who provide home care for half-days. Mastenbroek (1986, p.29) refers to the problem of recruiting home helps in Amsterdam and The Hague because of the emigration of younger residents to the satellite towns and suburbs. There are shortages in these cities, a matter not mentioned by most commentators.

The home care workers serve some 159,000 older people annually, either short-term or long-term (Van den Heuvel and Gerritsen, 1991, p.217). The users' contributions cover about 10% of the costs. The Ministry of Welfare, Health and Cultural Affairs provides a budget; this plus social security payments in the case of illness help to defray expenses. Since 1989 the home help services have been financed through the AWBZ; in addition, the user has usually to pay towards the cost on an income-related basis. For the older population there are two types of home care assistance:

1 'Home carers for the aged' (*bejaardenverzorgsters*). These receive more training and are involved in fewer domestic tasks.
2 'Home helpers for the aged' (*bejaardenhelpsters*). These are more involved in domestic tasks, and constitute the majority (there are more than five times as many helpers as carers).

Mastenbroek (1986, p.30) and Van den Heuvel and Gerritsen (1991, pp.218–20) explain what is known as 'alpha care': this consists of purely domestic private helpers allocated to the applicants by a private institution. There are over 46,000 users of such a service (see Mastenbroek, 1986, p.30). Home help is made available for a maximum of 16 hours per week, and on average amounts to 4.5 hours per week, spread over one or two part-days (see Mastenbroek, 1986, p.30). Some may be involved at all hours, seven days a week, in which case their work is referred to as 'tailor-made care' (*zorg op maat*). This round-the-clock call-out system, as described by Van den Heuvel and Gerritsen (1991), is designed to keep people out of institutions. The home carers often provide home support for those recently discharged from hospital or assist the dying.

Cover in the evening, night and early morning is provided by 'community/district care for the aged' (Wijkbejaardenverzorging). An intake criteria system, known as the LIER (Landelijk Inicatie en Registratiessysteem), determines the allocation of care, as explained by Van den Heuvel and Gerritsen (1991, pp.219–20). However, as the same authors state, there is considerable variation between regions with regard to the usage of the LIER. In addition, there are religious agencies, which have been guaranteed considerable leeway and autonomy. In assessment for home care needs, the Dutch also use the ADL (the elementary activities) and ADLI (the instrumental activities), as used in Central/Western Europe (for example, see Jamieson, 1991c, p.325).

In the Netherlands, according to Van den Heuvel and Gerritsen (1991, pp.231–3), the provision of home help may be more expensive than district nursing, social services and GP intervention. In addition, when more than ten hours of home help are provided each week, it can cost more in the long term than residential home care, as the same authors point out (p.231). Clearly, the estimate must be based upon the travel costs of the home help, as well as the costs attached to the intensive care. The payment by the users and by the health care agency, as determined by the General Act on Extraordinary Medical Expenses (Compensation) 1968 (AWBZ), for the care provided is described as a 'co-payment'. There is also a real possibility, because of rising needs and costs, that the services will only deal with low-risk older people; home care of high-risk older people necessarily means higher costs for the private home help agencies.

Mental health care

Thirty-five per cent of persons in psychiatric hospitals in the Netherlands are aged 65+. The number of hospital beds per 1,000 population in the Netherlands ranks third in the EU after Ireland (3.2) and Luxemburg (2.6) (Eurostat, 1991b, p.88). The Ministry of Welfare, Health and Cultural Affairs plans to transfer many hospital patients to sheltered residential units attached to institutions or in the surrounding locality. One example of an increasing number of extra-mural mental health caring units is cited by De Leng (1991). This is a 'near-home' care project, consisting of a small-scale multifunctional housing unit for dementia sufferers in De Gooyer – a kind of halfway house. The residents mix with other people who drop in for meals or snacks, and bus outings for the residents and local people are also arranged. Mental health care is attempting to link this type of innovative caring unit with the psychiatric and mental health staff in hospitals. Mastenbroek (1986, pp.39–40) describes the ambulant mental health service, which consists of the Socio-Geriatric Services (SGS) and the Socio-Psychiatric Services (SPS); the latter refers and acts as a clearing house for mentally ill people, some of whom are older people. Pijl (1992a, p.16) states that there are 24,046 places for psychogeriatric patients in nursing homes.

Rosdorff and Vollering (1991, p.298) refer to the Mental Health Advisory Service (RIAGG), which consists of regional units for ambulant mental health care. Psychiatrists, social workers, social psychiatric nurses and psychologists in these units provide ongoing care, supportive counselling and prevention for many older people.

Institutional care

With regard to institutional care, the Netherlands has one of the best reputations in Europe for high-quality residential and nursing care. Van Poppel and Van der Wijst (1987, p.113) point out that 8% of the older population live in residential homes, and just over 2% in nursing homes. Tunissen (1993, p.71) states that the proportion in residential homes now stands at 7%.

The Residential Homes for the Elderly Act 1963 was one of the first measures of its kind in Europe. It established quality controls for residential care. It has been amended and updated over the years, with the most radical change in 1985. Half of the cost of running the homes is provided by the state. The government allocates funds for the running of the homes annually, but has handed over the administration of these funds to the provinces and the four major cities of Amsterdam, Rotterdam, The Hague and Utrecht. Provincial complaints boards have been set up. Murray (1993, p.21) refers to the larger 'caring homes' (*versorgingstehuis*) built during the 1970s, which was the period when the proportion of older people in the Netherlands was the highest in Europe. Murray (1993) also refers to the 9.3% of those aged 65+ who lived in residential homes and the 2.2% in nursing homes in 1975 (see also Rosdorff and Vollering, 1991).

A high percentage of older people continue to reside in institutions in the Netherlands. In the mid-1980s there were approximately 150,000 places in residential homes, which for a small country with approximately 1,709,000 people aged 65+ was impressive (see Ministry of Welfare, Health and Cultural Affairs, 1986, p.1; Driest, 1988, p.159; Lunn, 1989, p.15). In the early 1990s there were as many as 132,000 older people in 1,530 residential homes (Pijl, 1992a, p.15). Three out of every four in institutional homes are women. In no country are so many older people cared for in institutions as in the Netherlands. It is not surprising that institutional care has been described as the 'pillar of Dutch policy' (Driest, 1988, p.159). The average age in these homes is 83; 50,000 residential staff care for the residents. The staffing ratios in the residential homes are very high, consisting of about one full-time staff member to each bed (see Ministry of Welfare, Health and Cultural Affairs,

1986, pp.2-3). The cost of running these homes with their day care facilities is met by a scheme set up under the AWBZ and from the fees paid by patients (which include unearned income).

Tunissen and Knapen (1991a), Evers (1991) and Baldock (1991b) describe the institutional care in the Netherlands in its earlier period as largely unco-ordinated, rather traditional and costly. However, in its day, institutional care in the Netherlands was regarded as comparatively progressive. Today the residential institutions that serve a dual purpose of community/day centre as well as residential establishment have broken the traditional mould. Certainly, older, fit and able people have been moved into residential homes when they could quite easily have stayed at home. Tunissen (1993) describes the residents' councils with their grievance committees which deal with residents' rights and complaints. They help to create changes.

In the early 1980s there were some 330 nursing homes (*verpleeghuis*) with approximately 30,000 non-psychogeriatric beds (Ministry of Welfare, Health and Cultural Affairs, 1986, p.3). In the early 1990s the number decreased: Pijl (1992a, p.16) states that there are about 26,651 somatic patients in the nursing homes.

There are three kinds of nursing home in the Netherlands: psychogeriatric, somatic and combined. The problem of the 'wrong bed' occurs from time to time (Driest, 1988, p.159). Attached to these homes are day care facilities, catering for about 4,500 older people. In collaboration with a local Stitching Welzijn Ouderen (co-ordinated work for the elderly unit) and agencies for home help, hot meals, alarm systems, assistance with bathing and showering, cultural activities, pedicure, hairdressing and emergency aid are provided by many residential homes (see Tunissen and Knapen, 1991a, p.11). Many of the homes have rooms for self-reliant and more independent older people, who may use the communal facilities if they please – a type of sheltered accommodation: the *aanleunwoningen* (see Tunissen and Knapen, 1991a, p.11).

Personal social services

Steijger (1986, p.405) describes the social services as a decentralized network of agencies under the Ministry of Welfare, Health and Cultural Affairs. The state has favoured private care over state intervention. The Churches have played a significant role in carrying out the tasks of the emerging plural welfare state.

The rather limited role of the municipalities calls for comment. Indeed, Pijl (1992b, pp.203–4) states that 'local government finds itself in a difficult position'. As stated above, it is not responsible for health, but is responsible for providing information and courses on health matters, and can set up special programmes for the older population. The municipality subsidizes community centres, generic social work, meals-on-wheels, counsellors for older people, transportation to and from day care, alarm systems, the adaptation of houses for older people, and voluntary organizations.

As stated earlier, the Municipal Public Health Services are also responsible for prevention. The rather centrist structure of the local services is further confirmed by the fact that the local social services offices, which administer income support, have to abide by national rules dictated from the capital.

Social services for older people in the Netherlands are described by Driest (1988, pp.156–66) and Pijl (1992a, pp.2–33). As is the case in the UK and many other European countries, social workers are seldom in direct touch with older people. Indeed, the social workers are employed by any one of hundreds of member organizations under the aegis of the Association of Enterprises in the Subsidized Sector (VOG), which in turn comes under the Secretariat for the Elderly, but whose role is merely consultative.

The profile of social service workers is low. Many workers have been incorporated within municipal offices. Social work for older people is sparse and mainly provided through home care agencies. Buis (1989), in an influential study which assesses with whom the older population are in contact in the Netherlands, gives the following rank order, which totally excludes social workers but does include informal carers and the 'cleaning lady', relatives, and the district nurse (11% are unaccounted for):

1 help from the offspring (30%);
2 help from a cleaning lady (19%);
3 help from neighbours, friends/contacts (15%);
4 help from a home help (12%);
5 help from other relatives (9%);
6 help from a district nurse (4%).

In 1987 a home care project was set up which was based on the Kent model of community care designed by Challis and Davies (1986). The project was designed to introduce the UK 'case management' programme to the sphere of home care in the Netherlands. The case manager is entrusted with the entire responsibility for providing care and services to older clients, but in partnership with them. A care plan is drawn up, and in partnership with the user an individual care package is provided. A major pilot 'case management' project was set up in Rotterdam, and is described by Koedoot and Hommel (1992). It was funded by the Ministry of Welfare, Health and Cultural Affairs. The costs of home care were kept to within two-thirds of the cost of care in a nursing/residential home, so that cost effectiveness as well as quality of care were maintained. The leading role of the older people was a central feature in the Rotterdam pilot scheme, which demonstrated that it was cheaper for the health and social services to keep them at home (if aged 75+). They also retained greater independence over a longer period.

However, other 'case management' projects in the Netherlands have not been as successful, and their costs have not been justified.

Amongst the successful schemes are those in which the home helps are directly employed by the old people themselves, who may well choose to be their own care managers. In addition, parish workers and Church volunteers account for many of the cleaning staff, for whom there is no payment. Many researchers continue to overlook the work of the Churches, especially important in the Netherlands with its strong religious community links (see Lunn, 1989). Clearly the home helps are of immense importance, especially to the increasing number of isolated older people who have neither family nor surviving relatives, nor the private means or the contacts to survive in their own homes without that help. The issue uppermost in the minds of social care managers in the Netherlands is the most cost-effective means of involving home helps.

The emphasis is upon community strategies rather than social service programmes. There are also the district carers (*wijkziekenverzorgenden*), who are part of the home help network. Central to community care provision is COSBO-Nederland, a central co-ordinating body which represents the major concerns and community interests of its members. Local community work for older people consists to a large extent of the work of Co-ordinated Work with the Elderly (GBW) projects (see Mastenbroek, 1986, p.30; Driest, 1988, p.158); this organization works chiefly through the service centres in the districts. In 600 of the 750 municipalities in the Netherlands there are several hundreds of projects with approximately 2,000 employees (Driest, 1988, p.159). The government supplies 80% of the GBW budget (see Mastenbroek, 1986, p.30). It concentrates on encouraging co-operation between voluntary groups and various organizations; setting up information networks and small local amenities such as libraries, chiropody facilities and meals services, and organizing various cultural and recreational activities. Along with other organizations such as the Volunteers' Union (UVV), the GBW organizes cooked meals, serving about 2 million meals a year. Older people have 30% of the seats on the board of the GBW.

Next, there are travelling shops, which 14% of the older population make use of. Milk deliverers, bakers and greengrocers call in their vans, and 1% have meals delivered (Mastenbroek, 1986, pp.32-3). As people get older, they use the travelling shop and meals-on-wheels more frequently.

Voluntary care agencies and support organizations

There is a sense in which the bulk of the formal caring systems of the Netherlands are run by agencies that are similar to voluntary agencies in the UK. For example, district nursing (*kruiswerk*) is done by the cross-organizations, which are the non-profit home nursing organizations. These are recognized by the government if they fulfil certain criteria.

Tunissen and Knapen (1991, p.13) refer to the 234 organizations with approximately 80,000 workers, mostly part-time, who run the home help services (Gezinsverzorging). They are subsidized by the state.

Amongst the most influential of these voluntary organizations is the Netherlands General Association for the Elderly (Algemene Nedetlandse Bond Voor Ouderen – ANBO), the Netherlands Gerontology Foundation (Stichting Voor Gerontologie) and the Dutch Institute of Care and Welfare (Nederlands Instituut Voor Zorg en Welzijn – NIZW).

Informal care

As Table 1 shows, the Netherlands will most probably have the highest increase in the number of older people in Europe by the year 2025, although Switzerland will have the highest proportion of older persons (see CPA, 1989, pp.108 and 142). This small country of 15 million inhabitants has a growing number of solitary older people, which will increase considerably (Pijl, 1991, p.97). Mastenbroek (1986, p.111), regarding the care of the older population generally in the Netherlands, says that 'the future does not look very rosy for the group of very elderly' because of the increasing costs of formal care; also, the 'young old' will be more vocal in their demands. As a result, there could be a polarization and intra-generational struggle for resources. Pijl (1991) says that very little is known about the older immigrants, but by the end of the century there will be over 950,000 of them.

As everywhere, it is the very old women who will be most in need and greatest in number. Knipscheer (1992, p.152), on the basis of Dutch research, states that in 1960, 57% of the unmarried older population were living alone; in 1970 the figure was 83%. In the early 1980s 64% of independent women aged 80+ lived alone. The percentage of men in the same age group was as low as 26% (Mastenbroek, 1986, p.7). When one considers women generally, Knipscheer (1992) says that in the Netherlands 33% aged 65–70 live alone; of those aged 75+, 61% live alone. However, there appears to be a tendency for the divorced or widowed to live with one of their offspring when they are aged 75+. The same author later adds that in the Netherlands, 'the family is the first and main resource for support of the elderly'.

Four-fifths of those needing help at home receive informal help. The Netherlands has one of the lowest rates of women in paid employment in the EU (see Tunissen and Knapen, 1991). With regard to ordinary daily chores, 43% get help from their partners, 15% from other household members, 19%

from a formal helper and 53% from someone else (Mastenbroek, 1986, p.26). There is evidence nationally of a significant informal circle of support for frail older people living at home, which is provided by kin, neighbours and friends.

On the positive side, Pijl (1991, pp.105–6) refers to the 33% of those aged 20–65 and the 20% of those aged 65 and over who give informal help; 72% of all carers support their parents or parents-in-law; in addition, 23% of the carers are friends. Not surprisingly, there are twice as many women as men carers. Most spouses receive help from their partner; next in importance are offspring, then neighbours, friends, and lastly, other relatives. On the negative side, women receive less help than men and are given least assistance when living alone. Buis (1989) also refers to the lack of support for the informal carers. Those who care for a family member or relative experience more stress than those who care for friends (Pijl, 1991, p.108).

The ability of older people to help each other within their own circles is a central element; they primarily give help to friends. At the same time, it must be said that the family in the Netherlands, as in Northern and Western Europe, is not as culturally significant in terms of filial support as in Central, Southern and Eastern Europe. There is a greater reluctance for older people to depend upon their offspring – they value their independence more. In addition, the family mantle of care is not always possible, and it is becoming less available. Van den Heuvel and Gerritsen (1991, p.221) state that approximately half of the older population live independent lives. On the basis of statistics provided by these authors, it appears that informal care has been almost static between 1975 and 1985.

Not uncommonly, older women form households of two persons who are unrelated by blood, and older men tend to form households of three or more persons not related by blood (Mastenbroek, 1986). For this minority, informal care is in great part not so much family care as 'home' care. Knipscheer (1992, pp.154–5) shows that the evidence of intimacy between older people and their offspring is contradictory: some research shows that intimacy is significant, other research does not. There is a need for caution and the avoidance of generalization.

The Dutch government has attempted to popularize the concept of the 'caring society', but the growing demand for care of older people, the decrease in the number of carers within the circle of the family, the reduction in the number of families, the smaller size of families, and geographic mobility have disenchanted the potential carers. As far back as 1983 the Welfare Division of the Ministry of Welfare, Health and Cultural Affairs found that its 'support policy for the elderly in the community' was not filling the gaps, and after 1985 it was more or less at a standstill in real terms.

The government is aware of the need to encourage informal care to effect a shift from intra-mural to extra-mural care involving self-help and informal care (Mastenbroek, 1986, p.79). The need was realized long before the UK's Griffiths proposals (Griffiths, 1988). A Dutch strategy known as the 'closed circuit' strategy was devised, which floated the idea of harmonizing extra-mural and intra-mural care. The strategy was devised in the Netherlands in 1975, over a decade before the so-called 'Griffiths initiative' in the UK. In addition, it is commonly said that these strategies are a copy-cat version of some US policies, whereas the European mainland also explored plural mixes in the 1970s. The debate within the Netherlands was in progress long before even the 1975 government memorandum entitled *Measures for the Elderly, 1975* (see Mastenbroek, 1986, p.66). However, the substitution of extra-mural care for intra-mural care was seen to be problematic if the older people and their immediate circle of care were not involved: the professional carers were felt to be taking over. This follows the findings of international research which emphasizes that the divide between the formal and the informal must always be respected. It was realized fairly early that when formal carers came up with choices or support systems, informal care ceased to function or withdrew from the interaction (Mastenbroek, 1986, p.67).

Years before the UK White Paper *Caring for People* (HMSO, 1989), the Netherlands had established a formula for plural welfare, well described by Mastenbroek (1986, pp.67–8) under the heading: 'The elderly have a say': 'In order to meet the individual needs of an elderly person, the most suitable solution should be sought in consultation with the person concerned and those immediately around him/her.' This is a highly relevant statement in the context of individual packages of care within the UK system, as was seen in Chapter 7 when assessing the informal domain within England and Wales.

Regarding informal care, by way of conclusion, it is clear that, in spite of the Dutch government's faith in the family and the significance to date of familial support, the mantle of care is now under severe strain in the Netherlands. The concern over the changing structures of families voiced within other European countries is also expressed within the Netherlands. Whether there is greater awareness of the dangers in leaning upon family support when it is tottering is another matter. The Dutch family is less resilient than most. As stated above, the future burden of care appears to be formidable for the authorities: smaller families increase in number as the birth rate continues to plummet; more and more single people continue to live independent lives within more *Gesellschaft*-like neighbourhoods; serial marriages fragment relationships and extra-familial contacts; the marriage rate drops, and greater distances between families develop, as European countries open up their borders and commerce.

The informal neighbourhood circles are not always there to fill the gaps. The research indicates that their support is dependent upon long-term rather than short-term contacts with neighbours.

Leisure pursuits and education

With regard to leisure interests (so important in dealing with boredom and the lack of stimulation) the Ministry of Welfare, Health and Cultural Affairs has established a welfare policy which encourages and supports adult educational courses. Only 8% of older people participate in such pursuits. The very active Interministerial Steering Committee on the Care of the Elderly formulates innovatory programmes. Grants are given to the Central Federation of Old People's Associations to organize training courses and fitness programmes (see CPA, 1989, p.110). Almost half of those born before the 1920s have only received primary education. Many of them have taken advantage of Third Age-type general education to update themselves.

Older Dutch people are generally fit and more conscious of the importance of responsible living, such as maintaining a healthy diet and regular physical exercises. Because of the flatness of the country and the minimal costs entailed, the bicycle is one of the most common means of travel for the older population.

Rural aspects

Before concluding, it is clear that, in contrast with Chapter 7 on the UK, little has been said regarding the care of older people in the rural areas of the Netherlands. Relevant research is not available. However, according to Groenendijk (1988, p.49), regional policy has mainly focused in recent times upon the city-regions in the north and south of the country. Priority is given to urban problems. Of the 10% lowest-ranked municipalities, the peripheral provinces of Friesland and Zeeland and the major river areas of the southern parts of Gelderland and Zuid-Holland have a considerable degree of rural deprivation, because of the many disadvantaged households in the remoter villages. The welfare services face greater welfare austerity in the rural areas because of the rationalization of services (Groenendijk, 1988, pp.51ff.). A weakness in the system is that there are no sectoral government agencies which deal specifically with the rural areas. The small rural municipalities lack power when competing for resources with the larger urban municipalities. The older people are vulnerable, and at the same time costly, consumers. The result is that the older rural population are amongst the most disadvantaged in the Netherlands, as they increasingly are throughout Europe.

Conclusion

In concluding, it is clear that the care of older people in the Netherlands provides a picture of an increasingly diversified plural system of care at the level of the municipality. The Dutch administrative system, however, is not as polycephalic as its Scandinavian neighbours. Although in flux, the structure veers towards being monocephalic. In spite of the localized collaboration between agencies and local authorities, and although the municipalities provide the older population with 'closer-to-home' facilities, the centre continues to decide what lump sums are to be given towards local need and how they should be allocated. Moreover, health services are not the responsibility of the municipalities. Although the local state, the voluntary agencies, the Church groups and private agencies have been interrelated for years within the formal triangle of social care, the part-government, part-Church and part-commercialized institutions are not. They do not pick up the major casualties, being involved mainly with diverse forms of prevention. The state has been firmly lodged at the apex of the triangle of care, because its central controls remain in place. The country is small, so that although the centre responds immediately to local needs, providing subsidies to fit the requests of the regional and municipal authorities, it is also able to interfere as speedily. As Baldock and Evers (1991, p.189) point out, access to choice in the care market and voluntary sector is hampered by the vestiges of central state control. Older people may also be confused by the discontinuities in procedures and by the chaos in local administration (see Tunissen and Knapen, 1991b, p.94).

9 Belgium

Demography

Belgium has the seventh-largest proportion of older people jointly with Switzerland. As shown in Table 1, the proportion will probably increase by 5% by 2025. As the CPA (1989, p.26; 1993, pp.44–5) and Eurostat (1991a) indicate, the percentage of children will remain steady. The potential caring ratio is good.

Belgium is divided into three distinct areas: Flanders to the north with its Flemish-speaking population; Wallonia to the south with its French-speaking population, and Brussels, the capital, with its bilingual population. Dooghe and Van den Boer (1986, p.9) state that in Flanders the present 17.5% of people aged 60+ will rise to 20% by the year 2000; in Wallonia, the present approximately 19% will remain much the same, and in Brussels the percentage will increase from 22.2% to 23% – a city with one of the highest percentages in all Europe. Since the start of the twentieth century, the average life expectancy has increased by some 30 years (Dooghe and Van den Boer, 1986, p.2). The life expectancy of women aged 65+ in Belgium is 18.2 years, the ninth-highest in Europe, while that of men is 14 years, the fourteenth-highest in Europe (Eurostat, 1990; UN, 1991). Belgium's proportion of children under 14 years of age will be 1.7% less than that of the population aged 65+ (see CPA, 1989, p.26). The highest proportions of older people are in the Brussels region (approximately 22%); in the Wallonia region (approximately 19%), and in the Flanders region (approximately 17%) (see CPA, 1993, p.47 for further details and Dooghe, 1992).

Socio-political and administrative background

Belgium is one of the smallest countries of Europe; however, it is also one of the most densely populated. Since 1944, Belgium has been part of the Benelux customs union, along with the Netherlands and Luxemburg. Belgium is mainly divided lingually, administratively and culturally into three regions – Flanders (Vlaanderen) in the north, which is Flemish-speaking, the Walloon (Wallonie) region in the south, which is French-speaking, and Brussels, the capital, which is bilingual. There are five provinces in Flanders and five in Wallonia, and there is also Eupen, a small German-speaking area in the east (approximately 350,000 inhabitants), which was incorporated into Belgium at the end of World War I. The main political parties are the Christian Social Party, the Belgian Socialist Party and the Liberty and Progress Party.

As is clear from the contents of this chapter, the state has been moving away from a universalist to a pluralist system. Leaper (1990) describes Belgium as a country with many faces. He regards it as almost a federal state, although conserving its formal unity through the Belgian monarch. Flanders and Wallonia are generally described as the 'communities'. Since 1980 the country's administration has become more decentralized. The provision of social care and the financing of services have been devolved from the state to the two major language communities. Baro et al. (1991, p.17) explain how the French and Flemish communities now have their own constitutions and are in effect parts of federal Belgium. These communities are governed by the 'executives'. With regard to matters concerning the person (*persoonsgebonden materies*), they often have autonomous authority. Outside of Brussels there are nine autonomous provinces, each headed by a governor, and a 'Permanent Deputation' which administers these provinces. The provinces are divided into 44 administrative districts (*arrondissements*) and 2,373 communes. The communes are headed by a burgomaster. Each commune has a local welfare centre.

The progressively polycephalic nature of the Belgian services has created greater contrasts between regions. These contrasts will be addressed once the nationwide factors – such as pensions, housing, the health system and social service provision – have been discussed. At regional (mezzo) level, a high council for senior citizens has an advisory role, facilitating the co-ordination of services.

Social security: pensions and benefits

All employees are covered by the Belgian social security scheme. However, there are separate arrangements for public employees and self-employed persons. The state pension is funded by the employee and the employer, in addition to being topped up by state subsidy (see CPA, 1989, p.26; 1993, p.48). The retirement pension is payable at 65 for men and at 60 for women. Pensions at an earlier age are available for miners and others engaged in certain demanding jobs. The full pension is equivalent to 60% of average earnings. There is a minimum pension, and the pensions are adjusted annually to the Retail Price Index (CPA, 1993, p.48). An interesting feature, like that of the Netherlands, is the yearly holiday allowance. Dooghe (1992, pp.152–2) states that the older populations – particularly very old people in Flanders – are generally in the lowest income brackets. In spite of improvements, 44% of the heads of such families belong to the 20% lowest income class. One out of every three older lone persons are reckoned to be in a state of social insecurity, according to research cited by Dooghe (1992, p.152).

All men aged 65+ and women aged 60+ have a right to a minimum income (pension) as from 1969, and reaffirmed in 1974, when the Public Centres were deputed to handle the management of the allocation of the income-related benefits. The minimum income is defined by Royal Decree after parliamentary discussion. The National Office for Wage-earners' Pensions administers the pension, which is paid by girocheque. The contributions of offspring towards the maintenance of their parent(s) and the amount of capital holdings are taken into account when determining the levels of payments.

Leaper (1990; 1991) describes how responsibility for the administration of the entire social security payments system resides with a network of public agencies, who deal with the occupational groups. Amongst other payments and benefits, they administer pensions and the costs of medical care. Applicants for income-related cash aid must be interviewed and assessed by a social worker at the local commune organization. This consists of the Openbaar Centrum Voor Pelijk Maatschap Welzijn (OCMW) in the north and the Centre Public d'Aide Sociale (CPAS) in the south, which have been in existence since July 1976. These centres also award the *minime*, the minimum income level necessary for subsistence. They also have other important functions which will be dealt with later. Those who use these facilities do not experience stigma. The centres are governed by an elected council in which there are local commune councillors (Leaper, 1990). The smaller centres are governed by an inter-commune joint council; 586 centres employ about 2,000 social workers and also about 7% of local authority staff. Leaper (1990) indicates that the Belgian general public regard these centres as providers of local hospital care and care for the older population, although they do perform others tasks, such as providing social services, institutional care, home help, meal services, and community care for mentally ill people.

Housing

Three types of housing for older people exist in Belgium. Firstly, there is 'service housing', which is as in the Netherlands (see pages 163–4). There is usually a common room for hot meals, and an alarm system. They are usually apartments in high-rise blocks of flats. Secondly, there is 'semi-dependent housing' – small units with common rooms, built near to a residential home or community centre for the more able-bodied older persons. Individual arrangements are made to suit their needs, such as hot meals and temporary care. Thirdly, there are the 'clustered housing schemes', specially adapted with alarm systems. These are grouped together closely. Hot meals may be provided, and there is a warden. These are very similar to the UK provision of sheltered accommodation (see pages 132–3).

The majority of older people live in ordinary housing, usually with their families. Dooghe and Van den Boer (1986, p.13) state that 40% of the older population in Flanders are accommodated in terraced houses, 34% in detached houses, 17% in flats (*bejaardenwoning*) and 9% in semi-detached houses. Similarly to the UK, two out of three older Belgians are either owners or joint-owners or leaseholders. Like Holland, most older renters are in the cities. The smaller the urban area, the smaller the number of older renters. Those at the bottom of the social scale spend about half their income on housing; this contrasts with those higher up, who spend about 31% of their income on housing. Twenty per cent live in houses built before 1915; about 40% in houses built between 1926 and 1956, and about 17% in houses built since 1965 (see Dooghe and Van den Boer, 1986, p.13). There is 'void space' (too many empty rooms, as in large houses) in about half of the houses occupied by older people.

With regard to amenities, 40% do not have inside toilets; 49% do not have bathrooms or showers indoors; 66% have no central heating, and 49% have no phone, as cited by Dooghe and Van den Boer (1986, p.14) on the basis of the 1981 census statistics. The same authors state that 18% of the accommodation is not adapted to suit the needs of older people. As stated many times in this study, most older Europeans live in older housing – the situation is no different in Belgium, however high its general standard of living (see Dooghe and Van den Boer, 1993).

Given that 10% are only semi-mobile and 4% are housebound, many older Belgians are greatly disadvantaged. Judging by the Eurostat (1991b, p.119) statistics regarding new housing from 1978–88, the country has the second-lowest increase of new houses after Italy (which is at the bottom of the EU countries for the rate of growth in new dwellings per 1,000 inhabitants) as well as the second-highest proportion of houses built before the end of the war after the UK.

Older people, along with other low-income groups, may apply for means-tested benefits. The older population in Belgium are the fifth-highest beneficiaries of social protection benefits after Italy, France, Spain and Luxemburg (Eurostat, 1991b, p.84). People aged 60+ have a 50% reduction on rail travel and on tickets for large cultural events; there are also telephone charge reductions for some categories of older people; subsidies are available for housing adaptations and for removal costs and rent subsidies are often negotiated (see Spinnewyn et al., 1991, p.95).

Health care

With regard to health, older people receive partially-free medical care through health insurance provided by means of the State Institute for Sickness and Invalidity Insurance. The institute also reimburses the costs of medico-physical nursing tasks within the domiciliary care provision. The Belgian system has always provided a mixed health and welfare system. Unlike most of its neighbours, Belgium has fewer major adjustments to make to its plural system of care, well established on a mixed basis long before Europe coined the phraseology of 'mixtures of care' and 'plural welfare systems'.

Health policy and health insurance are ultimately the responsibility of central government. The Ministry of Public Health and Family Affairs provides the largest slice of funding for health care (see CPA, 1989, p.26). However, the French and Flemish cultural communities administer the health services. In general, about 37% of health costs are covered by insurance; 35% are covered by the consumer, and about 25% by the state via the communities and local authorities (see Mangen, 1985a, p.45). Baro et al. (1991, pp.17–18), commenting upon the Flemish community system, describe the 'Administration for Health Care and the Administration for Social Welfare and the Family', each of which is headed by a Community Minister; the former is responsible for hospitals, rest and nursing homes, and home nursing; the latter is responsible for the social services for older people, which includes home help.

Hospital care and medical services

According to the Eurostat (1991b, p.88) statistics, Belgium has 4.7 general hospital beds per 1,000 inhabitants and comes eighth in rank order out of the EU countries; it comes fourth, however, with regard to psychiatric beds; 31% of its general hospital patients are aged 60+ (Dooghe and Van den Boer, 1986, p.22). However, Spinnewyn et al., 1991, p.90) state that the average age of patients in the geriatric wards is 75+, and the average stay is less than thirty days. There are as many as 140 specialists in internal medicine in geriatrics in Belgium, which must be the highest number in any European country.

As stated above, the health system is mixed: 60% of building and equipment costs come from the state and 40% from the hospital and the Medico-Social Institutions Building Fund (see Mangen, 1985a, p.42). Hospitals receive a global annual sum of money for in-patient health care. Sickness and insurance funds indemnify 75% of patient costs and the state indemnifies the other 25%. Patients usually pay a fixed sum for hospital bed and board. They pay a *ticket modérateur* (a regulatory ticket; see page 201) for the hospital doctor's services, but most of the fee is covered by insurance funds. Out-patient services are financed on an item-of-service basis.

With regard to extra-mural general medicine, there are 2.8 doctors per 1,000 Belgian inhabitants, which is the fourth-highest ratio in the EU. Belgium's household consumption of health services is the third-highest in the EU (Eurostat, 1991b, p.89). The family doctors, dentists, chiropodists, pharmacists and specialists are independent contractors, to whom part-payments are due, in the manner explained above. Belgium has the highest ratio of pharmacists per person in the EU (see Eurostat, 1991b, p.88). As in Italy, they are often consulted, and in many instances are in effect substitute doctors, especially within poorer neighbourhoods.

Nursing

With regard to nursing home care, one of the biggest community nursing organizations is the White and Yellow Cross, with about 1,350 full-time nurses, about 3,150 part-time nurses and 132 different services, all of which are well distributed throughout Belgium. This voluntary nursing organization provides almost 80% of all home care nursing. However, Belgium has a variety of other smaller voluntary and private nursing agencies. About two-thirds of those who use them are aged 65+; over a quarter are 80+ (Dooghe and Van den Boer, 1986, p.35). The less there is in terms of informal care (*mantelzorg*), the more often is home care required and the more costly it becomes. The Flemish administration sets itself a limit of subsidies for 9 million hours per year.

The nursing care is intensive: over half of the older people cared for at home are visited at least once a day. The nursing home care appears to be more generous in the Flemish than the French community. Dooghe and Van den Boer (1986, p.22) and later Baro et al. (1991, p.25) cite empirical evidence that there is an approximate margin of about 3.9 million extra units of home nursing care between the Flemish north (15.4 million) and the French south (11.5 million). The major reason for home nursing care is to administer injections; the next most important is to provide hygienic care and dress wounds (see Dooghe and Van den Boer, 1986; Baro et al., 1991). The biggest gap in home care, as identified by the users of services, is the lack of domestic work, which echoes the complaints of older people in the UK.

With regard to the more intensive nursing for older people living at home, the greater part of the funding is provided by the State Institute for Sickness and Invalidity Insurance (RIZIV).

Mental health care

The mental hospitals are known as 'neuro-psychiatric institutions', providing 0.3 beds per 1,000 inhabitants (see Dooghe and Van den Boer, 1986, p.23). These cater for dementia sufferers amongst other types of patients. About 22% of the 80+ age group are suffering from dementia, in contrast with only 2–3% of those aged 65–9. As will be shown below, the services cannot provide appropriate care for most of this group of older patients.

Mangen (1985a, p.48) refers to the 196 *dispensaires* linked to the hospitals serving the mentally ill, amongst whom are older people. These are privately managed units run by multidisciplinary teams offering containment at home, prevention and boarding out (see Mangen, 1985a, pp.48–51). However, the co-ordination and liaison between these and the hospitals to date has not been good. The patients have to provide a certain proportion of their income towards treatment costs at the *dispensaires'* rates, or apply for social assistance to pay their way. The Health Ministry provides 95% towards the salaries of the formal carers and the community costs, whereas the communities subsidize the building costs, as reported by Mangen (1985a).

A significant amount of the care given to mentally ill people in the non-statutory sector is provided by religious orders (in 1985, Mangen put it as high as 90%). The psychiatric colony at Geel has catered for chronically sick persons for almost a millennium (see Mangen, 1985a, p.44). As everywhere, the religious organizations are decreasing, although they progressively employ more and more lay persons to fill the gaps. Side by side with this reduction in the number of trained religious carers there is also, according to Davids (1992), a parallel decrease in nurses (as is so in Germany).

Spinnewyn et al. (1991, p.92) refer to the shortage of care provided for older people suffering from dementia or other neuro-psychiatric problems. As a result about a quarter of older people with dementia are placed in long-stay wards (*V-diensten*); of the rest about 17% are placed in rest homes and 15% in psychiatric hospitals.

Institutional care

With regard to institutional care, there is the 'rest home' (known as the *maison de repos* in the Walloon community, and the *rusthuis* in the Flanders community). Leaper (1990) indicates that there are probably about 84,031 rest homes in Belgium, of which 49% are in the northern community and 36.6% in the south, together with 14.4% in Brussels. Probably about 4% of the older population are in rest home care. There are more public centre-run rest homes than there are voluntary agency and religious rest homes; however, there has been a small increase in the voluntary and religious homes in the past two decades. The homes must be registered, and are subject to inspection by the regional administration. The rule is that there must be 1 nursing home bed per 1,000 inhabitants.

The residential homes in the south must be approved by the Ministry of the French Community. There has to be one member of staff for every five residents; one personal and health assistant for every ten residents, and one nurse for every thirty residents (Wanlin, 1992, p.9).

The rest and nursing homes in the north provide a care package to avoid hospitalization. The average age of residents is about 82. The ratio for rest homes is 4 beds per 100 senior citizens; 1 dementia patient bed per 100 older people; for rest and nursing home beds the ratio is 2 beds per 1,000 inhabitants. If the residents are unable to pay, the family or the Public Centre for Social Welfare steps in to cover costs (Mostinckx, 1992, p.20).

Personal social services

Wanlin (1992) describes the social services in the south and Mostinckx (1992) describes them in the north.

Social services in the southern provinces

Public Centres of Social Help (CPASs) are set up in every district. These have been referred to under 'Social security, pensions and benefits', but they deal with a great deal more than benefits and welfare payments. Older people receive advice and help in making decisions about entering rest homes or making use of day care. At least one social worker must be one of the managers of the centre. The centre is the first point of contact for older people when they find themselves in critical circumstances.

Social services in the northern provinces

Moenaert (1991) outlines the 'cash and caring' system in Bruges within an OCMW. Options are discussed regarding the care of older people by the social workers in terms of domiciliary, extra-mural and residential care. In addition to a domestic cleaning service, other services are available, such as day centres, baths, hot meals, chiropody, films, theatre programmes, coach trips and a variety of exercises.

The service centres (*dienstencentra*) also offer information, advice, meals, leisure activities and personal hygiene services. There are also housing services and electrical as well as house repairs, and the need for residential care is examined by the social workers. Financial assistance is also available at the service centres.

In addition to the social workers, there are less professionalized aides: the *aides seniors* in the French communities and their equivalent, the *bejaarden-helpster*, in the Flemish communities (see Leaper, 1990). Of all the Western European countries, the Belgian caring arrangements appear to be the most complex, but also the most flexible and highly adaptable to a mixed welfare system.

In an attempt to bring the services together, Flemish community-subsi-dized co-operation initiatives (*samenwerkingsinitiatieven*) have been set up. There are about 45 of these. Spinnewyn et al. (1990, p.97) describe them. They are multidisciplinary schemes made up of social workers, GPs, home nurses and home help assistants, and managed by a co-ordinator to meet the individual needs of older people in the area.

Amongst recent innovations are the 'S-O-S triangles' which are set on the older person's window-sill to alert passers-by in an emergency. Pink 'postman cards' are also placed in the window by the older residents when help is required. The postman then alerts the OCMW or CPAS. Sickness Funds loan older people alarm systems. Tele-Alarms Care Systems have been installed in many places: for example, there are between 10,000 and 20,00 in Flanders (see Spinnewyn et al., 1991, p.97).

Home care/help within each of the regions

Home help tasks in the Flanders community are arranged by the older person's social worker who, as seen above, is contacted at the service centre, as described by Leaper (1990). Home helps have been providing care in Belgium for at least forty years.

The home help services have become more comprehensive, offering more intensive care. For example, in Flanders, the home help hours increased by about 29% between 1975 and 1985, and the number of home helps by 2,168; but the number of users decreased by as much as 4,422 (based on statistics cited by Baro et al., 1991, referring to Steyaert, 1986). Not surprisingly, most of the users are women aged over 75, living alone and widowed. The home helps in Belgium are well-trained: in the Flemish community the basic training amounts to 650 hours. In addition to providing cooking, washing and cleaning services, a personal care service is also given, and moral support, counselling and giving advice are part of the amalgam of home care made available to consumers.

The formula for the costs is a mix of payments in line with the plural welfare model adopted by Belgium years ago: 70% from the state; 30% from local government and consumers, as described by Baro et al. (1991, p.22). The same authors refer to the recent innovation of utilizing unemployed persons as cleaners (an additional 3,800 persons).

Voluntary care agencies and support organizations

Belgium has had a long tradition of voluntary care for older people. The country was noted for its Beguine almshouses. Spinnewyn et al. (1991, p.89) refer to voluntary work and community work (*buurtwerk*) providing for the needs of older people in Belgium.

Much of the work carried out for older people by the parishes is not mentioned. Research into the work of the St Vincent de Paul Society for the poorer older people, especially in the thousands of parishes in the southern French community, is called for. The visiting of isolated older persons and the financial support offered ought to be surveyed. However, much that is done for older people, especially in terms of nursing and home care, is carried out by the secular voluntary organizations. These have been referred to earlier, such as the White and Yellow Cross providing domiciliary care services (since 1937). It employs about 4,500 nurses working in 140 areas (see Spinnewyn et al., 1991, p.94). There are also the home help services (*gezins-en-bejaardenhulp*), which are non-profit organizations operating particularly in Flanders.

Informal care

Eighteen per cent of the older population live in a multi-generational household, which Dooghe and Van den Boer (1986, p.9) state may lead to tension. However, more of the disabled, more of the widowed, and the frailer older parents tend to live with their family. In fact, one in two disabled older people receive assistance from their offspring with regard to washing and foot treatment; seven out of ten receive help with regard to going out and dressing. Baro et al. (1991) draw our attention to the fact that help provided by the family, neighbours and friends in Flanders is described as *mantelzorg* – 'the mantle of support/care'.

Dooghe and Van den Boer (1986, p.3) state that the number of widows is four times that of widowers in Belgium. Many more older women than men live alone and have no one to look after them. However, the authors add: 'It is striking to note that there is still a relatively large number of elderly people, more perhaps than might be expected, who live together with one of their children' (1986, p.5). The dependency ratio is calculated on the basis of the 'old age index' – the proportion of people aged 65 and over to younger people aged under 15. This has risen from 25% in the 1950s to 30% in the 1980s, rising probably to 65% by the year 2025 (Dooghe and Van den Boer, 1986, p.8). The authors observe that in cases of emergency and illness 43% will first turn to a spouse for help, and 46% to offspring or children-in-law. Moreover, in 80% of cases, offspring are cited as the first or second source of support and help.

With regard to those older people who are not living with their offspring, three out of ten are none the less assisted with the shopping, cleaning up and washing by their offspring (Dooghe and Van den Boer, 1986, p.28). They cite Belgian research which shows that in 52% of the cases offspring provide assistance with five domestic activities: washing up, cooking, shopping, cleaning and putting out the dustbins; 27% receive help with performing between three and six main domestic activities; 10% in performing two activities, and 15% in performing just one activity. More than nine out of ten married people turn to their spouse when they fall ill, and in the second instance to their children. Where there is no spouse the offspring will generally step in. They describe the offspring and the spouse as 'the pillars of the assistance process' (p.29).

More recently, Spinnewyn et al. (1991, p.84) point out that in the case of the sick older people, the most supportive person is the partner (49%), then the daughter (29%), the daughter-in-law (8%), the son (7%), or a sister (4%). These percentages, however, should be considered alongside the number of older people who have no family. Dooghe and Vanderleyden, as far back as 1976 (when familial and kinship care were more prevalent), stated that 28% of older people living on their own needed help in performing weekly cleansing activities, but their needs were not met. Also, Dooghe and Vanderleyden (1986, p.36) cite another survey in Wallonia and Brussels in which 137,000 older people were not assisted by their relatives, neighbours or friends.

The study of Dooghe and Van den Boer (1986, pp.38–9) identifies the following features which create difficulties for informal carers where older people at home are chronically sick or are suffering from dementia. These factors significantly affect the structure of the authoritarian nuclear family:

1   Household carers are physically overworked and mentally stressed: 'the stress is often felt to be worse than that resulting from a death in the family'.
2   Nursing care provided by the family compels the family member(s) to alter the family lifestyle: 'fear, frustration and disillusion provide a seed-bed of conflict'.
3   Making room for the older person alters the spatial arrangements within the household.
4   The carer can become a 'sort of secondary patient'. The wife conceals her difficulties from her husband. She is expected to be the linchpin and to hold out whatever the pressures.
5   The carer as domestic nurse runs the risk of becoming isolated.
6   Long-term domestic nursing of the chronically sick 'may result in a rising financial burden in some families'.

Dumon et al. (1994) discuss aspects of these characteristics of informal care in the context of need. These factors have been itemized because they present a fuller picture of the stress and burden of care experienced within Belgian households. Neighbourhood care is less evident here, and familial care is more apparent, as is the case generally in the Latin cultures, which I shall return to in Part V.

The traditional practice of adult foster care in Belgium deserves a mention. This is a domestic provision of care which has been little researched and which is hardly mentioned in the academic literature. McCoin (1983) and Bogen (1979) both refer to the ancient European practice of placing unrelated dependent adults in the care of private families. This was begun in the thirteenth century in Geel, Belgium, for persons who were mentally ill, and then extended to older persons in the 1940s (Aptekar, 1965). The large residential units of Scandinavia and the UK were never an attraction to Continental Europeans. In any case, residential care was totally eclipsed by the status of family care. With the contraction of European families into smaller and smaller units, it remains to be seen whether the option of adult foster care may become a major European feature in the next century, outside the Scandinavian countries and the UK, alongside more extensive domiciliary services.

Leisure pursuits and education

With regard to leisure interests, many pensioners' clubs exist, particularly Sports-Seniors and Seniors Horizons (see CPA, 1989, p.26); the latter arrange holidays abroad for older people. There are branches of the Union of

Christian Pensioners, which are also very active. The Third Age (Derde Leeftijd) also exists in most cities.

Rural aspects

The rural areas are contracting within a country where the agricultural production for many years has been less than 5% of GDP. No studies on caring arrangements in rural Belgium are available in English.

Conclusion

The Belgian system is 'one of many faces', to quote Leaper (1990). The federal nature of the political structure and the polycephalic service centres have brought the formal service agencies closer to the older population. The centres have managed to offer both health and social care options within one office. The centre users do not generally experience stigma, perhaps because they provide such a wide selection of services for all ages, as well as infor-mation. The multidisciplinary team also enlarges its flexibility and adds to its extensive resources.

Within this flexible and complex model, the local state and the private and voluntary/Church agencies or organizations are well balanced. The local state is the significant factor in the delivery of care within a polycephalic structure. Adapted to the needs and demands of two cultures, the local state maintains equilibrium and status through the government's acceptance of autonomy and 'closer-to-people' systems. As Table 6 indicates, the Belgian administrative welfare structure is essentially polycephalic. Family circles are at the centre of the informal modes of care. However, there are signs that the family is in decline.

The concern expressed over the transitional changes occurring within the family, due mainly to the higher incidence of divorce and the decline in the marriage rate, will dog the Belgian governments of the first decades of the 21st century. The number of divorces is 4.5 times higher in Belgium than in 1960 (Eurostat, 1991b, p.25), and the proportion of single households is also four times as great. Who will take care of the single and the separated married women in particular, twenty to thirty years from now? The reliance upon the family – a haven for most older Belgians today – may not be a viable option if the unity and permanence of the Belgian family progres-sively wane and decline. It will hardly be a fall-back for social workers in the OCMWs of Flanders and in the CPASs of Wallonia thirty years from now.

10 France

Demography

The proportion of the population aged 65+ in France is likely to increase by about 5.3% by the year 2025, constituting one of the largest increases in Europe (see Table 1). The proportion of older people in France is much the same as in Luxemburg and Belgium. France will probably have the twelfth-highest proportion of persons aged 65 and over in Europe by 2025. Leaper (1989) refers to the fact that France had the highest proportion of older people in the world in 1939, whereas it came seventh in the 'elderly league' in 1985.

The life expectancy of French women, which at 19.8 years at 65+, is the highest in Europe; for French men, in contrast, it is 15.4 years, joint third highest with Spain (see Eurostat, 1991a). The UN (1991) projections state that in the year 2025 there will be 2,915,000 persons aged 80+ in France – the highest of the European countries.

Over two-thirds of older French people live in the more urbanized areas. A third live in the very rural, often remote, parts of France, where provisions are necessarily scant; 10% of older French people living at home may have mobility problems (Pitaud et al., 1991, p.31).

Socio-political and administrative background

The French parliament is composed of two houses: the National Assembly and the Senate; the former is made up of 485 deputies; the latter is made up of 283 senators. Legislation is shared by the government and parliament. The President appoints the Prime Minister and his Ministers. The presidential office is supreme.

The Socialist Party to the left, the various Gaullist 'unions' to the right, the Christian Democrat Mouvement Republicain Populaire to the right, and the Radical Party usually dominate the political scene. The swing to the right in recent years has affected welfare policies.

There has been a recent move in France towards decentralization and polycephalic arrangements. However, at the same time, it is necessary to keep in mind the monocephalic tendency created by an earlier Napoleonic ethos. France is in two minds about decentralization (see Table 6), as is clear especially in the case of the uneasy restructuring of the rural areas within the *aménagement du territoire* (adjustment of the region).

Decentralization, which had begun in the post-war years in the field of mental health, was later to be official policy for all services from 1982, especially after the promulgation of the Decentralization Act (see Mangen, 1985a, pp.124–5). The country is made up of 22 regions, within which are the 96 *départements*, and within these the 36,000 *communes* (Ely and Saunders, 1992, p.4). A consultative body, CODERPA, advises on all aspects of health and welfare (see Leaper, 1990; 1991).

At national level, health and social protection is the responsibility of the Minister of Social Affairs. Next in line is the Minister Delegate, who deals with matters affecting older people. Within this ministry there are twelve directorates (*directions*), amongst which are the General Inspectorate of Social Affairs, and the Directorates of Social Action, Social Security, and Populations and Migrations.

At regional level, the Regional Directorate of Social Affairs is the representative of the national ministry. The Regional Directorate has only planning and monitoring roles since decentralization, and comes under the Prefect of the Region.

Health and social services are administered at departmental level. Decision-making and control have been devolved to the 96 *départements*. Here, the Commissioner of the Republic, assisted by the Departmental Director of Health and Social Affairs, has authority over the health institutions. The President of the elected General Council of the *département* has executive authority, holding responsibility regarding all welfare matters affecting older people. The executive determines the social service fees, and the rents in both housing and public institutions. It contracts with the voluntary associations with which residential costs are shared, pays home help charges and subsidizes the cost of meals for older people in the community.

The *commune* is the basic unit of government. In each *commune* the mayor has executive authority in certain affairs, including the domain of social care. Of significance in terms of the care of older people is the Centre Communal d'Action Sociale; this provides social assistance in kind or in cash. It manages services for older people, particularly old people's homes, hostels and home helps. The mayor's authority does not stop with social care, but extends into a variety of health-related services, such as health centres and health promotion programmes. Funds for these health-related activities are provided by National Health Insurance, or from the Commissioner of the Republic at regional level.

Social security: pensions and benefits

As stated previously, the level of income for older people is critical if they are to cope with the demands of community living and conserve their dignity and independence.

The French social security system is different to any other in Western Europe (see Segalman, 1986, p.30). Under the Directorate of Social Security, three great national insurance funds (*caisses*) are organized. These provide the following coverages:

1   old age and survivors' insurance (Caisse National d'Assurance Vieillesse des Travailleurs Salaries);
2   illness, invalidity, disability, accident and health insurance (Caisse National d'Assurance Maladie);
3   family protection (Caisse National d'Assurance Famille).

The first provides pensions to families, even when the parents have never been employed. Supervising agencies check this threefold complex system for maximum and minimum payments, which even the most experienced often find confusing.

Henrard and Brocas (1990, p.123) describe the cash benefits for older people in more detail. Firstly, through the National Old Age Insurance Pensions, older people can receive Social Insurance benefits in cash or in kind. These typically consist of half the cost of home help, and a small cash subsidy for home renovation. Secondly, through National Family Insurance, the main housing allowance is secured. Thirdly, through National Health Insurance, the following are covered: the major part of hospitalization costs and ambulatory care, and prescription costs by means of reimbursement. The level of social security is determined by the claimant's occupation, and the particular regime handling the older person's income and benefits.

Rollet (1991, p.193) describes the regimes which govern pensions and benefits by explaining what these are and drawing attention to the interrelationship within the French system of the 'regime' and the 'branch'. The regime denotes the organization, which in this case is an occupational group which acts to secure social security for its members, active or retired, and their families. The branch denotes the particular arrangements within the regime which, amongst other benefits, provide cover for risks such as sickness and old age. There are 150 regimes which deal specifically with particular occupations, such as farmers, railway workers, clerks, and so on.

It is clear from research in other countries that the more complex the social security system, the less understood it is, and the less the claims and uptake. The system is designed to fit into the complicated French superstructure, but does not facilitate the workings of the large French infrastructure of care. Somewhere in the middle, officers may be confused, and somewhere at the bottom, the pensioners may be disadvantaged.

When the income from insurance-based pensions or other sources does not reach the stipulated level, older people are entitled to a supplement to bring it up to that level. This is known as the *minimum vieillesse* ('old age minimum').

In France, three principles have dominated the evolution of the pension scheme (Pitaud et al., 1991, pp.31–3). These are: the principle of 'capitalization'; the principle of 'mutualization', and the principle of 'sharing'.

Before 1910 the principle of 'mutualization' was invoked. The retirement income was managed by the mutual benefit societies. In 1905 the provision of benefits for the old, disabled and sick who could not provide for themselves was made compulsory. After 1910 the state took over by laying down compulsory contributions, bringing in the notion of maximum income, by which the future income in retirement was paid for during people's working life. Implicit within this system is the notion of providence. Contributory old age pensions and the provision of supplementary benefits were put in place. The contributory pension scheme was extended in 1930 to employees in industry and commerce, by which time the capitalization system had been fully applied.

In 1935 this capitalization process was to be combined with the notion of sharing people's contributions to lighten the burden of providing an adequate income. This mixed system prepared the ground for the creation in 1945 of 'social security', which was similar to the notion of 'sharing' in terms of Beveridge's social welfare notions of universality, unity and uniformity (see page 129), but strongly influenced by the French traditions of social security prior to 1939.

'Sharing' moved from providing necessities within a survival model to that of releasing people from the need to work to the need for self-fulfilment in the second half of life. The Laroque Report (1962), referred to as *Policy for the Elderly*, advocated the merits of early retirement and opened the door to the positive and potentially creative aspects of retirement. Already, in the 1950s, old age had become the 'Third Age'. Pensions were not simply designed to cover the essential needs of food and shelter. A decrease in the retirement age and an increase in early retirement was now an increasing social phenomenon. There was a cost to this process: earlier retirement carried with it a decrease in contributions and an increase in the benefit that accompanied early retirement. Pitaud et al. (1991, p.35), along with others, see the strong possibility of antagonism between the young unemployed, who receive few benefits, and the 'young old', who are out of work but receive the benefit of paid free time, which some might describe as 'stolen rest'.

In spite of the new-style emphasis on providing people with the means of a creative retirement, there are those older people who have not made contributions, or whose pension is too low. They do not receive a national minimum, therefore the government's Fonds Nationale de Solidarité partially supports these people, along with contributions from the old age pension scheme, to make up their income to the national minimum level (see Collot et al., 1986, p.137ff.; Henrard and Brocas, 1990, pp.123–5). This government 'solidarity' fund provides for their basic needs (Leaper, 1990). In addition, they receive housing allowances to cover rent costs, and, if suffering from severe disability, a 'third-person allowance' is also provided. The real value of the pensions has fallen during the late 1980s and early 1990s. Although the 9.5% incidence of poverty in France is described by Dooghe (1992, p.160) as middle-range, the older French pensioners have slipped from the upper-range and appear still to be falling.

Housing

Turning from the income of older people to their housing, the European tendency for a significant proportion of the population to live in older houses is borne out in France. Dooghe (1992, p.173) refers to surveys which indicate that 22% of the houses occupied by older people were built before 1871; 53% were built before 1962, and 25% afterwards. As in most Western European countries, a significant number of houses occupied by older people are under-occupied. On the positive side, Delbes and Gaymu (1990, p.6) state that there has been a 53% increase in the proportion of older French people with running water, bathing facilities and toilets within their houses/apartments; none the less, one out of every four older persons in France does not have an indoor toilet. There was also a 16% increase of the proportion of housing units for older people with central heating in the same period. However, one-third of the older population in France are living in substandard houses, as reported by Dooghe (1992, pp.177–8). Only 46% of the older population have central heating (Delbes and Gaymu, 1990), in a nation where 67.6% of the general population have it (Eurostat, 1991b, p.121). Amongst those aged 85+, only 38.5% have centrally heated accommodation.

Fogarty (1986, pp.28–9) refers to the French regulation that new large estates of rented houses must reserve 20% of the units for single people, favouring older single persons. The tendency is for the older person to stay where they are, even in the largest of under-occupied houses. In any case, moving house requires income and assets beyond the reach of most older French people. Collot et al. (1986, pp.32–7) point out that older people are not eligible for long-term loans. Also, in those cases where the older person has assets, the capital of parents may be locked in, because of the pressures of the offspring, who have an eye on their inheritance, rather than the immediate welfare of their parents.

Collot et al. (1986, pp.32ff) provide examples of imaginative and success-ful schemes. There are the grouped dwellings with service facilities and supervision, variously provided in different *départements,* known as the Résidences Arcadie; these cater for about 5% of the older population, and are similar to the service dwellings and sheltered dwellings in most Western European countries. There are also the grouped retirement houses (*villages-retraités*) with communal facilities. Next, there are the 'sunshine houses' (*foyers-soleil*), which are situated close to residential homes and share some of the facilities.

The local authorities provide payments towards the costs of accommoda-tion at the bottom end of the housing market for persons with incomes below a certain level. In addition the state, by means of the Ministry of Social Affairs, provides local subsidies, which pay for the larger part of home reno-vation costs (see Henrard and Brocas, 1990, p.124). Premiums or subsidies are also available for emergency repairs and living improvements, which the same ministry may provide, or housing management associations, grouped under the umbrella organization the National Federation for Improvement, Preservation and Transformation of the Home (Pitaud et al., 1991, p.38; Henrard et al., 1991, pp.111–12), which assists about 45,000 householders annually.

Health care

The Ministry of Social Affairs is responsible for the delivery of hospital and social services and for the supervision of social security. There is a Secretary of State for Elderly People, in addition to a Secretary of State for Health. The health services are resourced by the social security system (or *caisses*) in France, and are funded by both employers and employees. They cater for 99% of the French population.

The French health and social welfare system is pluralist – more so than in Belgium. However, there is an uneasy tension between the state's bureau-cratic controls and the medical profession's commitment to clinical freedom. About 260,000 doctors (half of them are GPs) have won for themselves considerable professional autonomy. Central to the bureaucratic and professional conflict are the levels of fees and the arrangements for their payment. The needs of older people have little relevance within the bureaucratic and professional tensions. The official collaborative image sets out to project a semblance of solidarity, pluralism and liberal medicine (*la médicine libérale*) between the public and private domains of care, but without much evidence of solidarity. Harmonization depends upon the quality of relationships between officials and doctors.

Hospital care and medical services

Co-ordination and harmonization between the hospitals and extra-mural care have been poor. As in the Republic of Ireland, the reliance in the delivery of formal care for older people has tended to be upon the hospital. It remains to be seen whether the intention to extend the health care of older people beyond the hospital and to strengthen the social care programmes will be successful, because of the half-hearted implementation of the Social Development Plans. This is not to deny that there have been developments, but they are patchy because of the persistent tension between the more centralized hospital administration and the decentralized extra-mural health and social care system. A description of the hospital system and of the government system at regional, departmental and commune levels will help towards elucidating the two-way pull to and from the centre. Older people in France and their formal carers can be caught in the middle of what must be the most complex system of administering health and social care in Europe.

The Hospital Law 1970 established a 'health map', into which the central authorities have placed the public and private hospitals. The 22 administrative regions are divided into 284 health sectors. Two-thirds of all the hospital beds are provided by the public health sector in 1,059 hospitals. About 60% of all hospital admissions are in the public sector. This legislation enables the regional health commissions to control the expansion of the proprietary hospitals in order to prevent expensive duplication. However, this has proceeded slowly.

Following upon the Braun Report (Braun, 1988), the post of Secretary of State for Elderly People was created within the Directorate of Social Services, and Theo Braun became its first holder. His report had advocated individualizing care and avoiding categorization. Today health and social care come within the jurisdiction of the one department, the Ministry of Social Affairs. Devolution has been taking place in what was once one of Europe's most centralized systems: various central functions have been devolved to the regions and the 96 territorial *départements*.

Since the Acts of 1983 an elected general council is responsible for the provision of health and social services at *département* level and the state ministry continues its role of inspection and subvention. The day-to-day running of the hospitals is carried out by administrative councils. Inspection and capital investment are left to the Commissioner of the Republic (the original *Préfet*). The Commissioner liaises and co-operates with the elected council and its president (see Leaper, 1991, p.181).

On the positive side, Rollet (1991, pp.193–4) describes the freedom of management enjoyed by the hospitals. Their management committee is chaired by the city mayor, and the state has only supervisory power (a *tutelle*) over the hospital. The state directorate continues to be responsible in each department for inspection, particularly of the public hospitals, which are required to provide a range of basic services. The control of beds is determined by indices of need dictated by the regional commissions, but increasingly by the Ministry of Finance. It is here that tensions arise.

The picture cannot be complete without placing these matters within the threefold government levels of authority. It is the workings of these and their interrelationship which will ultimately determine the quality of care provided for older people in France.

As Spinnewyn and Jani-Le Bris (1991, p.185) explain, there are no short-stay geriatric wards in France, only long-stay or medium-stay. The use of the hospital bed is paid for by the user, who is reimbursed by the social security *caisses*. For the use of the bed and consultancy, the users have to pay 20% of the bills, unless exempted by reason of low income. The chronically sick and those who are in receipt of social assistance are not charged, their costs being met from the *aide sociale*. However, many older persons marginally beyond the determined threshold of exemption are made to pay.

The remaining hospital beds are in the 1,921 private sector *cliniques*. These consist of proprietary hospitals and non-profit hospitals (see Hunter, 1986, pp.24–5). There are twice as many proprietary hospitals as non-profit hospitals; the latter are large, the former, on average, have about 38 beds. Whereas the practice is to move patients out of hospitals and to have the briefest period of care, in contrast, the proprietary hospitals prolong the treatment period. Obviously, a two-tier system of care emerges and doctors tend to spend more time where there are more emoluments. Misallocation of older people to beds in inappropriate institutions has been a big problem in France, running to 28% of older people's bed allocations (Spinnewyn and Jani-Le Bris, 1991, p.186).

When older people go for consultation, like any other patient, they pay the doctors at the surgery. As in most of Europe, the doctors are *in* the extra-mural system, but not *of* the system: they are contracted, not employed. There are 130,000 GPs, 90% of whom are contracted to the National Health Insurance scheme, and others are private; the former charge standard fees, whilst the private GPs fix their own charges. Patients pay and are then reimbursed for some of the charges. The proportion that is not reimbursed (which is in effect the real payment at access) is the *ticket modérateur*, which is the part paid by the patient/user. There is also the *tiers payant*, which exempts from paying in advance, when the doctor or hospital is directly paid by the fund to which the patient/user subscribes. Currently, the *ticket modérateur* amounts to a 25% payment for the consultation and 40% for the medication, varying according to patient need or costs of medicines.

Recently the amounts of reimbursements to patients have been reduced. Hospital day charges have gone up in price. It is becoming more and more costly to be sick in France, especially if you are old.

Nursing

The home medical services consist of nurses, auxiliary nurses, chiropodists and physiotherapists. They act upon doctors' prescriptions or referral by social workers, whenever older people are ill.

Hospitalization at home (*hospitalisation à domicile*) serves about 19,136 older patients, but is at present confined largely to Paris. Although promoted by the government, about half of the services are provided by the private and about half by the public sector (see Spinnewyn and Jani-Le Bris, 1991, p.190).

Nursing services may be established and run by several centres or agencies: the social service centres of the municipal authority; health centres or municipal nursing care centres; private or public residential homes, and by home help associations (Henrard et al., 1991, p.108).

Domiciliary nursing (*service de soins à domicile*) is referred to by Ely and Saunders (1992, p.16). They point out that most domiciliary nursing is provided by self-employed nurses (*infirmières libérales*) on a fee-paying scheme. Sickness insurance covers the costs entailed within a fixed ceiling within a 12-hour day. In practice, as in Italy, many of these nurses have not been trained specifically to carry out this care. The ratio is 8 places per 1,000 people aged 75+ (Henrard et al., 1991, pp.109–10). There are about 780 services, at least 1,400 nurses and at least 3,500 care assistants. Henrard's (1987) research indicates that the average age of the users is 81. Most receive help with getting up, washing, being dressed, and eating. About 40% suffer from psychiatric conditions such as dementia and states of disorientation; about 43% suffer from incontinence. However, 'real nursing' is judged only to be necessary for one person out of six.

Integrated services

The report of the General Planning Commissariat (1982), *Vieillir Demain* ('Ageing Tomorrow'), complained that the policy of maintaining people at home had not been working. By the time Braun reiterated the policy of *'soutien à domicile'* in his report of 1988, the community care plans continued to work slowly and sometimes badly. The Braun Report recommended that various fiscal measures be implemented to facilitate the care of older people at home. Co-ordinated nursing, adult foster care of older people and domiciliary care were urged once again, and financial help was argued for strongly. Clearly, in the eyes of the Ministry, the local need for these community facilities validates cutting back beds in institutions, which, as shall be seen shortly, are the remit of the local authorities. More facilities for one means less facilities for the other. Getting the balance right may be the axiom, but other competitive political and administrative interests may foil the attempt to accomplish this.

Pitaud et al. (1991, pp.36–9) identify and discuss the nature of the alternative home care services, most of which are public or private provisions. The principal 12 services are as follows:

1   home medical care services (*services de soins à domicile*);.
2   home helps (*aides ménagères*) for people aged 65+ and for disabled people aged 60+;
3   meals-on-wheels provided by catering services;
4   hospitalization at home, public or private;
5   day centres run from non-profit or public hospital units;
6   urgency help systems such as *télé alarme* and *télé assistance*;
7   live-in carer services for those aged 70+;
8   cleaning and repair work at home;
9   laundry;
10   chiropody;
11   care within a family for those aged 65+ with low incomes;
12   consultations regarding allowances and health insurance.

Many of these services are carried out by the staff attached to the Centre Communal d'Action Sociale (the CCAS), or private association (see Pitaud et al., 1991, p.36), which in many ways resembles the OCMW and CPAS in Belgium (see page 181). The CCAS serves the neighbourhood or locality within the *commune* on a 'price per day' basis (Pitaud et al., 1991, p.36). Leaper (1990) describes the CCASs as local social care centres, as do most commentators, but the centres include certain services which would be regarded in the UK as health care. The CCASs are responsible, either by delegation or directly to independent bodies, mainly for residential care, sheltered housing, home care assistance, home nursing assistance, meals-on-wheels and post-operative home care.

The policy at the level of the *communes* of maintaining older people at home (*maintien à domicile*) has been proposed and discussed widely by French politicians, civil servants and experts for over thirty years. As in Germany and Austria, the family is responsible for the maintenance of their older relatives (*l'obligation alimentaire*). The natural tendency, therefore, is to lean heavily upon the family, where it exists. The introduction of extra-mural services has been a slow process.

It is clear that some of the above services are strictly speaking neither medical nor nursing; however, they are part of an integrated holistic approach, hence their inclusion here. The home help service will be dealt with shortly under 'Personal social services'.

Mental health care

Community psychiatric care made early advances in terms of community care. France has the lowest proportion of psychiatric hospital beds in Europe, even lower than in Italy (see Eurostat, 1991b, p.88). This is of interest because France was the first European country to introduce the practice of 'mental medicine', in 1838 (see Mangen, 1985a, p.114). 'Extra-hospital services' for the mentally ill have been in place within France, in a 'revolving door' system of care, since 1945.

Since 1960 there has been a policy of psychiatric sectorization, which encouraged the re-orientation of services from the hospital to the community. Multidisciplinary teams care for the mentally ill within 750 geographical sectors, and establish locally-based in-patient units. How the care of depressed older French people is being conducted has not been researched sufficiently, but there is some cause for concern when considering the number of suicides among them in France. According to Pritchard's (1992, p.129) findings, France has the highest number of known suicides per million inhabitants among persons aged 75+ of any country.

Institutional care

Dooghe (1992, p.106) states that about 5% of older people in France reside in old people's homes. However, the percentage rises to 8.4% if long-stay wards or psychiatric hospitals are included. Apart from the hospitals, the major institutions are the retirement homes and the older *invalide* almshouses.

The Ministry of Social Affairs acknowledges several types of homes, which are funded by the National Health Insurance institutions, National Family Insurance or by local authorities. These are described by Pitaud et al. (1991, pp.40–1). Firstly, there are the homes for able-bodied older people. These homes may be public or private. Secondly, there are old people's residences, which are often flats using communal services such as a common restaurant, care room and activities centre. Thirdly, there are the old people's homes with health treatment services. An example of this is the CANTOU, which usually accommodates 12 people who have (non-psychiatric) problems. These are highly integrated units involving families and neighbours in their activities and recreational pursuits. Fourthly, there are the medical treatment residential homes, known as MAPA (40–80 places), usually urban, and the MARPA (7–20 places), usually rural. Spinnewyn and Jani-Le Bris (1991, p.183) indicate that there are about 2,041 hospices and old people's homes; 2,001 institutions for sheltered housing (*logement-foyer*), and 518 long-stay hospitals.

The residents of sheltered accommodation pay rent. Board and lodging in the medico-social institutions is paid for by the older person; the medical treatment is covered by health insurance. If the older people cannot pay the medico-social costs, the relatives to the first and second degree of consanguinity are charged. Failing this, the welfare system (*l'aide sociale*) covers the cost.

Private institutions have recently created a market in residential care; about eighty have been created recently. Family *pensions* and hotels are being refurbished to accommodate the more mobile older French population.

Personal social services

The importance of the personal social services has been increased by the recent policy which encourages social care alternatives to institutionalization. Cutting across the central tendency to control facilities and the local tendency to resist it is the increased importance given to extra-mural care for older people by creating more local day centres and domiciliary care, in accordance with the five-year Economic and Social Development Plans: in particular that of the Seventh Economic and Development Plan (1975–80) and the ninth Plan (1983–8).

Social workers

The social workers attached to the *départements* are responsible to the *Direction Départementale des Affaires Sanitaires et Sociales* (DDASS) (Departmental Directorate of Health and Social Affairs), as described by Louatron (1986). They are also employed in a variety of agencies responsible for social insurance, family allowances, industrial welfare and pension funds, in private agencies and in the CCASs (the Communal Centres for Social Action). There are probably about 34,000 social workers in France, judging from recent statistics (see Leaper, 1991, p.181). These social workers often work closely with health visitors, playing their role in extending and increasing the domiciliary services within decentralized teams. The social workers play a critical role in identifying social need and determining social care for older people in the public, semi-public and private sectors, and in diverse associations (see Brauns and Kramer, 1986, p.147).

Day care

The CCASs are also responsible for day care, which, according to Pitaud et al. (1991, p.37), has been a failure in France. There are six in France, serving less than a thousand older people (see Spinnewyn and Jani-Le Bris, 1991, p.190).

Home care/help

The French home help (*aide ménagère*) system deserves special comment. This service was first established 35 years ago (see Henrard et al., 1991, p.104). There are about 4,000 home help service facilities in 90% of French districts, provided by the municipalities, consisting of about 70,000 home helps (Pitaud et al., 1991, pp.36–7). There appears, however, to be some considerable discrepancy regarding these statistics, because Henrard et al. (1991, p.105) put the figure at 100,000 home helps. The service benefits about 500,000 older people, according to the calculations of Pitaud et al. (1991, p.36) and Spinnewyn and Jani-Le Bris (1991, p.187).

The service is limited to a maximum of 30 hours per month by a doctor's prescription or by a local social worker. Most of the users live alone, as is the case in most countries that run the service. Pitaud et al. (1991) and Henrard et al. (1991), as well as several other studies cited by the former, agree that the home help service needs to be overhauled in France. The service takes too long to set up and does not respond to emergencies (Pitaud et al., 1991, p.36). Only 36% of those in need receive the help, and 40% of those who do receive it do not require it (Henrard et al., 1991, p.107). They add that people with severe disabilities rarely benefit from home help.

A recent innovation in many parts of France has been the creation of the *postes de coordonnateurs* (co-ordinators), which operate between residential and home care; 500 now exist (Spinnewyn and Jani-Le Bris, 1991, p.191).

Other services

Ely and Saunders (1992, p.8) describe the first stage of the 'open for all preventive services' which are available to older people. Through the Minitel television text system, subscribers can have access to lists of services for older people. The central points of access are the CCASs, which are financed by the General Council. They provide information, but also co-ordinate social action and deal with claims for financial support. Each CCAS has its own council of administration presided over by the mayor. Its agency workers are employed by the Council of Social Action. They work alongside the nurses and help to co-ordinate care strategies.

Voluntary care agencies and support organizations

There are many voluntary sector groups and co-operatives in France. In just over a decade there has been a 29% increase of social associations, as recorded by Pitaud et al. (1991). They mainly consist of older people working for older people. They are, in general, the humanitarian associations, with an average age of 60–70; political groups, with an average age of 45–65, and consumer associations, with an average age of about 65 (see Pitaud et al., 1991, p.52).

Informal care

There are indications that the familial obligation may be wearing thin. Marin (1992) refers to this when she identifies the drain and strain within families in Alsace, who have to provide for their aged parents from their income.

Great concern is expressed within government departments over the one-third of the older French population who live in rural areas in a country which has one of the lowest population densities in Europe. The rural aspects of care will be dealt with below.

Spinnewyn and Jani-Le Bris (1991, pp.178–9) cite the 30% of French persons aged 65+ who live alone, the 40% living with a partner only, and the 24% living with others. It is the high percentage of older women living alone that is a matter of greatest concern. Fogarty (1986, p.15) refers to the rising proportion of French women living alone, increasing from 30% aged 65–69 to 48% aged 80–84, but falling to 31% after the age of 90 because the greater percentage of the oldest are cared for in institutions, and to a far lesser extent within their offspring's households. Collot et al. (1986, p.11) says that there are 2.7 million women aged 60 and over living alone, almost three times as many as the number of men over 60 living alone. There are also an additional 1.1 million women aged 75 and over, approximately five times as many as there are men of the same age. Spinnewyn and Jani-Le Bris (1991, p.179) do not share the pessimism of Marin (1992). They point out that family bonds are strong in France. They state, on the basis of their findings, that more than half of the older people receive at least one weekly visit from family members.

The French report *Ageing Tomorrow*, cited by Pitaud et al. (1991), states that 'the family is the social element which presents in a concrete and immediate way the contradiction between fundamental social realities and the changing of behaviour'. However, the state's involvement in helping to establish domestic solidarity and familial support systems has been decreasing in France. Both the formal and informal systems of care are deteriorating. Firstly, the state system is weakened due to lack of sufficient funds; and secondly, social relations within kinship infrastructures of care are also less supportive due to the progressive dilution of family life. However, as Henrard et al. (1991, p.113) show, the most recent surveys in France indicate how significant and effective the support of the family continues to be, whatever the sociological familial changes.

There is a continuing belief in the family as the prime 'natural' caring unit in French society. Pitaud et al. (1991, p.47) refer to the moral value of solidarity: 'the family is the first place for solidarity'. They refer to the family as the 'natural support'. Likewise, Dumon (1991, p.124) describes informal care, which is mainly familial, as 'natural care'.

Citing recent surveys, Pitaud et al. (1991) state that family values are the most essential values in life (p.48). Henrard et al. (1991, p.99) refer to the political emphasis upon caring for older people at home for the past thirty years (*maintien à domicile*). Solidarity between the welfare and family systems and 'co-ordination' appear to be the major focuses of these French authors.

Pitaud et al. (1991, p.39) refer to provisions for care within the household for those of low income aged 65+ (Article 157, 'Code of Social Help', Law No. 89.475, 10 July 1989). It is not left to chance. The code deals with the formalities surrounding informal home care. As in Belgium, much of the care is domestic or familial informal nursing; however, it does not always appear to come naturally. Again, there is little research to build upon. Fogarty (1986, p.46), commenting upon the Collot et al. (1986) French report, presents a picture of not infrequent domestic stress, as found in almost all European research, whatever its geography, its political and administrative system or culture of care. Collot et al. (1986) indicate that there are certain features which mar the domestic informal care of housebound or bedridden older persons:

1   The domestic support may be from a spouse who is also old and also in need of care.
2   The carer may be a single woman caring for her mother or father and who is also in employment.
3   There is often a shortfall in support for the carers who are at their wits' end.

Selby and Schechter (1982), over a decade ago, cited the need for support for the carers after reviewing the caring arrangements in a number of countries, including France. They identified the gap then, which others have since picked up. The family in France has been expected to cope because caring is 'natural'. As has been illustrated, formal care is threadbare, and respite care still seems to be regarded as a novel suggestion, even at international conferences organized for experts, where respite care has been on the agenda for well over a decade. The emphasis put forward years ago by Selby and Schechter (1982), and since then by more and more experts, is upon the need for tax relief for families caring for older relatives; time off from work similar to maternity leave; respite programmes; emergency assistance, and holiday relief for the tired and overworked carers, who are mainly women, and many of whom are over 75. Apart from the holiday schemes, the care of the carers as a strategy hardly features within the triangle of care in France, in spite of the activities of their CCASs. A French government official at an international conference in Pisa (1990) summed up the situation, when discussing caring arrangements, in the following terms: 'Respite care has never really been on the social policy agenda. Local governments have had it on their back-burners which they turn on when politically expedient and then off when costs are rising. The recession has now blown it out in most European regions.' Leaper (1989) has pointed out that France, through Pierre Laroque, set the general lines of future policies in 1962, well ahead of most European states. Inter-generational solidarity has been the major emphasis, as has the idea of older people as givers as well as receivers in society. The family features as a major caring entity within the French schema of care. It is treated as a major provider alongside the market and the state. As Leaper (1989) points out: 'Family responsibility is much emphasised both in French law on the obligation to maintain needy relatives, and in current family practice.'

The family is Europe's mainstay, wherever one travels, as stressed earlier. There is no doubt that it is regarded as the so-called 'natural safety net'. There is no doubt that it has been and remains the major caring resource for most of France's older population, as it does in the rest of Europe, but for how long? That is the recurring question throughout this exploration of care in Europe. The expectation at every level is that the family is the back-stop, whilst at the same time European families are in the throes of social change. It is clear from the research that, in France, the care of older people, like child care, is regarded as a prime domestic natural duty. It is also clear that the goodwill of so many women is prostituted by managers and formal carers. As commentators keep repeating, as does this study, care by the family is in effect care by women.

Leisure pursuits and education

The CPA (1989, pp.61–2) refers to the 20,000 clubs which cater for older people's leisure needs. The Universities of the Third Age are a French innovation, now extending throughout Europe. About half of the French Universities of the Third Age adopt the structure of a traditional university. Their educational programmes are usually run on university campuses. They are often subsidized, but depend mainly upon subscriptions (see CPA, 1993, pp.86–7). There is also a wide network of clubs and societies, generally co-ordinated in each *département* by an Offices des Personnes à la Retraite (OPAR).

The holders of the senior rail card (*Carte Vermeil*) are often granted concessionary admission to theatres and cinemas. Disabled people and persons aged 60+ are entitled to half-price admission tickets. In Paris the *Carte Emeraude* entitles persons aged 60+ to free admission to museums and the Louvre. Some insurance schemes via the Caisse Régionale d'Assurance Maladie and Caisse Retraité Complémentaire provide holidays at a discount for older people (see CPA, 1993, p.86).

Rural aspects

Care of older people in rural France requires special comment, because France is one of Europe's largest rural countries. As Clout (1988, p.99) points out, nine-tenths of France is still occupied by farmland and forests, and 93% of its *communes* are still classified as 'rural'. Rokkan and Urwin (1983) refer to *'les deux Frances'* – the second France, which lies in the west and the south-west of France, constitutes an extensive area of peripherality. Collot et al. (1986, p.10) identify eight largely rural regions with more than 22% of persons aged 60 and over, with Limousin's proportion as high as 26%. In contrast, metropolitan France has 18% of its people within the same age band. Physical isolation in rural areas constitutes one of the most expensive factors in delivering care. The additional lack of stimulation is more likely to bring about a deterioration in physical and mental health. With the exodus of younger French people to the urban areas, the older population are rendered more vulnerable within threadbare rural networks. There is a similarity here (though to a far lesser degree) with peripheral areas in Southern and Eastern European countries. Almost half the *communes* have fewer than 300 inhabitants. From the late 1960s, groups of between 15 and 20 adjacent *communes* have been amalgamated administratively under a market town to form a viable service entity. Catering for older people from such poorly-resourced administrative centres is presenting the authorities with many problems. Clout (1988, p.116) observes that a major problem for rural France is the plight of the older population (*la France fragile*) in remoter parts of the countryside, where the services are often almost non-existent. Fortunately, two-thirds of older French people live in the more urbanized areas, but the concern is for the third that remain in these poorly-resourced, peripheral, rural regions.

Conclusion

The monocephalic structures of France have been giving way, since the mid-1980s, to a decentralization process which has brought the services closer to the older population. However, the complexities of the historic centralized French system remain, as does the rural geography, both of which slow down the whole process of establishing polycephalic systems of care (see Table 6). The state is being pulled in two directions.

The triangulation of care is one in which the central state regime has increasingly frustrated the local collectivities (*collectivité*). The plural ends of the triangle of care within the microsystem or infrastructure of care have challenged the major public services, the private agencies and the social associations. French logic has established a mix of welfare and health services on paper to meet the exigencies of theoretical models, but in practice the social and health needs of the older population are not being met effectively and efficiently by the extra-mural services. The complexity puzzles the users and often bewilders the providers of care.

The solidarity of interdependent parts is made more difficult because, unlike the UK, France lacks a rich heritage of volunteering. Its social associations are relative latecomers. Harmonization is also thwarted by the clash of interests and the unchanged attitude of the doctors, who remain entrenched, or rather bogged down, within the *ancien régime* of their dominant profession.

One facet of services for older people in France, which has had little if any commentary in the literature of social gerontology, has to do with the needs of the older ethnic minorities. A problem for France, as for Germany and the UK, will be to take into account the diverse health and social needs of a growing number of older black Africans and various white ethnic minorities. Eurostat statistics (1991a, pp.18–19) indicate that France has the second-largest proportion (3.8%) of extra-EU immigrants after Germany (5.2%). According to Ely and Saunders (1992, p.29), amongst others, the major ethnic groups consist of Algerians (15%), Moroccans (15%) and Turkish (4%). Many return to their country of origin, but more and more have settled down. The government has not really taken the growing number of these older immigrants and their special needs into account; neither have the major texts on older people in Europe commented upon the ethnic dimension: for them Europe is 'white'. The older black Europeans are not given a mention; even the excellent texts published by the experts fail to comment, such as Dooghe (1992), Jamieson (1991a; 1991b), Jamieson and Illsley (1990) and Evers and Svetlik (1991). The recent book, *The Coming of Age in Europe* (Davies, 1992), which is confined more or less to the EU countries, provides one page on pre-retirement courses for black and white minority migrant workers. The book's demographic survey and its 'rich map of change' fails to acknowledge the cosmopolitan mix in European countries and the emergence of black Europeans. In the well-presented glossy Eurostat (1991b) publication, *A Social Portrait of Europe*, there is not a single black face on any of the many coloured photographs, whether young or old. Hugman's (1994) study stands out as an exception, identifying the relative isolation of older migrant people in France and the myth of extensive family care which exists concerning their family support systems.

11 Luxemburg

Demography

According to the statistics presented in Table 1, 13.4% of the population in Luxemburg are over 65. The present proportion of older people is amongst the top 12 in Europe; by the year 2025, Luxemburg's proportion will probably rank fifth in the whole of Europe, after Switzerland, Sweden, Denmark and the Netherlands. The Grand Duchy's very low birth rate accounts for the disproportionate number of older people and the high rate of immigrant retired people. For example, between 1970 and 1986 the proportion of outsiders rose from 18.4% to 26.2%, many of whom were aged 55+.

The country's priority is coping with the significantly high numbers of lone older people. Over 50% of citizens living alone are aged 60 years and over, most of whom are women (CPA, 1989, p.98; Bemelmans, 1986, p.5). The proportion of women aged 80+ is more than double that of their male counterparts (CPA, 1993, p.159). The life expectancy of Luxemburg women at 65 is 17.2 years, which ranks sixteenth in Europe; that of men at 65 is 13.1 years, which ranks eighteenth in Europe (Eurostat, 1991a; UN, 1991). Given the high standard of living, one would have thought that life expectancy at 65 years would have been higher. Pollution may help to explain the discrepancy, as will be discussed under 'Health care'.

Socio-political and administrative background

The Grand Duchy of Luxemburg, which celebrated its 150th anniversary in 1989, is most probably the most prosperous European haven for older Europeans. This sovereign state about the size of a middle-sized European city has hung onto its own distinctiveness, as well as its dialect (Letzeburgisch).

Luxemburg is a constitutional monarchy. Sovereign power is invested in its people; executive power lies with the Grand Duke and Cabinet (Ministerial Council). It is responsible to the 56 members of the Chamber of Deputies. A second legislative chamber consisting of 21 members is consulted on all draft legislation. Health is one of the responsibilities of the 118 *communes*, which are governed by elected councils. The mayor, alderman and council are the local agents of the central government. There is a strong political will and a well-established consensus to create a co-ordinated and integrated service for older people.

The Duchy, occupying only 999 square miles, has a remarkably high standard of living, as can be seen by the following 11 EU 'firsts' (Eurostat, 1991b, pp.67–80):

1   the highest national income per capita;
2   the highest disposable national income per capita;
3   the highest GDP per capita;
4   the highest gross monthly employment earnings per capita in Purchasing Powers Standards (PPSs);
5   the highest gross and net earnings per capita;
6   the highest use of net national income per capita;
7   the highest level of saving and consumption as a proportion of net national income;
8   the highest consumption of fuel and power per capita in PPSs;
9   the highest consumption of food and beverages per capita;
10   the highest consumption of household equipment and furnishings per capita;
11   the highest consumption of transport and communications per capita.

The development of socio-medical care in the Duchy goes back to the care provided by the religious bodies of the seventh century and the later contribution of the Catholic organizations. Later, at the beginning of the twentieth century, at a time described as 'the period of social foresight' (Hartmann-Hirsch et al., 1992, p.2), the need of protection was duly incorporated into the notion of social concern but at a non-state voluntary care level, so the voluntary contribution was added to that of the vocational contribution of the Church. The voluntary arm of care has since been a source of strength within the Duchy's system. It fashioned the two key associations: the Luxemburg League of Socio-Medical Action and Prevention (which can be traced back to 1908) and the Luxemburg Red Cross.

So 'vocationalism' and 'voluntarism' have been a salient feature within the genesis of welfare and medical care in the Duchy. To this has been added the 'professionalism' of the various statutory and professional bodies that emerged within the twentieth century. The mix of 'vocationalism', 'voluntarism' and 'professionalism' has been and continues to be a feature of social and medical care in Luxemburg, which is evident in the Duchy's provision of care for older people.

The foundation of the 'social state' really took place after World War II, when ministries were set up to complement the associations. This was inspired by the UK Beveridge welfare scheme (see page 129). The Ministry of Social Assistance and Public Health was established first. Next, the Ministry of Family Affairs was created. The associations referred to above were then regrouped into the Caritas Federation and organized into the Social Family Services. A strong family value system clearly dominated the sphere of care and social concern. The Ministry of Family Affairs set up the *services des personnes agées* in 1985, backed by the diverse parties. All political parties in Luxemburg are agreed about the priority which ought to be given to care of the older people in the Duchy. On 23 July 1984 the government declared its intention to maintain older people in their own homes and localities for as long as possible, which set the stage for the establishment of intermediate community services to attain this objective. The policy was formulated about nine years before the UK launched its very similar strategy in 1993.

Unlike the UK strategy, the residential home is at the centre of the Luxemburg scheme, and acts as a locality centre with open care facilities, respite care and a day centre. There was to be a regional centre (the CERPA, see page 219). This co-ordinates residential and community services as well as volunteer care for older people. The centre comes under the Entente which is an overall co-ordinating body. The idea is to integrate the various local efforts and largely voluntary groups and agencies working for older people into a more effective scheme.

Social security: pensions and benefits

The CPA (1989, p.98) says that the Duchy has one of the most generous pensions and social insurance schemes in the world. Retirement does not bring with it such a drop in income as in the UK, because the pension is almost 85% of the pensioner's final salary/wages (see CPA, 1989; 1993; Dickson, 1989, p.i). Since 1986 the Ministry of Social Security has established the right to a guaranteed minimum income which secures a decent pension.

There are two old age pension schemes: contributory and non-contributory; the latter, which is index-linked, caters for the public servants. Eligibility begins at 65. The government pays the entire contribution in accordance with the number of years of service and level of the employee's last salary. Retirement is not mandatory for these employees. Regarding the contributory scheme, both the employer and employee make contributions, in addition to government funding; it is index-linked to a combination of earnings and prices (Walker, 1992a, p.168). In contrast with the non-contributory pension scheme, retirement is mandatory, and can be taken at 60 for wage-earners (both men and women) with at least 10,800 days of contributions. Salaried male employees may retire on pension at 60, and women at 55, provided they have had at least 15 years of paid-up insurance. The full pension requires at least 15 years' residence in Luxemburg.

There are four contributory pensions: two pension schemes exist for waged or salaried employees, and another two exist for self-employed persons, such as for business people and farmers. The bottom of the pension scale is equal to the minimum social wage; the top of the scale is equivalent to four times the minimum social wage (Bemelmans, 1986, p.15). Because unemployment benefits decrease progressively over time, many older workers in heavy industry retire early.

The Ministry of Family Affairs provides grants for the economically disadvantaged. A means-tested low-income allowance provides for residents of at least 15 years, which is administered by the National Solidarity Fund. Those who are aged 65+ and in receipt of assistance from the fund are exempt from paying fares on public transport. The fund also pays additional allowances to certain groups of retired people and pensioners (see Bemelmans, 1986; CPA, 1989). The older population are expected to contribute towards almost all services in Luxemburg, but their contribution is related to their ability to pay.

Since July 1986 the Ministry of Social Security can top up a pension where the total income is less than the fixed, guaranteed minimum wage (called the RMG), and since May 1989 it can also allocate a care grant when a person in urgent need of care can no longer be admitted into a nursing home; the resident in the Duchy must be at least 65. The grant is conditional: their physical or mental condition ought to require constant care, and their income singly or together with that of a partner ought to add up to less than 2.5 times the minimum wage (see Hartmann-Hirsch et al., 1992, p.20).

Housing

With regard to accommodation, Bemelmans (1986, p.9) points out that 95.3% of the older population live outside institutions; about 67% are home-owners, and about 38% live in rented accommodation; three-quarters live in family households. The Duchy has the highest proportion of houses with central heating in all of Europe (see Eurostat, 1991b, p.121). About 90% of the older population have a telephone (94.9% of all households have a telephone). Costs of connections, rental and even calls may be covered by the local authorities in certain circumstances.

Government grants are available to enable older people to improve their properties; like other countries, the government subsidizes the adaptation of houses. Under what is known as 'the G-D Regulation' of 25 February 1979, premiums and interest repayments may be claimed when making such adaptations (Bemelmans, 1986, p.9).

Special accommodation for the older population is minimal. The government only provides 0.9% of serviced flats within the housing sector. However, the quality of the housing is generally excellent, with 97% having access to an indoor lavatory and 83% equipped with a bath or shower. The concern is about the less well-furbished older houses, where, as in all major European cities, the oldest people reside; some of these are amongst the 26.6% who live alone (see CPA, 1993, p.164). Research has not identified their number nor their household conditions.

Health care

Roulleaux (1986, p.402) refers to the socio-medical centres in 114 out of 118 *communes*. These have been in existence, in a slightly modified form, since 1920. They serve a clearly defined geographic area, addressing both medical and social aspects of care.

In spite of the high rates of consumption and excellent standard of living, the health profile of Luxemburg's older people lags behind most of the European countries. As already stated, the life expectancy of persons aged 65+ is not impressive. How can this be explained? As Bemelmans (1986, p.1) and Waterplas (1991, p.265) point out, there is little detailed information about the care of the older population in Luxemburg, because of the lack of research in this sphere, which is surprising given that Luxemburg is so visible and centre-stage in the EU, and given that it is a small nation. One possible reason for the lower life expectancy might be the fact that many of the retired in the Duchy are recent immigrants who bring their bad health with them. The iron ore industry has also been a major pollutant (although it produces 26% of GDP). A cleaner environment exists today, but this was not so in the earlier lives of many of the older people.

With regard to health services, the older population have access to virtually free medical and paramedical care within the social security system. Waterplas (1991, p.266) cites a recent survey indicating that the average outlay per capita on health care among older people in Luxemburg is almost three times that of the population in paid employment.

Hospital care and medical services

With regard to the infrastructure of health care available for older people, there are 1.8 doctors per 1,000 inhabitants (see Eurostat, 1991b, p.88). There are fewer doctors within the hospital services, and more in primary care. Almost all the doctors are in private practice. On average, there is 1 family doctor to serve every 705 patients, one of the lowest patient loadings in Europe. The heavy loading of doctors in hospitals which exists in other European countries is not replicated here. In such a small country it is also cost-effective for the family doctors to practise both outside and inside the hospitals.

The proportion of pharmacists is higher, standing fourth in rank order within the EU at 0.8 per 1,000 inhabitants. However, the dentists' ratio is 0.5 per 1,000 people: seventh out of the EU countries.

Nursing

There is free choice of nursing services. Approximately twelve nuns run home nursing services in their small neighbourhood practices. Waterplas (1991, p.272) states that home nursing has been provided locally for over a hundred years. Today, a non-profit organization known as Hellef Doheem employs 16 home nurses. In addition, there is the Luxemburg Red Cross, which employs 11 nurses and one aide. Any registered nurse may apply to the Ministry of Health to act as a home nurse (*soins à domicile*).

Domiciliary care is offered by six associations under the Ministry of Health for those who have paid into the Sickness Savings Fund. The Red Cross and five other agencies serve the scheme (Hartmann-Hirsch et al., 1992, pp. 19–20).

Mental health care

Outreach services under the aegis of the Ministry of Health are available for mental health intervention/care, as indicated by Hartmann-Hirsch et al. (1992, p.19), but there is no information regarding their scope. There is a day centre for patients with Alzheimer's Disease, but here again no details are provided by either Waterplas, Bemelmans or Hartmann-Hirsch et al.

Institutional care

The Ministry of Family Affairs deals with reception into residential care and the provision of institutional care. Waterplas (1991, p.264) states that 7.9% of the older population aged 65+ live in institutions, as does the CPA (1993, p.164). However, Hartmann-Hirsch et al. (1992, p.18), on the basis of information provided by the Ministry of the Family, state that only 4–6% are institutionalized. None the less, there are 33 homes, 10 of which are provided by the Department of the Family; 7 by the municipalities, and 16 by private organizations, mostly run by nuns. More than half of the residents occupy private beds, which have been increasing rapidly, whereas those who occupy public beds in the public sector residential and nursing homes are decreasing proportionately: in residential homes by 3%; in nursing homes by 0.8%.

Waterplas (1991, p.268) states that there are 2,353 beds in residential homes, of which 68% are private. All applications for public beds go through the Ministry of Health. The Duchy has only nine nursing homes, which provide 713 beds for older people. These vary in size, providing between 137 and 410 beds. In addition to the beds in the residential and nursing homes, there are 636 beds in the Centres de Logement et d'Accueil (Board and Lodging Welcome Centres) which provide social housing to older people. These institutions are opening their doors to the local communities. For example, some residential homes provide an *amicale* – a network of people supporting home carers (Waterplas, 1991, p.265).

Personal social services

The country is divided into five areas, each with a Centre Régional pour Personnes Agées (CERPA), as described by Hartmann-Hirsch et al. (1992, p.18). The Ministry of Health and the Ministry of Family Affairs are both involved in supervising these and their co-ordination. These centres provide for the 'third and fourth age'. The Service des Personnes Agées (SPA), accountable to the Ministry of Family Affairs, deals with the problems presented by older people.

The government is committed to the principle of subsidiarity, which it interprets as leaving the intervention to the various utilities, associations and other private agencies within the *communes*. If it cannot be managed at these levels, only then will the social workers take up the case. A great deal is left to discretion and to circumstances. Hartmann-Hirsch et al. (1992, p.6) state: 'To our knowledge, there are very few legislative texts which refer explicitly to social services.' The SPA is responsible to the Department of the Family for the implementation of care of older people (see Hartmann-Hirsch et al., 1992, p.18).

Since 1843, welfare bureaux have been set up to deal with social care and provide information in the *communes*, under the authority of the Ministry of the Interior. In 1986 these bureaux were renamed 'Communal Social Offices'. However, they only exist in four of the 118 *communes* (Hartmann-Hirsch et al., 1992, p.9).

Social workers

Roulleaux (1986) and Hartmann-Hirsch et al. (1992) comment upon the public sector social workers. Social workers have cared for older people since 1935. A major organizational problem over the years has been the lack of professional cohesiveness – social workers have their own divisions within several ministries: that of the Family, Labour, Social Security, Justice, and Health (see Roulleaux, 1986, p.394). Some have the status of civil servants; others are local authority employees; others are religious; others are employed by non-profit organizations. It is difficult for older people to know their way through the diverse systems. About 55.5% of the social service workers are engaged in generic services, and about 4.4% in work associated with older people's needs, usually in institutions (see Roulleaux, 1986, p.396).

Meals services

Meals-on-wheels are delivered to the housebound or bedridden on a daily basis; this service is organized by the local authority. The Red Cross or AMIPERAS (Amicale des Personnes Retraitées Agées ou Solitaires, mostly made up of older volunteers) may also be deputed by the local authority to provide the meals. Hartmann-Hirsch et al., (1992, p.20) state that meals-on-wheels operate in the 118 *communes*. These provide 1,500–1,600 meals a day. Meals-on-wheels are also provided by public utility organizations, private catering firms, residential institutions, restaurants and hospitals in 91 localities (Waterplas, 1991, p.274). Half of the recipients are living alone, and their average age is 78 years. The social worker assesses how much the user is able to pay in accordance with the level of their income; the balance is met by the local authority, which can recoup most of the subsidy from central government (Bemelmans, 1986, p.11).

Day care services

The Ministry of Family Affairs deals with day care services and night shelters for older people (Hartmann-Hirsch et al., 1992, p.6). The first day centre was opened in 1986. By 1991 there were 17 day centres catering for about 300 older people; 13 of these are state-run centres (Hartmann-Hirsch et al., 1992, p.18).

Home care/help

The Ministry of Family Affairs is responsible for the provision of home help (Hartmann-Hirsch et al., 1992, p.6). Home help is mainly run by the voluntary sector, which will be discussed under 'Voluntary care agencies and support organizations'. In 1989, as cited by CPA (1993, p.167), 29 home helps visited 454 households. One-third of older people visited by these helps were men and two-thirds were women. On the basis of a survey in 1988, about 60% were aged 75+ and about 31% aged 80+.

Other services

There is a well-co-ordinated network of community services for older people, which includes a day and night emergency call-out scheme to the residences of older people. Also, a telephone alarm system for older people was first started in the Luxemburg *commune* (Hartmann-Hirsch et al., 1992, p.20). Before passing on to the next section, it must be said that, at times, the manner in which these are made available reflects the paternalism of the nineteenth century, according to the observations of Roulleaux (1986, p.397). Also, as in the UK and other parts of Europe, there is some confusion over the professional boundaries of the *assistant d'hygiène sociale* and the *assistant social*; the former is very similar in function to the social nurse in Belgium (*infirmier gradué social*); the latter is basically a social worker.

Voluntary care agencies and support organizations

The voluntary agencies, as stated earlier, are described as the 'utilities' or 'associations'. As in other Catholic countries, Caritas plays a central role in providing recreational and leisure pursuits and holidays for older people; it also provides home help. Home help (*aide à domicile*), also known as *aide familiale* or *aide senior*, is delivered by about 29 helpers in close partnership with the social workers (Bemelmans, 1986, p.11). Most of the clients are over 80, and most live alone. The social workers calculate how much the user is able to pay. Caritas pays part of the difference, and the rest is paid by the Ministry of Family Affairs.

AMIPERAS is another vigorous voluntary agency with about 25,000 older people in 93 branches, for whom 'self-reliance' is all-important. The organization also runs a holiday home.

Waterplas (1991, p.264) refers to the small voluntary agencies in Luxemburg who assist older people. Of particular note are the following three networks:

1   the Association Femmes du Nord, who help with transporting older people; accompanying and visiting them; helping in the house, and assisting with carrying out administrative tasks, such as form filling;
2   the Premier Secours de la Croix de Malte, who provide meals-on-wheels and manage a telephone alarm scheme in the city of Luxemburg;
3   the Christian Equipes d'Entraide, who provide older people with moral support, visit them and accompany them to the doctor's surgery.

There is also a 24-hour emergency service for older people, staffed by volunteers. This facility provides information regarding hospital or extra-mural care, as well as a call-out number for ambulance services.

It is clear that Luxemburg provides a wide mix of utilities and associations in a relatively small area. The co-ordination of these services is a formidable task.

Informal care

Bemelmans (1986, p.6) states that 21% of older people in Luxemburg live with their offspring, and 2% with their partner and children.

There is concern about the future modes of care for older people because of the fourfold increase in divorces, which often results in women being left alone. Therefore, although there is currently a great deal of dependence upon informal care in comfortable circumstances, the care of the older population in the twenty-first century will present the government of the Grand Dutchy with considerable problems. However, looking at the contemporary scene, the older population in Luxemburg are certainly amongst Europe's most fortunate pensioners.

Bemelmans (1986) cites the lack of research into the needs and care of older people in Luxemburg. As late as 1983, even the Ministry of Family Affairs had no hard facts as to how many older people lived alone, and their living arrangements. Bemelmans's contribution does not cover the modes of familial or neighbourhood care. The picture of familial and kinship care which emerges is very similar to the Belgian situation, and counterbalanced by much the same infrastructure of care and cultural norms.

Leisure pursuits and education

Educational programmes, and sometimes holidays, are increasingly provided by AMIPERAS. The older people in Luxemburg have generous pensions; most are fairly well-off. Subsidies and concessions for the vast majority are neither necessary nor culturally acceptable to a people wedded to paying their way, hence such concessions are few (CPA, 1993, p.166).

Rural aspects

No research findings appear to exist with regard to the care of older people in the more rural areas of Oesling or the Bon Pays.

Conclusion

It is clear from the above details that this small Duchy has a high density and a very varied panoply of services under various ministries and organizations. But, there appears to be an apparent lack of clear guidelines and adequate regulations. There is also considerable state interference at local level, in spite of the stress upon subsidiarity (see Roulleaux, 1986, p.395). The confusing and loose authority structure requires considerable reorganization and co-ordination. The multiplicity and the overlaps of spontaneous and haphazard services must bewilder the older population. The government, in an attempt to address this problem, introduced a White Paper (Luxemburg Grand Duchy, 1991b) dealing with legal structures. Hartmann-Hirsch et al. (1992, p.7) refer to three major intents behind the White Paper: to create a legal framework within which organizations may interrelate; to define the baseline for action/agreement, and to cut out the overlaps and the non-regulated action.

Small countries tend to be monocephalic. However, this 'land-locked island of prosperity' is a supreme example of a 'closer-to-people state', where the central state and local state are in effect one administrative entity. The macrospheres, the mezzospheres and the microspheres, as it were, collapse into one. The state administration (see Table 6) tends to be centralized, but it is in transition as it is pulled in the direction of subsidiarity by the associations. There is therefore a two-way pull, as shown in Table 6.

The state can be run as a village, bringing together within a small area, through a plural welfare system, the services of the associations or utilities, the statutory agencies and the private organizations within a 'cash and caring service', much like that of Belgium, within a land-locked mini-country.

Part III

Central Europe

Chapter 12 will deal with the care of older people in Switzerland, where an open care (i.e. provided outside of institutional care) system and communitarian model of welfare have been well established in one of Europe's more affluent and stable countries. The influence of Röpke's (1943) 'middle-way' between the market welfare and the socialist welfare models has been considerable (Girod et al., 1985; Giarchi, 1996). Writing in Geneva, he argued for a welfare system that advocated a more localized service that fitted the polycephalic structure of a country where the cantons provided services that were 'closer to people'.

The following two chapters will deal with care for older people in Austria and Germany. Along with Switzerland, the services in these two countries have much in common, particularly federalism and the principle of subsidiarity. They adopt a more asynchronic and communitarian model of care, which contrasts sharply with the modes of formal care in Northern and Western European countries.

As stated elsewhere in the introduction, the precise identification of a Central Europe is problematic and debated by many. Schöpflin and Wood (1989) have provided a comprehensive discussion about the controversy and lack of consensus over its identification and location (see also Giarchi, 1996).

Esping-Andersen (1990) refers to 'corporatist regimes', which stand for regimes founded upon subsidiarity and Christian democratic political philosophy, with emphasis upon family support. Esping-Andersen regards Germany and Austria as the major corporatist states (and to a lesser extent Italy, France and Poland). Whatever the merits of these observations, preference is given here to Röpke's 'middle way' and to the emergence of a communitarian model. This is user-led and springs from civil and religious roots within society.

12 Switzerland

Demography

As shown earlier in Table 1, Switzerland will probably have the highest proportion of older people in Europe by 2025. According to Eurostat (1991a) and UN (1991) life expectancy at birth in Switzerland for women (80.7 years) is the highest in Europe, and for men (73.9 years) is the third-highest in Europe. At 65, life expectancy for Swiss women is 19.5 years, and for Swiss men is 15.3 years.

Socio-political and administrative background

The basis of social policy is a collective responsibility which attempts to cut across ethnic and parish boundaries. Galbraith (1977) commented upon the community-based Swiss welfare system, which also reflects the ideas of Röpke, as stated earlier. However, in spite of the positive aspects in the system, problems do exist in Switzerland, which certainly affect the older population. It has one of Europe's highest standards of living and yet 5–10% of the population are poor; many of these are older people, as cited by Modena-Burkhardt (1986, p.507). There is also a great deal of disillusionment with politics, as evidenced by the drop in the proportion of Swiss voters. Therefore, the tendency is for the health and social care systems to remain largely unchanged. Up to the 1960s the canton welfare laws had changed little since the nineteenth century.

Switzerland (Schweizerische Eidgenossenschaft or Swiss Confederation) is one of the smallest countries in Europe (half the size of Scotland). This state is the supreme European example of a polycephalic system. It is one of the most diversified of administrations, with 26 cantons (*kantone, cantons, cantoni*) or states. Each has its own constitution and laws. The cantons impose and spend most of the taxes, and come under the Federal Assembly, the Federal Council and the Federal Supreme Court. Legislative power rests with the Federal Assembly. It has two chambers: the Standrat, which has two representatives from each canton, and the Nationalrat, which is made up of the nationally elected members; the representatives can raise matters which concern the older local population directly at the federal level.

There are 3,000 small *communes* at the next level. These are largely autonomous. Switzerland is the epitome of decentralization. According to Segalman (1986, p.55) the country has the most decentralized system in the world. Röpke's ideas on community-led systems, referred to earlier, are clearly shaped by the commune networks. Unity through diversity characterizes this communal approach to social and health care, going back to Article 2 of the Swiss Constitution of 1874, which declared that the constitution was established 'for the promotion of common welfare' (Modena-Burkhardt, 1986, p.508). The Swiss canton-based systems of care are generally regarded as being eminently flexible, adapted to the varied needs of the older population, who lead very diversified lives, in varied environments. The systems of care have to be flexible, given that the Swiss are made up of many different peoples: German Swiss, Italian Swiss, French Swiss, Rhaeto-Romanic Swiss, of different Christian Churches and a small Jewish community. In addition, there are the migrant workers (*Gastarbeiter*), amounting to 16% of the population (see Modena-Burkhardt, 1986, p.507), many of whom have settled down over the years and now constitute ethnic minorities requiring special care in their retirement.

Social security: pensions and benefits

Financial assistance for the older population in Switzerland was first provided in 1929. The pension scheme was introduced in 1948, and updated in 1963 and 1972 (see CPA, 1989, p.142; Gross and Puttner, 1987, pp.615–21). The Swiss social security scheme is founded upon three pillars. The first pillar is federal social security, the universal old age and survivors' programme, principally based upon employer or self-employed and employee contributions. The pension is payable to men aged 65+ and women aged 62+. There are two pension levels: a minimum, and a maximum which is twice the minimum. An older couple receive 150% of the single pension. The expenditure on the public pension is around 8% of Gross Domestic Product (CPA, 1989, p.142). The second pillar is an occupational pension programme, which is compulsory for all those earning above a basic threshold, funded by contributions from both employers and employees. Both these schemes are subsidized by the government. The third pillar consists of the private and additional pension schemes. Over half of the older population enjoy the same standards of living as they did before retirement.

Studies have shown that Switzerland provides higher old age insurance benefits than the USA, Belgium, France, Austria, the Netherlands, the UK and the former Federal Republic of Germany (see Segalman, 1986, pp.49–50). The first and second pillars provide the older population with pensions which are 50–80% of their previous income. In the case of survivors' benefits, these exceed those of other European nations by at least 50%. Swiss health insurance benefits are also far in advance of the international average. However, there is a wide gap between the poorest 10% and the better-off pensioners. A means-tested supplementary pension arrangement exists, which is paid by the canton to bring the older person's income up to the declared subsistence level.

Housing

Gross and Puttner (1987, p.635) provide an overview of Switzerland's housing policies, which is relevant to older tenants in particular. Housing legislation is a federal responsibility. Public subsidies and loans for land development and for housing construction are part of the federal provision in accordance with housing and property legislation.

Low-priced housing is made available for special needs groups, and provision is made within social policy for the low-income groups. In what must be one of Europe's most generous systems, the state guarantees and mediates mortgages of up to 90% for installation costs.

The federal system provides capital and loans to community development projects. Federal loans are available for houses in the mountainous areas. Aid is also available for houses declared to be unhealthy by the surveyor's office, whether these are old or new properties.

The rights of tenants are safeguarded by the accredited rent tribunals. The tenants and landlords are given equal hearing and representation. In accord with the federal resolution (the *Bundesbeschluss* of 1977) the tenant is protected against unwarranted notice to quit the rented house. Rents may also be reduced by the authorities.

There are also state subsidies for sheltered apartments in an attempt to slow down the entry into residential care. However, Segalman (1986, p.134), in examining social care in Berne, identifies the unsuitable accommodation and the inadequate housing for some of the older population, in spite of the aid available.

Health care

The public health system administers hospitals, medical and nursing home care, and food hygiene (Gross and Puttner, 1987, p.631). Health care and welfare provision are administered and managed by the governing bodies in each canton. There is no national health service. Hospitals are usually run by the cantons and the *communes*, as well as by voluntary and private agencies, such as associations, foundations and joint-stock companies. Public or cantonal health officers are responsible for the treatment of infectious diseases and strive to maintain a healthy environment. Health insurance is optional, although some cantons make medical insurance compulsory, either for all or only for certain groups of people. None the less, most of the older population are insured against sickness. Insurance covers doctors' fees, treatment and up to 720 days of in-patient care out of every 900 days. Those who are not insured turn to the local welfare offices, which pay hospital and other medical fees (see CPA, 1989, p.142). Funeral grants are provided in the form of a lump sum (Gross and Puttner, 1987, p.622).

Hospital care and medical services

Health provision for the older population includes geriatric and psychogeriatric centres, which may contain day hospital facilities. In the cities there are 'polyclinics' where the family doctors provide primary care; these are situated in centres of population and convenient for most of the older urban residents. Rural mini-hospital facilities are usually accessible for most older rural residents.

Nursing

Nursing old people is a specialism within the geriatric and psychogeriatric centres, but there is no welfare state counterpart to the district nurses of the UK (see page 136).

Home care/help

There are pedicurists and home nurses, but the domiciliary services are scarce and costly. However, the policy is to avoid or shorten hospital care for older people (see Gross and Puttner, 1987, p.631). Home care is the responsibility of the private non-profit agencies, such as the Swiss Red Cross, Caritas and other Church organizations. Home care is financed by subsidies from the cantons and *communes*, which cover half the costs. Voluntary insurance payments make up for a quarter of the costs, and patient fees make up the remainder.

Mental health care

Psychiatric care is the sole responsibility of the canton and health authorities at local level. There is no central government ministry responsible for mental health. An extensive in-patient and out-patient psychiatric service exists, linked to nine voluntary mental health associations (see Segalman, 1986, pp. 170–1). Segalman indicates, on the basis of World Health Organization calculations, that Switzerland has an average of 2.4 out-patient facilities per canton. The Swiss out-patient facilities are better than those of Belgium and Luxemburg, and in the same range as those of France and the Netherlands, but inferior to Sweden and Denmark. Its in-patient psychiatric facilities are also inferior to Sweden's, better than those of Denmark, France and Norway, but comparable to those of England and Wales. Although the proportion of older depressed and psychiatric patients is not stated, it is clear that facilities are well-distributed and readily available. The community care policy endeavours to maintain older people at home whenever feasible: there are fewer beds and fewer admissions than in most Western European countries (Segalman, 1986, p.171).

Institutional care

The Protestant ethic, with its emphasis upon self-reliance, still provides the basis for Switzerland's social policy. The voluntary sector, inspired by the Churches, fills the gaps in formal care. Ambulatory residential care has been a concern (Segalman, 1986, p.134). It is not possible to assess the extent and nature of nursing home care, except that when the city of Berne faced the need to provide 300 of its older residents (1% of the older population) with nursing care in 1980, Segalman states that they simply built two sanitoria providing some 170 beds! The 1980s saw less emphasis on the larger establishments in the more developed countries, but the CPA (1989, p.143) states that 6–8% of those over 65 require places in homes. The increase in the number of older people in Switzerland by 2025 will surely lead to even greater demands upon what appears to be an underdeveloped residential sector. Nursing home care and respite care appear to be more advanced in the French cantons; respite care is provided in the residential homes (CPA, 1989, p.143).

Personal social services

The principle of subsidiarity is invoked (as in Germany and in some Latin countries), so that the canton will only come to the rescue when the family and the voluntary agencies are no longer able to assist. The whole system is administered locally and does not draw upon national capital, unlike the major welfare states of Europe. Welfare support is not a right in Switzerland. Older people and any other client groups are regarded as essentially independent and self-reliant until need is demonstrably required. Rehabilitation is the first aim when the usual informal caring arrangements break down; formal care is the last resort. The federal government is not responsible for social assistance (see Segalman, 1986, pp.107–8). Only after all other measures have been attempted and failed do the public services step in. At that point the canton is obliged to provide social care for those who require help. In fact, should the client move into another canton, the canton of previous domicile will reimburse all costs for social care for the first five years. Means-testing is carried out simply on the basis of the citizen's annual income and wealth tax statement, so no searching personal questions are asked.

Social workers

In the Central European countries relatively few older people are in contact with or assisted by social workers. As Modena-Burkhardt (1986, p.509) has observed, social work agencies tend to exist only in the larger towns and cities. There are about 5,300 social workers, not including those who are state-employed (see Modena-Burkhardt, 1986, p.510). In the smaller towns and villages, the politicians or canton officers make social work decisions and decide upon the merits of the older persons' appeals for help and assistance. The state depends more upon voluntary groups and private organizations, so is slow to subsidize the social services.

The services

No description or evaluation is available of home help or other social care services, such as day care, within the remit of the personal social services. Home help, meals services and laundry services are available from the voluntary organizations, but this often involves social workers (see below).

Voluntary care agencies and support organizations

The major voluntary agency for the elderly is Pro Senectute, a legal trust operating through largely autonomous sub-organizations in the cantons. This organization runs pre-retirement courses (see CPA, 1989, p.143). There is also Pro Infirmis, a national organization for the disabled, operating locally through specialized branches for particular forms of disability. These are financed through charity and the canton. Most voluntary agencies depend entirely upon charity to meet their costs.

Private agencies have also been contracted to assist the older people in the cantons. Working *with* the older population (rather than *for* them in a paternalistic fashion) and providing them with multiple choices are features of the voluntary provision. Domiciliary care is also available from the voluntary organizations; it includes home help, meals services, house repair schemes and laundry services, some of which are co-ordinated by trained social workers within the voluntary agency (see CPA, 1989, p.143).

Informal care

With regard to family in Switzerland, Segalman (1986, p.150) says that: 'Unlike the condition of the family in many other Western countries, the position of the family as a functioning institution is robust in Switzerland.' More marriages occur at a later age in Switzerland, and divorces have not increased at the same pace as in other advanced European nations. Families are more intact in Switzerland, according to Segalman (1986), than in most other European nations. There is no doubt that the principle of subsidiarity matters in Switzerland. Segalman (p.153) observes: 'Nothing is relegated to the community or to community agencies that the Swiss family believes belongs to it.' The organization Pro Familia, which was founded in 1931, sponsors research and constitutes a pressure group in defence of the family. It has been successful, for example, in exerting influence upon the Swiss Ministry of the Interior to initiate a Swiss family policy (see Luscher, 1982). However, even Calvinist Switzerland cannot easily escape from the social changes affecting the structure and nature of family life and its caring function. There are signs that in Zurich and Berne the traditional Swiss family is less evident. There is also evidence that about 12% of families are those of single parents (see Segalman, 1986, p.151). In addition, at least 30% of families have no children, so that familial care is not a viable option for many of the survivors in their old age.

Geriatric and gerontological research have been slow to take off in Switzerland. The CPA (1989, p.142) points out that geriatrics in that country is not recognized as a speciality. It is interesting that Todd (1985) does not mention Switzerland in his overview of family types in Europe, except to state in passing that the dominant family type in that country is the authoritarian nuclear family. The pride taken in the family providing care may have insulated the older Swiss against the need for formal care. Indeed, the mantle of informal care often covers the privacy and quality of familial and kinship care in secrecy.

The challenge facing Swiss families, kinship circles and single households in the first half of the twenty-first century will be formidable. Firstly, the projected proportion of older people in Switzerland by 2025, as shown in Table 1, will be 23.8%. Secondly, the proportionate increase of persons aged 65 and over will also constitute the second-highest after that of the Netherlands. Since the 1980s the number of vulnerable older women living alone has increased significantly; 44% of women and 15% of men lived alone in 1980 (CPA, 1989). That situation is worsening all the time. As the CPA reports, formal care has been slow to catch up with need. The reliance upon the family has halted the development of welfare arrangements. Switzerland faces the critical years ahead ill-prepared to cope, because alternatives to informal care have not been developed.

Leisure pursuits and education

Universities of the Third Age exist in most cantons. There are also many leisure associations for older people – even a Gymnastic Federation. About half of those in the urban areas make use of their centres, but in the rural areas only one-fifth do (see CPA, 1989, p.143).

Rural aspects

Rural studies are not available. The discussion of care has tended to concern itself with what is going on within Switzerland as a whole.

Conclusion

It is clear that the formal caring arrangements for the older population in Switzerland have been slow to develop. The family has been the mainstay, and currently continues to be the major support, for older people within a system that is dictated by the principle of subsidiarity. The welfare system is localized and closer to the older population than in most European countries, but developments are hardly innovative, with institutions tending to adopt more traditional practices.

Segalman (1986, p.194) sums up the importance of local involvement when discussing the provision of welfare in Switzerland:

> Experience has shown that only at the local level is it possible for everyone to know one another. It is also possible at this level to ask questions and to receive clear answers. It is possible at local levels to understand the issues and the people affected. And at the local level the citizen either gets involved [in the issues] or has to suffer with the results of someone else's activity.

The local state is the critical factor within a federal and polycephalic Switzerland. The federal interaction is between the local state at canton level, the voluntary agencies and the Church organizations. The asynchronic system, referred to in Part I, operates at 'closer-to-people' levels within the voluntary agencies, and in many cantons with the Churches, establishing local caring systems for the older residents within the relatively small areas of administration. The administrative systems and the health and social care programmes tend to be polycephalic. In addition, the civic decisions regarding the care of older people are regulated in accordance with the principle of subsidiarity, which will be shown to be a paramount factor in Austria and Germany, the two major Central European neighbours of Switzerland.

13 Austria

Demography

The proportion of older people in Austria ranks sixth in Europe, but will probably drop to tenth place by 2025, as can be calculated on the basis of Table 1. Since the mid-1960s one in five Austrians have been over the age of 60 (UN Austrian Report, 1982). The proportion of women over the age of 75 has more than doubled since 1951. In the 1980s there were approximately 1,000 older women to every 600 men, due to the high proportion of male fatalities during World War II, and the higher mortality rate amongst the men who survived it. This particularly affected Vienna, where the higher proportion of older people in the capital is cited by the CPA (1989, p.22).

The life expectancy of Austrian women at 65 is 17.7 years, and that of men is 14.5 years. The women's life expectancy at birth is ranked twelfth in Europe; that of Austrian men is ranked fifteenth (Eurostat, 1991a).

A certain demographic stability has been attained for at least a decade, but this is mainly urban, as shall be seen below. Comparatively speaking, the increase in the proportion of older people in the urban areas will not be as critical a welfare factor as in other countries. The national report cited above does emphasize the constant demographic level for some time to come.

Socio-political and administrative background

Badelt and Pazourek (1991, p.13) refer to the authoritarian regime established within Austria after the demise of the monarchy. The people have been accustomed to leave the responsibility to provide care to the authorities and to the Church. Professionalism and vocationalism have been all-important in an authoritarian welfare system; voluntarism less so. As this section will show, there has now been a turnabout in which the authorities have initiated schemes involving the people, but supported by state subsidies.

Austria now has a polycephalic administrative structure. Until recently the systems of government, management of social security, and health and social care were monocephalic. However, Pohoryles et al. (1988, p.169) describe the Austrian social security network as both 'over-centralized' and 'splintered'. The traditional authoritative and centrist system is officially being replaced, but anachronisms may slow down the transition by which the various institutions are given more responsibilities in a devolved programme of networking social health care. In Austria the central state, the local state and the market are still in uneasy balance, as are the private agencies, the national voluntary organizations, the Church and the local grassroots voluntary agencies, with the household/family at the centre in an unsteady state. In spite of the unease and some splintering, the provision of care within the provinces and the local communities in Austria provides a good example of a decentralized, plural personal service system for older people.

Currently, the federal authority exercises almost no legislative power in relation to the care of older people. The public sector is made up of nine provinces (*Bundesländer*), within which are the districts, communities and associations of communities. The provinces legislate for finance and organize the necessary services, and formulate regionalized services. These operate differently. 'There is not one Austrian welfare triangle, but at least nine of them', according to Badelt and Pazourek (1991, p.22). These consist of the nine provinces (the *Bundesländer*).

Within the current consensus between the central and provincial governments regarding the decentralization programme, the strengthened social and economic partnerships and the self-administered social insurance system aim to establish a grand coalition, which is in effect a social partnership. The move is towards changes in the system of need, so that neighbourhood and self-help activities can be subsidized; the latter are not termed 'community care', rather they are identified as 'extra-mural care'. As in other major European countries, the principle of subsidiarity operates, but in a modified form, as will be discussed later. Badelt and Pazourek (1991) are somewhat pessimistic regarding both the welfare system as a whole and the dangers inherent in pursuing the 'care-by-contract' approach now adopted in Austria.

Social security: pensions and benefits

Weigel and Amann (1987, p.532), refer to the Federation of Austrian Social

Insurance Institutes (established in 1955), the supreme co-ordinating institution which negotiates with the health services and the professionals and acts on their behalf when called to do so.

There are two distinct monetary support systems in Austria: social security or social insurance, and social welfare. Each requires some commentary because they are of considerable significance for older Austrians.

The social security scheme

This caters for over 90% of the people, providing the retirement pension, and health and accident insurance. Entitlement to a pension requires at least 180 months of contributions in the previous 30 years, payable at 65 for men and 60 for women. The minimum number of 180 monthly payments is referred to as the 'waiting time' (*Wartezeit*). The minimum number of 60 payments for survivors' and invalidity pension, respectively, is referred to as the 'short waiting time' (*kürze Wartezeit*) (see CPA, 1989, p.22; Weigel and Amann, 1987, p.536). The 'full pension' (after 45 years of contributions) is equivalent to almost 80% of assessed earnings. Early retirement pensions are available from the age of 60 for men and 55 for women, on condition that they are long-term unemployed with 180 months of contributions. Long service pensions are also granted at 60 for men and 55 for women, provided that they have made 420 monthly contributions, of which 24 have been within the preceding 36 months. Widows receive 60% of the insured man's basic pension. Some 20% of the pension is safeguarded as pocket money, etc.

The compulsory health insurance scheme covers medical aid, including hospital fees and any prescribed medication; 10.5% of the pension is contributed towards the health insurance scheme. Home care is not covered, but it is an option.

Social insurance is administered by 24 Social Insurance Institutions. The multi-administrative network of social insurance illustrates the polycephalic system. The Director General of the Federation of Austrian Social Insurance Institutes is the mouthpiece of the 24 independent institutions. They call for changes in the regulations and legal principles regarding health and pension benefits and contributions. The demands for changes from the bottom up have been effective.

The social welfare scheme

This is mainly implemented at provincial levels, invoking the principle of subsidiarity. It caters for people with disabilities and establishes care and various other allowances; it provides institutional care such as nursing homes and other social services.

When the private and voluntary sectors cannot help, the state welfare system steps in. Badelt and Pazourek (1991, p.16) indicate that an area of concern for many older people is the distinction between 'treatment cases' and 'care cases' (as is also the case in Germany). In the 'treatment cases' the physician judges that the condition is curable; in the 'care cases' either treatment is not called for, or it will not make any notable difference, so the patient must turn to the private or state welfare system. If the price of care exceeds the older person's income, support is provided by civil servants in the provincial social assistance office. Welfare workers are also available through the local health services.

Housing

Housing is centrally controlled by the Austrian government, which finances the major housing programmes. However, devolution is under way in Austria: the provinces are increasingly implementing their own housing laws and supplementary programmes. They promote construction, improve stock and administer housing allowances and land regulation. Today, three-quarters of expenditure on housing is federal, one-sixth is provincial, and the remainder is municipal. On the basis of data provided by Weigel and Amann (1987, pp.568–9), at least 50% of Austrian accommodation (41% houses, 9% apartments) is owner-occupied. The rest are rented properties. The public authorities provide at least 8% of the housing stock, and the building associations (*gemeinnützige Bauvereinigungen*) provide about 34%. From 1940, non-profit building associations, amounting to at least 252 organizations, have administered at least half a million dwellings in Austria. Under the Housing Construction Promotion Act 1968 (WFG), small and medium-sized dwellings are constructed for low-income groups, such as certain older people who cannot afford to stay on in larger properties. The modernization of housing stock has been legislated for by the Housing Improvement Act 1967 (WVG), which provides for 40% subvention of interest payments on loans. Since 1975, supplements have been available for housing improvements. These financial options enable some families and older parents to carry out improvements on older properties when they are called for, such as new sanitation and heating. Housing supplements are also available for those who cannot meet their WFG or their WVG monthly payments. The full rent is waived in favour of an 'acceptable rent', if the claimant meets the conditions.

Health care

The public health services are mainly legislated for and administered by the provinces or the local communities; only a small number of services are the responsibility of the federal government. In their overall evaluation of the care of older people in Austria as a whole, Badelt and Pazourek (1991, p.16) are more critical than other recent commentators, especially regarding health care. They state that provision for older people who are at risk is inadequate. They also point out that there is a stigma attached to 'care cases'. Also, according to their appraisal, Public Health Insurance does not provide for rehabilitation. The supply of both institutional and extra-mural care, as seen by Badelt and Pazourek (1991, p.20), is less than in Switzerland and Germany, and generally inadequate, particularly in rural areas.

Hospital care and medical services

Hospitals are mainly administered by the provinces. Hospital care is well resourced, with almost as many beds per capita as in Germany, the Netherlands and Luxemburg, the countries with the greatest number of beds per capita in the EU (Eurostat, 1991b, p.888).

Geriatric care, as in Germany, has only developed lately. As in most European countries, medical care of older people lacks professional prestige.

Nursing

As in Germany, the nurse does not enjoy the same status as in the UK. The hospital nurses have greater standing than the extra-mural nurses, who are employed by the social services, Caritas (Caritasverband) and the Red Cross.

However, in addition to the nurses, older people may be assisted by 'care-helpers' (who are trained and qualified to work within the hospital system) or by a variety of new formal carers such as 'geriatric helpers', 'geriatric nurses' and 'geriatric assistants' (see Badelt and Pazourek, 1991, p.21).

Home care/help

Extra-mural care chiefly consists of home care. Qualified nurses provide the domiciliary health care, semi-professional staff provide meals-on-wheels, and home helps provide domestic assistance, in much the same way as in many other European countries.

Home help is provided in Vienna by eight non-governmental organizations (NGOs), employing 2,655 home helps serving almost 11,000 clients each month. Self-help groups are assisted by a centre established by the Municipal Health and Social Welfare Office in Vienna. It provides advice and information as well as financial assistance to groups of older people providing help for each other. The Vienna arrangement is not typical: home helps are usually employed by the social services.

Mental health care

Mentally ill older people make use of the Fund for Psycho-Social Services, an extra-mural system of care. Within a decade this system of care halved the number of places in the psychiatric institutions. However, there is a movement to de-institutionalize and to democratize the mental health services further, activated by the Group for the Democratization of Psychiatric Services (Gruppe Demokratische Psychiatrie).

Institutional care

Although the provinces are not legally bound to provide residential or nursing homes, they run 68% of the residential homes and 48% of the nursing homes. These are usually large, and mainly care for persons lower down the social scale. There are approximately 22,000 people aged 60+ in Austrian nursing homes. About four times as many reside within private households. The nursing home patients are mostly single women. About a quarter moved from single households, and about a third from older households (Badelt and Pazourek, 1991, p.18).

Although the public sector is not legally obliged to provide institutional care, about 64% of nursing homes and about 68% of retirement homes are provided by government organizations (GOs), according to Badelt (1989). However, the GO institutions are generally larger and less comfortable. They cater mainly for the poorest older Austrians.

The largest provision of residential homes and extra-mural services (community care) are provided by the non-profit organizations (NPOs). It is this type of non-profit provision which is being developed most to meet increasing state welfare and health costs, which are often heavily subsidized. Pohoryles et al. (1988, pp.187–92) refer, for example, to the co-operation that exists between the public and the voluntary agencies in the provinces. They cite how non-government residential schemes are subcontracted and/or their extra-mural costs are reimbursed. Firstly, in Vienna, with an above-average large proportion of older residents, the local authority financially supports or assists in the management of The Fund for Vienna Pensioners' Homes, which provides 5,500 places in city apartments and 670 nursing units. The private institutions, although relatively few, are growing in number. A nationwide audit conducted by Badelt (1991) stated that about 4% of the retirement homes were private, providing 2% of all places for older people in Austria; approximately 13% of the nursing homes were also private, providing about 2% of nursing places. Most of the private residential and nursing homes are located in the urban areas, and they usually cater for the more affluent older population.

The institutional care provided for the older population nowadays consists mainly of apartments, supporting the need for people's independence. The average apartment unit caters for some 250 people. Nursing wards are also contained within the building complex. To all intents and purposes many of the apartments are similar to geriatric hospitals (see CPA, 1989, p.22).

Personal social services

Hoffmann (1986, p.47) states that the welfare worker has eclipsed the social worker in the history of social care in Austria. The old 'care worker' (*Fürsorger*) for many years catered only for unmarried mothers and their children. Only in the 1960s were social workers formally accredited by the state. Older Austrians, therefore, are less aware of the role of social workers than are older people in most of Western and Northern Europe.

With regard to social services available to the older population, it is important to distinguish between the monetary supports listed above and social assistance (*Sozialhilfe*), the so-called 'second social net' against the risks of life, which is designed to assist the disadvantaged who have fallen through the social insurance net (Hoffmann, 1986, p.44). This service replaces the old 'care of the poor' (*Armenpflege*). The province is responsible for social assistance, not the federal government.

There are nine provincial legislatures with their own Social Assistance Acts. These differ greatly, in much the same way as the regional social services differ in Italy. Personal social services and benefits for special contingencies are provided within and by the provinces. Basic social assistance is a right in certain circumstances (Hoffmann, 1986, p.45).

Voluntary care agencies and support organizations

In Austria, there is no term which has the same denotation as 'voluntary sector', as pointed out by Badelt and Pazourek (1991, p.26). The umbrella category of the non-profit organization is the nearest equivalent to the English 'voluntary sector'. There are three types of NPO:

1   the *Wohlfahrtsverbande* – the social welfare organizations such as Caritas or the Red Cross, which have both paid and volunteer labour;

2   the *Vereine* – the local associations, which may or may not be affiliated to major or political organizations, run by both paid and volunteer labour;
3   the grassroots groups and self-help initiatives, which are run and supported by volunteers only.

The NPOs often exploit their workers, who are frequently on part-time contracts. They are mainly untrained. In addition, the NPOs are in competition, so that joint or inter-agency action seldom occurs. Non-statutory agencies run by the Churches, such as Caritas, other political party-run welfare agencies and the Red Cross provide personal social services for older people. An important point to note is that grassroots welfare agencies are usually run by the political parties (see Badelt and Pazourek, 1991, p.14), and the public as well as the private agencies are driven by party politics.

The private market organizations (PMOs) are relatively few, because the NPOs have overshadowed them. In spite of some recent developments, the Church organizations, supported by public funds and assisted by independent sources, continue to be major providers of care for older people.

The social services subcontract work to voluntary agencies. This is often carried out within largely decentralized neighbourhood systems, which also link with self-help groups; this co-operation is particularly important in rural Austria. For example, in Lower Austria, the largest Austrian province, which is mainly rural, personal social services consist of 74 different decentralized service stations. An additional 32 contact offices provide the bulk of care. Most are subcontracted non-profit organizations. These are staffed by 60 registered nurses; 35 family helpers, some for the aged; 70 home helps, and about 720 voluntary workers. Another example is Eastern Austria, an even more rural province, which is well known for its Burgenland Neighbourhood Help scheme (Pohoryles et al., 1988, pp.188–9). Local people living near older people assist them, providing home help, nursing and family help. They are given a subsidy by the provincial welfare office, as well as being supported and supervised by social workers.

A third example of local ventures providing social care is in the Tyrol, around the city of Innsbruck. Here, eight surrounding administrative districts are divided up into smaller sectors (similar in many ways to the UK 'patch' system). Within these sectors, private entrepreneurial schemes are encouraged, providing neighbourhood help, home nursing and neighbourhood care, and support for self-help groups.

Within the triangulation process the NPOs exert the greatest pull upon the state, and the PMOs are less likely to provide an alternative to the GOs and the NPOs.

The care provided in Austria is decentralized, but is highly disorganized at local levels, having been allowed to develop in a somewhat *laissez-faire* fashion. In an attempt to meet the rising costs in the face of both the population explosion of older people and recent scandals in the residential sector, the Federal Ministry of Affairs, the Federal Ministry of Health Care, the provincial authorities, and the various representatives of the NPOs and the PMOs have been instrumental in introducing new measures to extend both the modes of care and the range of choices for the older population. The major new recommendations are as follows:

1 attendance allowances are to be introduced, consisting of seven rates in accordance with levels of need;
2 extra-mural services are to be further developed.

In addition, the federal authorities have initiated a nationwide scheme to integrate the fragmented provision of care, to rationalize the muddle that exists, and to bridge the gaps between the GOs, the NPOs and the PMOs. The scheme, known as the Integrated Health and Social Areas (IGSs), consists of an infrastructure of co-ordinated social and health care within small areas. The plan incorporates many of the best features of the local co-ordinated schemes cited by Pohoryles et al. (1988). These initiatives are indicative of the convergence of European ideas in and around the need to rationalize care and to extend community care (extra-mural care) provision to enable people to stay at home for as long as possible. The Austrian situation also shows how decentralization may be disastrous if it is uncoordinated. The lack of collaboration between agencies and the overt competition between them often block any possibility of partnership. The older population often suffer as a result.

Informal care

Badelt and Pazourek (1991, pp.26–7) refer to the 22% of the population aged 60+ in households who require help, and the 6% in need of care.

The duty of caring for older family members has been proverbial in Austria, where, like Germany, it has been recognized as a major familial (usually filial) duty within its authoritarian nuclear families. The traditional concern is epitomized by the *Ausgedinge* (the old person's portion), which provided a household social security system. In Vienna, one in five people aged 60+ live in inter-generational families, according to the 1982 national report (UN Austrian Report, 1982); but Mitterauer and Sieder (1982, p.153) say that the proportion of the non-peasant population of Lower Austria who live with one of their married offspring is as low as 14%, and the proportion of persons aged 60 and over is as low as 3%. They also add that more than 50% of single women over 65 live alone in Vienna, as opposed to only 7% in the rural population of Lower Austria. Badelt and Pazourek (1991, p.19) describe the 'singularization' process in Austria, accompanied by the progressive break-up of families and the spatial mobility and increased paid employment of women. To date, more than 80% of informal care is provided in Austria by women.

Urbanization has altered family values. Greater mobility has added to this, with the consequent isolation of the older rural population, according to Amann (1980).

The impact of modern developments upon the provincialism and style of living in the villages of Austria has been researched by Pevetz and Jauch (1985). Forty-five villages were studied by Austrian researchers between 1945 and 1972, followed up by others between 1972 and 1982. In what must be the most comprehensive village studies in Europe, the geographers and sociologists contrasted the closed mountain villages in the inner Alpine region with the more open lowland villages in the east, north, south-east and extreme west (Pevetz and Jauch, 1985, p.1).

The word *Dorf* (village) signifies a relatively closed rural settlement, but the influx of outsiders to the lowland villages has threatened and changed much of the traditional life and values of the *Dorf*. Life in the rural areas has changed, and is often characterized by insecurity and depopulation, followed by repopulation, particularly affecting the household traditions, and the advent of the 'industrial villages'. In the mountainous areas the people 'among themselves' are characterized by large, sound farm families. Here the traditional care of the older population is maintained in spite of modernity. However, the impact of tourism on the Tyrolean mountain region is cited in several studies.

A major development is the greater exodus of women to find work within the tourist industry, leaving behind larger proportions of men. The need to tend thus falls increasingly upon fewer and more heavily burdened women carers, especially in the mountain villages.

Moreover, the farms in the mountains are generally run by men over 60; in some areas only 10% of farms are run by farmers below 40 years of age. Encroaching modernity has also reduced the average size of household rural dwellings: the typical new flat consists of three rooms. The inter-generational families are decreasing, as in other parts of rural Europe. Also, traditionalism, provincialism and modernity polarize the villagers. Household lifestyles contrast and progressively diversify. The impact upon the older people in a world of change must therefore be severe: 'the family is no longer the '"germ cell of society"' (Pevetz and Jauch, 1985, p.16), surely affecting the traditional expectations regarding the extent and nature of caring responsibilities.

Leisure pursuits and education

Leisure and educational opportunities for older Austrians are well-developed (see CPA, 1989, p.23). There are 350 adult education colleges and 2,400 local institutes funded by the state, the trade unions, the Churches and various private organizations. Also the Federal Ministry of Education, Arts and Sports aims to provide older people with opportunities to extend their education. Many had only an elementary or very limited education in their youth. Every three years all persons aged 65+ are informed through an outreach service of all facilities, including leisure facilities, available to them within their province. Social clubs, country holidays and recreational facilities are provided by the provincial authorities.

Rural aspects

The orientation of the existing studies is essentially urban. There do not appear to any major rural studies of caring arrangements for older Austrians in English.

Conclusion

The triangulation of care in Austria is essentially held together by the province, which may act as provider and purchaser in what is Europe's most complicated and most diversified system. The government organizations, the non-profit organizations and the private market organizations referred to above have their merits, but they also have their drawbacks, and are considered by more and more carers to be of less importance than extra-mural care.

Badelt and Pazourek (1991, p.31) identify and discuss the major arguments regarding the perspectives on the triangle of care in Austria. The government organizations (GOs) are too large and offer less privacy. It is argued that the non-profit organizations (NPOs) are smaller and more private, and so should be preferred to the government organizations. Although they are cheaper than all the private market organizations, they are not always utilized. Also, the non-profit organizations generally have a large percentage of less well-trained volunteer staff.

The arguments for and against one or other forms of institutional care, however, are less relevant, as the state and professional carers prefer to encourage and support extra-mural care. This policy has been strengthened, especially after the publicity given to the public scandal of 1989, when four nurses were alleged to have murdered more than forty older patients. The extra-mural alternative to institutional care, which upholds the dignity and independence of the older person, is receiving increasing professional and electoral support. But can the informal carers support the growing numbers of older Austrians?

14 Germany

Demography

The demographic explosion of the older population in Germany has been created in part by the increased life expectancy. While in the years 1970–2 the average life expectancy at birth was 73.8 years for women and 67.4 years for men, more recently the life expectancy has been 79 years and 72.6 years respectively (Eurostat, 1991a). Contributions to state funding will diminish with the decrease in the number of people in paid employment, while at the same time the escalation in the number of older pensioners will reach critical levels by 2030 (see Evers and Olk, 1991, p.60). Older women outnumber older men by two to one (Eurostat, 1991a). One in five of these are widowed, the highest proportion in the EU. Because German women are living longer – usually alone, and many without offspring – they constitute a major concern for the health and social services, especially in Eastern Germany. There are almost four times as many people aged 65+ in Western Germany as there are in Eastern Germany.

A major concern is the shrinkage in the numbers of potential carers between the ages of 45 and 59 (see Evers and Olk, 1991, p.61). As can be seen from the data presented in Table 1, both East and West Germany combined are ranked fifth in Europe in terms of proportions of older people. In line with major EU countries, the percentage of women aged 80+ is more than double that of men of the same age (Eurostat, 1991a; CPA, 1993, p.97).

The demography of Germany does not include black ethnic and white outsider groups. They are amongst the most marginalized people in Germany, a growing number of whom are reaching retirement age. Politically they are invisible, but socially they are visible in a white Europe, where racism has stereotyped the vulnerable migrants. Over the centuries, black slaves and ethnic white minorities built up nations. The Europeans spread worldwide from their militarized countries, in the spurious cause of 'developing' the Third World. In contemporary Europe, the migrant-workers are the current slaves who have built up commercial empires at great cost to themselves and their families. Muslims, Sikhs and North Africans have poured into the heart of Europe, particularly into Germany.

In Germany, *Gastarbeiter* (guest workers) have neither civil rights, social security nor the right to own a business (Edwards, 1990, p.150). Large numbers of those who have taken up residence in Germany are amongst the unknown vagrants and homeless people, many of whom are black people and other ethnic minorities, from either the troubled areas of Southern Europe or deprived areas of North Africa. They do not feature in statistical tables because they are eliminated from the citizens' register. Added to this are the white migrants from Eastern Europe, whose presence has sparked off a right-wing backlash: Germany is a threatening place for most refugees, drifting there from landward East-Central regions.

Socio-political and administrative background

In spite of reunification, in terms of the quality of life and the provision of social and health care, there are still two Germanies. During the period of transition there will necessarily be delays in the integrational process. One must avoid looking too far back in the attempt to explain this. It will probably be some five to ten years before a unified federal polycephalic system is fully established. This perilous transition process is exacerbated by an unprecedented nationwide increase in the demand of older Germans for services in the eastern and western *Länder*.

It might be assumed that the retired now exert considerable political leverage within Germany, especially through the efforts of the Grey Panthers. However, Dieck and Garms-Homolová (1991, pp.125–6) question the political impact of the older population. They see the response of the government to the needs of older people as simply one of appeasement.

The reunification of Germany presented the authorities within the *Länder* federal structure with enormous problems, particularly in the eastern areas where values and principles of welfare and health care needed to be adapted and modified, and at times eliminated, to make possible an integrated, federal, decentralized system.

According to the *Grundgesetz* (Basic Law) (Paragraph 1, Article 20), the state is obliged to provide the financial means of care and welfare, but is not obliged to provide either care or welfare provisions. The state is essentially the purchaser of care – the provider of finances to meet needs – rather than the provider of care. In addition, social care has traditionally been financed and provided by the Churches, the charity associations and voluntary organizations locally. The *Länder* are represented in the second chamber of parliament. They are responsible for social assistance costs. These they often attempt to shift onto the state's federal budget, but without success, as Dieck indicates (1990, pp.108–12). It is a 'Catch 22' situation, because the *Länder* jealously hold onto their polycephalic systems and the municipalities cling to their 'closer-to-home' strategies of care: to shift costs might easily shift the *Länder*'s regional fulcrum.

According to the *Grundgesetz* (Paragraph 2, Article 28), the municipalities within the *Länder* are responsible for the local legal infrastructure and monitoring of social care and welfare, but not for local provision, which it increasingly purchases.

The Federal Social Assistance Act 1961 is the main basis for the three major support systems: domiciliary, institutional and semi-institutional. Responsibility for the older population rests mainly with the local bodies. This takes the form of assistance for subsistence and for specific situations of need. The possible forms of help are: assistance with nursing, running the household, and providing support for the blind and the deaf; integration for the disabled; preventative health measures and social care for older people, and also the provision and maintenance of suitable housing for older people. Because as few as 22,500 people claim this assistance, information systems are now at the top of the German *Länder*'s agendas.

There is also a national umbrella organization, which meets in Bonn, which includes within its committees representatives of the municipalities and the *Länder*; officers of the six large non-profit welfare organizations, and representatives from relevant research institutions and centres. It is advisory, and as pointed out by Dieck (1990, p.108), its recommendations have recently been ignored by the federal government.

Social security: pensions and benefits

The retirement age for men and women in Germany is 65. Early retirement for men and women can be taken at 63 (or 60 if disabled). The conditions are 35 years of contributions. The option for women to retire at 60 is being phased out (see Walker, 1992a, p.169). The German pension is earnings-related, as in most of Europe, in contradistinction to the flat-rate pension scheme in the UK, Denmark, the Republic of Ireland and the Netherlands. The earnings-related scheme originated in Germany in 1889. In keeping with the Bismarckian legislation, the German social security system is stratified and differentiated on the basis of the contributions of the employees and the employers, under the direction of the state. The FRG's social policy regarding social security in the post-war years decided the nature of a united Germany's pension after reunification. The welfare reform in the Federal Republic of Germany in 1957 updated the earnings-related scheme and indexed pensions to the general rise in wages.

The pension in Germany, as a proportion of overall social security benefits (45.9%), is the second-highest in the EU (Eurostat, 1991a, p.84) after Italy. Walker (1992a, p.162) states that in terms of old age benefit expenditure per capita in the EU countries, West Germany ranks third with Italy (112%), after France (131%) and Denmark (164%). However, there is considerable concern regarding the viability of the German pension over the next few decades. Tax levels have become a major political issue, as almost everywhere in the First World.

The main pension is the public state pension. The demands of the many non-earning Eastern Germans will necessarily increase welfare expenditure within the new Germany for many years to come.

The state pension provides for approximately 90% of the population. However, the current overall carers/older people dependency ratio of 100:82 will increase to 100:116 by 2023, as Dieck (1990, p.102) observes. The present pension system must be changed to meet the situation. An income-related statutory pension system is favoured by the Social Democratic Party and the trade unions, whom one would imagine would prefer a minimum or basic pension. This indicates the new challenge facing Germany, as the economic demands of adequate pensions begin to shake and then rock the welfare system. After 3 October 1990 the monetary union of East and West Germany, resulting in a debt of billions of Deutschmarks, has exacerbated the problem of establishing a pension scheme which Germany can afford in the twenty-first century.

The Federal Social Assistance Act 1961 legislated for the provision of money, goods and personal assistance to older people in need. These were extended in 1974 in line with a more positive appreciation of the social needs of older people on the basis of more positive images of the senior citizen.

In spite of the improvement in the general standard of living for most pensioners, old age poverty has not been eliminated. Older women suffer the most, receiving smaller pensions generally. They have usually made fewer contributions, having had an interrupted 'working life biography' because of unemployment, child-raising and familial care. Unmarried women, divorcees and widows are badly hit in retirement. Married couples who depend upon rebates from the workers' pension scheme are also amongst the poorest. They need to apply for the minimum *Hilfe zum Lebensunterhalt* (Help for Everyday Maintenance), and they often need to apply for *Hilfe in Besonderen Lebenslagen* (Help in Specific Life Circumstances). For those over 60, there is also 'aid for care'.

In spite of these support systems, the older German population are receiv-

ing 'second best' treatment, according to Dieck (1990). The increases in benefits do exist, but they are compensatory at less important levels of provision,
whilst mainstream injustices and redistribution gaps in social welfare
remain.

One of the most comprehensive surveys, commissioned by the Federal
Ministry for Labour and Social Welfare, is cited by Steinack and Dieck (1986,
p.58). Although the survey is dated, the conditions represent recent ongoing
trends. It points out, with regard to the older population, that both husband
and wife have an income in 46% of the older households, and that the only
income is the husband's statutory pension in 26% of married wage-earner
households and in 19% of married salary-earner households. This survey
also points out, with regard to the single, that 45% of single men and 39% of
unmarried and 31% of divorced women require an income from supplementary security systems to top up their statutory pension; 35% of widows
depend solely upon their Widow's Pension; 6% of the men and 14% of the
unmarried, 15% of the widowed and 35% of the divorced women draw upon
the Housing Allowance or social assistance.

On the basis of this and other surveys, as well as Evers and Olk's (1991,
p.60) observations, it is clear that unmarried German women are more likely
to be on a low income, as is the case throughout Europe. These two authors
also point out that there has been a decrease in the number of social insurance contributors and in the number of carers, both formal and informal,
whilst the number of users of services and claimants for benefits are on the
increase.

Beck (1995) indicates that the number of people contributing to the
pension fund is falling. For example, the population will decrease by 10.9
million in 2030 and the older population (60+) will increase by 8.4 million
(Beck, 1995, p.2).

Housing

From 1982–92, approximately 33.6% of older households have been owner-
occupied (see CPA, 1989, p.65; Steinack and Dieck, 1986; Dooghe, 1992);
about 64% have been rented, and around 2.4% have been sub-tenanted.
According to Dooghe (1992, p.172), the majority of older Germans are
tenants, in contrast with Belgium and England. The highest proportion of
home-owners in Germany have been former self-employed persons or
farmers. Their houses are typically oversized and under-occupied. Thirty-
nine per cent of German people aged over 65 live alone, second only to
Belgium (see Steinack and Dieck, 1986, p.23; Dooghe, 1992, p.100; Eurostat,
1991b); 41.6% of the older population live in single-generation households,

and almost 90% live in private households; only 14% live with their offspring. Their houses are often among the oldest properties, more difficult to maintain and heat (Dooghe, 1992).

In an earlier but more detailed commentary, Steinack and Dieck (1986, pp.23–38) describe at length the housing arrangements of the older German population. In this, they include the homeless and vagrant old people. In keeping with other studies, it is clear that the older the person, the older the household facilities and the fewer such facilities. As is the case throughout most of Europe, almost half of the oldest people live in the oldest housing (see Steinack and Dieck, 1986, p.63). At the height of the FRG's prosperity, approximately 44.3% houses of the older population were without central heating, although the nation as a whole had the second-highest proportion of houses with central heating amongst the 12 EU countries (see Eurostat, 1991b, p.121). In contemporary Germany, approximately 6% of the older population have no inside WC, although the nation as a whole has the third-highest proportion of houses with an internal WC amongst the EU countries; approximately 14.3% have no bath, although the nation as a whole has the third-highest proportion of houses with a bathroom or shower on the premises in the EU (Eurostat, 1991b, p.121). Special housing for older people in Germany is under 5% of the housing provision (see Steinack and Dieck, 1986, p.68). Germany, along with Northern Ireland, Scotland, the Netherlands and Greece, has the highest percentage of rented accommodation (see Eurostat, 1991b, p.118). There has also been a steady decline in the construction of new and cheaper housing in Germany.

Some older people are homeless, but the numbers are unknown. By the 'homeless' Steinack and Dieck (1986) mean those who live temporarily in a communal hostel; those who live in rundown accommodation, and those who are about to lose their homes. The German single homeless are given vouchers when seeking shelter in hostels. Many are prematurely aged at 50, due to over-exposure to the extremes of cold and the heat, and poor diets. The number of homeless people over 60 is increasing (Steinack and Dieck, 1986, pp.38–40). On the basis of a survey cited by Steinack and Dieck (1986, pp.70–2), approximately 22,100 older people in the western *Länder* live in cold, dingy shelters. They constitute as much as a third of the total number of people using the shelters. In addition, hundreds of older men are living in cheap lodging houses. Most of them cannot move out into residential care because the managers are afraid of their socially unacceptable behaviour, and because of exaggerated fears of the effect upon the other residents. In any case, the financial rates in the residential and nursing sectors are far higher than those in the shelters and other cheap lodging houses. Many prefer to spend their money on other things. Alcohol abuse amongst older males is a matter of grave concern for the social and health services.

Some vagrants refuse to use the hostels – they generally sleep in the open, sometimes using the shelters or tents provided for them on colder nights. They not only have a right to social assistance, but they are also offered help and counselling in most of the *Länder* in order to return to mainstream life. Many are rootless men who take up places within the special sections created for them, in the so-called 'workers' colonies' (see Steinack and Dieck, 1986, p.71). These are located mostly in the federal *Land* North Rhine Westphalia, outside the urban areas and outside the villages, out of sight. With regard to women, according to the Register of the Federal Association for Assistance to Vagrants and later evaluations in 1984, women vagrants over 60 have a disproportionately high rate of re-appearance. None the less, as elsewhere in Europe, the majority of older vagrants are men: probably 23,000 vagrant men over 50 (Steinack and Dieck, 1986). The additional poorer and more unhealthy older vagrants within the *Länder* of Eastern Germany will add significantly to their number within the 1990s.

Health care

Since the Health Reform Laws of 1989 and 1991, the provision for the well-being of older German people should have vastly improved. However, Evers and Olk (1991, p.73) are pessimistic; they state that the new measures only benefit 600,000 out of over 2 million frail older people who are in need of care. Others, like Dieck and Garms-Homolová (1991), want to give the system time before commenting. It is interesting that the proportion of annual household consumption on health services in Germany is the highest in the EU (Eurostat, 1991b, p.89). However, the percentage spent *on* the older population and the percentage spent *by* the older population are two quite different things.

Older people are covered by the statutory National Health Insurance Scheme (see CPA, 1989, p.65; Hunter, 1986, p.33: Matzat, 1989, p.3). The older population were not covered by health insurance until 1941. Today, the costs of the comprehensive health services are borne not so much by the state as by the collective German community. Almost half is paid by the contributions of the employers, and the other half by the employees. Approximately 92% are covered by the national scheme, and about 8% by private insurance schemes. GP care, specialist medical consultations, dental care, medicines and appliances, hospitalization and annual health check-ups are provided, with some cost-sharing. The major focus is upon hospital provision. Home care is regarded as a substitute for hospital care. Over a thousand insurance funds, which are voluntary bodies, manage the scheme. A care insurance scheme set up by act in 1994, was implemented in 1995. As discussed in the conclusion to this chapter, its cover is only partial.

Hospital care and medical services

Turning now to medical provision, there are 2.5 doctors (approximately 83,000) per 1,000 people, the sixth-highest ratio in the EU (Eurostat, 1991b, p.88). They are paid on a fee-for-service basis, rather than on a per capita basis as, for example, in the UK. Most are located in the urban areas, serving 33% of the population, whilst the other 67% of the population, in the rural areas, are under-provided (see Hunter, 1986, p.35).

Other health-related items demonstrate the commitment of the country to health matters. Germany has 0.6 dentists per 1,000 – ranked fourth of the EU countries, alongside Belgium and France. It has 11 hospital beds per 1,000 – third in rank order in the EU. It has 0.5 pharmacists per 1,000 inhabitants – ranked the fifth-highest in the EU (Eurostat, 1991b, p.88). Moreover, although Germany does not rank top in Europe for its medical provision, it has more users and more forms of intensive care than most European countries. For example, in terms of health expenditure as a proportion of total household expenditure, Germany spends more than ten times as much on health as the UK (Eurostat, 1991b, p.89). None the less, as stated above, the care of older people is not a top priority in Germany.

Nursing

There are two types of community nursing in Germany:

1   specialist nursing (*Behandlungspflege*), such as giving intravenous injections, dressing leg ulcers, inserting catheters, or attending to post-operative dressings;
2   basic nursing (*Grundpflege*), such as carrying out personal tasks like bathing or taking temperatures, administering medication, assisting in toiletry, etc.

Although home help (*Haushaltshilfe*) such as house cleaning, shopping and some cooking, etc., have been linked with home nursing, it will be dealt with in the next section.

Up to 1995, insurance on a discretionary basis did not always pay for nursing care, whether at home or in nursing institutions. However, in Germany these provisions came under the social welfare system. Payment will be met by the welfare system if the older person cannot meet the expenses and costs. Before 1984, ailments which did not respond to treatment were referred to as 'decrepitude', and could not come under health insurance cover.

The statistics are meagre regarding the number of open care or extramural nurses. The nationwide ratio of nurses to those aged 65+ in 1986 was

2.4 per 1,000. Today it varies in the cities, where there are more nurses: from 1.4 per 1,000 in Düsseldorf to 5.4 per 1,000 in Berlin (Baum et al., 1989).

Nursing in Western Germany, especially of the older people, has less status than in many of the other European countries, especially in Northern and Western Europe. Turkish women, who are less concerned about the low salaries of the nursing profession in Germany, are filling the gaps left by the indigenous women seeking better pay and better career prospects in other occupations.

Nursing in Eastern Germany was provided solely by the state. There the conditions in nursing are even less attractive to the younger generation. For the older population, the nursing provision in Eastern Germany was primitive and one of the worst-resourced in Europe, and extra-mural nursing care was almost non-existent.

Home care/help

Clearly, of the two republics before reunification in October 1990, the GDR had less resources to provide care for older people. Leaper (1991, p.185) cites the 25,000 paid workers and volunteers providing domiciliary care in the FRG. Today the older people in the eastern half of Germany carry the scars of years of neglect. They will continue to do so for years to come. One of the major deficits was the lack of home care, especially rehabilitation.

Since the 1970s, both the former FRG and the GDR have had a policy of providing support to enable older people to stay in their own homes. According to recent estimates, 87% of Germans aged 75 and over prefer to live at home; 70–80% of those aged over 75 who are in bad health and living alone do not want to move from their home into an institution (see Evers and Olk, 1991; Thiede, 1988; Haag and Schneider, 1989).

The two Germanies which existed prior to reunification have left different legacies to the *Länder* authorities. With regard to the *Länder* of former Eastern Germany, extra-mural services consisting of social and health care provision are very slim and do not operate everywhere (see Backhaus-Maul and Olk, 1991). Domestic services and hot meals under the old regime were organized and delivered by *Volkssolidarität* (People's Solidarity). Industry also supported this semi-government enterprise, but the gigantic losses endured by them have cut into the once-generous subsidies.

The public expectations established in the former GDR still persist and may be accentuated as a reaction to the economic stringency facing the new Germany during the transitional period. The Health Reform Laws of 1989 and 1991 have gone some way to alleviate the burden of care on the family or members of the household, who provide the bulk of care. The Health

Insurance Reform of 1988, implemented in 1991, has brought together two services into one system: a home nursing service and a home caring service within the system of household care for older people. The extra-mural nursing provision is complex and has always been highly diversified and mixed in the FRG, which is establishing similar mixes in the former GDR. Home care service is located within a decentralized and plural infrastructure. Before distinguishing between the types of home nursing and home care generally, it is necessary to become familiar with the structure within which they are located and in which they are interrelated.

Dieck and Garms-Homolová (1991) explain the development of home care services generally and the community nursing system in particular. Protestant and Catholic parishes have traditionally provided home care in Germany, but this was originally confined to basic nursing tasks and home help. The work was vocational rather than voluntary. Today the community nursing and home care services are not run by the health authorities, but by one or other of six central associations. However, there are restrictions on the amount of time given to attending to older people and the costs entailed. Those older people who live at home, whose needs for extensive or intensive care have been measured and tested, may choose between 25 hours of professional care per month, within cost limits, and an allowance paid to the carers, also within a stipulated ceiling (see Evers and Olk, 1991, p.73; Dieck and Garms-Homolová, 1991, pp.124–7).

Cash payments for those in need of nursing care at home has been a central issue regionally. There has been a groundswell, backed by the Green Party and social carers, in support of the view that health insurance should be extended beyond the medical criteria. Benefits within the existing social welfare arrangement should not be related to material need.

Only after incessant discussions and parliamentary debate did the federal government permit a new health bill in 1988, which would allow for the incorporation of service provision for older chronically ill people cared for within households. This did allow for payments for substitute nursing to be made when a key carer was on holiday. This Health Insurance Reform Law 1988 marked a singular concession in the hitherto inflexible health insurance system. Since 1989, very sick older people living at home could apply for substitute care for up to four weeks of respite, and a refund of money (currently up to DM 1,800), provided that the person has been receiving care at home for at least 12 months. There was a price, however: costs in other fields of care would have to be reduced. The reduction of acute hospital beds within the *Länder* had been one such part of the federal government's deal. The Green Party has been struggling, along with social carers, voluntary agencies and social gerontologists, to initiate reforms in which smaller nursing units would replace the larger nursing homes and extend the day care and other ambulant home nursing facilities. As stated later, the new

Care Insurance Scheme 1994 extended the ambit of the 1988 law.

Mental health care

Mangen (1985a) and Dieck (1986; 1990) comment upon psychiatric provision in Germany. Between 1975 and 1985 reforms of the old systems of care were carried out in 14 German regions within the FRG, inspired by the commission of inquiry known as the *Psychiatrie Enquête*. There had been dissatisfaction with the deterioration of care within institutions which housed large numbers of older mentally ill patients. These were reduced in size. Psychogeriatric units were opened in hospitals. Boarding-out schemes were established. Day clinics were set up. The Gerlsenkirken, an extra-mural clinic, provided advice and care within an open-door policy.

The 1975 programmes have been criticized because many of the older people were simply transferred to the residential and nursing home sectors, which were also large, and where the worst features of institutionalization were replicated. The day care was an improvement, but not enough care centres have been created. The extra-mural social-psychiatric services introduced for crisis intervention, offering counselling and managing admissions into hospitals etc., were poorly resourced except in the Kassel region (see Dieck, 1986, pp.160–1).

Institutional care

Firstly, with regard to conventional residential services for older people in Western Germany, as cited by Vollering and Börsch-Supan (1991, pp.137–40), there are institutions for permanent residency and for temporary residency.

With regard to permanent residency, there are five major types of provision:

- Old age homes (*Altenheim*): These provide for those older people who are unable to manage on their own. Eighty per cent of residential staff have nursing skills.
- Service apartments/housing attached to support services (*Altenwhohnheim*): These are similar to the old age homes except that for a supplementary payment they offer more privacy.
- Nursing homes (*Altenpflegeheim/Altenkranenheim*): These provide for those who need extensive care, therapy or medical attention.
- Multilevel homes for older people (*Mehrgliedrige Einrichtungen*): These are complex institutions that offer a combination of two to three of the above facilities.

- Nursing homes for demented older people (*Gerontopsychiatrisch Pflegeheim*): These are government-recognized, offering psychiatric care in addition to health care.

With regard to temporary residency, there are five types of services:

- Geriatric units in general hospitals (*Geriatrische Ableilung in Sonderkrankenhäusern*): These are specialized hospitals offering temporary medical care.
- Geriatric day or night hospitals (*Geriatrische Tages-oder Nachtkliniken*): These offer further care after hospital discharge.
- Day care nursing homes (*Tagespflegeheime/Tagesheime*): These provide daytime nursing care.
- Communication centres for older people (*Altentagesstätten/Altenbegegnungsstätten*): These provide activities and leisure programmes and tea parties etc.
- Short-run nursing homes (*Kurzzeitpflegeheim*): These offer respite care and/or rehabilitation or post-hospital care.

About 4% of the older population in Germany reside in some 6,000 permanent homes. The provision is changing: the social services have been behind the move from large post-war homes to 'boarding homes for the aged'. The homes are larger than in the UK, and usually provide a ward for the bedridden. Some are becoming mini-hospitals, as older people require more and more nursing care (see surveys conducted by the Kuratorium Deutsche Altershilfe, 1991). The biggest gap is in the inadequate provision of semi-institutional care (Schumann, 1988, p.67).

In the former GDR the situation was far worse for most older people. For the vast majority, the only option for those whose condition became too difficult for the household/family to manage was residential accommodation in the *Feierabend* (relaxation-after-hours) homes and the large residential institutions. Evers and Olk (1991, p.71) state that these homes were so cheap (because of massive state subsidies) that living in them cost older people far less than staying at home. Inevitably, this meant that many preferred to be cared for in them than at home, but their condition deteriorated in these large institutions, where they tended to vegetate.

Emerging from this bleak background is the inevitable bad health and greater debility of many older people in Eastern Germany. The costs of residential and nursing care will necessarily increase significantly in the new Germany, especially in the first decades of the twenty-first century, as a disproportionate number of older people will require care.

Personal social services

There are probably about 182,000 qualified social workers employed in West Germany working in statutory or voluntary agencies (see Leaper, 1991, p.183). As Nijkamp et al. (1991b, p.28) observe, there are about 55,000 full-time employees in the social service sector who are *Zivildienstleistende* (conscientious objectors to military service), who are obliged to serve in caring agencies instead of being in the German armed forces.

The social services in Germany can only be fully understood within the context of subsidiarity. This concept was first conceived by the Vatican. Jarré (1991) cites the words of Pope Pius XI, who proposed and formulated the notion in his second encyclical, *Quadragesimo Anno* (1931). The drift of the text is that duties previously carried out by smaller communities may now be carried out by larger ones, but individuals/smaller subsidiary communities ought to be allowed to manage themselves if they have the means to do so. The state is then freed within the hierarchy of social organizations to deal with more important duties and demands.

The principle of subsidiarity is central to social theory and practice in Germany. Jarré (1991, p.212) cites the German Federal Social Assistance Act:

> The bodies responsible for social assistance shall collaborate with the public-law churches and religious communities and with the voluntary welfare associations, acknowledging in so doing their independence in the targeting and execution of their functions. Collaboration shall be so directed that social assistance and the activities of voluntary welfare effectively complement one another for the benefit of those seeking assistance. The social assistance bodies shall support the voluntary welfare associations appropriately in their activities in the field of social assistance. If assistance in individual cases is ensured by voluntary welfare, the social assistance bodies shall refrain from implementing their own measures: this does not apply to the provision of cash benefits.

Clients cannot be assisted by the social services unless they have first tried all other means of support and social care, beginning with their families, the Churches, the voluntary welfare organizations and, where they exist, the co-operatives and until recently the social stations (*Sozialstationen*).

Social stations provided mainly social care. They were established in the 1970s and the 1980s. Inside the former FRG are also the religious centres, providing personal social care, known as the *Evangelische Diakoniestationen* (the Protestant centres) and the *Katholische Sozialstationen* (the Catholic centres). Although the Church agencies have contracted in numbers, they still maintained the major local resources. In Stuttgart, for example, there are 8 Catholic stations and 15 Protestant ones alongside the 2 *Sozialstationen der Arbeiterwohlfahrt* (Workers' Welfare Social Stations). These agencies will be discussed further in the next section.

The stations encountered regional problems, as Dieck and Garms-Homolová (1991, p.143) have indicated. These centres have been wound down. They failed to become popular and even met with some resistance from doctors. The stations also moved from mainly providing short-term support to long-term care. The average age of the clients in Berlin is 75. In addition, the private agencies are in direct competition. Indeed, as pointed out by Brauns and Kramer (1989, p.133), private welfare agencies are consulted before laws are passed. Some persistent difficulties encountered, as listed by Dieck and Garms-Homolová (1991), are: poor service co-ordination; GPs' lack of co-operation; arbitrary allocation of care, and low standards of community care, often due to the lack of adequate training. Although these difficulties are identified in Berlin, they reflect the general weaknesses of the social stations elsewhere as they existed in the 1970s and 1980s.

The general social services offices (*Sozialamter*) are described by Brauns and Kramer (1989). Their remit includes assistance to and supervision of homes for older people; recreational and leisure facilities for them; the training of volunteers; the disbursement of welfare payments to adults; personal help for older persons in institutions; court-ordered guardianship for adults, and care of the homeless and vagrants. The social services are almost exclusively offered at local government or *Land* level. At federal level there are no government services for the older population, although it supports and finances the German Centre for Questions of Ageing.

Social work care for older people is commented upon by Schumann (1988) at greater length. However, there is relatively little to expand upon in terms of the contribution of social workers to the care of older people nationally. As Brauns and Kramer (1989, p.137) state: 'More accurate statistics are available on the different species of cattle grazing in West German pastures than on the social workers employed by the various agencies.'

The specific aims of the personal social services regarding older people are enshrined within the Federal Law of National Assistance 1961:

1   to secure the integration of older people into society;
2   to maintain independent living in an environment of their own choice as long as this is possible;
3   to establish and support suitable facilities and institutions for those older people who are incapable of maintaining an independent household.

Clearly these principles resemble those behind the recent UK strategy of community care, but antedate the Griffiths (1988) objectives by over two decades!

Voluntary care agencies and support organizations

The Poor Laws did not cater for home care services – these were left to the Churches. Other humanitarian and secular agencies emerged and established themselves which had the same concern for those in need. Out of these roots have grown the current six non-profit organizations in Germany, constituting some 6,000 voluntary organizations. These had their origins in the following six entities:

1 the *Arbeiterwohlfahrt*, the federal Workers' Welfare Association (1870);
2 the *Diakonisches Werk*, the Service Agency of the Protestant Church in Germany (1848);
3 the German Caritas Federation (1887);
4 the *Deutsches Paritätischer Wohlfahrtsverband*, the German Welfare Parity Association (1920);
5 the *Deutsches Rotes Kreuz*, the German Red Cross (1888);
6 the Central Office of the Jews in Germany.

In Western Germany there are 62,000 legally independent organizations, employing 760,000 professionals, which is more than the total number of employees in German banks, and double that of the employees in the German railways. The turnover of these voluntary welfare organizations is DM 50 billion. They are assisted by 1.5 million volunteers. About 42% of the hospital beds and 64.1% of the residential and nursing homes belong to them (see Jarré, 1991, p.216). The aggregate workforce of the associations constitutes approximately 2.8% of the total German workforce.

The situation in the former GDR, although somewhat different, is also characterized by an emphasis upon plural non-state agencies. Church organizations have formed on the one hand and secular agencies on the other, the latter merging with the pre-reunification *Volkssolidarität*. The Federal Association of Voluntary Welfare Services in Bonn, represents their interests in political and economic terms at national level. In addition to lotteries and Church collections, the Catholic and Protestant associations receive most of their income from the Church income tax.

Up to the 1970s these non-profit organizations were the major providers of an integrated health and social home care system. They mainly consisted of Protestant and Catholic local centres. Between the 1950s and 1970s their staff fell by 24%, and the number of nurses, who were mainly nuns, fell by a dramatic 41%, according to Dieck (1990). Other social organizations were developed alongside the Church agencies. The other four organizations, listed above, were beginning to take on more of the social care tasks, but the Churches still provide major services and are primarily staffed by professional and trained or qualified lay persons, in addition to their volunteers.

Leichsenring and Pruckner (1993) describe the increasing number of voluntary counselling support services, such as in Augsburg and Marburg. These assist the carers and mediate between the formal and informal domains. There are also the small private agencies which are part of 'the caring business'. These are increasing, and amount to 30% in the cities (Evers and Olk, 1991, p.87).

Informal care

Some 2 million persons aged 65+ are cared for by members of their family. Most of those who are in need of care are categorized as being in a state of 'decrepitude'. Many of these people are unsupported by the *Länder*. As stated already, the health insurance organizations/funds have refused (since 1926) to include nursing services within their remit (see Dieck and Garms-Homolová, 1991, pp.134–9), unless the services provide care for people undergoing medical treatment, and then only on a voluntary basis. Home nursing has always been recognized as a purely discretionary service of health insurance when it is used as a substitute for hospital treatment.

Within the principle of subsidiarity, the older person's sons and daughters are obliged to pay for the formal care of their parents. The insurance organizations and the medical profession have constantly pointed to the need for families to care for their own older relatives on the basis of their moral obligation (the *sittliche Verpflichtung*). The sons and daughters are means-tested. Informal care is therefore preferred, in order to avoid dipping into the family funds. However, there are some *Länder* which provide allowances purely on the basis of the older person's disability rather than upon any means-testing, such as Berlin, Rhineland-Palatine and Bremen (Dieck and Garms-Homolová, 1991, p.124).

In commenting upon the *Länder*'s measures to cope with poverty, Evers and Olk (1991, p.64) identify the 19% of those aged 65+ who live alone, without a partner, relatives or living offspring; they are particularly vulnerable. The older women in the new federal areas of Eastern Germany are worse off still. In the old GDR, women carers were fewer because of the high proportion of women in paid employment. None the less, 80–90% of the care of older people was provided by their families. The old GDR, like all Eastern Bloc countries, relied heavily upon family care. The formal macro, mezzo and micro care links did not tie up with the informal circles of care: in effect, the household/family circle of care was often a yawning hole into which all the problems facing the older population were tossed.

Although now united, the two Germanies have contrasting informal care arrangements. More is known about West Germany. With regard to West Germany, Fogarty (1986, p.12) says that its authorities and planners will have an enormous problem in coping with the needs of its ageing population by 2030. And the total dependency ratio of over-60s and under-20s to those aged 20–59 will soar to 116% in 2023 (Fogarty, 1986, p.8). Currently, the potential family support is reckoned to be adequate. On the basis of the German report of the European Foundation for the Improvement of Living and Working Conditions (see Steinack and Dieck, 1986), as cited by Fogarty, the contact between older people and their families is 'astonishingly high'. How it will remain so, given the demographic facts identified above, remains to be seen.

Steinack and Dieck (1986) state that a major concern in West Germany was the number of older people living alone. Fogarty (1986, p.15) refers to the high proportion of one-person older households, which stood as high as 43% in 1982, and leapt to 55% by 1985, most of whom were women, usually widowed. The independence of the 'young old' is very apparent; the concern is, what will happen in 20 years' time? As in all of Europe, the men fare better than the women: 60% of all men over 75 still have their wives when needing assistance, but 70% of the women who are widowed live alone and are the most vulnerable (Steinack and Dieck, 1986, p.11).

There are rural and urban demographic differences. A disproportionate number of lone older people reside in Hamburg, Bremen and Berlin, where the indiscriminate bombings of World War II decimated the populations. In the rural areas, probably around 22% of those over 65 are living in a multi-generational household. The reasons for the setting up of such households are interpreted as: loneliness after the death of a spouse; shrinking income; increasing age, and onset of chronic illness and with it the need for care (Steinack and Dieck, 1986, p.27). These multi-generational families, however, are only about 3% of all private households in urban and rural West Germany. Although the number of older people has increased, the number of inter-generational households has steadily decreased in the past ten years. Howe (1992) refers to the decrease in potential helpers in the rural areas of Germany.

Schumann (1988, pp.68–9) states that politicians and associations constantly refer to the family as being the prime German institution to care for its older citizens: 'the socially and most inconspicuous and cheapest solution'. As Jamieson and Illsley (1990, pp.14–15) point out, on the basis of Alber (1986), family responsibility is sovereign within German welfare legislation:

> Family responsibility is stated explicitly and dominates attitudes and feelings in such a way that help from outside the family is not taken for granted. Indeed, it cannot be taken for granted, because any need for care which is not a need for strictly medical treatment, is not covered by insurance.

If older people cannot pay for residential, nursing or domiciliary care, their family is often made to pay. The carers are usually spouses or family members, 80% of whom in recent years are women. Citing Steinack and Dieck (1986), Jamieson and Illsley (1990, p.15) refer to the anxiety, stress, uncertainty, pity, guilt and duty which are said to be prevalent amongst the informal familial or kinship circles of carers. There are signs that families in the western *Länder* are less close than they once were. Harding et al. (1986, p.136) observe, on the basis of their European values research findings, that 25% of West Germans state that their parents were not particularly close; 34% that they had not been close to their fathers, and 18% that they had not been close to their mothers. The authoritarian nuclear family of Germany appears to be losing its strong ties, in spite of the fact, as Todd (1985, p.97) says, that it is *the* authoritarian family of Europe. Steinack and Dieck (1986) refer to the fact that:

> the family is ceasing to function as a unit. In Germany, welfare associations, churches and public authorities since the 1960s have warned of a deficit in welfare provisions, firstly because of the demographic upturn in the number of elderly people; secondly, because of sharp decline in the number of formal carers in the traditional, mostly denominational community nursing organisations; and thirdly, the growing changes in family and household structures. (pp.82–3)

The moral imperatives identified by Kant are muted now because the German family appears to be losing its strong sense of duty. The traditional behavioural norms transmitted by the German authoritarian family (see Todd, 1985, p.64) are weakening in contemporary Germany. And at the same time, it is calculated by Steinack and Dieck (1986) that there has been a 400,000 increase in the number of older people needing *Nachbarschafthilfe* (neighbourhood help) in the past twenty years. (The German people do not use the term 'community care'.)

Probably about 2.5 million older people living at home require care. Evers and Olk (1991, p.61), on the basis of German surveys, point out that in West Germany 11.1% of those aged 65+ and 28.4% of those aged 74+ are in need of some form of care, and 15.4% are in need of extensive and intensive care. These same authors state (p.65) that 80–90% of the older population are cared for within the family in both the old Federal Republic and the German Democratic Republic (p.71). The burden has increased for the families because the numbers of potential carers are decreasing. In fact, the average household size has dropped from 4.63 members in 1871 to 2.28 in 1987 (see Evers and Olk, 1991, p.66). The majority of carers are women of the same generation as the older person in need of care. As in almost all of Europe, the carers are often mutual carers. Evers and Olk (1991, p.66) state that in West Germany, household informal care usually lasts about ten years and involves considerable emotional strain. Evers and Olk (1991, p.71) point out that the state did not directly support the carers in the old German Democratic Republic.

As the 80-year-olds increase disproportionately in Germany as a whole, the demand will necessarily create a state of crisis for the formal providers in a Germany that has one of the greatest imbalances in the care ratio. Dependence on the household and informal networks is discussed by Dieck and Garms-Homolová (1991, pp.137–8). The care provided at home by persons related to the client by blood or marriage, up to the second degree of consanguinity, is not reimbursed. They are regarded as carrying out a natural task. Reimbursement may be granted with discretion on a temporary basis in terms of travel costs and loss of earnings.

Self-help groups are beginning to play a significant role within parishes in providing parish support for the older frail people within their neighbourhoods. However, there is a particular problem surrounding both the social policy of the old FRG and the meaning of 'self-help' in Germany. The emphasis has been upon the responsibility to care for oneself. The principle is codified in the *Bundessozialhilfegesetz* (the Federal Social Assistance Act 1961), so self-help is meant in individual not collective terms. The German Non-Denominational Welfare Association assists in creating citizens' initiatives in line with the UK's use of the term 'self-help groups'. Matzat (1989) refers to the new wave of citizens' initiatives which have multiplied in Germany within the past fifteen years. Nearly 2 million social insurance pensioners are involved.

The German Association for the Support of Self-Help Groups (Deutsche Arbeitgemeinschaft Selbsthilfegruppen) emerged in the 1980s. It operates from Berlin as a national clearing house for self-help groups. Municipalities now set aside budgets to assist in the creation of local initiatives, providing facilities such as premises for meetings. The political parties are broadly in support of the self-help groups, but not all of them consider them to be of primary importance. The Christian Democrats emphasize the importance of self-responsibility; the Social Democrats focus upon the principle of solidarity, whereas the Green Party upholds the grassroots principle of collective action. The unions are afraid that the self-help groups may take over the roles and functions of the health and welfare workers.

The growing interest and investment of money in the self-help groups echoes the significance given to the idea of client and patient involvement by the World Health Organization within the Alma-Ata Declaration (1978). A centre in Hamburg is described by Estorff (1989) which is a support centre for self-help initiatives. In Baden-Württemberg the 'self-reliance' of self-help groups providing support and various initiatives for older people has been guided by Hummel (1991).

An Office for Senior Co-operatives has been set up in Stuttgart. Hummel, who heads it, has stated that hitherto the service providers have gone to the older people with answers; now they approach them with questions, seeking answers. The aim is to create vertical and horizontal networking; they interrelate in the middle ground. Linking the efforts from below with those from above means that social policy is related to everyday life, and the plural welfare groups can establish collaboration between themselves and the self-help organizations which represent the views of older people.

The emphasis is upon the fact that the third phase of life represents, for most of the older population, a quarter of their lives. They ought to take charge of their own affairs. Co-operatives enable them to do precisely that. Pilot schemes in the Waldshut, Ostfildern and Ludwigsburg districts are demonstrating the importance of co-operatives run by older people for older people – the 'active seniors'. The efforts of Hummel and his colleagues in the Stuttgart area are being studied, along with the co-operative ventures in Rhône-Alpes, Catalonia, and Lombardy.

In an attempt to destroy the negative stereotypes of the aged, the 'liberty of the late years' (*die späte Freiheit*) has been supported by the media and nationwide re-education programmes. This imaginative venture is financed by the *Länder* ministries, which have attempted to introduce positive images of retirement and many creative educational programmes. The point made by Dieck (1990, p.99) is that at the end of the day the older population are less and less represented in the municipal, *Länder* and federal parliaments. Since 1974, councils of the older people have been formed in the municipalities. On the negative side, although there are now 150 (Dieck, 1990, p.99), they do not have any voice within the formal local system of government.

Leisure pursuits and education

Since 1975, 'Studies for Seniors' have been run at German universities, notably at Dortmund University (see Norton, 1992, p.55). Many attend as associate students. The CPA (1989, p.66) cites the survey evidence that 9% of the over-55s had participated in education courses within the past five years.

Rural aspects

In common with most of the Central European countries, the rural dimension has not been a feature in studies of the care of older people. However, the University of Osnabrück *Institut für Interdisziplinäre Gerontologie* has specialized in carrying out research into the care of older people in rural areas, especially in Western Germany. Hiller (1992) describes the caring arrangements for older rural residents in Lower Saxony. There has been an increase in lone older people, many without relatives. Well-trained paramedics provide the coverage. What is needed is an affordable care insurance system. The cost of care often exceeds the pension of people in rural areas. A discount system for the poorer older people is being planned. Short-term care stations providing holistic care which are accessible and run by well-trained carers are now part of Lower Saxony's rural strategy.

Howe (1992) identifies the many diversities in European rural areas. He points out that planning is difficult because the authorities lack precise information regarding sizes of households in areas that are not only remote but which attract incoming new residents, many of whom are retired. Resources can scarcely be allocated when there is uncertainty over numbers of users/consumers. There are also local rural perceptions and biases which, for example, block the delivery of care in Lower Saxony. There is shame associated with an older person having recourse to the local rural social stations. The client's family or household are looked upon locally as 'failures'. The local stations are not in any case well-equipped because the urban stations take precedence.

Every seventh rural family in Lower Saxony is caring for an older person. The old custom of bequeathing property in exchange for care is the major insurance against isolation and ending one's days in an institution. The major concern in families is the rise in the numbers of people suffering from one of the dementias, mostly requiring 7–9 years of nursing. But the number of potential carers is decreasing. More resources are needed for home care. Howe sees a need for smaller municipalities in German rural areas. It is also imperative to shift money from the nursing institutions to community care.

The rural service infrastructures are not up to national standards. The lack of transport is a major problem, affecting frail older people more than any other group. Much of what Howe identifies as problematic in attempting to care for older people in rural Germany reflects the same problems in rural parts of the UK.

Conclusion

In concluding this chapter on Germany, it is clear that the richest country at the centre of Europe's 'golden egg' has not provided the older population in many of the *Länder* with a golden retirement. This country with the lowest birth rate in Europe faces an unknown future, with one of the worst caring ratios in the developed world. Neighbourhood care and support (*Nachbarschafthilfe*) is dependent on commitment, but also upon the ratio of caring persons to frail older people.

There is concern nationally about the numbers of older, depressed single women. Although, according to Pritchard (1992, p.132), the number of reported suicides of older people of both genders has fallen in West Germany, none the less, the proportion in Germany remains the fifth-highest in Europe.

The German system is federal and essentially polycephalic. The delivery of services is decided by 'closer-to-people' welfare systems. These are part of an integrated welfare partnership, as laid down in the German Federal Social Assistance Act 1961, with its emphasis upon 'collaboration'. The 'German Social Code', as described by Jarré (1991, p.212), with its emphasis upon 'effective complementarity', pre-dated the Griffiths (1988) UK emphasis upon joint multidisciplinary action. Germany's community social work strategies, its pluralist policies, its introduction of caring co-operatives and the 'bottom up' delivery of services, backed by the policy of subsidiarity, indicate how the triangle of care in Germany is essentially asynchronic. It remains to be seen how the older people of the eastern *Länder* will fare, and how the government will meet the additional costs of caring for older people that reunification has visited upon the new Germany.

One attempt by the government to meet rising costs has been implemented in 1995. This consists of the Care Insurance Scheme 1994 (*Pflegeversicherung*). It aims to provide cover for home care and residential costs. The former was implemented on 1 April 1995 and the latter on 1 July 1995. Contributions are compulsory for all employees over a basic minimum and their employers. However, the scheme provides only for those in 'considerable need for care', which requires strict assessment, and even when granted does not cover the full costs (Beck, 1995, p.2). Those under the minimum wage and those who were unemployed, will still need to be catered for at federal cost. Immense problems remain in spite of this new scheme, with health insurance companies having the power to decide on 'the need for care' (see Ruppel and King, 1995).

Part IV

Eastern Europe

This part of the study of the care of older people in Europe will start with a general view of the conditions facing older people within the Czech and Slovak Republics (the former Czechoslovakia), then in Bulgaria, followed by a commentary upon the care and the nature of contemporary support of older people in the Commonwealth of Independent States (CIS) within the transition from 'Homo sovieticus' to 'Homo democraticus'. This leads on to an overview of formal and informal care provided for older people within Poland, Hungary and Romania. There are inevitable gaps in the information required to put together a total picture of the care of older people in Eastern Europe because the countries of the former USSR and its former satellite countries are in transition, undergoing massive socio-economic changes.

As Table 6 indicates, the administration of welfare and care for older people is also in flux within the former Eastern Bloc countries. The totalitarian macro welfare systems will not be replaced immediately because other priorities must first be implemented. Laczko (1994) indicates that at times the older populations are confused and uncertain about their future within the new regimes.

15 The Czech and Slovak Republics

Demography

According to the UN (1991) and Eurostat (1991a) the life expectancy of men at age 65 in the former Czechoslovakia is the lowest (11.6 years) and for women is the second-lowest (14.8 years) in Europe. There appears to be less urgency to provide care for the older population in the Czech and Slovak states, because their proportion is relatively small, as can be deduced from Table 1. The projected increase by 2025 within the two old post-1918 federal states will probably not be significant, when taken in comparative terms. However, within the former country of Czechoslovakia there has been a 35.7% increase in those aged 60 and over between 1960 and 1985, as cited by Hartl (1991, p.28). In the Czech Republic, the retired population (women aged 55+, men aged 60+) constitute 20.3% of the population, and in the Slovak Republic they constitute 17%. Taking both women and men aged 60+, the proportion overall in the two republics is 16.6% (see Laczko, 1994, p.60). The Eurostat (1991a) data refers to the 11.3% aged 65+ in the former Czechoslovakia, which proportion will increase by about 4.9% by 2025. Of the two republics, the major increase will be more apparent in the Czech Republic.

Socio-political and administrative background

Both parts of the former Czechoslovakia lie in the heart of Europe, where the ancient major trade routes once converged upon some of the oldest settlements in Europe. The Czech people have always been in more direct communication with Western Europe. The former Czechoslovakia influenced and was influenced by approaches to health care in the West – for example, Sweden and France (Hartl, 1991, p.27). The state of Czechoslovakia created in 1918 had two quite separate human geographies: the western half, which is Bohemian, and the eastern half, which comprises Slovakia. It also has had two histories, two cultures, and now two separate political states.

In the former Czechoslovakia, Prague held the reins of the central government administration (*hlavni mesto*); it directly managed the services of seven regions (*kraje*) in the west, whereas Bratislava managed those of the three regions in the east. The state was dominated by the monocephalic, oppressive communist administration. There was a reluctant acknowledgement of the separate Slovakia which did not minimize the centrist and absolutist rulings of Prague. After liberation, the hold has been loosened, but it will necessarily take time to dismantle the former regime and create two separate monocephalic states. The regions in both parts of the former Czechoslovakia are divided into districts (*okresy*), and these in turn are divided into communes (the *obce*) within centralized structures.

In spite of unification in 1918, the western and eastern regions, as indicated above, have always been two contrasting socio-economic and cultural entities with their different spheres of life. The Czech west is more urbanized, more secular, less rural and traditional. The services also contrast, as will be demonstrated below. To date, no study is available of such differences in the context of the care of older people; the studies that do exist are generalized. Potucek (1992) is well aware of the differences between the Czech and the Slovak areas in sociological terms, when he cites the more liberal values in Bohemia and the more egalitarian ones in Slovakia. Potucek sees these values affecting the social policies in these two contrasting spheres. The Church also has greater standing in the eastern *kraje*, and has greater potential in providing social care in the *obce*.

Modern Czechoslovakia came into being after the collapse of the Austro-Hungarian Empire. The relevance of this to the life of older people will be referred to below. Two generations suffered under the oppressive communist regime before the revolution of November 1989. Potucek (1992) describes the relatively advanced Czechoslovakian social security system before World War II, as does Hartl (1991).

As far back as 1916, the old pre-communist ideas in Czechoslovakia spoke of 'welfare pluralism', referring to it as a mix between state, corporate and private organizations, and an institutional network of formal and informal care (see Hartl, 1991, p.27; Englis, 1921). However, the totalitarian regime in the aftermath of World War II brought great miseries for the population, especially older people. Hartl (1991, p.26) refers to the shabby egalitarian system as having a high degree of 'nivelisation' (levelling out), which was paternalist, restrictive and statist.

Social security: pensions and benefits

In putting together a communist pension scheme, the state officials sought to surpass the old Bismarckian insurance system adopted in Austria, Hungary and Czechoslovakia. Under the communist regime, national insurance was introduced in 1948. The full old age pension was available to men aged 60, provided they had worked for at least 25 years (CPA, 1989, p.48). For women, the retirement age ranged from 53, and included in the calculation the number of children they had. As an incentive for parents to continue working, those who carried on had two options. Firstly, they could choose to receive an enhanced pension when they retired; secondly, they could receive their pension, but add to it by working. Paid employment was a condition for a pension, except in certain cases with regard to women working at home. Chronically sick older people who required attendance at home, and those solely dependent upon the minimum and disability pension, received a pension supplement.

Laczko (1994, p.15), on the basis of research findings in the 1990s, found that 10% of the working population in the two republics had retired early, which was the highest proportion in the former Eastern Bloc countries. Many took their pension and topped it up by working; 6% of those aged 65+ were in paid employment in the Czech Republic, and 9% of these had a second job. In the Slovak Republic, in contrast, 2% had a regular job, although probably about 9% worked sporadically. In spite of the fact that the regime has changed, the pension scheme for many beneficiaries still operates along the same lines as before, but there are uncertainties as the new governments tinker with the pensions and propose updated schemes. Older people are in the throes of uncertainty, especially regarding housing.

The average pension equals about 45–50% of the average wage in both republics (see Laczko, 1994, p.23). Of course, the purchasing power is reduced by the unstable economy, resulting in a frenetic inflation rate. Women lose out because the men's pension is about 30% higher than that for women (Laczko, 1994, p.23). The old structures endure, in spite of promises of reform.

Housing

Housing in the former Czechoslovakia reached a higher standard than in most communist regimes. The supply of housing in Bohemia and Moravia was more plentiful after World War II because 3 million Germans had to move out (Adam, 1991, p.17). However, as in other Eastern European countries, the housing programmes slowed down to make way for the creation of industrial plants (Adam, 1991, p.17). However, Castle-Kanerova (1992, p.102) describes how, as far back as 1970, 98.6% of households had electricity, 76.7% had running water, 57.2% had an integral bath suite, 30.3% had gas, and 29.4% had central heating.

In the former Czechoslovakia, special housing for the older population was provided earlier than in the other Eastern European countries. By 1986, 10,000 sheltered units were established in the former Czechoslovakia (CPA, 1989, p.49). Hartl (1991) describes these as council house flats into which the older people take their own belongings. There are four forms of housing provision in the CSFR (the Czech and Slovak Federal Republics): state housing, co-operative housing, enterprise houses and houses built by individuals. Although there is a lack of adapted and special needs housing for older people, there are 500 hygiene centres, which provide baths, and 300 laundries, which are mainly designed to serve older people. These provide a community care facility for the older underclass.

Castle-Kanerova (1992, p.112) states that in the transition period from the communist welfare state to that of a market welfare system, housing is most likely to suffer. The rents are on an upward spiral and will certainly increase by more than 100% within months of the privatization of Czech and Slovak properties. The properties and dwellings confiscated by the state after 1948 may now be reclaimed, as declared by parliament in 1991. Many expatriates are now returning to move into their old properties or to demand rents from the occupiers. There is to be compensation for those who have to leave such dwellings. The move will necessarily have detrimental psychological effects upon older people, whatever the level of compensation. The terse language of a CSFR administration statement (*Zachranna Socialni Sit*, as cited by Castle-Kanerova, 1992, p.112) reflects the indifference of the new administration: 'Temporary lowering of people's legal and social guarantees is most probably an unavoidable expression of the new conditions in the sphere of housing policy.' According to Castle-Kanerova's observations, about 1.5 million people will be penalized by the increased rents. They will drop down the socio-economic scale (many of them pensioners) to a position just above the poverty line, but not low enough to receive supplementary social assistance. Many older residents will move into crowded and rundown properties, which, together with the trauma of being forced to move, will result in a further deterioration of their health.

Health care

The extent of ill health in the Czech and Slovak Republics has been commented on by the World Health Organization (see Hegyi, 1992). Ill health is more apparent amongst the men, whose life expectancy at birth is about 67.3 years, one of the lowest in industrialized societies (see CPA, 1989, p.48; Castle-Kanerova, 1992, p.101). It is necessary, wherever possible, to identify the welfare and social provision of the older populations in the separate Czech and Slovak Republics, rather than simply refer to welfare and health care in the CSFR. A comparative study of both republics is not yet available. However, Hegyi (1992) cites a study which examines the health status of 237,596 older persons in the Slovak Republic, as assessed by GPs and geriatric nurses, between 1987 and 1990 in a national research project. This large sample constitutes one-third of the older Slovak population. The cited report states that of those aged 60+, 38.1% enjoy good health and require no care. On the other hand, 30% experience multiple risks and are chronically ill, but they can cope at home because they are self-reliant, and many have someone to care for them. In addition, there are 20.3% who likewise suffer from graver chronic illnesses and are more at risk. The remainder suffer from the severest illnesses and are largely immobile, lonely and in dire need of formal care and outside support; most of these people are aged 80+.

Hegyi (1992, p.3) describes primary care in both republics. Patients are free to consult any GP. Providing the funds to run the CSFR health services is a major problem for the new regimes. Some of the health service costs are covered by the state; others are to be paid from the new, independent social fund resourced by the contributions of employers, employees, the self-employed and from individually insured persons. In the context of the care of older people, health insurance (see Castle-Kanerova, 1992, p.114) is planned to cover treatment for illness; support for the carers of a sick family member, and burial costs. There is a rigid division between the health care sector run by the Ministry of Health and the social care run by the Ministry of Labour and Social Affairs (Hegyi, 1992, p.5).

It is likely that opting out of state insurance will occur (Castle-Kanerova, 1992, p.114). Devolution of health decisions to the regions will almost certainly privatize health insurance. Health care will therefore be two-tier: those who pay their way through private schemes will profit by securing more expensive forms of care; those who cannot meet the private costs will lose out.

Reban and Bayer (1993, pp.176–8), commenting on Czech and Slovak systems, describe in general how important in the new regimes is a prior medical assessment, followed by social and psychological evaluations, and that these should be co-ordinated by a single authority. Given the rigid division, problems must occur.

Hospital care and medical services

The hospital stock is old: only eight of the hospitals have been built since 1948 (see Castle-Kanerova, 1992, p.101). There are long-term beds for older patients in the 115 hospitals within the CSFR (see Castle-Kanerova, 1992, p.101; Hegyi, 1992, p.4); 79 of these hospitals provide long-term care for older people in the Czech Republic, and 7 in the Slovak Republic. In the Slovak Republic there are 476 beds within special geriatric hospital departments, which have been set up since 1980. In the Czech Republic, hospital policy is not to make separate provision for older people, so that increasingly they are treated as patients along with the others within integrated wards. The best medical services are in the regional and district hospitals of the Czech Republic; there are 30 geriatric specialists in the Czech Republic and 49 in the Slovak Republic. In both republics, geriatricians serve in out-patient departments within the polyclinics. Most of the hospitals and sanatoria are in the west, and so too are the famous spas of Karklovy Vary, Marianske Lazne and Frantiskovy Lazne. These benefit older Czechs more than the Slovaks. The former Czechoslovakia, which had great internal variations, clearly has two contrasting populations, within which the needs of the older populations will necessarily be qualitatively different. Along with other citizens, the post-World War II generation suffered from a modernized form of slavery.

Hospital day care provides a service for 1,008 patients in the Czech Republic and only 476 in the Slovak Republic. These day care hospitals also have beds for short-term care and are therefore known as 'semi-institutional care units'.

The debate over what is 'health' and what is 'social' care of older people, as in almost all other parts of Europe, confuses the formal carers. Home care/help appears to be a largely voluntary programme, where it is available in an organized form in either of the republics. Health authorities pass the cost of home care to the social welfare services, and they in turn pass it on to the voluntary sector.

Nursing

There are 1.3 professional nurses and 6.2 voluntary nurses per 1,000 older people in the CSFR as a whole. The number of fully qualified nurses who serve older people is minimal. There are relatively few trained and qualified nurses. On the basis of the Czech and Slovak Ministries of Labour and Social Affairs, as cited by Hartl (1991, p.31), there are approximately five times as many voluntary nurses as there are professional nurses serving older people. Geriatric nurses are each responsible for a specific district and work with more than one GP. There are generally more professional health carers in the Czech Republic than in the Slovak Republic. In the former there are 2,799 professional nurses and 5,242 volunteer nurses, and in the latter there are only 384 professional nurses and 7,019 volunteer nurses (Hegyi, 1992, p.4); 3.2% of their patients are people aged 60+ in the Czech Republic, compared with 2.1% in the Slovak Republic.

Home care/help

Keeping people at home in both republics is at a premium. Approximately 4% of those aged 65+ are in receipt of home care services, but, as stated above, the provision of home help is largely left to the voluntary organizations and provided for those without families. Laczko (1994, p.45) cites recent findings which indicate that only 4.5% of those aged 65+ have some rudimentary home help in the former Czechoslovakia.

Mental health care

Little is known about mental health provision in the former Czechoslovakia, apart from the large institutional centres provided for mentally ill people.

Institutional care

As in the other communist regimes, the former Czechoslovakia provided large institutions for the care of older people; non-hospital institutional care mainly consists of nursing homes and boarding houses. These were first incorporated within a national social work strategy in the early 1970s; 0.7% of the older population are cared for in over 300 big nursing institutions catering mainly for older people in the CSFR; 254 of these nursing homes are in the Czech Republic, each with about 126 beds. In the Slovak Republic, there are 79 nursing homes, each with about 114 beds (see Hegyi, 1992, p.5). About 94% of the beds are occupied at any one time. These large nursing homes are largely occupied by women in a country where older lone women are increasing in number, becoming frailer and in greater need of nursing care. The CPA (1989, p.49) states that there are 41,121 persons in these nursing homes (see also Laczko, 1994, p.47). Boarding house care is paid for by mobile and healthy older persons. Currently, there are probably 14,000 people in these boarding houses – less than 1% of the older population. There are about 41,121 places in 329 nursing homes (CPA, 1989, p.49) – approximately 2.2% of the older population. Those aged 70+ constitute 3.5% of the residents in these homes (Hartl, 1991). The majority consist of the 'young old'; however, they are in need of residential care, and most require extra help because support can no longer be given by family or by home care services. Payment for residential care is paid out of their pension. Many have to provide a certificate providing evidence that their family cannot provide them with care.

There are 80 boarding houses in the CSFR; 51 of these are in the Czech Republic, each with about 106 beds; in the Slovak Republic there are 29 boarding houses, each with about 102 beds. About 90% of the beds are occupied at any one time. Many mentally ill and disabled persons have been incarcerated in these boarding houses along with older people who are neither mentally ill nor disabled.

The CPA (1989) states that a 10–15% growth in boarding house and nursing care had been planned in the former Czechoslovakia. This was never attained.

Personal social services

There were two major concerns in the former Czechoslovakia which continue to challenge the services within the two republics. The first is the number of lone women aged 75 and over. Within this age band, there are twice as many women as men, according to one calculation (see CPA, 1989; Hartl, 1991, p.28); 50% of men aged 80–85 are still married, whilst only 10% of women are; 77% of women aged 75–79 are widows, as are 80% of women aged 80+. The second concern is about providing support and care for a very divided older ethnic population: 63% is Czech; 31% Slovak; 4% Hungarian, and 2% Polish, German and others, including Gypsies (Borrell, 1990, p.9). Regarding the marginalized older minorities, the Gypsies suffer disproportionately from deprivation and ill health. The ethnic minorities, as elsewhere in many parts of Europe, are marginalized and stripped of political and national identity. Only in 1965 were the Gypsies included within the national census (see Castle-Kanerova, 1992, p.102).

Cafeterias offer meals to older local people, as is the case in Italy and parts of the UK. Hartl (1991, p.31) describes an impressive community care programme in which meals and personal services are provided for 30 out of every 1,000 persons aged 65+.

Voluntary care agencies and support organizations

Voluntary workers are few and far between in spite of the pre-communist tradition of voluntarism. The Bolshevik *subbotniks* (brigades) had taken over to provide planned care, which disenchanted the formal carers. Volunteers are usually paid. The Slovaks are more committed to voluntary work than their fellow citizens in the western regions (see Potucek, 1992, p.3). Social workers in the CSFR hardly feature in the research reports.

Informal care

The vast majority of the older population are cared for by their families (Hartl, 1991, p.32). Throughout the transition from the *ancien régime* of communist socialism to the new pluralism, the conservative protagonists of the family have asserted themselves. The revival of 'primary mutual solidarity' and 'family sovereignty' is referred to by Castle-Kanerova (1992, p.115). In effect, within this domestic welfare idyll, CSFR women are to be the front-line social workers in a conservative regime, where 'virtue' and 'merit' are the moral substitutes for adequate care allowances. A social wage has been designed for women caring for their children under 3 years of age, and health insurance is to cover caring for the sick at home, but not for the social care of older, frail parents.

A lower marriage age and a higher life expectancy, plus a shortage of housing, have resulted in an increase in four-generation families; 80% of the older population are cared for by offspring (Hartl, 1991, p.29). The lone widowed, divorced and other lone older people constitute the majority of those who have to turn to neighbours, voluntary agencies or the public services.

The home care services provide approximately 4% of the frailer older population with domiciliary care given by paid volunteers. Most of these people lack kinship care. Domiciliary care is often only available for those without family. It is presumed that families can cope.

Leisure pursuits and education

Whatever the gaps in personal social services for older people, and the burden carried by women carers, the 1,100 clubs for older people point to a vigorous leisure market involving them as consumers and producers (see CPA, 1989, p.49). These also provide some respite for the carers during the day. In addition, there are highly subsidized cinema and leisure tickets and public transport, and educational or tourist events, which have been of benefit to many. Older people have had to spend as much as 53% of their income on food. Telephones and washing machines are a rarity, being such expensive items (Hartl, 1991, p.32).

Rural aspects

There are no studies available that deal with the provision of care for older rural Czech and Slovak people. The Czech and Slovak countrysides are highly polluted, especially the latter, bordering as it does upon the Ukraine and Poland, with inevitable negative effects upon the health of older people. Older Czech and Slovak people may be respected, but their needs in rural areas are not on the state's current welfare agenda.

Conclusion

The Czech Republic, rather than the Slovak Republic, is likely to warrant a place within the Central European systems of care, but the reforms will take 15–20 years to be fully developed, as cited by Castle-Kanerova (1992, p.115). In the mean time, the older population are caught between the ambiguities and contradictions of the state's new westernized social care and health schemes. Monocephalic welfare structures are largely still in place. Bolting market systems and cash onto the old paternalistic system is not going to work. Hartl (1991, p.38) describes the older population as still 'feeling blue' under the bureaucratic weight of the 'rigid, sterile, autocratic, monolithic' *ancien régime*. As Table 6 indicates (see p.29), the Slovak Republic in transition tends to be polycephalic, whereas the Czech Republic in transition veers towards being polycephalic. Ringen and Wallace (1993) have explored the critical stages of transition.

Solidarity based upon family care, freedom of choice and the rights of individuals also entails an inherent contradiction, because the feminization of labour and the rights of women are flouted in placing the burden of caring for older people upon the family, where care is in effect 'care provided by women'. The incomplete, insecure markets and the lack of capital and management skills, together with the volatile political scene in the two republics, have created great uncertainties for older people. Regarded as non-producers, the pensioners could easily be overlooked in an anarchic, individualistic state system. There was the lack of money to support a sea-change in welfare provision for older people in the Czech and Slovak Republics at a time when the respective economies were concentrating upon take-off. Laczko (1994, p.52) observes:

> there is perhaps too great an expectation that social services provided by the voluntary sector will grow as the state seeks to reduce its welfare responsibilities in Eastern Central European countries. Such growth is unlikely to happen, however, without substantial further funding from the government.

The future looks bleak for millions of older people in the Czech and Slovak regions.

16 Bulgaria

Demography

Amongst the former Eastern Bloc countries, Bulgaria has the highest proportion of older people, with 12.0% of the general population aged 65+ (Eurostat, 1991a; UN, 1991). At the same time, the dependent children aged 0–14 constitute 22.3%: twice as high as the proportion of persons aged 65 and over (CPA, 1989, p.32). By the year 2025, however, the projected proportion of older people will probably increase by about 4.7%, whereas that of the children will probably decrease by about 2.3%. The average life expectancy for women at 65 is 14.6 years, the lowest in Europe, and that for men is 12.7 years, the fourth-lowest.

The country's people are largely homogeneous: 85% are Bulgarians; 9% are Turkish; 3% are Gypsy, and 3% are from other ethnic groups (Borrell, 1990, p.9; see also Laczko, 1994, p.59). The major religion is Eastern (Bulgarian) Orthodox. There are small numbers of Catholics, Protestants and Muslims.

Socio-political and administrative background

The modern state of Bulgaria dates from the Treaty of San Stefano (1878); it was part of the Ottoman Empire. The Bulgarian nationalist element is antagonistic towards the Turks. This will be relevant when considering the attitudes of the majority regarding the Turkish ethnic minorities, which particularly affect older Turkish people.

The state became a people's republic in 1947. In 1989, the old communist regime was removed and the country joined the other Eastern European countries on the road to democracy, under the leadership of Peter Mladenov. However, the country did not break with communism entirely: the Bulgarian Communist Party (BCP) simply changed its name to the Bulgarian Socialist Party. The party won the elections in December 1990, in competition with the Union of Democratic Forces Party (the UDF) and the Movement for Rights and Freedom Party (the DPS): their political agendas created a new climate and the makings of a social market economy (Deacon and Vidinova, 1992, p.77). However, the changes the Bulgarian Socialist Party introduced were forced upon it because of the pressures coming from the younger people and the urban voters in the ten major settlements. It was the rural voters and the older people who clung to the old regime and returned the party to power. There is an inter-generational political divide in Bulgaria, which cannot be overlooked when considering any shifts in the policies and caring arrangements for older Bulgarians. After initial unrest, political stalemate was resolved by the election to the presidency of Zhelyu Zhelev, the leader of the major opposition party (the UDF). The Socialist Party agreed to 'decommunization'. Application was made to the World Bank and the IMF for membership, and a co-operation agreement with the EU was put forward.

Bulgaria consists of the city commune of Sofia (*gradska obshtina*) and 28 districts (the *okruzi*). The proportion of urban territory in the country was 25% in the 1950s; about 50% in the 1970s, and about 69% in the 1980s. This rapid expansion has inevitably affected what was largely a peasant society before World War II.

Bulgarians constitute the majority and have at times made life difficult for the 800,000 Turks, and the smaller populations of Gypsies, Armenians and Jews (Economist Intelligence Unit, 1990a, p.6). The harassment and the persecution of the Turkish people in particular (described as 'Bulgarization') made life difficult during the former Zhivkov regime. Today the cause of minority people is defended by the 23 politicians of the new Movement for Rights and Freedom Party, who were elected to the Grand National Assembly in the 1990 election.

Power, ideologically, according to the constitution of 1971, resided in 'the working people in town and countryside'. However, power and administration in Sofia was sovereign, as it remains today. Under central administration in Sofia are the districts, which are subdivided into the municipalities which are in turn divided into the urban constituencies (the *rayoni*). There are also the rural constituencies (the *obshtini*).

The welfare state has penetrated the familial support system. The CPA (1989, p.32) has nothing to say about either the older population or their welfare systems in Bulgaria. This is hardly surprising, given the huge gap in both the literature and research available to UK scholars. Even well-known histories of Europe or its national development, such as that of Hobsbaum

(1990), say little about contemporary Bulgaria.

Social security: pensions and benefits

Pensions in Bulgaria have been safeguarded to date in spite of political wranglings and shifts of power. The commitment to a decent pension for all is supported in principle, but there is concern over the costs entailed in providing an inflationproofed pension. The post-communist government, in round table negotiations with the opposition parties and the trade unions, determines people's income levels and provides protection for the older population, along with other dependent groups. The Social Insurance Fund provides for the population outside paid employment. The retirement age is nominally 55 for women and 60 for men.

A new social security bill was formulated in 1991, to become law in 1993. The flexible retirement scheme determines the pension level on the basis of age and length of employment. All things being equal, the aim is to provide a pension which is at least 75% of the minimum worker's salary. The length of employment must be at least 15 years; women with more than 25 years and men with more than 30 years of employment receive a pension increment of 1.5% for each year. Men may retire at 57 if they have 30 years' employment, and women may retire at 52 after 30 years' employment. There are generous arrangements for people engaged in hazardous and at-risk occupations, who may retire at 50, provided they have at least seven years' service.

The non-market economies have broken down and the Bulgarians have been and still are dependent upon a 'shadow economy'. Rose (1991, p.16) cites a nationwide survey where 76% of Bulgarians stated that their income from their regular job was insufficient to cover their family and personal needs; the average Bulgarian requires more than one job to survive. Rose cites the Bulgarian proverb, 'If you have to live from one job, you will die.' Most of the older population have no job. Households often have to rely upon a mix of several part-time jobs. The older population are worse off because they have less opportunity to access the 'shadow economy', and the one-person household is doomed to suffer multiple deprivation. Deacon and Vidinova (1992, p.75) refer to the Communal Service Bureaux, which provide the services of women for housework.

According to Deacon and Vidinova (1992, pp.84–8), the new Bulgaria is adopting a corporatist mould within which social protection is safeguarded at the expense of economic growth. However, the post-communist corporate control of costs in practice has been more successful with regard to such primary commodities as gas, electricity, coal and butane/propane, which have not been privatized. The prices of some goods are reviewed and social bonuses are provided within a compensation scheme to safeguard incomes. The prices of such goods, particularly of food, soared by 25–30% within the first six months of 'liberalization', putting a strain upon the government's compensation scheme.

The increase in the price of bread since the introduction of the free market in post-communist Bulgaria has been as high as 600% and that of food as high as 700%, the highest increases of these commodities of the Eastern European countries, as demonstrated by the statistics provided by Deacon (1992c, p.169). Payments to older people inevitably constitute an expensive drain upon the state's revenues. The Social Insurance Fund needed 300 million leva to meet its payments within twelve months of the liberalization of prices and the introduction of privatization.

In July 1991 a minimum income level was introduced in order to protect the incomes and basic standards of living of dependent and socially vulnerable groups, such as older people, and children. The minimum income was to be determined centrally. As of 1 February 1991, prices have been liberalized, except those of heating and lighting. These commodities are of particular importance to the older population. In addition, the state budget protects the purchasing power of old age pensions, so there is a measure of protection for older people, provided the state can afford to compensate them by increasing the purchasing power of the pension at regular intervals. The speed of price rises is likely to overtake these periodic adjustments to pension levels.

An income support system is available to pensioners who have no savings, no adequate means of income, and cannot cope with their household expenses. Deacon and Vidinova (1992, p.88) cite the benefits in kind provided for those aged 70+ whose income falls below the basic level necessary for subsistence. They receive free lunches, electricity and heating, together with half-price water. The disabled who do not own a car are eligible for free travel through a vouchers system, and may have a spell within a sanatorium at the state's expense. Six times a year they receive social bonuses to help them purchase clothes, expensive medicines and domestic cleaning materials.

These schemes hang precariously in the balance. The future of the older population in Bulgaria depends upon the uncertain economic outcome resulting from the volatile market and the political struggle between post-communist corporatism and non-communists, led by the Union of Democratic Forces and the centre-right Podkrepa Labour Confederation, which have called for rapid liberalization and total privatization.

Housing

The provision of housing in Bulgaria is a matter of the greatest social concern. The exogamous families are contracting in the face of increasing urbanization everywhere. In particular, the older population in the rural areas are becoming more and more isolated as the younger families move to the industrial areas, as is the case in other parts of Europe, especially the Southern and Eastern European countries – but few with the same disastrous effects as in Bulgaria, which will be discussed further below.

The Economist Intelligence Unit (1990a, pp.19–20) states that the housing programme has fallen behind because of pressure on the public construction sector to complete work on productive investment projects. About 45% of the housing stock is built by the state, the rest is provided by co-operatives and private individuals. The housing needs of older people are hardly likely to be prioritized.

Health care

Bulgaria lies at the tail end of the 'long shadow' that hangs over the polluted Eastern European landscape. Although the ecology is less affected by acid rain than the other Eastern European countries, seven thermal plants south of the Balkan Mountains are strung across southern Bulgaria from west to east, interspersed with outdated chemical and metallurgical plants that poison the environment for the vulnerable older people living in the surrounding crowded urban areas. In the rural areas, 70% of the farmland is polluted by industrial waste and 85% of the river water is contaminated (see Thompson, 1991, p.45). Public health measures are non-existent.

The government prioritizes health provision, but within the gross constraints of a country slipping further and further into recession. The health services are run and administered by the Health Ministry. Health care is free, but there are prescription charges for everyone except children under 6. Private health care was abolished in 1972.

Hospital care and medical services

In the 1970s there were 180 hospitals in Bulgaria, with an impressive ratio of 1 bed to every 180 persons (Carter, 1979). By the 1980s, on the basis of data cited by Deacon and Vidinova (1992, p.72), the ratio had risen to 1 bed to every 55 persons, which was probably the best in Europe. There are 38.1 doctors per 10,000 inhabitants (Laczko, 1994, p.59). Medical social services are backed largely by an insurance scheme funded by the Central Council of Trade Unions and Co-operatives. The two best hospitals and the best health service technology are located in Sofia. Over 60% of the country's patients are catered for in the city.

Nursing

There appears to be an even spread of nurses and doctors, except in the rural areas. The Economist Intelligence Unit (1990a, p.7) stated that the numbers of nurses have almost doubled in the last two decades.

Home care/help

Home help is not provided by the state in Bulgaria. As in other Eastern European countries, home care has been left to the family, whatever the communist rhetoric about 'total state welfare provision'.

Mental health care

Caring arrangements for mentally ill older people have not been referred to in the English-language commentaries upon older Bulgarians to date. The mentally ill are regarded as 'misfits': people whose behaviour is unacceptable are thrown together into large institutions, often without medication and usually without dignity.

Institutional care

Residential and nursing homes are virtually non-existent. There are limited numbers of long-term beds in the hospitals. What passes by the name of 'nursing home care', is provided in large, Dickensian institutions providing board and little else, combining the miserable features of the rundown hospital and the uncomfortable and stigmatized old-fashioned workhouse. This contrasts with the *prophylactoria*, which are a feature of the Bulgarian health system. These are run by private enterprises and trade unions, providing accommodation and various treatments, particularly for workers.

Personal social services

Personal services did not fit into the old communist ideology. In accordance with Leninist rhetoric, the family was not recognized as part of the welfare system, and yet the reality has been that families have been burdened with the total load of care and support in Bulgaria, in common with all Eastern European countries, because personal social services constitute a neglected sector.

Voluntary care agencies and support organizations

Orthodox Church workers and volunteers constitute the backbone of care for roughly 2,155,000 older people. The older population are now more isolated than they were when Carter (1979) commented upon the rural problems facing older Bulgarians.

Informal care

In Bulgaria the family has been undergoing rapid changes which have accompanied the rapid urbanization of the country. The increased divorce rate has created rifts between parents and their offspring. Serial marriages, as elsewhere in Europe, create difficulties as to who is responsible for the care of the older relatives, so older people will increasingly need to turn to formal care.

Little more can be said about the informal care of the older population in this country. Carter (1979) refers to the exodus of the young from the rural areas to the major cities and the high numbers of older people left behind – the urban areas have doubled in size within a period of about thirty years. The paid employment of women has increased so that about 47% are not tied to the home. Consequently the Bulgarian domestic household, which was traditionally an exogamous community type, has undergone considerable social changes.

Leisure pursuits and education

Policies and social welfare programmes to provide leisure and education for older Bulgarians are not part of current developments in post-communist Bulgaria.

Rural aspects

The older rural population are the most disadvantaged, and the rural areas are badly serviced. Few rural areas are provided with local social care and health agencies. The people have to travel into the major towns and cities to consult their GPs. The housebound and bedridden depend upon the infrequent visits of medical specialists and mobile nurses. Here, the services are almost non-existent.

The communications and transport systems are poor. The Economist Intelligence Unit (1990a, p.21) states that neither rail nor road networks are being extended, apart from some work on the motorways. The road network length (36,908 km) is less than that of Greece (40,395 km), but more than that of Portugal; there are about 400 cars per 1,000 households, which is lower than the figure for Ireland (717) (Eurostat, 1991b, p.110; Economist Intelligence Unit, 1990a, p.21). Older isolated people have little contact with doctors or nurses in Bulgaria.

Approximately 10% of the villages do not have a water supply. Until fairly recently about a quarter of the houses were constructed of lath and plaster. During the period of stabilized communism, the mortality rate of the older population was higher in the rural areas than in the urban districts, as pointed out by Carter (1979, p.472). Given the considerations set out above, it is likely to remain so.

Conclusion

The Bulgarian regime has been paternalistic, restrictive and corrupt. The former communist officers at middle levels still remain. The vestiges of imposed systems take years to replace when bringing in freedom (Rose, 1991). The centre does not reach out to respond to people in social need. To get things done, the people need to reach to the centre from the *rayoni* and the *obshtini*. Do-it-yourself welfare, in the mean time (better described as 'grab-for-yourself' welfare), is the only alternative for a beleaguered people. Rose (1991, p.23) cites a survey which indicates that 34% of Bulgarians are paying to secure social services. Over 90% of the older population have neither the energy nor the means to join in the illegality and bribery of an 'uncivil society' (see Rose, 1991): two-fifths of Bulgarians, according to Rose (p.19), are involved in bribery and illegality; more than four-fifths of the older population cannot do so.

This 'uncivil' welfare and health system is located within a blighted, unhealthy environment, where public health is not addressed, and older women's life expectancy at 65 years of age is the lowest in Europe and that of men the fourth-lowest. The older Bulgarians are amongst the least protected and the most insecure people in greater Europe.

17 The Commonwealth of Independent States

Demography

The former USSR countries of Estonia, Latvia, Lithuania, Belorussia, the Ukraine, Moldavia, Georgia, Azerbaijan, Armenia and the Russian territories up to the Urals constitute the major part of the Eastern European countries, adding richly to the cosmopolitanism of Europe. Covering more than half of Europe, these countries extend across 11 time zones, comprise a sixth of the planet's earth surface and contain more than a hundred ethnic strains. More than 70% are Slavs.

It will be several years before the care of the older population in these countries has been adequately researched, not only because of the challenge of exploring the many varied systems currently serving over 25,974,000 persons aged 65 and over, but because of the political and administrative changes affecting these systems and the uncertainties overshadowing the Eastern extremities of Europe before 2025, when the projected older population will probably total 56,641,000 (CPA, 1989, p.151).

The current Russian life expectancy at birth, as presented by Ryan (1991, p.233), is 62.7 years for men and 72.7 years for women, in contrast with 70.7 years for men and 77.7 years for women in the USA, France, UK, Japan and the former Federal Republic of Germany. As shown in Table 1, only 9.6% of the population in the former USSR were aged 65 and over in the late 1980s. The projected proportion by the year 2025 will probably be 14.8% (CPA, 1989, p.151).

This chapter focuses upon the former USSR countries up to the Ural Mountains which now constitute the Commonwealth of Independent States (CIS). Geographically, the countries of Estonia, Latvia and Lithuania are Baltic, and are now free from the Moscow regime; none the less, they are included here because most of the data that is available on these countries is included under the former USSR.

The ethnic composition of the CIS countries and territories enshrines some of Europe's oldest traditions and longest-established religious groups. Formal caring systems can hardly be understood without first taking into account the divergent and contrasting cultures; at the same time, the systems can hardly begin to serve the older people without identifying the ethnic groups, nor communicate meaningfully and effectively without understanding their needs and wants and respecting their traditions and values. An appreciation of the magnitude of this task can be gained when listing the ethnic diversities within the European countries in the former USSR (Lloyd, 1990):

- Russia: 82.6% Russian; 3.6% Tartar; 2.7% Ukrainian; 1.2% Chuvash; more than a hundred other nationalities;
- Armenia: 89.7% Armenian; 5.5% Azeri; 2.3% Russian; 1.7% Kurd;
- Azerbaijan: 78.1% Azeri; 7.9% Russian; 7.9% Armenian;
- Belorussia: 79.4% Belorussian; 11.9% Russian; 4.2% Polish; 2.4% Ukrainian; 1.4% Jewish;
- Estonia: 64.7% Estonian; 27.9% Russian; 2.5% Ukrainian; 1.6% Belorussian; 1.2% Finnish;
- Georgia: 68.8% Georgian; 9.0% Armenian; 7.4% Russian; 5.1% Azeri; 3.3% Ossetian; 1.7% Abkhazian;
- Latvia: 53.7% Latvian; 32.8% Russian; 4.5% Belorussian; 2.7% Ukrainian; 2.5% Polish;
- Lithuania: 80.1% Lithuanian; 8.6% Russian; 7.7% Polish; 1.5% Belorussian;
- Moldavia: 63.9% Moldavian; 14.2% Ukrainian; 12.8% Russian; 3.5% Gagauzi; 2.0% Jewish; 2.0% Bulgarian;
- Ukraine: 73.6% Ukrainian; 21.1% Russian; 1.3% Jewish; 0.8% Belorussian; 0.6% Moldavian; 0.5% Polish.

This list conveys the enormous cultural plurality within the ten countries. Serving the needs of older people satisfactorily given these ethnic divides within a monocephalic system was inevitably a near-impossible task. In the midst of this cultural and multi-racial maelstrom, welfare systems are difficult to find. The only way forward is to deal in generalities, while picking out specific examples of welfare care.

Socio-political and administrative background

A fully comprehensive study of the social changes and problems facing the formal carers of older people in the CIS west of the Urals would be an impossible task. In addition, it is difficult to fully explore the transition from '*Homo sovieticus*' to that of '*Homo democraticus*', the massive reconstruction of welfare systems, and the accompanying adaptations and shifts within the acculturation process. Predictions regarding eventual outcomes are also virtually impossible to make. Moreover, replicating Western systems in Eastern European countries would be impracticable. Judging CIS welfare policies by the standards of the rest of Europe requires considerable circumspection. Recognition of the needs of older people, their inclusion in consultative processes, and their participation in decision-making regarding modes of care, cure and domicile must be the salient features of any set of criteria. The evidence to date implies that none of these were respected under the old regime, and that in the current transition period they are generally overlooked.

Manning (1984) provides the student of former Soviet welfare policies with a conspectus of socio-political developments divided into four periods. An understanding of past developments enables the student to identify the vestiges of older systems enduring within newer systems of care.

The first period (1917–21) was the Utopian phase. The state prioritized the introduction of public health and an education system. The former dramatically altered the lives of older people, who were crushed by extreme deprivation and illiteracy, and threatened by widespread epidemics. Currently, frustrated older people – who in the past were more fully socialized and integrated into the communist value systems – look back at the first years of the post-revolutionary period as the years of promise, when social needs received immediate attention.

The second period (1921–9) established urban programmes throughout the USSR. Economic and social developments were first established in the urban areas. Resistance to change alienated the rural people and caused immense suffering. The older population saw the collapse of their traditions. The various ethnic cultures rooted in religious belief were threatened by the rough, secular arm of an atheist state. Towards the close of this period, state pensions were introduced in 1928 for workers in the Soviet textile industry, and then later for other occupations (Adam, 1991, p.7). It was some time before there was parity between the industrial and the rural workers.

The third period (1929–57) was the period of industrialization. The supply of adequate living standards for older people and other social concerns were set aside in the rush to create an industrial society, and, after World War II, Eastern European superiority over the Western countries. Manning (1992, p.34) states with regard to this period that 'debate about the problematic nature of social conditions withered'.

The fourth period (1957–84) was the period of welfare and productivity. This era was punctuated by Khrushchev's (1957–64) revival of old socialist ideals, but in spite of a relatively brief urban housing programme, the USSR slipped back into inter-bloc rivalry and distanced itself from the people, amongst whom were the senior citizens. However, the introduction of a better pension scheme was to lay the foundation for later generations, which will be dealt with next.

Social security: pensions and benefits

Today there are wide disparities within the pension schemes of the CIS, which originate from the system within the former USSR. Men are eligible for their pension at 60 if they have at least 25 years' employment, and women are eligible at 55 with at least 20 years' employment. The pension is funded by the state, the collective farm funds and employees' contributions (CPA, 1989, p.151). The old age pension appears to be generous, being on average 60–70% of the pre-retirement salary. There is a special scheme for farmers. Approximately 16% of budget expenditure under the old regime was allocated for social insurance and security. However, the pensions have been devalued since the 1950s, as has the real value of salaries. Chapman (1991, p.38) states that in the late 1980s pensioners made up about one-fifth of the 36 million persons with monthly incomes less than 75 roubles per month – 3 roubles below the official poverty line.

Manning (1992, pp.50–1) refers to the improvements in pensions under *perestroika*. The minimum pension was upgraded to the level of the minimum wage. It was referred to by some as 'the small pension law' because it was brought forward as a short-term measure to meet the soaring costs of inflation. Many older people were experiencing 'food poverty' (see Manning, 1992, p.50).

Kampfner (1992) refers to Yeltsin's scheme aiming to turn 150 million people into a nation of shareholders. The introduction of the privatization voucher has been a premature gesture, more politically than socially significant in the early Yeltsin years. Each member of the family is provided with one voucher, which can be sold, invested or exchanged for shares. Older people are confused by the scheme, and most are more than likely to hand the voucher over to anyone who can offer anything which they cannot afford with their basic but meagre pension. Kampfner refers to wry cynicism in the streets, where the people refer to *privatisatsiya* (privatization) as *prikhvatisatsiya* (snatch and grab).

Housing

Housing provision for most of the older population has been deplorable for many years. The widespread destruction of World War II provided the state with the opportunity to rebuild houses adapted to the needs of the older and the disabled population, but older people, as 'non-producers', lacked the privileges of the active Communist Party members. The various countries which have gained their independence after the breakdown of the former USSR have inherited a stock of primitive houses, the worst of which are inhabited by older people.

The poor social conditions facing those over the age of 70 in at least five of the ten CIS countries have been examined by the Goskomtrud Research Institute; in a sample of some of the poorest older people within the Ukraine and four other countries, cited by Helgeson (1989, pp.59–60), 30% of the older population have no running water (90% in the rural areas); 58% have no hot water, bath or shower; 57% of the older urban population have no central heating, and about 87% have no telephone. In Heikkinen et al.'s report (1983, pp.63–76), these adverse conditions for older Russian people contrast with those in the more prosperous city of Kiev. However, by Western standards, the older residents in Kiev hardly surpass their counterparts in the northern, western, central and most of the southern cities: 10–20% of Kiev's older residents have no bath; 10% have no hot and cold water; approximately 72% have no automatic washing machine; 42% have no telephone; 10% have no TV set, and 20% live on upper floors without a lift. Chapman (1991) cites the findings in a typical central Russian industrial area, in which 8% of the population have no running water; 18% no hot water; 10% no sewage; 11% no central heating; 12% no gas, and 16% no baths. Older people have an unfair share in such urban deprivation.

Housing designed to suit the needs of older people is almost non-existent in the CIS. Adam (1991, pp.15–16) states that the massive destruction of World War II had not been tackled by a vigorous national rebuilding programme. Older people, faced with their ruined homes, suffered greatly due to exposure and disorientation. Basic housing is lacking, not to mention specially designed dwellings. By the early 1990s, with the exception of Kiev and St Petersburg, there was no sheltered housing in all of the old Soviet countries, even in Moscow (Gilbert, 1990). With regard to housing generally, investment has been slow and minimal in the countries within the former Soviet Union. Chapman (1991, pp.41–2) states that 22.7 million people were on housing waiting lists. Newly-married couples had to live with their parents for the first twenty years before they could move out. As much as 15% of the adult population lived in communal apartments, often in dormitories (Narodnoe, 1987, p.517; Chapman, 1991, p.42). Even in the better-provided Russian cities, older people have had few household comforts. Heikkinen et al.'s 1983 study indicates how the majority of urban older people in Kiev lived in one room only. They usually had to share other people's cooking facilities. These conditions persist for the poorer older population: a fifth of those in Kiev live on the upper floors in dilapidated buildings without lifts.

Less has been invested proportionately in housing than in Hungary, Italy, Spain, Portugal, Greece, the UK, France, Sweden, Austria and the former Federal Republic of Germany (see Deacon, 1983, p.70). This has been so in spite of the success of the small-scale housing co-operatives (the *zhakty*). However, rents have been very low, only 5–10% of income, which is clearly important. The 27th Communist Party Congress in 1986 set up a programme to provide flats for all by the year 2000. In 1988 the government decreed that housing ventures could be set up, backed by bank credit, to provide private and co-operative houses. However, the liberalization of the housing market was to benefit people with money, not the older population.

Bezrukov et al. (1993) describe the lack of hot water, gas, telephone and other amenities facing many single older people in Kiev. Half of the single people in such dwellings need constant social and medical attention.

Health care

Feschbach and Rubin (1991, p.81) cite the fact that the death rate amongst able-bodied males in the former USSR was 2.8 times the rate in the West, and that 70 million citizens are currently living in cities where the permissible level of pollutants is exceeded at least fivefold; 50 million in cities where it is exceeded tenfold or more, and 43 million in cities where it is exceeded fifteenfold or more. This is the context of health care provision in the countries of the CIS, and it has thwarted efforts to combat ill health and the morbidities of retirement for thousands of poorer older people.

Regarding the post-Khrushchev period, Deacon (1983) refers to the 'numbers game', in which the numbers of doctors, nurses, flats and the early retirement age were publicized as indicators that the former USSR was a caring society. Manning (1992, pp.36–7) indicates how residual the social welfare system was, citing Aganbegyan (1988) to demonstrate how socially deprived the people were in the period leading up to the demise of the USSR. This was particularly true in terms of health care for the older population.

The ideals were high, but the old regime was short on cash to bring them into effect. Deacon (1983, pp.70–81) describes the former Soviet health system, citing the six factors that were part and parcel of the ethics of care under the old Bolshevik regime:

1   comprehensive qualified medical care;
2   availability of health care to everyone in the population;
3   a single, unified service provided by the state;
4   a free service;
5   extensive preventative care, with the aim of creating a healthy population;

6 full workers' participation in the health service.

Ryan (1991, p.227) also refers to the universalism and equal treatment for all, as contained within Article 42 of the old Russian Constitution of 1977. However, there has never been a full realization of the former USSR's health policies. Deacon (1983) shows how the USSR spent a smaller proportion of its Gross Domestic Product on health care than the EU countries. There were signs that the Soviet system was succumbing to the marketing of health in the late 1980s. The first fee-charging hospital was established in 1987 (CPA, 1989, p.152), and charges for health care were on the cards. Ironically, under Gorbachev (see Manning, 1992, p.53), the purchaser–provider split was introduced in Russia before the UK, in April 1988. This was in Leningrad (now St Petersburg). However, the older modes of care have remained as vestiges of the Marxist health system, which will take years to replace. Environmental pollution also remains the major cause of higher mortality and morbidity rates. Also, alcohol abuse affects a disproportionate number of older people.

Hospital care and medical services

According to the pre-1989 indicators of health services, presented by Ryan (1991), the ratio of doctors to patients was, and remains, impressively high, but quality of care is another matter. On the basis of the SSSR Statistical Yearbook (1990) as cited by Ryan (1991, pp.232 and 237), there have been claims that the former USSR had more hospital beds, doctors and nurses than most of the other major industrial countries. However, the partially-trained nurses/midwives and practitioners – what have been called the 'second class doctors' – or the *feldshers* – the doctor surrogates in the rural areas – mean that in effect there has been a two-tier system; this goes back to the pre-revolutionary days, and is not likely to end now, given the switch to privatization and the lack of state educational and training funds, in an attempt to make savings following upon the widespread collapse of economies within the CIS. In the early stages of *glasnost*, the former Minister of Health, Yevgeniy Chazov, complained that 40% of medical school graduates did not know how to read an electrocardiogram and, worse still, that about half of the medical institutions did not have hot water or sewerage (Feschbach and Rubin, 1991, p.72). Clearly older people are very vulnerable in these circumstances, especially so because of increased nosocomial (in-hospital) infections in overcrowded insanitary hospitals and the inadequate supply of medicines, as described by Feschbach and Rubin (1991). A few hospital day centres exist, but mainly in Moscow (Gilbert, 1990, p.15). Personal care in hospitals is usually provided by the family on a rota basis, as in many parts of the Mediterranean countries.

The system within the former USSR was totalitarian, as Ryan (1991, p.228) shows. The medical/health service was in effect an industrial workforce subject to the specifications of the state system. Labour and health were inter-related. In fact, the state-run hospitals and clinics on factory sites and centres of employment are described by Ryan as the world's most extensive industrial health service. However, the health system has not always been 'universal'. Thirty per cent of the general hospital beds are taken up by people over 60 years of age.

Nursing

There are no established community nursing services in the CIS, although, as shall be shown below, there are a few experimental programmes involving community nurses. Pilot programmes have been set up in the Baltic republics to provide a district nurse support service for single older persons in their own homes; 15 such people have been assigned to each of the nurses, who carry out home help tasks for them. This is a departure from the policy of running a 'pension service' which provides older people with enough cash to buy care for themselves, and is in keeping with the 'Continental pattern' in Belgium, France, Luxemburg and the Netherlands.

Home care/help

As Helgeson (1989, p.61) states, home care services for older people in the former USSR were largely uneven and slow. The Red Cross and the Red Crescent offer limited domiciliary care for disabled people within the CIS. In addition, polyclinic visits provide some home cover, half of which visits are to the older population. Home care is only provided in a few major cities such as Moscow. The CPA (1989, p.152) cite the home help service organized by the Consumer Services Production Combine; however, these are expensive, have long waiting lists and offer a limited service. This situation continues to disturb the 60 million pensioners in the CIS countries (see Kravchenko, 1990).

Mental health care

A major concern in the former USSR was the misuse of the mental health hospitals to punish non-conformists.

With regard to mentally ill older people, the Ministry of Health and the social security services do not provide specialist care, except when treating some of the older clients in the psycho-neurological dispensaries within some administrative districts. 'Social administrative sisters' (*meditsinskaya sestra sotsial'noy pomoshchi*) serve mentally ill people from these out-patient clinics, which are well described by Helgeson (1989, pp.66–7). The nurses are backed by a multidisciplinary team. They are able to combine social and health care support in liaison with the 'patron', who is in effect the equivalent of a 'key worker' in the UK. They sometimes run day care facilities at these centres. In many respects there is a certain similarity between this service and that of the Italian local centres for mentally ill people, although the old-type mental hospitals remain – a dark side of the old, oppressive Soviet regime. It remains to be seen what happens to these now in the post-1991 era.

Institutional care

Since 1963 the Ministries of Health and Social Security have run the residential homes. According to Gilbert (1990), there are 350,000 older and physically disabled people living in residential homes in Moscow; 35,000 are on the waiting lists. Most of the payment comes from the residents' pensions; they are permitted 10% of it as pocket money. The general conditions for residents are a matter of great concern, especially when one considers that the best services are usually provided in Moscow.

The official provision of 3.2 beds per 1,000 people aged 65 and over compares badly with other European figures cited by Sinclair (1988a, p.248): 28.5 in England and Wales, 43 in West Germany and 112.5 in the Netherlands. Helgeson (1989, pp.62–63) describes these homes as very large, with as many as 86% bedridden residents. Gilbert (1990) indicates that there are seven large institutes in Moscow providing places for more than 600 older people. These homes are usually run for both older and physically disabled people; age is seen to be a disability in such circumstances. The Ministry of Health stipulates how much should be spent on each resident. Central control has been a salient feature here, as in almost all welfare provision within the countries of the CIS.

Gilbert (1990) describes a Moscow residential home and Bezrukov et al. (1993) describe a Kiev home. Although two rare examples, they provide a glimpse of conditions said to exist in most such institutions. In the Moscow residential home there were 300 bedridden older people, and 200 suffering from dementia. They were served by 7 doctors, 44 nurses and 96 auxiliary nurses; 45% of these posts were vacant when the home was visited by Gilbert and his colleagues in 1990. The training in gerontology lasts three months for doctors and two weeks for nurses. In the Kiev home there were 85 flats in a six-storey building with a cinema hall and a large dining room. Most of the 20 other homes in Kiev catered for 100 to 300 people.

Personal social services

In almost all of the former Soviet republics, apart from a few cities such as Moscow (Gilbert, 1990, p.15), there are no day centres, no luncheon clubs, and no meals-on-wheels. However, since May 1985, social security departments have been keeping registers of pensioners who have special needs or are at risk, so that officers may provide services and support through local catering organizations and residential homes (Helgeson, 1989, p.58). One unusual feature of the services in these countries is the fact that there are no social workers, as we understand the term. Manning (1992, p.39) refers to the quasi-social work activities carried out by the doctors within the polyclinics attached to local housing estates.

Helgeson (1989, pp.58–9) has indicated that *perestroika* has brought with it certain localized innovations following upon a heightened awareness of the disintegration of the traditional family and the significant increase in older persons living alone. The establishment of local personal social services is now on the CIS welfare agenda.

Voluntary care agencies and support organizations

The voluntary agencies in the former USSR were greatly varied, according to Helgeson (1989, p.61), consisting mainly of the Red Cross, trade union groups, societies for the blind and deaf, the Pensioners' Councils and various charities run by the Churches, which mainly serve those older people who live alone and/or have no family ties.

Informal care

Kravchenko (1990) describes the general conditions of the older people in the former USSR. There were some 60 million pensioners, mostly cared for by the family. Although the USSR has been replaced by many states, the culture of care of at least fifteen major ethnic minorities will have remained constant, whatever the colours of the national flag on their civic centres. The point to stress is that the Eastern totalitarian state had to abandon its earlier aim of the abolition of the family as a social institution. Since the early 1930s the Soviet state had to rely on the diverse types of ethnic families to provide care. Article 66 of the old USSR Constitution (1977) states that offspring are ultimately responsible for their parents' welfare. It is difficult to identify the informal care of neighbours or befriender circles in the studies available.

Helgeson (1989, p.53) refers to the three recognized institutions which provide welfare assistance: the state, the place of work and the individual family.

Distrust of the bureaucracies, government policies and all officialdom have thrown the older people of the CIS on low incomes back into the arms of the family. Deacon (1983) cites the statement by George and Manning (1980, p.33):

> The Soviet insurance scheme is clearly comprehensive but it undoubtedly leaves a variety of groups either partially covered or not covered at all. For these groups a comprehensive public assistance scheme is necessary to provide allowances according to their circumstances. No such scheme exists in the Soviet Union. Spouses, parents, children and grandchildren are legally required to support their relatives who are in financial need. Thus old and disabled people in need must be supported by their family; only if this is not possible will the state provide help.

Leisure pursuits and education

There is no source of information regarding leisure and education provision for older people in the CIS. However, educational, craft and leisure pursuits are open to all residents in the major urban areas. Inter-generational interest in the arts and general education have been stressed ideologically by the former regimes and, given the rich cultural heritage of the nations that make up the CIS, it is likely that further educational art and music courses will continue to be developed. To what extent they will be subsidized by the state is another question, especially during the current transition.

Rural aspects

It took fifty years for rural workers to gain a share in the health scheme (Adam, 1991, p.10). These health care measures and the highly centralized system are still in place and, given the need to rationalize costs associated with inputs and outputs, it is clear that the care of the 'unproductive' older population will remain a family matter and an unprioritized sector of health provision.

Today, 65% of all rural hospitals have no hot water and 17% have no running water at all.

Azarkh and Ryvkina (1985) also provide ethnographic glimpses of the three-/two-generational and single-family households in the rural areas of the Baltics, Belorussia, the Ukraine and Moldavia, amongst other areas beyond the Urals. On the whole, the rural families are larger than those in the Mediterranean states, but as with other Eastern European countries, families/households are less exclusive, so that single older people are less likely to be as isolated as some of their counterparts in the Mediterranean regions.

Azarkh and Ryvkina (1985) refer to the rural studies carried out in Kalinin, Voronezh, Oriol, Penza, the Moscow provinces, Tavropol and Krasnodar. Although these authors do not specifically deal with the familial and kinship care of older people, they indicate that the traditional exogamous community families have largely broken down with the advent of collective farming and the loss of smallholdings, together with the exodus of the younger people from the rural areas to industrial centres. However, kinship ties still endure. The relatives keep in touch with the elders and the people back home. Care of the dependent members of the family is a major responsibility. The older family members play a very full role within the households, many still working fields vacated by younger workers within the kinship networks. They are influential but not oppressive members of the family circle. Under the new regimes, the villages may change and the familial solidarity may give way to narrow individualism. Azarkh and Ryvkina (1985, p.149) describe the influence of the older people in the villages, where: 'The elders in the family are influential but they do not suppress the independence and initiative of other family members, especially of the young generation.' It is hardly likely that the Russian authoritarianism of the elders in the pre-communist era will ever return.

Conclusion

Clearly, the countries which made up the former Soviet Union have inherited many health services, but of poor quality. They are also bereft of appropriate and sufficient geriatric and psychogeriatric health and nursing care services, without trained social workers and any semblance of a community care system. In effect, the family members provided care without respite or day care support. Article 66 (1977) simply stated: 'Children are obliged to care for their parents in their old age.'

Although the old totalitarian regime has been supplanted in favour of more democratic systems, populist preferences and political rhetoric do not match economic realities. The plain fact is that the new monocephalic administrative structure has become even slimmer, and controls the benefits and pensions of older people more rigorously. In the mean time, the liberalization of prices and the privatization of welfare marginalize many older people. The residual social and health services of the state cannot match the social and health care of the welfare market.

In introducing an open market system of health and welfare, the Eastern European state welfare systems have become even more restrictive and highly selective mechanisms of care. The restrictions will inevitably affect older people because the negotiation involved in establishing their rights will demand more administration and means-testing. If half of the older population in Europe do not at present claim their benefits, it is likely that in the future more and more of them will not wish to cope with the bureaucratic, highly selective, monocephalic welfare systems.

Helgeson (1989, pp.58–62) describes the traditional Slavic family and the other nationalities within the former USSR's boundaries. A place in an old people's home is only countenanced when the family can no longer cope or if there are no family or close kin to offer support. The *babushka* (grandparent) is an asset to any household within three-generation families. Housework and caring for the children are the major tasks of the grandparent, in return for care, board and lodging.

Helgeson (1989) draws upon a survey in four separate provinces and the Ukraine, where the living arrangements read like those of a Third World country – 30% of the older population in urban areas and 90% in rural areas had no running water in their homes.

As stated above, there are signs that nuclear families are increasing and the traditional three-generation families are decreasing. As they do so, the chances of being supported by kin lessen. The alternative institutions providing care for older and physically disabled people are crowded, dilapidated dwellings which are often dens of drunkenness, as cited by Helgeson (1989, p.62). Relatively few specialist care services for older people and inadequate institutions provide a highly questionable safety net for households which cannot cope. All of this augurs ill for the 60 million pensioners in the CIS countries.

18 Poland

Demography

According to the data presented in Table 1, Poland is ranked twenty-third in greater Europe in terms of its proportion of older people. By the year 2025 the projected figures suggest that Poland will probably be ranked eighteenth. However, this belies the fact that the country's older population will increase by 7.1% – amongst the highest increases in Europe. According to the UN (1991), the life expectancy of women at 65 is 16.2 years, which is ranked nineteenth in Europe; that of men at 65 is 12.5 years, which is ranked twenty-second in Europe.

Socio-political and administrative background

Poland is difficult to place within the rest of Europe because of its chequered history. It has a sad record, having been split asunder or overrun by Russia, Prussia and Austria over the centuries. For almost 150 years Poland was not an independent state (see Tryfan, 1992, p.160). Some of its past and more recent miseries have rubbed off onto the older population.

The Polish welfare and health systems have shifted from their former bureaucratic collectivist mode to that of a capitalist market economy, best described as a 'liberal welfare state' in Esping-Andersen's (1990) terms. However, this is blunted by the corporatism of Catholic welfare values and the stress upon family obligations. Subsidies for agencies and subcontracting, as well as market welfare arrangements, create a welfare system in which means-testing establishes who needs help and who can afford to pay their way within the services available. The state only intervenes when the family members can no longer support their older relatives.

The demise of the paternalistic socialist state is well described by Flakierski (1991). In addition, Piasek (1989, pp.182–4), counsellor to the Minister of Health, states that her country is facing two tasks: to enable the country to recover from the disaster of experimental socialism, and to address the socio-economic needs of two Polands – rural and urban.

As in a disaster, there are the immediate, urgent tasks. Piasek enumerates the priority groups: these are mainly the retired with low pensions; members of numerous and incomplete families, and disabled people. Hunger, cold, misery and homelessness are amongst the conditions affecting the weaker citizens of a liberated Poland attempting to deal with the transition from the communist to more capitalist systems. Piasek is concerned that, whilst the government must at first be engaged in crisis intervention, it ought not to turn its back on older people in the name of long-term planning. Providing fuel, food, paying the rent and introducing various financial concessions are all part of Poland's immediate programme of intervention. Following upon these short-term measures, there must be long-term programmes, so Piasek sets out five aims to tackle the crises facing the weaker groups in Poland's transitional society:

1   Everyone should be given equal opportunities rather than equal goods.
2   The monopoly of state health should be broken.
3   Legal and organizational conditions necessary for setting up networks of non-governmental bodies should be established.
4   Conditions for the development of local governments, responsible for local social policy and social order, should be created.
5   The durability of the Polish family should be strengthened by social policies.

Each is immediately relevant to the modes of formal care and the mixes of care for older people, but the most formidable challenge is the need to decentralize.

The communist regime stressed the need to centralize, keeping a tight rein on formal welfare services, leaving the family to provide substitute welfare and personal social services. Changes in welfare relief and building up localized services will necessarily make demands upon a Treasury already in enormous debt. Existing benefits and pensions are already expensive items of expenditure (Flakierski, 1991).

Social security: pensions and benefits

An adequate and fair income for older people is a first requirement, if they are to enjoy the opportunities available to others and have access to resources within a plural welfare system. However, the old Polish pension system is still in place. Any radical change would affect many millions and shatter their established rights and expectations. The CPA (1989, pp.123–4) comments upon the Polish pensions. The legal retirement age is 65 for men and 60 for women. Workers in teaching, railways and mining have the right to retire five years earlier. In a largely rural country, farmers and their spouses are entitled by legislation to a retirement pension. According to the Gdansk Accord (1980) and several Solidarity documents, pensions were to be raised to the level of the social minimum, and the old portfolio of pensions was to be abolished. Also, pensions were to be increased annually in line with the lowest wages. It was hoped that pensions in the 1980s would represent 75% of the average salary, but these measures were never fully carried out, as cited by Flakierski (1991, p.98). The average pension paid by the Office of Social Insurance (ZUS) constituted 58% of the average wage in 1987; 52% at the end of 1988; 48% at the close of the first quarter of 1989, and 36% after the first six months of 1989 (see Fallenbuchl, 1991, p.121). Millard (1992, p.134) describes the diminishing value of the pensions and benefits.

In reality, almost 50% of Poles aged 65 and over are in paid employment (see also Laczko, 1994, p.18). High proportions of farmers aged 70+ are working: 97% of men and 87% of women in rural Poland. In the 1980s, 40% of the older population were not living on retirement benefits and pensions. Today, many work to supplement their inadequate pensions: 18% of those aged 65+ have second jobs (Laczko, 1994, p.20). Many others do not claim their entitlement, or for one reason or another do not have a pension to draw upon in their old age. The situation is particularly bad in the rural areas. According to Hrynkiewicz et al. (1991, p.63; see also Laczko, 1994, p.23), a farmer's pension is approximately 30% lower than the average pension for any other worker. Almost 20% cannot meet the conditions for eligibility. Selby and Schechter (1982, p.139), looking to the future, stated that 'retirement income will improve in general, but landless retired farmers will lack assistance'.

In the 1990s a social assistance system does provide some support for people who are unable to meet their everyday needs and cannot cope independently. Pensions do not cover the basic needs of clothing, food, rent and health services (Hrynkiewicz et al., 1991, p.64). Older people may claim welfare support grants, but most pensioners do not apply for them. The big problem is the depreciation of the Polish pension. In 1990, the real value of pensioners' savings dropped by as much as 75%.

Subsidized food constitutes a large part of the benefits system for the general population, particularly for needy groups such as older people on low incomes. However, as Flakierski (1991, p.102) points out, the poorer groups gain less than the more affluent groups. Moreover, the marketization of food prices has not been well received by the Polish people generally, and the increased prices especially affect the older population. When the Solidarity-led Mazowiecki government reduced subsidies in January 1990, the increased costs of running a home hit older people in particular: the price of coal increased fivefold, and rent and heating increased significantly, while the pension was a fraction of the social minimum income. Attempts to establish economic stability in an erratic economy and equilibrium in the social market have been at a price: groups such as the older population have been badly hit. Flakierski describes the remedy for Poland's economy as 'strong medicine'.

Housing

The issue of decent housing for older Polish people within the deprived inner cities requires urgent attention. The more rundown the city neighbourhoods, the more old people reside there, in dilapidated houses close to polluted, industrial centres. Examples of this exist in Katowice, Lodz, Warsaw and Krakow, where concentrations of older people in such areas reach approximately 35% (see Hrynkiewicz et al., 1991, p.62).

Millard (1992, pp.123–4) describes the legacy of poor-quality housing handed down by the communist regime in Poland, pointing to the shortage. The state passed the provision of housing to the co-operatives from the 1960s onwards, and state housing ceased to be built as of 1976. On average, people were on a 24-year waiting list. The wretched accommodation conditions facing older people prompted the housing co-operatives in the 1980s to construct houses with specially designed apartments for the frail older people (see Piotrowski and Oleszczynska, 1980, p.151); there are relatively few of these. As pointed out by Fallenbuchl (1991, p.127), matters grew even worse between 1980 and 1989. The former Soviet-styled local government housing bureaux (the *kwaterunek*), in control of the housing stock and its allocation, had failed to provide a high-quality or just service for local people, and the construction industry built 22% fewer dwellings than it did in 1980 (Fallenbuchl, 1991, p.126).

Heikkinen et al.'s report (1983, p.11) provides a glimpse of urban Polish houses in the city of Bialystok, at a time when the Polish economy was stronger than at the end of the 1980s, and when great strides forward were supposed to have been achieved. Not all the houses had a water tap in their apartments; about half of those aged 75+ had neither a bath nor shower;

about 78% of those aged 60 and over had no telephone; between 93 and 96% of those aged 60 and over living above the second floor had no lift (Heikkinen et al., 1983, pp.63, 66 and 67). By 1988, many rural houses still lacked running water and indoor lavatories: even 22% of urban dwellings lacked bathrooms, as cited by Millard (1992, p.123). Those who suffered most were the older population, who occupied the oldest houses.

Since Heikkinen et al.'s Polish report (1983), the deplorable domestic conditions for older Poles have not changed. Hrynkiewicz et al. (1991, pp.62–3), commenting upon the contemporary scene, state that 15.5% of the older urban population do not have running water in their homes; 57.9% have no flushing toilet, and 84% have no phone (however, 99% have a TV). Of the older rural population, 60.1% have no running water; 80.4% no flush toilet and 99% have no phone. The accommodation of older Poles is amongst the most rundown, and usually consists of older properties, a situation facing most older Europeans, especially in Southern and Eastern Europe.

Housing in Poland not only compares badly with that of the West, but also with that of the rest of Eastern Europe. The housing stock is worse on the whole than in the former USSR, Hungary and the former Czechoslovakia, according to Adam (1991). Fallenbuchl (1991, p.127) cites statistics which indicate that in Poland in 1988 there were 284 houses per 1,000 inhabitants, compared with 417 in Austria; 446 in Denmark; 477 in the Federal Republic of Germany; 359 in Bulgaria; 366 in Hungary; 370 in Czechoslovakia, and 417 in the German Democratic Republic.

Millard (1992, pp.135–7) refers to the debate over the withdrawal of the state from the responsibility of providing and subsidizing housing. The construction of houses is privatized. Housing for older people and other disadvantaged groups continues, at least in principle, to be regarded as a state responsibility to which such groups have a right as vulnerable citizens. By 1993, full-cost charges had replaced the old subsidized housing system. In 1990, about 60% of the older population required help with interest payments in the public sector, and even more required such help in the co-operative housing sector; it is not possible for these people to meet the full costs of housing. Whatever the grand statements as to rights, arrangements for older people and deprived groups will not be in place in the foreseeable future, for several reasons. Higher building costs and the refusal of banks to extend credit to the co-operatives mean that about half a million houses have been left uncompleted – a social blot on the landscape of the new liberal welfare state. Any hopes of sheltered accommodation and special needs housing have been dashed, at least in the medium term, because the state has other priorities in its pursuit of solvency and emergence from deep recession. Improving the overall standard of houses provided by the local authorities will have to wait (see Millard, 1992, p.136).

Health care

The environment in which older Polish people live is being ravaged, not only by the emissions from the country's own outdated industrial plants, but also by pollutants from other countries in the West. Sulphur dioxide from the nearby steel mills shrouds the city of Krakow; as reported by Thompson (1991, p.44), the nearby Nowa Huta plant emits 170 tons of lead per year. Dirty high-sulphur brown coal pollutes the city air from thousands of chimneys. Cadmium-laden dust and fluorine gas from 19 factories poison the air, affecting the older residents particularly. Almost 35% of the residents in the deprived inner city areas of Katowice and Krakow are old (Hrynkiewicz et al., 1991, p.62). The Katowice mining and urban industrial development area is another example of the high levels of pollution which affect thousands of residents for miles around, where zinc, lead and coal are mined; here black dust covers the inner rooms and the furniture of thousands of homes. In Upper Silesia, high levels of cadmium and lead in the soil add to the poisoned environment. In addition, beyond the urban areas, the forests of south-west Poland are dying. It is ludicrous to attempt to examine the needs of older Europeans and the responses of welfare and health authorities without identifying the major causes for ill health in these central highly-populated areas. Seldom do gerontological studies refer to such matters, even in passing. Various other factors conspire to ravage the older population's waning state of health; in addition to the water and air pollution, overcrowded housing, unbalanced diets and depression take their toll (see Fallenbuchl, 1991, p.117). Reviewing the health of 2,440 people aged 60+, Fratczak (1989) in her analysis of the *Polish Retrospective Survey* (1988) reported that 34% of men and 43% of women claimed that their state of health was 'bad' or 'very bad'; only 18% of men and 9% of women evaluated their health as 'very good' or 'good' (see also Fratczak, 1992, p.11). According to the national censuses of 1978–88, the number of disabled people among those aged 60+ increased by 62%. The major reason was the decline in the health of the population as a whole, especially morbidity because of circulatory diseases, cancer, accidents and poisoning. The results of Dooghe and Helander's (1989) comment in their book on the survey, *Using Health Services*, demonstrated that the usage of the health services increased significantly from the age of 60. Older people used hospital services twice as much as the general population. Many of them were the victims of the alarming levels of pollution described by Millard (1992, p.125).

There is free medical care, but it is largely the Red Cross which both administers and runs care programmes and general domiciliary assistance for infirm and old people. The need is great because the proportion of dependent people over 65 amounts to about one-third of the population; 60% of those over 80 are not self-sufficient. The state cannot afford the costs involved in updating the rundown health services. Underfunding has led to under-provision and equipment failures. In 1989, health costs rose by between 40 and 60%, and within twelve months by almost 900% (see Millard, 1992, p.139).

The next major cutback was the removal of free prescriptions in September 1991, although the state did continue to subsidize the basic drugs. Rural pharmacies were being closed down and older people in remote areas were cut off from health care centres.

The plan to run a national health service funded by compulsory health insurance contributions has been shelved, at least in the medium term, on the advice of the World Bank (see Millard, 1992, p.140). The state's attempt to introduce such an insurance scheme was also unpopular, because people felt that they would only be paying for a little more of much the same. The pre-war self-governing medical councils have been re-introduced to help reduce the cumbersome bureaucracy and the tiresome centralization (see Fallenbuchl, 1991, p.121). The system has had to run on charges and private tenders. Millard (1992, p.141) states that the older population are particularly disadvantaged.

Against this dismal background, the provision of health care and ancillary services for older Polish people is certainly inadequate.

Hospital care and medical services

Although the country has 20.9 doctors per 10,000 patients (a higher ratio than in the UK, Australia or Japan), the primary care doctors have been criticized for the poor quality of their service and the low regard shown towards their older patients.

Hrynkiewicz et al. (1991) describe the geriatric beds. In the mid-1970s there were about ten geriatric centres in 49 *voivodeships* (counties). Millard (1992, p.126) refers to the extended periods of health care required by older patients because of inadequate facilities and the lack of either the appropriate equipment or medication. Clinics had such long waiting lists that the older local population had to travel miles to consult another doctor. The prescriptions were often useless because the pharmacists could not provide the medication. Even insulin was difficult to come by. The hospital specialist geriatric services and the relatively few geriatric clinics have progressively deteriorated since Selby and Schechter (1982, p.55) first identified the deficiencies in their World Health Organization study. There are 69.7 hospital beds per 10,000 inhabitants (see Laczko, 1994, p.62), and the demand for hospital beds has been one of the highest in Europe. This has been exacerbated by the lack of alternatives and any well-planned community health and social care programme. As many as 40% of hospital beds at any one time are taken up by older patients (see CPA, 1989). Brach (1989) comments:

> A free national health service was established as one of the basic principles at the time when the People's Republic of Poland was created. However, a long time ago it ceased to be free and accessible to all. To an increasing extent it depends on whom you know and who recommends you.

Nursing

As many as 9,000 older people with chronic conditions occupy beds in inappropriate units unfit to deal with their specialist nursing needs. The Polish experts reported back to Selby and Schechter (1982, p.99) that the adaptation of short-term hospitals for nursing rehabilitation was a special need. Very little was done to improve the situation. A small step in the right direction was the creation of the *hospicjum* (hospice), inspired by the Catholic Church, which was created in 1981 by the Association for Aiding the Sick. Apart from the fact that some of these are wretched centres far below World Health Organization standards, the more pressing need is for post-operative and medium-term nursing in local clinics, as well as domiciliary nursing care. In the autumn of 1989 there was a brave attempt to swing policies from institutional to domiciliary care, which ushered in a rationalization of health care, and the closure of certain hospital wards and clinics – a thing unheard of in Poland – but the lack of resources and the long process of recovery have delayed these measures.

Mental health care

Little information and analysis of current mental health provision in Poland is available in the literature, apart from the work of Tryfan (1992) and Hrynkiewicz et al. (1991). Tryfan (1992, p.167) cites the large institutions catering for the chronic psychiatric patients, many of whom are old, and mentally handicapped older people. These resemble the large institutions so prevalent in the CIS countries. The official estimated shortfall in providing places for older mentally ill people is 39%, but in reality this could be as high as 76%. There are some 93 homes for mentally ill people, providing 11,000 places, but the proportion of older people occupying them has not been made known (see Hrynkiewicz et al., 1991, p.68).

Any shift from institutional care to a community mental health programme is currently thwarted by the lack of psychogeriatricians, or their equivalent, and the lack of community mental health nurses. In addition, there are the costs entailed in providing local mental health centres.

Institutional care

Relatively fewer older people than in most other European countries have places in residential or nursing homes. Residential care and community care programmes are also poorer in quality when compared with those of other nations outside the Eastern European countries.

Hrynkiewicz et al. (1991, pp.67–9) describe six types of homes apart from those which cater for the mentally ill:

1 pensioners' homes;
2 departmental homes;
3 homes for the chronically sick;
4 homes for those with nervous system deficiencies;
5 homes for alcoholics;
6 homes for the blind.

Hrynkiewicz et al. (1991) explain these categories. The pensioners' homes cater for the retired who are not able to cope alone, but are not in need of any special social care or nursing. These were mainly built since World War II, and they are usually located in the cities. There are 109 pensioners' homes catering for 10,000 older people. There are also 175 long-term voluntary/private homes run by Caritas (see Laczko, 1994, p.47). The CPA (1989) also indicates that the waiting lists for residential care are in excess of 14,000. The residential homes usually exist in the cities (Hrynkiewicz et al., 1991, p.68), and older rural people have to be uprooted from their localities when moved into them, away from their social circles of family and friends. These meet approximately 65% of client demand for such care.

The departmental homes mainly provide for special occupational groups. In Warsaw there are the Health Care Service Employees' Homes, the Homes for Workers' Movement Veterans, and the Homes for Builders. Elsewhere there are Homes for Meritorious Teachers and Veterans' Homes.

The homes for the chronically sick are available for those people who have chronic somatic diseases and disabilities requiring nursing and constant attention; 80% of the places are taken up by women aged 60+ and men aged 65+. These meet approximately 61% of client demand for such care.

The homes for those with nervous system deficiencies are designed to provide for those suffering from chronic senile somatic disease, central or peripheral nervous system deficiency or serious handicaps. There are 82 homes providing 9,000 places. These meet approximately 25% of client demand for such care.

The homes for alcoholics cater for those suffering from alcohol dependency, but who do not require treatment. Over-dependency on alcohol is a major social problem in Poland, affecting many older people.

The homes for the blind cater for those whose impaired sight renders them incapable of living independently.

Until recently, according to the CPA (1989, p.124), there were 534 social welfare institutions providing beds/places for 59,346 older persons – approximately 1.7% of the total number of older people (3,484,000) – of which 9,464 were in 104 retirement homes and 21,949 in 164 institutions catering for persons with chronic diseases. The rest of the older people were in hospital beds or geriatric centres, which were not suitable for their nursing needs. Piotrowski and Oleszczynska (1980) described the drab, anonymous dormitories where thousands ended their days. These dormitories still exist in the larger institutions.

Older people have to pay 80% of their disability or old age pension towards care and lodging in the pensioners' homes, according to Tryfan (1992, p.167). Hrynkiewicz et al. (1991, p.69) say that care in the state social welfare homes (items 2–6 in the list above) has been free of charge, but many older people are encouraged (they say 'coaxed') to pay voluntary fees.

Within the last decade there has been a policy swing to pensioners' homes with *en suite* accommodation, and to other smaller homes. However, most older people have had to be content with large homes, because the economy cannot cope with the costs of a massive national de-institutionalization and refurbishment programme. In spite of progressive thinking, the situation in the residential sector continues to be a major problem. The emergence of some private homes and a few co-operative homes can scarcely replace the large institutions which obstinately defy the Polish health reformers. In any case, they are usually too expensive for most older Polish people.

Personal social services

The Ministry of Health and Social Welfare runs both the health and social care services. Social care for the older population is guaranteed (see Selby and Schechter, 1982, p.72). However, it is the actual services available in the final analysis which determine the care provided. These continue to be slim, although improvements have been considerable since Selby and Schechter's report.

In spite of the liberalization of Poland, the post-communist era, which is intent on creating a non-centralized system and introducing plural provision, has been hampered by splits and confusion. Hrynkiewicz et al. (1991, p.60) state that 'Agreement on social policy in Poland is extremely difficult – if at all possible.' Fallenbuchl (1991, p.114) also states that 'Poland has practically no sensible social welfare system.'

As Millard (1992, p.131) states, some of the former systems still survive in spite of the persistence of the 'myth of the market'. Agreement is made difficult because of the increase in the number of single older people, which poses enormous problems for a country which depended heavily upon informal familial care. The high costs borne by the older population during the years of war, together with the Stalinist Marxist oppression and enforced deportations, etc., have resulted in older single people, mostly women, suffering multiple loss and meagre incomes. Every fourth woman and every tenth man lives alone. The personal social services have little to offer the frail and lonely older people.

Day care services

The CPA (1989, p.124) refers to the 86 day centres in the urban areas, which for a small fee provide meals, rehabilitation and physical exercises. Approximately 90 day centres existed in 1982, and the Ministry of Health and Social Welfare managed to double the number within just five years (there were 190 in 1987), but these were largely confined to the urban areas. Between 1971 and 1987 the number of day care places rose from 150 to more than 6,000 (Hrynkiewicz et al., 1991, p.70), but these had to serve 9.4 million people aged 65 and over. These day centres are similar to day centres elsewhere in Europe. For a low fee, social and health care are provided, plus leisure activities.

Home care/help

The household care of older people is largely a familial obligation and is carried out by the voluntary sector, as will be described in the next section.

The lack of rehabilitation, and a weak community care strategy, have been of major concern. Selby and Schechter's report (1982, p.72), however, presents a more positive picture of the beginnings of a planned strategy, but the authors perceptively add: 'in fact, serious problems compromise the design'. Later, the authors note (p.93) that Polish feedback indicates that 'there are too few social workers and they are not well trained', and later (p.94) that mutual aid in the communities is poorly developed.

Voluntary care agencies and support organizations

As in many Southern European countries, male volunteers in Poland outnumber female ones. The Polish Red Cross, the Union of Pensioners and the Disabled, the Polish Social Welfare Committee (PSWC), the Union of

Disabled Veterans, the Warsaw Charity Association, the trade unions, and the Polish Scouts Association help to fill the gaps in social care provision, especially in the rural areas where there are fewer welfare workers. The PSWC deserves further comment because of its significant contribution to social care.

The PSWC is subsidized by the state. It provides a network of carers who assist the frailer older people with housekeeping. It provides home helps who assist in many ways similar to home helps in the UK, such as bringing meals from cafeterias, carrying coal from cellars and lighting fires, gardening, arranging laundry services, hygiene, escorting to the surgery or clubs, etc. Volunteers are paid by the PSWC to carry out these tasks (as they are by the Red Cross). One innovation has been the agreement for an active person, such as a student, who needs accommodation to occupy one of the rooms of the older person's apartment in exchange for social care (Hrynkiewicz et al., 1991, pp.69–70).

The Churches also provide home help at local levels, drawing mainly upon the ancillary back-up services of the women's parish groups. Until 1950 the Catholic Church led the social sector; afterwards its influence in terms of social policy and provision was diminished. Pensioners have voiced their demands for a better pension through the trade union Solidarity.

In theory the market is a major provider, but in practice it is weak, and so too is market welfare. In any case, people do not have adequate pensions, even for the basics.

Frysztacki (1991) describes Poland as a marginal country facing the tensions between the macrostructural demands of state social policy and the microstructural demands of the people in need. Like Piasek (1989), Frysztacki (1991) identifies 'localism' as the way forward for Poland; it runs between the macrostructural deliberations of the unwieldy state system and the microstructural everyday world of health and social needs. It establishes community developments (echoes of Röpke, 1943, once again). Frysztacki (1991, p.6) states that there is a widespread deterioration of trust 'in broad processes and large-scale agencies', accompanied by 'macrosocial and macroeconomic pessimism'. He fears that the village mentality will create insularity and not push forward to alleviate the condition of vulnerable people like the older population. The solidarity and partnership between local agencies and local carers is required to mediate between the macro and micro systems of welfare. He sees the parishes as one vehicle for the restructuring of destroyed social structures.

Informal care

Although politically, economically and geographically Poland lies in the East, culturally, like Romania, its families and domestic values are more akin to those of France (Todd, 1985, p.106). Poland's egalitarian nuclear family system distinguishes the nation from the authoritarian nuclear families of Central European countries, and at the same time its families contrast with the exogamous community families of other Eastern European countries. However, it has shared the totalitarian welfare experience of the other countries which came under the communist heel in the aftermath of World War II. In reaction to the oppressive and overtly atheist communist regime, Polish households have become even more Catholic, upholding the sovereignty of familial obligations. The domiciliary care undertaken by the traditional family suited the communist regimes – it constituted a money-saver.

As stated earlier, Frysztacki (1991) emphasizes the importance of 'localism' in the Poland of today, a nation which is 'still largely rural and peasantlike'; 40% of the population is rural. He then adds that families and the kinship networks are 'the fundamental integrated groups and institutions of the social structure'. Both tradition and necessity determine this. He adds (1991, p.137): 'What is decisive is the prevailing belief that family mechanisms are the most appropriate to solve particular human problems', and then refers to the 'deteriorating faith in broad processes and large-scale agencies'.

Under the communist regime the state claimed to provide a comprehensive welfare system. Older people had to work to contribute towards the family. Almost 50% of those aged 65 and over were in the labour force (see CPA, 1989, p.123). There was also a lack of suitable accommodation for older people. In 1966/67, 55% of the older population in the towns and 77% in the rural areas lived with their families (Piotrowski and Oleszczynska, 1980, p.148). Although more recently two-thirds of those aged 65+ stay at home (CPA, 1989, pp.123–4), Piotrowski and Oleszczynska (1980, p.148) refer to the modified extended family, where 74% of white-collar workers, 84% of manual workers and 92% of farmers usually have at least one offspring living within easy walking distance from their home. The authors also identify the friction that often exists when older people live with their families, and the farmwork and childminding they have to provide.

The Council for Family Affairs came into being in 1979 (Selby and Schechter, 1982, p.44) but achieved little, especially in the rural areas because of the mistrust of authority; 70% of the 60–74-year-olds require support, and 85% of those aged 75 and over are dependent. In Heikkinen et al.'s comparative international report (1983, p.42), the largest percentage of those who considered their health to be 'bad' or 'fairly bad' was among the older Polish population.

Polish households have been unable to provide sufficient care for chronically sick, disabled and mentally confused older persons. The mantle of care can only sustain a burden which is commensurate with its limited human resources. The change-over to a capitalist regime merely sustains the same system, the only difference being that the rhetoric has changed; the family continues to carry the burden of care, and older people continue to work in the fields or as childminders, as Fratczak (1992) explains on the basis of a national survey of older Polish households.

Fratczak (1989) draws most of her study from the findings of the *Polish Retrospective Survey, 1988: Life Course – Family, Occupational and Migratory Biography*. This study evaluates the living arrangements within families, household composition, inter-generational transfer, occupational activities and life satisfaction of those aged 60+; 2,440 people were included within the survey. Every fifth person in the survey was living in a single-person household, every third person being female and every twentieth male. About 60% of households consisted of a married couple. There were twice as many married males aged 60+ as married females. One-fifth of offspring were living either with a single old parent or old mother and father. The offspring were usually females. The older rural households were more extended than the urban households. The inter-generational transfer of care was significant: offspring caring for parents and parents caring for their children, and/or providing other household services.

With regard to support provided by parents, 28% provided financial support, 26% material support, and 26% took care of their grandchildren. However, the traditional support was not universal: every fourth individual from a two-person household did not support the children or the grandchildren (Fratczak, 1992, pp.9–10). There was more material support of the younger family by their older relatives in the rural than the urban areas. The support provided by the offspring was less than that provided by their older kin; however, 21% provided nursing, 15% material help and 15% housework. As is the case almost everywhere in Europe, older males were assisted more than older females. In a difficult life situation, 56% would depend upon a spouse, 67% on offspring, 24% on family or relatives and only 9% would depend upon friends or neighbours. The old regime encouraged family care in spite of the communist ideology that the state is the total provider. Today's state also relies upon informal home care.

According to Piasek (1989, p.184), the Polish regime which has taken over from the totalitarian welfare system declares that its social policy aims to create 'the conditions for the family to fulfil its final goals. Society regards the durability of the family to be an essential value. Thus social policy should aim at consolidating this value, for example by strengthening family bonds so peculiar in Poland [various generations living together, etc.].' Synak (1987, p.140) points out that the Polish family is much closer to the traditional model. However, whereas 47% shared a household with their children in 1967, only 35% did so in 1985; 18% lived alone; 42% were older lone couples;

70% of the older population were women; 61% were widows. World War II helps to explain these statistics. Every tenth man and every fourth woman lives alone (Hrynkiewicz et al., 1991, p.60).

The demography of Poland is in line with that of the UK twenty years ago, according to Synak (1987, p.141). In the north-eastern agricultural regions the households are very traditional.

The Polish 'reconstructed extended family' is cited as a relatively new phenomenon in the urban areas. This consists of migrant older people who come into the city to join their offspring. They not only assist in the caring of the children and the running of the house, but also share their savings with their offspring. They often live in crowded flats. Unlike some Eastern European families, the older relatives have little status. Synak (1987, p.142) states that every third woman and every third grandparent expresses dissatisfaction with this arrangement. His research shows that older people living with their offspring feel more lonely than those who are living separately. In fact, there is less feeling of loneliness amongst older people in the countryside, where more of them live alone than in the urban areas. Here, however, it is the lack of long-standing peer group associates which creates a social vacuum in a situation where the offspring are out at work for most of the week.

The irony is that support and care of offspring or grandchildren by older people within the urban family has increased, whereas the care of older people has decreased, according to Synak. Domestic care by spouses has increased in the past twenty years. Nursing care by neighbours and siblings has remained largely the same, as has the nursing care provided by offspring. Synak (1987, p.145), having pointed out that only 2% of the older population receive care from nurses, adds:

> To a great extent, the Polish family still fulfils the nursing function towards its old and disabled members. This results not only from scarcity of professional nurses, social services and shortage of places in hospitals and old people's homes, but also from the deep sense of moral obligation to provide family help.

Several times she refers to euthanasia, and ends with the statement, 'social policy for the old could be faced with harsh alternatives, as extreme as euthanasia, unless family members accept their duty to protect and support their older members' (p.149). Other Polish writings share the pessimism of Synak over the negativity of life for older Polish people. Amongst these critical writers are Hrynkiewicz et al. (1991). They conclude that Polish society is dominated by stereotypical negative images of older people which are perhaps amongst the worst in Europe. These authors report that they are pictured as sick, poor, badly dressed, untidy, alone, depressed, confused, empty-headed and poorly housed (p.71). They are also blamed for all that is wrong with Polish society. The older people feel that they are hard done by, which engenders mistrust, and in a spiral of self-fulfilling prophecy makes them more depressed still, and adds yet more to their negative responses.

Leisure pursuits and education

Although 88% of the older population have only basic primary education, there have been major advances in providing leisure activities and post-retirement education programmes. The Women's League organizes leisure activities in the towns and cities. The CPA (1989, p.124) cites the Senior Citizens' Clubs (the *Klub Seniora*), of which there are about 1,000 (see also Selby and Schechter, 1982, p.117). Hrynkiewicz et al. (1991, p.71) indicate that there are 1,700 such clubs. At first these clubs were managed by the National Social Welfare Committee, almost as a symbol of the centralist controls; later they were organized by local people's co-operatives.

Rural aspects

Rural deprivation is a major concern in Poland. There are 2.5 times as many older people in the rural areas as there are in the cities. The more backward the agricultural regime, the more older persons there are in that area. Hrynkiewicz et al. (1991, p.62) refer to the high proportion of the older population who are far removed from the health clinics and have no access to public transport. Those older people who have their own farms are the worst off in terms of conveniences, and are usually abandoned by the younger people who seek work in the cities; 97% of the older men and 87% of the older women continue to work on the land. The CPA (1989, p.124) refers to the rural youth who assist the older farmers with the harvest and the older women with the washing. However, once they leave school they leave the rural areas. In the rural areas only 2% of the women and 6% of the men received secondary education; in the urban areas only 20% of women and 40% of men (Hrynkiewicz et al., 1991, p.62).

Conclusion

The available evidence indicates that Poland's welfare system faces increasing demands for formal care for older people and decreasing revenues with which to fill the gaps and extend the services. The administration of welfare is in transition. The state now leans towards polycephalic structures, but vestiges of the monocephalic system drag the reformers backwards. The politicians have been slow to democratize and bring the decision-making machinery closer to the people, because money is scarce. The traditional egalitarian nuclear family, governed by its Christian conscience, is slow to pass on its responsibilities to the state. Those families who have shaken off this sense of guilt have to choose between the state and the market. The Polish state is passing the responsibilities back to them; the market costs deter most of them. Sadly, Tryfan (1992, p.161) observes that the conflict of social interests relegates the needs of the poor older population to the bottom half of the government's list of priorities. The burden of caring for older people remains where it has remained for centuries – within the mantle of familial care – but, as stated throughout this study, this mantle is becoming threadbare.

Old age in Poland is a social problem (Hrynkiewicz et al., 1991, pp.71–2). Much of the pessimism results from the post-war trauma affecting the many who suffered from multiple loss: 6 million Poles died during World War II: 220 out of every 1,000 (in the UK only 8 per 1,000 and in France only 13 per 1,000 died). In addition, older Polish people are amongst the most deprived in Europe; for many the state pension is inadequate, so that many rural people in their seventies are forced to work. Last, but not least, many older people are unhealthy because they have been forced to work in some of the worst industrial and mining conditions in Europe, in areas that are amongst the most polluted in the world, especially in Silesia, where life expectancy is generally six years shorter because of pollution (see Laczko, 1994, p.62).

19 Hungary

Demography

According to the data presented in Table 1, Hungary has only the joint twelfth-highest proportion of older people in Europe, but it has the highest proportion amongst the Eastern European countries. Judging by the projected figures presented in Table 1, the increase in this proportion will be 5.6% by 2025. The life expectancy at 65 for women (15.4 years) is ranked twenty-second in greater Europe; that of men at 65 (12.2 years) is ranked the second-lowest life span in greater Europe (UN, 1991; Eurostat, 1991a). But, of the Eastern European countries, Hungary has the highest percentage (5.5%) of persons aged 75+ (UN, 1991). There are four ethnic minorities: Roma (600,000), Germans (220,000), Slovaks (100,000) and South Slavs (100,000), as cited by Laczko (1994, p.61).

Socio-political and administrative background

After the euphoria following upon the democratic elections of April 1990, Hungary, like Poland, has had to face the sober challenge of dismantling and reconstructing its state welfare and health care infrastructure. The country is in the throes of transition. Its aim is to create an up-to-date European social market economy, based upon the right to private property and the need to establish a plural market welfare system. Needless to say, these formidable changes will call for fundamental administrative changes during the next twenty years. Pickvance (1992) describes the Hungarian developments and the trends since the post-war years. Ferge (1991, p.136) refers to the swing away from the moneyless, universal and abstract principles of collective justice to the dominance of money over needs and care.

Although the political and social welfare systems have been highly centralized, there has more recently been a tendency towards 'apparatus pluralism'. However, it is also clear that in the Kadarist period (1957–88) the classical Marxist welfare system was being gradually broken down into a more liberal system. Unlike other Eastern European countries, the change to a more liberal welfare system has not been sudden, because the reinterpretation of Hungary's economic and welfare system had been going on for some years, although mammoth changes still had to be introduced in the post-communist era. Szalai and Orosz (1992, p.149) describe the state engaged in this reformist development as 'Janus-like'.

The earlier reaction of the institutions in Hungary to the bureaucratic burden of totalitarianism has come about as a reaction to the monocephalic system in the Kadarist and post-communist era, showing itself at first in quasi-democratic forms. The tendency is towards creating welfare pluralism, but the real power lies with the bureaucratic ministerial systems, so that the formal welfare apparatus tends to hamper attempts to create a more liberal system. As a result, the vulnerable groups, such as the older population, are frustrated. Széman and Sik (1991, pp.43–4) state that the revolution from above in the communist era left no room for civil society: people were excluded from public affairs and central decision-making.

Although pluralization has been introduced, in the post-communist era the National Planning Office is still engaged in making decisions from above. It will not be easy to transfer power, nor will the restructuring of government administration be workable within the medium term. Building up a new infrastructure of care will take many years. It must be realized that about 80% of the annual Gross Domestic Product was devoted to the preservation of the state welfare system.

There is also the 'lost half' of the nation, referred to by Szalai and Orosz (1992, p.144), which consists of those who cannot survive without support from the state, and who cannot afford to pay 'gratitude money' to the underpaid state welfare workers, nurses and doctors, let alone any contributions to a state health system.

Széman and Sik (1991, p.48) point out that there are two obstacles to the restructuring of the welfare system:

1   the powers that be are becoming impatient with long-term planning;
2   the family has always been there to care, and provides a cheap alternative to formal care in keeping with the utilitarian logic within a context of scarce resources.

The challenge facing the state is enormous. As shown in Table 1, Hungary has the highest proportion of older people amongst the Eastern European countries, and will probably have more older people, proportionately, than the UK by 2025; with 12.5 million, it is currently amongst the countries with an 'old demographic structure'.

The administration has been highly centralized and monocephalic. There are three regions centred upon Budapest: the Alfold (lowland region), the Dunantui (Danube region) and the Eszak (northern region). The northern region contains the capital. The regions are subdivided into counties (*megyek*). Over 30% live within the Budapest metropolitan area and the surrounding industrial belt. It is here in the Alfold region that the major health and welfare schemes are located. The interests of the people have been voiced over the years through the 19 trade unions. Village, urban and metropolitan district councils have had increased status since the liberation of the system of government following upon the crash of the Hungarian Communist Party (Magyar Szocialista Munkaspart).

Social security: pensions and benefits

In principle there is a basic pension scheme (although it does not cover everyone) providing for 95% of the older population (for men aged 60+ and women aged 55+). The replacement rate (the ratio of average pensions to average wages) increased from 22% to 55% between 1950 and 1988 (see Ferge, 1991, p.139). A residual tight rein on benefits for poorer older people and a means-tested approach has embittered those who have retired. Ferge (1991, p.135) states that totalitarian logic has turned the welfare schemes into agents of political domination. In addition, as pointed out by Dooghe (1992, pp.157–8), pensions have not been able to keep up with inflation. He states that from 1982–7 the value of the average pension in real terms had only increased by 3%, compared with the 21% increase in the preceding five years. The pension scheme has not been inflationproof. For example, during the 1980s, when inflation was between 17 and 20%, pensions only increased by 2% (see Széman and Sik, 1991, p.49; Dooghe, 1992, p.157).

The pension has been so inadequate in Hungary that many pensioners (as elsewhere in the Eastern European countries) have had to supplement it with part-time work, as indicated by the CPA (1989, p.74); 30% of pensioners aged 60–69 and 12% of those aged 70+ have had to work to make ends meet. During the days of the communist regime, Szeben (1980, p.105) stated that 20% of the older Hungarian population were not entitled to a pension nor an allowance. In this situation, they could go to the local councils for 'complementary social aid', but it is clear from the low number registered in Hungary (approximately 22,000 per year) that many did not receive such a grant. The Churches have had to help out (see Szeben, 1980, p.106). Worse still, families caring for older relatives have received no welfare state allowances. Considerable debate exists about alternatives and about the merits of a compulsory social security system.

There are three major alternatives to the present state-dominated scheme, as presented by Szalai and Orosz (1992, p.156):

1   The retention of a state-owned scheme, but converted into a Western welfare model funded by the contributions of the state, employers and employees. This model is supported by the Federation of the Free Democrats, the major opposition party, and by the new free trade unions.
2   The addition of a network of enterprise-based insurance schemes. This suggestion is supported by the Entrepreneur's Party.
3   Replacing the present scheme with a national pension fund and health insurance fund, which is contribution-based and managed centrally. The welfare aid, support and services would be organized locally within a decentralized welfare system, funded by local and central taxation. The costs would be reduced by the involvement of charitable organizations, the voluntary non-profit agencies, co-operatives and Church organizations, operating within the various localities.

The care of the older population under the old Kadar regime was monocephalic; the new order still consists of centralized government systems. These long-established controls will be difficult and costly to shift. In addition, in a financial crisis the state is reluctant to release its hold on the welfare providers: the second alternative could be worse than the first. It is always possible that diseconomies might multiply further. The third alternative goes some of the way towards a decentralized welfare system. However, the local machinery to handle the system must first be in place, and the expertise within Western-style management structures must be established. The plight of the older Hungarians is bad enough now; since the demise of the totalitarian regime, 70% of them state that they are having serious problems in making ends meet. To be on a pension is synonymous with being poor in the estimation of many Hungarians. Dooghe (1992, p.157) says that in 1987, 26% of the older population were living under the official social minimum income level. Many seek employment, and many fail to find it. For the rest, for those with money, the local state has been turned into a purchaser of care, rather than a provider. The recent cutbacks in the Hungarian state budget have more adversely affected pensions: cash benefits are easy prey when the government is hunting for a solution, when hard-pressed for survival.

Controversy surrounds changes to the 1975 Hungarian pension scheme. The earnings-related scheme which is company-based and financed by compulsory contributions is feared by many because it is seen as helping to create a dual welfare system. For the same reason there is unease over yet another tier, consisting of voluntary insurance schemes to be contracted individually, or as part of a corporate pension scheme, created by employers/ firms and professional bodies (Ferge, 1991, p.141).

The basic universal flat-rate pension financed by taxation has gained support, but will the finances stand the strain? Ferge (1991, p.141) observes that no international comparisons have been made regarding the viability of any possible changes. There appear to be no proper financial assessments related to the Hungarian budgets, either medium- or long-term. In addition, the financing of social insurance falls heavily upon employers, being as high as 43% of the wage fund. From January 1990 a clear distinction has been made between services and benefits covered from the budget (general taxation) and contributions of employers and employees (the payroll); the former constitute social policy benefits, and the latter constitute social insurance benefits. It is clear that the muddle needs to be cleared by a further rationalization of the Hungarian pension scheme.

In the light of the present public debate about pensions, older Hungarians are confused, uncertain and fearful. They are caught in the middle, not knowing what their present pensions are really worth, whatever the promises of better pensions in the future. In addition, according to *The Book of Facts* (1990), cited by Szalai and Orosz (1992, p.157), pensions have been grossly devalued. For example, the purchasing power of the Hungarian pension between 1980 and 1987 dropped by between 25 and 30%.

Most of the older Hungarian population are poor. The vast majority of the 0.5 million Hungarians on assistance are old (Széman and Sik, 1991, p.55). Approximately 63% of the entire welfare policy funds are spent on older people, but the purchasing power of the money, as stated earlier, has been eroded. The state now turns to charities: the Churches and other non-profit organizations are expected, in the name of the old Hungarian values, to provide care when government money runs out within its restricted welfare system. Széman and Sik (1991, p.54) describe this as 'having your cake and eating it', because the government has made few changes to its centralized welfare and health system, but leaves the real provision increasingly to alternative, plural providers. The state's rights over control and decision-making remain in place; 30–40% of the listed measures for older people have not been carried out. However, there is a strong reaction against the old hegemonistic state social policy.

Széman and Sik (1991, pp.44–6) state that care for older Hungarians amounts to care for the poor. This was especially the case from 1988 onwards. On the eve of the new Constitution of 1989, 25% of the people were around or below the poverty line, particularly single older persons (see also Dooghe, 1992, p.157). Széman and Sik (1991) describe how older people began to steal essentials like milk, bread and soap; 30–40% of the sick or residential beds were occupied by older people during the winter cold spells. Hungry and angry older demonstrators began to protest outside the parliament buildings in Budapest because so many of them were suffering from multiple deprivation. To get any type of relief or assistance took months of negotiation. Even securing the installation of a telephone was an immense exercise, taking many older people 25 years (Széman and Sik, 1991).

Housing

Housing in Hungary has been designed almost exclusively to provide homes for the young; housing for older people has been at a standstill for many years. The housing stock has deteriorated and not been refurbished, especially in the rural areas. It must be noted that as much as 72% of housing under the old regime was privately owned, a surprising anachronism in a communist state. The worst housing was private, and disproportionately located in the rural areas outside the Alfold region.

Ferge (1991, p.151) says that the current housing problems are most serious and intractable. The favouritism that accompanies public housing decisions made by monocephalic corrupt regimes has made a mockery of the principles of equality. In 1960 an ambitious plan aimed to provide 1 million flats, 60% of which were to be state-owned. The flats were completed, but only 36% were supplied by the state. Older people were not the major beneficiaries of the programme, and suffered most from housing shortages in the urban areas. A family-based second economy in the rural areas contrasted with the situation in the urban areas. Applying for cheap state-owned flats became twice as difficult for older people after 1980. From the 1980s onwards the state did not provide cheap flats.

Hungarian housing policies have always been notorious for their contradictory nature or dual ethic. For example, the local authorities built houses for sale (*oroklakas*) as well as for rent (an interesting factor that might suggest that the communists were doing what Thatcher's government was later to do in putting public housing on the market). The co-operative housing sector (*szovetkezeti lakas*) is a major provider of apartment houses of no more than ten flats (*tarsashaz*). Subsidies were granted from 1971, as well as 30–35-year mortgages at low rates of interest, but chiefly to families with young children, or to couples who agreed to have children within five years; this obviously cut out the older population.

Health care

The health of older people has been badly affected during their working lives in the major industrial areas, particularly those who resided and worked in and around Budapest. The health of older people is largely determined by their earlier lifestyle, their diet and environment. The pollution may help to explain the fact that Hungarian women at 65 have the third-lowest life expectancy in Europe and men the second-lowest life expectancy at 65 (UN, 1991). Hygiene and pollution are critical factors, as is the quality of water. Half the Hungarian population is without any sewerage system; in fact, three-quarters of Budapest's sewage runs into the Danube. In addition, irresponsible dumping of toxic waste substances since the late 1960s has polluted the groundwater of much of rural Hungary: 5–6 million tons of toxic waste is produced and dumped each year in Hungary. One in ten Hungarians lack access to safe drinking water. Nitrates and phosphates coming from human sewage, fertilizers and pig farms have contaminated the groundwater and promoted the growth of algae in lakes and rivers (Thompson, 1991, p.59). Safe drinking water in plastic bags has had to be supplied to the 800 villages that have a high nitrate content in the local water. Public health authorities face a major problem. Their success will determine how healthy the future generations of older Hungarians will be.

With regard to health and social care needs in Hungary, Dooghe (1992, p.81) provides some important indicators. Although based on a rather dated 1981 morbidity survey, it was carried out when the health services and other support systems were superior to those that operate now. About 56% of the men and about 66% of the women aged 60+ suffer from some chronic disease or impairment. Their smoking habits and poor diet partly explain their ill health (Dooghe, 1992, p.82). Health education is almost non-existent. Ferge (1991, p.144), in a more updated survey of health, points out that the mortality rate in Hungary is the worst in Europe. The country has the highest percentage of heart and arterial disease and suicides. Nearly two-thirds of pensioners have some chronic illnesses, according to the CPA (1989, p.74). By any measure the situation presents an enormous challenge to the formal carers. The state's health care provision under the old regime failed the older population completely; the signs are that the present state of affairs is little better than the previous one. In addition, Szalai and Orosz (1992, pp.159–60) state that the life expectancy of males is the same as it was in the 1930s and the mortality rate of Hungarian women, contrary to that of almost all women throughout Europe, is increasing.

Szalai and Orosz (1992) describe the dual Hungarian health care system set up to deal with the ill health of the nation and to initiate healthy living habits. The National Health Plan was extended free to the entire population in 1972. However, as the amendments of the Social Security Act 1975 were later to show, some of the most vulnerable disadvantaged people could be left out of the health insurance scheme. The new regime has not brought equity to the health schemes. Szalai and Orosz (1992, p.161) criticize the health system on several counts, all of which adversely affect older people. They state that the new market-led ideas concerning health care are founded on the principle that the citizen has no absolute or universal right to health care. Extreme ideological stances to the far left are now being supplanted by others to the far right. The authors' general criticisms are worth noting, because the current design of the health care strategy will further disadvantage older people, destined to be in the 'slow lane' of health care; worse still, they might be better described as 'going backwards' as they follow the signposting of a regressive system. Perhaps the situation is best described as a 'ban' on most of the older population, because of their inability to pay the 'toll' to be on the 'main thoroughfare'.

The specific criticisms of Szalai and Orosz (1992, p.161) are worth noting. Firstly, the health system lacks a consumer voice, and there is a total lack of user participation. Secondly, the processes of bargaining and bringing about changes are unregulated. Thirdly, the health facilities that are run locally are under central control, with central plans in mind and unrelated to local needs. Fourthly, there is a dependency on state revenue, a lack of incentives and the abuse of 'gratitude money'. Fifthly, physicians are low-paid. Sixthly, the hospitals overshadow the importance of primary care. Lastly, there is a lack of user choice. Medical treatment is free under the Ministry of Social Affairs and Health. However, only certain medicines and therapeutic equipment are free for certain eligible older people.

An alternative pluralist welfare and health care model has enjoyed some support in Hungarian academic and political circles for some time (Manchin and Szelenyi, 1984). Already Ferge (1982; 1984) and Zavada (1983) had critically questioned government claims regarding the standards of Hungarian state health care. The older population shared these criticisms.

Schemes tend to be centralized. For example, Gergely (1993) describes the Gerontology Centre at the Budapest Semmelweis University of Medicine, where thousands of older people receive complete check-ups and where an advisory service directs healthy living.

The post-communist Hungarian government is facing a crisis regarding adequate health provision. Top-heavy centralization and obsession with mega-plans exacerbate the problems facing rundown local services. There is an urgent need to change, but the monocephalic structures of the past will take time and funds to replace. In the mean time, demands for more sophisticated and advanced forms of health care raise expectations. Alongside the need for better health care, more funding for social care is required to alleviate the burden carried by the families.

The government, with money in short supply, has shown a preference for adopting a market health model. A reactionary conservatism appears to have asserted itself. The ruling Democratic Forum made much of 'traditional Hungarian values' in its successful election campaign in 1990. Together with its political ally, the Smallholders' Party, it continues to uphold the conservative values of the 'one-thousand-year-old Hungarian order': a return to religion, discipline and family life (see Borrell, 1990, p.13). Deacon (1987) has shown and documented the 'marketization' of state welfare via charges and contracts, indicating a marked similarity of welfare strategies between Hungary and the UK. There is also evidence that it is the 'better-offs' in both countries who favour the market and restricted welfare. The poorer older population are a major special needs group who will never be able to pay their way within a market health care system.

To underline the chaotic and uncertain state of the health services in Hungary, Szalai and Orosz (1992, p.163) refer to a few major problems facing the Ministry of Social Insurance, much of which are of its own making. They refer to the new legislation of October 1990 which promulgated that local health facilities were now the property of the local authority. However, the follow-up legislative measures needed to implement this measure have not been put into place. Also, they refer to the Act of Properties of the Churches which grants the religious bodies the right to take over their properties which had been confiscated when the Marxist regimes were set up. Some of these are health centres and hospitals run by local government. Confusion abounds. As always, the older population are caught out, along with other vulnerable groups, not knowing who is running what, nor what the possible costs, merits and staff credentials are within the new forms of provision.

Hospital care and medical services

The CPA (1989, p.74) states that persons aged 60+ occupy every third hospital bed in Hungary. They require about 32.5% of hospital treatment in the country as a whole, and about 41.8% in Budapest. There are about 93.6 hospital beds per 10,000 and about 33.8 doctors per 10,000 inhabitants (see Laczko, 1994, p.61); 63% of men live to the age of 65, in contrast with 74.6% in England and Wales and 77.4% in Sweden (Laczko, 1994, p.35).

Alarming inequalities in health are highlighted by the fact that the expenditure on health as a proportion of GDP has for some years remained at less than 4%. Laczko (1994, p.37) refers to the 2.7% expenditure on the basis of a 1991 citation. Whereas the health systems in almost all other countries in the 1960s, outside the Eastern European countries, were updated and considerably expanded, that of Hungary remained outdated and was almost at a standstill. When the services do respond, their intervention is thwarted because they lack medication and updated equipment.

The demands upon the medical and nursing professionals have been high: 77 million visits in 1987 to out-patient departments: eight per citizen, whilst the number of hospital patients was 2.2 million (Ferge, 1991, p.144). The older population make up a significant proportion of these sick people. This is not surprising, given that for over thirty years older Hungarians have had the longest working hours in Europe, in obsolete, unhealthy and dangerous working conditions and high levels of pollution.

Szalai and Orosz (1992, p.162) refer to the health policy rhetoric. Ferge (1991, pp.142–5) also comments critically upon the state of the health system, concluding that it is in crisis. It has been under-financed for at least thirty years. From 1945 onwards, only 3–4% of GDP on average has been spent annually upon the health system. Low-paid medical staff, who are amongst the worst-paid in Europe, have had to rely upon tips, described by Ferge (1991, p.143) as 'money of gratefulness' and by Szalai and Orosz (1992, p.160) as 'gratitude money', which is common in Eastern Europe and in parts of Southern Europe.

Nursing

A major problem for the Hungarian health services is the difficulty of providing adequate and effective nursing care. As cited by the CPA (1989, p.74), a quarter of the Hungarian population aged 75+ are living alone. Laczko (1994, p.43) refers to the 22% aged 65+ who are living with their offspring. Many need to be supported and nursed. Domiciliary care is critical, yet it is in short supply. The need for special nursing skills, adapted to the needs of the older patients in hospital, is underlined by the fact that patients over 60 years of age occupy every third hospital bed, nearly two-thirds of retired Hungarians suffer from some chronic illness, and a tenth require hospital care.

Home care/help

The demands of older Hungarians for domiciliary care are great. Széman and Sik (1991, pp.50–1), on the basis of current surveys, say that probably 22% of older men and 32% of older women want home help. The healthier want 2–6 hours of help with shopping and domestic assistance per day; those partially confined to bed require 4 hours of help and care per day; and bedridden people at home need 10–14 hours per day. These high and expensive expectations could hardly be met in full by the formal services, even in developed social and health care systems. The Ministry of Health prioritizes care on the basis of criteria for delivery of services established in 1986.

In the 1980s, under the communist regime, the shortfall in providing community care was considerable. Szeben (1980, p.101) indicates that only 23,000 older Hungarians were provided with any form of domiciliary care. Approximately 70% of requests for some form of domiciliary care were not met by the authorities (see Szeben, 1980, p.103).

Mental health care

The recent publications and research projects do not provide any commentary upon the mental health needs and response of the services in Hungary. Laczko (1994, p.61) indicates that Hungary has the highest number of suicides in the world. There are no reliable statistics regarding depression and suicides amongst the older Hungarians.

Institutional care

Residential provision is in short supply (Széman and Sik, 1991, p.52); 40,000 older people reside in social welfare homes and 29,000 in Church-run institutions (see citation by Laczko, 1994, p.47). There has been an enormous increase in the past few years (contrast Széman's data with that of the CPA, 1989, p.74). Many lodge in these homes for the winter because they lack either the fuel or the heating facilities to keep warm; in the late spring they move back home. These homes are in need of repair, being older dwellings; however, the Hungarian homes are reported as providing certain worthwhile services. The staff are aware of the need to rehabilitate and to use beds as respite so as to alleviate the burden on carers. The residents are given a six-month trial period during which they may change their minds and return home or move to another residential home.

A significant proportion of the population have negative feelings about residential care. This is not surprising because the institutions tend to be large, often consisting of converted premises such as country homes, barracks, stables and mills. These only cater for an estimated 1,200 older people. One important type of residential care is to be found in the rural areas, known as 'the isolated area care centres'. These are centres for older farmers living in isolated farms, serving the residents from autumn to spring (Széman and Sik, 1991, p.49). The plight of the older population is more critical in the rural than in the urban areas, due partly to 'distance decay' and to the scant provision of services.

Personal social services

With regard to social services, there has been little change since 1968 (Dooghe, 1992). Voluntary social workers have always been paid by an honorarium. There are under 1,000 voluntary and state social workers in a country with millions of older residents. The total expenditure on social services and social security amounts to about one-third of the national budget. Restricted welfare services exist, but they are means-tested.

Of interest is the fact that social workers, along with semi-skilled paid helpers, come under the supervision of district medical officers and district nurses (CPA, 1989, p.74). The CPA (1989, p.75) states that in the early 1980s, 25% of those aged 75+ living alone and 60% of those aged 80+ were attended by social workers. The UN Hungarian Report (1982) prepared for the UN World Assembly on Ageing stated that there were 16,000 home care service workers catering for older people, of whom 14,600 were volunteers.

Diverse mixes of social care are emerging. Banfalvi (1990), the Secretary of State for Social Affairs and Health in Hungary, interrelates social and family policy. He comments on the change of the Constitution in 1989. This supports a multi-party parliamentary democracy based upon mixed ownership and a social market economy. For the older population, local welfare provision by the state is seen to be necessary, and consists of local care centres and services, home social care, meals, and old folks' clubs with attached accommodation.

Day care

With regard to day care (some Hungarians have named it 'day shelter'), the UN Hungarian Report (1982) stated that there were 835 day care centres in Hungary which catered for 24,000 people. Older people and commentators refer to the stigma attached to attending the day centres (see Széman and Sik, 1991, p.51). The provision is primarily designed for those who have inadequate heating, few contacts and who have no family support. The centres are regionally located, but their use is limited because of their relative scarcity. In addition to the stigma attached to attending day centres in Hungary, there is also evidence that the distance of the day centre from home is a major deterrent, as well as the lack of information about what it has to offer, as cited by Széman and Sik (1991, p.51). In 1986 the Ministry of Health also set up 'care centres' within the day centres. These care centres would cater for the social needs of the older people in the locality, and also provide them with 'social food'. Respite care and financial support for families/households caring for their older relatives are urgently needed.

Growing numbers of older people are increasingly underfed (Széman and Sik, 1991, pp.51–2). Expenditure on food often amounts to 40% of the older person's personal income. In addition, a costlier diet is required for more than a million older people suffering from gastric, digestive and circulatory disorders as well as diabetes.

Voluntary care agencies and support organizations

The new state system also openly supports the social services of the Churches (Banfalvi, 1990, p.172). The Red Cross and the voluntary agencies are also favoured, which for forty years, in many instances, provided the only assistance offered to the older poor. Without them, even the new government could hardly cope with the many social demands made by the older poor.

Although there has been dialogue about creating a mixed welfare programme involving the Churches and the non-governmental organizations, and although there have been many meetings to negotiate partnerships between the authorities and the Church groups, their contribution has to date been negligible, according to Sik (1988, p.283).

Informal care

Although about 69% of women and 85% of men aged 75+ live with kin (see citations in Laczko, 1994, p.43), there is great concern that 40% of marriages are breaking up, and concurrently the traditional informal caring structures catering for the aged frail or infirm are affected. Serial marriages and short-term partnerships create difficulties in the long term with regard to who within the shifting kinship circle will care for the serial partners when they are in need of care.

The familial and kinship situation in Hungary is much the same as in Poland and Finland, but the demands on resources will be higher than in Poland, but less than in Finland (see UN Hungarian Report, 1982). In the 1980s, home care only catered for the 25% of those older people who were living alone. The CPA (1989, p.74) points out that approximately two-thirds of the older population live with their adult children, and adds 'Family law outlines the obligations of children towards their parents.'

Social changes have made the implementation of this law difficult. Firstly, progressively since the 1950s, offspring have left home to set up independent homes. Secondly, those who stay on to care for their older parents usually go out to work. As in the Southern European nations and the other Eastern European countries, the exodus of the young from the countryside leaves older people in vulnerable isolation, and cuts down the village networks of informal care. Szeben (1980, p.104), however, does refer to the practice of urban children spending their summer holidays with their rural grandparents – an example of care in the 'reversed direction'.

As in the rest of Europe, there is concern that the family may no longer be able to fill the demographic gaps. There has been a dramatic fall in the marriage rate and a significant rise in the number of single parents, which has doubled since 1960. The proportion of single parents will reach 10% by the year 2000, and 40% of marriages will probably end in divorce (Banfalvi, 1990, p.169). The period since World War II has seen enormous familial changes. It was usual for three-generation families to live together in one flat, in keeping with the traditional Hungarian exogamous community family. Respect for older people was also a Hungarian characteristic, but, according to Szeben (1980, p.103), this is also changing. She states:

> Old people who find no intimacy in their families, who constantly crouch between four walls and are eternally criticised, and feel more at home among their own age-group than with their own blood relations who, however, in their way of thinking and perhaps also in their affection, behave like distant relatives.

On the basis of Széman and Sik's report (1991), it can be calculated that, over a decade later, Hungarian families have become even more mobile. Probably about 62% of the older Hungarian population live apart from their offspring, and 90% cook for themselves; 47% of the retired live alone, although 35% of them live near at least one of their offspring. There may well be many who experience the bleak conditions described by Szeben (1980), but as many as 73% of the older population expect one of their household to care for them in infirmity, and 20% of those living alone count upon their family or friends living apart from them providing them with home care (Széman and Sik, 1991, p.53). As has been made clear repeatedly, the state welfare system in Eastern European countries has offered few alternatives to informal home care, relatively little support and virtually no respite to caring households.

Sik (1988) describes 'self-welfarization' in Hungary. He sees the household as the unrecognized major provider within Hungary (p.283), but this cannot be verified because of the lack of comparable sociological data. He identifies the 'externalization strategy', which consists of shifting care out of the formal sector when the burden of expensive formal care reaches a point where it can no longer function; substitute cheaper forms of care are introduced and encouraged instead. This has been an integral part of social policy in Hungary since the recession of the 1970s. The shift is facilitated when there is an existing cultural tradition which values modes of care such as those provided by the family. This has been a 'hidden exploitation', says Sik (1988, p.288). He foresees a new 'peasantization' – the household as a sub-economy will be charged with all the burdens of welfare and care. The net result would be growing morbidity, domestic tensions and greater deprivation.

Leisure pursuits and education

As reported by the CPA (1989, p.74), educational programmes for the 'third stage of life' were first set up in 1983 in Budapest. Little is known at present about the success of these. The familial life of the older generations tends to cloister the women within the home, and usually within the kitchen. However, since the introduction of half-fare concessions on the railways in Hungary, older people have been able to go on occasional trips and visit friends, relatives and families.

Rural aspects

There are no major sources to draw upon with regard to the life of older rural Hungarian people and the nature of their services in the remoter areas, but a few observations may indicate some of the drawbacks encountered by them.

The lack of communication has been a problem facing older Hungarians, especially in more than a thousand small rural settlements, as cited by Széman and Sik (1991, p.52). The proportion of telephones in Hungary is one of the lowest in Europe (Széman and Sik, 1991, pp.45–6). In fact, tens of thousands have been on the waiting lists for some 25 years. This affected the older people in the peripheral rural settlements more drastically. In addition, the roads have deteriorated, making communication with the older people more difficult. As in almost all parts of Europe, the younger people have left the older people behind in their search for work or better living conditions in the cities. The lack of cars and public transport has also cut people off from major resources. The decline of the service network of the village is mentioned by the CPA (1989, p.74). Although day care, described as 'the day time home', under the former regime was supposed to be well established in the rural provinces, there were only 14,927 users in the rural areas, according to the data cited by Szeben (1980, p.100). This overlapped the scheme set up in the late 1960s, described as the 'isolated area care centres'. These provided farmers with havens from autumn to spring, in an effort to combat rural deprivation during the colder months of the year (see Széman and Sik, 1991, p.49).

Conclusion

Older Hungarian people suffer principally because pensions have not kept up with inflation. By the late 1980s, because of the cost of inflation, the pension had only one-seventh of its original value as it stood in 1980. Over 70% of the older population have suffered from hardship in Hungary within the past few years (Dooghe, 1992, p.157), and 26% have had to cope with an income below the social minimum. Forty per cent of personal income is spent on food; in addition to the hunger, there is the frailty and ill health which accompany poverty, which is endured by thousands of older Hungarians. Major difficulties exist because their pensions are inadequate and not inflationproof. In addition, it has been noted that, in any case, 20% of Hungarians are not entitled to a pension.

Mistrust bedevils the relationship between the state and the older population. The state was once paternalistic, and is fast becoming an anarchic money-led system. This chapter has indicated that most proposed state measures have not been carried out. As stated above, 70% of requests for domiciliary care go unheeded. Older Hungarians have lost faith in their health system. Although Hungary has one of the lowest life expectancy rates at birth in Europe (66.2 years for men and 74.0 for women – UN, 1991 and Eurostat, 1991a), the needs of the older population are largely overlooked, with the emphasis upon 'Janus-like' reforms and expensive innovatory health care for the young. A monocephalic welfare state system has been in place for years; the administrative structure is now in transition, shifting towards polycephalic structures. Older people, as recognized above, are the 'lost half' of the population.

20 Romania

Demography

According to the data presented in Table 1, the proportion of older people in Romania is ranked twenty-sixth in greater Europe. The projected figures for 2025 suggest that this rank order will drop by one, with an increase of only 5%; given the high level of pollution and the consequent escalation of morbidity, this increase may even be less. According to data compiled by the UN (1991), Romania has the lowest percentage of persons aged 75+ in greater Europe. Romanian women have the lowest life expectancy at birth (72.1 years) in Europe, and Romanian men the third-lowest (67.4 years) (UN, 1991; Eurostat 1991a).

Of the ethnic minorities, the Gypsies constitute about 2 million; the Hungarians 1.8 million, and the German Lutheran Saxons and Roman Catholic Swabians 363,000. Then there are the smaller groups (each no more than 0.5% of the population) consisting of Turks, Ukrainians, Serbs and Jews (see the Economist Intelligence Unit, 1990b, pp.8–9). Few of the Gypsies have had access to decent social welfare and health services.

Socio-political and administrative background

Romania is linked with the general malaise and socio-political chaos facing Bulgaria. More than the Friendship Bridge between the Romanian city of Giurgui and the Bulgarian city of Ruse links the two countries. The two nations share many of the post-communist problems: both are 'uncivil societies', as will be explained below.

Romania was able to retain its independence from Moscow's rule under

Gheorgiu-Dej, and later under Ceausescu, but the Romanian Communist Party's ideology and the government's welfare system were in line with those of the other communist countries. The older people suffered under the regime in much the same way as their counterparts elsewhere in Eastern Europe. The large network of secret police, the Securitate, protected the regime and spied on people.

After Ceausescu's execution on Christmas Day 1989, the National Salvation Front took over. It was made up of dissidents and religious leaders, but many were survivors of the communist regime.

In Romania, as in Bulgaria, the veneer of democracy after the fall of the previous totalitarian regime is thin; vestiges of the old regime's oppressive monocephalic administration remain, as do those of the Securitate, centred upon Bucharest. Ion Iliescu, the current President and head of state, was part of the old machinery of government.

According to the data provided by Turnock (1987), the investment in the central administration of Bucharest was higher than that on administration in the rest of the country as a whole, including industry, agriculture and forestry, transport and distribution services, education and science services, and the construction services. The centralized administrative system is perhaps all the more evident in these days of scarce resources as the regime holds tightly onto the purse strings and allocation system. There are approximately 2,706 communes, of which 150 are suburban. These largely rural communes are small, consisting of about 4,500 persons each, and are located within 39 counties (*judete*). There are about 47 municipalities (*municipiu*), of which Bucharest is the principal one.

The Romanian regime shows every sign of being an 'uncivil' administration rather than a civil one, to use Rose's (1992, p.5) distinction. Respect for legal rights and legal obligations, for the vulnerable segments of society, and for the common good are features of a civil society, which is accountable to its electorate. The former monocephalic and totalitarian Romanian regime officially no longer remains in place, but in effect there is little change administratively. In addition, the former power 'connections' remain, as they do to a large extent in Slovakia.

The economy and the provision of care and health services in the 'uncivil' societies at times is also determined by what is given 'in kind' by way of exchange by those who have possessions and highly prized commodities. These modes of informal exchange take over where, for many underprivileged people, deprivation has become the norm. On observational visits to Romania I have witnessed the Romanians exchanging fruit and agricultural produce, TVs, transistor radios and watches for medicines in the north-west of the country outside urban areas by the major roadways (Giarchi, 1989).

Social security: pensions and benefits

Significant numbers of rural older Romanian people have no pension. Rose (1992), on the basis of a nationwide representative survey of 1,000 adults in February 1992, observes that older Romanians are below average in material conditions, and also in terms of subjective indicators of need. According to the survey, family size and age are two salient factors. One-income families are more than three times as likely to have a minimum income than two-income families. Those aged over 60 are more than four times as likely to have a low income than middle-aged and younger households (see Rose, 1992, p.25). The poorest older people are disproportionately rural, poorly educated and lacking motivation. They also live in one of the most polluted environments in Europe (see also Turnock, 1987; 1989; Thompson, 1991).

The pension system is far from adequate. The Romanian pension usually lasts no more than a week. As in other Eastern European countries, apart from goods and food received from kin and friends, the people depend upon a portfolio of sources of income: one source is not enough. Rose (1991, p.9) refers to the need for participation in different economies for the household to survive. The median Romanian family is involved in four economies (Rose, 1992, p.12). As Rose (1992, p.38) also points out, four-fifths of people are dependent upon three or more economies. There is a vulnerable 13% of the older population who do not have more than one source of income, and who lack consumer durables to exchange for food and drink.

About 46% of the older people interviewed in a nationwide Romanian survey (IRSOP, 1991) reported being in the lowest income category (see Rose, 1992). Laczko (1994, p.63) refers to a recent poll in which 41% of Romanians 'think they are poor'. For example, many older people spend much of their day in queues: 68% of people in Bucharest spend eight hours or more queuing for food – more than double the national average. As night sets in, Romanian and Hungarian cars virtually become mobile shops and pharmacists' exchange centres. These 'boot' markets are part of an anarchic export/import system, because the Romanian leu has lost its place amongst the acceptable stable currencies of greater Europe. The older population are hardly able to compete in this bartering system. There is no supplementary system of support for the countless older poor people, so they must look for substitute sources. I have spotted them scavenging for food and 'cast-offs' etc. What surprised me was the fact that the troupes rummaging in bins and tips were not an embarrassment – their quest for the left-overs was taken for granted.

Housing

Expenditure on housing almost doubled between the 1950s and the 1980s (see Dawson, 1987, p.231). Ceausescu attempted to 'systematize' the country by building urban apartments in the countryside in a drive to promote 300–400 villages to urban status by 1990 and create 'agro-industrial' centres. In the quest to realize his ideological dream, Ceausescu and his planners halted all programmes related to upgrading the dilapidated homes of many older urban residents; those in rural areas, however, like their neighbours, moved into the new apartments. These apartments often lacked electricity supplies, and their toilets, bathrooms and water supply did not function properly, as I was to learn to my cost whilst staying in one within a Bihor rural commune. The city high-rise flats also encountered problems, especially when the electricity supplies were limited to certain times of the day, so that lifts and water pumps ceased to function. Older people longed for the old houses where they did not need to walk down many flights of stairs for water to fill their cisterns.

Health care

Older people age rapidly in Romania. Until this was explained to me by a local family doctor in north-west Romania, I was several years out in my estimation of older people's ages on my Romanian visits. The environmental conditions endured by older people are extreme in the cities.

The polluted environment is a major health concern. Turnock (1987, p.235) identifies and assesses the groups of Romanian counties, and, using Trebici's (1976) scale, Turnock identifies the worst-resourced areas. These also fall into the unhealthy zones within Thompson's (1991) most polluted European areas – the 'long shadow' cited in the Introduction, which, as has already been shown, is notorious for water and air pollution (see Turnock, 1989). Older Romanians are particularly vulnerable in the shadow of the chemical plants in or close to Cluj-Napoca, Oradea, Copsa Mica, Lasi, Timisoara, Giurgiu, Galati and Bucharest. The population is not protected from the fumes, and older people live in the older properties closer to the plants. Metallurgical plants are mainly scattered down the centre of the country, and the oil refineries run mainly from the lower reaches of the Transylvanian Alps just north of Bucharest to areas just west of where the Carpathian Mountains join up with the Alps (Thompson, 1991, p.45).

The lack of resources and the continuing deprivation suggest that the older Romanian population will be amongst the most unhealthy in Europe.

The media coverage of the HIV-positive children in Romania has eclipsed the problems facing older people near to starvation, many of whom have no pension. With the exception of the older diabetic population, there is no free medication. The CPA (1989) has nothing to say about the conditions facing older Romanians, simply presenting the statistical tables. Romania is close to being a Third World country in Europe.

Little research has been published regarding the social/health needs and formal/informal caring provisions for contemporary Romanians aged 65+. The World Health Organization socio-medical survey in Bucharest was confined to one area of the city (Heikkinen et al., 1983). Widespread deprivation and the progressive deterioration of social and health care provision in Romania is affecting the most vulnerable people (Sweeney, 1991), which is a matter for international concern. Romania and Albania are described as 'the poor men of Eastern Europe' (Dawson, 1987, p.237). Significant numbers of older Romanians have neither a pension nor free medication. In addition, Romania is almost entirely outside the major relief schemes and overseas development programmes, unlike Poland, Hungary and the Czech and Slovak Republics.

Officially, medical services are provided free by the state. In practice, as referred to above, these services are frequently paid for, sometimes with US dollars or in kind, chiefly within the municipality of Bucharest and the other urban areas of the 39 counties. Heikkinen et al. (1983) have commented upon the quality of health care provided in Bucharest, which has the highest proportion of older people in Romania. Here the resources are greatest. The researchers report (Heikkinen et al., 1983, pp.113–14) that doctors' visits to older patients are amongst the lowest of the cities and rural areas studied in 11 countries. However, there is evidence that older women in Bucharest (as also in Florence) contact their doctor most frequently, chiefly by phone. However, the number of doctors per 1,000 people in Bucharest, in spite of it being the best-resourced area in Romania, is seven times lower than in Kiev, five lower than in Bialystok and Brussels, and three lower than in Belgrade. Perhaps this explains why Bucharest has the highest percentage of older women visiting public health nurses out of the 11 countries commented upon by Heikkinen et al. (1983, p.114).

Every commune has its own clinic and dispensary, but electricity has been in short supply so that the use of equipment is heavily curtailed. There is a lack of antibiotics and other medicines, especially in the remoter rural areas, where the doctors' petrol allowances run out, and older people die unattended in dire conditions. In addition, I came across doctors who did not have stethoscopes and painkillers, and hospitals without anaesthetics (Giarchi, 1989). The only free medication for older patients in practice amounts to that required by diabetics. Pharmacists lack medical supplies, as evidenced by the many voluntary European groups bringing in supplies of antibiotics to the various health centres. There is a 'shadow' medical and health infrastructure and trade in medicines. For this reason, the medication brought by relief agencies in many instances is entrusted to the local clergy, whose Church Council controls its distribution within the commune by setting up a contractual arrangement with local doctors to prevent abuses. Volunteers have told me that at times they came across older patients selling off their own prescribed medicines.

Hospital care and medical services

The health service is free, but the quality of care and the standards of hospitalization have rapidly fallen behind the rest of Europe. Little has been done to improve the care of older people in hospitals since the mid-1950s, certainly outside Bucharest. The Romanian health services are under-resourced and underdeveloped in a country which Holzmann (1992) and Rose (1992) regard (on the basis of official statistics and health expenditure as proportion of GDP) as one of the poorest of the Eastern European countries. The media have opened the door upon such factors. I and my colleagues have witnessed operations, even amputations, without general anaesthetic in some of the town hospitals. Doctors also use textbooks that are out of date.

Nursing

Community nursing of the type known in the UK hardly exists. However, there are public health nurses serving out-patients at clinics, chiefly within the cities; 21–44% of the women's World Health Organization sample in Bucharest had visited the public health nurse during the previous 12 months (see Heikkinen et al., 1983, pp.120–21).

Hospital nurses are not specially trained to provide care for older people. The nurses do not enjoy the professional status of their counterparts in most of Europe.

Home care/help

Within the capital of Bucharest, the home help system is impressive. Back in the early 1980s, according to Heikkinen et al.'s report (1983, p.129), the majority of people aged 80+ 'occasionally or regularly' received home help.

Outside the capital, there is no national, systematized home help scheme providing for the older population in Romania. In general, neighbours and relatives assist in cleaning the homes of older people. Bringing in paid outsiders is alien to the largely rural Romanian families or neighbourhood circles in most of the districts.

Mental health care

Little is known outside of Romania about the mental health care provided for older people. Balaceanu et al. (1987), of the Institute of Gerontology and Geriatrics, Bucharest, studied depression, anxiety and obsessional ideas in older Romanians. They found that the incidence of depression was equal in both older men and women aged 60+. However, anxiety appeared to be greater amongst grandmothers, associated with their concerns over the welfare and health of their grandchildren.

Institutional care

The older people, the mentally ill and people with learning difficulties are herded together in large institutions without trained staff and totally unsupervised, in probably the worst residential homes in Europe. Gorman et al. (1992) state that there are 19 'homes for pensioners'. Even in the 1990s the semi-dressed and unwashed older residents have been housed indiscriminately, along with the chronically sick and the mentally ill, often alongside psychotic patients, in large dormitories, where they lose their dignity as human beings and pitifully regress. These homes are chiefly in the north-east of Romania and the remoter rural areas north of Bucharest. As cited by Laczko (1994, p.47), pensioners' homes cater for 2,105; homes for old people cater for some 4,146, and 'home hospitals' cater for the chronically ill, housing some 11,023, including younger people. Gorman et al. (1992) state that there are 66 such hospitals. Fortunately, only 1.8% of the older population are in Romanian institutions (Laczko, 1994, p.46).

Personal social services

Personal social services hardly exist in the rural areas. Such services are mainly centred upon the cities, especially Bucharest (Heikkinen et al., 1983, pp.135–9). The urban social services include meals-on-wheels, day care, laundry and chiropody. The use of day centres and chiropody services are commonest, and the best are found in urban areas.

Voluntary care agencies and support organizations

The Orthodox Churches maintain support networks and monitor the health and social needs of their older worshippers. The family is the major provider of care. Reliance upon outside agencies is seen as an admission of failure, much like the familial attitudes of Italian, Polish and French kinship groups. However, as the next section will show, that pride is tempered by the absence of family because of the greater mobility of the younger people.

Informal care

The Romanian family, as in the rest of Europe, is in the throes of social change. Younger people move in droves to seek part-time or temporary work. Stable relationships decrease. Rural families break up as younger people move out to live in the cities. Under the repressive rule of Nicolae Ceausescu, the traditional family was lauded and held up as the rock of society. Following his overthrow, the counter-reaction has shaken the traditional family and its values. Within these processes, older people are now more isolated. It is 'every person for her/himself'. They have neither the strength to cultivate crops nor the means to repair the old, crumbling family dwellings. One Romanian lecturer explained, when I was visiting the north-western counties of Romania:

> The family was identified as a Ceausescu dream. We heard so much about the family from him and his wife that we came in time to see it as an evil. It was about having children to provide tomorrow's workers; it had nothing whatsoever to do with providing care. The family members were suspicious about each other within a system which rewarded disclosures about disloyalty to the regime and its warped ideology.

Leisure pursuits and education

The only leisure activity that I identified in Romania amongst older people was the enjoyment of having a conversation. Older people were not very visible within households: they were the backroom helpers. It was unthinkable for them to run in tracksuits like some of their luckier European counterparts, or stretch themselves in leotards. Neither did they appear to indulge in cards or other table games, listen to music, or go on outings. Little appeared to break the monotony of their ageing, often silent years behind shuttered kitchen windows.

Rural aspects

No contemporary study of the quality of life of rural Romanians has been published. However, on the basis of Dawson (1987), Turnock (1987) and Zeman (1991) and the researchers' observational visits to Romania it is clear that older rural Romanians are amongst the most deprived Europeans. Rural family life in Romania is very similar to that of Poland (see Todd, 1985, regarding family types). As in Bulgaria, travel is restricted, and rural people have few transport services or their own cars to get to the hospitals and other support services. According to the Economist Intelligence Unit (1990b, p.25), there are only 11.2 cars per 1,000 people, the lowest proportion in Eastern Europe after Albania. The number of buses was almost halved during the 1980s. Petrol is expensive, and doctors' allowances run short about halfway through the month, with disastrous results for older people in rural areas.

My observations during my stay in the rural north-western areas in 1989 indicated that older people were marginalized within the multi-generational families. The grandparents were silent and hidden. Whilst the mothers were working the stubborn soil or tending the sheep and cattle, the grandmothers were working in the kitchens, minding the children and collecting the firewood. When the evenings came, the older people either confined themselves to the back kitchens or went off to bed. In the summer evenings they stood outside in the garden or street, and, leaning on the ledges of the open windows, they listened in to the conversation going on within. They were outsiders, backroom people and domestic helpers. It was not surprising that they also preferred to eat with their peers. Caring for the older housebound or bedridden Romanians was a task carried out exclusively by women. When the older people were chronically sick there was nowhere for them to go, nor nurses to attend to them. As for the doctors, they seldom had medication to offer or prescribe.

Conclusion

In conclusion, older Romanians, along with their counterparts in Bulgaria, are more deprived than most of those in the rest of Europe. It is difficult to see whether a triangle of care exists, because it presupposes a relatively stable state within an established, recognizable structure. Formal social care is hard to find; formal health care is concentrated in the cities, especially Bucharest. Unlike Poland and Hungary, Romania has not been in receipt of European Union aid. Alongside Albania and Bulgaria, Romania lags behind the rest of the former communist regimes because its own regime has been suspect.

Whatever the outcome of the political situation, the late start in one of Europe's most underdeveloped economies and outdated health and social care systems means that it will be many years before older Romanians will enjoy a comparable lifestyle to that of Hungary and Poland, and the more progressive Czech Republic. Widespread deprivation and the progressive deterioration of social and health care provision are affecting the vulnerable older Romanian population (Sweeney, 1991). Within Romania, older people are forgotten and deprived, kept out of sight and out of mind, behind an 'uncivil' curtain of suspicion and mistrust, especially the older people of the minority ethnic groups, such as the Gypsies.

Part V

Southern Europe

Of the Southern European countries, Italy stands out as one of the most affluent nations, especially its northern regions, which are within the European 'golden egg'. The less well-resourced social and health care systems in Spain and Portugal are considered next, followed by the Balkan regions of Greece, the former Yugoslavia and Albania. Finally, there is the island system of care in Malta, followed by mainland Turkey, and another island system, Cyprus. Malta has built up a creditable body of research upon which I was able to draw. Cyprus is characterized by a split culture, where conflicting communities reflect mainland Greek and Turkish systems of care, but where familial care is sovereign. Only the Greek systems will be considered, as less is known about the island's Turkish arrangements for older people.

21 Italy

Demography

According to the data presented in Table 1, the proportion of older people (65+) in Italy ranks ninth within Europe, in terms of its proportion of older people. By the year 2025 the nation will probably rank eleventh, but the proportion of older people will increase by 5.1%.

According to Bianchi (1991, p.102), more than 18% of the Italian population is over 60. The birth rate is decreasing, and will probably drop by 2.6% by the second decade of the twenty-first century. The caring ratio will be considerably reduced because of the significant decrease in the number of younger people and the rapid increase of the number of older people. At birth, the life expectancy of women is 79.7 years, which is the seventh-highest (jointly with Iceland) in Europe; that of men is 73.2 years, which is the sixth-highest (jointly with Spain) in Europe (Eurostat, 1991a; UN, 1991). Grundy and Harrop (1992, pp.26 and 28) state that almost twice as many women (12.7%) as men (6.6%) are single. There are about three times as many widows (51.1%) as widowers (16.9%).

The highest proportions of older people are in the northern regions of Liguria, Piedmont, Tuscany and Trieste. In contrast, the southern regions have a significantly lower percentage, such as Naples, where the standards of living are lower and the social and health care services are scarcer and of a poorer quality.

Bianchi (1991, p.103) refers to the growing number of single older people. Older disabled persons with health problems and with lower incomes are a particular concern in a nation where 10% of households consist of a single person aged 65+ on a low income. In the cities of the north the proportion of single people is about 25% – in Genoa 29%.

351

Socio-political and administrative background

The north of Italy is within the 'golden egg', but most of the Italian regions are outside it, along with the other countries of the Mediterranean rim. Its administrative systems are largely polycephalic. Italy is a relative latecomer among European welfare states (Balbo, 1986, p.24). Ascoli (1986, p.107) says that the welfare state was a marginal topic in both the Italian academic world and political agenda until the second half of the 1970s. Hitherto, the state provided assistance as problems arose over time – a type of provision which is termed 'incremental' – which in Italy took the form of what was described by Ascoli (1986, p.108) as a 'particularistic-clientelistic' model.

Until about 1877, social policy in the Italian peninsula was almost exclusively managed by the Catholic Church, centred upon Rome (Ferrera, 1986, pp.388–93). The state was happy to leave the care of older people and other vulnerable groups to the parishes and religious institutes of Italy. Only in the last two decades of the nineteenth century did the 'social question' figure in the government's agenda. The emergence of the Italian Socialist Party in 1892 and concern over the Mezzogiorno (the south of Italy) sparked off political debate.

The papal encyclical *Rerum Novarum* of Pope Leo XIII also marked a greater awareness in the Roman Catholic Church of contemporary social issues. The Liberal government, following upon the example of Germany, began to put together some primary, basic measures of social protection. Next, the various charitable and voluntary Christian agencies (the *opere pie*) involved in poor relief were to come under state control. In 1898, compulsory insurance was introduced, and a state-supported voluntary scheme for old age and invalidity insurance was established.

In the first decades of the twentieth century, principally through the Liberal politician Giolitti, interventionist policies began to emerge and the state began to subsidize voluntary insurance funds. Life insurance was also nationalized. It was only after World War I, however, that social policy became a major issue. Compulsory insurance for old age was introduced in 1919.

The Fascist corporatist state from 1927 began to establish welfare programmes, characterized by selective benefits for certain vulnerable sectors, such as the older population. The beginnings of a complex Italian insurance system were ushered in by the establishment of three large national insurance agencies and a variety of smaller institutes (*enti*) catering for special categories of clients.

In 1931, Pope Pius XI's celebrated encyclical *Quadragesimo Anno* was promulgated, which formulated the now much-quoted EU principle of 'subsidiarity', referred to earlier. The social concerns of communities should first be dealt with at local levels and only passed on for solution to higher levels of the welfare or political hierarchy when the families or neighbourhoods are unable to provide a remedy.

On the eve of World War II, social expenditure in Italy was as high as 15–17% of the state budget. The Church also provided poor relief at parish level, as did various local charities. As shall be shown later, these provided a local community with its mantle of care, described by some Italians as *campanilismo* (after the parish church bell, *campanile*).

Before passing on to pensions, housing, health and social care provision in Italy, the administrative structure within which the services are provided ought to be outlined. Since 1970 the state's welfare responsibility has been delegated by law to the 20 Italian regions, divided into the provinces, communes and the smaller *circoscrizioni*, within which local care is administered, organized and delivered. The political and welfare systems are polycephalic. A decentralization programme has been assiduously followed, much of which reflects the principle of subsidiarity. Locality-based systems bring formal care closer to the older Italian population. To what extent the regional regimes have been successful is another matter.

Reorganization and decentralization shifted the administration of social assistance, health care and housing to the regions, passing responsibilities on to the local authorities. Client participation and populist control were encouraged. Finally, the National Health Service was introduced in 1978. By the end of the 1970s, the secularization of the nation had separated the notion of welfare from that of Christian charity (see Ferrera, 1986, p.393). The Church was still to provide care, but it was independent and characterized by being voluntary, much of which continues to be provided by the St Vincent de Paul Society and Caritas.

Two things need to be emphasized regarding the implementation of the care of the older population in Italy: Italian bureaucracy (the *burocrazia*) gets in the way of operational management, creating organizational stagnation, and Italian party political power games (the *partitocrazia*) bring about sporadic changes involving reversals and wastages for the sake of scoring political points. Older people have become suspicious about political reforms. Locked between these, and often in opposition, are the families constituting the *famiglialismo*, the domestic lobby.

Social security: pensions and benefits

After World War II a consensus regarding 'reconstruction' helped the nation to piece together new welfare policies, much of which were directed to establishing a sound social security scheme for older people. Unfortunately, the more integrated social security scheme put forward by the Parliamentary Commission chaired by the Socialist senator D'Aragona in 1947 was overtaken by the new centre coalition led by the Christian Democrats in 1948. The complex pre-war institutional social security framework was reinstated. For much of the 1950s, social policy consisted of marginal adjustments to the pre-war welfare system, and a welfare incrementalism emerged. However, in 1952 the pension reform did establish a basic pension (the *minima*) which was to improve the lot of older Italians considerably.

Following upon the institutional inheritance of the post-war regime, social security is divided into three parts:

1   social insurance (*previdenza*);
2   health and sanitation (*sanità*);
3   assistance (*assistenza*).

Social insurance contains six schemes for pensions, which are administered mainly by three agencies that were set up under the Fascist regime. These are: Instituto Nazionale della Previdenza Sociale (INPS) for social insurance; Instituto Nazionale per l'Assicurazione contro le Malattie (INAM) for sickness insurance, and Instituto Nazionale contro gli Infortuni sul Lavoro (INAIL) for occupational injury insurance. Most benefits were only for employees, not the self-employed. Myriad public agencies provided social assistance for those in need at national, regional, provincial and local levels.

The 1960s and 1970s witnessed major welfare changes, which were to alter the nature of social security for older people. In 1969, earnings-related and social pensions were introduced, as well as cost of living indexation. The Pensions Act No.153 of 1969 came about through collaboration between the political parties and the unions in the struggle to procure a better pension. The unions (CGIL, CISL and UIL) secured majority participation on the Italian National Institute for Social Security's management board.

Pensions are the largest single item within Italy's social expenditure budget. In the 1980s, expenditure on pensions represented about 24% of total expenditure and about 11% of GDP (see Ferrera, 1986, p.397). Since the mid-1980s the Italian state welfare system has provided generous social insurance coverage. Old age insurance, together with sickness, unemployment and accident insurance, are now comparable with those of the Scandinavian countries. The Continental pattern of providing people with incomes with which they may purchase services also characterizes the Italian welfare system, along with that of Belgium, France, Luxemburg and the Netherlands. Income maintenance has been the largest component of welfare provision in Italy. Italian pensions constitute almost a quarter of total public expenditure, at least 10% of GDP, and about 80% of income maintenance expenditure. The Eurostat statistics (1991b, p.84) indicate that Italy has the highest percentage (59.4%) of old age survivors' benefits in the EU. But, although the pension scheme is generous at present, many of the oldest pensioners are still relatively poor because they had made few contributions. Bianchi (1991) states that 21.8% of the total number of the poor in Italy are over 65; indeed, one-fifth of the older population are defined as 'poor'. For the beneficiaries, the pension scheme aims to provide the retired with a major proportion of the employee's previous income by means of the earnings-related pension. It also aims to provide older people with a basic and viable subsistence income by means of the pensions *minima* and social pensions. Dependent workers (women aged 55 and men aged 60) with 40+ years of contributions receive a pension that amounts to about 80% of previous earnings up to a ceiling after 40 years of contributions. The minimum period of contributions is 15 years. Certain civil servants receive 100% of their former income as a pension. Survivors' pensions range from 60–100% of the deceased person's entitlement.

Perhaps the most comprehensive taxonomy of Italian pensions is provided by Bianchi (1991, p.105). This serves to present the relevant old age pensions in summary form. She describes the four that concern older people and their families, which have been touched upon in part above:

1   The Occupational Pension (*la pensione di vecchiaia*): on the basis of recent discussion, it is likely that the pensionable age will be increased for women from 55 to 60, and for men from 60 to 65, and the number of years' contributions required to qualify will be increased from 15 to 20.
2   The Seniority Pension (*la pensione di anzianità*): workers registered with INPS who have paid their pension contributions for at least 35 years may retire early.
3   The Transferable Pension (*la pensione di versabilità*): upon the death of a pensioner or insured person, the survivors receive part-payment, such as the spouse, who receives 60%; the offspring up to 18 years of age, or if at university up to 26, who each receive 20%, or 40% if sole beneficiary; and the parents aged 65+ in the absence of an eligible spouse or children, provided they were supported by the recipient and have no pension of their own, who receive 15%.
4   The Non-Contributory Pension (*la pensione sociale*): this is paid to those over 65 who have little or no other means of support. It is usually topped up by a supplementary allowance.

A critical aspect of the politics surrounding the Italian pension scheme is the involvement of the unions in the deliberations of the INPS national board. This board pays out more than 90% of all non-civil-service pensions. Eighteen national representatives of the workers' trade unions are members of the board. The other members consist of nine employers' representatives;

nine representatives of the self-employed, and three state officials. No country in Europe matches this involvement of union representatives at such a high level.

It would appear that the Italian programme of *tutto per tutti* ('everything for everyone') should provide older people with a generous pension and excellent benefits. However, as Segalman (1986, pp.33–5) indicates, the programmes have been bogged down by clumsy legislation and an abundance of red tape. On paper the system is one of the best in Europe; the reality is that claims take months to settle, and even years. On the positive side, there has also been a redefinition of 'disability', which in Italy now means 'reduced earning power capacity'. However, the door has been flung open to millions of claimants. Millions of able-bodied pensioners in the more deprived areas are able to claim they are disabled merely because of the areas they live in. In addition, the recession in Italy has brought high inflation, and the pension costs have increased taxation. Castellino (1976, p.50) stated, in the midst of rapid welfare changes, that the assumption is that every pensioner is in need, and that the Italian system 'has a dose of Mediterranean lightheartedness'. It has continued unabated.

Certainly, pensioners are held in high regard by most organizations and the general population, especially by the unions; for example, they are accustomed to lead the May Day processions in the foremost place of honour throughout Italy under a banner proclaiming '*Forza ai pensionati*' – 'Power to the pensioners'.

An especially helpful and supportive feature in the Italian system are the *patronati*. These are offices which are in some respects like the Citizens' Advice Bureaux (CABs) in the UK. They are manned by advisers and a lawyer, who not only provide information to the pensioners and others regarding their welfare rights, but also take over the form-filling and act as advocates for their clients. There are proportionately more of these than there are CABs or welfare advisory services in the UK; for example, there are 25 such offices in the province of La Spezia, with about the same population as in West Devon, which only has about half that number. What use are benefits if 'information deprivation' blocks access? (Giarchi, 1990c).

Housing

In spite of the fact that Bianchi and Saraceno (1988, p.104) state that one-fifth of the older Italian population live in conditions of poverty, they do not explore their housing conditions, nor do any other major Italian studies in the English language.

Housing in Italy, according to Ascoli (1986, p.111), has generally suffered from the lack of government planning. In addition, intervention on behalf of persons with special needs and within low-income groups has been minimal. The tax concessions to builders and purchasers alike up to the end of the 1950s favoured the higher-income households. There were a few regional exceptions.

There are three social policy principles governing housing in Italy which usually affect the older population in terms of control and making properties available for them: firstly, the state controls rents; secondly, it subsidizes public housing, and thirdly it subsidizes private housing. Four national procedures have been in place which often assist older people:

1   The state controls all rents under the Fair Rents Law (*regime dell'equo canone*), and all expropriation of land and construction by means of the Land Use Law (*regime sull'uso dei suoli*).
2   The state provides low-cost public housing (*edilizia sovvenzionata*) for low-income families and households, such as those houses built by the Instituti Autonomi Case Popolari (IACP).
3   The state grants special low-income loans to private builders on condition that the 'aided housing' meets certain criteria of size and numbers.
4   The state has the power to reduce taxes and grant direct subsidies to private builders when creating large economic housing schemes.

These principles and salient state procedures are generally evident in northern, central and southern Italy. There are also geographic disparities in the way these are implemented in response to local housing needs. For instance, in a comparative EU study, I have identified the various housing arrangements which provide for the elderly in La Spezia, Liguria, north-west Italy (Giarchi, 1987a). The area has one of the highest proportions of older residents in Italy. Some occupy the *case popolari* that were built after the war and which originally catered for the poorer bombed-out families. In addition, some reside in the *mini-apartamenti*, owned by the communes, and managed by the social services in some neighbourhoods, which offer lower-rental municipal accommodation for older people. Local authority housing is also provided for local authority employees, and is not quite the same as the UK's council housing. There are also the IACP houses, which are run by co-operatives under a state arrangement, and provide lower mortgages for lower-income families; 65.5% of those aged 65+ in Italy own their accommodation (Bianchi, 1991, p.104), which usually consists of much older dwellings; 21.7% live in rented accommodation.

In the north the majority of the long-established middle-class people live in urban apartments, many re-built and modernized since the war, provided with lifts and electronic door controls, as indicated by Giarchi (1987a, p.26). Depaoli et al. (1986, pp.3–7) refer to the closer proximity of the wider family living in private (usually rented) apartments close to each other in Milan. Often the immediate family and relatives occupy adjoining floors, taking up several flats in the same block, as in the north-west city of La Spezia (Giarchi, 1987a, p.25). More older people live alone in mini-apartments in these northern cities, particularly in Milan, where about 20% of older males and about 80% of older females are living alone (see Depaoli et al., 1986, p.21).

According to an earlier comparative study, covering 16 nations, proportionately more Italians identify housing as the number one priority. However, at the same time they complain that housing is in short supply and beyond their means (Selby and Schechter, 1982, pp.37 and 61). In the province of La Spezia the urban housing was generally excellent, but relatively few older people owned their apartments or houses. If it were not for their relatives and immediate family many of the poorer older people would be unable to find a home of their own. Rents were high. The *case popolari* were often occupied by older single persons and lone older couples. The house was often a gift *inter vivos*: the house of the older person was bequeathed in exchange for an assurance of care by the family (the 'gift economy').

Within the rural areas of the province of La Spezia the 27 older rural interviewees whom I visited were living in homes inhabited by their ancestors for centuries. Permission was given to examine the baptismal registers in the sacristies of the mountain churches. Through this means I was able to piece together the interviewees' background and check out their provenance. At one house where I interviewed an older lady, there was an inscription inside the door *'rinnovamento 1651'* ('renovation 1651'). In the central belt of Italy (sometimes described as 'third Italy') the 'extended family' is widespread, consisting of several generations and/or related nuclear families living under the same roof, as for example in Forli, on the east side of the country. Here fewer older people live alone (see Depaoli et al., 1986, p.28).

In the south the extended family occupies more crowded and straitened accommodation. According to Depaoli et al. (1986, p.29), almost 75% of those aged 60+ live with a spouse and/or children, and 45% live with their offspring. Only about 15% of the older population live alone in Naples.

Sheltered housing is provided as small flats for single and married older couples. A warden keeps in touch with the older residents. Meals are available in an adjoining canteen. Waiting lists in Bari, Bologna, Udine and Modena testify to the growing demand for such accommodation (Bianchi, 1991, p.109). However, the price of private sheltered accommodation, where it does exist, is high and prohibitive for most older people in most regions. The local authority in some areas pays almost a half in subsidy towards the rental for public sheltered accommodation.

Health care

The Italian health service (Servizio Sanitaria Nazionale) is the equivalent of the UK's National Health Service. Italy's health policy at the close of the 1970s was designed to conform to a universalist health model. Towards this end, and to extend the decentralization of care, in 1978 the government created the Local Health Units (LHUs). Citizen participation has also been incorporated within the management structures (Piperino, 1984; Ascoli, 1986). The territorially based units are run by an assembly of elected members within districts. There are 673 local health units (each comprising approximately 50,000–100,000 persons). The health services are equivalent to those of the UK in terms of autonomy, whereas the social services come under the local authorities (the *comune*), ruled from above by the Ministry of the Interior (see Hunter, 1986, pp.54–9). Under the 1984–6 National Health Plan, the health care of the older population was given national priority (CPA, 1989, p.85). The health system is organized by regions, provinces and sectors (*settori*). The actual provision is within municipalities or the communes, where the local health units constitute the USL (Unità Sanitaria Locale) (see Palma, 1986).

Hospital care and medical services

Italy has the fifth-highest number of hospital beds per 1,000 inhabitants in the EU (Eurostat, 1991b, p.88). Bianchi (1991, p.109) states that there are about 2,655 private and public hospitals and 172,310 hospital beds for older people. Proportionately more persons aged 55+ use these beds, the proportion increasing with age (see Bianchi, 1991, p.106). Women and men aged 65+ make equal use of the health services. There is a historical bias towards hospital provision in Italy, as in Luxemburg, the Netherlands and Germany. For example, in La Spezia, a city of about 115,000 people, there are approximately 162 hospital beds for older sick people and about 68 for long-term care of the chronically sick in the province. There are ten hospital-based consultants for older patients (Giarchi, 1987a). More older men than women go into Italian hospitals. Older women appear to make more use of home care than do older men (see Bianchi, 1991, p.106).

Day hospitals are few in number in Italy. Bianchi (1991) and other recent commentators do not list them. For example, even in the south of Liguria, one of Italy's best-resourced regions, there were still no day hospital services for older patients in the early 1990s. Giarchi (1987a, p.25) describes how the consultants had written to the Assembly requesting that the urgency of such a service be addressed. They wrote three times, receiving neither a reply nor even an acknowledgment. The consultants explained that the notion of formal community support was alien to a health service that lagged behind the Northern European countries in terms of community support for older people, and there was a pressing need for rehabilitation.

In particular, the polyclinics provide the older population with a handy, comprehensive, local unit of health care; for example, there are five in La Spezia, which are well-situated within highly-populated areas. The specialists organize consultations at these polyclinics, which are centrally located within most localities, providing extra facilities for tests and pre-operative or post-operative consultation, often paramedical care and dentistry, plus X-ray facilities and eye tests. This contrasts with the system in the UK and in most other European countries, where older patients often have to travel great distances at great cost to visit consultants in the major central hospitals. The Italian USL specialists work on a fee-for-service basis. Although the frailer older patients rely heavily upon their family practitioners within the districts, many often prefer to consult their local pharmacists: probably a relic of the days when they had to pay for medical consultations.

According to Eurostat (1991b, p.88), Italy has the highest ratio of pharmacists per 1,000 inhabitants in the EU; for example, there are approximately 31 in the city of La Spezia, a small city, 12 in the local towns of the province of La Spezia and 29 in the rural areas of southern Liguria.

Under the USL, the doctors generally have small practices, limited by law to 1,500 patients. Italy has a ratio of 4.2 doctors and dentists per 1,000 inhabitants (Eurostat, 1991b, p.88). The family doctors are private contractors as in the UK, receiving per capita fees. However, they may receive payments from non-registered patients. Giarchi (1987a) learned from interviews in Liguria with older persons aged 75 and over that many of them were paying their local doctors for medical consultations on top of their state contributions. They agreed that they were not obliged to pay for the services, but the majority of interviewees stated that it helped to procure a better service! On one occasion, in the mountains of Varese, I observed a visiting paramedic accepting payment when collecting an older woman involved in an accident in the vineyard. The villagers said this was usual practice.

Nursing

Although Vollering et al. (1991, p.251) state that nursing services cater for older people in all the districts of Italy except six (Basilicata, Calabria, Molise, Piedmont, Umbria and the province of Trento), Italian extra-mural nursing is poor. Moreover, private nursing agencies employ nurses with dubious qualifications, if any (Giarchi, 1987a). In southern Liguria, in spite of the area having one of Europe's highest concentrations of older residents, there are only about twenty-seven community nurses serving the city, and four in the rural areas within the province of La Spezia (Giarchi, 1987a), only ten of whom serve older clients. In La Spezia, Liguria's second city, fewer than twenty nuns assist both the older residents and the housebound sick with domiciliary care.

There appear to be only three USL community nurses in La Spezia, one in nearby Lerici and one at Porto Venere, all working from the three centres for older people and the handicapped. Both groups of patients are unhappy with the fact that the centre serves them both (Giarchi, 1987a): the older patients stress that they are not disabled because they are old, and the disabled patients stress that they are not old.

There is great diversity over the running of the home care nursing services in Italy. The same confusion that exists in the UK over what is 'social care' and what is 'health care' is found in Italy. However, the regional disparities exacerbate the confusion even further in Italy, because home care in some regions includes home nursing, home help, occupational therapy, cooked meals services and chiropody, etc., run by the commune and often involving social workers. In other regions the home nursing services and the other domiciliary services are run by USL centres. Bianchi (1991, p.113) refers to the division of duties between the commune and the USL within home care in some regions, and in others, the integration of home services such as nursing and home assistance of various kinds. There is evidence that in the north, especially in Veneto and Genoa, there is a stronger welfare–health integration at home care levels than in the south of Italy. (In keeping with the division of topics within this book, home nursing is separated from home help. So that, although they are sometimes jointly administered and provided by multidisciplinary teams in some Italian regions, they are separated out within this discussion.)

Mental health care

Italy's mental health service is essentially a community care system in keeping with Basaglia's (1968) model. In La Spezia, Giarchi (1987a) accompanied the psychiatric team on its rounds, observing the home visits paid to depressed older people. The province of La Spezia is divided up into five territories. Each day the small van from the Mental Health Centre (Centro per la Salute Mentale) goes out to the homes of the depressed or psychiatric patients. The psychiatrist, the social worker and a mental health community nurse pay joint visits. There are 11 mental health community nurses and 6 psychiatric community social workers (nurses and social workers are on the same salary scale).

Infrasca (1987) identified that approximately 20% of the mentally ill were old in this area. About 8% of the older population suffer from some form of dementia, which is in keeping with other European statistics. Mangen (1985a) deals with Italy's innovations along with those of other EU countries. The Italian model propagated by the Psychiatria Democratica (PD) challenges the traditional clinical and ideological psychiatric models in Europe (Mangen, 1985a, p.14). The psychiatric institutions built as asylums were closed down on the basis of the Psychiatric Reform Law No.180 of 1978.

There are critics of the Italian system (for example, Jones and Polatti, 1984): the quality of the care is declared to be uneven, depending upon regional diversities, as well described by Fasolo and Frisanco (1991). The most efficient services are located in the north-east regions – Emilia Romagna, Umbria, Friuli and parts of Tuscany – noted for their social programmes and non-pharmacological outreach services.

Depression amongst older people in Italy has been commented upon by Infrasca (1987). As elsewhere in Europe, these depressed older people are often single women, widows or widowers, who are isolated, alienated and disengaged. According to the data provided by Pritchard (1992, p.129), 494 Italians aged 75+ per million are reported to have committed suicide – which ranks only ninth of 16 European countries, after Austria, Switzerland, France, Finland, West Germany, Denmark, Portugal and Sweden. However, the suicide rate is three times as great as it is in the UK (Pritchard, 1992).

Institutional care

The greatest problem is the lack of resources for bedridden chronically sick older people who require long-term nursing care, and for those who are suffering from dementia (the *non-autosufficienti* – 'non-self-sufficient'). Few regions have suitable institutions and trained staff to provide suitable specialist care for them. Until recently the practice was for the family to care for them within their household for as long as possible, supporting them with an attendance allowance (*assegno di accompagnamento*), and if care became too onerous to send them to institutions; these, however, have always been relatively few in number in Italy, so that often the non-self-sufficient have had to be sent to institutions in other regions at the other end of the country, as has been the case for many in Liguria (Giarchi, 1987a, p.30). Older people have been separated from their nearest relatives. However, as cited by Bianchi (1991, p.111), a piece of national legislation in the late 1980s identified the need for more regional centres and legislated for the establishment of residential homes for non-self-sufficient older people. The increase in the number of those aged 80+ and the high costs of home care have prompted the government to build more residential homes, when the rest of Europe is closing them down.

On the basis of data provided by Bianchi (1991, p.109), there are probably about 2,462 institutions for older Italians, such as the rest homes (*case di riposo*); Vollering et al. (1991, p.250) state that there are 2,656, serving 172,319 older persons. The residential homes have been given the name 'health care homes' (*residenze sanitarie assistentiale*). In Liguria, which, as stated, has one of the highest proportions of older residents, there are only 157 residential establishments, nursing homes and sheltered housing units of one kind or another, serving a regional population of over 326,560 older people aged 65 and over. The government, realizing the shortfall in residential nursing care, has provided funding for 140,000 places, either in these homes or in day hospitals. These are to cater for the non-self-sufficient, and also for the 'prevalently non-self-sufficient'. The Health Ministry, by decree (1989) and presidential decree (December 1989), established new regulations for the health care homes in a nationwide attempt to step up the number of residential units to cater for the growing number of dependent single older people, and those who could no longer be catered for in their own homes; so the nationwide policy of de-institutionalization cited by Depaoli et al. (1986, p.43) has to a large extent been diluted. Unlike other parts of Western and Northern Europe, there is an urgent need for more residential places. This situation is exacerbated by the fragmentation of family life referred to earlier. To date, the residential nursing sector has been largely run by religious institutions. For example, in Milan, a city that has probably the highest proportion of residential homes for older people in Italy, just over half are run by religious orders (Depaoli et al., 1986, p.50). However, the number of nuns is dropping and there are signs that the religious institutions, as elsewhere in Europe, are facing a rapid contraction of vocations to the religious life.

Not surprisingly, the residential homes are concentrated chiefly in the north of Italy, within Lombardy, Marche, Emilia Romagna, Valle d'Aosta, Piedmont and Trentino-Alto Adige.

Local authorities determine the different modes of payment for residential care. In the communes of Modena, Bari, Udine and Bologna, older residents pay for their residential care from their pension, as discussed at the SYSTED (Systems Science in Health and Social Services for the Elderly and Disabled) International Conference in Bologna in 1990 by the various Italian commentators. Most of the pension goes to the institution, sometimes at least 80–85% of it; the local commune pays the rest on the basis of an assessment requiring some means-testing. In all regions, older residents retain a part of their pension as an allowance or pocket money.

Personal social services

The only national law which regulated social service was the Legge Crispi, passed at the end of the nineteenth century. In Italy, social services are provided by the commune. As Cavallone (1986, p.359) observes, the function of social workers has not enjoyed the level of public support found in other countries. In fact, the term 'social worker' was dropped in Italy, and replaced with *'operatore sociale'* ('social operator'); it applies to all professionals, such as psychologists and sociologists, who are engaged in social care. The social operators turned from 'caseworking' older clients to fighting the marginalization of people such as the aged, as well as the institutionalization of the care of the older population. There was also concentration upon the need for integrating social and health care and promoting citizen participation. There is no doubt that the integration of younger and older people in welfare, health, leisure and work schemes has been furthered by the involvement of the new cohorts of Italian social operators, inspired by the Women's Movement and the Movement for Democratic Psychiatry.

The social services within the communes are usually run by an *assessore* (alderman), who is appointed by the council. The *assessore* can be consulted by the public on two mornings a week at the local office. Public accountability rates highly, as it does with the President of the USL, who is also available to the public at the central office. Settling disputes and receiving complaints are major duties of the president and the *assessore*.

At the same time it must be stressed that the regions each have their own structures: for example, in Tuscany the social services usually have a full-time appointed co-ordinator, much the same as the director's post in the UK, whereas in Liguria and most of Italy, the *assessori* are appointed by the reigning majority political party. No matter what the systems, there is no doubt that the provision of social and health care in Italy is highly politicized.

Social workers

The social work profession has been criticized within academia and by the media because it was seen to fulfil a function of social control, rather than provide care for the needy. In fact, as mentioned earlier, the title of 'social worker' was dropped in Italy following upon the dissolution of the Association of the Italian Schools of Social Work in 1973, in favour of the new term, *operatore sociale* (Cavallone, 1986, p.359).

The social operators employed by the commune are not as available as social workers are elsewhere in Europe. They usually adopt the same hours of work as civil and government workers. For this reason, the voluntary workers and the co-operatives have a significant role to play. With a few exceptions, the social work offices close down for the rest of the day at lunch from Friday to Saturday inclusively. On Sundays the caring co-operatives take over.

The number of social operators in Italy is considerably less than the number of social workers in the Northern, Western and Central European countries; for example, in Genoa there are 26 care teams within the *assistenza domiciliare*, consisting of approximately one social worker, six home helps and two nurses per team. In La Spezia there are approximately 14 field workers (*assistenti domiciliari*) and 24 home helps for the entire province (approximate population 240,000: see Giarchi, 1987a, p.5), in a region with the highest proportion of older people in Italy.

Meals services

The social work staff in Liguria, Abruzzo and Valle d'Aosta organize meals (*pasti caldi*) at home. In my Italian study (Giarchi, 1987a, p.30) these meals were delivered to about a hundred older households in La Spezia twice weekly. The staff sometimes ordered meals at local *trattorie* and had them delivered by a waiter to older people in the same street.

Day centres

There are day centres for older people (*centri diurni per anziani*) in the more highly-populated regions which are very similar to those in the UK. As cited by Vollering et al. (1991, p.251), there are only 5 districts (Campania, Emilia Romagna, Molise, Toscana, and the province of Trento) out of 21 which do not provide day care.

The day centres date back to the early 1970s. In Milan they were opened at the request of the older people themselves. However, the number of local authority day centres within 13 provinces is relatively small, with the exception of Rome, where there are about 60. Depaoli et al. observe that there are only about ten day centres in Milan and about seven in Forli; none are provided in Naples and other major centres of population (1986, pp.52 and 66). Only Lazio and the province of Bolzano appear to provide information at the day centres. Rehabilitation is offered in Lazio, Liguria and Puglia (see Vollering et al., 1991, p.251).

Home care/help

Home help is sometimes provided by the *assistenza domiciliare*, a service within the commune. It may also be provided by multidisciplinary teams, as in Genoa. The survey carried out by SYNERGIA (1990) cites the multiplicity of home care workers who answer to a variety of names, but who are basically home helps:

- 'domestic assistants' (Liguria and Lombardy);
- 'home helps' (Tuscany, Campania, Sicily and Calabria);
- 'home help centre staff' (Lazio);
- 'socio-health auxiliaries' (Lombardy);
- 'auxiliary helpers' or 'geriatric and household assistants' (Alto Adige);
- 'assistants' (Emilia Romagna);
- 'home help and care staff' (Marche).

No country in Europe has such a diverse set of labels to describe home care, but whatever the title, home care users are usually subject to means-testing. However, the older person's income must not exceed the minimum state pension (as determined by the National Institute of Social Security). According to a national survey carried out by the Department of the Interior (1985), 8 out of the 88 authorities reported that they ask their clients for contributions in accordance with their ability to pay. In all but five districts in Italy (the provinces of Trento, Molise, Umbria, Friuli and Calabria) home care of one kind or another is on offer (Vollering et al., 1991, p.251).

Even where the helpers are available, they are often few in number. In La Spezia, for example, I was informed that there were approximately 24 home helps for the whole province. In addition, there is a flexible roster of trusted parish women, acting in collaboration with the St Vincent de Paul Society. Night cover is only provided by eight Italian health authorities. Eligibility for the various home care services is not standardized; for example, the minimum age for eligibility varies between 55 and 70 years. In Bari the older person must be living alone and have an income below the poverty line. National requirements do exist; for example, the pensioner's income must not exceed the minimum state pension granted by the National Institute of Social Security. Discretionary powers determine whether the older person's state of mental or physical invalidity or disability is sufficient to merit local authority support at home, but only about one-fifth of Italian authorities have introduced an assessment procedure. The aims and objectives behind the regional laws regarding the home care system are to prevent older and/or disabled people from going into residential/nursing care. In practice, it is the *instituto famigliare* (the 'institute of the family') which cares and provides, as will be discussed below.

Depaoli et al. (1986) provide a comparative urban study of home care in Milan, Rome, Forli and Naples; Bianchi (1991) provides a view of the Italian home help scheme in Modena, Bari, Bologna, Rome, Udine and Trieste, and Costanzi (1991) presents a general description of the home care system in Italy and a particular study of home help in Genoa (the capital of Liguria). I have also provided a view of home care in the province of La Spezia (Giarchi, 1987a, p.30). It is clear that, of the diverse home care services, home help is not always the major provision. Also, in each of the above areas the backing provided by occupational therapists and physiotherapists is minimal, and private chiropody is expensive and not usually part of the commune's provision.

The various forms of home help are mainly provided in the northern regions of Italy by subsidized co-operatives and voluntary agencies, and between approximately 10–80% of the communes. However, uptake is not impressive: between 0.7% and 2.8% of the older population in the various Italian regions make use of home help. Most Italian home helps are employed in the north. As one moves southwards, the home care systems deteriorate, and they are worst in Sardinia and Calabria (Fasolo and Frisanco, 1991, p.224). Where the scheme does exist, the ratio is usually 1 home help to every 2,000 residents (see SYNERGIA, 1990, pp.22–3). However, in the only two southern regions which provide home help, significantly more older persons use the service. Costanzi's (1991) description of home care in Genoa indicates that only 743 older people were in receipt of home care from three centres, the majority of whom were living alone. Only nine regions in all of Italy provide home help, within which about 47% of the communes provide it.

However, it must be stressed that home help usually provides for the mentally ill, the disadvantaged families, the disabled, the chronically sick and persons with learning difficulties. Three regions restrict the home help service to older people: Abruzzo, Sardinia and Campania (SYNERGIA, 1990).

Bianchi (1991, p.116) identifies the three aims of the home help system in Italy:

1   protection from institutional care;
2   prevention from physical, psychological and mental deterioration;
3   promotion of healthy living.

Protection from institutional care is the foremost aim. The second and the third aims are not as evident in implementation of home help or nursing care policies, as has already been addressed above.

The diversities between major cities are exemplified by contrasting the home help systems of these areas. In the city of Genoa, as reported by Costanzi (1991, p.195), there are 26 multidisciplinary teams run from home care centres, all of which have their own management committees. Within each of the teams there are about six home helps. Such an integrated system contrasts with those of Milan and Rome.

In Milan, there are 22 home assistance service departments run by the commune. The services in Milan are diversified, but within a unitary central system. They are co-ordinated by the Office for the Distribution of Welfare and Social Security. Each department has health workers, social operators, rehabilitation therapists, general and professional nurses, family helpers and chiropodists (Depaoli et al., 1986, pp.46–7). The Milan system offers domestic assistance, nursing services, social assistance, rehabilitation, information and arrangements for leisure or holidays and an emergency service for older residents. The uptake of nursing care is twice that of social care, but domestic care is by far the most-used service.

In Rome, home assistance is not run by the commune, but by about 19 co-operatives in agreement with the commune (Depaoli et al, 1986, p.58). Here again, there is a multidisciplinary team made up of nurses, home assistants, physiotherapists and psychologists. The services include the delivery of hot meals and the collection and return of laundry, as well as a phone-in facility.

In Forli there are about ten workers. Home care does not include nurses. The service is run by a private co-operative and emphasizes the importance of older people running things for themselves. In Naples the home helps are employed by the Welfare Services Department. They provide social assistance for those living alone, preparing meals and organizing summer holidays. However, home assistance is not well used (see Depaoli et al., 1986, p.75).

In spite of the widespread provision of the home help services, many older Italians are not aware of them or what they have to offer. A recent national survey, cited by Bianchi (1991, p.121), states that about one-fifth of older Italians have never heard about 'home help'. Once again, information deprivation hinders the welfare enterprise and take-up.

Other services

Vollering et al. (1991, p.252) also describe an innovative system in Milan, described as *anziano in famiglia* ('older people in family'). This consists of monthly payments made to people to care for their older relatives at home whilst they are on waiting lists. The older person must be 'self-sufficient'. The scheme caters for about 250 older people per year.

Voluntary care agencies and support organizations

The voluntary agencies, amongst which are the major voluntary programmes implemented for older people, are run by Caritas, the St Vincent de Paul Society or parish groups and various small social solidarity co-operatives. Donati and Colozzi (1988) describe these as the 'third sector'.

They are mainly voluntary health or social relief agencies and semi-market social solidarity co-operatives. It comes as a surprise to Northern Europeans that the majority of Italian volunteers in the voluntary health care sector are men, not women. In contrast, the majority within the social relief sector are women, which is in line with most European voluntary groups. Over 78% of these agencies work in partnership with the local authorities. On the whole, the social relief sector, however, works independently.

The formal voluntary sector in Italy falls roughly into three formal clusters, emanating from three social policy orientations, reflecting the left parties, the lay centre parties and the Christian centre party (which others might identify as the party of the right). Donati and Colozzi (1988, pp.75–95) describe them, basing much of their analysis upon a nationwide investigation into 7,024 voluntary associations by Colozzi and Rossi (1983). On the basis of their remarks and my own observations, there are three recognizable types of welfare mixes, which open up alternatives to older people in accordance with their circumstances.

Firstly, there are the agencies which supplement the welfare state. They reflect its universalist values and are non-selective. These voluntary agencies constitute the 'other arm' of welfare. When the social services close down in the middle of the day, the voluntary sector takes over. Their regulations and conditions of service differ from region to region; for example, in Milan the weekly commitment is 5–10 hours' work. Many are over retirement age, and their expenses are paid by the local authority (see Depaoli et al., 1986, p.54). In Forli there are about 40 voluntary agencies, which are brought together by a Voluntary Council. There is also the Italian Red Cross, which, although it manages its work for older people independently of the commune, none the less complements the local authority services and extends the provision of care locally.

Secondly, there are the agencies which uphold the rights of everyone to health care and social relief, but also the right to choose between mixes, some of which may be bought from private or co-operative welfare agencies. This is basically founded upon partnership, rather than seeing the agency as an extension of state welfare. This partnership, however, is at arms'-length. Their local involvement reflects the community welfare model, in line with the ideas of Röpke, referred to in the introductory remarks to Part III, conserving the principles of neither state nor market welfare.

Thirdly, there are the agencies which are inspired by the Christian concept of care. The Catholic voluntary sector (motivated by vocationalism) is the largest provider (see Depaoli et al., 1986). Caritas is prominent everywhere, as is the St Vincent de Paul Society, which is also active in other countries in Europe. There are also Catholic Action (Azione Cattolica) youth groups engaged in working for older people locally. Local parish care is often referred to as the *campanilismo* (after the campanile – the church steeple).

These and the other non-statutory lay agencies are competitive providers who complement state provision but resist control. They subscribe to a welfare society model, and in the main conserve democratic individualism.

There are many other major Church organizations – for example, in La Spezia there is the Egidio Bullesi Association, which builds villages based upon integration of younger and older persons, and is Church-inspired; in Rome there is the Associazione Cultura e Assistenza Popolare (People's Culture and Welfare Association: ACAP), which is made up of about 200 volunteers who care for older people, working within teams under co-ordinators. Many of them are professional nurses and doctors, and they work independently of the secular welfare organizations. Also, there is the Gruppo Socializzazione Anziani (Elderly Socialization Group: GSA). These volunteers also include many trained and professional persons who work within day centres. In Naples, in addition to voluntary Church-inspired organizations such as Caritas and the St Vincent de Paul Society, there are the Daughters of Charity and the Caterina Volpicelli social centres, in addition to the many other voluntary organizations for which Naples is well known in Italy.

With increasing secularization, there are signs that these organizations are diminishing in number. However, during the recession the state has looked increasingly towards these non-profit agencies and the co-operatives to fill the gaps in care and provision. Referring to the voluntary sector in general, Depaoli et al. (1986, p.98) state that the welfare activities provided by volunteers are characterized by a relatively non-specialist range of services, and a tendency to attach importance to the person, rather than to the recipient of welfare – 'making a gift of part of one's time and resources'.

The specialist care provided by Age Concern, for example, is not replicated in Italy. The formal voluntary carers tend to be generic, with the notable exceptions of the leisure agencies and the Third Age educational centres.

Informal care

De Luca and Valgimigli (1983, pp.19–20) help to complete a national picture of older people in Italy. They say that there are six types of older Italians:

1   the honoured: (10% of the older population), revered and loved;
2   the neglected: (28%), victims of a callous society;
3   the useless: (16%), put away in institutions;
4   the failures: (11%), abandoned by their family, living in isolation and resignation;
5   the withdrawn: (20%), not able to make sense of life;

6 the ever-young: (15%), on the ascendancy.

The authors warn against romantic images of the 'new age elderly', and also, at the other extreme, the negative stereotypes which abound in Italy. The picture which emerges runs counter to the expectations of the casual tourist or visitor to Italy, as well as the idealized image of the Italian family as an extended haven where age is revered and older relatives sit in a place of honour.

English-language literature and research into the informal care of older Italians is minimal. The influential World Health Organization-sponsored work of Kendig et al. (1992), dealing with family support of older people internationally, does not fill this gap. Jamieson's (1991a) edited readings provide a picture of formal home care in Genoa, but not of the informal supports. Giarchi (1987a) does explore some of the informal caring arrangements in southern Liguria.

Magnani (1982, pp.894–5) states that the family in Italy is no longer the place in which to be socialized, nor the functional institution which helps to establish society. In fact, the family at times gets in the way by perpetuating ideas which run counter to the values of today's society. The older relatives are pushed out and marginalized – the older spinners of yesterday's tales are now redundant because the fables are futurist, not stories from an unexciting past. Magnani (1982, p.897) comments that inactive older people are less acceptable, because today 'non-production equates with *"male"* [badness]'. These are challenging comments, just as those of De Luca and Valgimigli (1983). The most significant early nationwide survey of family structures in Italy was carried out by the Instituto Centrale di Statistica (ISTAT) in 1983. The picture it presented of older people in the Italian household has not changed significantly. The need for informal carers is growing apace: 66.3% of those living alone in Italy are aged 60+; out of ten older people, about eight are single women, and about six are aged 70+. The highest proportions of single older persons are in the north-western cities, and the lowest in central Italy. The survey has demonstrated that singleness does not necessarily mean isolation. Many are assisted by their offspring's families, especially the men. Also, single older women are often the local helpers, and have a central role within the inter-family circle of care. The networks of care are more evident and are strongest in the smaller neighbourhoods and in central Italy.

The ESRC (Economic and Social Research Council) -funded research project which I carried out in Liguria (Giarchi, 1987a) explores the nature of family support within an area with one of the highest concentrations of older people. The proportion of older people in the province was as high as 21.5% (women 60+/men 65+). One of my interviewees was a witty woman of 106, living in the mountains above La Spezia. In addition to her, 73 persons were chosen at random, aged 75 years of age and over, whom I interviewed in some depth within their homes; 47 were in local towns or the city of La Spezia, and 27 in the rural communes. The sample brought me into contact with established households of the *Spezzini* (as the people of La Spezia are called) and with incomers, giving me the opportunity to take a long look at the family life of typical urban families; 10% of households were outsiders, mainly from the south of Italy. I also visited many rural families north of the city. The urban and the rural interviews in southern Liguria provide some important observations about contemporary care of older people in Italian households. A more detailed commentary is under preparation for a forthcoming publication.

There was a surprising 35.3% population of single older people in the province of La Spezia. The stereotypical large Latin family household was not evident; in fact, the average number of dependent children in Liguria was as low as 0.5 per family. According to the local lawyers, the divorce rate was rising rapidly, amounting to about one in three, usually of couples under 30 years of age. However, in the rural areas the traditional attitudes regarding home care and family life prevailed, but the rural population was rapidly decreasing. It was clear that many of the younger families had different expectations regarding the nature of family life and familial responsibilities. Family life in Italy was in transition, but not without a moral struggle, taken up by the leading Italian Church magazine, *La Famiglia Cristiana*, a popular national magazine which propagated the traditional ideals of the Italian family.

In the city, 62% of the interviewees lived with their families, usually in private rented accommodation; the rest either lived alone or were lone couples. Most of the older parents who did not live with their offspring did, however, live either close by in the same block of apartments or in a nearby house. Approximately 40% of these had weekly visits by their immediate family, and approximately 38% had weekly contact with their relatives (down to third cousins). Only 2% had no contact with their offspring, and only 1% had no contact with their relatives at all. The Italian family circle was more intensive and extensive, and also more exclusive, than the Irish and UK counterparts which I had interviewed in County Cork (Ireland) and Devon (UK). The interviews with the 33 professional or voluntary sector carers did indicate that there was great concern as to whether the families of the future could be relied upon to provide the same comprehensive care. However, the tight family circle was a veritable halter for some of the women I talked to, creating a form of benign oppression within semi-closed and sometimes even cloistered, almost impassable, households.

Tight bonding was the significant factor, particularly for the Italian women, which often amounted to a type of bondage. There were moments in the interviews which picked up the sense of imprisonment of grandmothers peering through half-opened shutters at the world outside, where their husbands, male relatives and friends were enjoying the *passegiata* (promenade), or were drinking and playing cards in the *trattorie* or enjoying a game of *boccia* (a popular game of bowls). Women went out occasionally to the garden of remembrance, to Sunday Mass (here the men stayed at home), to do the shopping with their daughters, or take the grandchildren for early morning or evening walks.

The tight family life had little patience with any attempt of the voluntary sector to involve the circles of relatives in its activities. During my three-month stay, the Italian families generally kept outside informal carers at bay. Families kept within their circle of relatives. However, Church visitors were welcome, as they are in Greece, especially those who came to pray with the sick or brought Holy Communion. Their visits did not carry with them any inference that the family was not coping. On the contrary, if the family arranged Church visits, the household status was enhanced. The 'cure of souls' is an old Latin expression: it is regarded as the supreme form of care ('cure' and 'care' are synonymous in the Italian language). Most of the interviewees explained that everyone had spiritual needs, especially the women. As one older man explained to me in a La Spezia *trattoria*, 'The soul comes direct from God; our body comes from the womb of the family.'

The family structure was so tight that the number of contacts with neighbours and friends was significantly less amongst the women than in the UK or the Irish family samples within the ESRC study (Giarchi, 1987a). Single, lone older people appeared to be marginalized. The Church organizations attempted to fill the gap, especially the Saint Vincent de Paul Society.

The professionals interviewed during the ESRC study (Giarchi, 1987a) spoke of the *famiglismo* ('the family institution'), which was a central cultural and historic feature within Italy. They explained that it was families which owned and ran Italian industries, agencies and even the Church. The culture of care was also dominated by family pride, and the rights of women within the family were a major political issue for all parties and unions. Party politics is a main topic of conversation in a country with Europe's highest turnouts of voters. The family was not only the primary care unit, it was also the primary political unit.

Within the triangle of welfare many different households and their grey-haired kinship circles resisted any formal intervention. When hospitalization was necessary, the kinship circle centred upon the patient, providing a continuous rota of bedside carers. Hospital staff expected such a rota to operate round the clock when an older patient was *in extremis*. The intimate care, even toileting, was carried out by relatives – always described as *famiglia*, whether granddaughter or great-niece.

The reliance upon the family to provide care is evident everywhere, in both the urban and rural areas. The CPA (1993, p.153) cites recent Italian research which indicates that 88% of older people are cared for by family members, in contrast with 9.8% who seek outside assistance. Significantly, of the 7,024 groups of volunteers in Italy, only 50 (0.7%) are involved with helping older Italians. Given the impact of social change upon Italian families, older Italians may not be cared for to the same extent by their own offspring nor near relatives in twenty years' time. (Given the oppressive nature of that care in some Italian families, the alternatives may be less oppressive.)

Leisure pursuits and education

The centres for older people are often run by the unions. In addition, there are the Universities of the Third Age, for example in La Spezia, a city of under 150,000 people, where there are three such educational courses. In Italy as a whole there are 176 learning centres (Golden Age Learning Centres), catering for about 48,230 older people; significantly, 112 of these exist in the north of the country. Also, the co-operatives run Open Universities in most of the cities, but relatively few of the millions of older Italians register. However, in my later research in Italy (Giarchi et al., 1992), I have been acutely aware of the more enclosed nature of family life for older Italians, which acts as a barrier to engagement. Disengagement is positively fostered: the women and the frailer men are often not permitted to enter into the social life of the locality. The further south one travels, the more are older people captive within households, especially women after retirement. The CPA (1993, p.149) refers to the Italian description of retirement as 'empty time' (*tempo vuoto*). Some authorities offer a 59% reduction to older people for holidays, but they are usually means-tested.

Rural aspects

Rural Italy is under-resourced in terms of community nurses and social operators, even in the more developed northern provinces. The more rural communes often have small populations of between 270 and 700. The younger people have been leaving the villages and hamlets since the 1930s to emigrate abroad or to work in the major cities, leaving the older people behind in the sparsely-populated areas. In the rural areas I visited, 18 out of the 29 communes had decimated populations. Neither nurses nor social workers visited the area, and even the priest's house stood empty. Church services and visits to the sick and frail at home were organized from the nearby city, and this was in the more prosperous and better-served north of

Italy. As stated earlier, the Egidio Bullesi Association in southern Liguria is committed to setting up villages for the family, which integrates older mountain regions. Many hundreds have gone back, even the third and fourth generations. I visited the first village set up in the late 1980s in Sorbolo di Follo. The association believes in both the family and the rural community. Much like the housing associations of the UK, this inter-generational agency provides for low-income families in the fight against homelessness. Vineyards and workshops have been established around the dwellings, with older people playing a vital role in the life of the village.

In the early 1990s, one of my studies of the lifestyle of older Europeans (Giarchi et al., 1992), sponsored by the EU in collaboration with SAGO (Società di Ricercha per l'Orginazzione Sanitaria) in Florence, compared Italian older people's groups in rural Chianti with those in rural Devon (UK) and County Cork (Republic of Ireland). Contrary to expectations, the older people in the rural areas of Chianti were more reserved and slow to join groups set up by the USL, and the Italian families in the rural areas were wary and diffident when invited to join such groups. Most families prided themselves on not requiring any outside support. Those that made up these rural groups were not as outgoing, nor as gregarious, as their Irish and English counterparts. The women particularly did not have the same freedom, and were kept at home to carry out household chores, much like older Greek and Romanian women. A peasant told me that 'In Italy we have been saying, even before the Romans, *La donna fa l'uomo* [The woman makes the man].' He then added: 'She's a helper – Adam can't exist without Eve.' The older women worked on the small farms, whilst their menfolk sunned themselves or sat drinking in the *trattorie*.

More studies in rural Italy (both in the north and south) are needed to establish the care systems, the needs of the older populations and their concerns.

Conclusion

The major interactive linkages within the Italian welfare system consist of: the market and the co-operatives; the local state and the highly politicized, regionally accountable, formal social and health care systems, backed by a variety of voluntary agencies, and the state's decentralized system of care and devolution to the regional assemblies and councils. The Catholic principle of 'subsidiarity' is in place, but not legislated for, as is the case in Germany.

The state welfare system leans heavily upon familial care. However, it is also clear that the structure of the younger Italian family is changing dramatically, and that the increase in the proportion of older people is making additional demands upon the country's already strained formal resources. In addition, the Church organizations are weakened in the wake of increasing secularization. The more significant these support systems have been to date, the more significant will be the gaps in the caring arrangements for older Italians in the next fifty years. Plans for alternative or substitute modes of care to the traditional one do not appear to be on the political agenda.

The market has now become a significant factor. Expenditure is the central Italian issue, often eclipsing the old ideological differences. The present home care schemes, often put in place by the Communist Party, such as in Bologna, are now giving way to a market welfare system. They have not been in place long enough to test their effectiveness, but the Italian electorate are restless.

Within the triangulation processes at macro and micro levels, families will face the responsibility of paying for services which until recently were provided in many areas by the *assessori*. Costanzi (1991, pp.190–1), along with Manoukian (1988), states that the social movement towards state welfare and restructured health services cuts across all party divides and is feminist-inspired. There is no doubt that the communist welfare thrust was so powerful that the other parties, reading the signs, had little choice but to go along with the changes that brought in universalist collective care if they were to win votes at regional and provincial levels. However, expediency rather than shared basic humanitarian ideals is uppermost. The pendulum has swung to the market, and in many areas to the right. Italy's New Right is making capital from the collapse of communism in Eastern Europe.

Costanzi (1991, p.194) observes that the private and the voluntary services are currently playing an ever-increasing role in the new welfare systems. The ability to pay is the central factor in determining who gets what. The voluntary sector, sustained by *famiglismo* and *campanilismo*, will cater for the poorer older Italians, but both are weakening.

It is hardly likely that the current pension system will survive the contemporary socio-economic and political upheaval that has struck Italy, and enable older Italians to buy care and conserve their dignity. The infrastructure of care is weak, and alternatives to family care are weaker still. It remains to be seen how strong family ties will be in the next 30 years.

22 Spain

Demography

The proportion of older people in Spain is lower than in most European countries, as can be seen from Table 1, principally because the birth rate is higher. By the year 2025 the proportion will be approximately 15.7%, which will be 3.2% lower than that of dependent children (0–14 years) (see CPA, 1989, p.135). As Table 1 indicates, the number of older people will increase by 2.4% by 2025. Spanish women at 65 have the sixth-highest life expectancy (18.8 years) in greater Europe, and men at the same age the second-highest (15.4 years), according to UN (1991) and Eurostat (1991a). The CPA (1993, p.201) points out that the country has one of the highest life expectancies at 75 (men: 9 years; women: 11). However, Spain has the highest proportion of single older people in Southern Europe, at 14% (Grundy and Harrop, 1992, p.28).

Many of the population gravitate towards the coasts, especially in the regions of the Basque country, Galicia, Catalonia, Valencia and the Balearic Islands. The single largest concentration is, of course, in and around Madrid.

Most Spaniards are now urban residents. The older rural people, as in so many parts of Europe, have been left behind. The study of older rural people is a very neglected field in European studies.

Socio-political and administrative background

Since the death of Franco in 1975 the unitary state he created has had to undergo immense changes. In 1978 a new territorial administrative structure was instituted. The new constitution of 1978 enshrined the ideals of the

377

welfare state within a shared programme of care between the Central State Administration and 17 'Autonomous Communities' (Comunidades Autónomas): 15 in mainland Spain and 2 outside it, in the Canarias and Ceuta-Melilla, North Africa. These are responsible for social aid (*assistencia social*). They also promulgate social service laws which have immediate relevance to the care of older people.

The national government outlines its policies regarding older people by means of its social security policy (Spinnewyn and Cabrero, 1991, p.173). The important central bodies are INSERSO (Instituto de Servicios Sociales) and the Ministry of Social Affairs, which was set up to complement the role of INSERSO. Support for older people is one of the ministry's five major priorities (Lishman et al., 1993, p.10). The ministry creates a partnership between the government and the older population.

The Spanish Constitution of 1978 grants authority to the public authorities to administer the social protection system at regional levels, but it also allows for private profit-making, private voluntary and charitable agencies to operate within a flexible scheme that is essentially polycephalic and pluralist.

Central government determines the basic law and the economic structure of the social services within the social security system with regard to older people and disabled persons. Most services for the immigrant/migrant populations are under central government control.

Although Autonomous Communities are invested with authority to promulgate laws regarding social services, in seven regions full authority is still in a transitional state. The system resembles Italy's regionalized social care structure, and to some extent those of Switzerland and Germany. Like Italy's social care structure, there are variations between the regions. Some consist of one province, such as Rioja, Navarre, Murcia and Madrid; others respect larger regional national identities, such as those of Catalonia, the Basque country and Galicia; others cut historic provinces in two, such as La Mancha, Castilla-Leon and Castilla (Rossell and Rimbau, 1989, p.121).

Social care in Spain has been commented upon in general introductory terms by Rossell and Rimbau (1989). After the Franco regime ended in 1975, the country swung towards public service provision and increased professionalism. Hitherto the emphasis had been upon vocationalism and voluntarism, particularly when it came to the care of older people. As indicated above, the swing has faltered somewhat, with the state bolstering up the very sectors which Franco had striven to maintain. Unfortunately for Spain, the end of the Franco era was shortly followed by the beginning of the European recession. The universalist intent of the new democratic regime of services for all, and not simply for the destitute and marginalized people, entailed enormous expenditure.

In spite of the recession of the 1980s and early 1990s, new primary care social services have been established. These have favoured the care of older and disabled people over other special needs groups. In contrast with the under-provision of community nursing, the social services are beginning to expand and diversify social care for older people, plus recreational and cultural activities (Rossell and Rimbau, 1989, p.111). Temporary unskilled work is offered to local people to manage the programmes within localities. Caritas and the Red Cross, prominent care providers as elsewhere in Europe, attempt to fill gaps within the caring systems, as reluctant partners to the public sector. However, welfare pluralism is the only alternative if Spain is to cope with its large number of older people.

As in Italy, the regions are the major loci of social care provision and statutory responsibility backed by regional laws, enjoying considerable autonomy. Spinnewyn and Cabrero (1991, p.173) describe the current administrative system that provides for older Spanish people. The regions are responsible for community integration programmes, rural environment and mental health programmes.

The local administration of care is carried out at the level of the provinces and municipalities. There are 51 provinces and 9,000 municipalities with their own mayors and councils. They organize home help services, day centres and sheltered flats, and are responsible for administering free travel for older people. The nature of these services will be dealt with in the appropriate sections below.

The private sector has been slow to develop, partly because of the many well-organized and creditable voluntary agencies. Casado (1992, p.6) states that there are relatively few profit-making agencies, apart from some residential homes. Spain's long tradition of co-operatives may also help to explain the apparent lack of enthusiasm for the development of private commercialized care.

Knapp et al. (1990, p.47) refer to the mixing of welfare in Spain. Whereas the process within the UK has consisted of decreasing the public provision of services, the process within Spain has consisted of increasing both the public and private sectors as complementary partners. At the same time, the Spanish government proceeds with caution in the wake of the collapse of large welfare systems elsewhere in Europe. As a Spanish theorist at a conference in Malta explained to me: 'Large welfare systems are still required, but not too large.'

Social security: pensions and benefits

In spite of the fact that Spain is one of the poorer countries in Europe, it spends proportionately more on old age social security benefits than the other countries within the EU apart from Germany. But, the country has a relatively low proportion of older people. However, the poverty amongst the older population in Spain is an embarrassment. The major reason is that Spain has had so much leeway to make up in providing for its long-neglected older people. During Franco's regime the country was in a welfare limbo, out of touch with economic and social developments in the rest of Europe. Its demise left Spain with the highest level of unemployment in Europe (see Burns, 1989). The problem of unemployment has since been the major focus of attention; this, together with the attendant problems affecting the younger families, leaves little room for the prioritization of the care of older people, but a major concern of the National Institute for Social Security has been to remove the immediate embarrassment related to their poverty (see European Programme to Combat Poverty, 1989).

Aid in the form of money to survive and to buy in necessary care in crises is the immediate provision. The state pension is earnings-related. There is universal cover for employees, and for the self-employed there is voluntary cover. For industrial and service workers there is a general scheme, with special ones for particular occupations, public service employees and the self-employed (CPA, 1989, p.135). Eligibility generally requires at least 15 years of contributions by the age of 65.

Housing

Housing in Spain has only recently been adapted for older people; the first modifications were made in the early 1980s (CPA, 1989, p.135). After Ireland, Spain has the highest percentage of owner-occupiers in the EU (Eurostat, 1991b, p.118). Older people occupy the oldest houses, which are often in bad repair and are not likely ever to be refurbished during their occupancy. Since 1988 the municipalities have introduced sheltered housing (*pisos protegidos*). Spain is a latecomer to this form of provision, and has a considerable gap to fill. Soria (1993) describes how rundown the properties are and the lack of modern conveniences, with 11% living in upper-level apartments without lifts.

Health care

The health service provides people aged 65 and over with a health identity card. The socialist health reform in Spain was a major breakthrough, but the country's health and statutory services still lag behind most of the other European welfare systems. Spain, along with Portugal, Greece, Yugoslavia and Albania, spends less on health than the more affluent countries of Northern, Western and Central Europe (De Miguel, 1990, p.39). Hospital beds in Spain are few, and the occupancy rate is the lowest in Europe (De Miguel, 1990, p.40). However, it is also pointed out by De Miguel that there is no correlation between the proportion of GDP spent on health and the status of a country's health.

Life expectancy is high in Spain – the highest amongst the Southern European countries (Eurostat, 1991a; UN, 1991; CPA, 1989). Because of this, the Spanish health providers have greater costs to meet after Spaniards reach the age of 75. De Miguel (1990, pp.44–5) makes the point that long-term care of older people includes not only health care but also economic assistance, social services, pensions and social welfare policies, rather than therapeutic or diagnostic medical interventions, 'which would have the greatest benefit potential'. None the less a very dependent 5% of the older population require residential and nursing care. It is here that Spain's health and social care systems, are under the greatest pressure. Soria (1993) describes how over half of those aged 65+ have untreated symptoms.

Hospital care and medical services

The hospitals have only recently set up special units (*unidades geriatrices*) for older people with handicaps; these cater for approximately 3,178 patients (Spinnewyn and Cabrero, 1991, p.167). These modern well-equipped hospital units sharply contrast with the older wards and their 'geriatric' beds. It is feared that the numbers of beds required in the next twenty years will be almost impossible to sustain. For example, Lishman et al. (1993, p.11) refer to the 14,000 beds in hospitals in Valencia, which it is predicted will increase to as many as 107,000 in ten years' time.

After Italy, Spain has the highest ratio of doctors: 3.3 per 1,000 inhabitants (Eurostat, 1991b, p.88); but, with Portugal, it has the lowest ratio of dentists: 0.1 per 1,000 inhabitants. Many older people have dental problems. However, the health of older people is generally much better than in other European countries.

Mental health care

Recently, occupational therapy centres outside psychiatric hospitals have been created in Spain, as reported by Casado (1992, p.14). The de-institutionalization of the large mental health hospitals, where many older people have languished and regressed for many years, has not been fully implemented. As has been the case in the UK, transfer programmes have been protracted, and at times have met with opposition. However, Spain, along with Italy, has only 0.9 psychiatric beds per 1,000 inhabitants, the lowest ratio in the EU (Eurostat, 1991b, p.88), so the programme of de-institutionalization has not been such a massive problem as in other parts of Europe (the UK ratio is 2.6 beds per 1,000).

According to law, the court can decide within the Spanish Civil Code that persons unable to care for themselves because of mental illness can be placed under the protection of a form of guardianship (Lishman et al., 1993, p.17).

Institutional care

Spain has lagged behind most of Europe in providing social care for older people. This is illustrated by the fact that the Ministry of Social Affairs has put forward a plan which proposes that there should be 107,588 new residential places by the year 2000 in order to meet the demand for 3.5 places for every 100 older people. Whilst other countries are closing down or blocking the further development of homes for older people, Spain is increasing their number. Lishman et al. (1993, p.13) cite the state homes (*residencias proprias*) which, for example, offer 2,020 places in 19 homes in Alicante, Castellon and Valencia. A further 20 will be provided to cater for 1,767 older people in the immediate future.

The old age homes (*residencias de tercera edad*) cater mainly for the able-bodied, and are available to those who have an income and are able to pay for their residence. Spinnewyn and Cabrero (1991, pp.167–8) state that there are 1,281 institutions for older people, providing 89,799 beds; 20.1% of the institutions are public sector homes; 79.9% are private, providing for 46,809 residents. About 4,289 residents do not pay, often because they have no pension. Half of the homes are below the standard requirements, which is another reason why Spain is building new homes.

Only 2.6% of Spaniards aged 65+ are in residential homes (Council of Europe, 1988, p.13). The government subsidizes the homes in the public and private sectors in order to make up the yawning gap in provision.

Knapp et al. (1990, p.51) describe 89 Catalonian homes in detail out of the total of 382 homes. Although Knapp et al.'s picture does not open a window on Spain as a whole, it does present a panorama of what is happening in one of Spain's more affluent and ancient regions, and an appreciation of government policy regarding priorities. The area, centred on Barcelona, has been redeveloped by the EU. The region attracts more than 40% of all foreign capital invested in Spain (Generalitat de Catalunya, 1992). The development of the infrastructure of care lags hopelessly behind, hence the subsidies to prop up the private and voluntary sectors of care. At least a quarter of the homes are private, but most are voluntary, and continue to be provided by the Church. Under the old regime these catered for the frail and destitute older people. The reliance upon the family has already been emphasized in Catholic countries where residential care is seen as an extended family provision. It is significant also that the monies paid to the residential sector are equivalent to about one-fifth of the annual amount paid in pensions by the Generalitat (the regional government).

Knapp et al. (1990) provide us with a closer look at residential arrangements and costs. The ten public sector Catalonian homes of the Generalitat have an average of 140 residents in each. They are managed by the counties and local authorities (Knapp et al., 1990, p.52). As much as 70% of the running costs are met by the residents' fees. As is the case in the UK, the public sector homes are more expensive to run than the residential homes in the private sector. Knapp et al. (1990, p.65) state that each public sector home costs on average 4,522 pesetas more per week for residence than does the voluntary residential home.

The voluntary homes are usually smaller, with about 42 residents in each, and generally situated close to the households within catchment areas that are amongst the most traditional neighbourhoods in Europe. The government policy of providing families with income so as to purchase this service when required is part of the strategy to bolster the so-called 'fourth sector' of the family. However, they are a cheaper option for the state than the public sector because they receive private donations which prop up the meagre payments of residents, which are in accordance with their means; the residents are often amongst the poorest, with low levels of state benefits. The contributions of the voluntary sector, which amount to almost 55% of costs, enable the homes to cope, but with great difficulty on a deficit payments basis, whereby they receive the state payments one year in arrears (Knapp et al., 1990, p.53). The voluntary social care services in Catalonia consume as much as 45% of all public expenditure, within which the care of older people forms a significant cost.

Knapp et al. conclude that the contracting-out of residential care bureaucratizes the voluntary sector unduly as the agencies get caught up within the state procedures and evaluation programmes. The state is also able to be in control through the mechanism of payments in arrears. The whole ethos of voluntarism and vocationalism is threatened by the state bureaucracies holding out the tempting offer of state-subsidized places in the so-called 'independent' sector.

The private homes are small businesses run by families; although small, they now provide about 25% of the available places. In other less prosperous parts of Spain the private provision is clearly considerably less.

Personal social services

The Spanish Constitution states that all citizens have the right to social services. Casado (1992) describes the nature and extent of the personal social services. As stated earlier, the Autonomous Communities are endowed by the Spanish Constitution with exclusive authority for the provision of 'social aid' (*asistencia social*), which is equivalent to 'social services' as generally understood in Europe.

Local offices

First-stage social work comes under various names in the Autonomous Communities, such as 'First Aid Social Services' (*Servicios Sociales de Atención Primaria*), 'Basic Social Services' (*Servicios Sociales de Base*) or 'Community Social Services' (*Servicios Sociales Comunitarios*). Whatever the names they are given, these intake facilities consist of small offices which may serve a whole district, several municipalities or just one municipality. They can serve anything from 5,000–25,000 people. They often only have one qualified social worker plus some specialist professionals and a back-up administrative staff. They provide information and deal with requests for residential care and home aid. The older populations in the cities of Bilbao, Barcelona and Madrid are better served by more experienced and qualified social workers.

Community care

Community care has been minimal in Spain (Estivill, 1984; Casado, 1985; Rossell and Rimbau, 1989). Striking the balance between open care and institutional care is a present concern of the government. These community services are mainly provided by the municipalities, some of which have introduced a wide variety of 'closer-to-home' facilities.

Day centres

There are 1,834 day centres (*hogares*) in Spain, according to Spinnewyn and Cabrero (1991, p.168); 28.3% (463) of these are provided by social security, and 30% (approximately 1.7 million) of the older population attend them.

Home care/help

The home help system (*ayuda a domicilio*) is in its early stages; none the less, there are 248 home help organizations in Spain, providing care for approximately 24,000 older people. According to Spinnewyn and Cabrero (1991, p.169), the home help resources are supported and run by 187 social security centres, by 22 Catholic service centres, by 13 town councils, by 12 regional government centres, by 11 private agencies and by three other undefined organizations (see Spinnewyn and Cabrero, 1991, p.169). Lishman et al. (1993, p.13) state that the provision of home help is increasing faster than any other service provision for older people in Spain; for example, in the Valencia community, 477 of the 539 Town Halls have agreed to home help services.

Other services

Some Autonomous Communities have set up Social Services Centres designed solely for older people. Others have also introduced a 'telephone aid system' to enable older people to communicate with their neighbours/friends, and especially their families/relatives. Another innovation is the 'tele-help' emergency help system organized for older people in distress.

In certain areas there are Medical Check-up Centres, staffed by psychologists, ophthalmologists, general practitioners and administrative staff. In others, there is also a Home Assistance Service, as distinct from home help, which provides respite for carers.

Voluntary care agencies and support organizations

During the Franco regime the trade unions still survived. The syndicalist system and trade union structure are an integral feature of Spanish life. It is not surprising that the caring co-operatives should be so active in Spain. The independent associations and the polycephalic nature of Spanish administration encourage and strengthen the autonomy of the voluntary sector. About 38% of the day centres are provided by the private non-profit organizations (see Spinnewyn and Cabrero, 1991, p.168).

As stated above, home helps are often volunteers within the Red Cross and other Church/voluntary organizations. For example, Lishman et al. (1993, p.16) describe the variety of support offered by the Red Cross in Alicante, such as transport for people with disabilities, the loan of wheelchairs, crutches and stretchers, an emergency ambulance service, and a home help service.

Informal care

The structure of the Spanish household is changing rapidly. Whereas in 1970 10% of older people lived on their own and 70% with partners, in 1990 the former increased to 19% and the latter decreased to 58% (Lishman et al, 1993, p.11).

Spinnewyn and Cabrero (1991, p.171) state that 'in Spain the family is still the main carer for the elderly. Volunteers are now beginning to play a relevant role. We could say that there has been a certain loss of importance in the role of the family which perhaps has been partly compensated by volunteers.' Although the family is beginning to be less important in the care of its older relatives, the next of kin are still expected to help them. However, there are at present inadequate back-up, benefits and allowances necessary to sustain household care.

The potential caring ratio is greater in Spain because the birth rate is higher. The older the families, the more matriarchal they become. The husbands are generally much older, and their domestic dependency is a feature within families. On the basis of the CPA (1989, pp.125 and 135), three-quarters of the over-65s live in the rural areas in Portugal, and just under half in Spain, where the traditions of the male chauvinist family are more prevalent.

In Spain, the family is 'the basic point of reference in the social structure', according to Rossell and Rimbau (1989, p.105). The welfare state has never been the mainstay of social care in Spain (see Casado, 1992). During the welfare crisis of the 1970s the families provided the safety net, particularly the women. The expectation is such that they must appear to be in control to uphold the traditional idealized Latin family image of caring, resourceful women. If supplementary care is needed, the supportive network still tends to include the family because it must oversee any mode of care. Substitute care is rare. Rubies i Ferrer (1992) confirms the points made by Rossell and Rimbau (1989) and Soria (1993).

Leisure pursuits and education

INSERSO promotes holidays ('old age tourism') for older people. There are also 'old age universities' throughout Spain. These are sorely needed as 92% of older people are either illiterate or only educated to primary school level (Soria, 1993, p.272). The CPA (1993, p.206) refers to 'social tourism', which has recently been created by local authorities. Subsidized holidays are provided for older people on low incomes. However, almost half of older people never go on holiday.

Rural aspects

Spinnewyn and Cabrero (1991, p.173) refer to the fact that it is in the cities that policies for the older population are more evident. Great disparities exist, as in almost all of Europe, between the general services for older people in rural as distinct from urban areas. Like France, Spain has some of the most remote rural areas in Europe. Mobility has created great imbalances in the caring ratios, so that with the dramatic drop in the availability of informal care, more formal care is necessary.

Conclusion

In the past the only formal care available for older people in Spain was residential care. The Franco regime created, by means of the Movimento Nacional, a traditional Church-led social care service system throughout Spain. In fact, Spain probably has one of the greatest shortfalls in welfare and social care to make up if it is to fall in line with the major EU countries. The formal community care services, like those in Italy, are slim, dependent as the country has been upon the informal care provided by the family, with minimal public care and maximum voluntary care. However, as this chapter demonstrates, the welfare and health systems have been greatly improved and expanded in a nation that has developed rapidly within the EU.

Research into the formal provision of care in Spain is fraught with the difficulties associated with studying the dominant cultures of care peculiar to totally separate nations within one country; these contrast more between the different regional ethnic groups than with peoples outside it. It is imperative that there be more research into the regional needs of the older populations in this vast geographic area with its very heterogeneous distinctive cultures and diversified values. A closer comparative examination of the services within the respective Comunidades Autónomas and municipalities is called for.

23 Portugal

Demography

As indicated in Table 1, Portugal's proportion of older people is ranked sixteenth in greater Europe. It is likely to drop to twenty-fourth place (jointly with Spain) by the year 2025, on the basis of projections (CPA, 1989, p.125). The life expectancy of older women at 65 years of age is 17.8 years, ranked twelfth in greater Europe; that of men at the same age is ranked sixth (jointly with Austria and Greece), at 14.5 years (Eurostat, 1991a; UN, 1991).

Socio-political and administrative background

Portugal is on the peripheral, seaward side of Europe, well outside the 'golden egg', and its population clings to the coasts. Like its Iberian neighbour Spain, Portugal has shaken off an authoritarian regime and created in its place a mainly polycephalic administrative system. Social policy regarding older people comes under the authority of the Ministry of Employment and Social Security in Lisbon. Many socio-economic and administrative changes took place after the dictator Salazar retired in 1968, which were to have an important effect upon the lives of older people particularly.

Under the old regime they were the victims of a patriarchal social structure in which care was provided by familes and when they did not provide, by the Church. The dictatorship was to be followed by social instability and political disorganization, with anarchists and other factions attempting to take over. After the revolution of 1974, three phases help to explain what older people had to face and the emergent system that would provide for them (Lisboa, 1986, p.439).

In the first phase, older people were expected to provide for themselves because the technocrats of the old regime were largely still in office. In the second phase, the social pendulum swung towards the concept of the universalist welfare state. But there were no resources to establish one, in spite of the passing of a national health service law (see Lisboa, 1986, p.440). The third phase is where my account begins, with the emphasis of Lisbon's Ministry of Employment and Social Security upon a pluralist welfare state.

The Constitution of the Portuguese Republic of 1975 (approved in 1976 and revised in 1989) guarantees citizens the right to social security and protection in old age, disability and in widowhood.

In 1977, the Unified Social Security System was introduced. The new law integrated social welfare and social assistance, and created regional social security centres. These regional entities were granted administrative and financial autonomy, and were empowered to set up local grassroots services. This was part of a policy of decentralization. The polycephalic structures emerged in reaction to the former authoritarian, centralist regime.

In 1979 the Statute of Private Social Solidarity Institutions (SPSSI) was established. The institutions had a moral duty to bring about solidarity and justice, provide social action or benefits, and recognize the role of organized social volunteers (Castelhano et al., 1992, p.3). In 1983 the Regional Social Security Centres were set up, as part of this massive shift to bring decision-making closer to vulnerable people in need, such as older people. In 1984 the law stipulated that 'social action' was the responsibility of the Private Social Solidarity Institutions (PSSIs). 'Social action' complements social security benefits; in broad terms it is the promotion of the wellbeing of people, and the provision of social services towards this end. In 1989, the government proceeded to extend the role of agencies in providing social action by legislating for the inclusion of the private sector in providing care. Rules were promulgated for the setting up, operational management and licensing of profit-making private institutions and homes for older people. By 1990, there were rules for the running of local services under the Regional Social Security Centres.

Since 1991, social action is regulated, evaluated and monitored by the General Direction for Social Action. This body is one of the three central departments in Lisbon, so that social services are organized and administered separately from the administrative social security system (see Castelhano et al., 1992, p.2). However, the Regional Social Security Centres (RSSCs), although answerable to the General Direction for Social Action, are responsible for carrying out social action, an important part of which is the care of older people. They promote social integration, develop community social action, support the PSSIs and license and supervise private profit-making institutions.

The PSSIs may consist of social solidarity associations, social action volunteer associations, mutual benefit associations, social solidarity foundations and Irmandades da Misericordia, a well-known organization which is responsible for social action in Lisbon. Unions, federations and confederations may be involved. All participant organizations etc. must be licensed by the RSSCs and agree to state supervision.

Portugal's administration has been divided for many years into 18 administrative districts (*distritos*), each with a civil governor, administered with the help of a board. The 18 districts now form the regions: 15 are mainland, the others are in the Azores and Arquipelago in the Atlantic Ocean. The Church organizations of the Misericordias used to be the major providers of social care at district levels. The old districts are subdivided into municipalities (*concelhos*) and parishes (*freguesias*). The municipality is headed by a town council (*camara municipal*). These age-old local entities are where decision-making is passed down from the central departments and the regional centres.

Before describing the various forms of care provided for older people in Portugal, it is important to understand that over the years there has been little co-ordination between the two key ministries governing the policies for the care of older people: the Ministry of Health and the Ministry of Employment and Social Security. These ministries have delegates in the 18 regions, so that conflicts tended to occur throughout the whole system; however, in 1988 the National Commission for Ageing Policy was set up, which is designed to bring the ministries and the PSSIs together.

Social security: pensions and benefits

The social security schemes are financed by contributions from employers and employees, and provide almost universal coverage for employed women aged 62+ and employed men aged 65+, provided they have paid 120 months' contributions (see CPA, 1989, p.125). There are schemes for the self-employed, for non-agricultural workers, for bank employees, transport workers, the other categories of employed and public employees. Those who have not contributed towards the pension have access to a 'social pension' which is means-tested and funded by the government. It is the only example of such a pension.

Within the benefit structure people are entitled to 2.2% of their pensionable salary for each year of contribution, subject to a 30% minimum and an 80% maximum. These must be seen within the context of poverty in Portugal: 31.4% of households and 32.4% of individuals receive 50% or less of the respective national average income (Eurostat, 1990; see Davis, 1992, p.22), putting Portugal at the bottom of the EU poverty league, and with it many of its older people.

Portugal has a high income replacement ratio (the pension expressed as a proportion of the last wage or salary received before retirement). For example, Walker (1992a, p.175) states that a Portuguese worker (who has a spouse) in a manufacturing industry receives 82% of his or her prior gross wages, in contrast to the 33% income replacement ratio of the counterpart in the UK. Whether single or married, the Portuguese upon retirement, after taxation and compulsory contributions, generally have a higher income replacement ratio than retiring pensioners in Belgium, Germany, France, Luxemburg and the Netherlands. However, the wages/salaries and standard of living are much lower in Portugal than in these countries. One of the major problems for older people in Portugal is that there is no formal indexation, so that older people can see the purchasing power of their pension plummet with inflation, or because of a dramatic increase in other people's earnings.

Housing

For many years, housing in Portugal has been financed by private enterprise. Socio-economic disparities and gaps in housing conditions between house-holders have appeared over time. Official schemes, such as low-cost but better-furbished housing, have been provided for public and civil servants, white-collar employees and trade union members. The government, the municipalities and the corporative organizations created this privileged stock of houses under the Salazar regime. These contrast with the houses for the poor once provided by the Salazar Foundation, which were funded by public benefactors; these constitute the worst of the Portuguese slums. Low-rent housing for fishermen's families also contrasts with the more modern properties in Lisbon. Portuguese housing is the worst in the EU countries, and amongst the worst in greater Europe. The poorest older people occupy the worst housing, so that the low level of household comforts is of significance. Only 58% of Portuguese households have a bathroom or shower on the premises (Eurostat, 1991b, p.121), and only 58.7% have an internal WC, the EU averages being 83.1% and 85.3% respectively. Portuguese households are also the most overcrowded in the EU (Eurostat, 1991b, p.121).

Weaver (1989) focuses upon examples of housing conditions which affect older people in some of Portugal's poorest areas. Firstly, there is the La Se study (see Weaver, 1989, pp.190–1), which describes the housing deprivation facing older people in the historical centre of Porto, where 22.9% of the population are aged 60+. The houses were designed in the Salazar regime to accommodate one family. In the vast majority of the houses several families are cramped in unsanitary and dilapidated properties. In the midst of such squalor and deprivation many people have grown old prematurely. Alcohol abuse is rife amongst the older inhabitants. A large proportion of the older women were once prostitutes. The next study presented by Weaver (1989, p.200) is also an example of severe housing deprivation, this time facing older people in Alfange, within the region of Santarem. Inadequate sanitation and deplorable conditions have lowered the morale of the people so that there is no community spirit. Self-help and self-reliance are minimal in such environments. Only better conditions can break the vicious circle of depression which sets in. Social housing is minimal in Portugal – both Portugal and Spain have the lowest stock of such housing (see Potter and Zill, 1992, p.115). Also, Portugal probably has the lowest provision of specialist accommodation for older people in the EU, with the exception perhaps of Greece (Potter and Zill, 1992, p.111).

Health care

The Portuguese government approved a plan for a National Health Service in 1979. The difficulty was that the state could not carry out the plan fully when facing deep recession and political instability. Since then the proportion of expenditure on older people has consistently been below the proportion of expenditure on the population as a whole (see Spinnewyn and Nazareth, 1991, p.312).

Hospital care and medical services

Portugal has only 2.9 hospital beds per 1,000 inhabitants, which is the lowest ratio in the EU, as also is its ratio of dentists (0.1 per 1,000). The ratio of doctors per 1,000 inhabitants is 2.4, the seventh-lowest in the EU, and its ratio of pharmacists (0.5 per 1,000) is the sixth-lowest (Eurostat, 1991b, p.88). The will to update and expand services is clearly demonstrated by the Health Ministry's attempts to construct a reputable health service. In the late 1970s, geriatric services within general hospitals were introduced (see CPA, 1989, p.125). Towers (1992, p.199) refers to the late start Portugal has made in constructing a national framework of health care, but points out that the country *has* invested in information technology and epidemiology. It is attempting to streamline the services it has, and to create a systems approach in establishing its care units nationwide.

Health expenditure increased from 8.0% of GDP in 1975 to 10% in 1988. However, the older persons' care budget was not significant, given that the older population in 1988 stood at 12.4% and the proportion of expenditure of the total health budget was 10.4% (Spinnewyn and Nazareth, 1991, p.312).

Child care has had a higher priority due to the pressure of demand in a country with a high birth rate. The CPA (1989, p.125) states that the proportion of children aged 0–14 is 24.6%.

Nursing

District nursing does exist in Portugal, but little can be said about this service except that much of the nursing is carried out by religious orders. Home help and district nursing are combined in Portugal. The tasks may be carried out by unqualified assistants, social workers and nurses. The government spent only 6% of the total community service budget on community nursing and home help in 1987, based upon statistics provided by Spinnewyn and Nazareth, 1991, p.312).

Mental health care

Portugal, together with Italy and Spain, has only 0.9 places in mental health hospitals (*psiquiatricos*) per 1,000 inhabitants (Eurostat, 1991b, p.88). Castelhano et al. (1992, p.18) refer to the collaboration between doctors, nurses and social service technicians in providing care and support for the mentally ill. This service is provided under the aegis of the Social Action Services. However, this is an area where mental health care lags behind the mental health services available in the rest of the EU and much of greater Europe. Support centres are said to be used in Lisbon and Pisao-Cascals (Castelhano et al., 1992, p.20). There is a floating population of homeless people, among whom there are prematurely aged people in need of psychiatric care and counselling. Emergency services for these persons appear to exist only to provide meals and lodgings for limited periods. The Social Action Services are ill prepared to cope with the psychiatric needs of older people. The containment of the disturbed is often left to their families, supported by their GPs. Many who cannot cope become drifters, of which Portugal is reputed to have a large number, including older men who seek temporary asylum in the night shelters of Lisbon and other major cities.

Institutional care

In Portugal only about 1.5% of the older population live in institutions (CPA, 1989, p.125). Approximately 19,794 older people are resident in one of two types of institutional provision:

1 'old age homes' (*lares para idosos*);
2 'service flats' (*residenciais para idosos*).

The 'old age homes' exist for older people who are either 'at risk' or suffering from a loss of autonomy (Castelhano et al., 1992, p.14). There are 411 state institutions for older people in Portugal. These are large establishments with 60–450 beds. The CPA (1989, p.125) states that there are 280 state-subsidized retirement homes owned and run by charitable organizations.

Groups of apartments or service flats exist for older people who are still independent (Castelhano et al., 1992, p.14); there are at present only six of these in Portugal, each with a capacity of 22–50 lodgers. They are supported by ancillary social care units, much like the SHARE units in the Cork areas of the Republic of Ireland (see pages 110–11), or those that I have visited in Rome. More than two-thirds of those who are admitted were living alone and on low incomes; all are aged 65 and over. It is planned to expand these units throughout Portugal. Half of the costs are met by the government, and half privately. In principle, at least, these flats/apartments are inspected, and have to abide by quality standards laid down by the authorities.

Personal social services

Local offices

The Regional Social Security Centres administer social action services providing 'open-for-all' generic assistance in the form of counselling. In Lisbon the Santa Casa di Misericordia provides the care and a 24-hour emergency service. Elsewhere, the emergency service is usually only run on a nine-to-five basis. The centres also provide information.

Social workers

Social workers in Portugal are called 'social service technicians'. In 1974 there was a crisis in social work, when the workers rose against the management, which was said to be made up of adherents to the old regime. For several years older people were caught between the two factions, and services tended to be at a standstill. The connections with the Roman Catholic Church were severed in 1974, and the profession was secularized (see Lisboa, 1986, pp.439–42), with the introduction of a professional qualification in 'social service'. None the less, as will be further explained shortly, the religious organizations provide a large proportion of community care for older people. Also, the Catholic University of Vizeu runs accredited courses in social service at licentiate, masters and doctorate levels.

Meals services

Meal distribution for older people living at home is organized by parish groups and by the day centres, but at present no study of its effectiveness and standards is available.

Day care

The day centres (*centros de dia*) are developing fast. They were established in 1976. In 1980, 76 were in operation, serving 3,000 people (CPA, 1989, pp.126–7). By 1991 there were 450 centres; they have a capacity to serve about 20,000 older people (Spinnewyn and Nazareth, 1991, p.316). The government provides 60% of the expenditure in running these centres, and older people pay one-fifth of the costs entailed. The centres have to meet certain requirements for official accreditation. They are managed and run by social service technicians and occupational therapists, and offer meals, hairdressing, social activities, laundry, health care and pedicure services.

Home care/help

Home help (*ajuda domiciliara*) provision is limited: less than 1% of persons aged 65+ in Portugal are receiving home help (Anderson, 1992, p.78). As stated above, home help and district nursing are a combined community service in Portugal. Spinnewyn and Nazareth (1991, p.315) cite the 4,240 clients who receive home help. These are served by 1,500 service teams, and 100% of the expenditure is met by the government.

Other services

There are 'get-together' service centres run by either Private Social Solidarity Institutions or the authorities. These social centres also cater for children (Castelhano et al., 1992, p.15).

Voluntary care agencies and support organizations

As stated earlier, the General Direction for Social Action oversees the voluntary and private profit-making sector of caring agencies and organizations (the Private Social Solidarity Institutions – PSSIs). The PSSI establishments are used by social security, receive state support, have autonomy and a private budget, and carry out social action activities for older people, with the assistance of organized volunteers.

There are many different types of organizations within the PSSI category. Unions, federations and confederations make up the heterogeneous spectrum of voluntary non-profit agencies. There are the social solidarity associations, the social action volunteer associations, the mutual benefit associations, and lastly the Irmandades da Misericordia. Most of the older people who require support are assisted by these agencies. Many of the associations are run by the Church.

The private profit-making organizations are referred to by Castelhano et al. (1992, p.7). These are licensed by the Regional Social Security Centres, provided they abide by the regulations and accept state supervision.

There are pressure groups for older people, such as MURPI, MODERP and Vida Ascedente (Spinnewyn and Nazareth, 1991, p.318).

Informal care

Informal care in Portugal is expected to stay at the same level in the near future (Nijkamp et al., 1991b, p.57), and households rather than public organizations are likely to continue to be the mainstay. Informal care is not on the political agenda in Portugal because it is taken so much for granted, as is the domestic role of women (Anderson, 1992, p.82).

Glasner (1992, p.76) refers to the impeded emancipation of women in Portugal because of the constraining influence of the Catholic Church, with its stress upon familial responsibilities. Along with Greece and Italy, the proportion of women in part-time work in Portugal is the lowest in the EU (see Glasner, 1992, p.89). However, the percentage of married Portuguese women in paid employment is relatively high, at 48.2%, as is the proportion of widows and divorced women in full employment (see Glasner, 1992, p.85). One explanation is that the poorer-paid agricultural jobs are carried out disproportionately by women, as are the worst-paid onshore fishing jobs, which are traditionally carried out by women. In spite of the high proportion of married women in paid employment, the majority are still at home, and where an older parent exists they provide the bulk of the caring. However, the number of family members caring for older people dropped from 80.8% in 1980 to 80.5% in 1986; the projection for the year 2000 is 77.1% (see Spinnewyn and Nazareth, 1991, p.310). The role of the family is being affected by the emigration of its younger members.

According to *Eurobarometer* (1987), Portugal has the highest proportion of older people residing in extended households (three generations, or second-order relatives, or unrelated persons). There are six times as many three-generation families living under one roof in Portugal as there are in the UK (on the basis of data provided by Potter and Zill, 1992, p.121); in southern Portugal these are generally exogamous families (see Todd, 1985). The rest of the country has a largely egalitarian nuclear family structure, where older parents live next door or close by their offspring. Portugal has the highest proportion of people aged 16–64 who maintain that caring for their own older relatives is an important family role, according to *Eurobarometer* (1989b).

Leisure pursuits and education

The CPA (1989, p.126) states that entertainment agencies organize and publicize shows and performances for older people. They also offer concessionary tickets for theatre-goers. The Department of Social Security arranges holidays for older people. In some of the metropolitan areas transport concessions are made available for those aged 65+.

Rural aspects

Many rural areas have suffered great population losses, firstly through younger people going abroad to find work (the emigration rate is one of the highest in Europe); secondly, many have moved from the rural hinterland to the coastal settlements, and the city of Lisbon towards the south and Porto in the north. The Beira Litoral and Estramadura have dispersed pockets of population, amongst whom are isolated older people left behind by the younger emigrants – a situation repeated in many parts of Europe, but particularly in Southern Europe. The older people have very few services. In most areas only the parishes and religious orders offer formal care, although these orders are now fewer in number than at the height of the migrations in late 1960s and early 1970s. Recently there has been a move to establish more day centres in rural areas (see Spinnewyn and Nazareth, 1991, p.317). However, at present rural day centres are scarce.

Conclusion

Portugal, like Greece, has been slow to develop its welfare and health systems. The socialist policies have recently attempted to update them. Only the recession and internal conflicts delayed the implementation of major new services for older people. Much has been accomplished at the planning level, but it remains to be seen whether implementation will occur.

The increases in pensions and social security benefits have been significant, probably the fastest-growing contributions in Europe, but with the biggest leeway to make up. In 1970 the total amount in 'bio escudos' was 1.5, and the total number of pensions was 165,530; in 1988 the total amount in 'bio escudos' had risen to 352.9, and the pensions had leapt to 2,042,120 (see Spinnewyn and Nazareth, 1991, p.311).

Portugal presents the classic Southern European example of the reliance on family support with relatively little formal domiciliary care. Institutional care is minimal. In fact, the family household is usually the sole caring unit in most of rural Portugal (Nijkamp et al., 1991a, p.33).

The proportion of expenditure on health care for older people has not been significantly higher than that on the population as a whole. Reliance upon the services offered by the local Church community/parishes is the only option available for older people who are no longer able to cope with disability and ill health.

Probably the greatest need for older Portuguese people is decent and appropriate housing. Here, even less proportionately has been spent upon extra provision and reconstruction. For example, there has been less than 1% increase in housing expenditure between 1975 and 1988 (Spinnewyn and Nazareth, 1991, p.313).

In addition to this bleak picture, the numbers of nurses and ancillary health staff have decreased, and the reliance upon unqualified staff has increased. This situation is exacerbated by the lack of trust in the services, and the reliance upon family care of older people, which is demonstrated by a survey where 80% of the respondents would rely upon the family for such care, and only 10% would turn to state provision (Nazareth, 1988).

Lastly, but not least, there is now an annual flow of about 40,000–50,000 returning migrants, who are settling down in their country of origin, according to information provided by the Portuguese Embassy in London. These people are adding to the demographic and consequent socio-economic imbalances, and to the increase in demand for welfare/health services.

24 Greece

Demography

As cited in Table 1, the percentage of older people in Greece is ranked eleventh in Europe. The proportion in 1989 was 13.7% according to Eurostat (1991a) and the UN (1991), but only 13.1% according to the CPA (1989, p.68) estimates. The predicted proportion of 17.8% by the year 2025 ranks fifteenth in greater Europe. The life expectancy of older Greek women at age 65 is 16.9 years, which is ranked seventeenth in greater Europe; that of men is 14.5 years and is ranked seventh, jointly with Portugal and Austria (UN, 1991; Eurostat, 1991a).

Socio-political and administrative background

Today there are 52 prefectures in Greece which implement the health and welfare policies of the directorates and the departments (see below). Since the mid-nineteenth century the day-to-day lives of older people have been run by municipal governments with elected mayors and urban and rural councils. The systems of welfare and health today are also highly localized and polycephalic. After the downfall of the short-term centralist rule of the military junta in 1974, the decentralization process, which was halted for a time, was resumed once again. However, indecision caused by political stale-mate has been reflected in the patchy social policies of recent years.

The Ministry of Health, Welfare and Social Security (MHWSS) has author-ity over health and social care. Amongst its 31 offices located in Athens, there are 8 central competences which are highly relevant with regard to the health and welfare of the older population. They are known as 'directorates' and consist of: the Directorates of Public Health, of Protection and Promotion of Health, of Mental Health, of Public Assistance, of Protection of Individuals with Particular Needs and of the Elderly, of Housing, of Social Work and of Social Welfare Professions (see Sokoly, 1992, p.3). These are in contact with the 52 prefectures at regional levels. Nijkamp and Giaoutzi (1991, p.216) sum up the administrative system well when they describe it as 'decentralized, but shaped according to hierarchical principles'.

A five-year plan (1983–7) aims to improve the living conditions of people by providing for substantial investment, particularly in health and social welfare (Kokkinaki, 1986, p.250).

At national level the policy, as formulated within the directorates and departments in Athens, is almost in line with the community care rhetoric and management strategy of the UK and other countries of Northern and Western Europe, where older people are maintained in their own homes for as long as is possible. This is described in Greece as 'open care', as opposed to 'closed protection' (Nijkamp and Giaoutzi, 1991, p.216). At regional level, the prefectures provide a co-ordinating role and budget brokerage.

It is at the local level of the municipalities that the Greek system has the greatest impact, and where it draws together the various strands of Greek social welfare and health care as provided by the state, the Orthodox Church and the Greek Red Cross, which will be described in more detail in the relevant sections of this chapter.

Unlike many other European states, the Greek government is concerned with educational and awareness programmes to reorientate the older people towards changes of careers and of occupations in the second half of their lives. The aim is to enable older people not only to be independent, but also if possible to enable them to be economically autonomous.

Social security: pensions and benefits

The state pension scheme is earnings-related. Average earnings are calculated over the whole insurance period. There is virtually universal coverage for Greek workers in industry, commerce and related employment categories (CPA, 1989, p.69). The system is characterized by special schemes for state employees, agricultural workers and the self-employed. The pensions are subsidized. The major source of funding is from the payments of individuals and employers. Public expenditure on pensions is around 10% of GDP (see CPA, 1989).

Eligibility for the state pension is achieved at 65 for men and 57 for women, but they must have made a minimum of 10,000 days' contributions. There are four situations when retirement may occur in Greece:

1   at 58 for men with at least 10,500 days' contributions, and 55 for women with unmarried children under 18, at least 5,500 days' contributions and no other pension;
2   at 60 for men and 55 for women, after arduous or unhealthy work with a minimum of 4,050 days' contributions;
3   at 60 for men and 55 for women, at a reduced pension rate, together with a 6% per annum reduction in the pension rate;
4   at 62 for women and 67 for men, after 27 years' contributions have been paid.

Nijkamp and Giaoutzi (1991, pp.204–5) cite the relative poverty endured by older Greeks, whom they describe as 'very weak', especially in the agricultural areas. If pensioners are in paid employment in Greece, the pension is reduced to the minimum wage level. The older Greek people are amongst the most active in Europe. The CPA (1989, p.68) cites the fact that in 1985, 18% of older men and 10.7% of older women aged 65–69 were economically active, as were 9.6% of men and 5.5% of women aged 70–74, together with 3% of men and 1% of women aged 75+. Many of these hard-working older people are rural agricultural workers. According to OECD statistics cited by Walker (1992a, p.162), Greece spends less than half of the EU average per head on old age benefits.

Special pensions/benefits and protection schemes have been devised to enable older people to remain at home. Sokoly (1992, p.14) refers to these in detail. These are:

1   pensions granted by the Farmers' Social Security Fund (OGA) to non-insured persons aged over 68, plus insurance cover;
2   housing assistance to non-insured and financially weak persons or couples aged 65+ who are homeless.

Housing

The Greek housing stock, like that of the former Yugoslavia, is generally inappropriate for older people. Only 2% of the government budget is spent on housing, as cited by Nijkamp and Giaoutzi (1991, p.208). After Portugal, houses in Greece have the lowest proportion (69.3%) of bathrooms or showers on the premises and the lowest proportion of inside WCs in the EU (70.9%), as cited in Eurostat (1991b, p.121). The major difference in housing standards within Greece is between the rural and urban dwellings.

In the cities, the increased demand within the housing market has increased the price of rents and repairs. The redeveloped housing schemes have been too expensive for most older Greeks. Many older people live in high-density districts of Athens, which is second only to Hong Kong for congestion. They are the principal victims of its pollution. The city of Athens has the smallest proportion of green space of all European cities (Hope, 1990). The brown layer of smog (the *nefos*) hangs over one of the unhealthiest cities in the industrialized West. The city environment is unsafe, with at least 700,000 cars (using the roads on alternate days according to their number plates) without catalytic converters, belching out black fumes in one of the hottest European cities. The CPA (1989, p.68) states that there is a demand for housing for older couples in the more populous, congested urban areas. Urban conditions are notoriously bad for older people living in older rented city flats. Central city decay stifles human identity and chokes human dignity.

In the rural areas about 20% have no running water in the house and over 60% have outside WCs (Malikiossi-Loizos, 1986, p.11). The fact that over 40% of the older population still live in rural areas underlines the housing problems facing large numbers of older people in the remoter areas of Greece. Repairs may be cheaper, being more rudimentary, but builders and joiners etc. are in short supply.

As well illustrated in Weaver (1989, pp.47–8), the provision of housing for older repatriated refugees is a pressing problem in northern Greece. This will be exacerbated by the influx of older war-weary and shocked people from the former Yugoslavia. Also, in the outskirts of Athens are the Gypsies and the Kazakhstan Pontians, who have returned from the Greek settlements on the shores of the Black Sea in Pontos in Turkey. As late as 1986 only 220 state-owned one-roomed flats designed for older people existed in all Greece, according to Malikiossi-Loizos. The Ministry of Health and Welfare has begun to build respite units. In addition, the Ministry of Health and Welfare, in association with the Workers' Housing Organization, has added to the stock of sheltered housing in recent years.

Health care

The health service system (ESY) was created in 1983 and progressively developed in the 1980s. It is described by Hunter (1986) and Malikiossi-Loizos (1986). The public system is run by the Ministry of Health and Welfare, and is advised by the Central Health Council. Because of its late foundation, there is a relatively large private health sector.

Hospital care and medical services

Nijkamp and Giaoutzi (1991, p.210) refer to the 30 chronic diseases institutes (*therapeuteria chronion patheseon*) which cater for 2,000 older people. These institutes are public. There is no special provision for older people in the general hospitals (*genika nosokomea*). Approximately 45% of hospital beds are private. The ratio of beds per 1,000 inhabitants in Greece ranks ninth of the 12 EU nations (Eurostat, 1991b, p.88).

The new health service is decentralized, as are most of the systems within the Southern European countries. It is run within eight health care regions and their 52 counties. Within these counties there are 264 municipalities, and in turn as many as 5,774 communities, as described by Hunter (1986, p.44). These are served by directly-elected councils which can establish the local health and social services. The system is clearly polycephalic. Like the Italian polyclinics, the health centres are outposts of the hospitals. Voluntary hospitals have had the choice of joining the public sector, if they wish to be subsidized.

According to Eurostat (1991b, p.88), the ratio of doctors per 1,000 inhabitants is the third-highest amongst the EU countries; dentists are the third-highest, with a ratio of 0.9 per 1,000; pharmacists are the sixth-highest, with a ratio of 0.6 per 1,000, along with the Republic of Ireland. Hunter (1986, p.47) refers to the high concentration of doctors in Athens and Salonica, three-quarters of whom are located there. There are approximately 1,000 doctors outside Athens and Salonica, serving 6 million people. The doctors within the health scheme must choose whether to be private or public practitioners. Unlike UK doctors, they cannot provide both private and public medical care. An embargo was placed upon the creation of any new private clinics.

The health and social care services are provided by the one centre. The old voluntary centres for older people, known as the KAPIs ('Open Care Day Centres'), have been integrated and become part of the formal public community care system (see Amira, 1990, pp.73–4). Each of the KAPIs has a doctor, a social worker, a physiotherapist, an occupational therapist, a visiting nurse and a home assistant. They offer vaccinations, examinations for diabetes and for heart diseases, electrocardiograms, diagnostic X-rays, and nutritional counselling (see Malikiossi-Loizos, 1986, p.23). Social events are also organized from these multidisciplinary centres. Each centre caters for 250–500 people aged over 65. They may provide domiciliary health care when required.

Nursing

The country has one of the lowest ratios of nurses in Europe: 1 nurse per 18,000 people. Although the medical profession has been slow to establish a specialism in geriatric medicine, there have been experimental geriatric units within the Centres of Health and Welfare in Greater Athens (see Malikiossi-Loizos, 1986, pp.22–3) offering free medical check-ups as well as health advice. In spite of these relatively recent innovations, the formal provision is mainly hospitalization, in common with other Southern and Eastern European countries. An area of great concern for the nursing services in Greece is the demand which will be made upon the institutional caring sector by the estimated 100,000 bedridden older people by the year 2000 (see CPA, 1989, p.69).

Private nursing domiciliary services for older people are available for the relatively few who have the means to pay. These consist of district nurses and also 'exclusive nurses', who are untrained, but who can carry out auxiliary nursing tasks (see Amira, 1990, p.74), similar to the services I came across in Italy (see Giarchi, 1987a). The nurses' night attendance is similar to the 'sitting' services of some private UK nursing organizations.

Mental health care

Mangen (1985a, p.30) describes the mental health situation in Greece, where half of the psychiatric patients are in the two largest cities. Three large hospitals account for 60% of the beds. In addition, 60% of psychiatrists practise in Athens. A community care scheme has been in operation since the late 1970s, but has been slow to develop. The first Greek day hospital for mentally ill patients was opened in 1977. Older depressed rural people have no support apart from the assistance of the family doctor. Referral to city psychiatrists is often out of the question because of the distances and expenses involved. As in Italy, there are also local mental health centres, although mental health hospitals still exist.

Institutional care

There are relatively few residential homes in Greece. They are described as 'old age homes' (*gyrokomia*), catering for some 5,000 older people. In the 1980s there were only ten public sector homes in all of Greece and 114 privately-run homes for older people (see Association of Greek Social Workers, 1982; Malikiossi-Loizos, 1986, p.14). Nijkamp and Giaoutzi (1991, p.208) state that there are 100 mainly public homes catering for 5,000 older people. There is a two-tier system: the public catering for the lower socio-economic groups, and the private for the middle and upper classes. There are also 11 institutions for the chronically ill (*therapeuteria chronion patheseon*), catering for some 2,000 persons; some are large. The Charitable Society of Athens accommodates about 800 older people.

Personal social services

The Ministry of Health, Welfare and Social Security provides care for the older people. Formal social care is minimal in Greece. When it is on offer, it is usually coupled with health and nursing care. It is also provided by the Greek Red Cross. For these reasons, much of the social care that is provided has been referred to in the above section on 'Health care' or in the section on voluntary care below.

Local offices

Because local social and health care are provided by the single office, social work involvement is covered under 'Health care' above.

Social workers

According to Kokkinaki (1986, p.253), there are 2,680 social workers in Greece. The largest percentage (48.7%) are employed in social welfare agencies; 14.3% are engaged in health institutes and 11.1% in residential care. More than half the staff in each of these forms of provision are working for older people, but most are not trained to specialize in this work.

Meals services

These are delivered by the KAPIs (Nijkamp and Giaoutzi, 1991, p.211), but further details are not available.

Day care

The day centre function is carried out by the 250 KAPIs. As described by Amira (1990, p.73), these are used by the relatively able older people. In many ways they match the UK model of day care. The state funds the KAPIs. They are organized by a council of representatives from the municipality.

Home care/help

This service is listed by Nijkamp and Giaoutzi (1991, p.211), but the numbers of users are not recorded, nor is its quality commented upon. Anderson (1992, p.78) states that less than 1% are receiving some sort of home help in Greece.

Other services

Summer holidays in camping sites are provided for older people aged 60+ at times in collaboration with younger groups such as the National Institute for the Young (see Sokoly, 1992, p.14). Adult foster care places for older people are now organized locally by the municipalities.

Housing improvements are also available for older people, but once again, further information is lacking at present.

Voluntary care agencies and support organizations

Voluntary organizations are surprisingly few in number, apart from the Church agencies, the Red Cross and the Foundation of Volunteers. Members of the pensioners' federations collect money on behalf of the unions and run some recreational activities, but the numbers of older people involved are minimal.

As in other Southern European countries, care provided by the Church is significant. Teperoglou (1980, p.84) describes the Greek Orthodox Church activities arranged by the Special Care for the Elderly programmes supplied by the Holy Archdiocese of Athens; Houses of Christ's Peace provide over a thousand older Athenians with food. The Church Centres for Parish Love (the KEAs) and the groups of Freely Living Elderly of the Greek Orthodox Church provide medicopharmaceutical consultation when required. One innovation has been the introduction of four mobile medical units run by the Church in Athens, which provide domiciliary care for bedridden older people (see Malikiossi-Loizos, 1986, p.23).

The older Greek population do not participate much in club events or voluntary organization activities; this is especially true in the rural areas. Malikiossi-Loizos (1986, p.25) cites the study in which only 6% of men aged 60–64 and 2% of men aged 75–79 were active members in clubs/associations/societies, and no women were active in any of them at all. In the urban areas there is greater participation, but the involvement is still significantly low. The city of Athens has been running Clubs of Friendship for older people, which are subsidized by the municipality, in an attempt to break the tight domestic mould into which older Greeks are forced, and to provide them with more external stimulation. Family reunions and socio-religious events are central in the life of older Greeks.

Informal care

Familial care is still the mainstay of the care of older people in Greece. However, as noted already, about one-fifth of older Greeks are economically active and independent; of the other four-fifths, those within the cities are more vulnerable in some respects than those in the rural areas. The older men are not seen as often in the *kafenions* because of the threatening anonymity within the urban landscape. Malikiossi-Loizos (1986) provides a picture of the close-knit familial care of older people within Athens when she describes the 56% living with their offspring or very close to them, and the 82% living quite close and in frequent contact with their relatives; only 8% do not see their relatives on a daily basis. Housework, house maintenance, grocery shopping and also cooking are provided within the family circle.

Malikiossi-Loizos (1986, p.19) observes that friends and neighbours support those older people who do not live close to their family or relatives. This confirms the view that the informal support of outsiders only operates when the family does not exist. Participation in non-family events is rare. She says (1986, p.25): 'It is true that the Greek elderly people participate primarily in family or socio-religious activities. Family ties are still very strong in Greece and it is interesting that when asked, the elderly mentioned that their best friend in most cases was a close relative.'

Most of the older men are cared for by their wives (see Amira, 1990) and the single and married offspring take care of their parents. Only about 1% of the older Greek population are in residential care. The burden of familial care falls heavily upon the daughters. The carers find support within the kinship network and want to have as little to do as possible with the hospital or professional agencies. These, in any case, are amongst the worst-resourced in Europe, so the family *has* to carry the burden. Of all European countries Greece probably has the least number of isolated, unsupported older people. Fogarty (1986, p.74) states that under 5% live alone, that 17% of bachelors live in households headed by brothers, and 27% in households headed by their sisters.

A quarter of those aged 60–64 and more than a third aged 85–89 live in households of more than four family members, according to Malikiossi-Loizos (1986). In her Greek Report for the European Foundation for the Improvement of Living and Working Conditions (Malikiossi-Loizos, 1986) she concludes: 'In Greece even the single elderly are not suffering much from isolation.'

Apart from the lack of housing and other statutory resources, the pensions are inadequate for most older people. This creates a greater dependency upon the younger earning population, and reinforces the significance of the family as a means of informal support. The grandparents, however, play an important role in providing child care because of the lack of crèches. Teperoglou (1980, p.87) reported that there are no cash benefits for families with older dependents, but since then dependent supplements have been introduced (CPA, 1989). Teperoglou (1980) refers to the impoverishment that results from the parents having to supply their daughters at marriage with a dowry – the house is the basic form of the dowry, so parents must sometimes move out of their own house and pass it on to their daughter, and move into rented accommodation. The dowry forces many parents into a situation where they cannot save for their old age, few recovering from the demands made upon them by their family.

Leisure pursuits and education

Travel concessions exist; for example, the Third Age Cards for travel within Greece and the Rail Europ Senior, which allows those aged 60 and over to travel in 20 European countries at less than half fares (Malikiossi-Loizos, 1986, p.17).

Rural aspects

The proportion of older people in the rural areas is half that of the urban areas, according to Malikiossi-Loizos (1986, p.5). The depopulation of rural areas, with the exodus of younger people, either to the cities or abroad, has had a considerable impact upon the older inhabitants, both within the cities and the countryside. Since 1988 the number of older rural people has decreased yet further. One consequence has been the need for older people to continue working to survive and to maintain their smallholdings. Over the years the percentage of actively employed older Greek people has been amongst the highest in Europe. In the study of Heikkinen et al. (1983, p.93), the proportion of the older population engaged in full/part-time work in rural Greece – both men and women – is the highest of their ten European samples: in Greece, Belgium, West Germany, Finland, France, Italy, Poland, Romania, USSR and the former Yugoslavia.

Although Heikkinen et al.'s report (1983) is dated, it presents a valuable, more detailed rural view than most Greek studies. The researchers examine the life of older people in 21 Greek villages and small towns in 12 departments. They state that doctors visit many of the villages once a week (p.30). They also refer to the less fortunate villagers, who have to travel over 10 km to the nearest medical centre over rough roads. The older rural population increasingly live in isolated dwellings as household members move out. They are also identified (p.95) as those who feel loneliness the most. Both men and women experience psychological isolation. In rural areas there is a marked difference between the freedom of the older men and the household captivity of the older women. Malikiossi-Loizos (1986, p.26) refers to the men meeting in the *kafenion*, where they play table games, drink and talk politics, in much the same way as older Italians (Giarchi, 1987a). Also as in Italy, the women spend most of their time with their families. The bonding created within these networks helps to establish the caring arrangements when older people fall ill or need domestic support. However, as already stated, the family circle has contracted because of the exodus of the younger members. This, added to a weak infrastructure in the rural areas, increases the vulnerability of the older rural population. Mauthner (1990) also refers to the higher costs of living in one of the poorest EU and OECD countries. In addition, tourism has not benefited older people; on the contrary, it has added to their cost of living by increasing the price of local goods – even groceries and fruit.

Conclusion

The strong cultural emphasis on familial support in Greece to date has tended to create a closed household pattern of care and involvement. The welfare system is residual. The triangulation of care has consisted of a state system that provides mainly hospital services and minimal institutional care, relying heavily upon informal familial care, with limited subsidies to a slim voluntary sector. There is also a heavy reliance upon the contribution of the Church. However, the caring systems are polycephalic (see Table 6), which facilitates the mix of local support in Greece.

Domiciliary care is now receiving more state support. For example, the government has created 125 'open protection centres', and the 227 localities have received state subsides for the care of older people (see Nijkamp and Giaoutzi, 1991, p.215). However, if the traditional family alters significantly, and if secularization continues to limit the involvement of the Church, the implications for household care will be extreme, given that the hospitals will have to cater for over 100,000 older people, and given that the levels of residential care and voluntary work in Greece are amongst the lowest in greater Europe.

25 The former Yugoslavia

Demography

According to Table 1, the percentage of older people in the former Yugoslavia ranks twenty-seventh in greater Europe. The projection that 17.3% of the population will be older people by the year 2025 must now be questioned, given the high death rate resulting from the internal war that has decimated the population. The life expectancy of older women aged 65+ is 15.5 years, which ranks twenty-first in greater Europe; that of older men is 13.1 years, which ranks eighteenth (jointly with Luxemburg) in greater Europe (Eurostat, 1991a; UN, 1991).

The likelihood is that the more northerly parts of Slovenia and Croatia will have higher proportions of older people than the central and southern territories, mainly because of the greater fatalities and migrants fleeing from the wars, or pushed out in the process of 'ethnic cleansing'. Rusica et al. (1991, pp.73–4) indicate that the populations of the north-western regions (Vojvodina, Croatia and Slovenia) are on average marginally older than those of the south-east (Macedonia and Kosovo). A higher standard of living may account for this. According to the Federal Statistical Institute of Yugoslavia (1987), more than 16% of the populations of Croatia, Serbia and Vojvodina were older people; the other regions had less. The wars will have depleted these proportions in a nation which has approximately 8.2% of its population aged 65+, and 13.8% aged 60+ (see Ruzica et al., 1991, p.75). The northern Balkan territories have always been more affluent, and the north has experienced less fighting.

Socio-political and administrative background

Because of the complexities surrounding welfare and health provision in Europe's most war-torn area, and the implications for older people living there, this section will necessarily deal at greater length with recent developments in the former Yugoslavia and with the consequences of recent ethnic conflicts. Older people in the former Yugoslavia have experienced internal wars intermittently over their lifetime. In 1919, many separate nations or ethnic peoples were brought together to constitute the independent state of Yugoslavia. Up to 1919, Serbia and Montenegro were two separate states; Slovenia, Croatia, Vojvodina, Bosnia and Hercegovina were part of the Austro-Hungarian Empire; in addition, Kosovo and Macedonia were once separate and dominated by Turkey, until World War I. The various peoples have also been subject to many polities and competing religious movements. The Austrian state governed Slovenia, Croatia and Vojvodina for many centuries. The Ottoman Empire ruled over Serbia, Macedonia, Montenegro, Kosovo, Bosnia and Hercegovina for some six centuries.

The three Slav languages spoken in the Yugoslav areas have a long history, although Serbo-Croat is the main language for most of the area. Ethnic mixes and uneven integration have also added to the very heterogeneous cultural texture of life in these territories. To add to these diversities and cleavages, three major religions have survived in an uneasy co-existence: Eastern Christian Orthodoxy, Roman Catholicism and Islam.

The state of Yugoslavia dated from the end of World War I, when it rose from the ruins of the Austro-Hungarian Empire and its border states. For a short time (1921–45) the country was served by a constitutional monarch. Tito (Josip Broz) took over when a federal people's republic was declared in 1945. During the years of World War II about a fifth of the population had been killed, when 1.75 million people were shot by rival ethnic and religious groups. These killings were to herald the massacres of the 1990s. Tito then severed his ties with the USSR, developing Yugoslavia's own internal systems of state welfare and social care in 1948.

The country's diverse ethnic groups were held uneasily together by Tito in his attempt to create brotherhood and unity (*bratsvo-jedinstovo*). However, the pseudo-unity he established under one flag was always on the verge of open conflict. Hundreds of years of ethnic hatred are not so easily forgotten. The recent internal wars indicate how the former Yugoslavia was in fact a dormant volcano ready to erupt. A spurious unity had been established, in which the citizens did not recognize themselves as Yugoslavs, but as separate ethnic people proud of their age-old racial identity, inspired by separate religious beliefs, and dedicated to the conservation of their distinctive linguistic and cultural heritage on the basis of blood and soil. The older people who had experienced the tensions between ethnic groups – some of whom had many scores to settle – were an integral part of the violent racist and ethnic groundswell, passing on the story of one atrocity or another, and keeping the memory of incidents of recent and past history fresh within their local enclaves.

The religious affiliations referred to above divided the older people from one another. For centuries, the eastern parts of the Balkans have been peopled by Serbs and Macedonians, while the western parts have been peopled by Croats and Slovenes; the former have been Eastern Christian Orthodox, and the latter Roman Catholic, and the Muslim Bosnians have been uncomfortably located in the middle. Their fears that they might be squeezed out were justified, as time was to show when the nightmare turned into reality.

Because of the historic, religious and cultural diversities, and the danger that racial and religious conflict might surface and destroy his dream, Tito had divided the former Yugoslavia into six main territories, recognized as socialist republics (*socialisticke republike*). The hope was that the ethnic and religious divides might be respected, and with time the antagonists would soften their attitudes, enabled by global communism to transcend their local-ized animosities, and in turn be protagonists of Yugoslavia's own system of 'market socialism', free from the control of the USSR.

The former Yugoslav territories corresponded to the major Slav-speaking national groups and two autonomous provinces. In terms of size of popula-tion, these territories were ranked as follows:

1   Serbia;
2   Croatia;
3   Bosnia and Hercegovina;
4   Slovenia;
5   Macedonia;
6   Montenegro.

Added to these were the provinces (*autonomne pokrajine*) of Kosovo and Vojvodina. The autonomous province of Kosovo was populated by mainly Albanian-speaking people, and that of Vojvodina by mixed populations of Slavs, Hungarians and Romanians. These two provinces came under Serbia. A greater Serbia always cast its eastern shadow over the western territories in its attempt to reach out to the Adriatic shores.

About nine-tenths of the older population speak Slavic languages in the lands which once made up the former Yugoslavia. About one-third are Roman Catholic, one-tenth are Muslim, and the rest are Eastern Orthodox. The religious differences and affiliations have divided the older populations, dictating their view of welfare and systems of formal and informal care.

In 1989, older people and their fellow citizens were freed from the oppressive monistic structure which had done nothing to soften the culture clash and age-old religious animosities. In fact, the people were to react to the faceless communism of Yugoslav officialdom by a reaffirmation of their diverse beliefs and renewed ethnic loyalty. The country was supposed to be federal, but its institutions were directly controlled by the party state. Ruzica et al. (1991, p.75) describe the pervasive system as 'polycentric etatism'. Although the communes were declared to be autonomous, the system of making decisions at federal level was very complex and bureaucratic. The pseudo-federalism was in fact a quasi-state network under the Federal Assembly (Savezna Skrupstina) which sat in Belgrade. Decentralization and 'destatization' were said to have taken place. Authority, it was boasted, had been devolved to the federal organs of the republics, provinces and communes, and self-government was encouraged. Self-managing worker councils elected their delegates to the political organs of the communes, the republics and the federations. The system was in fact a subtle scheme whereby centrism was clothed in the garb of political pluralism. However, in emphasizing these negative elements, one cannot overlook the positive aspects of social welfare and health care provision, which have been highly beneficial for the older population during the period leading up to 1989, especially in the north.

As stated above, decentralization in political terms was bogus, but in the sectors of social welfare and health care provision, decentralization did take place. As part of the bid to sell a 'market socialism', the regime aimed to provide a welfare and health system which would be second to none in the socialist countries, and which would bolster the image of a government which truly cared for the vulnerable and the needy.

There is no doubt that the social welfare and health system of the former Yugoslavia was sometimes on a par with those of the more democratic states of Europe. Apart from pensions and housing, and the systems were often superior to the Marxist socialist welfare and health schemes in Eastern Europe, as the following sections will demonstrate. Ironically, when liberalization took place in 1989 the welfare and social care schemes for older people were put in jeopardy. And with the ensuing internal wars, the infrastructure of care was to be completely destroyed in the battle zones of the western and central areas.

Liberalization took place in 1989–90 for Slovenia and Croatia; the market welfare state supplanted 'market socialism'. The likelihood is that social welfare and health care provision in Slovenia and Croatia will survive, albeit modified by a greater mix of public and private provision, in line with most of Europe. However, doubts and uncertainties hang over the southern and western territories, where the internal war has destroyed services and households and exterminated thousands of people. The scars of war in the southern and western areas will take years to heal, if ever.

In the turmoil of the political whirlwind of the early 1990s, Milosevic's Serbian nationalism fanned the simmering hatreds that were always close to the surface. These hatreds and accompanying racial negative stereotypes have divided the various ethnic and religious groups in this mountainous corner of the Balkans for more than a millennium, creating in turn intra-generational conflicts between older people. Throughout the troubles, children, mothers and older people have been caught in the cross-fire, and the informal networks of care provided the only support. The exogamous community family system described by Todd (1985) has been the mainstay for the vulnerable, such as the older population. During the troubies there was little else for the dependent to turn to, and in the future in the Bosnian and Serbian territories it will be those who still have surviving families who are more likely to cope within a region that will lack adequate infrastructures for years to come. How long will it take before the health and social welfare systems destroyed in the gunfire return to the Bosnian, Serb and Muslim populations?

According to the Constitution of 1974, the member states regulated the social welfare services. They made the laws and allocated public funds. The federal institutions co-ordinated services and made recommendations.

Social security: pensions and benefits

A universal disability pension was introduced under the old regime for the employees of the nationalized industries. For agricultural producers/farmers, the self-employed and some professional occupations there were separate insurance schemes (see Ruzica et al., 1991, p.81). They were voluntary. They were introduced for agricultural producers/farmers in 1972. Compulsory insurance for agricultural producers/farmers was made obligatory in 1983, but some member states did not introduce the scheme. The state pension was compulsory in all parts except Slovenia. Needless to say, people are neither able to pay contributions nor to receive payments in a war-torn area. A 'full pension' requires 40 years' contributions, when the pension may be 85% of the average annual earnings within the last ten years of employment; it is payable for men at 60 and for women at 55 (Ruzica et al., 1991, p.82). There are early retirement opportunities for men at 55, provided they have worked for 35 years, and for women at 50, provided they have worked for 30 years. Problems occur because 15 years' contributions are required for a minimum pension, so that there are underemployed people without one; for example, in 1988 there was only 1 pension per 2.8 employees (Republican Institute for Social Planning, 1990).

Thousands of older people have been on low incomes; others are without any income at all. Hundreds of the oldest people in the war-torn area will be without a home or a pension in the aftermath of the fighting.

Ruzica et al. (1991, pp.82–3) explain the predicament of the pensioners. Poverty existed amongst many of the older population in the former Yugoslavia because of low pensions. They were particularly vulnerable after 1979, when real income decreased annually: in 1985, real income was 20% lower than in 1979. The pensions were therefore greatly devalued, dropping by 6% annually in the 1980s. The income of older people reached an all-time low in 1989, when inflation stood at 1,365%. At least half of the pensioners were below the poverty line. Those aged 65+ and without a pension or children to support them have a right to receive what is known as the 'permanent subsidy', which is a means-tested regular monthly payment.

In 1985, 38% of the older population were on old age pensions; 34% were on disability pensions, and 27% were on other pensions (as cited by Ruzica et al., 1991, p.82). One-fifth of the older population continued working, particularly in the rural areas. Half of the older workers were in full-time employment.

Housing

The housing stock is poor in the territories of the former Yugoslavia. Given the massive destruction in Bosnia and Hercegovina particularly, the country's depleted and wretched housing stock must be the worst in greater Europe. Over the years the under-provision of housing created an unacceptable shortfall in supply, particularly in public housing. In 1981, according to the Federal Statistical Institute of Yugoslavia (1987), there was a shortfall of 600,000 dwellings in the housing market. From the mid-1980s the production of houses has been almost at a standstill.

Svetlik (1988, pp.336–7) points out that 42% of adults in the former Yugoslavia have built their own houses or apartments; 71.1% of adults in Slovenia were assisted by their parents, relatives or friends. Moreover, just under twice as many people turned to their relatives than turned to the authorities when faced with housing problems. The increase in housing costs, plus the spiralling rents, affected many older people, particularly in the cities (Ruzica et al., 1991, p.77). In 70 cities there were approximately 978,000 local authority flats or apartments available at very cheap rents; 6.6% of the residents also received rent subsidies.

Another social housing venture has been the creation of 'residential units', which are a form of collective living in old age, similar to the local authority sheltered accommodation in the UK. They were started in 1966 in

Macedonia. Ruzica et al. (1991, pp.88–9) describe them and their eventual failure to take off in other territories. There were 36 such units, one in each municipality and four in the city of Skopje, which in total housed some 1,188 older people. The venture proved to be too expensive to run.

The exogamous community families are characteristic of the Eastern European countries (Todd, 1985). Throughout the Balkans the living arrangements and housing structures have been determined over time by the ancient *zadruga* family type, which is essentially a variant of the exogamous community family structure. It has been a salient feature in former Yugoslavia up to the 1960s, which will be explained further under 'Informal care'. Suffice it to say here that these large households of 9–15 persons (sometimes even 20+) were eroded by rural migration and urbanization in the 1960s, when families were fragmented by the extensive migrations of younger people seeking jobs in Central Europe and within the major cities of the north of the former Yugoslavia (Erlih, 1966). However, more recently unemployment has stemmed the flow from home, with a return to the congestion of families in small city apartments or in semi-dilapidated rural houses. In addition, for those less traditional families, alternative housing has been so expensive that the younger members have tended to stay with their parents. The more affluent homes consist of smaller households, and the poorer ones of larger households. During the wars the larger and more complex families have been a support to each other, as they moved around in larger units.

The housing in the rural areas prior to the wars was generally inadequate and unhygienic. The recent fighting has exacerbated the housing crisis in the Yugoslav territories, making it the most deprived housing area of greater Europe. Some of the northern communes have been building housing complexes, where the generations are encouraged to interrelate and integrate. In this way, they are replicating and conserving much of the *zadruga* family structure and the collective values of tightly-knit ethnic groups.

If the principle of subsidiarity epitomizes much of the care provided in Southern European Catholic countries, the principle also epitomizes care in those countries where the exogamous community is a dominant cultural feature. This, of course, has also been reinforced by the communist political system during the post-World War II period of Soviet influence, with its emphasis upon collectivism.

Health care

On the whole, when compared with the neighbouring Balkan countries and communist regimes, the health care systems in the former Yugoslav territories were impressive, constituting a rich mix. However, the boundaries of care have been shaken by the recent hostilities which have developed after the collapse of the old 'market socialism', with long-term implications in an uncertain future. None the less, many of the caring arrangements of the former Yugoslav schemes appear to be still in place in the north and in the less battle-torn areas.

Today, 80–90% of the older population are covered by health insurance. However, Svetlik (1988, p.348) refers to the 38% (and increasing) of the older population in Slovenia who pay for health treatment at centres there. The effect of 'marketizing' health care in Slovenia has been a decrease by at least 4% in out-patient care and a drop of 1.2% in the average hospitalization period (Svetlik, 1988, p.348). However, in Macedonia and Serbia, those aged 65 and over have a right to free health care, regardless of their means. Free medical care is available on demand for all the older population in most of the old established district health centres, within areas whose current administrative boundaries adhere in the majority of cases to those of the former provincial scheme. Health screening and home care are organized from these health centres (CPA, 1989, p.195). Farmers had their own health insurance scheme.

Heikkinen et al. (1983, p.30) indicate that there are at least three times as many doctors in the urban than the rural areas of the former Yugoslavia. Also, Belgrade has about three times as many doctors per 1,000 of its population as there are in Louvain, Belgium. A countrywide Yugoslav programme on ageing was inaugurated in 1985, which was preventive and not problem-centred, in keeping with the World Health Organization's adage of not simply adding years to life, but life to years. Unfortunately the country was soon to be thrown into civil war.

Before the internal wars there were cuts in free medication for older patients (Ruzica et al., 1991, p.80). Today the supply of medicines for most of the former Yugoslavia is minimal, and is reserved for emergencies only. It will take more than a decade to restore any semblance of a health system available to the general public on the basis of need and not simply survival.

Nursing

Heikkinen et al. (1983, pp.120 and 122) indicated that in Zagreb and Belgrade the older people were visited by nurses. Community nurses paid more visits to the older people of Belgrade than were paid by nurses in the other 14 European countries sampled. Nursing homes provide home care for older people in the locality, but little has been published regarding the numbers involved, eligibility, and the extent and quality of the work.

Mental health care

There are no reports available regarding mental health services for older people in the territories of the former Yugoslavia.

Institutional care

Kavar-Vidmar et al. (1980, p.161) describe the three types of institutions provided for dependent older people who cannot be cared for within their families:

1 homes for the frail, which offer placement, food and health care;
2 homes for the physically and mentally disabled, which offer placement, food and medical care;
3 combined homes for younger and older pensioners who need a placement for other purposes.

There are under 200 homes for older people in the Yugoslav territories, catering for over 30,800 potential residents. In 1986 there were 160 institutions. With the exception of homes in Serbia and in a few northern areas, they are generally large establishments, run like hotels, with between 150 and 200 residents. According to Ruzica et al. (1991, p.84), the average number of residents is as high as 190. By 1986, for every 1,000 people in the former Yugoslavia, there were only 1.3 beds in homes for the aged, and as few as 0.4 in Macedonia. The former Slovenia had the highest ratio, with 5.7 per 1,000 people.

Before the civil war broke out in Yugoslavia, the number of places in residential care were being cut back, and the very dependent were transferred from the formal sector to the informal domain of domestic care. The ultimate principle underlying social policies seemed to have been the belief in the utilitarian principle that older people not only preferred to be at home, but that it was also a cheaper alternative. However spurious that belief, there is no doubt that the planners believed that open care was a cheaper option (see Milosavljevic and Ruzica, 1989).

The institutions are served by medical staff, nurses, social workers and technical staff. The payment schemes are complex: the residents may be self-payers; self and family part-payers; self, relatives and social services part-payers, or payments may be provided solely by relatives. About 80% of the residents are either bedridden or in need of special care. The places are in short supply, with at least 5,400 on the waiting lists (Ruzica et al., 1991, p.84).

From the late 1970s the homes for older people extended their facilities to include what became known in the former Yugoslavia as the 'gerontological centres'. These were in effect community care centres, which delivered meals locally, organized home help, and also provided day care on their premises. They were more common in Slovenia (see Ruzica et al., 1991, p.90).

Personal social services

As Svetlik explains (1988, p.333), according to the Constitution of 1974 the welfare system was to be completely separate from the state. So, instead of bureaucratic state regulatory bodies overseeing the social services, a mediating professional and user representative group was to carry this out. From 1974 to 1990 the social services, along with other major providers such as health care, social security and social assistance, came under an intermediary body, the Self-managed Community of Interest (SCI). Svetlik (1988, pp.333–6) and Ruzica et al. (1991, p.78) describe the function of the SCIs, which were located in the republics in communes, towns and regions. The SCIs had their own executive and expert teams, which also consisted of elected representatives who included users/clients. The SCIs made decisions to be implemented at local levels, which they backed by resources/finance. The SCIs also developed and determined standards of care/service, and supervised care delivery for a whole spectrum of users/clients at the level of the communes, towns and regions. The SCIs did not exist at the federal levels. However, in the first six months of 1990 the SCIs were abolished so that the control of personal social service spending might be transferred wholly to the member states. The authorities, it must be remembered, were facing one of the highest inflation rates in Europe. Greater central control heralded measures such as the withdrawal of access to free medication for those aged 70+. It was ironic that just when the territories threw off 'market sccialism' they also had to expose the needy and the older population to the vagaries of Church politics, the slack voluntary sector and the profiteering entrepreneurs of the new market welfare system.

Local offices

The composition and purpose of the Social Work Centres (SWCs) ought to be described because they are very dissimilar to social work offices in most European countries. The SWCs are composed of multidisciplinary teams, consisting of social workers, psychologists, pedagogues, lawyers and sociologists, plus administrative staff (Milosavljevic and Ruzica, 1989, pp.158–63). They plan local welfare schemes, keep records, run preventative programmes, offer protection to persons in need, assume guardianships, supervise institutional care and co-operate with charities and other organs associated with social policy. There is supposed to be one SWC in every municipality; in fact, 20% are without one. They are generic centres, catering for all types of clients, including older people. In this way, they are greatly assisted in avoiding the marginalization of particular client/user groups. Their work includes social assistance. It remains to be seen what will become of the SWCs once the rebuilding programmes begin after the cessation of the internal war.

At the start of the recent wars the state welfare systems were in the process of being dismantled and remodelled. The wars have turned the attention of the authorities away from social welfare and health to the immediate task of prioritizing the economy. The provision of care has been handed back to the informal sector, the Churches, the voluntary sector, and to a lesser extent, the market. Part of the 'saving process' is the development of community care provision (described as 'open care') rather than institutional care. The policy reflects the same rationalization conducted in other parts of Europe, and in the UK in particular. Svetlik (1988, p.352) describes the new modes of care as the 'externalization of service production'. He means by this the transfer of modes of care and support from the professionals to lay persons; from the public to the private sector, and from formal to informal care. One Yugoslav social scientist at an international conference at Kent University in 1992 described this in conversation with me as: 'the great community care "con". It's wiped out the triangle of formal and informal care by pushing most of the care loading to the informal sector.'

Social workers

Social workers enjoyed high status under the former Yugoslav regime (Pesic and Jovanovic, 1986, p.558). They worked in social security as well as in social intervention. Social workers were employed mostly in Bosnia and Hercegovina, Macedonia, Slovenia and Serbia. However, the provision of care by the personal social services has been very limited even before the wars (Milosavljevic and Ruzica, 1989, pp.158–63).

Meals services

Heikkinen et al. (1983, p.136) found that 7% of older people in their sample were in receipt of meals-on-wheels in Zagreb. However, Slovenia has the most progressive system of meals-on-wheels, although it is too expensive for the poorest older people (Ruzica et al., 1991, p.86).

Svetlik (1988, p.354) refers to the meals provided for older people by the Red Cross and neighbours, together with fuel. They may also buy in food for the housebound and help with the cooking.

The 'public community kitchens' provide facilities for older people, which have been utilized more during the recent troubles when homelessness has reduced families to penury and extreme deprivation.

Day care

Neighbourhood help systems are organized by the Red Cross, chiefly in the northern communes. Youths participate in laying on outings, helping in the home, reading and writing letters, acting as shopping escorts, bringing newspapers, etc. Most of these activities have been ended.

Home/care help

The home help system is run by health authorities or the voluntary sector. The community care system mainly consists of a comprehensive home care programme provided for those who are not able to care for themselves and who have nobody to help them manage in their own homes (Kavar-Vidmar et al., 1980, p.162). The most progressive home care schemes appear to have been run for over 20 years in Slovenia. They are usually only successful in the cities (Ruzica et al., 1991, p.85). The home care usually provides a range of options, the main ones being:

1   bodily hygiene and laundering;
2   assistance in managing a medicine regime;
3   help in taking and preparing meals;
4   information about services available;
5   housework.

Home care has existed in Vojvodina since 1971 (Kavar-Vidmar et al., 1980, p.163), operating from a community centre which provides comprehensive care, such as giving advice on general matters, dispensing medicines, providing massage, escorting people to clinics, running a drop-in centre and lunches and snacks, organizing and administering a home care outreach service, and providing a laundry centre on site. Such a community centre was one of the earliest of its kind in Europe.

In Belgrade and Slovenia generally, day care centres are also run by the residential homes. These were established years before the practice took off in the UK and in other European countries. An interesting feature are the club-day-hospitals for chronically ill older people, who each have an escort to take them to and from the club. These are co-managed by the older people themselves, alongside some professionals.

Other services

Neighbourhood care is fired by slogans such as 'Care for the elderly is every-body's duty' (see for example Kavar-Vidmar et al., 1980, p.165). In many communes a 'Senior Citizens' Week' is organized periodically during the year, providing leisure and educational programmes. At the great national festivals, pupils and representatives of the local organizations involve older people, run parties for them and bring them gifts. Few such events survive.

Foster care of adults, which, as seen earlier, exists in Belgium (see page 190), is also available in many communes. This arrangement is particularly important in providing care for older, depressed or mentally ill persons who have no family.

All of these activities are organized or facilitated by the communes. Social workers and the Red Cross also collaborate with employment agencies, unions and with self-managed voluntary groups.

Voluntary care agencies and support organizations

Voluntary organizations are a relatively recent innovation in the former Yugoslavia. The few non-Church agencies which do exist receive very little support in the way of state subsidies. However, self-help groups are currently on the increase in the former Yugoslavia, especially in the war-torn zones.

The major voluntary organizations are the Red Cross, Caritas and the associations for the deaf, blind and the pensioners. Until recently, these third-sector organizations were relatively few in number. They now play an ever-increasing supportive and often critical role within the welfare system. A prime example is the work of the Red Cross in Croatia, which has organized as many as fifteen services employing 159 people, who attend older or sick people at home (Svetlik, 1988, p.355). About 30,000 older or disabled people are assisted by the young people who are trained and employed by the Red Cross, which has provided clothing and fuel, and heightened awareness of the needs of the older people by running the 'Senior Citizens' Week'.

Ruzica et al. (1991, p.89) describe a number of voluntary efforts which are worth noting here. A voluntary scheme providing a counselling service for the old has been set up in Belgrade, providing afternoon advice services and telephone helpline networks. These are described as 'hot lines' for those older people suffering from stress or loneliness. In Zagreb, Caritas has provided kitchens and shelter which the older people have been using to great advantage. In Ljubljana, the youth group The Goodness of the Young Service, run by Franciscan friars, cares for older people in the city. They have nurses and physicians within the group. In Subotica the Fund for Social Care of the Old has activated various community resources, both private and public, on behalf of older people since 1983. In Belgrade the Counselling Service for the Old has pioneered a successful telephone support network for older people in distress.

Clubs which cater specifically for older people are chiefly a feature in the urban areas. These were first set up in the 1960s, notably in Novi Beograd. Other local clubs make their facilities available for older people at set times at cheap or nominal rates. Lastly, in Slovenia and Croatia, monasteries and religious institutions provide care for older people. Their work has not been documented, although they have often been the only source of help in emergencies, or when state support either ran out of resources or could not help. The silence can be explained in terms of the bias and sectarianism that surrounded any alternative provision to that of the secular regime.

Informal care

The studies in the former Yugoslavia until the recent internal wars have referred to one country, whereas this territory within the Balkan peninsula has always represented several distinctive cultures and diverse ethnic groups. Instead of one nation, there were eight distinctive territories: Slovenia, Croatia, Bosnia and Hercegovina, Serbia, Montenegro, Macedonia, Vojvodina and Kosovo. The populations of the north-western territories (Vojvodina, Croatia and Slovenia) are on average slightly older than those of the south. There are three Slav languages, although 70% speak Serbo-Croat. Three major religions – Eastern Orthodoxy, Roman Catholicism and Islam – compete for worshippers, determine values and shape traditions. Contrasting modes of informal domestic support and care of older people are inevitable in one of Europe's most diversified areas.

Milosavljevic and Ruzica (1989) set out the historical context of today's divisions and the misfortunes and fortunes of the Yugoslav peoples under the various regimes. One thing stands out within that troubled history: the extent and strength of familial care. The CPA (1989, p.194) states: 'The family still provides most of the support needed for elderly people, especially in the rural areas of Yugoslavia.' According to law in all the republics of the former Yugoslavia, all offspring were obliged to take care of their parents. For example, Article 124 of the Law of Marriage and Family Relations in Slovenia laid down the following injunction:

> Children of age are obliged to maintain their parents who are incapable of work or do not have enough means for their living. Both parties make an agreement about the level of alimony at the social welfare community agency responsible. Should an agreement not be possible the entitled person may claim it through the law court.

Indeed, after the recession of the 1970s, most social responsibilities, apart from the basic ones, were transferred to the family (Milosavljevic and Rusica, 1989, p.171). Smolic-Krkovic (1977) refers to the reluctance of older people to report their offspring for non-support. However, the social pressures are considerable and difficult to resist in a cultural setting where the standing of the family is judged by its self-reliance and its measure of assistance, not only to the older people but to the wider family, in accordance with the traditional values of the exogamous community family.

As stated above, one form of exogamous community family in the former Yugoslav territories is the *zadruga*. In terms of informal care, the household variants are significant. Vincent and Mudrovcic (1992, pp.10–13) refer to two forms of *zadruga*. The first exists in rural Croatia, and consists of 'big households' (*veliko domacinstvo*) where smaller households come together. Here, the kinship ties are not a key factor. The second type is found in Serbia, in parts of Bosnia Hercegovina and Montenegro, as well as in some areas of Greece and Bulgaria. Here, the kinship ties are on the father's side (agnatic) in which the sons and parents stay together. These extended households have a larger ratio of males to females. In either case, older people have greater support.

The migrations and the increase in urbanization referred to above meant that there were more isolated older people, without status and the support of the extended households. During the wars, because of the exodus of the younger males to join in the fighting, older people, women and children have come together in matriarchal and supportive groups. Ironically, the old *zadruga* value systems have been recreated, but with a lower ratio of men to women, and more in the form of the 'big households' as the refugees cluster together to survive. An area of growing concern is the plight of the widows. Even before the fighting, 57–60% of the older women and 20–26% of the older men had lost their spouses (on the basis of CPA, 1989, p.194; Grundy and Harrop, 1992, pp.26 and 28). Since the wars, the number of widows will have escalated. Isolated men and women have neither social status nor much support. Their number is greatest in the large urban areas.

The older men are more involved in outside events than the women, and seek company generally within associations, particularly in the cities (over half of the sample of Belgrade men are members of associations in Heikkinen et al., 1983, p.83); whilst over a quarter of the oldest women in Heikkinen et al.'s study (p.109) felt lonely in Belgrade, under 14% of the oldest women in Zagreb did not. The difference between localities is difficult to explain. Isolation is less in one city and more in the other. However, cutting across the diverse areas of the country is the increasing loneliness of those aged over 75. In spite of the greater family integration in 1980, Kavar-Vidmar et al. (1980, p.168) cite the 32% who felt lonely. Recent atrocities increase loneliness.

As reported by Heikkinen et al. (1983, p.74), over 45% of those in the sample in Belgrade live in crowded households. In contrast with the isolated widows and widowers, these suggest other stressful difficulties for families caring both for older relatives and for children in cramped households. The eulogistic reference to the strength of familial care of older people cited earlier must be somewhat modified in the light of other observations made by other researchers. Already in 1980, Kavar-Vidmar et al. (1980, p.167) cited four major changes affecting the open care of older people in Yugoslavia (p.167):

1   The socialization of family functions: the welfare systems progressively take over familial care as the care of older people becomes the problem of the entire society. However, older rural people, especially farmers, are on the breadline, forced to depend upon their offspring for social help, especially their sons.
2   Structural changes in 50% of families with the gradual disappearance of the extended family: the emotional and economic integration of families lessens.
3   Modified extended families constitute 30% of Yugoslav families: emotional ties and financial help still exist in spite of the distances created by migration, but for progressively fewer families.
4   Nuclear families become isolated, constituting 10% of Yugoslav families: emotional and financial connections are largely dropped: older people are left on their own; life for them is the most difficult of all. Offspring more frequently abandon their mothers than their fathers.

These factors are still in place, at least in Bosnia, on the basis of Vincent and Mudrovcic's (1992) findings. The rural areas throughout the regions of the former Yugoslavia are in the throes of change, and lag behind the social texture of life in the urban areas. Kavar-Vidmar et al. (1980, p.168) commented upon this in 1980; the transitional phase has been slow to run its extended course:

> On the one hand, the role of the traditional forms of assistance within the framework of the patriarchal family and village community is weakening, while on the other, the system of organized care and protection has not yet been shaped so far that the responsibilities of the traditional family can be taken over smoothly without noticeable lags.

In addition, the recession and the subsequent destruction of the villages and the countryside, particularly in the northern areas, have slowed down the formalization of supportive care of the older population. The problem is that the traditional families are not likely to return to fill the yawning gaps in local caring arrangements. The rural areas need to be looked at further in the light of the available research, but to date there is a lack of studies into the caring arrangements in the villages, except that Stambuk and Zupancic (1985, pp.169–204) identify a rift between the older and the younger people over the status of women within the family and the preference for urban as opposed to rural living.

Ruzica et al. (1991) present one of the most comprehensive pictures of informal care within the former Yugoslav territories, which confirms the above descriptions of informal care and the general conditions facing the older population, but also adds to the store of knowledge regarding informal care of older people in these parts of the Balkan peninsula.

The patriarchal *zadruga* family structure in some rural areas and the shortage of houses have forced many younger men to stay with their parents even after marriage. These families are described by Ruzica et al. (1991, p.74) as 'forced communities'. They also add that more than 50% of pensioners are below the poverty line (p.83); many have neither pensions nor savings. They receive the so-called 'permanent subsidy', which is very often not taken up because it is means-tested; about 5% of the older population are in receipt of this payment. Those who have no family nor relatives to support them are a major problem, especially in rural areas. Half the population is rural, and older people reside in about 10–25% of the rural households (Ruzica et al., 1991, p.89).

Leisure pursuits and education

Clubs for older people have existed for over twenty years in most of the smaller towns or communes within the former Yugoslavia. As stated above, these were often social care centres rather than leisure centres, although care and leisure often went hand in hand. Universities of the Third Life Period have existed in Belgrade, and also in Ljubljana and in some towns of Slovenia, since 1986, with groups of as few as 30 to as many as 300 students (Ruzica et al., 1991, p.90). Lastly, the Pensioners' Association provides contacts and solidarity for a growing number of older people (Ruzica et al., 1991, p.87).

Svetlik (1988, p.355) describes the Pensioners' Associations, and the educational programmes run by the Red Cross. Firstly, the Pensioners' Associations are set up in localities or the communes. These organize sport, cultural activities, recreation, outings, holidays and exhibitions. There are about 325 such associations in Slovenia, organizing some 461 sports circles, 71 choirs and over 3,000 outings. Secondly, the Red Cross runs health education courses. Within a period of four years in the mid-1980s, as many as 2,780 courses were provided; 113,000 people took part, many of them older people.

Rural aspects

Eighty per cent of farmland is family-owned, and 50% of people still live in villages, according to Ruzica et al. (1991, p.74). Approximately 11% of the over-65s in the rural areas are economically active, forced to continue working to make ends meet in much the same way as older people are in Greece.

Depopulation of the villages is a feature, particularly in the hilly areas of Slovenia, where at least 600 villages have less than ten residents (see Ruzica et al., 1991, p.74). The areas nearest the heart of Europe are the more urban and the more affluent, where the older people are better-served and healthier. The proportion of older people in the agricultural sector of Slovenia is only 9.4%, whilst in Serbia it is 27.6% and in Macedonia 27.7%. The ratio of older persons aged 60+ to younger persons in the rural areas was 18:1 in 1980. It was predicted that by the year 2000 the ratio will be 30:1, and by the year 2025 it will be 43:1. However, tragically, the civil war will have totally altered that projection (see Ruzica et al., 1991, pp.74–6).

Conclusion

The former Yugoslavia has had a history of decentralization which created localized infrastructures over time, but they were seldom integrated. The surviving regional systems of the former Yugoslavia are a conglomerate of ethnic and religious systems. For years these antipathetic territories have been diametrically opposed to any form of lasting solidarity; 1.3 million people are homeless, and millions more are in trauma of one kind or another. In their midst are countless older people for whom there is no security and nowhere to go. In these unresolved situations, alienation is rife, and any hope of a permanent socio-political solution is likely to remain elusive for years to come. It is against such a bleak and brutal environment, in Bosnia and Hercegovina particularly, that the care of older people today has to be set. There are probably six emergent triangles of care in the diverse territories and republics of the former Yugoslavia. It is not possible at this stage to predict what will constitute the emergent patterns or resultant triangulation processes of care and welfare systems, once the tanks, guns and troops have cleared the streets and fields of this war-torn region. In the mean time, older people will continue to languish, then die.

26 Albania

Demography

As shown in Table 1, the proportion of older people in Albania ranks second-last in greater Europe, at only 4.9%. By 2025 the projected proportion of older people is 9.8%, which will still rank second-last (see CPA, 1989, p.14). The life expectancy of women at birth is 74.9 years, and that of men is 69.4 years (UN, 1991). The life expectancy for women is higher than that in the former Czechoslovakia, the former Yugoslavia, Hungary, Bulgaria and Romania (see UN, 1991); the life expectancy for men is above that of Portugal, the former Yugoslavia, Bulgaria, Romania, the former Czechoslovakia, Poland and Hungary.

The demand for care for older people is outweighed by that of children; the percentage of children aged 0–14 years is 35.4% (CPA, 1989, p.14), whereas that of the Republic of Ireland is 29.6% (CPA, 1989, p.81). The predicted proportion of children in Albania by the year 2025 is 25%, and that in Ireland is 21%, so the imbalance will persist. On the positive side, the caring ratio will be maintained.

Socio-political and administrative background

Albania, the smallest member of the former socialist communities of Europe, has been secluded from the mainstream of European life, and aptly known for years as Shqiperi ('Eagles' Country'). Its formal systems of care have never been adequate and are currently in chaos, in what is regarded by almost all commentators as a Third World country in Europe, probably the continent's most underdeveloped country. Its 4.9 million older people must be amongst the most deprived in Southern Europe.

There are about 20 towns and 26 small provinces (*rrethi*), each averaging about 90,000 people, with the highest concentration of people in Tirane. The largest centralized administration, ruled by the Albanian Labour Party (Patria e Punes se Shqiperise), had in effect no social policy on the care of older people. Home care has largely been left to the Albanian family, which traditionally belongs to the exogamous community family type. Albanians hold older people in high regard, in much the same way as in China.

About 95% of the population are Albanians, the balance is made up of small ethnic minorities: Greeks, Romanians, Macedonians, Gypsies and Montenegrins. The majority are Muslims, of which there are about five times as many as the Orthodox Christians and six times as many as the Roman Catholics. The imperatives of the Qur'an hold sway here, so that caring for older people within the household is regarded as a holy duty. The largely agricultural nature of Albanian society also reinforces the traditional role of the family as sovereign carer. Hence the reliance of the government upon the goodwill of the family: during the Hoxha regime, great reliance was placed upon the largely Muslim family structure, whilst at the same time the government provided very few services for older people, and officially declared the family 'outmoded'. Formal care is only provided when the health of the older person or the support provided by the family/household breaks down completely. Even when the state's formal care is called for, its intervention is largely symbolic.

What remains of the health and welfare care systems of the old regime cannot be dismantled overnight. On paper, the Soviet-designed health and social welfare model introduced by the Albanian Labour Party was committed to equality and justice for all. A universal health insurance scheme was free for all Albanians. Since liberation in 1989, Albania, the 'last true European Stalinist state' (Sjoberg and Wyzan, 1991b, p.1), has not immediately and resolutely entered into dismantling the old welfare and health systems by means of a transitional programme (Deacon, 1992c, p.168). Instead there is a hiatus because of uncertainties over which steps to take; in the mean time, the older systems remain.

The political and administrative systems in Albania continue to be centrist. Pashko (1991, p.128) describes the *status quo* as 'hypercentralization'. Departmentalism has become the rule. This is illustrated by the proliferation of procedures which have simply reproduced shortages; for example, older people along with the general population had to face rationing in the towns (Sjoberg, 1991, p.118), and life was generally bleak in the 1980s and early 1990s for vulnerable groups.

In the late 1980s the proportion of consumer expenditure on food was 62.1%, whereas that of non-food was 37.9% (Pashko, 1991, p.135). In his commentary on the state system, Pashko describes the situation in the late

1980s as 'a pathology of structures and mechanisms'. The way out of such a debilitating malaise is described as a 'slow therapy'. The Tenth Central Committee Plenum (1990) passed legislation to reduce the bureaucracy, which although it was directed mainly at liberating the economy, applied also to the whole process of state administration.

Removing the centre of gravity from the ministerial level to that of the localities is the first major task for the provision of welfare and health care. Additionally, the freeing of practitioners from the 'unrestrained supervision' of the authorities has had to run parallel to the whole liberating process in industry and the market economy. Increased sectoral autonomy is the goal in industry within contemporary Albania; it will be some time before a parallel process will occur in health and social care.

Social and health care for older people are regarded as enterprises within the emergent market systems currently being sold to purchasers in many parts of Europe. In a nation where the adoption of a market orientation is proving to be very difficult (see Sjoberg, 1991; Pashko, 1991), the adoption of a plural welfare system is proving to be more difficult still.

Social security: pensions and benefits

After World War II, Albania introduced a universalist non-contributory state pension. Many of the 4.9 million Albanian older population are now concerned because of uncertainties surrounding their future pensions and benefits. The emphasis upon commercial viability is totally foreign to the older people who have been conditioned and socialized for years within a socialist welfare state.

Housing

Housing is poor but rents are cheap. The old systems did provide some of the best models of formal networks. The statutory, professional and voluntary agencies were interwoven. The open system lent itself to plural integration. Unfortunately the same cannot be said about the sectarian and ideological splits which have reduced the standard of living and services to the level of many Third World countries. Older people stand in the bread queues, relying upon the support of the wider family in emergencies, or upon the local Church or religious groups.

Health care

Nothing can be said about hospital care and medical services as they now exist. In the circumstances, it may help to throw light upon the resources in Albania by going back to earlier, reliable sources. According to the edition of the *Encyclopaedia Britannica* (1979, Micropaedia, Vol.I, p.191) there were 0.7 doctors and 0.9 hospital beds per 1,000 inhabitants. This ratio was lower than any of the other European countries; for example, Portugal – one of the poorest countries – had a ratio of 0.9 doctors per 1,000 (see Eurostat, 1991b, p.88).

In spite of the inferior health systems, the life expectancy in Albania has been superior to some of its neighbouring countries. However, hospital care is underdeveloped: geriatric consultants do not exist; there are no teams of qualified community nurses nor organized home helps, and no strategy or policy of domiciliary care exists.

The rush to privatize in the name of democratization will only make matters worse because the scarce health facilities and medication that do exist will be siphoned off from general consumption to be bought by the affluent few.

Mental health care

Albania has no mental health care system comparable with other European caring systems; still less is there any psychogeriatric care.

Institutional care

Official sources indicate that institutional care consists of large multi-bed hospital establishments with well over 100 occupants each. Details are not available.

Personal social services

The claim is that the old regime spent two-thirds of its net national income on social care (*Encyclopaedia Britannica*, Micropaedia, Vol.1, 1990). However, in the government's *Statistical Yearbook of Albania* there is no separate section concerning services, so there is no way of assessing the country's social product to confirm this claim. The lack of services and the secrecy surrounding welfare and health provision in Albania suggest that the country has not been able to provide a supportive welfare system nor organize social care for vulnerable groups such as older people. Taking into account the economic analyses of Sjoberg (1991, pp.115–27) and of Pashko (1991, pp.128–46), it is not possible to see how the state could afford to spend two-thirds of its net income on social care. In addition, the notion of social service as an agent of the citizen/user/consumer rather than an agent of the state is not easily assimilated into the consciousness of the formal Albanian care providers, who are still in control and who remain statist, whatever the rhetoric and current Albanian 'market speak'. It is difficult for them to break the Hoxha mould. It will take several years to dismantle the former social philosophical tenets and to construct new ones.

Voluntary care agencies and support organizations

The voluntary sector does not really have a post-war history in Albania. The Muslim families provided care and support for their older relatives. The Orthodox Church and the Roman Catholic parishes did not openly establish a social outreach policy. The state was the sole provider of formal care.

Informal care

Struggling families, especially in the 'Fourth World economy' of Albania, will have less spare time to care for their older relatives, as they strive to supplement their meagre incomes with longer hours at work. The domestic time they do have will be largely claimed by their children. The demands of resources for the care of dependent offspring will be maintained well into the twenty-first century. The birth rate in Albania is the highest in Europe and is likely to remain so up to the year 2025, as predicted by the UN (1986), and as cited by Simons (1992, p.56). As stated earlier, on the positive side, the high caring ratio within families will mean that, in the event of the Albanian family retaining its prime caring role, the family circle will retain its strength.

Leisure pursuits and education

Any counterpart to the leisure and adult learning provision in other countries, such as that of the University of the Third Age, is out of the question.

Older people are often in employment, especially as farm labourers. The motivation of those with spare time is low, and many are illiterate. Only in 1946 was education made compulsory, and it was confined to only eight years of elementary education.

Rural aspects

Many older people reside in the rural areas, unable to compete in the new monetarist labour system, and unsure about the value of their pension within an unfamiliar market welfare scheme.

Older people in the rural areas of Tropoje, Puke, Mirdite and Kolonje often live in remote areas without health and social care services. Lack of transport and poor telecommunications in the country as a whole (Pashko, 1991, p.136) cut off the remoter countrysides from the markets and the health centres. The government was concerned about the exodus of the people to the urban areas, so it attempted to halt it by its urban–rural equalization measures of the 1960s and 1970s (see Sjoberg, 1991, p.117).

Conclusion

Backwardness and centralization are salient factors that block any possible welfare progress in Albania. Smith (1991a, p.155) states that Albania has more in common with the rural areas of Russia just after the death of Stalin than with Europe in the 1990s. Population growth outstrips agricultural output. The system is inert and the obstacles to developing a viable mix of welfare and health provision for vulnerable groups such as frail and needy older people are formidable. The health system is the worst in greater Europe; the welfare system is virtually non-existent, and there is no voluntary care ethos nor army of volunteers to fill the gaps in formal care. In addition, the government's strategy for care of older Albanians is hard to identify.

Analysis is thwarted by the difficulty of receiving information from this deprived country, particularly commentaries about the modes and quality of informal and formal care. The state is committed to modernization and democratization, but cannot presently take the steps necessary to move in their direction.

The fact is that, with the changeover from the old regime to the new, the Albanian people, particularly the older population, are deprived of the little succour the welfare state had offered them in the past. At the same time, in the current confused regime they are denied the largesse which market welfare promises them.

Aslund (1991, p.165) makes the point that Albania needs to establish a civil society before democratization and marketization take place. A truly civil society will take more than a decade to establish. In the mean time, 'plural welfare' in Albania will be little more than a vain hope.

The care system will never be more than hollow rhetoric, unless the essential hardware requirements of hospital care are installed; unless qualified and experienced personnel are provided, and unless centres of social care are equipped to serve both older people and their carers.

27 Malta

Demography

According to the data presented in Table 1, Malta is currently ranked twenty-second in Europe in terms of its proportion of people aged 65+, but will probably rank sixteenth by 2025, judging by the projections (UN, 1991). Malta passed the 10% benchmark used by demographers to identify an old population structure in 1989 – a small island population with a great age imbalance. According to Troisi (1988, p.6), the proportion of persons aged 60+ in Malta will be 23.8% by the year 2025, which exceeds the UN (1991) prediction. The increase in those aged 65+ will be the tenth-highest (7.6%) in Europe. The life expectancy of women in Malta at 65 is 16.8 years, which is ranked eighteenth in greater Europe; that of men is 13.7 years, and is ranked fifteenth (UN, 1986, 1991; Eurostat, 1991a).

Socio-political and administrative background

Administrative systems in small islands are mainly monocephalic. However, Malta's parish structure tends to create polycephalic entities, so that there is a local tension between parochialism and centrism. The government is committed to dismantling the centrist system. Galea et al. (1990) describe the 'Malta experience' and the government's aim to create an integrated social policy centred upon the formal care of the island's older population in partnership with families and the Catholic Church. In the past the Catholic Church and the state have jointly provided the bulk of the care of older people within this small country with a population of approximately 393,000.

All matters related to the care of older people are dealt with by the

Ministry for Social Policy, and two main government departments are answerable to the ministry: the Department of Social Security and the Department of Social and Family Welfare. The first is concerned with the financial aspects, the second is concerned with the delivery of services. Effective strategy and efficient operational management rest upon five key ideas, as expressed by the Ministry for Social Policy:

1   participation;
2   solidarity;
3   empowerment;
4   subsidiarity;
5   decentralization.

These are the major elements in the restructured system (see Ministry for Social Policy, 1990, p.4). In addition, a Social and Family Welfare Council has been set up as an advisory body to the Minister for Social Policy to see that the five elements inform practice. The government has also bunched together health, housing, labour and welfare under the ministry. The workings of the system providing care is determined by recent legislation, the Family and Social Welfare Act (see Ministry for Social Policy, 1990, p.5).

The Central Social and Family Welfare Agency (CSFWA), answerable to the Director of the Department of Social and Family Welfare (under the Minister for Social Policy), co-ordinates all statutory welfare and all non-government organizations providing care. One of these is the Welfare Unit for the Elderly, which has been well described by Troisi (1988).

The care of the older population is integrated within a system that facilitates multidisciplinary assessment and breaks down the old ministerial and professional barriers that often block the pathways to appropriate caring arrangements. Like Greece, Malta has had a strong tradition in familial care. In keeping with the country's concern for the growing number of older people, in May 1987 the Maltese government created the post of Parliamentary Secretary for the Care of the Elderly – a unique appointment.

There are six regions in Malta. The island has no first-order political sub-divisions. Physical and administrative links with the Ministry for Social Policy are perhaps the closest of any in Europe, in a small island community with a sharp eye for swift decision-making and immediate action.

Social security, pensions and benefits

Malta has a comprehensive social insurance scheme and retirement/old age pension packages. Income support systems have existed on the island since

1921, and were followed by the Old Age Pensions Act 1948 and the Universal Pension Scheme 1956, based upon contributions. The 1956 Act was amended in 1979, granting a two-thirds pension for all contributors to the National Insurance Fund, at 60 for women and 61 for men. There is also a non-contributory pension scheme, and a twice-yearly bonus.

There has been an anomaly regarding equity within the pension scheme because persons who retired before the instigation of the two-thirds pension scheme of 1979 receive substantially less. This particularly disadvantaged those who retired before 1959. The government is forced to provide pension supplements, but these do not adequately redress the imbalance. The savings of older citizens have in any case fallen in value, whilst their expenditure has increased, alongside health and housing/property maintenance costs. Another difficulty within the system which has concerned the government has been the fact that widows have had their pensions reduced on reaching the age of 60.

The government is committed to protecting the purchasing power of the older population by regulating prices. Indirectly, this cuts down on their payments/benefits. A screening body, the Advisory Committee, regulates the prices of virtually all items, particularly the staple food items such as bread, pasta, dairy products and meat.

The levels of income support and the range of social security benefits are linked to the Retail Price Index.

Housing

Government policy is to provide independent flatlets and sheltered accommodation (CPA, 1989, p.102). Troisi's report (1988, pp.14–15) does not provide any detailed information regarding housing for older Maltese people. Most pensioners own their own homes. The rents for the non-owners are controlled. There are inferences that there are some houses without running water and with restricted sanitation, which are also cold in winter. The thrust of the new policies has been to provide special ground-floor state housing flats for the older people in the worst housing.

Health care

Hospital care and medical services

Hospitalization, health services and home help care are free. There is an acute geriatric hospital system providing rehabilitation. Chiropody and remedial services are free (CPA, 1989, p.102). There is a free drugs distribution service for the low-income patients, which is means-tested (see Troisi, 1988, p.14). All medication is provided without charge in hospitals.

There are two GP services: a public medical service, which is free of charge, and a private fee-paying alternative. The public GP service is provided at six health centres. There is no payment for either consultation at the centres or the doctors' home visits. The centres (formerly named 'polyclinics') were established in 1980 within specified catchment areas. The size of these is worth noting: the Floriana centre caters for 96,956 persons in 14 settlements (towns/villages); the Gzira centre caters for 53,580 persons in 7 settlements; the Paolo centre caters for 70,232 persons in 11 settlements; the Conspicua centre caters for 17,547 persons in 4 settlements; the Mosta centre caters for 60,352 persons in 9 settlements, and the Rabat centre for 21,069 persons in 4 settlements. They therefore have huge commitments. They are served by at least 85 GPs and at least 110 nurses; the staffing levels of doctors and nurses at these centres are not published within the official statements regarding services in Malta. The aims of the centres are to provide curative, rehabilitative and preventive services for all, regardless of means. The people of Gozo do not have a centre, instead they consult their GPs at the local hospital. A matter for concern is the fact that the patients are not seen by the same doctor at every visit.

There are about 200 GPs in private practice in Malta. Their charges are said to be moderate. There are 43 dispensaries, 6 of which are included within the health centres. There is almost one dispensary to each village. The prescription charges are in accordance with the patient's means.

The hospital service is free for the whole population. There are six hospitals providing a total of 2,095 beds. St Luke's on the main island is the principal hospital, which specializes in caring for the older population. An acute geriatric teaching hospital with 100 beds has recently been established. Two other minor hospitals provide nursing care and respite care for periods of less than three weeks. The policy is to reduce the number of older people in long-term care in line with hospital policy in most of Europe. However, there are 'social emergency cases' where older people have blocked beds for months. They have had neither people to care for them at home nor suitable accommodation to return to. There is a lack of hospital day centres.

Nursing

As stated above, about 110 nurses provide care at the health centres. Domiciliary nursing services were started in 1973 (Troisi, 1988, p.37); these are now free of charge irrespective of the patient's level of income. The nurses are a mix of government nurses and private Malta Memorial

District Nursing Association (MMDNA) nurses; there are 31 of the former and 12 of the latter. The operational management for all the community nurses comes under the MMDNA in liaison with the Community Services Centre, on behalf of the Secretariat for the Care of the Elderly. The arrangement is a good example of a public–private mix. The nursing is prescribed by the GP. The 43 nurses operate within a 'patch' system, providing a total of 860 visits each day. The caseload averages 1,547 a month (Troisi, 1988, p.38). There is also a 24-hour, seven-days-a-week emergency 'out of hours' service.

Home care/help

Home help in Malta comes under the auspices of the nursing services; it is also contracted-out to the MMDNA. The workers are known as 'Health Assistants'; 22 of them serve about 113 housebound older people a month. The service provides fortnightly house cleaning and is free, and it operates from Mondays to Saturdays, inclusive. Requests come via the GP or a registered social worker.

Another parallel scheme has been introduced in four of the major towns, which provides fuller assistance at a nominal fee. The workers are known as 'Casual Social Assistants'. They provide services such as shopping, bed-making, ironing, dressing or cooking meals. Above all, they are befrienders. They each work solely for four older persons; 94% of those assisted are over 70 years of age, and half of these are octogenarians.

Mental health care

Mental health care is provided principally at two hospitals: at Mount Carmel Hospital on the main island, and at Gozo. There are five psychiatric social workers at Mount Carmel Hospital and 89 psychogeriatric beds in the St Vincent de Paul Residence, which is described under 'Institutional care'. There are also psychiatric units at the four major health centres of Floriana, Gzira, Mosta and Paola (Troisi, 1988, p.16). Apart from the psychogeriatric service unit at the St Vincent de Paul Residence, there appears to be little mental health care specifically for older patients. In view of this, the government is in the process of setting up psychiatric support in sheltered accommodation and supporting volunteer or self-help groups. Little is known about the quality of the care provided and the extent to which the new emphasis upon the community care of mentally ill and confused older patients is progressing.

Institutional care

There are two major public institutions: the larger, the St Vincent de Paul Residence, is a complex establishment providing multiple forms of nursing care, or simply residential care, with 1,048 beds, of which 884 are geriatric beds, in addition to the psychogeriatric beds mentioned above. There are also 75 beds in flatlet units, whose occupants are mainly in receipt of residential care; 61% are women. There are 237 nurses and 71 health assistants. The residence is an old *imgieret* or 'poor house' on the island; thus, in spite of being upgraded, stigma is often associated with this large establishment. The other institution is a residential home providing 57 beds.

The majority of private homes are run by religious orders. There are 16 such homes, served by 136 nuns who are qualified nurses, catering for 596 persons with a waiting list of 2,000 older people; 78.5% of the residents are women. In 1979 a Commission of Church Homes for the Elderly was established to provide co-ordination and formulate policies for them (Troisi, 1988, p.32). Although the average number of residents is about 37, there are two with over 70 residents and one with 127.

The government is now acutely aware of the number of older people who should not be in institutional care: 40% of the older residents at the major nursing home should be at home or in sheltered accommodation (Troisi, 1988, p.44). The policy is to offer alternatives and smaller units.

Apart from the traditional institutional homes, there are small, community-based, hostel-type homes. Smaller homes for older people have been built in each locality close to the residents' former household, and the residents have participated in the planning of these homes (Galea et al., 1990, p.198). Those who wish to live independently have a choice between the independent flatlets and sheltered housing.

There is a concerted drive to enable older people to stay in their own homes. The emphasis is upon 'inter-generational family solidarity'. The older population are very much involved in designing a strategy of care tailored to suit their needs and in discussions within the family circle. The aim is to complement familial care, not replace it. Those without family are obviously handicapped by the lack of household support and status.

The CSFWA determines who gets a place in a state residential home. The policy is to encourage the maintenance of family solidarity (Vella, 1990b). Institutional care is the last resort (Troisi, 1988). To carry this out, the islanders are backed by a community care scheme under the eye of a Parliamentary Secretariat for the Care of the Elderly (since May 1987). Much of the back-up care for the household carers is provided by the Church. However, such vocations are generally dropping in number: older nuns are themselves requiring care. Also, there are signs that in spite of far-seeing social policies, the added strains of caring for older relatives upon house-holds will increase. Where will frailer older people go for support, and how will the household carers themselves find support in the first quarter of the twenty-first century?

In spite of the emphasis upon alternatives to institutional care, people still choose to end their days in a traditional residential home, hence the 2,000 persons on the waiting list for just 596 beds in the 16 homes run by the Church. The safety net is currently stretched. On the basis of the Nationalist Party's manifesto in the 1987 elections, there is a shortfall of about 53 homes for older Maltese people. However, in line with policies in most of Europe, the government is now more convinced of the need to provide alternatives to the traditional type of residential or nursing home; 'more of the same' would be a step backwards. In liaison with such agencies as Caritas, the government is engaged in providing and servicing smaller units or apartments, and facil-itating/maintaining the back-up of a grassroots support system in line with its five key ideas referred to above.

Personal social services

The Director of Social and Family Welfare is responsible for the provision of the personal social services, within which the care of older people forms a major area of work.

Social workers

These are qualified and graded in much the same way as social workers in the UK. There are also Assistant Social Workers and Care Workers; the latter are employed within community homes. Unlike the UK, the majority of resi-dential social workers are qualified. A key social worker is attached to each referred older person.

Meals services

As stated earlier, older people may be provided with meals at home. There are 'one-off' deliveries from day centres in response to particular requests, but there is no organized meals-on-wheels scheme equivalent to that of the UK.

Day care

The CPA (1989, p.102) refers to day care in Malta, but no further details are provided. The Ministry for Social Policy (1990, p.15) states that 'There are only a few centres functioning as the organizational base for the supply of lunches to the residences of the elderly who request it, and in some cases for occupational therapy.'

The Ministry for Social Policy is in the process of setting up centres much like those of the UK, where people can meet and engage in leisure pursuits and have access to certain services. However, there is one difference: the centres are designed to cut across age groups in order to encourage greater solidarity between generations and to reduce marginalization.

Other services

A 'Home Maintenance Service' is provided, which is a form of 'care and repair' assistance, providing home repairs, but also a 'Life Line Service' in direct communication with the Emergency Department at the major hospital and a stand-by GP.

Voluntary care agencies and support organizations

Through its district committees the Association of Pensioners (established in 1970) has built up a broad-based association for older Maltese people. Over 3,500 members have been influential in several ways: in helping to reshape community health and domiciliary care; in arguing for a lighter tax burden and more concessions for older people; in improving the National Insurance Act, and in setting up more effective residential homes and social care centres.

According to the Ministry for Social Policy (1990), there are at least 3,500 volunteers who work with over 40,000 people in need, a large proportion of whom are older people. Caritas set up Helpage Malta in 1980 (CPA, 1989, p.103). This runs various packages/programmes. Firstly, it has a consultancy role; for example, it advises on social care strategies at parish level. Secondly, it has a training role for students and carers regarding modes of assisting older people. Thirdly, it has a counselling and support role, running an independent-living advice centre, a counselling service for older people, and a referral service for those needing and seeking residential/institutional care. Fourthly, it is a fundraiser and raises public awareness about issues affecting the older Maltese population.

Since 1986, Caritas also runs the island's Good Neighbour Schemes, which serve the housebound or the quasi-housebound (see Buhagiar, 1993). Under the leadership of a Caritas worker, seven trained parishioners form a group to provide a free visiting service as befrienders. There are also two volunteers. They also set up, where necessary, intercom systems/emergency alarms, and provide daily check-ups for 'at risk' older people. Caritas helps to create social clubs for older people. At present there are 30 in 27 parishes (Troisi, 1988, pp.50–1) with 15–40 club members. They are served by about eight volunteers; most are older people themselves, and receive training by Caritas. The most imaginative work of Caritas is the educational programme (the Schools Programme on the Elderly) they run in at least 19 schools. The purpose is to raise the pupils' awareness and introduce them to voluntary work for older people.

The Welfare Society for the Sick and the Aged, set up in 1964, serves the housebound. People are taken out to entertainment, and laundry facilities are provided. There are eight other major voluntary organizations working for older people in Malta (see Troisi, 1988, p.53). Also, the Churches and the St Vincent de Paul Society assist needy older people by providing visits on request. The St Vincent De Paul Society also provide older people with pecuniary assistance. There is also the Independent Living Advice Centre (Buhagiar, 1993).

Informal care

There can be few European nations with such a family-oriented welfare policy as Malta. The Maltese Department of Information has issued a booklet, *Family Wellbeing: Government Measures for a Better Quality of Life* (1989). It states: 'The welfare of the Maltese family is a primary political commitment of this government.'

The Maltese Ministry for Social Policy report (1990) clearly adopts a family focus and from the outset reflects Catholic family welfare principles (with the words of the old Latin hymn as its opening text, '*Ubi caritas et amor Deus ibi est*': 'Where there is love and care God is there'). Malta's high birth rate (very much like that of the Republic of Ireland) reflects the welfare family policies of a Catholic country. Its percentage of older people is one of the lowest in Europe; its proportion of children is one of the highest. However, the situation is altering.

The government is well aware of the breakdown of the traditional family; for example, Troisi (1988, p.34) reports that the fall in the average size of the Maltese family has reduced the number of available family carers: whereas in 1948 there were 7.7 available to each person of retirement age, in 1969 there were only 5.4, and this reduced to 4.3 in 1986. In addition, more older people are immigrating to retire in Malta, creating an increase in demand for support when frailty sets in. With the easing of migration controls between European countries, younger Maltese emigrants are likely to be seeking work in mainland Europe, leaving their older relatives behind and cutting back the number of potential carers still more. Also, increasing numbers of older people are living alone: approximately 19% (Troisi, 1988, p.34).

The living arrangements for the older Maltese are in keeping with the general European picture of rundown properties, especially evident in the inner city. The influx of retired outsiders referred to above puts up the prices/rents of houses and flats, especially the costs of repairs. Most of the islanders have to contend with apartment stairs; these prevent older more disabled people getting out. Troisi (1988, p.43) states that 'the level of comfort in dwellings inhabited by the elderly tends to be below the average for the general population'.

There has been a scarcity of sheltered housing and purpose-designed flats for older people. As stated above, the government is in the process of altering this. Reliance upon family care has to be founded upon adequate housing arrangements. Fifty-three hostel-type homes are being provided for older people dispersed throughout Malta and Gozo (near to their present homes or apartments) which I have been able to visit. These houses are close to shops and relatives.

Keeping pace with the increasing numbers and needs of frailer older people is high on the government's agenda. However, there appears to be little emphasis upon caring for the carers within the Maltese documents, nor in the planning process. The reliance is upon the family/kinship networks picking up the pieces and providing support. Perhaps because of the island culture, the cosmopolitan nature of Malta's busy port of Valletta, and the Anglo-Saxon impact of the colonial days, the support networks are not exclusively familial.

Several senior social service officers explained in my discussions with them that the familial culture of the island is essentially characterized by openness. The Maltese are also renowned in Europe for their hospitality. So the networks have a richer mix, with the involvement of friends and neighbours in the household support available, although the more personal and intimate care is reserved for the next of kin. The supplementary support of the neighbourhood network tends to be jointly managed, as in most Southern European countries. As in Italy and Greece, the men enjoy more contact with people beyond the family circle, although the demarcation between the genders is not as rigid as in other countries within the Mediterranean rim.

The awareness and the planning of innovative community care outstrips that of Greece. However, the reliance of both government and people upon Maltese families continues to be the central element; reliance upon formal care is minimal. For how many and for how long will the family be able to cope, given the above considerations?

Leisure pursuits and education

In order to co-ordinate policies at the highest level a National Commission on Ageing has been created. Louis Galea, the Minister for Social Policy, at the international conference in Malta, 'Integrating Social and Family Policy for the 1990s', described education as the 'living water for human and social development' (Galea et al., 1990). However, there is little evidence of any major, well-patronized educational and leisure schemes for older Maltese people.

Rural aspects

Malta has the highest population density in Europe, and is essentially urban. Studies which focus upon the care of rural older people are not available.

Conclusion

Malta chaired the Preparatory Committee and the Main Committee of the World Assembly on Ageing in 1982. Although a small nation, it has been very positive in prioritizing care for older people, and enshrined concern for the growing number of older Maltese within recent legislation. This has been backed up by a reorganized structure designed to target needy older people.

Being a small country, governance on the island tends to be centralized. On the other hand, in keeping with the influential ethos of the Catholic parish, the preference is for a polycephalic system, so the country's administration is pulled in two directions (see Table 6). The family is regarded as the basic unit of society, providing primary care (it is not coincidental that Malta has the lowest proportion of women in paid employment in Europe). Accordingly, the Maltese welfare administration has unified its services on the basis of the agreement between the electorate and the government that the family is the primary unit of care. Social welfare policies are regarded as family policies. Where there is no family, the Churches, the voluntary agencies and the state welfare system step in – usually in that order – to assist the older population.

28 Turkey

Demography

According to Table 1, Turkey has the lowest proportion of older people in Europe, which it appears will remain the case for years to come. However, the projected drop of the proportion of children aged 0–14 by over 10% by the year 2025 will also be the greatest in all Europe (see CPA, 1989, pp.14 and 149). The projected decrease will shift the major burden of informal care from younger householders to the middle-aged population. In addition, the former will continue to leave the smaller settlements, and so reduce the rural ratio of care still further.

Europe's Gregorian Calendar was not adopted in Turkey until 1923, so that there is some confusion over the age of many of the older rural people. The percentage of older people may well be understated as a result.

Socio-political and administrative background

Geographically, Turkey is partly inside the European rim and partly outside it; hence it is partly European and partly Asian. Turkey in Europe is separated from Turkey in Asia (Anatolia) by the Bosporus, the Sea of Marmara and the Dardanelles, which link the Black Sea to the Mediterranean. Turkey's landmass is pivotal: economically and politically it looks westwards; culturally it looks eastwards. One cannot overlook Turkey's application in 1987 to join the EU, which will most likely be granted once the stipulated conditions are met in full. None the less, there is no consensus over the inclusion or exclusion of Turkey in Europe; for example, Kendig et al. (1992), in their commentary on family support of older relatives, locate Turkey within the

451

Middle East and Africa. However, on the basis of the political, economic and historical links Turkey has with the West, and its well-established connection with the regions of the 'golden egg', and in particular with Germany, a case can be made in support of including Turkey within greater Europe.

The vast distances in a country of 780,576 square kilometres and the cultural mix of the peoples within the provinces in a country which is both European and Asian present the Turkish administration with considerable problems, especially for the peripheral and remote areas, as is demonstrated by the many research projects cited and commented upon by Sertel and Planck (1985).

The great unifying factor in this otherwise very heterogeneous country of largely Mediterranean-Turkic people is the predominance of the Muslim religion, whose followers constitute over 90% of the population. In addition, there is the Asian emphasis upon the wisdom of the elders.

About half of the country is urbanized. Ankara, Istanbul and Izmir can be designated as metropolitan. More and more older people reside within these polluted cities. Wherever older people reside, meeting their needs takes a protracted period of time. They have to deal with a highly bureaucratized officialdom via bureaux accustomed to administering in the old style. The Grand National Assembly in Ankara and its lower chamber of the National Assembly rule over eight vastly different regions, consisting of 67 provinces (*il* or *vilâyet*), with their governors (*vali*). Within these are the districts (*ilçe* or *kaza*) with their prefects (the *kaymakam*); within these are the communes with their district officials (the *nahiye müdürü*).

The provinces have tenuous administrative links with Ankara and the other 19 large cities with more than 100,000 inhabitants. Five of the provinces have populations of more than a million (Tomanbay, 1986, p.529). A provincial council is elected for four years, headed by a provincial president. It debates questions of local administration, passes laws and makes decisions regarding the running of the services. The *vali* (non-elected) also act as chief administration officers of the province, representing all the national departments (except that of law and justice).

Towns of over 2,000 inhabitants have a municipality (the *beledye*), with its mayor assisted by its elected council and a committee. The commune comprises a number of villages, each of which is run by a headman (a *muhtar*) and a council of elders (the *ihtijararlar meclisi*). Five to twelve older people make up the council, which attends to local matters (see Temir, 1974). Perhaps the best commentary on the workings of the Turkish Grand National Assembly is provided by Kalaycioglu (1990). The government did not adequately address itself to the contemporary social problems from the time of the coup in 1960 until 1980, because legislation was clogged by unstable coalitions (see Kalaycioglu, 1990, pp. 186–8). However, the 1982 Constitution heralded a period when the process of democratization established greater stability. Improvements were made in provision for older people in the early 1980s, especially during Turkey's fifth five-year development plan (1985–9), when care for the older population was set up as a priority. However, only 2.1% of the commissions dealing with health and social services between 1983 and 1988 had the relevant expertise (Kalaycioglu, 1990, p.207).

The administrative structure is essentially monocephalic. The country's administrative structure is 'strongly centralized' (Tomanbay, 1986, p.529) via the governors who are appointed by the president on the recommendation of the Minister of the Interior. Although Turkish is the main tongue, Arabic, Kurdish and Yiddish are also spoken, creating communication problems for the administration and the clients when settling pensions and benefits, with regard to which there is a great shortfall in take-up (see CPA, 1989, p.150).

Social security: pensions and benefits

The high regard the Turkish people have for older people has been commented upon by Kagitçibasi (1985). Added to this is the injunction of the Qur'an to care for the needy (see Ruthven, 1991, p.65). The irony is that, in practice, respect and social justice are not reflected in the pension schemes, especially with regard to the older rural population.

The social security systems are best described by Heisel (1992). There are three social security schemes. The first, established in 1949, is the Government Employee Retirement Fund (GERF). This caters for public service employees, and the contributions come from the civil servants themselves and the state. By 1986 the GERF had 1.5 million members in paid employment, and 720,000 recipients of retirement, dependents' or survivors' benefits.

The second scheme is the Social Insurance Organization (SIO), which was established by the Social Security Act 1964. The premiums are paid by the employers and employees. The scheme covers most employees, but at first excluded agricultural workers. However, in 1984 they were included. By 1986 a quarter of the population was covered by the SIO (Heisel, 1992, p.196). The SIO provides long-term retirement and disability benefits, and also pharmaceutical benefits. The survivors' pensions are in addition to short-term medical benefits payable for up to 18 months for the insured, their dependents and survivors. In 1988 the State Planning Organization (Devlet Planlama Teskilati) reported that over 1.5 million persons were in receipt of monthly retirement, disability or survivors' benefits.

The third scheme is provided by the Social Security Institution for the Self-Employed and Independent Workers (the BAG-KUR). Established in 1972, the scheme is mandatory and contributions are compulsory. At first it excluded those employed in agriculture, but in 1984 it was extended to self-employed agricultural workers. Although the scheme was limited to providing retirement, disability and death benefits, it now includes health services and benefits within certain provinces.

The CPA (1989, p.150) describes the pensions. A general scheme covers industrial and commercial workers. Special schemes exist for public employees, agricultural workers and the self-employed, and funding comes from the employees and employers. Eligibility begins at 55 years for men and 50 years for women. Significantly, prematurely aged men and miners may retire when they have made 1,800 days' contributions. However, anyone may acquire a retirement pension if they have 25 years of insurance contributions (20 for women) and 5,000 days of contributions after the age of 18. The total worth of the pension is equivalent to 70% of the contributor's average earnings during the last five years of employment. The pension is adjusted every two years in line with wages and prices nationally. The problem is that many are not in receipt of pensions, particularly in the rural areas (as is the case in Eastern European countries such as Romania). Invalids aged 65 and over who are without pensions are means-tested.

Tomanbay (1986, p.531) and Gurkan and Gilleard (1987, p.153) state that agricultural workers are not in receipt of the three contributory pension schemes. They are not eligible for welfare payments, unless they can demonstrate that they have no means of support. Modernization has reduced the status of older people because they are regarded as 'non-producers', who consume welfare and health resources, and are at best the 'storytellers'. The studies of Gurkan and Gilleard indicate that more older males are working in the rural areas of Turkey than in the urban areas because of the migration of the younger population, because they are on lower pensions, or simply because they do not wish to claim as a result of wounded pride and stigma. Independence is valued by the older Turkish generation.

Heisel refers to the non-contributory and means-tested social assistance programme – the Universal Old Age and Disability Pension (introduced in 1976); 25% of people aged 65+ received such a pension in 1986 (Heisel, 1992, p.197). Though this pension is fully financed by the state, it remains highly inadequate.

Housing

By European standards, housing standards are low. The older population live in overcrowded cities or in the shanty towns (the *gecekondu*). In the mid-1960s the shanty towns constituted a large proportion of the city inhabitants: 45% of Ankara, 21% of Istanbul, and 18% of Izmir, according to Temir (1974, p.791); this has since escalated. By 1985, approximately 60% of the population of the large cities resided in the shanty towns, according to Tomanbay (1986, p.530). A Ministry of Reconstruction and Resettlement was established in 1958 to meet the needs of many migrant peoples and to update the houses. The housing need continues to demand large programmes of reconstruction. The older people suffer most, residing in some of the oldest rundown properties in cities and near-primitive rural settings.

Health care

The Ministry of Public Health and Social Welfare was established in 1921, two years before Turkey became a republic. However, its legal mandate was not adopted until 1936 (see Tomanbay, 1986, p.532).

Hospital care and medical services

Since 1975 the Ministry of Health and Social Services has been responsible for the hospitals, clinics and many of the residential homes. There are no geriatric hospitals, and only the beginnings of a geriatric medical/health service. Medical provision is free for invalid older people and other poor clients. In the 1970s there were only 0.4 doctors and 0.5 hospital beds per 1,000 inhabitants in Turkey (*Encyclopaedia Britannica*, 1979, Micropaedia, Vol.X, p.195).

Nursing

There are no studies available regarding the extent and type of nursing care in general, and for older people in particular.

Mental health care

There are no psychogeriatric hospitals nor community mental health units. Older people with psychiatric illnesses are not permitted admittance to non-hospital mental health care (Heisel, 1992, p.198).

Institutional care

Heisel (1992, p.198) describes the retirement institutions, which are the *huzurevi* ('homes for peace of mind'). These provide accommodation, meals and housekeeping and, when necessary, personal care. These institutions were established by the Ministry of Health and Social Services in 1966. In 1986 there were only 20 such establishments in Turkey, and they tended to be large, with about 150 residents on average. Between 1975 and 1985 the number of residential places doubled. However, taking into account the UK's number of places at that time of approximately 62,000, in a country with half the number of older people as in Turkey, the UK had 77 times as many places. This conveys some idea of the large gaps between the provision of residential care in the two countries.

The Turkish government's 1985–9 five-year plan, cited by the CPA (1989), prioritizes care of the older population. The policy sets out to encourage private residential care. In addition, there are the local municipality or district residential homes. Private medical institutions exist side by side with the statutory provision. About 30% of places are provided by the local authority (the 'ministry'), according to the CPA (1989, p.150). These offer lower rates and single rooms. An estimate in the mid-1980s indicates that there is a two-year waiting list for the residential homes run by the ministry. Private sector provision is encouraged and growing, and is probably now providing a third of the residential places in Turkey.

Personal social services

The Turkish Republic, founded in 1923, is a late starter in providing statutory services. In 1959 a law established the Institute for Social Work, which in 1963 was integrated into the General Directorate for Social Work. This body dealt with the care of the older population, along with generic training needs. Only approximately 1,000 qualified social workers provide care for vulnerable groups throughout the whole of this large country. The Office of Social Work and Child Protection, founded in 1983, replaced the old directorate, and orchestrates social care everywhere in Turkey. The emphasis, as the title of the organization suggests, is upon child care, which is understandably prioritized. All homes for older people come under this office; however, community care and personal social services for older people are almost non-existent. The only significant task that appears to be carried out by the office is the inspection of private homes for older people (see Tomanbay, 1986, p.533). Social workers are employed in the ministry's residential homes.

Secularization has been slow to progress in this Islamic country. According to statistics cited by Tomanbay (1986, p.529), social spending accounts for only 3% of government expenditure. Personal accountability, stressed by the Qur'an, has slowed down the need for a family policy and social protection for older people that is provided by a collective, responsible state body.

Voluntary care agencies and support organizations

Little is known about the Turkish voluntary sector's provision for older people. The institution of the family has provided the bulk of care, as will be further explained in the next section.

Informal care

The traditional Turkish family is the major provider of care for older people. As stated above, the Qur'anic obligation of the family to care helps to explain why state provision is minimal, constituting a slim residual support system when called upon to intervene. The main recipients of formal care are single and isolated older people. There are relatively few of these aged 65+: 2.1% of men and 1.3% of women (Grundy and Harrop, 1992, pp.26 and 28).

In contrast with other neighbouring family systems, which are exogamous, the Turkish family is Islamic and consists of the endogamous community family type (see Todd, 1985), in line with that of North Africa, the Middle East, Iran, Iraq and Pakistan. The Islamic household, as Todd (1985, p.144) demonstrates, recognizes only religion and the family. The dynastic Islamic families resist the notion of a Western-style welfare state, and the family strives to be the sole provider for its children and older relatives.

Gurkan and Gilleard (1987, p.154) cite the 'widespread values of respect for the elderly by their families in Turkey', on the basis of influential research carried out by Kagitçibasi (1985). The old and the new face each other, in a land of paradoxes, often in stormy conflict. Heisel (1992) cites a study carried out by Emiroglu (1985) in a typical village where only a quarter of the respondents stated that they would like to live with their sons in their old age. At the same time, three-quarters of the heads of families perceived the young as having less respect for their elders. None the less, all the older people were living with their sons, but the daughter-in-law bore the burden of personal care. A quarter were seen to have difficulties in getting along with their families, particularly with their sons. Almost all those who resided within a household where an older family member was cared for regarded old age negatively, and as many as 87% regarded ageing as being entirely bad. In urban studies by Sevil (1984) and Danisoglu (1988), it is clear that in the city/town areas of Turkey the tensions referred to above were aggravated by the pressures of modernity. The older population felt more and more pushed out of affective family ties. Those who provided child care were more fortunate because they could at least be regarded as being of some use.

It would therefore appear that informal care of the older population is in a state of tension in Turkey, and that the family is often the reluctant carer, particularly in the urban areas. There is little evidence that either friends or neighbours are able to fill gaps in providing social care. If the older people suffer from dementia or are severely disabled, there is very little that the formal services can offer. The stress and frustrations in these circumstances, particularly for the daughters-in-law, are as a consequence horrendous.

Leisure pursuits and education

Leisure and educational provision for older people are non-existent in Turkey. Many older Turkish people lack basic education and did not even have the benefit of elementary schooling (*ilkokul*). In the 1970s, only 40.9% of women and 69.6% of men were literate (*Encyclopaedia Britannica*, 1979, Micropaedia, Vol.X, p.195). Today only elementary schooling is obligatory. Community education schemes and literacy tuition for older people are required, particularly in the rural areas.

Rural aspects

More than 60% of the population in Turkey live in rural areas, and higher proportions of older people exist in the rural areas, in common with most parts of Europe. The CPA (1989, pp.149–50) identifies the larger proportions of older people in the underdeveloped rural regions, which have risen significantly in most parts (less so in the eastern regions) because of the exodus of the younger people since the 1950s (Heisel, 1992, p.188). Turkish migrant workers have constituted the largest proportion of migrant workers in Europe, particularly in Germany. The migration from the rural to the urban areas is as marked in Turkey as in Greece and other agricultural parts of Europe. However, the migration of persons aged 55 and over is as low as 5% within any five-year cycle (CPA, 1989, p.150).

Older rural people have had to be self-sufficient. As in Greece, the emigration of the younger males especially has left the burden of agricultural work in the family settlement to the parents. In sharp contrast with most of the European countries, over 33% of the older population in Turkey are economically active. The proportion of older men in paid employment in the rural areas of the southern regions is 50%, but in the rural areas of the central region of Turkey the proportion of older men in paid employment is as high as 61% (see Gurkan and Gilleard, 1987, p.154).

Heisel (1992, pp.192–5) describes the traditional predominant family types in the rural areas of eastern, south-eastern and central Anatolia. Their traditional structure and caring arrangements are in sharp contrast with the more modern urban families in the western and southern coasts of Marmara, the Aegean Sea and the Mediterranean. There is a dearth of social and health care for vast numbers of older people in the rural areas, especially for those living in the *mahalle* (the single rural settlement units) and the small *koms* (the settlements in between hamlet and village size). There are also the nomadic peoples with their winter quarters (*kislas*) and their temporary pastures (*yaylas*).

In the rural areas the endogamous community family, described so well by Todd (1985), essentially dominated by the eldest male in the direct line, still exists, with its pool of carers.

Conclusion

Turkey's older population rely heavily upon the family. Islam inculcates a great respect for older people, and the Qur'an also establishes the familial imperatives which have secured for most of the retired population a sheltered old age. Only 1.7% (1.3% women/2.1% men) of the population are single, the lowest percentage in Southern Europe (based on Grundy and Harrop, 1992, pp.26 and 28). Having outlined the familial and kinship care that exists in Turkey, it is clear that there is a heavy reliance upon the informal care provided by the family circle. Support provided by neighbours and friends is not referred to in most of the studies.

The care of older people is overshadowed by the care of children, as in the rest of Europe. Indeed, as also in most of Europe, older people are themselves the major household carers, either of children or of their frailer and sick peers. Turkish social care policies and most social work tenets are purely symbolic, according to Tomanbay (1986).

The care of the older population in Turkey is essentially informal. The formal provision of the state constitutes a residual infrastructure, which in effect is no more than a cardboard facsimile for display in Turkey's European shop window. The special report of the Expert Committee on the Family, submitted to and requested by the State Planning Organization (1988), indicate that a significant number of Turkish families were in acute need of care and protection, particularly the older members (Heisel, 1992, p.194). In the second half of the 1980s about 56.4% of the older population received old age and health benefits, although they were eligible for National Insurance schemes (State Planning Organization, 1988). Perhaps the very low life expectancy at birth of 60 years for men and 63.3 for women (CPA, 1989, p.149), reflects the much lower state of health and the high degree of deprivation in this large nation, once with a claim to large parts of Europe, now hanging on to its south-eastern apron strings.

29 Cyprus

Demography

This third-largest island of the Mediterranean has a population of approximately 706,900 people. As indicated in Table 1, the proportion of older people in Cyprus (9.9%) is ranked twenty-fourth in greater Europe. By the year 2025 it is estimated that the proportion will increase by approximately 6.2%, but in comparative terms its rank order will remain more or less as it is.

Life expectancy on the island at birth, according to the CPA (1989), is 78.3 years for women and 73.9 years for men. These estimates cover the years 1985–9. On the basis of the life expectancies published by the UN (1986, 1991) and Eurostat (1991a), the life expectancy of women at birth in Cyprus would rank thirteenth in greater Europe, higher than that of women in Luxemburg, Portugal, the UK, Denmark, Greece, Malta, the Republic of Ireland, Poland, Albania, the former Czechoslovakia, the former Yugoslavia, Hungary, Bulgaria and Romania. The life expectancy of the population as a whole would rank ninth-highest in greater Europe, above Denmark, Belgium and the UK.

Socio-political and administrative background

Cyprus, located in the south-east corner of greater Europe, sits uneasily on the edge of the Mediterranean basin. The island is also immersed within the East-West contraflows of divergent values and customs. Cyprus's culture and family structures are part-Greek and part-Turkish. The island is split between the Kipriaki Demokratia (Greek) and the Kibris Cumhuriyeti (Turkish). Here the exogamous and the endogamous community families contrast, and Islam and Orthodox Christianity stand opposed. Cyprus has been a cosmopolitan island, but split by ethnic antagonisms. In 1974 the Turkish invasion took over 37% of the island. About two-thirds of the Greek Cypriot population lives in the four (free) towns. A third of the population is displaced (approximately 200,000). Older people, along with their families, had to move out of the north at the time of the Turkish invasion, about 50,000 people living in camps. The island's economy and services were badly affected, the island's economy being set back by C£3.5 million. Because of reduced public revenues, developments to improve the social and health care services were set back many years, and chronic shortages in health and housing badly affected the vulnerable older population (see Cyprus Press and Information Office, 1992, p.46).

Older Cypriots conserve their Greek folklore and the antipathies between the two island communities in which cultural and sharp religious divides create distrust and a tendency for older people to be cocooned within their own immediate social world, unsure of change and cynical about welfare bureaucracies. In a land of great diversity and recent struggles, the infra-structures of welfare are unstable. Older people fall back upon the ancient institution of the family and their local religious network of worshippers. The care of the older population is the last item on the island's political agenda, but fortunately for them, familial care is the prime value on the agenda of the island's kinship groups.

The House of Representatives has a two-thirds elected Greek Cypriot representation and one-third Turkish Cypriot representation. The Maronite, Armenian and Latin minorities elect representatives who act as advisors, and are able to inform the authorities of matters pertaining to the cultural needs of the older population. There are two important government organs which are more immediately relevant to care of older people in Cyprus: the Ministry of Health and the Ministry of Labour and Social Insurance. The former, apart from other medical matters, is responsible for medical and public health services, and the latter, apart from other social concerns, is responsible for social insurance and social welfare services.

The administration of services affecting older people is spread across six districts. There is a three-tier local authority administrative structure: the Municipal Districts at the top which cater for the towns; Improvement Boards in the middle which cater for larger villages, and the Village Commissions at the lowest level which cater for the small villages (Cyprus Press and Information Office, 1992, p.39).

Kyriazis (1992) refers to the leeway the island has had to make up in welfare and health care, reminding mainland Europeans that until 1924 Cyprus was a nineteenth-century country, and it has tended to be out of touch with major welfare and health care developments. In the context of innovative care for older people, it lags behind many other European countries, including Greece. None the less, in the 1980s, older Cypriots were to gain by the 7.5% growth in tertiary services; by the 8.5% growth in transport, and by the drop in inflation from 10.1% in 1981 to 1.2% in 1986 (Cyprus Press and Information Office, 1992, p.49). The 1988/9 Development Plan concentrated upon measures which were to improve the living conditions of the older population, such as health and housing, and in this the government succeeded, but the poorer older people did not gain as much as the more affluent older population.

According to the Cyprus Press and Information Office (1992, p.48), by 1981 Cyprus claimed it had launched a welfare state with a creditable range of social services. This claim is doubtful because the private sector is dominant in the major sectors of need, as the following sections will demonstrate.

Social security: pensions and benefits

A social insurance scheme was introduced in 1980; the contributions and the benefits are earnings-related. It is compulsory for all except the unemployed; they may join, but only on certain conditions. The contribution adds up to 15.5%: 6% is paid by the employee (6% of gross earnings), 6% by the employer, and 3.5% is paid out of the general revenue of the republic. The self-employed's payment varies according to the individual's occupational category. If the income is lower than the notional one, the individual is assessed on her/his actual income. Cypriot nationals and non-nationals enjoy the same rights within the scheme. The social insurance scheme covers old age pensions, invalidity pensions, widows' pensions, funeral grants, and disablement and death benefits. The scheme also provides free medical treatment to invalidity pensioners. The benefits are also payable outside Cyprus.

Housing

As stated above, the housing programme was set back some years by the Turkish invasion. The 200,000 dispossessed, who included many older people, also had to be accommodated. The republic lost 26.3% of its housing, which had to be replaced. By the mid-1980s the government, heartened by the 6% rate of growth in the economy, set in motion a massive housing programme. Government Housing Estates and Self-Help Housing Estates were created, and helped to replace and further improve existing stock under surveillance of the new Planning Board. These developments were backed by schemes such as rent subsidies and low-interest long-term loans.

Overcrowding is a problem in a country where accommodating older parents is encouraged both culturally and politically. To provide more space, the Cyprus Land Development Corporation and the Housing Finance Corporation, supported by government grants, supply long-term loans and building plots at low prices. Urban Development Plans established the type of housing, based upon the principles of health, welfare and amenity within Local Plan Areas; in this the needs of older people were considered. Applicants have made use of the 'grants-in-aid and low-interest long-term loans' to acquire property plus additional accommodation for their older family members: wide use was made of grants for extensions or building in a nearby plot to accommodate older relatives in the 1980s. The housing policy has taken into account the ethnic mix, and the programme has striven to maintain equity in accordance with need.

In 1992, 59.6% of housing was owned by Greek Cypriots; 12.3% was owned by Turkish Cypriots; 1.4% by other minorities, and 26.7% was owned by the government (see Cyprus Press and Information Office, 1992, p.118).

Health care

The government's introduction of a general health scheme within the new Development Plan of 1988/9 was a big step forward to improve the health of older people along with that of the rest of the population. The average rate of growth of GDP of 6.5% in 1989–90 enabled the government to pursue its original aim.

There are three medical systems in Cyprus:

1   the government health sector;
2   the private health sector;
3   special health schemes.

The government health sector services are mainly available to those of low or middle income. These services are provided free or at reduced rates. Many of the poorer older people receive health care free of charge. Accident and emergency services are free for all, irrespective of level of income, excluding subsequent hospitalization. In fact, most people make use of some kind of private medical care in Cyprus (see Cyprus Press and Information Office, 1992, pp.151–2). Special schemes are provided by the trade unions for their employees. There are also special employer-sponsored arrangements which provide free medical care through public health services. The public services mainly provide for the rural population, and the private services mainly for the urban population.

Hospital care and medical services

The proportions of private medical beds and private practitioners are probably among the highest in Europe (see Cyprus Press and Information Office, 1992, p.153). The beds' ratio, 6.4 to 1,000 inhabitants, is a higher ratio than that of seven EU countries: Belgium, Denmark, Greece, Spain, the Republic of Ireland, Portugal and the UK (see Eurostat, 1991b, p.88).

Public hospital provision is of three kinds. Relatively speaking, older people on the island appear to be well provided for. Firstly, there are the general and district hospitals. These provide 1,110 beds and admit about 39,400 patients annually; the Geriatric Department has 24 beds and admits about 302 patients annually (Cyprus Ministry of Finance, 1989–90, pp.105 and 109). Secondly, there are the rural hospitals, which provide 94 geriatric beds and admit about 1,114 patients annually. Here the turnover is greater because the presenting cases are less severe and the care mostly consists of public provision. Thirdly, there are the Rural Health Centres, which have increasingly had fewer and fewer patients, sometimes under ten per centre.

However, being ill in retirement is expensive because the public service has so little to offer, and the private so much more to provide in terms of expertise and quality of care. With regard to private hospital/clinic provision, there are 1,458 beds – about 13% for orthopaedic care/surgery, and 105 specialist consultancies. There is 1 doctor to every 482 persons, which is a higher ratio than in the Republic of Ireland, Luxemburg and the UK, but most of Cyprus's doctors only provide private care. There is 1 dentist for every 1,356 persons (Cyprus Press and Information Office, 1992, p.153), which is a better ratio than in most EU countries except Denmark, Greece and Italy (see Eurostat, 1991b, p.88), but, as with doctors, the majority only provide private care. In the private sector there are 819 doctors, whereas in the public there are 353. Similarly, in the private sector there are 384 dentists, whereas in the public there are 33 (Cyprus Ministry of Finance, 1989–90, p.106). Lack of planning is a matter of great concern, according to Kyriazis (1992), especially for the needs of older patients when they are discharged from hospital.

As can be gathered from the life expectancy ratio presented above, Cypriots' health rating is higher than that of older people in some of the more progressive European countries. Judging by the recent improvements in the health services, there is every possibility that the standards of living and general health will improve yet further. One can only be concerned about the poorer older Cypriots, given the two-tier system described above.

Nursing care

There are only 1,850 community nurses in the public sector and 600 in the private sector (Cyprus Ministry of Finance, 1989–90, p.106), although there are plans to introduce specialist nurses. Many of the public sector nurses are involved in the private and public mix of care, as is so in the UK NHS scheme. Those who can afford to pay make use of private nurses through the agencies when they require home nursing. The majority of public health nurses are engaged in the hospitals. However, in recent years there has been a move within the public sector to provide a personal care assistant to monitor the older person's progress and to supervise the household care provided by the family.

Mental health care

In the public health sector there are 50 psychiatric beds in the general and district hospitals and 790 in the Athalassa Psychiatric Special Hospitals (Cyprus Ministry of Finance, 1989–90, p.109). About 879 persons are admitted and about 878 discharged per year, but no reference is made to the care offered, and no mention of how many of the patients are older people.

Institutional care

The skeletal institutional provision that does exist tends to be a mixture of social and health care. There are long queues for entry to the few residential and nursing homes (Kyriazis, 1992).

There are seven homes for older people (Cyprus Press and Information Office, 1992, p.174). Wall (1989, p.124) indicates that only 2% of the older population are cared for in institutions within Cyprus; this is in keeping with the general trend in the Southern European countries. Because older Cypriots are less likely to live on their own or in households consisting only of older persons (Wall, 1989, p.135), the traditional familial or household cover lessens the need for the state welfare or health system to provide care or support. However, one wonders about the needs of the solitary older people without family support.

Kyriazis (1992) refers to the preference for sheltered housing and the grants that the government has provided for the inhabitants to build accommodation for their parents. It is here that the authorities recognize the polycephalic local structures. For expediency's sake, and because it is the cheaper option, they support the local inhabitants' self-help and 'do-it-yourself' provision, be it buildings or grassroot programmes of care within the two communities.

Personal social services

The Department of Social Services is administratively divided into four areas of work (Cyprus Press and Information Office, 1992, p.173):

1   Child Care and Family Welfare;
2   Public Assistance and Services for the Elderly;
3   Community Work;
4   Youth Protection and Development.

Only the second of these concerns us here. This service division provides counselling, financial benefits, day care services and residential institutions. However, neither details nor studies are available with regard to care provided by social workers/assistants in day centres, or whether there are meals-on-wheels and home care/help.

Since January 1990 a Service for the Care and Rehabilitation of the Disabled has been set up within the Department of Labour. Although most of the beneficiaries of this service are younger, the needs of older people are also addressed in a more concerted manner, and allowances are provided for the severely disabled to cover their special needs. Also, technical aids and equipment come under the remit of the service.

Voluntary care agencies and support organizations

The Orthodox Church, as in many parts of Eastern and Southern Europe, provides local care, but there is no study available regarding its role and the nature of the support it provides.

Informal care

The familial informal caring arrangements are very similar culturally to those of Greece and Turkey. However, there are no studies of the informal modes of care in Cyprus.

Leisure pursuits and education

As in other areas, information is lacking regarding the leisure interests of older Cypriots and the provision of further education to meet their needs.

Municipal authorities are responsible for public health and health education generally. More older people are becoming better acquainted with healthier lifestyles, particularly through health education provided by nurses.

Rural aspects

The Cyprus Press and Information Office (1992, p.152) refers to the network of rural hospitals and rural health centres, subcentres and dispensaries, which are said to be staffed with nurses, dentists, pharmacists, health inspectors and health visitors, but it does not indicate how many there are or where they are located, nor does it comment upon the quality of their services and to what extent the older patients are cared for, if at all.

Conclusion

It is clear from the above account that the older population in Cyprus enjoy a high degree of good health and a rising standard of living. The development of formal modes of state care has been slow, whereas the private sector has developed quickly. The result has been that a two-tier system has evolved. The systems of care tend to be dictated by anarchic individualism. The poorer older people, especially the single, have to turn to the public sector and cope with the stigma that dogs the system. Kyriazis (1992) refers to the dislike Cypriots have of being called or regarded as 'old'. The authorities in recent years have become aware of the anachronisms in the health and welfare programmes, and have recognized the inequities for the older poorer population and the marginalization created.

It is also clear that the triangle of care is dominated by the private sector in Cyprus. Market welfare is the major feature. At each stage of the development of welfare and health provision, the changes have come about in response to the fluctuations of the market and to major events affecting the economy of the island. Economic action plans undertaken at regular intervals determine what, when and how welfare and health services should be modified and new ones introduced. Apart from a general awareness of the need to respect the citizens and respond to their needs, the politicians appear not to have had any welfare model in mind, nor any overall proactive welfare and health care strategy.

Epilogue

We need a compass in order to orient ourselves among the myriad of social
processes going on. We need a map to localize ourselves and other forces and
events. (Therborn, 1995, p.7).

This book has set out to present a panoramic view of the nature and extent of
the diverse forms of care provided for older people within greater Europe.
The research is necessarily thin in places. In addition, the fluctuating transitions, changing structures and reforms in welfare with the shift towards a
mixed welfare system in a 'new Europe' make it more difficult to analyse
developments. Also, because of the lack of space, the sociological implications and the political ramifications have not been addressed; these are dealt
with in another text (Giarchi, forthcoming).

It is also clear that at present the division of Europe is indistinct and the
debate of what constitutes the 'new Europe' is under discussion. None the
less, the focus adopted here assumes there is a north/south split and a
geopolitical core to Europe flanked by Western countries on the seaward side
and by Eastern countries to the landward side, although some of the latter
may be regarded as Central-Eastern countries. Clearly the Anglo-Saxon view
of Europe will not find it easy, politically, to acknowledge Germany as the
European fulcrum, which along with the adjacent countries of Austria and
Switzerland make up a geographic European centre. The point made in this
text is that welfare and caring policies cannot be established without first
structuring the European setting in which policies and care for the older
populations are determined. Most studies of caring provisions for older
Europeans have ignored European settings. The EU provides a structure, but
once the analysis shifts to greater Europe complications exist. None the less,
the 'spacing of our continent' helps towards understanding what occurs
within it (Therborn, 1995).

469

Whatever the future, the designation of five European segments provides a geographical and welfare framework, albeit inchoate, for presenting the diversities of care for older people. The former Eastern Bloc countries are not as yet integrated into the rest of Europe, so they are generally described in this text as Eastern (with the exception of Albania, which is geographically in the south). In the context of welfare, it will take many years before the social and health care systems in the former Eastern Bloc countries will fall into line with the eventual economic and political infrastructures of a 'new Europe'. Clearly, events indicate that the political future in the Eastern regions is volatile. Many older Europeans in the former Eastern countries complain that they are worse off now than before, because of the uncertainties and the anarchic market welfare system which appears to be getting out of hand.

In addition to establishing the setting in which older Europeans reside, and the regional structures that determine their destiny and programmes of care, it is also essential that studies of older Europeans take into account the ecological settings in which they live. Most commentaries omit any mention of environment. Certainly, policy-makers and local practitioners can ill afford to overlook the ecological milieux in which older people reside. The pollution that affects Eastern Europe (see Introduction) is a significant factor affecting older people's health and quality of life. In many research projects the retired are assumed to be living in an ecological vacuum. Yet, as social history has demonstrated, it is public health and the epidemiological advances which have dramatically altered the health of older people, hence the need for an environmental dimension to social gerontology.

Many studies of care have an urban bias and few (with the exception of writers such as: Harper, 1987, 1991; Lishman, 1984; Wenger, 1982, 1984, 1989; Tout, 1993) have included the rural aspects of care, or sufficiently addressed the rural setting in which millions of older Europeans live. There is the isolation of older rural people and their lack of social and health care facilities. 'Distance decay' has disadvantaged them, which is worsened by the grand exit of younger people to the cities, almost everywhere in Europe.

The provision of care is determined in the last analysis by a philosophy of care, which provides both the value base and the principles of intervention. Ken Tout (1992) was asked by the UN to provide a mission statement which would encapsulate the fundamental principles of care upon which UN strategy for the care of older people could be based. He coined the acronym 'DESIR', which embraced both the basic values and the primary principles of care strategies for older people everywhere, as follows:

D Dignity   'preserving/restoring older persons' dignity;
E Education   through education of elders/carers/public/nation;
S Support   leading to family and community support assurance;
I Independence   encouraging independence achieved or enhanced

R Rehabilitation   by rehabilitation, in physical, mental and
                    socio-economic condition'.

However, these noble sentiments and salient aims are not so easily identified
in the formulation and implementation of care for older Europeans, because
similar declarations or mission statements made by officials or directors of
care are in short supply. European policy-makers in most of Europe tend to
implement money-led pragmatism, rather than be value-led altruists. For
this reason, Parts I–V do not indicate to what extent humanitarian principles
have inspired welfare legislation or the many social and health care schemes
and modes of formal care. We do not have an exposé in the research literature
of the value statements which have inspired the systems of care, but structures and outcomes speak much louder than manifestos.

Examining the welfare state systems of the past, it is clear that welfare
administration and care policies have often been managed within oppressive, paternalist structures. In the post-war years until the 1980s, bureaucratization of welfare created the ethos of the expert, which dictated care and
therapy, with scant regard for preferences and choices or user/client consultation. The clients or users had little, if any, say, and almost no choice of individual packages of care. The matching of provision to personal need within
mega-bureaucratic systems was often clumsy. The norms of management
and the ethos of professionalism generally dictated the outcomes. For
example, the centralization of welfare within largely monocephalic structures dominated the care of older people in the Northern and Western
European countries for many years. Capitalist structures, west of the former
Eastern Bloc countries, generally viewed older people as 'non-producers'
and as a tax burden. This view continues to prevail, in spite of the fact that
over a period of thirty years millions of older Europeans have paid taxes and
national security subscriptions towards state welfare and the maintenance of
health care systems.

Also, until the mid-1980s, state care systems in Northern and Western
Europe have tended almost everywhere to be both top-down and procedure-
led. The organizational principles engendered by bureaucracy created
controls, which minimized older people's self-determination, choice and
independence. As stated above, the formal carers were 'the' experts. Their
views predominated and few complaint procedures existed. Their judgment
within the dogma of professionalism determined outcomes for millions of
older people, in which neither the client nor the informal carer had much of
a say. This was true especially where the welfare state was sovereign in the
more northerly and westerly regions of Europe and particularly in Eastern
Europe. Moreover, there was a greater likelihood in the post-war years until
the early 1980s, for older Europeans in the Northern, Western and Eastern

countries to be incarcerated or 'put away', often with no regard for their rights, independence or freedom.

Community care in Northern and Western Europe, particularly, has progressively swung towards subsidiarist and polycephalic structures. Patient and user charters are a recurrent feature. However, the swing to the community or open care structures has often been expedient and money-led as governments have had to face the costs of institutional care. The charters have generally lacked teeth. Sanctions are almost non-existent or difficult to exercise. Moreover, as recent developments have indicated, community care is proving to be an intensive means-testing exercise.

It might be suggested that voluntarism, rather than professionalism, has determined outcomes for most older Europeans. However, voluntary provision for older people in Europe is uneven. In the Northern countries, voluntarism has played a less significant role than it has in most of the rest of Europe. In the Western countries, although government support for the voluntary sector has been minimal, voluntary agencies have stepped in to fill the gaps in the provision of care for older people, particularly in the UK. The significant role of non-government organizations (NGOs) has been most apparent in the Central European countries, where voluntarism has provided a major support for older people. In addition, welfare providers in Germany, Austria and Switzerland have generally upheld the importance of asynchronic communitarian principles of care. These countries have valued subsidiarity and federalism, and have attempted to establish a participatory citizenship, co-management systems and, more recently, caring co-operatives for older people. In the Southern European countries, the voluntarism of the well-established co-operatives, particularly in Italy, Spain and Portugal, have helped to counter the inadequate state systems, but these are often not identified in the literature and European commentaries. More needs to be researched at this level.

There is an upsurge everywhere in the former communist countries of alternative welfare and support structures, which runs side by side with the dismantling of the state's totalitarian system. Although the role of the local non-government organizations (along with that of the Churches) in providing social, and sometimes health, care has increased, their resources have been sparse. Indeed, many have relied upon assistance from the West in terms of resources and social and health care training, especially Romania and Bulgaria.

In contrast with the Northern and Eastern regimes, the Southern European countries have provided a residual welfare system, because the care of older people was regarded as a family and religious obligation. The local churches organized care for their frail older parishioners, which they identified first and foremost as a virtuous act rather than a civic responsibility. With the secularization of society, virtue and merit have progressively lost their meaning, leaving gaps in welfare and care, in a world where policies are now increasingly driven by monetarism and expendiency. If this continues and increases, younger people today will face a bleak old age when it is their time to retire.

Elsewhere in Europe, in an attempt to utilize all possible avenues and to save costs, the Northern, Western and Central countries are turning to the Church to fill welfare gaps. Ironically, such a reveille is not matched by a religious revival in these highly secularized parts of Europe. Some Churches are able to respond, but their involvement is marginal, due to diminishing resources and dwindling congregations. Moreover, side by side with the dismantling of the state, many churches of Europe have been and are being demolished in a widespread religious sell-out, especially in the major cities of Northern and Western Europe. It remains to be seen to what extent the Protestant, Catholic and Orthodox Christian Churches of Central and Eastern Europe will fill the welfare gaps and provide a significant response to the social needs of older people. The impact of Islamic values upon the care of older immigrant people in Europe has yet to be assessed comparatively in research programmes.

Today, most administrative structures and modes of formal care in Europe's welfare centres increasingly reflect a pragmatic approach, prompted mainly by cost-effectiveness and assessed less in terms of resultant benefits. The increasing privatization of welfare in all of Europe (except in Denmark) clearly allows the care of older Europeans to be profit-based. Indeed, as stated several times, the Eastern countries are heading towards anarchic monetarist systems. Community and home care are increasingly being privatized. Means-testing is being introduced in more and more European countries to determine who pays, how much, and for what care packages. A market welfare system is now being set up, making a mockery of the very notion of a triangle of care. Even where the current level of privatization is marginal, the ageism that has blighted the history of care in Europe for centuries has led to the low priority given by the state to care for older populations, in contrast to that provided for younger people. Younger Europeans, especially the unemployed, question the welfare payments provided for the older citizen. Certainly, in the present crisis in welfare, the cut-backs almost always begin with a debate about the cost to taxpayers of the state pension. The EU's attempt in 1993 to create a 'solidarity between generations' could well fall flat on its face.

Most countries are engaged in a debate as to whether state pension schemes should be undercut or even waived altogether. It is doubtful whether any country in Europe (with the possible exception of Denmark) will provide a state pension in 30 years' time. Moreover, loopholes in the formulation of laws governing recent private pensions schemes have allowed entrepreneurs (as happened with the Robert Maxwell affair in the

UK) to make use of the monies invested by older people for their own ends.

The most significant factor is that care for older European people is mainly provided by families. This is borne out by research everywhere throughout Europe. Informal carers may often be reluctant, but their contribution has been the mainstay for older generations. Home care has been provided chiefly by women, whose goodwill has been prostituted by governments everywhere – although to a lesser extent in the Scandinavian countries. But there are signs that this may now change. Care by neighbours comes second everywhere to familial care and indeed is less apparent in some Southern countries, where families take over home care, often not through obligation but because of family pride.

The diverse formal and informal provision and modes of care which I have collated and which I myself have researched in several regions of Europe are at times impressive and often innovative, but besides falling short of the needs of over 100 million older people, significant cracks in the edifice of welfare systems are appearing. In recent years, governments have faced a moral crisis due to the following well-established factors, which impact upon greater Europe as a whole. First, the welfare state is being dismantled everywhere, except in Denmark (for the present). Second, the virtual abdication of state responsibility has taken place side by side with the fragmentation of each of the traditional European family types. The nature and extent of family obligations towards older parents is now more difficult to determine because there is a blurring of the duty to care for grandparents and great-grandparents within fragmented household/family structures. More women are employed and rightly look to men to share the obligation to care, but without significant success. Third, the ratio of younger carers to older frail people has dropped, with the exception of the former Eastern Bloc countries and Ireland in the West. In addition, the dramatic rise of the number of older people has challenged the welfare values of all European countries besides the considerable strain upon resources. These multiple factors must be set against persistent ageism in a Europe in which older people have lacked status for centuries. As a consequence, discrimination against older Europeans, elder abuse, neglect and deprivation have increased for those aged 75+ (see Bytheway, 1995).

Tout's (1992) mission statement may appear to be well-nigh impossible to accomplish, given the above concerns and bleak portents. Certainly, the storm clouds are gathering on the dark horizon. The winds of change carry with them concerns over balancing the moral responsibility of the state, the social and collective responsibility of civil society and the cost/benefits of social and health care required, not only to protect older Europeans from poverty and sickness, but also to enable them to enjoy life to the full.

Bibliography

Abelson, R. (1968), 'Computers, Polls and Public Opinion', Transaction, September.

Abrahamson, P. (1989), *Postmodern Welfares: Market, State and Civil Society, Towards Year 2000*, Research Report No.6, Roskilde: Institute of Economics.

Abrahamson, P. (1990), 'Future Welfare: Solidarity Toward Year 2000', conference paper, Helsinki: The Finnish National Board of Welfare.

Abrahamson, P. (1991), 'Welfare for the Elderly in Denmark: From Institutionalization to Self-reliance', *Eurosocial Report*, Vol.40, No.2, pp.35–61.

Abrams, M. (1979/1980), 'Beyond Three Score Years and Ten', First and Second Reports for Age Concern, Mitcham: Age Concern.

Abrams, P. (1980), 'Social Change, Social Networks and Neighbourhood Care', *Social Work Service*, No.22, February, pp.12–23.

Abrams, P., Abrams, S., Humphrey, R. & Snaith, R. (1981), *Action for Care: Review of Good Neighbour Schemes in England*, Berkhamsted: The Volunteer Centre.

Abrams, P., Abrams, S., Humphrey, R. & Snaith, R. (1982), *A Handbook of Good Neighbour Schemes in England*, Berkhamsted: The Volunteer Centre.

Abrams, P., Abrams, S., Humphrey, R. & Snaith, R. (1985), *Patterns of Neighbourhood Care: Case Studies in their Social Context*, Durham: Department of Sociology and Social Policy, Rowntree Research Unit Working Paper.

Abrams, S. & Marsden, D. (1988), 'The Costs of Care: A Survey of Daughters Caring for Mothers', mimeo, London: Department of Social Science and Administration, Goldsmith College, University of London.

ACO (Albanian Consulate Office) (1993), *Fact Sheets*, Risborough/Aylesbury: ACO.

ACORA (The Archbishops' Commission on Rural Areas) (1990), *Faith in the Countryside*, Worthing: Churchman.

Adam, J. (ed.) (1991), *Economic Reforms and Welfare Systems in the USSR, Poland and Hungary*, Basingstoke/London: Macmillan.

Adams, C.T. & Winston, K.T. (1986), *Mothers at Home*, London/New York: Longman.

Ade-Ridler, L. & Brubaker, H. (1983), 'Quality of Long-Term Marriages', in Brubaker (1983), pp.21–30.

Aganbegyan, A. (1988), *The Challenge: Economics of Perestroika*, London: Hutchinson.

Agh, A. (1989), 'The Triangle Model of Society and Beyond', in Gaty, L. (ed.), *State and Civil Society: Relationship in Flux*, Budapest: Institute of Sociology.

Agh, A. (1990), *Transitions to Democracy in Central Europe: A Comparative View*, Budapest: School of Economics.

AISA (Association for Independent Social Analysis) (1992), *Czechs and Slovaks Compared*, Prague: AISA.

Alber, J. (1986), 'Germany', in Flora (1986), pp.1–154.

Aldcroft, D.H. (ed.) (1993), *The European Economy*, London: Routledge.

Alestalo, M. & Uusitalo, H. (1986), 'Finland', in Flora (1986), pp.199–292.

Allan, G. (1989), *Developing a Sociological Perspective*, London: Harvester Wheatsheaf.

Allan, P. (1991), 'The New Islamic Presence in Europe', *Geography Review*, Vol.5, No.5, January, pp.2–6.

Allen, I., Kellaher, L. & Peace, S. (1986), *The Impact of Social Cohesion and Time Available on Assistance to the Elderly in the UK*, London: PSI (Policy Studies Institute).

Amann, A. (ed.) (1980), *Open Care for the Elderly in Seven European Countries*, Oxford: Pergamon Press.

Amira, A. (1990), 'Family Care in Greece', in Jamieson & Ilsley (1990), pp.72–9.

Amministrazione Provinciale della Spezia (Provincial Administration of La Spezia) (1984), *La Realtà Demografica Spezzina*, La Spezia: Provincial Administration.

Anderson, R. (1992), 'Health and Community Care', in Davies (1992), pp.62–84.

Anttonen, A. (1991), 'Care for the Elderly in Finland and the Future of the Scandinavian Caring State', *Eurosocial Report*, Vol.4, No.2, pp.63–82.

Aptekar, H.H. (1965), 'Foster and Home Care for Adults', in Lurie (1965), pp.13–50.

Arber, S. & Gilbert, G.N. (1989a), 'Men: The Forgotten Carers', *Sociology*, Vol.23, No.1, pp.111–18.

Arber, S. & Gilbert, G.N. (1989b), 'Transitions in Caring, Gender, Life Course and the Care of the Elderly', in Bytheway et al. (1989), pp.72–103.

Arber, S., Gilbert, G. & Evandrou, M. (1988), 'Gender, Household Composition and Receipt of Domiciliary Services by the Elderly Disabled', *Journal of Social Policy*, Vol.17, No.2, pp.153–76.

Arber, S. & Ginn, J. (1991), *Gender and Later Life*, London: Sage.

Ascoli, U. (ed.) (1985), *Welfare State all'Italiana*, Bari: La Terza.

Ascoli, U. (1986), 'The Italian Welfare State', in Balbo & Nowotny (1986), pp.107–41.

Ascoli, U. (1987), 'The Italian Welfare State: Between Incrementalism and Rationalism', in Friedman et al. (1987), pp.110–50.

Ashford, S. & Timms, N. (1992), *What Europe Thinks*, Aldershot: Dartmouth.

Aslund, A. (1991), 'Conclusion: The Socialist Balkan Countries will follow East Central Europe', in Sjoberg & Wyzan (1991a), pp.161–6.

Association of District Councils (1986), *The Rural Economy at the Crossroads*, London: ADC.

Association of Egidio Bullesi (1987), *Villaggio Famiglia: Sorbolo di Follo*, La Spezia: Association of Egidio Bullesi.

Association of Greek Social Workers (1982), 'Living Conditions of the Elderly in Greece', *Social Policy Memorandum, Eklogi*, Athens, No.59, December, pp.137–50.

Atkin, K. (1992), 'Similarities and Differences between Informal Carers', in Parker (1992), pp.30–58.

Attila, A. (1989), 'The Triangle Model of Society and Beyond', in Gaty, L. (ed.), *State and Civil Society: Relationship in Flux*, Budapest: Institute of Sociology.

Attila, A. (1990), *Transitions to Democracy in Central Europe: A Comparative View*, Budapest: School of Economics.

Audit Commission (1986), *Making a Reality of Community Care*, London: HMSO.

Audit Commisson (1992a), *Homeward Bound: A New Course for Community Health*, London: National Health Service.

Audit Commission (1992b), *Developing Local Authority Housing Strategies*, London: HMSO.

Azarkh, E.D. & Ryvkina, R.V. (1985), 'Rural Community Studies in the USSR', in Durand-Drouhin et al. (1985), pp.125–67.

Backhaus-Maul, H. & Olk, T. (1991), 'Intermediare Organisationen und Kommunale Sozialpolitik und Deutschen Einigungsrprozeb', *Zeitschrift furt Sozialreform*, Vol.11, No.12.

Badelt, C. (1989), 'The Role of Non-Profit Organizations in Social Service Provision: A European Welfare State Perspective', unpublished paper delivered at Chicago Conference, cited in Badelt & Pazourek (1991), p.25.

Badelt, C. (1991), 'Stationare Altenpflege in Osterreich, Profil eins Markes', in Kytir, J. & Munz, R. (eds) (1991), *Pflege und Hilfsbedurfligkeit in Alter*, Vienna: Blackwell.

Badelt, C. & Pazourek, J. (1991), 'Care for the Elderly in Austria', *Eurosocial Report*, Vol.40, No.2, pp.13–33.

Bahry, D. (1980), 'Measuring Communist Priorities', *Comparative Political Studies*, Vol.13, No.3.

Bailey, J. (ed.) (1992), *Social Europe*, London: Longman.

Bailey, J.M. & Layzell, A.D. (1983), *Special Transport Service for Elderly and Disabled People*, Aldershot: Gower.

Balaceanu, C., Vrabiescu, M. & Manoiu, A. (1987), 'Peculiarities of Psychic Ageing', unpublished paper 56.20, 'Ageing Well' International Conference, Brighton.

Balbo, L. (1982), *Crazy Quilts*, Maastricht: European Institute for Social Work.

Balbo, L. (1986), 'The Culture of Caring and the "New Daily Rights"', in Balbo & Nowotny (1986), pp.19–26.

Balbo, L. (1987), 'Crazy Quilts: Rethinking the Welfare State Debate from a Woman's Point of View', in Sassoon, A.S. (ed.), *Women and the State: the Shifting Boundaries of Public and Private Care*, London: Hutchinson.

Balbo, L. (1990), 'The Strategy of Social Citizenship', conference paper delivered to the First European Dialogue on Social Policies, Helsinki, Finland, 15–19 March.

Balbo, L. & Nowotny, H. (eds) (1986), *Eurosocial Report: Time to Care in Tomorrow's Welfare System*, Vienna: European Centre for Social Welfare Training and Research.

Baldock, J. (1991a), 'Strengthening Home-based Care – England and Wales', in Kramm, J.R. et al. (eds), *Care for the Elderly*, Frankfurt: European Centre for Social Welfare and Policy and Research, Campus Verlag and Colorado: Westview Press, pp.141–85.

Baldock, J. (1991b), 'The Welfare Mix and the Elderly in Britain', in Evers & Svetlik (1991), pp.125–41.

Baldock, J. & Evers, A. (1991), 'Concluding Remarks on the Significance of the Innovations Reviewed', in Kraan et al. (eds) (1991), pp.186–202.

Banfalvi, I. (1990), 'Hungary: Shaping Policy to Accept Various Patterns of Family Lifestyles', in Vella (1990b), pp.169–75.

Barclay Report (1982), *Social Workers: their Role and Tasks*, London: Bedford Square Press.

Barnat, J., Pereira, C., Pilgrim, D. & Williams, F. (eds) (1993), *Community Care: A Reader*, Basingstoke: Macmillan and the Open University.

Barnes, J.A. (1954), 'Class and Communities in a Norwegian Island Parish', *Human Relations*, Vol.7, No.1.

Baro, F., Moorthamer, L., De Bruyne, G., Van den Bergh, H. & Magits, K. (1991), 'Home Services in the Flanders, Belgium', in Jamieson (1991a), pp.15–37.

Barraclough, B. & Hughes, J. (1987), *Suicide: Clinical and Epidemiological Studies*, London: Croom Helm.

Barrett, M. & McIntosh, R.M. (1991), *The Anti-Social Family*, London: Verso.

Basaglia, F. (ed.) (1968), *L'Istituzione Negate: Rapporto da un Ospedale Psichiatrico*, Turin: Einandi Editore.

Batley, R. & Stoker, G. (1993), *Local Government in Europe*, London: Macmillan.

Baum, C., Koch, M. & Seeger, M. (1989), *Verlichbare Strukturdatem des Sozial und Gesundheitswesensansgewählter Grosstadte der Bunderepublik*, Senator für Gesundheit und Soziales, Berlin.

Baxter, C. (1988), 'Ethnic Minority Carers: the Invisible Carers', *Health and Race*, No.15, pp.4–8.

Bayley, M. (1973), *Mental Handicap and Community Care*, London: Routledge and Kegan Paul.

Bayley, M. (1978), *Community Oriented Systems of Care*, Berkhamsted: The Volunteer Centre.

Beck, R. (1995), 'Social Insurance and Elderly People in Germany', paper presented at International Social Work Conference, University of Plymouth, Plymouth.

Beedle, P. & Taylor-Gooby, P. (1983), 'Ambivalence and Altruism', *Policy and Politics*, Vol.11, No.1.

Bell, P. & Cloke, P. (1991), 'Public Transport in the Countryside: the Effects of Bus Deregulation in Rural Wales', in Champion & Watkins (1991), pp.125–43.

Bemelmans, Y. (1986), *The Impact of Changing Social Patterns on the Services for the Elderly*, Maastricht: Europees Centrum Voor Werk en Samenleving.

Benzuri, A. & Brauns, H.J. (1986), 'Social Work Education in France', in Brauns & Kramer (1986), pp.141–67.

Berger, P. and Luckmann, P. (1967), *The Social Construction of Reality*, Harmondsworth: Penguin.

Bernard, M. (1993), 'A Foundation for Good Health', in Tout (1993), pp.112–20.

Bernardes, J. (1992), 'The Role of Sociology in Family Policy in Europe', paper delivered at the BSA National Conference, University of Kent, Canterbury.

Beveridge, W. (1942), *Social Insurance and Allied Services*, London: HMSO.

Bezrukov, V.V., Podust, L.A. & Chaikovskaya, V.V. (1993), ' A Home in Kiev', in Tout (1993), pp.149–54.

Bianchi, M. (1991), 'Policy for the Elderly in Italy: Innovation and Modernization', *Eurosocial Report*, Vol.40, No.3, pp.101– 24.

Bianchi, M. & Saraceno, C. (1988), 'Changes in Labour Market Regulations – Three Italian Case Studies', in Evers & Wintersberger (1988b), pp.97–131.

Binstock, R. & Shanas, E. (1985), *The Handbook of Aging and the Social Sciences*, New York: Van Nostrand Reinhold.

Black Report (1980), 'Inequalities in Health', in Townsend, P. & Davidson, N. (eds), *Inequalities in Health: The Black Report*, Harmondsworth: Penguin.

Blum, P. (1990), 'Pressures of Integration', *Financial Times*, 24 October, pp.vii–ix.

Bochel, M. (1988), 'Public Policy and Residential Provision for the Elderly', *Geoform*, Vol.19, No.4, pp.467–77.

Boeva, I. & Shironin, V. (1990), *Soviet Arms Manufacturers' Response to Change*, Moscow: Academy of Sciences.

Bogen, H. (1979), 'The History of Adult Home Care', in Nash, K.H. & Tesiny, D.J. (eds) (1979), *Readings in Adult Foster Care*, New York: Continuing Education Project, School of Social Welfare, State University of New York and Albany.

Booth, T. (1985), *Home Truths: Old People's Homes and the Outcomes of Care*, Aldershot: Gower.

Borrrell, J. (1990), 'Face to Face with Old Demons', *Time International*, Vol. 136, No.6, pp.8–14.

Bosanquet, N. (1983), *After the New Right*, London: Heinemann Educational Books.

Botev, N. (1990), 'Nuptiality in the Course of the Demographic Transition: The Experience of the Balkan Countries', in *Population Statistics*, (44), pp.107–26.

Bott, E. (1971), *Family and Social Network*, London: Tavistock.

Bourdieu, P. (1979), *La Distinction*, Paris: Minuit.

Brach, B. (1988), *Zycie Gsapodarze*, Nos 40,44.

Brach, B. (1989), *Zycie Gsapodarze*, Nos 7,15,17.

Branckaerts, J. & Richardson, A. (1989), 'Politics and Policies on Self-Help: Notes on the International Scene', in Humble & Urell (1989), pp.29–50.

Brasier, M. (1992), 'We Think We've Got Problems', *Daily Telegraph*, 19 May, p.17.

Brasier, M. & Johnston, P. (1992), 'Sweden Puts Interest up to 24% as Strains Begin to Take Their Toll', *Daily Telegraph*, 2 September.

Braun, T. (1988), *Les Personnes Agées Dépendantes: Rapport au Secrétaire de la Sécurité Sociale*, Paris: La Documentation Française.

Brauns, H. & Kramer, D. (eds) (1986), *Social Work Education in Europe*, Mainz: Eigenverlag des Deutschen Vereins für Öffentliche und Private Fürsorge.

Brauns, H. & Kramer D. (1989), 'West Germany: the Breakup of Consensus and the Demographic Threat', in Munday (1989), pp.124–54.

Breslauer, N. (1978), cited in Tsagarousianou (1992), p.2.

Brody, H. (1973), *Inishkillane*, London: Norman & Hobhouse.

Brody, J.A. (1979), 'Prospects for an Ageing Population', *Nature*, Vol.6, pp.315 and 463.

Browne, M. (1990), 'Innovation and Linkage in Service Provision for Elderly People in Ireland', in Jamieson & Illsley (1990), pp.157–67.

Brubaker, H. (ed.) (1983), *Family Relationships in Later Life*, London: Sage.

Bruszt, A. (1988), cited in Tsagarousianou (1992), p.5.

Buhagiar, M. (1993), 'The Caritas Malta Good Neighbour Scheme', in Tout (1993), pp.41–6.

Buis, M. (1989), *Mantelzorg voor Ouderen en Verkennende Studie bij Drie Woontussenvoorzieningen*, Tilburg: Katholieke Universiteit Brabant Studierichting Sociale Zekerheidswetenschap.

Buis, M. (1990), *Onderstenning van Mantelzorg. Een Staalkaart van Initiatieven*, Utrecht NIZW: Commissie Structuur en Financiering Gezondheidszorg, 1987 Bereidheid tot Verandering Dop Den Haag.

Bulmer, M. (1986), *Neighbours: the Work of Philip Abrams*, London: Cambridge University Press.

Bulmer, M. (1987a), *The Future of Informal Care*, London: Unwin Hyman.

Bulmer, M. (1987b), *The Social Basis of Community Care*, London: Unwin Hyman.

Bulmer, M. & Warwick, D. (eds) (1984), *Social Research in Developing Countries*, London: Wiley.

Bundesministerium (1993), *Information zum Gaetzentwurfzur Pflege-versicherung*, Bundesministerium für Arbeit und Soziallordnung, July BAS.

Burgess, R. (1982), *Field Research: A Sourcebook and Field Manual*, London: George Allen & Unwin.

Burgess, R. (1984), *In the Field*, London: George Allen & Unwin.

Burgess, M. (1986), *Federalism and Federation in Western Europe*, London: Croom Helm.

Burns, T. (1989), 'Spain', *Europe Review*, London: World of Information, WI, pp.153–7.

Bytheway, B. (1987), 'Care in the Families of Redundant Welsh Steelworkers', in Di Gregorio (1987), pp.177–87.

Bytheway, B. (1989), 'Poverty, Care and Age: A Case Study', in Bytheway et al. (1989), pp.93–103.

Bytheway, B. (1995), *Ageism*, Buckingham: Open University.

Bytheway, B., Keil, T., Allatt, P. & Brymen, A. (eds) (1989), *Becoming and Being Old*, London: Sage.

Carey, S. & Carroll, B. (1986), *Patch Work*, Dublin: Glendale Press.

Carroll, B. (1991), 'Developments in Care for Elderly People in Ireland', *Social Policy and Administration*, Vol.25, No.3, September, pp.238–48.

Carter, F.W. (1979), 'Bulgaria', in *Encyclopaedia Britannica* (1979), Macro-paedia, Vol.3, pp.468–75.

Casado, D. (ed.) (1985), *El Bienestar Social Acorraledo*, Madrid: Promoción Popular Cristiana.

Casado, D. (1992), 'Spain', in Munday (1992), pp.1–25.

Casey, J. (1989), *The History of the Family*, Oxford: Blackwell.

Casey, J. (1990), 'Our Housing: The Task Ahead,' paper presented at Annual Conference of the British Society of Gerontology, Durham.

Castelhano, M.G.P., De Lurdes Vas Abrantes, M., Do Amaral, A. & Gomes, M.V.B. (1992), 'Information on Social Services in Portugal', in Munday (1992), pp.2–27.

Castellino, O. (1976), *Il Labirinto delle Pensioni*, Bologna: Il Molino.

Castle-Kanerova, M. (1992), 'Social Policy in Czechoslovakia', in Deacon et al. (1992), pp.100–16.

Cavallone, D. (1986), 'Italy', in Brauns & Kramer (1986), pp.355–90.

Cawson, A. (1982), *Corporatism and Welfare*, London: Heinemann Educational Books.

Cecil, R., Offer, J. & St Leger, F. (1987), *Informal Welfare: A Sociological Study of Care in Northern Ireland*, Aldershot: Gower.

Challis, D. & Davies, B. (1986), *Case Management in Community Care*, Aldershot: Gower.

Champion, A.G. (1981), 'Population Trends in Rural Britain', *Population Trends*, No.26, pp.20–3.

Champion, A.G. & Townsend, A.R. (1990), *Contemporary Britain*, London: Edward Arnold.

Champion, T. & Townsend, A. (1990), Appendix D, in ACORA (1990), pp.349–59.

Champion, T. & Watkins, C. (eds) (1991), *People in the Rural Countryside*, London: Paul Chapman.

Chance, F. & Bradley, C. (1985), 'Social Services in Crisis', *Relate*, Vol.2, No.5, pp.18–20.

Chapman, J. (1991), 'Changes in the Soviet Social Contracts', in Adam (1991), pp.26–51.

Cheal, D. (1991), *Family and the State of Theory*, London: Harvester.

Clark, D.M. & Woollett, S. (1990), *English Village Services in the Eighties*, London: ACRE, Rural Development Commission.

Cloke, P.J. (1977), 'An Index of Rurality for England and Wales', *Regional Studies*, Vol.II, No.1, pp.31–46.

Cloke, P.J. (ed.) (1988), *Policies and Plans for Rural People*, London: Unwin Hyman.

Cloke, P. & Edwards, G. (1986), 'Rurality in England and Wales 1981: A Replication of the 1981 Index', *Regional Studies*, No.20, pp.289–306.

Clout, H.D. (1984), *A Rural Policy for the EEC*, London: Methuen.

Clout, H.D. (1988), 'France', in Cloke, P. (ed.) (1988), *Policies and Plans for Rural People*, London: Allen & Unwin, pp.89–119.

Cohen, A.P. (ed.) (1982a), *Belonging*, Manchester: Manchester University Press.

Cohen, A.P. (1982b), 'The Experience of Culture', *Belonging*, Manchester: Manchester University Press, pp.1–49.

Collot, C., Jani-Le Bris, H. & Le Beguec, J. (1986), *L'Impact de la Solidarité Active et du Temps Disponible Pour Venir en Aide aux Personnes Agées'*, Paris: Centre de Liaison, d'Étude, d'Information et de Recerche des Problèmes des Personnes Agées; and Dublin: European Foundation for the Improvement of Living and Working Conditions (EFILWC).

Colozzi, I. & Rossi, G. (1983), cited in Donati & Colozzi (1988) p.83.

Commission of the European Communities (1987), *Eurobarometer Survey*, November, Brussels: Commission of the EC.

Commission of the European Communities (1993a), *Eurobarometer Survey*, No.1, Brussels: Commission of the EC.

Commission of the European Communities (1993b), *Eurobarometer Survey*, No.2, Brussels: Commission of the EC.

Community Care (1989), 'Public Ends; Private Means' (Feature Articles), 30 November, *Community Care*, pp.15–17.

Coombe, V. (1986), 'Ethnic Minority Elderly', in Coombe, V. & Little, A. (eds), *Race and Social Work*, London and New York: Tavistock, pp.220–5.

Cork Diocese (1984), *Social Care: Commission Report*, Cork: Cork Diocese.

Costanzi, C. (1991), 'Home Care Services in Italy with Special Reference to Genoa', in Jamieson (1991c), pp.188–212.

Council of Europe (1986), *The Provision of Medical and Nursing Care for the Elderly Home*, Strasbourg: Council of Europe.

Council of Europe (1988), *Surveillance and Screening Techniques for the Elderly*, Strasbourg: Council of Europe.

CPA (1989), *World Directory of Old Age*, Sussex: Longman.

CPA (1993), *The European Directory of Older Age*, London: Centre for Policy on Ageing.

Cumberlege Report (1986), *Neighbourhood Nursing: A Focus for Care*, London: Department of Health and Social Security.

Curry, J. (1980), *The Irish Social Services*, Dublin: Institute of Public Administration.

Cyprus Ministry of Finance (1989–90), *Statistical Abstract, 1989–90*, Nicosia: Printing Office of the Republic of Cyprus.

Cyprus Press and Information Office (1992), *Cyprus*, London: High Commission of the Republic of Cyprus.

Dail Debates (1975), *Dail Debates*, Col.60, Vol.281, No.1, Dublin: Stationery Office, 20 May.

Dalley, G. (1984), 'Rural/Urban Differences in Health Care. Some Research Evidence', in Lishman (1984), pp.114–34.

Daly, M. & O'Connor, J. (1984), *The World of the Elderly: the Rural Experience*, Dublin: The National Council for the Aged.

Damiankos, S. (1985), 'Rural Community Studies in Greece', in Durand-Drouhin et al. (1985), pp.73–124.

Danish Statistical Department (1988), *Ten Year Statistical Compendium*, Copenhagen.

Danisoglu, E. (1988), *Sosyal Yapi – III Nufus Gruplari: A Yash Nufus*, State Planning Organisation, pub. no. DPT: 2135-SPB 415, Oxford: Oxford University Press.

Daunt, P. (1992), 'Transport and Mobility: A European Overview', in Davies (1992), pp.132–60.

David, J. (1981), 'The Housing Question: Market and Norms', *Volosag*, No.8.

David, J. (1984), 'Recent Developments in Housing Policy in Hungary', paper delivered at Critical Social Policy Conference, Manchester.

Davids, F. (1992), 'Die Lage der Altenpflege in Belgien', paper at International Conference, University of Osnabrück, Standort Vechta.

Davies, A.M. (1990), 'Prevention in the Aging?', in Kane et al. (1990), pp.316–37.

Davies, L. (ed.) (1992), *The Coming of Age in Europe*, London: Age Concern.

Davis, H.H. (1992), 'Social Stratification in Europe', in Bailey (1992), pp.17–35.

Davy, R. (1990), 'The Central European Dimension', in Wallace (1990b), pp.141–54.

Dawson, A.H. (ed.) (1987), *Planning in Eastern Europe*, Beckenham: Croom Helm.

De Beauvoir, S. (1970), *La Vieillesse*, Paris: Gallimard.

De Laubier, P. (1985), 'Three Forecasts for Our Time', in Girod et al. (1985), pp.13–26.

De Leng, N. (1991), 'Life in de Gooyer', working paper, Netherlands: A Dapperbuurt Report.

De Luca, G. & Valgimigli, C. (1983), 'La Condizione degli Anziani Oggi In Italia', *Il Pensiero Scientifico*, Vol.20, pp.17–48.

De Miguel, J. (1990), 'Funding Health Care: Implications for Harmonisation', in Mangen et al. (1990), pp.37–49.

Deacon, B. (1983), *Social Policy and Socialism*, London: Pluto Press.

Deacon, B. (1984), 'Medical Care and Health Under State Socialism', *International Journal of Health Services*, Vol.14, No.3.

Deacon, B. (1987), 'The Comparative Analysis of Policy in Britain and Hungary', in *Comparative Social Research: the East–West Divide*, No.4, Cross-National Research Paper, Aston University, Birmingham, pp.15–27.

Deacon, B. (1992a), 'Past, Present and Future in Comparative Context', in Deacon et al. (1992), pp.1–30.

Deacon, B. (ed.) (1992b), *Social Policy, Social Justice and Citizenship in Eastern Europe*, Aldershot: Avebury.

Deacon, B. (1992c), 'The Future of Social Policy in Eastern Europe', in Deacon et al. (1992), pp.167–91.

Deacon, B. & Vidinova, A. (1992), 'Social Policy in Bulgaria', in Deacon et al. (1992), pp.67–90.

Deacon, B., Castle-Kanerova, M., Manning, N., Millard, F., Orosz, E., Szalai, J. & Vidinova, A. (eds) (1992), *The New Eastern Europe*, London: Sage.

Deacon, B., David, J., Gyori, P., Jacobs, S., Szalai, J. & Williams, F. (1984), 'Welfare in Crisis: East and West', paper delivered at Critical Social Policy Conference, Manchester.

Deitch, B. (1979), *The Legitimation of Regimes*, London: Sage.

Dekker Commission (1987), *The Dekker Plan*, The Hague: Ministry of Social Welfare.

DeKok, A.C.M. (1989), 'Social Innovation – The Rotterdam Approach', paper presented at Malta Conference, 'Integrating Social and Family Policy for the 1990s', November.

Delaisi, R. (1929), *Les Deux Europes*, Paris: Payot.

Delbes, C. & Gaymu, J. (1990), 'L'Univers Domestique des Anciens', *Gérontologie et Société*, No.52, pp.6–18.

Dellenbrant, J. (1992), 'Finland and Estonia, 1940–1990: A Comparison of Economic and Social Performance', in Deacon et al. (1992), pp.19–33.

Depaoli, P., Florea, A., Gipollone, P., Colombini, L., Della Valle, F., Fatello, M., Ginnelli, G., Montanari, F. & Truffi, C. (1986), *Impact of Social Cohesion and Time Available on Assistance to the Elderly*, Rome: ARPES (Analisi, Ricerche, Piani Economici e Sociali).

Department of the Environment (1987), Cmd 214, *Housing: the Government's Proposals*, London: HMSO.

Department of the Environment (with the Department of Health) (1992), *Housing and Community Care*, Circular 10/92, London: HMSO.

Department of the Environment (1993), *Annual Report*, London: HMSO.

Department of Health (1988), *Residential Accommodation for Elderly and for Younger Physically Handicapped People: All Residents in Local Authority, Voluntary and Private Homes, Year Ending 31 March, 1988*, London: HMSO.

Department of Health (1989), *Caring for People: Community Care in the Next Decade and Beyond*, London: HMSO.

Department of Health (1990), *Community Care in the Next Decade and Beyond: Policy Guidance*, London: HMSO.

Department of the Interior (1985), *A Survey on Every Residential Institution for Elderly People*, Rome: ISTAT (Istituto Centrale di Statistici – Central Bureau of Statistics).

Di Gregorio, S. (ed.) (1987), *Social Gerontology: New Directions*, London: Sage.

Dickson, T. (1989), 'Financial Fizz of the Festival', *Financial Times*, 25 October, pp.i–iv.

Dieck, M. (1986), 'Society Structures and Socio-Political Innovations in Society to Date and Public Debate', in Steinack & Dieck (1986), pp.143–76.

Dieck, M. (1990), 'Politics for Elderly People in the FRG', in Jamieson & Illsley (1990), pp.95–119.

Dieck, M. & Garms-Homolová, V. (1991), 'Home Care Services in the Federal Republic of Germany', in Jamieson (1991a), pp.118–56.

Directorate General for Employment, Industrial Relations and Social Affairs (DGEIRS) (1993), *Social Europe*, Brussels: Commission of the EC.

Dominelli, L. (1991), *Women Across Continents*, London: Harvester Wheatsheaf.

Donati, P. (1991), 'The Development of European Policies for the Protection of Families and Children: Problems and Prospects', plenary paper, EC Conference, 'Child, Family and Society', Luxemburg, May.

Donati, P. & Colozzi, I. (1988), 'Institutional Reorganization and New Shifts in the Welfare Mix in Italy during the 1980s', in Evers & Wintersberger (1988b), pp.63–95.

Donnison, D.V. (1979), 'Social Welfare After Titmuss', *Journal of Social Policy*, Vol.8, No.2.

Dontas, A.S. (1986), 'Primary Social and Health Services for the Aged in Greece', paper delivered at the National Conference of the British Society of Gerontology (BSG), University of Glasgow, Glasgow.

Dooghe, G. (ed.) (1992), *The Ageing of the Population in Europe*, Brussels: Commission of the European Community.

Dooghe, G. & Helander, J. (1989), *Family Life in Older Age*, The Hague: NIDI, CBGS.

Dooghe, G. & Van den Boer, L. (1986), *Care for the Elderly in Belgium*, Brussels: European Centre for Work and Retirement.

Dooghe, G. & Van den Boer, L. (1993), *Sheltered Accomodation for Elderly People in an International Perspective*, Amsterdam: Swets & Zeitlinger.

Dooghe, G. & Vanderleyden, L. (1986), 'Levenvootwarden en Benoeften Van Bejaarden', Studies en Documenten 7, *De Nederlandsche, Bockhadel*.

Doyal, L. & Gough, I. (1991), *A Theory of Human Need*, Basingstoke: Macmillan.

Driest, P.F. (1988), 'Social Services and the Elderly in the Netherlands', in Hokenstad & Kendall (1988), pp.153–66.

Drury, E. (1992), 'Employment and Retirement in Europe', in Davies (1992), pp.85–108.

Drury, E. (1993), *Age Discrimination Against Older Workers in the EC*, London: Eurolink-Age.

Dublin Hospital Initiative Group (1990), *Interim Report*, Dublin: Stationery Office.

Dublin Stationery Office (1968), *Care of the Aged*, Dublin: Stationery Office.

Dumon, W. (ed.) (1989), *Family Policy in EEC Countries*, Louvain: Catholic University of Louvain.

Dumon, W. (1991), 'Families and Policies: Evolutions and European Trends in 1989–90', *Observatory in National Family Policies*, Brussels: Commission of the European Community.

Dumon, W. et al. (1994), *Revue Belge de la Sécurité Sociale*, Brussels: Ministère de la Prévoyance Sociale.

Durand-Drouhin, J.L., Szwengrub, L.M. & Mihailiscu, I. (eds) (1985), *Rural Community Studies in Europe*, Oxford: Pergamon Press.

Eastman, M. (1984), *Old Age Abuse*, Mitcham: Age Concern.

Economist (1993), *World in Figures*, London: Century Business.

Economist Intelligence Unit (1990a), 'Bulgaria, Albania, 1990–91', *Business International*, information bulletin.

Economist Intelligence Unit (1990b), 'Romania', *Business International*, information bulletin.

Edgell, S. & Duke, V. (1983), 'Gender and Social Policy: The Impact of the Public Expenditure Cuts and Reactions to Them', *Journal of Social Policy*, Vol.12, No.3.

Edwards, D.L. (1990), *Christians in a New Europe*, London/Glasgow: Collins.

EFILWC (European Foundation for the Improvement of Living and Working Conditions) (1987), *Greek Report: 1986*, Shankhill: Office for Official Publications, EFILWC.

Eichler, M. (1981), 'The Inadequacy of the Monolithic Model of the Family', *Canadian Journal of Sociology*, No.6, cited in Cheal, D. (1991), *Family and the State of Theory*, London: Harvester Wheatsheaf, p.175.

Elliot, L. & Cowe, R. (1992), 'Sterling Hit as Finland Devalues', *Guardian*, 9 September.

Ely, P. & Saunders, R. (1992), 'Social Services in France', in Munday (1992), pp.1–35.

Emiroglu, V. (1985), 'Cekirdekesiz Koyde Yaslilar' (The Elderly in Cakirdeksz Koy), *Antropolji*, 12, pp.87–120.

Encyclopaedia Britannica (1979), Micropaedia, Vols I–X, Chicago: H.H. Benton.

Encyclopaedia Britannica (1979), Macropaedia, Vols 1–19, Chicago: H.H. Benton.

Encyclopaedia Britannica (1990), Chicago: University of Chicago Press.

Engels, F. (1884), *The Origin of the Family, Private Property and the State*, Chicago: Charles Kerr (1902 edn).

Englis, K. (1921), *Socialm Politika*, Praha: F. Topic.

Erlih, V. (1966), *Porodica u Transformacyi*, Zagreb: Naprijed.

Ermisch, J. (1990), *Fewer Babies, Longer Lives*, York: Joseph Rowntree Foundation.

Esping-Andersen, G. (1986), 'Life Cycle Policy as the Emergent Model of Scandinavian Welfare States', in Balbo & Nowotny (1986), pp.71–8.

Esping-Andersen, G. (1990), *The Three Worlds of Welfare Capitalism*, Cambridge: Polity Press.

Estivill, J. (1984), *La Politica Social a Debat*, Catalonia: Generalitat de Catalunya.

Estorff, A. (1989), 'The Contact and Information Centre for Self-Help Groups in Hamburg: How It was Set Up', in Humble & Urell (1989), pp.99–108.

Estrin St Pierotin, V. (1988), 'Privatisation by Default: Old Age Homes in Britain and France', *Welfare State Programme Research Notes*, No.11.

Eurobarometer Survey Report (1987), 28, Brussels: The Commission of the European Community (CEC)/Directorate General for Information, Communication and Culture (DGV).

Eurobarometer Survey Report (1989a), 31(a), Brussels: CEC/DGV.

Eurobarometer Survey Report (1989b), 32, Brussels: CEC/DGV.

Eurobarometer Survey Report (1992a), 37(a), Brussels: CEC/DGV.

Eurobarometer Survey Report (1992b), 37(b), Brussels: CEC/DGV.

Eurobarometer Survey Report (1993), 38, Brussels: CEC/DGV.

EC (1989), *Europe Review*, Brussels: Commission of the EC.

Eurolink-Age (1989), *Eurolink-Age Bulletin*, March, London: Age Concern.

Eurolink-Age (1990), *Eurolink-Age Bulletin*, March, London: Age Concern.

European Commission (1988), *Proposal*, Brussels: EC Com. 87, 494, Article 10.

European Commission (1989), *Community Charter of the Fundamental Social Rights of Workers*, Brussels: EC Com. 89, 568, final.

European Court of Justice (1990), *Occupational Pension Schemes*, Strasbourg: European Court of Justice, 17 May, implemented 1 January 1993.

European Programme to Combat Poverty (1989), *Second Programme of the European Communities to Combat Poverty*, Cologne: ISG Institute.

Eurostat (1990), *Populations and Social Conditions, 1990–1997*, Rapid Reports, Brussels: EC.

Eurostat (1991a), *Demographic Statistics, 1991*, Luxemburg: Office for Official Publications of the European Community.

Eurostat (1991b), *A Social Portrait of Europe*, Luxemburg: Office for Official Publications of the European Community.

Evers, A. (1988), 'Shifts in the Welfare Mix', in Evers & Wintersberger (1988b), pp.7–31.

Evers, A. (1990), 'Shifts in the Welfare Mix: the Case of Care for the Elderly', paper presented in Montreal, 14–19 May, cited by Svetlik (1992b).

Evers, A. (1991), 'Concluding Remarks on the Significance of the Existing Policy, Frameworks and Planned Reforms', in Kraan et al. (1991), pp.73–85.

Evers, A. & Olk, T. (1991), 'The Mix of Care Provisions for the Frail Elderly in the Republic of Germany', *Eurosocial Report*, Vol.40, No.3, pp.59–100.

Evers, A. & Svetlik, I. (eds) (1991), *New Welfare Mixes in Care for the Elderly*, Vols 1–3, Vienna: European Centre for Social Welfare Policy and Research.

Evers, A. & Svetlik, I. (1993), *Balancing Pluralism: New Welfare Mixes in Care for the Elderly*, Vienna: European Centre for Social Welfare Policy and Research.

Evers, A. & Wintersberger, H. (1988a), 'Main Findings and Common Orientations: the National Reports', in Evers & Wintersberger (1988b), pp.389–409.

Evers, A. & Wintersberger, H. (eds) (1988b), *Shifts in the Welfare Mix*, Vienna: European Centre for Social Welfare Policy and Research.

Exile Report (1992), 'Yugoslavs Flee Terror', *Exile*, Annual Report, London: Exile Refugee Council.

Fallenbuchl, Z.M. (1991), 'Economic Reform and Changes in the Welfare System in Poland', in Adam (1991), pp.110–31.

Family Policy Studies Centre (1989), *Family Policy Bulletin*, No.6, Winter.

Fasolo, E. & Frisanco, R. (1991), 'Mental Health Care in Italy', *Social Policy and Administration*, Vol.25, No.3, pp.218–26.

Featherstone, M. (ed.) (1990), *Global Culture*, London: Sage.

Federal Statistical Institute of Yugoslavia (1987), *Statistical Yearbook of Yugoslavia*, Belgrade.

Fenton, S. (1987), *Ageing Minorities: Black People as they Grow Old in Britain*, London: Commission for Racial Equality.

Fenton, S. (1991), 'Ethnic Minority Populations in the UK', in Squires, A. (ed.) (1991), *Multicultural Health Care and Rehabilitation of Older People*, London: Edward Arnold, pp.3–16.

Ferge, Z. (1979), *A Society in the Making*, Harmondsworth: Penguin.

Ferge, Z. (1982), 'Proposals for the Modification of the Organisational System of Social Policy', unpublished manuscript, Budapest: University of Budapest.

Ferge, Z. (1983), 'The Impact of the Present Economic Crisis on Hungarian Social Policy', paper given at the European Centre for Social Welfare Training, Vienna.

Ferge, Z. (1984), 'Social Policy and Inequality in Hungary', paper given at the National Conference of the Social Administration Association, University of Kent, Canterbury.

Ferge, Z. (1991), 'Recent Trends in Social Policy in Hungary', in Adam (1991), pp.132–55.

Fernández-Armesto, F. (1994), *Guide to the Peoples of Europe*, London: Times Books.

Ferrera, M. (1985), *Il Welfare State in Italia*, Bologna: Il Molino.

Ferrera, M. (1986), 'Italy', in Flora (1986), pp.385–499.

Feschbach, M. & Rubin, A. (1991), in Adam (1991), pp.68–84.

Finch, J. (1989), *Family Obligations and Social Change*, Cambridge: Polity Press.

Finch, J. (1990), 'Women, Equal Opportunities and Welfare in the EC: Some Questions and Issues', in O'Brien, M., Hantrais, L. & Mangen, S. (eds) (1990), *Crossnational Papers: the Implications of 1992 for Social Policy*, Birmingham: Crossnational Research Group.

Finch, J. & Groves, D. (eds) (1983), *A Labour of Love: Women, Work and Caring*, London: Routledge and Kegan Paul.

Flakierski, H. (1991), 'Social Policies in the 1980s in Poland: A Discussion of New Approaches', in Adam (1991), pp.85–109.

Flora, P. (ed.) (1986), *Growth to Limits: The Western European States Since World War Two*, Vol.1, Berlin: Walter de Gruyter.

Flora, P. (ed.) (1987a), *Growth to Limits: The Western European States Since World War Two*, Vol.2, Berlin: Walter de Gruyter.

Flora, P. (ed.) 1987b), *Growth to Limits: The Western European States Since World War Two*, Vol.3, Berlin: Walter de Gruyter.

Fogarty, M.P. (1986), *Meeting the Needs of the Elderly*, Dublin: European Foundation for the Improvement of Living and Working Conditions (EFILWC).

Foot, P. (1965), *Immigration and Race in British Politics*, Harmondsworth: Penguin.

Fratczak, E. (1989), 'Life Course – Family, Occupational and Migratory Biography', SGIS, GUS, Warsaw, as cited in Fratczak (1992), p.12.

Fratczak, E. (1992), 'Living Arrangements of the Elderly in Poland', *Bold*, Malta: International Institute on Ageing (UN), pp.6–12.

Frankenberg, R. (1966), *Communities in Britain*, Harmondsworth: Penguin.

Fremouw, W.J., Percel, M. & Ellis, T.E. (1990), *Suicide Risk: Assessment and Response Guidelines*, Oxford: Pergamon.

Friedman, M. (1978), *Tax Limitation, Inflation and the Role of Government*, Texas: The Fisher Institute.

Friedman, M. & Friedman, R. (1980), *La Liberté du Choix*, Paris: Belfont.

Friedman, R.R., Gilbert, N. & Sherer, M. (eds) (1987), *Modern Welfare States*, Brighton: Wheatsheaf.

Fries, J.F. (1980), 'Ageing, Natural Death and the Compassion of Morbidity', *Journal of Medicine*, 303(3), p.130.

Frysztacki, K. (1991), 'Social Work and Social Policy in Poland: Contradictions and Perspectives', in Toscano, M. (ed.) (1991), *Scienza Sociale, Politica Sociale, Servizio Sociale*, Milan: Angeli.

Galbraith, J.K. (1977), *The Age of Uncertainty*, Boston: Houghton Mifflin.

Galea, L. (1989), *Selected Speeches*, Malta: Department of Information, Valletta.

Galea, L., Naudi, J.R., Hyzler, G., Cassar, J., Gonzi, L., Borda, B. & Sciberras, M. (1990), 'The Malta Report', in Vella (1990b), pp.193–212.

Gamble, A. (1979), 'The Free Economy of the Strong State', in Savilles, J. & Milliband, R. (eds) (1979), *Social Register*, London: Merlin Press.

Gant, R. & Smith, J. (1991), 'The Elderly and Disabled in Rural Areas: Travel Patterns in the North Cotswolds', in Champion & Watkins (1991), pp.108–24.

Gavilan, H. (1992), 'Care in the Community, Issues of Dependencies and Control – the Similarities between Institution and Home', *Journal of the British Society of Gerontology*, Vol.2, No.4, December.

General Act (1968), *Extraordinary Medical Expenses* (AWBZ), The Hague: Ministry of Social Welfare and Cultural Affairs.

General Planning Commissariat (1982), *Vieillir Demain* (The Lion Report), Paris: Documentation Française.

Generalitat de Catalunya (1992), *Catalunya*, Barcelona: Department of Trade, Centre of Information and Business Development, CIDEM.

George, J. & Young, J. (1991), 'The Physician', in Squires (1991), pp.97–107.

George, V. & Manning, N. (1980), *Socialism, Social Welfare and the Soviet Union*, London: Routledge and Kegan Paul.

George, V. & Wilding, P. (1976), *Ideology and Social Welfare*, London: Routledge and Kegan Paul.

George, V. & Wilding, P. (1984), *The Impact of Social Policy*, London: Routledge and Kegan Paul.

Gergely, I.A. (1993), 'Advised to Live Longer', in Tout (1993), pp.121–6.

German Federal Social Assistance Act (1961), as cited by Jarré (1991), p.215.

Gershuny, J. (1986), 'L'Innovation Sociale: Nouveaux Modes de Présentations de Services', *Futuribles*, February, cited in Evers & Wintersberger (1988b), p.29.

Giarchi, G.G. (1984), *Between McAlpine and Polaris*, London: Routledge and Kegan Paul.

Giarchi, G.G. (1987a), *A Comparative Study of Very Older People in Europe*, Swindon: ESRC, No.90023 2397.

Giarchi, G.G. (1987b), 'Building for the Future', *Youth in Society*, No.129, pp.14–15.

Giarchi, G.G. (1989), 'Visit to Romania: Observations', unpublished report, Plymouth: Community Research Centre, Polytechnic South West.

Giarchi, G.G. (1990a), 'Community Care of the Very Elderly in Three EC Zones', in Puliafito, P.P. (ed.) (1990), *Care of the Elderly*, SYSTED (Science Systems in Health and Social Services for the Elderly and the Disabled), Regione Emilia-Romagna, pp.493–8.

Giarchi, G.G. (1990b), 'Distance Decay and Information Deprivation: Health Implications for People in Rural Isolation', in Abbot, P. & Payne, G. (eds) (1990), *New Directions in the Sociology of Health*, London: Falmer Press, pp.57–69.

Giarchi, G.G. (1990c), 'Information Deprivation in a Cornish Setting', unpublished report for the Citizens' Advice Bureau (CAB), Plymouth and Cornwall: CAB Southwest.

Giarchi, G.G. (1991a), 'Bleak Winter or Second Spring', paper delivered at the National Conference of the British Association of Science, Plymouth: Polytechnic South West, August.

Giarchi, G.G. (1991b), 'Community Care of Older People in Europe', in Toscano (1991), pp.191–217.

Giarchi, G.G. (forthcoming), *Ageing in Europe: Bleak Winter or Second Spring?*, London: Longman.

Giarchi, G.G. & Lankshear, G. (1993), *Choice With Care*, Devon Social Services Report, Plymouth: Community Research Centre, University of Plymouth.

Giarchi, G.G. & Lankshear, G. (1994), *Care of Older People: The First Year of the Community Care Programme'*, research study for Somerset Social Services, Plymouth: Community Research Centre, University of Plymouth.

Giarchi, G.G. & Sharp, G. (1993), *Turning the Barque Around*, Exeter: Plymouth Diocese – The Roman Catholic Diocesan Trustees Registered.

Giarchi, G.G., Lordon, N. & Regnieri, A. (1992), *A Comparison between the Lifestyles of Older People in the County of Devon, Cork and Chianti*, Plymouth: Community Research Centre, University of Plymouth.

Gibson, M.J. (1992), 'Public Health and Social Policy', in Kendig et al. (1992), pp.88–114.

Giddens, A. (1990), *The Consequences of Modernity*, Cambridge: Polity Press.

Giddens, A. (1993) *Sociology*, Cambridge: Polity Press.

Gilbert, J. (1990), 'Perestroika in Residence', *Social Work Today*, January, p.15.

Gilroy, D. (1982), 'Informal Care: Reality behind the Rhetoric', *Social Work Service*, No.30.

Girod, R., de Laubier, P. & Gladstone, A. (eds) (1985), *Social Policy in Western Europe and the USA, 1950–80*, Basingstoke: Macmillan.

Glasner, A. (1992), 'Gender and Europe: Cultural and Structural Impediments to Change', in Bailey (1992), pp.70–105.

Glendinning, C. (1992), *The Costs of Informal Care: Looking Inside the Household*, London: HMSO.

Glennerster, H. (1983), *The Future of Social Welfare*, London: Heinemann.

Goffman, I. (1961), *Asylums: Essays on the Social Situation of Mental Patients and Other Inmates*, New York: Doubleday.

Gorman, M., Hobson, J., Watt, G., Dumitrescu, G., Georgescu, A., Lungu, L., Olteanu, T. & Vladu, V. (1992), *Report on the Elderly in Romania*, London: Helpline International.

Grambs, J.D. (1989), *Women over 40: Visions and Reality*, Springer Series, Vol.4, New York: Springer.

Graubard, S.R. (ed.) (1991), *Eastern Europe ... Central Europe ... Europe*, San Francisco: Westview Press.

Gray, M. (1988), 'Living Environments for the Elderly Living at Home', in Wells & Freer (1988), pp.203–16.

Green, H. (1988), *Informal Carers*, OPCS Series GHS, No.15, Supplement A, London: HMSO.

Greengross, S. (1988), *Results and Prospects: Elderly People and Poverty in Europe*, Brussels: Commission of the European Community.

Griffiths (Sir Roy Griffiths) Report (1989), *Community Care: Agenda for Action*, London: HMSO.

Groenendijk, J. (1988), 'The Netherlands', in Cloke (1988), pp.47–67.

Gross, P. & Puttner, H. (1987), 'Switzerland', in Flora (1987), pp.611–70.

Grundy, E. & Harrop, A. (1992), 'Demographic Aspects of Ageing in Europe', in Davies (1992), pp.14–37.

Guibernau, M. (1992), 'Nationalism in Nations without a State: Catalonia, a Case Study', paper delivered at the BSA National Conference, 'A New Europe', University of Kent, Canterbury.

Gurkan, M. & Gilleard, D. (1987), 'Economic Activity of the Elderly: an Analysis of Urban and Rural Populations', in Di Gregorio (1987), pp.152–60.

Gurland, B.J., Mayeux, R. & Meyers, B.S. (1990), 'The Effectiveness of Intervention for the Mental Health of the Elderly', in Kane et al. (1990), pp.262–72.

Haag, G. & Schneider, U. (1989), 'Armut und Alter: Einkommrn, Wohnen, Gesundheit und Soziale Kontakte alter Menschen in der Bundesrepublik', *Blätter der Wohfahrtspflege*, Vol.11, No.12, pp.321–48.

Habermas, J. (1976), *Legitimation Crisis*, London: Heinemann.

Hadley, R. & Hatch, S. (1981), *Social Welfare and the Failure of the State*, London: George Allen & Unwin.

Hakim, C. (1982), *Secondary Analysis in Social Research*, London: George Allen & Unwin.

Halonen, T. (1990), 'Finland, New Approach to Social Welfare Policies', in Vella (1990b), pp.163–8.

Halsey, A. (1981), 'Some Lessons from the Debates: a Sociologist's Viewpoint', in *The Welfare State in Crisis*, Paris: OECD.

Hammett, C. & Mullings, B. (1991), 'The Distribution of Public and Private Residential Homes for Elderly Persons in England and Wales', paper delivered at the British Association of Science Annual Meeting, Plymouth: Polytechnic South West, 25–30 August.

Handy, C. (1989), *The Age of Unreason*, London: Business Books.

Hankiss, E. (1990), *East European Alternatives*, Oxford: Clarendon Press.

Hantrais, L., Mangen, S. & O'Brien, M. (eds) (1991), *Caring and the Welfare State*, Cross-National Research Papers, Birmingham: Aston University.

Harding, S., Phillips, D. & Fogarty, M. (1986), *Contrasting Values in Western Europe*, Basingstoke: Macmillan.

Harper, S. (1986), 'The Kinship Network of the Rural Aged: a Comparison of the Indigenous Elderly and the Retired Immigrant', paper presented at the Annual National Conference of the British Society of Gerontology, University of Glasgow, Glasgow.

Harper, S. (1987), 'The Kinship Network of the Rural Aged: a Comparison of the Indigenous Elderly and the Retired Immigrant', *Ageing and Society*, Vol.7, No.1, pp.303–27.

Harper, S. (1991), 'People Moving to the Countryside: Case Studies of Decision-making', in Champion & Watkins (1991), pp.22–37.

Harris, A. & Seldon, R. (1981), *Overruled on Welfare*, London: Institute of Economic Affairs.

Hartl, J. (1991), 'Social Policy, Social Care, and the Case of the Elderly in Czechoslovakia', in Evers & Svetlik (1991), Vol.1, pp.25–39.

Hartmann, J. (1985), 'Social Policy in Sweden', in Girod et al. (1985), pp.91–100.

Hartmann-Hirsch, M., Welter, C. & Neyens, E. (1992), 'The Grand Duchy of Luxembourg', in Munday (1992), pp.393–404.

Harvey, D. (1973), *Social Justice and the City*, London: Edward Arnold.

Hashimoto, A. & Kendig, H.L. (1992), 'Ageing in International Perspective', in Kendig et al. (1992), pp.1–14.

Hashimoto, A., Kendig, H.L. & Coppard, L. (1992), 'Family Support to the Elderly in International Perspective', in Kendig et al. (1992), pp.293–308.

Haskey, J. (1990), 'The Ethnic Minority Populations of Great Britain: Estimates by Ethnic Group and Country of Birth', *Population Trends*, No.60, pp.35–8, cited in Squires (1991), p.15.

Hatland, A. (1986), 'The Right to Care in Norwegian Social Policy', in Balbo, L. & Nowotny, H. (eds) (1986), *Time to Care in Tomorrow's Welfare Systems*, Vienna: European Centre for Social Welfare Training and Research, pp.53–69.

Hayek, F.A. (1944), *The Road to Serfdom*, London: Routledge and Kegan Paul.

Haynes, A.C.W. (1983), *The State of Black Britain*, London: Root Books.

Haynes, R.M. & Bentham, C.G. (1982), 'The Effects of Accessibility on General Practitioner Consultations, Outpatient Attendances and In-patient Admisssions in Norfolk, England', *Social Science and Medicine*, Vol.16, pp.561–9.

Heath, A., Jowell, R. & Curtice, J. (1985), *How Britain Votes*, Oxford: Pergamon.

Hedstrom, P. & Ringen, S. (1987), 'Age and Income in Contemporary Society: A Research Note', *Journal of Social Policy*, Vol.16, Part 2, Cambridge: Cambridge University Press.

Hegyi, L. (1992), 'Current Aspects of Old Age: Age Care in the Czech and Slovak Federal Republics', *Bold*, Malta: International Institute on Ageing, Malta, pp.2–5.

Heidenheimer, A.J., Helco, H. & Adams, H.C.T. (1983), *Comparative Public Policies*, London: Macmillan Press.

Heikkinen, B., Waters, W.E. & Brzezinski, Z.J. (eds) (1983), *Public Health in Europe*, No.21, Copenhagen: Regional Office for Europe, World Health Organization.

Heisel, M.A. (1987), 'Women and Widows in Turkey, Support Systems', in Lopata, H.Z. (ed.) (1987), *Widows, Vol.1: The Middle East, Asia and the People*, Durham: Durham University Press, pp.79–105.

Heisel, M.A. (1992), 'Support of the Elderly in Turkey', in Kendig et al. (1992), pp.188–202.

Helgeson, A. (1989), 'USSR: The Implications of Glasnost and Perestroika', in Munday (1989), pp.51–80.

Henrard, J.C. (1987), 'Blocage des Filières de Soins', *Revue d'Epidémiologie et Santé Publique*, Vol.35, pp.298–308.

Henrard, J.C. & Brocas, A.M. (1990), 'Financial Barriers to Health', in Jamieson & Illsley (1990), pp.120–32.

Henrard, J.C., Anki, J. & Isnard, M.C. (1991), 'Home Care Services in France', in Jamieson (1991c), pp.99–117.

Hernes, H.M. (1986), 'Care Work and the Organisation of Daily Life', in Balbo & Nowotny (1986), pp.41–51.

Higgins, J. (1981), *States of Welfare*, Oxford: Blackwell.

Hildeng, B. (1986), 'Norway', in Brauns & Kramer (1986), pp.425–36.

Hiller, W. (1992), 'The Rural Problems Facing Older People', paper presented at International Conference, University of Osnabrück, Germany.

Hirschtfeld, M.J. & Fleishman, R. (1990), 'Nursing Home Care for the Elderly', in Kane et al. (1990), pp.473–90.

HMSO (1989), *Caring for People: Community Care in the Next Decade and Beyond*, London: Government White Paper (in Northern Ireland, *People First*, 1990).

HMSO (1990), *National Health Service and Community Care Act*, London: HMSO.

HMSO (1991), *Options of Equality in State Pension Age*, London: HMSO.

HMSO (1992), *Social Trends, 1992*, Central Statistical Office, London: HMSO.

HMSO (1988), (1989), (1990), (1991), (1992) & (1993), *Regional Trends*, London: HMSO.

Hobsbaum, E.J. (1990), *Nations and Nationalism Since 1780*, Cambridge: Cambridge University Press.

Hoffman, D.M. (1986), 'Austria', in Brauns & Kramer (1986), pp.43–63.

Hokenstad, M.C. & Kendall, K.A. (eds) (1988), *Gerontological Social Work: International Perspectives*, London: Haworth Press.

Holland, M. (1965), *Report of the Committee on Housing in Greater London*, London: HMSO.

Holstein, B.E., Almind, G., Due, P. & Holst, E. (1988), *The Elderly in Denmark: Health and Social Situation*, Copenhagen: Institute of Social Medicine, University of Copenhagen.

Holstein, B.E., Due, P., Almind, G. & Holst, E. (1991), 'The Home Help Service in Denmark', in Jamieson (1991c), pp.38–62.

Holzmann, R. (1986), *Reforming Public Pensions*, Paris: OECD.

Holzmann, R. (1992), 'Adapting to Social Change: Social Policy Issues in Transition from Plan to Market', *Journal of Public Policy*, Vol.12, No.2.

Hope, K. (1990), 'Greece', *Financial Times*, 7 October, p.15.

Hoshi, I. (1989), *The Work of Sex, Vol.2: Sex and Marriage*, Woodchurch: Norbury Publications.

Howe, J. (1992), 'Probleme und Perspektiven der Atlenpflege in Ländlich Strukturierten Regionen der Bundesrepublik Deutschland', paper presented at International Conference at University of Osnabrück, Standort Vechta, Germany, 21–22 May.

Howe, J. (1993), *Altenpflege auf dem Lande*, Heidelberg: Roland Asanger Verlag.

Hrynkiewicz, J., Starega-Piasek, J. & Supinska, J. (1991), 'The Elderly and Social Policy in Poland', in Evers & Svetlik (1991), Vol.1, pp.59–72.

Hugman, R. (1994), *Ageing and the Care of Older People in Europe*, Basingstoke: Macmillan.

Hummel, K. (1991), 'Self-Reliancy of Course', paper presented at EC Conference, Stuttgart.

Hunter, D. (1986), *Care Delivery Systems for the Elderly*, Bath: Age Care Research, Europe (ACRE).

Hunter, D. (1991), 'An Overview of Community Care in Britain: Mixed Experiences and Mixed Economies', in Ulas, M., Black, S. & Hambleton, P. (eds) (1991), *Community Care*, Edinburgh: Social Services Research Group, pp.5–9.

Hunter, D. & Wistow, G. (1987), *Community Care in Britain*, London: Kings Fund Publishing Office.

Huntford, R. (1972), *The New Totalitarians*, New York: Stein and Day.

Hytti, H. (1983), *Vanhuus-ja Työkyvyttömyyseläkkeensaajien Tulot, 1980*, Helsinki: Kansaneläkelaitoksen Julkaisuja M: 42.

Infrasca, R. (1987), 'Gli Anziani nella Comunità Spezzina: Una Analysi Sociopsichiatria', *Prospettive Sociali e Sanitarie*.

Interdepartmental Committee (1968), *Care of the Aged*, Dublin: Dublin Stationery Office.

International Expert Meeting (1992), 'Towards a Competitive Society in Central and Eastern Europe: Social Dimensions', Vienna, 20–22 September, cited in *Eurosocial*, 61/63, pp.15–30.

International Labour Organization (ILO) (1989), *From Pyramid to Pillar – Population Change and Social Security in Europe*, London International Labour Organization.

IRSOP (Romanian Institute for Public Opinion) (1991), *The Economic Behaviour and Political Attitudes of the Romanian Population*, Bucharest: New Democracies Barometer.

ISTAT (1983), data published by the Istituto Centrale di Statistica, as cited by Bianchi (1991).

Jamieson, A. (1990), 'Informal Care in Europe', in Jamieson & Illsley (1990), pp.3–21.

Jamieson, A. (1991a), 'Care of Older People in the European Community: Caring and the Welfare State in the 90s', in Hantrais, Mangen & O'Brien (1991), pp.32–45.

Jamieson, A. (1991b), 'Community Care for Older People', in Room (1991), pp.107–26.

Jamieson, A. (ed.) (1991c), *Home Care for Older People in Europe: A Comparison of Policies and Practices*, Oxford: Oxford University Press.

Jamieson, A. & Illsley, R. (eds) (1990), *Contrasting European Policies for the Care of Older People*, Aldershot: Avebury.

Jani-Le Bris, H. (1992), *Family Care of the Dependent Elderly*, Dublin: European Foundation for the Improvement of Living and Working Conditions (EFILWC).

Jarré, D. (1991), 'Subsidiarity in Social Services in Germany', *Social Policy and Administration*, Vol.25, No.3, pp.211–17.

Jerrome, D. (1989), 'Virtue and Vicissitude: The Role of Old People's Clubs', in Jefferys, M. (ed.) (1989), *Growing Old in the Twentieth Century*, London: Routledge, pp.151–65.

Johansen, L.N. (1986), 'Denmark', in Flora (1986), pp.293–381.

Johansen, L.N. (1987), 'Denmark', in Flora (1987), pp.194–246.

Johansson, L. & Thorslund, M. (1991), 'The National Context of Social Innovation', in Kraan et al. (1991), pp.28–44.

Johansson, L. & Thorslund, M. (1992), 'Care Needs and Sources of Support in a Nationwide Sample of Elderly in Sweden', in *Zeitschrift für Gerontologie*, 25, pp.57–62.

Jolliffe, J. (1989), 'Portugal', in *The Europe Review*, London: World of Information, Kogan Page, pp.155–77.

Jones, C. (1985), *Patterns of Social Policy*, London: Tavistock.

Jones, K. & Polatti, A. (1984), 'The Mirage of Reform', *New Society*, Vol.69, No.2, pp.10–12.

Jònsdòttir, G. (1986), 'Iceland', in Brauns & Kramer (1986), pp.279–92.

Jowell, R. & Airey, C. (eds) (1984), *British Social Attitudes*, Aldershot: Gower.

Judge, K. (1981), 'Is There a Crisis in the Welfare State?', *The International Journal of Sociology and Social Policy*, Vol.1, No.2.

Judge, K., Smith, J. & Taylor-Gooby, P. (1983), 'Public Opinion and the Privatisation of Welfare: Some Theoretical Implications', *Journal of Social Policy*, Vol.12, No.4.

Julliard, E. & Noin, H. (eds) (1976), *Espaces et Régions en Europe Occidentale*, Paris: CNRS, cited in Toscano (1991), p.215.

Kagitçibasi, K. (1985), 'Intra-Family Interaction for Models of Change', in *Turkish Family Society: Sociological Legal Issues*, Social Science Association, Ankara: Moya.

Kahn, R. & Antonucci, T. (1980), 'Convoys over the Life Course: Attachment, Roles and Social Support', in Baltes, P. & Brim, O. (eds) (1980), *Life Span Development and Behaviour, Vol.3*, NY: Academic Press.

Kahn, V.A. & Kamerman, S.B. (1978), *Family Policy: Government and Families in 14 Countries*, NY: Columbia University Press.

Kalaycioglu, E. (1990), 'Cyclical Breakdown, Redesign and Nascent Institutionalization: the Turkish Grand National Assembly', in Liebert, U. & Cotta, M. (eds) (1990), *Parliament and Democratic Consolidation in Southern Europe*, London and NY: Printer Publication, pp.184–222.

Kampfner, J. (1992), 'Will She be Better Off?', *Daily Telegraph*, 28 September, p.19.

Kane, R.L., Grimley Evans, J. & Macfadyen, D. (eds) (1990), *Improving the Health of Older People: a World View*, Oxford: Oxford University Press.

Kavar-Vidmar, A., Mesec, B., Milosevic, V. & Tamaskovic, M. (1980), 'Open Care for the Elderly – Yugoslavia', in Amann (1980), pp.155–77.

Kellas, J.G. (1975), *The Scottish Political System*, Cambridge: Cambridge University Press.

Kempen, G.I., Van Sonderen, F.L.S., Suurmeijer, T.B.M. & Van den Heuvel, W.J.A. (1986), 'Formele en informele hulpverlenig bij ouderen. Een onderzoek naar de taaverdeling tussen bejaarden, informele hulpverleners en de gezinsverzorging', *Tijdschrift voor Gerontologie en Geriatrie*, 17, pp.227–32, cited in den Heuvel, W. & Gerritsen, H. (1991), 'Home Care Services in the Netherlands', in Jamieson (1991c), p.235.

Kendig, H., Hashimoto, A. & Coppard, L.C. (1992), *Family Support for the Elderly*, Oxford: Oxford University Press on behalf of World Health Organization.

Kennedy, K.A. (1981), *Who Should Care?*, Dublin: Turoe Press.

Kennedy, K.A. (1986a), *Ireland in Transition*, Cork and Dublin: Mercier Press.

Kennedy, K.A. (1986b), 'The Family in Transition', in Kennedy (1986a), pp.91–100.

Kilarska-Bobinska, L. (1992), 'Civil Society and Social Anomy in Poland', in Deacon et al. (1992), pp.56–70.

Kirk, H. & Leather, P. (1991), *Age File: The Facts*, London: Anchor Housing Trust.

Knapp, M., Montserrat, J. & Fenyo, A. (1990), 'Intersectoral and International Contracting out of Long-Term Care: Evidence on Comparative Costs and Efficiency from Britain and Spain', *Cross-national Research Papers*, Vol.2, No.2, pp.46–73.

Knipscheer, K.C.P.M. (1992), 'The Netherlands in European Perspective', in Kendig et al. (1992), pp.147–59.

Koedoot, N. & Hommel, A. (1992), '"Home, Sweet Home": Care Meditation for the Elderly', paper presented at the 21st Annual Conference of the British Society of Gerontology, University of Kent, Canterbury.

Kokkinaki, S.K. (1986), 'Greece', in Brauns & Kramer (1986), pp.249–78.

Konopasek, Z. (1992), 'Escape from State Socialism: Which Way?', in Deacon et al. (1992), pp.245–60.

Koskiaho, B. (1988), 'Yhteiskunnallistettu Vanhuskysmys', *Sosiaalihallituksen Julkaisuja*, No.11, Helsinki.

Kraan, R., Baldock, J., Davies, B., Evers, A., Johansson, L., Knapen, M., Thorslund, M. & Tunissen, C. (eds) (1991), *Care for the Elderly: Significant Innovations in Three European Countries*, Frankfurt: Campus Verlag and Boulder, Colorado: Westview Press.

Kravchenko, M. (1990), 'USSR: Main Options of the National Policy in the Social Sphere', in Vella (1990b), pp.189–92.

Kristinsson, V. & Matthiasson, B. (1979), 'Iceland', in *Encyclopaedia Britannica* (1979), Micropaedia, Vol.9, pp.170–5.

Ksiezopolski, M. (1992), 'The Prospects for Social Policy Development in Poland', in Deacon et al. (1992), pp.228–44.

Kuhnle, S. (1986), 'Norway', in Flora (1986), pp.119–96.

Kuhnle, S. (1987), 'Norway', in Flora (1987a), pp.67–122.

Kuratorium Deutsche Altershilfe (1991), *Wieviele alte Menschen Leben im Heim?* Köln: Presse und Informationsdienst.

Kyriazis, M. (1992), 'Care for Older People in Cyprus', conference paper delivered at the International Conference, 'The Marginalization of Elderly People', University of Liverpool, Liverpool.

Laczko, F. (1989), 'New Poverty and the Old Poor: Pensioners' Incomes in the European Community', paper delivered at the Annual National Conference of the British Society of Gerontology, Nottingham University, Nottingham.

Laczko, F. (1992), *Social Policy and Elderly People: The Role of Community Care*, Aldershot: Avebury.

Laczko, F. (1994), *Older People in Eastern and Central Europe*, London: Helpage International.

Laczko, F. & Phillipson, C. (1991), *Changing Work and Retirement*, Milton Keynes: Open University Press.

Lagergren, M. (1986), 'Time to Care in the Advanced Welfare State', in Balbo & Nowotny (1986), pp.27–40.

Lagergren, M. (1988), *Folkhemmets Framtider*, Stockholm: Institutet for Framtidsstudier.

Larder, D., Day, P. & Klein, R. (1986), 'Institutional Care for the Elderly: the Geographical Distribution of the Public/Private Mix in England', Social Policy Papers, No.10, Bath: University of Bath.

Laroque Report (1962), *Policy for the Elderly*, Paris: Commission for the Study of the Problems of Old Age.

Lawson, R. (1979), *Social Assistance in the European Community*, Brussels: report presented to the European Commission.

Leaper, R.A.B. (1989), 'French Elderly Social Care', *This Caring Business*, No.25.

Leaper, R.A.B. (1990), 'The Many Faces of Belgium: Analysis Feature', *This Caring Business*, No.24.

Leaper, R.A.B. (1991), 'Elderly People and Social Services in Four EC Countries', in Hill, M. (ed.) (1991), *Social Work and the European Community*, London: Jessica Kingsley, pp.178–97.

Leat, D. (1992), 'Innovations and Special Schemes', in Twigg (1992b), pp.95–125.

Leat, D. & Gay, P. (1987), *Paying for Care: A Study of Policy and Practice in Paid Care Schemes*, London: Policy Studies Institute.

Lee, J.J. (ed.) (1985), *Ireland: Towards a Sense of Place*, Cork: Cork University Press.

Leeson, G.W. (1993), 'Congregate Housing: the Multifunctional Centre – the Danish Experience', in Tout (1993), pp.160–5.

LeGrand, J. (1984), 'The Future of the Welfare State', *New Society*, No.7, June.

Leibfried, S. (1991), *Towards a European Welfare State?*, Bremen: Zentrum für Sozialpolitik.

Leichsenring, K. & Pruckner, B. (1993), 'Using Counselling Services to Mediate between Formal and Informal Care', in Tout (1993), pp.195–202.

Lennon, J. (1991), *Cornwall: Rural Deprivation*, Truro: Social Services Department.

Levin, E., Sinclair, I. & Gorbach, P. (1989), *Families, Services and Confusion in Old Age*, Aldershot: Gower.

Lewis, A. (1980), 'Attitudes to Public Expenditure', *Political Studies*, Vol.28, No.2.

Lingås, L. (ed.) (1970), *Myten an Velferdsstaten*, Oslo: Pax.

Lipset, S.M. & Rokkan, S. (1967), *Party Systems and Voter Alignments: Cross-National Perspectives*, NY: Free Press.

Lisboa, I.M.A.F. (1986), 'Portugal', in Brauns & Kramer (1986), pp.437–50.

Lishman, Y. (ed.) (1984), *Social Work in Rural and Urban Areas: Research Highlights 9*, Aberdeen: Aberdeen University Press.

Lishman, G., Morall, L. & Wilkins, N. (1993), *Older British People Resident in Spain*, London: Age Concern.

Lloyd, J. (1990), 'A Melting Pot Rapidly Coming to the Boil', *Financial Times*, 8 April, Spring Politics Section.

London Edinburgh Weekend Return Group (1980), *In and Against the State*, London: Pluto Press.

Long, J. (1989), 'A Part to Play: Men Experiencing Leisure through Retirement', in Bytheway et al. (1989), pp.55–71.

Lorenz, W. (1994), *Social Work in a Changing Europe*, London: Routledge.

Louatron, S. (1986), 'France', in Brauns & Kramer (1986), pp.141–67.

Luker, K. (1988), 'The Nurse's Role in Health Promotion and Preventative Health Care of the Elderly', in Wells & Freer (1988), pp.155–61.

Luker, K.A. & Perkins, E.S. (1987), 'The Elderly at Home: Services, Needs and Provision', *Journal of Royal College of General Practitioners*, cited in Wells & Freer (1988), p.161.

Lunn, T. (1989), 'Public Ends, Private Means', *Community Care*, 30 November, pp.15–17.

Lurie, H.L. (ed.) (1965), *Encyclopaedia of Social Work*, New York: National Association of Social Workers.

Luscher, K. (1982), 'Fifty Years of Family Policy in Switzerland', in *Pro Familia*, paper presented at the Lucerne Family Conference, 21 November.

Luxembourg Grand Duchy (1991a), *Sozialporträts Europas*, Luxembourg: Statistisches Amt Füramtliche Veröffentlichungen der Europäischen Gemeinschaften.

Luxembourg Grand Duchy (1991b), White Paper No.3571, Luxembourg, cited by Hartmann-Hirsch et al. (1992), p.12.

Ma Mpolo, M. (1982), *The Church and the Ageing in a Changing World*, Office of Family Education: World Council of Churches.

MacFadyen, D. (1990), 'International Demographic Trends', in Kane et al. (1990), pp.19–29.

Magnani, P. (1982), 'Che Fare degli Anziani?', *Il Ponte*, Anno 38, No.9, 30 September, pp.880–95.

Malikiossi-Loizos, M. (1986), 'The Impact of Social Cohesion and Time Available for Assistance to the Elderly', Dublin: European Foundation for the Improvement of Living and Working Conditions (EFILWC) and Paris: CLEIRPPA.

Malta Report (1990), 'The Malta Report', in Vella (1990b), pp.192–212.

Maltese Department of Information (1989), *Family Wellbeing: Government Measures for a Better Quality of Life*, Valletta: Maltese Department of Information.

Manchin, R. & Szelenyi, I. (1984), 'Social Policy Under State Socialism', in Esping-Andersen et al. (eds) (1984), *Comparative Social Policy*, Wisconsin: Sharpe.

Mangen, S.P. (ed.) (1985a), *Mental Health Care in the EC*, London: Sage.

Mangen, S.P. (1985b), 'The Psychiatric Enquete and its Aftermath', in Mangen (1985a), pp.73–113.

Mangen, S., Hantrais, L. & O'Brien, M. (eds) (1990), *The Implications of 1992 for Social Insurance*, Cross-National Research Papers, Birmingham: Aston University.

Manning, N. (1984), 'Social Policy in the USSR and the Nature of Soviet Society', *Critical Social Policy*, No.11, Winter, pp.74–88.

Manning, N. (1992), 'Social Policy in the Soviet Union and its Successors', in Deacon et al. (1992), pp.31–66.

Manoukian, F.O. (1988), *Stato di Servizi: Una Analisi Psicosociologica dei Servizi Sociosanitari*, Bologna: Il Molino.

Marin, Y. (1992), 'Helping Old People to Stay at Home', paper delivered at the International Conference, 'The Marginalization of Older People', University of Liverpool, Liverpool.

Marshall, M. (1991), 'Proud to be Old', in McEwan, E. (ed.) (1991), *The Unrecognised Discrimination*, Mitcham: Age Concern, pp.28–42.

Mastenbroek, J. (1986), *The Impact of Changing Social Patterns on the Services for the Elderly in the Netherlands*, Maastricht: European Centre for Work and Society, and Dublin: European Foundation for the Improvement of Living and Working Conditions (EFILWC).

Matzat, J. (1989), 'Some Remarks on West Germany's Health and Welfare System and the Position of Self-Help', in Humble and Urell (1989), pp.3–13.

Mauthner, R. (1991), 'Greece', *Financial Times*, 9 October, Survey, pp.15–19.

McCafferty, M. (1985), 'Family and Kin in North Antrim and South Derry Villages – a Geographic Perspective', unpublished M.Phil. thesis, Coleraine: University of Ulster.

McCleery, M. (1991), 'Population and Social Conditions in Remote Areas', in Champion & Watkins (1991), pp.144–89.

McCoin, J.M. (1983), *Adult Foster Homes: Their Managers and Residents*, NY: Human Science Press.

McKeigue, P. (1991), 'Patterns of Health and Disease in the Elderly from Minority Ethnic Groups', in Squires (1991), pp.69–77.

McLaughlin, B.P. (1985), *Rural Deprivation Report*, London: Department of the Environment, HMSO.

McLaughlin, B.P. (1986), 'The Rhetoric and the Reality of Rural Deprivation', *Journal of Rural Studies*, 2, pp.291–308.

McLaughlin, E. (1989), 'Women, the Extended Family and Poverty in Northern Ireland', Women and Social Policy Series, Coleraine: PSI, Belfast Centre for Research on Women.

Means, R. (1985), 'Older People in British Housing Studies: Rediscovery and Emerging Issues for Research', *Housing Studies*, pp.82–98.

Means, R. & Smith, R. (1994), *Community Care: Policy and Practice*, Basingstoke: Macmillan.

Meny, Y. & Wright, V. (eds) (1985), *Centre–Periphery Relations in Western Europe*, London: George Allen & Unwin.

Mewett, P.G. (1982), 'Associational Categories and the Social Location of Relationships in a Lewis Crofting Community', in Cohen (1982a), pp.101–30.

Milano, S. (1989), *Poverty in Europe: Poverty in Europe Report*, Dublin: International Council on Social Welfare and Combat Poverty Agency.

Millard, F. (1992), 'Social Policy in Poland', in Deacon et al. (1992), pp.118–43.

Milosavljevic, M.J. & Ruzica, M. (1989), 'Yugoslavia: the Effects of the Economic and Political Crisis', in Munday (1989), pp.155–80.

Ministry for Social Policy (1990), *A Caring Society in a Changing World*, Valletta: Ministry for Social Policy.

Ministry of Health Working Party (1988), *The Years Ahead: Report*, Dublin: Ministry of Health.

Ministry of Housing and Local Government (1969), *Sheltered Housing*, Circular 82/69, London: HMSO.

Ministry of Internal Affairs (1984), *Gli Operai Sociali: Urgenza di una Normativa*, Rome: Direzione Generale dei Servizi Civili.

Ministry of Social Affairs (1980), *Delrapport: Aldersforand-ringer-aeldrepolitikkens Forudsaetninger*, Copenhagen: Aeldrekommissionen.

Ministry of Social Affairs (1990), *Denmark*, as cited in Abrahamson (1991), p.61.

Ministry of Social Affairs and Health, Finland (1982), *Aging in Finland: Finnish National Report for the World Assembly on Aging*, Helsinki: Finnish Ministry of Social Affairs and Health.

Ministry of Welfare, Health and Cultural Affairs (1986), *Fact Sheet on the Netherlands*, Rijswijk: International Relations Directorate.

Minois, G. (1987), *History of Old Age*, Chicago: University of Chicago Press.

Mishra, R. (1984), *The Welfare State in Crisis*, Brighton: Wheatsheaf Books.

Mitterauer, M. & Sieder, R. (1982), *The European Family: Patriarchy to Partnership, From the Middle Ages to the Present*, Oxford: Blackwell.

Modena-Burkhardt, E. (1986), 'Switzerland', in Brauns & Kramer (1986), pp.507–28.

Moenaert, P. (1991), 'Cash and Caring in Brugge', *Social Policy and Administration*, Vol.25, No.3, September, pp.202–10.

Morewood, S. (1993), 'Eastern Europe in Transition, 1970–90', in Aldcroft (1993), pp.253–78.

Moser, C.A. (1970), 'Some General Developments in Social Statistics', *Social Trends*, Vol.2, No.1, pp.7–11.

Mostinckx, J.E.F. (1992), 'The Flemish Community of Belgium', in Munday (1992), pp.1–38.

Muintir-na Tire (1985), *Towards a New Democracy*, Dublin: Institute of Public Administration.

Muller, W. (1993), 'Community Work in Western Germany', seminar paper delivered at the University of Plymouth, Erasmus seminar, February.

Munday, B. (ed.) (1989), *The Crisis in Welfare*, Hemel Hempstead: Harvester Wheatsheaf.

Munday, B. (ed.) (1992), *Social Services in the Membership of the European Communities*, Canterbury: University of Kent.

Murphy, E. (1986), *Dementia and Mental Illness in the Old*, London: Macmillan.

Murphy, M. (1984), *Social Care Commission Report*, Cork: Cork Diocesan Report.

Murray, B. (1993), 'Housing Elderly People in England and the Netherlands', conference paper delivered at the International Conference, 'Community Care of the Elderly', University of Plymouth, Plymouth, April.

Myrdal, A. & Myrdal, G. (1935), referred to by Sundström, G. (1988), 'Social Work and Old Age Care in Sweden', in Hokenstad & Kendall (1988), p.167.

Narodnoe, K. (1987), *SSR: ZA 70 LET*, Moscow: Finansy i statistiki.

National Association of Teachers in Further and Higher Education (1994), 'Third Age', in *NATFHE Journal*, Vol.40, London: NATFHE Union.

National Consumer Council (1977), *The 4th Right of Citizenship: A Review of Local Advice Services*, London: NCC.

National Council for the Aged (1988), *The Years Ahead*, Dublin: Report of NCA.

National Council for Voluntary Organisations (1990), *Caring for People: A Rural Perspective*, London: NCVO Rural Unit.

National Economic and Social Council (1987), *Community Care Services: An Overview*, Dublin: NESC Publication.

National Federation of Housing Associations (1991), *The Future of Sheltered Housing: Who Cares? Practice Guide*, London: NFHA.

National Institute for Social Work (1990), *The Kaleidoscope of Care*, London: HMSO.

National Social Service Board (1989), *Entitlement for the Over 60s*, Dublin: NSSB.

Nazareth, J.M. (1988), 'Portugal: Os Proximos 20 Anos', *Unidade e Diversidade da Demograpia Portuguesa no Final de Seculo XX*, Vol.III, Lisbon: Fundaco Calouste Gulbenkian, p.398.

Nijkamp, P. & Giaoutzi, M. (1991), 'Greece', in Nijkamp et al. (1991c), pp.203–18.

Nijkamp, P., Vollering, A. & Wilderom, C. (1991a), 'Country-Comparative Analysis of Care for the EC Elderly', in Nijkamp et al. (1991c), pp.23–77.

Nijkamp, P., Vollering, A. & Wilderom, C. (1991b), 'Introduction', in Nijkamp et al. (1991c), pp.3–20.

Nijkamp, P., Pacolet, J., Spinnewyn, H., Vollering, A., Wilderom, C. & Winters, S. (eds) (1991c), *Services for the Elderly in Europe: A Cross-National Comparative Study*, Louvain: Catholic University of Louvain.

Nilsson, I. & Wadeskog, A. (1988), 'Local Initiatives in a New Welfare State: a Fourth Sector Approach', in Evers & Wintersberger (1988b), pp.33–62.

Norman, A. (1985), *Triple Jeopardy: Growing Old in a Second Homeland*, Policy Studies in Ageing, No.3, London: Centre for Policy on Ageing.

Norregaard, C. (1986), *Social Cohesion of Time Available for Assistance to the Elderly in Denmark*, Maastricht: European Foundation for the Improvement of Work and Society.

Norton, D. (1992), 'Social Provision for Older People in Europe in Education and Leisure', in Davies (1992), pp.38–62.

Norwegian National Survey (1970), *The Myth of the Welfare State*, cited by Kuhnle (1986), p.160.

Norwegian Social Care Act (1964), Oslo: Storting.

Novak, M. (1989), *Catholic Social Thought and Local Institutions*, NY: Transaction Publishers.

Nove, A. (1983), *The Economics of Feasible Socialism*, London: Allen & Unwin.

Nowotny, H. (1986), 'The Public and Private Uses of Time', in Balbo & Nowotny (1986), pp.11–17.

Oakley, A. (1980), *Women Confined*, London: Routledge and Kegan Paul.

O'Connor, J. & Ruddle, H. (1988), *Caring for the Elderly – Part 3: the Caring Process: a Study of Carers in Homes*, Dublin: National Council for the Aged.

OECD (1985), *Measuring Health Care*, Paris: Organisation for Economic Co-operation and Development.

OECD (1987), *Financing and Delivering Health Care*, Paris: Organisation for Economic Co-operation and Development.

OECD (1988a), *Employment Outlook*, Paris: Organisation for Economic Co-operation and Development.

OECD (1988b), *Iceland, Economic Survey*, Paris: Organisation for Economic Co-operation and Development.

OECD (1988c), *Reforming Public Pensions*, Paris: Organisation for Economic Co-operation and Development.

OECD (1988d), *Finland, Economic Survey*, Paris: Organisation for Economic Co-operation and Development.

OECD (1992), *Urban Policies for Aging Populations*, Paris: Organisation for Economic Co-operation and Development.

Offe, C. (1984), *Contradiction of the Welfare State*, London: Hutchinson.

Official Statistics of Finland (1983), 'Social Welfare, 1983', XXI B 45, in *Yearbook of Social Welfare Statistics*, Helsinki: National Board of Social Welfare Planning Department.

O'Higgins, M. (1983), 'Rolling Back the Welfare State', in Jones, C. & Stevenson, J. (eds) (1983), *Year Book of Social Policy 1982*, London: Routledge and Kegan Paul.

Oldman, C. (1993), 'Review of Current Literature', *Ageing and Society*, Vol.13, Part 1, March.

Olsen, R. (1986), 'A Social Support', *British Journal of Social Work*, 16, Supplement, pp.15–22.

Olsen, H. & Gregersen, O. (1988), *De Aeldre og Hjemmehjaelpen*, Copenhagen: Socialforsknings Instituttet, rapport 88:1.

Olson, S. (1986), 'Sweden', in Flora (1986),Vol.1, pp. 4–116.

Olsson, S.E. (1992), *Social Policy and the Welfare State in Sweden*, Lund: Arkiv Förlag.

OPCS (1985), *General Household Survey*, London: Office of Population Censuses and Surveys.

OPCS (1987), *General Household Survey*, London: Office of Population Censuses and Surveys.

OPCS (1989), *General Household Survey*, London: Office of Population Censuses and Surveys.

OPCS (1992), *1991 Census: Great Britain*, London: National Monitor, Office of Population Censuses and Surveys.

OPCS (1993), *National Population Projections (1991-based)*, PP2, 93/1, London: Office of Population Censuses and Surveys.

O'Shea, E., Donnison, D. & Larragy, J. (1991), *The Roles of Future Development of Nursing Homes in Ireland*, Dublin: National Council for the Elderly.

Owen, D. (1979), 'Reflections of the Royal Commission', the Trevor Lloyd Hughes Memorial Lecture, unpublished mimeo.

Pacione, M. (1984), *Rural Geography*, London: Harper & Row.

Palma, R. (1986), *Le USL Nel Sistema Sanitario Italiano*, Genova: Maggi.

Parker, G. (1985), *With Due Care and Attention*, London: Policy Studies Institute.

Parker, G. (1992), 'Counting Care: Numbers and Types of Informal Carers', in Twigg (1992b), pp.6–29.

Parker, R. (1980), *The State of Care*, Israel: Brookendale Institute of Gerontology and Adult Human Development in Israel.

Pashko, G. (1991), 'The Albanian Economy at the Beginning of the 1990s', in Sjoberg & Wyzan (1991a), pp.128–46.

Pasquino, G. (1986), 'The Italian Case-commentary', in Balbo & Nowotny (1986), pp.91–8.

Pearson, M., Lansley, J. & Pick, J. (1989), 'Preparation for Retirement in Europe: the Preserve of the Privileged Few?', *Journal of Educational Gerontology*, Vol.4, No.2, October.

Pedersen, O.R. (1993), 'Altenpflege in Dänemark: ein Modell für Europa auch für den Ländlichen Raum?', in Howe (1993), pp.25–39.

Pesic, V. & Jovanovic, S. (1986) 'Yugoslavia', in Brauns & Kramer (1986), pp.557–76.

Pevetz, W. & Jauch, D. (1985), 'Rural Community Studies in Austria', in Durand-Drouhin et al. (1985), pp.1–21.

Phillips, D., Vincent, J. & Blackwall, S. (1986), 'Petit Bourgeois Care: Private Residential Care for the Elderly', *Policy and Politics*, Vol.14, No.2, pp.189–208.

Phillipson, C., Bernard, M. & Strang, P. (eds) (1986), *Dependency and Interdependency in Old Age*, London: Croom Helm.

Piasek, J.S. (1989), 'Poland: Social Policy – Its Results and Goals', in Vella (1990b), pp.182–4.

Pickvance, K. (1992), 'The Development of Social Movements in Context', paper presented at the Annual National BSA Conference, 'A New Europe', University of Kent, Canterbury, pp.6–9.

Pijl, M.A. (1991), 'Netherlands', in Evers & Svetlik (1991), pp.97–121.

Pijl, M.A. (1992a), 'Information on Social Services in the Netherlands', in Munday (1992), pp.2–33.

Pijl, M.A. (1992b), 'Netherlands Policies for Elderly People', *Social Policy and Administration*, Vol.26, No.3, September, pp.201–25.

Piotrowski, J. & Oleszczynska, A. (1980), 'Open Care for the Elderly: Poland', in Amann (1980), pp.143–53.

Piperino, A. (1984), cited in Ascoli, U. (1986), *La Politica Sanitaria*, Milan: Angeli.

Pisa International Conference (1990), *Le Politiche Sociali*, Pisa: University of Pisa.

Pitaud, P., Vercauteren, R. & Dherbey, B. (1991), 'France', in Evers & Svetlik (1991), pp.29–58.

Platz, M. (1989), 'Gamle i Eget Hjem I: Levekar', Rapport 89:12, Copenhagen: Socialforsknings Instituttet.

Platz, M. (1992), *Laengst Muligt i Eget Hjem*, publikation nr.157, Copenhagen: Socialforsknings Instituttet.

Pohoryles, R., Hoffmann, D.M., Rauscher, B. & Wintersberger, H. (1988), 'The Limits of Consensus and Continuity? A Challenge for the Austrian and Welfare State', in Evers & Wintersberger (1988b), pp.169–96.

Polish Retrospective Survey (1988), *Life Course – Family, Occupational and Migratory Biography*, Warsaw: Institute of Statistics and Demography, the Central School of Planning and Statistics and the Department of Social Research at the Statistical Office.

Potter, P. & Zill, G. (1992), 'Older Households and their Housing Situation', in Davies (1992), pp.109–31.

Potucek, M. (1992), 'Dilemmas of Social Policy in Post-November Czechoslovakia', paper delivered at the Annual National BSA Conference, 'A New Europe', University of Kent, Canterbury.

Powell, D. & Powell, A. (1980), 'Too Fit for Hospital', *Community Care*, 16 October, pp.19–21.

Power, B. (1980), *Old and Alone in Ireland: A Report on a Survey of Old People Living Alone*, Dublin: St Vincent de Paul Society.

Poznan, A. (1992), *Poland: Results of a Survey of Economic and Political Behaviour: War*, Glasgow: Strathclyde University, Centre for the Study of Public Policy.

Press and Information Office, Republic of Cyprus (1992), *Cyprus*, London: High Commission of the Republic of Cyprus.

Pritchard, C. (1992), 'Changes in Elderly Suicides in the USA and the Developed World, 1974–87: Comparison with Current Homicide', *International Journal of Geriatric Psychiatry*, Vol.7, pp.125–34.

Pusic, E. (1987), 'The Development of the Welfare State in Yugoslavia', in Friedman et al. (1987), pp.151–73.

Ramhoej, J. (1992), 'Denmark', in Munday (1992), pp.1–33.

Reban, J. & Bayer, A. (1993), 'Integrating Services in a Changing Europe', in Tout (1993), pp.175–80.

Republican Institute for Social Planning (1990), *Analysis for Development Possibilities of the Slovenia Republic*, Ljubljana: Republican Institute for Social Planning.

Rex, J. (1992), 'Race and Ethnicity in Europe', in Bailey (1992), pp.106–20.

Ricknell, L. (1986), 'Sweden', in Brauns & Kramer (1986), pp.479–505.

Rigby, T.H. & Feher, F. (1982), *Political Legitimation in Communist States*, London: Macmillan.

Rijswijk White Paper (1990), *Social en Cultureel Rapport, 1990*, Rijswijk: Social Cultureel Planbureau.

Ringen, S. & Wallace, C. (eds) (1993), *Societies in Transition: East-Central Europe Today*, Prague: Central European University Press.

Ritsafakis, A. (1988), 'Research and Policy Making in Greece with Special Reference to Care of the Elderly', paper delivered at the BSG Spetses Seminar, Greece, May.

Rodgers, B.N. (1979), *The Study of Social Policy: a Comparative Approach*, London: Allen & Unwin.

Rodgers, B.N., Greve, J. & Morgan, J.S. (1968), *Comparative Social Administration*, London: Allen & Unwin.

Rodota, S. (1986), 'The Italian Case', in Balbo & Nowotny (1986), pp.99–100.

Rokkan, S. & Urwin, D.W. (1983), *Economy, Territory and Identity*, London: Sage.

Rollet, C. (1991), 'Problems of Health Services Finance in France', *Social Policy and Administration*, Vol.25, No.3, pp.193–201.

Room, G. (1979), *The Sociology of Welfare*, Oxford: Blackwell.

Room, G. (1990), *Final Report of the Programme Evaluation Team*, Brussels: European Commission.

Room, G. (ed.) (1991), *Towards a European Welfare State?*, Bristol: School of Advanced Urban Studies.

Room, G., Berham, J. et al. (1989), 'New Poverty in the European Community', *Policy and Politics*, Vol.17, No.2, pp.165–76.

Röpke, W. (1943), *The Social Crisis of Our Time*, London: W. Hodge (translation, 1950).

Rosdorff, S. & O'Shea, E. (1991), 'Ireland', in Nijkamp et al. (1991c), pp.219–41.

Rosdorff, S. & Vollering, A. (1991), 'The Netherlands', in Nijkamp et al. (1991c), pp.289–320.

Rosdorff, S. & Wright, K.G. (1991), 'United Kingdom', in Nijkamp et al. (1991c), pp.321–40.

Rose, R. (1985), *The State's Contribution to the Welfare Mix*, Glasgow: University of Strathclyde.

Rose, R. (1991), *Bringing Freedom Back In*, Glasgow: University of Strathclyde.

Rose, R. (1992), 'Identifying Needs for Social Protection in Romania: Constrained Empirical Analysis', paper presented at the Conference,

'Social Responses to Political and Economic Transformations in East-Central Europe', May, pp.1–44.

Rossell, T. & Rimbau, C. (1989), 'Spain: Social Services in the Post-Franco Democracy', in Munday (1989), pp.105–34.

Roulleaux, M. (1986), 'Luxembourg', in Brauns & Kramer (1986), pp.393–404.

Roy, A. (ed.) (1986), *Suicide*, Baltimore: Williams & Wilkins.

Rubies i Ferrer, J. (1992), 'Altenpflege auf dem Land in Spanien', in Howe (1993), pp.109–13.

Ruppel, F. & King, A. (1995), 'German Care Insurance and British Community Care: Comparative Perspectives', *Social Work in Europe*, Vol.2, No.1, pp.12–17.

Ruthven, M. (1991), *Islam in the West*, London: Penguin Books.

Ruzica, M., Hojnik–Zupanc, I. & Svetlik, I. (1991), 'Yugoslavia', in Evers & Svetlik (1991), pp.73–93.

Ryan, M. (1991), 'Policy and Administration in the Soviet Health Service', *Social Policy and Administration*, Vol.25, No.3, September, pp.227–37.

Satka, M., Korkeakoulu, L. & Rovaniemi, Y.O. (1986), 'Finland', in Brauns & Kramer (1986), pp.115–39.

Schöpflin, G. (1989), 'Central Europe: Definitions Old and New', in Schöpflin & Wood (1989), pp.7–29.

Schöpflin, G. & Wood, N. (eds) (1989), *In Search of Central Europe*, Oxford: Polity, Blackwell.

Schumann, J. (1988), 'Social Services and Social Work Practice with the Elderly in the FRG', in Hokenstad & Kendall (1988), pp.61–76.

Schumpeter, J.A. (1942), *Capitalism, Socialism and Democracy*, NY: Harper.

Schwelder, M. (1985), 'Rural Community Studies in Denmark', in Durand-Drouhin et al. (1985), pp.61–80.

Seabrook, J. (1980), *What Unemployment Means*, Oxford: Martin Robertson.

Seed, P. (1984), 'Residential and Day Services', in Lishman (1984), pp.95–113.

Seers, D. (1979), 'The Periphery of Europe', in Seers et al. (eds) (1979), *Underdeveloped Europe*, London: Harvester Press, pp.12–35.

Segalman, R. (1986), *The Swiss Way of Welfare*, NY: Praeger.

Selby, P. & Schechter, M. (1982), *Aging 2000*, Geneva: Sandoz Institute.

Sertel, A.K. & Planck, U. (1985), 'Rural Communities in Turkey', in Durand-Drouhin et al. (1985), pp.149–89.

Sevil, T. (1984), *Yaslilarin Psiko-Sosyal Sorunlari* ('Psychosocial Problems of the End'), Ankara: Harcettepe Universitesi Saglik Bilimleri Fakultesi.

Shanas, E. (1963), 'Some Observations on Cross-Cultural Surveys of Aging', *Gerontologist*, 31, pp.7–9.

Shanas, E., Townsend, P., Wedderburn, D., Friis, H., Milhoj, P. & Stehouwer, J. (1968), *Old People in Three Industrial Societies*, London: Routledge and Kegan Paul.

Sheedy, O.M. (1985), 'Residential Care for the Elderly', unpublished dissertation, Cork: University College.

Shepherd, G., Kellam, S.G., Ensminger, M. & Turner, J. (1977), 'Family Structure and the Mental Health of Children', *Archives of General Psychiatry, American Medical Association*, pp.10–36.

Sheppard, H.L. & Mullins, L.C. (1989), 'A Comparative Examination of Perceived Income Adequacy among Young and Old in Sweden and the USA', *Ageing and Society*, Vol.9, No.3, pp.223–39.

Shucksmith, M. (1991), 'Still No Homes for Locals? Affordable Housing and Planning Controls in Rural Areas', in Champion & Watkins (1991), pp.53–66.

Sihvo, T. (1988), *Arki ja Apu. Sosiaalihallituksen Väestötiedustelun*, Raportti I, Helsinki: Sosiaalhallituksen Julkaisuja, 14.

Siim, B. (1990), 'Women and the Welfare State, between Private and Public Dependence', in Ungerson (1990), pp.80–109.

Sik, E. (1988), 'New Trends in the Hungarian Welfare Mix', in Evers & Wintersberger (1988b), pp.281–96.

Sik, E. & Svetlik, I. (1988), 'Similarities and Differences', in Evers & Wintersberger (1988b), pp.273–9.

Simmel, G. (1908), *Soziologie*, Berlin: Dunker & Humblat (1968 edn).

Simonen, L. (1990), *Contradictions of the Welfare State: Women and Caring*, Acta Universitatis Tamperensis, ser. A., Vol.295, Tampere: University of Tampere.

Simons, J. (1992), 'Europe's Ageing Population – Demographic Trends', in Bailey (1992), pp.50–69.

Sinclair, I. (1988a), *Residential Care: The Research Reviewed*, London: National Institute of Social Work.

Sinclair, I. (1988b), 'Social Work and Personal Social Services for the Elderly in Great Britain', in Hokenstad and Kendall (1988), pp.77–95.

Sinclair, I. (1990), 'Carers: Their Contribution and Quality of Life', in Sinclair, I., Parker, R., Leat, D. & Williams, J. (eds) (1990), *The Kaleidoscope of Care: A Review of Research of Welfare Provision for Elderly People*, London: HMSO.

Sixsmith, A. (1986), 'Independence and Home in Later Life', in Phillipson et al. (1986), pp.338–47.

Sjoberg, I. (1985), *Pensioner/Pensioners*, Rapport, Centralbyran 43, Levnadsforhallanden, Stockholm: Statistka Centralbyran.

Sjoberg, O. (1991), 'The Albanian Economy in the 1980s: Coping with a Centralised System', in Sjoberg & Wyzan (1991a), pp.115–27.

Sjoberg, O. & Wyzan, M.L. (eds) (1991a), *Economic Change in the Balkan States*, London: Pinter.

Sjoberg, O. & Wyzan, M.L. (1991b), 'The Balkan States: Struggling Along the Road to the Market from Europe's Periphery', in Sjoberg & Wyzan (1991a), pp.1–15.

Sjoholt, P. (1988), 'Scandinavia', in Cloke (1988), pp.69–97.

Smith, A.H. (1991a), 'The Implications of Change in East Central Europe for the Balkan Socialist Economies', in Sjoberg & Wyzan (1991a), pp.147–60.

Smith, T. (1991b), 'Health Services and Community Care: Experiences from Northern Ireland', in Ulas, M., Black, S. & Hambleton, P. (eds) (1991), *Community Care*, Edinburgh: Social Services Research Group, pp.20–3.

Smolic-Krkovic, D.N. (1977), 'Aging, Bureaucracy and the Family', in Shanas, E. & Sussman, M.B. (eds) (1977), *Family, Bureaucracy and the Elderly*, Durham, North Carolina: Duke University, pp.81–2.

SOEC (Statistical Office of the European Community) (1988), *Demographic Statistics*, Brussels: European Community.

Soero de Brito, R. (1992), 'Familiare Strukturen und die Vorsorgung Pflegebedürftiger alter Maschen in Ländlichen Regionen in Spanien', paper delivered at the International Conference, 'Altenpflege auf dem Lande', University of Osnabrück, Vechta, May.

Sokoly, M. (1992), 'Greece', in Munday (1992), pp.2–19.

Sorensen, G.E. (1986), 'Denmark', in Brauns & Kramer (1986), pp.91–114.

Soria, R.P. (1993), 'Outline of the *Plan Gerontólogico* for Integrated Services in Spain', in Tout (1993), pp.271–6.

Southern Health Board (1987), *Care of the Elderly in the North Lee and South Lee Community Care Areas*, Cork: Southern Health Board.

Spicker, P. (1991), 'Solidarity', in Room (1991), pp.17–37.

Spinnewyn, H. & Cabrero, G.R. (1991), 'Spain', in Nijkamp et al. (1991c), pp.159–75.

Spinnewyn, H. & Jani-Le Bris, H. (1991), 'France', in Nijkamp et al. (1991c), pp.177–202.

Spinnewyn, H. & Nazareth, J.M. (1991), 'Portugal', in Nijkamp et al. (1991c), pp.309–20.

Spinnewyn, H., Winters, S. & Pacolet, J. (1991), 'Belgium', in Nijkamp et al. (1991c), pp.81–112.

Squires, A. (ed.) (1991), *Multicultural Health Care and Rehabilitation of Older People*, London: Edward Arnold.

SSSR Statistical Yearbook (1990), 'Goskomstat SSSR', *Narodnoe Khozyaistvo SSSR v 1989, Statisticheski Ezhegodnik*, Moskva: Finansy i statistika.

St Leger, F. & Gillespie, N. (1991), *Informal Welfare in Belfast: Caring Communities?*, Aldershot: Avebury.

Stacey, M. (1969), 'The Myth of Community Studies', *British Journal of Sociology*, Vol.20, No.2, pp.134–47.

Stahl, A. & Ahlund, O. (1992), 'The Life of the Elderly in Sparsely Populated Areas', conference paper delivered at the International Conference, 'The Marginalization of Elderly People', University of Liverpool, Liverpool.

Stambuk, M. & Zupancic, M. (1985), 'Rural Community Studies in Yugoslavia', in Durand-Drouhin et al. (1985), pp.169–204.

State Planning Organization (Devlet Planlama Teskilati) (1988), *Besinci bes Yillik Kalkinlasma Plani 1985–1989, 1988 Yili Programi* (Fifth Five Years' Development Plan, 1985–1989, Programme for 1988), Ankara, as cited in Jamieson (1991c), p.201.

Stearns, P. N. (1977), *Old Age in European Society – the Case of France*, London: Croom Helm.

Steijger, K. (1986), 'The Netherlands', in Brauns & Kramer (1986), pp.405–23.

Steinack, R. & Dieck, M. (eds) (1986), *Social Integration, Social Interaction, Material and Non-Material Resources: Aspects of the Situation of the Elderly in the Federal Republic of Germany*, Berlin: Berlin German Centre of Gerontology.

Stenhouwer, J. (1970), 'Living Conditions of the Aged', *Family Contacts*, Vol.VI, Copenhagen: Socialforsknings Instituttet.

Steyaert, R. (1986), 'Home Huishoudhulp op Mensenmaat. Aaanzet tot een Niew Beleid Inzake Gezins – en Bejaardenhulp' ('Humanizing Home Care – a New Policy'), Brussels: Kabinet van de Welzijnszorg, cited in Jamieson (1991c), pp.15–37.

Stovall, S. (1980), 'Denmark's Welfare System Proving Costly', *Los Angeles Times*, 1 December, Part 1, B, p.2.

Stromgren, E. (1985), 'Devaluation and Reform of Psychiatric Services in Denmark', in Mangen (1985a), pp.55–72.

Study Commission on the Family (1983), *Values and the Changing Family*, London: Study Commission on the Family.

Sundström, G. (1988), 'Social Work and Old Age Care in Sweden', in Hokenstad & Kendall (1988), pp.167–84.

Svetlik, I. (1988), 'Yugoslavia: Three Ways of Welfare System Restructuring', in Evers & Wintersberger (1988b), pp.331–87.

Svetlik, I. (1992a), 'The Future for Welfare Pluralism in Yugoslavia', in Deacon (1992b), pp.211–27.

Svetlik, I. (1992b), 'The Future of Welfare Pluralism in the Post Communist Countries', in Evers & Svetlik (1993), pp.13–23.

Swedish Institute (1989a), *The Care of the Elderly in Sweden*, Stockholm: Sverigehuset, Kungstradgarden.

Swedish Institute (1989b), *Fact Sheets on Sweden*, Stockholm: Swedish Institute.

Sweeney, J. (1991), *The Life and Evil Times of Nicolae Ceausescu*, London: Heinemann.

Synak, B. (1987), 'The Elderly in Poland: an Overview of "Selected Problems and Changes"', in Di Gregorio (1987), pp.131–51.

SYNERGIA (1990), 'Servizi di Aiuto Domiciliare in Alto Adige', *Synergia*, Bolzano: Autonomous Province of Bolzano.

Szalai, J. & Petrella, R. (1977), *Cross-National Comparative Survey Research*, Oxford: Pergamon Press.

Szalai, J. (1983), 'Use and Abuse of Social Benefits in Hungary', *New Hungarian Quarterly*, Vol.84.

Szalai, J. (1984a), 'Inequalities in Access to Health Care in Hungary', *Social Science and Medicine*, No.1.

Szalai, J. (1984b), 'The Crisis of Social Policy for Youth in Hungary', *Critical Social Policy*, Vol.3, No.3.

Szalai, J. & Orosz, E. (1992), 'Social Participation in Hungary in the Context of Restructuring and Liberalization', in Deacon et al. (1992), pp.144–66.

Szeben, E. (1980), 'Open Care for the Elderly: Hungary', in Amann (1980), pp.95–116.

Széman, Z. (1992), 'New Policy for the Old', in Deacon (1992b), pp.131–57.

Széman, Z. & Sik, E. (1991), 'Why Social Innovations are Needed in Care for the Elderly: The Hungarian Case', in Evers & Svetlik (1991), Vol.1, pp.43–57.

Taylor, R. (1988), 'The Elderly as Members of Society: an Examination of Social Differences in an Elderly Population', in Wells & Freer (1988), pp.105–29.

Taylor-Gooby, P. (1982), 'Two Cheers for the Welfare State', *Journal of Public Policy*, Vol.2, No.4.

Taylor-Gooby, P. (1983a), 'Moralism, Self-Interest and Attitudes to Welfare', *Policy and Politics*, Vol.11, No.2.

Taylor-Gooby, P. (1983b), 'Legitimation Deficit, Public Opinion and the Welfare State', *Sociology*, Vol.17, No.2.

Taylor-Gooby, P. (1984), 'Pleasing Any of the People Some of the Time', paper delivered at 'Government and Opposition: Workshops on the Politics of the Welfare State', Manchester.

Taylor-Gooby, P. (1985), *Public Opinion, Ideology and the Welfare State*, London: Routledge and Kegan Paul.

Taylor-Gooby, P. & Dale, J. (1981), *Social Theory and Social Welfare*, London: Edward Arnold.

Temir, A. (1974), 'Turkey', in *Encyclopaedia Britannica*, Macropaedia, Vol.18, pp.782–91.

Teperoglou, A. (1980), 'Open Care for the Elderly – Greece', in Amann (1980), pp.81–93.

Therborn, G. (1995), *European Modernity and Beyond*, London: Sage.

Thiede, R. (1988), 'Die Besondere Lage der Älteren Pflegebedurftigen Empirische Analysen und Sozialpolitische Uberlegungen auf der Basis Aktuellen Dateumaterials', *Sozialer Fortschritt*, 11, pp.250–5.

Thompson, J. (1991), 'East Europe's Dark Dawn', *National Geographic*, Vol.179, No.6, June, pp.37–68.

Thorne, B. (1982), 'Feminist Rethinking of the Family', in Thorne, B. & Yalom, M. (eds) (1982), *Rethinking the Family*, London: Longman.

Thorslund, M. & Parker, M.G. (1992), 'Care of the Elderly in the Changing Swedish Welfare State', paper delivered at the Annual National BSG Conference, University of Kent, Canterbury.

Timar, J. (1991), 'Economic Reform and New Employment Problems in Hungary', in Adam (1991), pp.156–76.

Timur, S. (1981), *Turkiyede Aile Yapisi* ('Family Structure in Turkey'), Ankara: Hacettepe University (Publication No.D – 15) .

Tinker, A. (1989), *An Evaluation of Very Sheltered Housing*, London: HMSO.

Tinker, A. (1992), *Elderly People in Modern Society* (third edn), London: Sage.

Todd, E. (1985), *The Explanation of Ideology*, Oxford: Blackwell.

Tomanbay, I. (1986), 'Turkey', in Brauns & Kramer (1986), pp.529–56.

Tönnies, F. (1955), *Community and Association*, London: Routledge and Kegan Paul.

Tornstam, L. (1992), 'Formal and Informal Support to the Elderly in Sweden', in Kendig et al. (1992), pp.138–46.

Toscano, M. (ed.) (1991), *Scienza Sociale, Politica Sociale, Servizio Sociale*, Milan: Angeli.

Tout, K. (1992), *Ageing: Programme Recommendations at the National Level for the Year 2001*, Vienna: United Nations, CSDHA.

Tout, K. (ed.) (1993), *Elderly Care: A World Perspective*, London, Glasgow: Chapman & Hall.

Towers, B. (1992), 'From Aids to Alzheimers: Policy and Politics in Setting New Health Agendas', in Bailey (1992), pp.190–215.

Townsend, P. (1962), *The Last Refuge: A Survey of Residential Institutions and Homes for the Aged in England and Wales*, London: Routledge and Kegan Paul.

Townsend, P. (1987), 'Deprivation', *Journal of Social Policy*, Vol.16, No.2.

Trebici, V. (1976), *Romania's Population and Demographic Trends*, Bucharest: Meridiane.

Troisi, J. (1988), *Organisation of Comprehensive Services for the Elderly in the Community of Malta*, Valletta: Working Group of the Organisation of Comprehensive Care in the Community.

Tryfan, B. (1992), 'Family Support to Elderly People in Poland', in Kendig et al. (1992), pp.160–70.

Tsagarousianou, R. (1992), 'Emerging Political Cultures in Post Communist Central and Eastern European Societies', paper delivered at the Annual National BSA Conference, 'A New Europe', University of Kent, Canterbury.

Tunissen, C. (1993), 'Residents' Councils in Homes for the Elderly in the Netherlands', in Tout (1993), pp.71–4.

Tunissen, C. & Knapen, M. (1991a), 'The National Context of Social Innovation – the Netherlands', in Kraan et al. (1991), pp.7–27.

Tunissen, C. & Knapen, M. (1991b), 'Strengthening Home-based care', in Kraan et al. (1991), pp.93–120.

Turner, B. (1984), *The Body and Society*, Oxford: Blackwell.

Turnock, D. (1987), 'Romania', in Dawson (1987), pp.229–73.

Turnock, D. (1989), *The Human Geography of Eastern Europe*, London: Routledge.

Tussing, A.D. (1985), *Irish Medical Care Resources: An Economic Analysis*, Dublin: Economic Social Research Institute (ESRI).

Twigg, J. (1990), 'Carers of Elderly People: Models of Analysis', in Jamieson & Illsley (1990), pp.22–36.

Twigg, J. (1992a), 'Carers in the Service System', in Twigg (1992b), pp.59–94.

Twigg, J. (ed.) (1992b), *Carers: Research and Practice*, London: HMSO.

Twigg, J. & Atkin, K. (1993), *Policy and Practice in Informal Care*, Buckingham: Open University Press.

Uldall-Hansen, B. (1980), 'Open Care for the Elderly – Denmark', in Amann (1980), pp.61–79.

UN (1969), *Declaration on Social Progress and Development*, United Nations General Assembly Resolution 254, (xxiv), 11 December, NY: United Nations.

UN Technical Meeting on Ageing for the European Region (1981), 10–12 June, Frankfurt: United Nations.

UN Austrian Report (1982), *Austrian National Report on Aging*, Vienna: United Nations.

UN Hungarian Report (1982), *Hungarian National Report on Ageing and the Situation of the Aged Population*, Budapest: United Nations.

UN (1986), *World Population Prospects*, NY: United Nations.

UN (1990), *Global Estimates and Projections*, Geneva: United Nations.

UN (1991), *Demographic Yearbook, 1989*, Geneva: United Nations.

UN (1993), *Conference of European Ministers Responsible for Social Affairs, Bratislava, Slovakia, 28 June–2 July*, Eurosocial Report 61/63, Vienna: European Centre for Social Welfare Policy and Research.

Ungerson, C. (ed.) (1990), *Gender and Caring*, Hemel Hempstead: Harvester Wheatsheaf.

Vajda, A. (1984), *The State and Socialism*, London: Allison and Busby.

Van den Heuvel, W. & Gerritsen, H. (1991), 'Home Care Services in the Netherlands', in Jamieson (1991c), pp.213–35.

Van Poppel, F.W.A. & Van der Wijst, C.A. (1987), 'The Demographic and Socio-Economic Situation of the Elderly in the Netherlands', *Tijdschrift voor Gerontologie en Geriatrie*, Vol.18, No.2a, May, pp.107–16.

Vella, G. (1990a), 'Introduction', in Vella (1990b), pp.11–14.

Vella, G. (ed.) (1990b), *Integrating Social and Family Policy for the 1990s*, Valletta: Ministry for Social Policy.

Vincent, J. & Mudrovcic, Z. (1992), 'Family Circumstances of Elderly People: Bosnia and Devon Compared', paper delivered at the Annual National Conference of the BSA, 'A New Europe?', University of Kent, Canterbury.

Vollering, A. & Börsch-Supan, A. (1991), 'West Germany', in Nijkamp et al. (1991c), pp.137–57.

Vollering, A., Belletti, F. & Senn, L. (1991), 'Italy', in Nijkamp et al. (1991c), pp.243–58.

Waerness, K. (1990), 'Informal and Formal Care in "Old Age"', in Ungerson (1990), pp.110–32.

Wagner Report (1988), *Residential Care: A Positive Choice*, London: National Institute of Social Work, HMSO.

Wahhab, I. (1989), *Muslims in Britain*, London: Runnymede Trust.

Walker, A. (1984), *Social Planning*, Oxford: Blackwell.

Walker, A. (1986), 'Progress in Private Sheltered Housing', *Housing and Planning Review*, Vol.41, No.3, pp.25–6.

Walker, A. (1991), 'The Benefits of Old Age?', in McEwan, E. (ed.) (1991), *The Unrecognised Discrimination*, Mitcham: Age Concern, pp.58–70.

Walker, A. (1992a), 'Pensions and the Living Standards of Pensioners in the EC', in Davies (1992), pp.161–80.

Walker, A. (1992b), 'The Poor Relation: Poverty among Older Women', in Glendinning, C. & Millar, J. (eds) (1992), *Women and Poverty in Britain*, Brighton: Wheatsheaf, pp.178–98.

Walker, A. (1993), 'Community Care Policy: From Consensus to Conflict', in Bornat et al. (1993), pp.204–26.

Walker, A., Guillemard, A.-M. & Alber, J. (1991), *Social and Economic Policies of Older People*, Brussels: Commission of the EC.

Walker, A., Alber, J. & Guillemard, A.-M. (1993), *Older People in Europe – The Public Dimensions*, Brussels: Commission of the EC.

Wall, R. (1989), 'The Living Arrangements of the Elderly in Europe in the 1980s', in Bytheway et al. (1989), pp.121–42.

Wall, R., Robin, J. & Laslett, P. (1989), *Family Forms in Historical Europe*, cited in Bytheway et al. (1989), p.142.

Wallace, W. (1990a), 'The Dynamics of European Integration', in Wallace (1990b), pp.1–24.

Wallace, W. (1990b), *The Dynamics of Human Integration*, London: Pinter.

Wallerstein, I. (1979), *The Capitalist World Economy*, NY: Cambridge University Press.

Walsh, D. (1990), 'Psychiatric Care in Ireland', in Gurland et al. (1990), pp.148–69.

Wanlin, P. (1992), 'The French Community of Belgium', in Munday (1992), pp.2–20.

Waterplas, L. (1991), 'Luxembourg', in Nijkamp et al. (1991c), pp.259–87.

Waters, W. & Brzezinski, Z.J. (eds) (1983), *WHO, Europe No.21 Sociomedical Survey*, Copenhagen: Regional Office for World Health Organization.

Watts, S. (1984), 'A Practice View', in Lishman (1984), pp.134–51.

Weaver, S.J. (ed.) (1989), *Second Programme of the European Communities to Combat Poverty*, Cologne: Commission of the EC.

Webb, A. & Wistow, G. (1982), *Whither State Welfare? Policy and Implementation in the Personal Social Services*, 1979–80, London: Royal Institute of Public Administration.

Weigel, W. & Amann, A. (1987), 'Austria', in Flora (1987b), pp.529–603.

Wells, N. & Freer, C. (eds) (1988), *The Ageing Population*, Basingstoke & London: Macmillan/Stockholm Press.

Wenger, G.C. (1979), *Report to DHSS on European Symposium on the Elderly and the Care System*, Poland: Jadwisin/Bangor: University College of North Wales, Social Services in Rural Areas Research Project.

Wenger, G.C. (1980), *Mid-Wales: Deprivation or Development: A Study of Patterns of Employment in Selected Communities*, Board of Celtic Studies, Social Science Monographs No.5, Cardiff: University of Wales Press.

Wenger, G.C. (1982), 'Ageing in Rural Communities: Family Contacts and Community Integration', *Ageing and Society*, Vol.2, No.2, pp.211–29.

Wenger, G.C. (1984), *The Supportive Network*, London: National Institute of Social Work.

Wenger, G.C. (1986), 'A Longitudinal Study of Changes and Adaptations in the Support of Welsh Elderly over 75', *Journal of Cross-Cultural Gerontology*, Vol.1, No.3, pp.277–304.

Wenger, G.C. (1989), 'Support Networks in Old Age', in Jefferys, M. (ed.) (1989), *Growing Old in the Twentieth Century*, London: Routledge, pp.166–85.

West, P., Illsley, R. & Kelman, H. (1984), 'Public Preferences for the Care of Dependency Groups', *Social Services and Medicine*, Vol.18, No.4, pp.287–95.

White Paper, Netherlands (1990), *Sociaal en Cultureel Rapport*, Rijswijk.

Whiteley, P. (1981), 'Public Opinion and the Demand for Social Welfare in Britain', *Journal of Social Policy*, Vol.10, N˅4.

Wicks, M. (1990), 'How Families Look at S˅cial Policies', in Vella (1990b), pp.107–12.

Wijkman, P.M. (1990), 'Patterns of Production and Trade', in Wallace (1990b), pp.89–105.

Wilderom, C. & Gottschalk, G. (1991), 'Denmark', in Nijkamp et al. (1991c), pp.113–57.

Willcocks, D., Peace, S. & Kellaher, L. (1987), *Private Lives in Public Places*, London: Tavistock.

Williamson, J., Stokoe, I.H., Gray, S., Fisher, M., Smith, A., McGhee, A. & Stephenson, F. (1964), 'Old People at Home, their Unreported Needs', *Lancet*, Vol.1, No.1, p.117.

Willmott, P. (1986), *Social Networks, Informal Care and Public Policy*, London: Policy Studies Institute.

Wintersberger, H. & Inglott, S.H. (1989), 'Integrating Social and Family Policy for the 1990s', report presented at the close of the European Conference, 'Integrating Social and Family Policies for the 1990s', Valletta, Malta, 1–5 November.

Woods, M. (1990), 'Ireland: Need for Integrating Economic and Social Policies', in Vella (1990b), pp.176–81.

World Health Organization (1978), *Alma-Ata Declaration: Primary Health Care*, Geneva: Report of the International WHO Conference.

World Health Organization (1982), *Psycho-Social and Psychiatric Emergency Services*, Copenhagen: Regional Office for Europe, WHO.

Wright, K. (1988), 'The Elderly Today, 1: An Economic Audit', in Wells & Freer (1988), pp.33–51.

Wrigley, L. (1985), 'Ireland in Economic Space', in Lee (1985), pp.66–83.

Young, P. (1986), 'Home Care for the Highly Dependent', *Geriatric Nursing*, Vol.10, No.1, pp.14–16.

Yvert-Jalu, H. (1985), 'Les Personnes Agées en Union Sorcetique', *Population*, 6, pp.829–54.

Zavada, P. (1983), 'Economic Reform, Social Reform', unpublished manuscript, Budapest.

Zeman, Z.A.B. (1991), *The Making and Breaking of Communist Europe*, Cambridge: Blackwell.

Ziomas, D. (1993), 'Greece', in DGEIRS (1993), pp.57–8.

Index

HOME CARE IN EUROPE

A country-specific guide to its organization and financing

edited by
Jack B. F. Hutten and Ada Kerkstra

"For anyone interested in comparing and contrasting the organisation and financing of home-care services across 15 European countries, this is the book for you. With the current emphasis on developing a primary-care-led NHS and bringing about a strategic shift from secondary to primary care the text provides a valuable reader for those nurses seeking to take a proactive stance in the debate." Nursing Times

Most countries in the European Union are confronted with an increasing demand for professional home care, due to demographic developments, socio-cultural changes and new policy goals in health care and social services. However, the organization and financing of services differ widely between the countries.

This book gives a systematic overview of the organization and financing of home care in the fifteen member states of the European Union: Austria, Belgium, Denmark, Finland, France, Germany, Greece, Ireland, Italy, Luxembourg, the Netherlands, Portugal, Spain, Sweden and the United Kingdom. Home care is defined as nursing care at home and home help services. Such an overview can be helpful to improve communication and co-operation between home care organizations as well as policy makers at European level.

1996   **328 pages**   **Hbk**   **1 85742 336 4**   **£35.00**

Pbk   **1 85742 337 2**   **£17.95**

Price subject to change without notification

arena

AGE AND DIGNITY

Working with Older People

Neil Thompson

Working with older people presents a number of important challenges. This book offers a successful blend of theory and practice to help staff in the caring professions to achieve high standards of practice in their dealings with older people.

Neil Thompson's text takes as its starting point the need to understand - and challenge - the role of ageism in constructing barriers to achieving a positive and dignified experience of old age. The implications of developing anti-ageist practice are drawn out to begin to equip practitioners for the challenges of empowering older people and their carers.

This is a book for all who wish to go beyond the confines of traditional approaches to working with older people.

1996   160 pages   Hbk   1 85742 250 3   £32.50
Pbk   1 85742 251 1   £16.95

Price subject to change without notification

arena

Parents' Duties, Children's Debts

The limits of policy intervention

edited by Hartley Dean

To what extent should we be responsible for our children? What is the nature of the debt we owe to our parents? How far should the state involve itself with these matters? This book sets out to examine these moral issues from a number of perspectives, but it is primarily concerned with the role of contemporary social policy in defining and enforcing the responsibilities of parents to their offspring during childhood and of adult offspring to their parents during old age.

The book adopts a critical stance which questions the extent to which reciprocal liabilities between parents and children are or should be biologically determined. It is argued that, while the function of social policy is to protect the vulnerable, it must also so far as possible enable people to define for themselves and to fulfil their familial duties and debts.

1996   196 pages   Hbk   1 85742 298 8   £29.50
Price subject to change without notification

arena

STUDIES IN EDUCATIONAL GERONTOLOGY 3

CHANGING CONCEPTS OF RETIREMENT

Educational Implications

edited by
JOANNA WALKER

This book successfully links contemporary thinking on older adult learning with social and psychological understandings of later life.

Professionals, who play an educational role with older people as clients, customers, students or employees, have often lacked a background understanding of how mature adulthood is experienced and perceived.

But what is retirement like today? Is it a deprived status or a privileged one? Who should pay for it, and how can it be afforded? What are the alternatives? The editor and her contributors explore the origins of the social institution that we call 'retirement', its current forms and its future directions.

The overall aim is to open up the possibilities of all kinds of learning and training in later life. This is because our current and future expectations of retirement will demand a range of new roles, new skills and new ways of living.

If society cannot update its view of retirement and of later life, then older people will not be the only losers.

1996   176 pages   Hbk   1 85742 259 7   £25.00
Price subject to change without notification

arena